CYCLING BRITAIN

Ian Connellan
Nicola Wells
Nicky Crowther
Ian Duckworth

LONELY PLANET PUBLICATIONS
Melbourne • Oakland • London • Paris

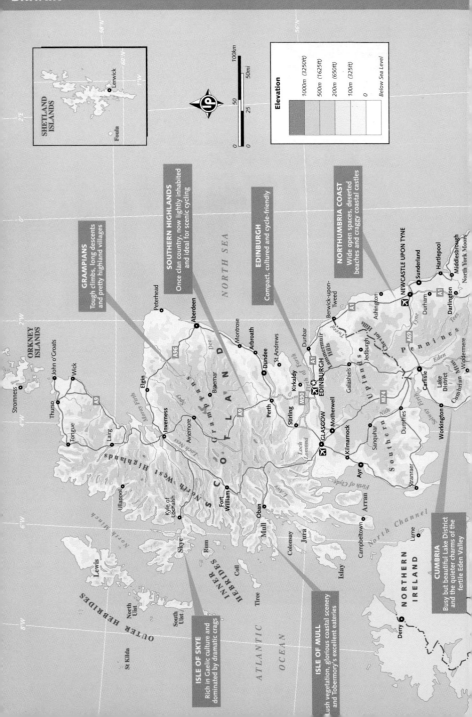

SHETLAND ISLANDS

Lerwick

Foula

Elevation

1000m (3250ft)
500m (1625ft)
200m (650ft)
100m (325ft)
0
Below Sea Level

GRAMPIANS
Tough climbs, long descents and pretty highland villages

SOUTHERN HIGHLANDS
Once clan country, now lightly inhabited and ideal for scenic cycling

EDINBURGH
Compact, cultured and cycle-friendly

NORTHUMBRIA COAST
Wide open spaces, deserted beaches and craggy coastal castles

ISLE OF SKYE
Rich in Gaelic culture and dominated by dramatic crags

ISLE OF MULL
Lush vegetation, glorious coastal scenery and Tobermory's excellent eateries

CUMBRIA
Busy but beautiful Lake District and the quieter charms of the fertile Eden Valley

NORTH SEA

ATLANTIC OCEAN

NORTH SEA

ORKNEY ISLANDS

Stromness
John o'Groats
Thurso
Wick
Tongue
Lairg

Peterhead
Aberdeen
Montrose
Arbroath
Elgin
Braemar
Dundee
St Andrews
Inverness
Aviemore
Perth
Kirkaldy
Dunbar
Stirling
EDINBURGH
Berwick-upon-Tweed
GLASGOW
Motherwell
Galashiels
Jedburgh
Kilmarnock
Sanquhar
Ayr
Dumfries
Stranraer
Carlisle
Workington
Lake District

Ullapool
Kyle of Lochalsh
Skye
Rum
Fort William
Oban
Mull
Coll
Colonsay
Jura
Islay
Campbeltown
Arran

Lewis
North Uist
South Uist
Tiree
St Kilda

SCOTLAND
GRAMPIANS
NORTH WEST HIGHLANDS
INNER HEBRIDES
OUTER HEBRIDES

Loch Ness
Loch Lomond
Firth of Forth
Firth of Clyde
Moray Firth
North Minch
Southern Uplands
Lammermuir Hills

NEWCASTLE UPON TYNE
Ashington
Sunderland
Hartlepool
Durham
Darlington
Middlesbrough
Hartlepool
North York Moors
Pennines
Cumbrian Mtns
Windermere

NORTHERN IRELAND
Derry
Larne

NORTH CHANNEL

A96
A9
M90
A1
M74
A59
A7

100km
50mi
50
25
0

NORTH YORKSHIRE
Bleak but beautiful moors and the delightful dales of James Herriot country

THE PEAK DISTRICT
Wild countryside full of fabulous challenges and great views

SUFFOLK & NORFOLK COAST
Peaceful haven for nature and people, good for visiting year-round

LONDON
Vibrant, rich in history and steadily improving for cyclists

SOUTH-EAST COAST
Chalk cliffs, historic fortifications and classic seaside resort towns

ISLE OF WIGHT
Quiet towns, great coastal scenery and plenty of sunshine

LAND'S END TO JOHN O'GROATS
Quiet roads, scenery and conquest from the extreme south to the extreme north of the mainland

NORTH-WEST WALES
The magnificent mountains of Snowdonia and a rich collection of medieval castles

THE MARCHES
Picturesque stretch of foothills full of lanes, history and atmosphere

BRECON BEACONS NATIONAL PARK
Superb mountain-biking and walking opportunities

SOUTH-WEST COAST
Charming towns, challenging climbs and peerless coastal scenery

FRANCE

NORTH SEA

Ostende
Dunkirk
Calais
Channel Tunnel
Boulogne
Dieppe
Cherbourg
Alderney

Great Yarmouth
Lowestoft
Norwich
Bury St Edmunds
Ipswich
Felixstowe
Harwich
Colchester
Southend-on-Sea
Margate
Ramsgate
Canterbury
Dover
Folkestone
Hastings
Royal Tunbridge Wells
Eastbourne
Brighton
Chichester
Portsmouth
Isle of Wight
Bournemouth

King's Lynn
The Wash
Boston
Peterborough
Ely
Cambridge
Harlow
LONDON
Crawley
Guildford
Winchester
Southampton
Basingstoke
Reading
Windsor
Oxford
Bedford
Luton

Scarborough
Bridlington
KINGSTON-UPON-HULL
Grimsby
Lincolnshire Wolds
Lincoln
Nottingham
Leicester
Northampton
Rugby
Coventry
BIRMINGHAM
Stratford-upon-Avon
Cheltenham
Gloucester
Swindon
Bath
Bristol
Salisbury
Weymouth
Exmouth
Torquay
Dartmoor
Exeter
Plymouth
Bude
Newquay
Truro
Penzance
Land's End
Isles of Scilly

York
LEEDS
Bradford
Halifax
Lancaster
Blackburn
Bolton
MANCHESTER
Sheffield
Peak District
Derby
Stafford
Stoke-on-Trent
Wolverhampton
Worcester
Hereford
Newtown
Merthyr Tydfil
Brecon Beacons
CARDIFF
Newport
Bristol Channel
Barnstaple
Taunton
North Dorset Downs
North Downs
South Downs
Chiltern Hills

Pennines

Barrow-in-Furness
Isle of Man
Douglas
Blackpool
Southport
LIVERPOOL
Birkenhead
Chester
Wrexham
Shrewsbury
Bangor
Holyhead
Anglesey
Colwyn Bay
Rhyl
Ffestiniog
Cambrian Mtns
Aberystwyth
Cardigan Bay
Llandovery
Llanelli
Swansea
Pembroke
Fishguard

WALES
ENGLAND

IRISH SEA
ST GEORGE'S CHANNEL
CELTIC SEA

IRELAND
DUBLIN
Cork

Yorkshire Wolds
Yorkshire Dales

Rivers: Ure, Ouse, Trent, Derwent, Witham, Nene, Gt Ouse, Stour, Thames, Severn, Wye, Exe, Tamar

Strait of Dover

Cycling Britain
1st edition – February 2001

Published by
Lonely Planet Publications Pty Ltd ABN 36 005 607 983
90 Maribyrnong St, Footscray, Victoria 3011, Australia

Lonely Planet Offices
Australia Locked Bag 1, Footscray, Victoria 3011
USA 150 Linden St, Oakland, CA 94607
UK 10a Spring Place, London NW5 3BH
France 1 rue du Dahomey, 75011 Paris

Photographs
Most of the images in this guide are available for licensing from
Lonely Planet Images (e lpi@lonelyplanet.com.au)

Main front cover photograph
English Lake District, England (M Evereton, The Image Bank)

Small front cover photograph
Route markers on Lôn Las Cymru ride, Powys, Wales (Ian Duckworth)

Back cover photographs (from left to right)
Touring cyclist in England (Chris Mellor)
Signs near Yarmouth, Isle of Wight, England (Ian Connellan)
Cycling through Hyde Park, London, England (Doug McKinlay)

ISBN 1 86450 037 9

text & maps © Lonely Planet 2001
photos © photographers as indicated 2001

The National Cycle Network Map © Sustrans

Printed by SNP SPrint (M) Sdn Bhd
Printed in Malaysia

**Although the authors
and Lonely Planet try
to make the informa-
tion as accurate as
possible, we accept
no responsibility for
any loss, injury or
inconvenience sus-
tained by anyone
using this book.**

Contents

2 Contents

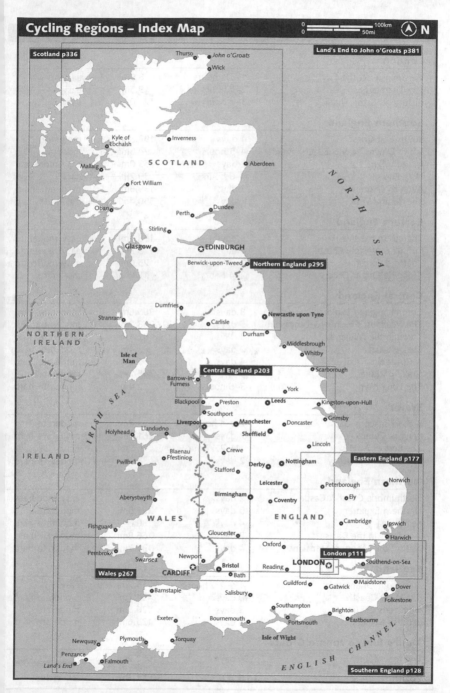

The Rides	Duration	Distance	Difficulty
London			
Westminster & the City	1–3½ hours	8.5mi	easy
The Thames East	2–5 hours	9.5mi	easy
Richmond & the Thames	3–4 hours	24.0mi	easy
Southern England			
South-East Coast	4 days	193.8mi	moderate
South Downs Way & Beachy Head	4–5 hours	24.8mi	moderate
Isle of Wight	2 days	53.0mi	easy-moderate
New Forest	4–6 hours	39.2mi	easy
Avon to Thames	3 days	139.6mi	moderate-hard
The South-West	7 days	350.4mi	moderate-hard
Eastern England			
Thames to the Wash	3 days	158.3mi	easy-moderate
Suffolk & Norfolk Coast	4 days	175.3mi	easy-moderate
Thetford Forest	2–3 hours	25.0mi	easy-moderate
Chipping Ongar Circuit	2–4 hours	12.0mi	moderate
Central England			
Central England Explorer	8 days	385.6mi	moderate-hard
The Marches, Cheshire & Lancashire	5 days	258.9mi	moderate
Through the Midlands	3 days	152.1mi	moderate
Peak District	2 days	83.4mi	moderate-hard
A Cotswolds Triangle	4 days	195.0mi	moderate
Chiltern Ridge	3–4½ hours	45.2mi	moderate
The Long Mynd	3–5 hours	12.4mi	moderate-hard
Wales			
Brecon Beacons Gap	2½–4 hours	21.4mi	moderate
Lôn Las Cymru	7 days	261.7mi	moderate-hard
The Best of Anglesey	1½–2½ hours	16.9mi	easy
Views from the Valley	2 days	36.2mi	moderate-hard
Northern England			
Northumbria Coast & Castles	2 days	107.0mi	easy-moderate
Northern Explorer	5 days	201.5mi	moderate
Sea to Sea	4 days	130.6mi	moderate-hard
Two Days in the Dales	2 days	66.8mi	moderate-hard
North York Moors & Mansions	4 days	139.7mi	moderate-hard
Scotland			
Edinburgh Orientation	1½–2½ hours	15.7mi	easy
The West Coast	10 days	424.7mi	moderate-hard
Highlands Circuit	3 days	126.8mi	moderate
Scottish Borders	3 days	125.6mi	moderate
Land's End to John o'Groats			
End to End	20 days	1051.2mi	hard
Totals	**119 days**	**5071.8mi**	**34 rides**

The Authors

Ian Connellan

Ian grew up in Sydney and currently lives there with his family; he spent several years ski-and-cycle bumming in Australia, the USA and Europe after completing university studies in literature, history and professional writing. Since the late 1980s he has worked as a writer and editor on magazines and books. This is his first book for Lonely Planet.

Nicola Wells

Nicola grew up in regional Victoria, Australia, and now lives in Melbourne. With an honours degree in ecology, she has had various writing and research-based jobs, worked for Bicycle Victoria – similar to Britain's CTC – and done a stint in a bike shop.

She rode a bike while living in Sweden, aged 12, and rediscovered cycling at university, where she became passionate about its environmental, social and health benefits. It is still her main transport, preserver of sanity and preferred mode for travel. Her other passions include classical music, especially choral singing (which, she regrets, is not terribly compatible with cycle touring) and food (which is). She has a particular weakness for good coffee.

Nicola has also toured in Australia and New Zealand. This is her second title for Lonely Planet.

Nicky Crowther

Having grown up cycling in London, Nicky toured in New Zealand, the Rocky Mountains, Scotland and Iceland before having another look at her home town. The result was a collection of cycle routes based on the city's green spaces and a new lust to discover other gems in unlikely places. A former national standard mountain bike racer, she's worked for 10 years as an editor and reporter for the national and international cycling press, researching routes and covering mountain bike racing, the highlight of which came at the Atlanta Olympics. She continues to race as an amateur, to commute by bike and to tour. This is her first title for Lonely Planet.

Ian Duckworth

Ian hails from Perth, Western Australia. He discovered the joys of cycle touring during a break from university when he traded in his train ticket for a bicycle, spending several months pedalling around the back roads of Europe. On his return to Australia he set about exploring his own back yard by bike, a journey that culminated in the publication of his first travel book. Having traded in a career in law to be a full time travel writer, Ian hopes to see a lot more of the world from his bicycle seat. This is his second title for Lonely Planet.

FROM THE AUTHORS

Ian Connellan Thanks to the home team – Jane, Tess, Adam, Claire and Norman and Heather – for their patience, support, deep pockets and good humour. In London, David and Anne Coombe, Jac Watson and Jaz, Richie, James and Rick provided price-is-right lodgings, pub companionship, riding partners and endless advice. Fellow author Nicky Crowther generously helped with mapping, research for London rides and answers to dozens of sundry questions. The crew at Bikepark, Chelsea, obliged with 'Ralph Raleigh the rental bike'; and friendly staff at the Cyclists' Touring Club, Guildford, helped with maps, books, reference material and advice. Thanks also to veteran cycle enthusiast David Scott, Sandy the international road-atlas courier, London riding partner Martin Gregory, of Perth, and Darren and Nick – thanks for the fun, chaps.

Nicola Wells Many thanks to wonderful hosts, Stuart and Neil, who put me up for so long, and Duncan and Polly at Ostaig House for their hospitality and gems of local knowledge.

Many other Scots assisted me with information: I'm indebted to Theresa Kewell and Sharon Rice-Jones from the Kingdom of Fife Millennium Cycle Ways, to Grace from Sustrans and, especially, to Katie and Tom for their advice (and Christopher who hooked us up). I'd also like to acknowledge Linda Johnstone from the Scottish Tourist Board; Cilla George from the End to End Club; Peter Butterworth from Edinburgh Cycle Hire; Ian Maxwell from Spokes; the staff at Braemar, Tomintoul, Portree, Glasgow, Edinburgh and Melrose TICs; Craig from the Portree Independent Hostel; Adrian from the Killin Youth Hostel; and the waitress at John o'Groats' Seaview Hotel.

Thanks to Ros at the Smithy, and Kai and Mike at the Crask, for being so hospitable (and serving good coffee) during an exhausting stretch – and to Tony, who appeared in my hour of need.

I'm grateful to the authors of Lonely Planet's *Scotland* guide and to Bryn Thomas; to Darren Elder at Lonely Planet for continued support and encouragement; and to Ian Connellan for his humour and solidarity.

And, of course, I'm ever thankful for the support and friendship of my dear friends and family. Special thanks to Heather, Matthew and Gael for teeing me up with friendly Scots.

Nicky Crowther Thanks to the basket-maker and needlemaker for their knowledge of Essex and the Cotswolds; Mrs Long-Cooldrink of Laxton, East Riding for her timely aid; the staff of York YHA for squeezing me in; the medieval stonemasons for their guiding spires; Chas Roberts for his framework; Ortlieb for their waterproof bags; Pace for their women's shorts; my family and friends around the country for their hospitality, particularly

Deb Murrell and family, Paul Watterson and family, Neil Simpson, Mel Allwood & Doreen Fedrigo and, of course, Judith Foster; and Sustrans for their sterling work on the National Cycle Network. Thanks also to the editorial crew at Lonely Planet, who realised the world needed a comprehensive cycle-touring guide to Britain and pushed the project through.

Ian Duckworth Special thanks must go to the hard-working folk at Sustrans, and the many volunteers behind the National Cycle Network. In particular from Sustrans I'd like to thank Bryn Dowson, Mike Collins and everyone else who generously offered their assistance. Heaps of other wonderful people also helped bring this project to fruition. My gratitude goes to Bryn Roberts, Richard Hernan, Steve Bailey, Molly Maddocks, Ralph and Betty Lamb, my parents Andy and Margaret, my brother Andrew and all the great cyclists and others I met on my travels who were only too happy to share their experiences and offer me advice.

Maps & Profiles

Most rides described in this book have an accompanying map that shows the route, services provided in towns en route as well as any attractions and possible side trips. These maps are oriented left to right in the direction of travel; a north point is located in the top right corner of each map. The maps are intended to stand alone but could be used together with one of the commercial maps recommended in the Planning section for each ride.

We provide a profile, or elevation chart, when there is a significant level of climbing and/or descending on a day's ride; most of the time these charts are included on the corresponding map but where space does not permit they accompany the text for that day. These charts are approximate and should be used as a guide only.

MAP LEGEND

Note: not all symbols displayed below appear in this book

CUE SHEET SYMBOLS

↑ Continue Straight	↰ Left Turn	✳ Point of Interest	⌷ Traffic Lights
↱ Right Turn	↖ Veer Left	▲ Mountain, Hill	◆ Roundabout/Traffic Circle
↗ Veer Right	↺ Return Trip	▲ Caution or Hazard	•• Side Trip

MAP SYMBOLS

[ON RIDE MAPS]

▨ Bike Shop	▣ Hostel	✳ Point of Interest
▤ Cafe, Takeaway or Pub Food	▤ Hotel, Motel, B&B	✖ Restaurant
▲ Camping	ℹ Information	▣ Store, Supermarket
✕ Airport		✛ Hospital
✝ Church	**[ON CITY MAPS]**	
	▢ Embassy	▭ Post Office
	▥ Gallery, Museum	

POPULATION

✪ CAPITAL National Capital	● LARGE Medium City	Town — Town, Village on Ride
◉ CAPITAL State Capital	• Town Village Town	Urban Area

ROUTES & TRANSPORT

═M1═ Motorway, Tunnel	─○ Train Line, Train Station
═A30═ Primary Road	──● Underground (Tube)
A45 Main Road	─▢ Tramway, Bus Terminal
B4530 Secondary Road	Bikepath, Bridleway, Track
Unsealed Road	Cable Car, Chairlift
Lane (one way)	Ferry

CYCLING ROUTES

Main Route
Alternative Route
Side Trip
Previous/ Next Day
← Route Direction

HYDROGRAPHIC FEATURES

Coastline, River, Creek	Spring, Rapids
Canal	Swamp
Lake	Waterfalls

TOPOGRAPHIC FEATURES

⌂ Cave
Cliff
▲ Mountain
)(Pass, Saddle

AREA FEATURES

Building	Beach
+++++ Cemetery	Glacier
National Park, Forest	Mall, Market

BOUNDARIES

International
State
Disputed

Cue Sheets

Route directions in this book are given in a series of brief 'cues', which tell you at what mile mark to change direction and point out features en route. The cues are placed on the route map, most of the time with a profile, or elevation chart. Together these provide all the primary directions for each route in one convenient reference. The only other thing you need is a cycle computer.

To make the cue sheets as brief as we can, yet still relatively simple to understand, we've developed a series of symbols (see the Map Legend on p9) and the following rule:

Once your route is following a particular road, continue on that road until the cue sheet tells you otherwise.

Follow the road first mentioned in the cue sheet even though it may cross a highway, shrink to a lane, change name (we generally only include the first name, and sometimes the last), wind, duck and climb its way across the country. Rely on us to tell you when to turn off it.

Because the cue sheets rely on an accurate odometer reading we suggest you disconnect your cycle computer (pop it out of the housing or turn the magnet away from the fork-mounted sensor) whenever you deviate from the route.

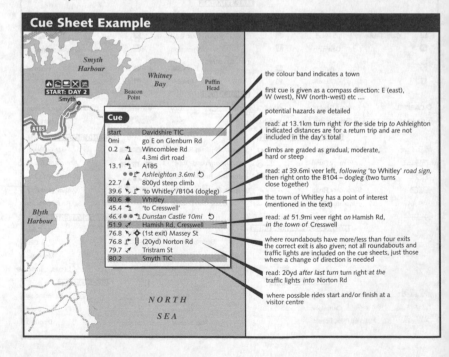

Cue Sheet Example

the colour band indicates a town

first cue is given as a compass direction: E (east), W (west), NW (north-west) etc ....

potential hazards are detailed

read: *at 13.1km turn right for the side trip to* Ashleighton indicated distances are for a return trip and are not included in the day's total

climbs are graded as gradual, moderate, hard or steep

read: *at 39.6mi veer left, following* 'to Whitley' *road sign, then right onto the B104 – dogleg* (two turns close together)

the town of Whitley has a point of interest (mentioned in the text)

read: *at 51.9mi veer right on* Hamish Rd, *in the town of* Cresswell

where roundabouts have more/less than four exits the correct exit is also given; not all roundabouts and traffic lights are included on the cue sheets, just those where a change of direction is needed

read: 20yd *after last turn turn right at the* traffic lights *into* Norton Rd

where possible rides start and/or finish at a visitor centre

Cue

start		Davidshire TIC
0mi		go E on Glenburn Rd
0.2	↰	Wincomblee Rd
	⚠	4.3mi dirt road
13.1	↱	A185
	●●↱	Ashleighton 3.6mi ↺
22.7	⚠	800yd steep climb
39.6	↖ ↱	'to Whitley'/B104 (dogleg)
40.6	✳	Whitley
45.4	↰	'to Cresswell'
46.4	●●↰	Dunstan Castle 10mi ↺
51.9	↗	Hamish Rd, Cresswell
76.8	↘ ◆	(1st exit) Massey St
76.8	↱ 🚦	(20yd) Norton Rd
79.7	↗	Tristram St
80.2		Smyth TIC

Smyth Harbour

Whitney Bay

Puffin Head

START: DAY 2
Smyth

Beacon Point

A185

Blyth Harbour

NORTH

SEA

Foreword

HOW TO USE A LONELY PLANET GUIDEBOOK

The best way to use a Lonely Planet guidebook is any way you choose. At Lonely Planet we believe the most memorable travel experiences are often those that are unexpected, and the finest discoveries are those you make yourself. Guidebooks are not intended to be used as if they provide a detailed set of infallible instructions!

Contents All Lonely Planet guidebooks follow roughly the same format, including the cycling guides. The Facts about the Destination chapters give background information ranging from history to weather. Facts for the Cyclist gives practical information on the destination. Health & Safety covers medical advice and road rules. Basic bicycle maintenance is addressed in Your Bicycle. Getting There & Away gives a brief starting point for researching travel to/from the destination. Getting Around gives an overview of the transport options when you arrive.

The peculiar demands of each destination determine how subsequent chapters are broken up, but some things remain constant. We always start each ride with background and getting to/from the ride information. Each day's ride is summarised and the highlights en route detailed in the text, and locations noted on the map and cue sheets. A selection of the best sights and places to stay and eat in each start and end town are also detailed.

Heading Hierarchy Lonely Planet headings are used in a strict hierarchical structure that can be visualised as a set of Russian dolls. Each heading (and its following text) is encompassed by any preceding heading that is higher on the hierarchical ladder.

Entry Points We do not assume guidebooks will be read from beginning to end, but that people will dip into them. The traditional entry points are the list of contents and the index. In addition, the cycling guides also have a table of rides and a map index illustrating the regional chapter break-up.

There is also a colour map that shows highlights. These highlights are dealt with in greater detail in the Facts for the Cyclist chapter, along with planning questions and suggested itineraries. Each chapter covering a geographical region also begins with a map showing all the rides for that region. Once you find something of interest turn to the index or table of rides.

ABOUT LONELY PLANET GUIDEBOOKS

The process of creating new editions begins with the letters, postcards and emails received from travellers. This correspondence often includes suggestions, criticisms and comments about the current editions. Interesting excerpts are immediately passed on via newsletters and the Web site, and everything goes to our authors to be verified when they're researching on the road. We're keen to get more feedback from organisations or individuals who represent communities visited by travellers.

Lonely Planet gathers information for everyone who's curious about the planet – and especially for those who explore it first-hand. Through guidebooks, phrasebooks, activity guides, maps, literature, newsletters, image library, TV series and Web site we act as an information exchange for a worldwide community of travellers.

Research Authors aim to gather sufficient practical information to enable travellers to make informed choices and to make the mechanics of a journey run smoothly. They also research historical and cultural background to help enrich the travel experience and allow travellers to understand and respond appropriately to cultural and environmental issues.

Authors don't stay in every hotel because that would mean spending a couple of weeks in each medium-sized city and, no, they don't eat at every restaurant because that would mean stretching belts beyond capacity. They do visit hotels and restaurants to check standards and prices, but feedback based on readers' direct experiences can be very helpful.

Many of our authors work undercover, others aren't so secretive. None of them accept freebies in exchange for positive write-ups. And none of our guidebooks contain any advertising.

Production Authors submit their raw manuscripts and maps to offices in Australia, USA, UK or France. Editors and cartographers – all experienced travellers themselves – then begin the process of assembling the pieces. When the book finally hits the shops, some things are already out of date, we start getting feedback from readers and the process begins again ...

WARNING & REQUEST

Things change – prices go up, schedules change, good places go bad and bad places go bankrupt – nothing stays the same. So, if you find things better or worse, recently opened or long since closed, please tell us and help make the next edition even more accurate and useful. We genuinely value all the feedback we receive. A well-travelled team reads and acknowledges every letter, postcard and email and ensures that every morsel of information finds its way to the appropriate authors, editors and cartographers for verification.

Everyone who writes to us will find their name in the next edition of the appropriate guidebook. They will also receive the latest issue of *Planet Talk*, our quarterly printed newsletter, or *Comet*, our monthly email newsletter. Subscriptions to both newsletters are free. The very best contributions will be rewarded with a free guidebook.

Excerpts from your correspondence may appear in new editions of Lonely Planet guidebooks, the Lonely Planet Web site, *Planet Talk* or *Comet*, so please let us know if you *don't* want your letter published or your name acknowledged.

Send all correspondence to the Lonely Planet office closest to you:

Australia: Locked Bag 1, Footscray, Victoria 3011
USA: 150 Linden St, Oakland, CA 94607
UK: 10A Spring Place, London NW5 3BH
France: 1 rue du Dahomey, 75011 Paris

Or email us at: e talk2us@lonelyplanet.com.au

For news, views and updates see our Web site: ⌨ www.lonelyplanet.com

Introduction

For many of the world's English-speaking peoples, Britain has an allure that's hard to define and impossible to resist. These are fabled lands of dragons, saints and kings; of fearless mariners, conquering regiments and pioneering settlers and merchants. Britain has a special place in cycling lore, too. British designers played a pivotal role in the evolution of the bicycle from an impractical plaything to a useful form of transport.

For bicycle tourists, Britain is a land of contrast. It is one of the world's most densely populated nations, and it harbours an astonishing complex of minor roads, some of which feel the wheels of no more than a handful of cars or trucks per day. These minor roads link the thousands of cities, towns and villages that make British bicycle touring an endeavour characterised by many small hops rather than large and lonely jumps. Population density also means that Britain's major roads – often the most direct route between major centres – are crowded with motorised vehicles.

This book provides general background to Britain and a detailed introduction to the British cycle-touring scene, including information about getting to and around Britain with a bicycle. The rides are broken into regional chapters, each of which offers tours from one to several days in length.

Multi-day tours will lead cyclists through countryside of surprising diversity and great beauty; Britain is a graceful and charming land, sublime under fair skies and enlivened by capricious weather that can have you drenched one day and reaching for sunscreen the next. Tours in England's south, east and Midlands have the advantage of proximity to big population centres, London in particular. The English north, Scotland and Wales have the attraction of greater isolation, higher terrain and, particularly in the case of the latter two, distinctive cultures.

Britain's excellent rail network gives cyclists with limited time the option of choosing several one-day rides in different regions; both road and off-road day tours are included in the book.

Wherever you choose to ride, you'll find a land rich in history and populated by hardy but welcoming and usually witty people. You'll wend your way along a network of mostly sealed minor roads, discovering en route that Britain has many hills but few real mountains. You'll also learn that, in all but a few isolated areas, it's usually only a short pedal to the next pub, cafe or guesthouse.

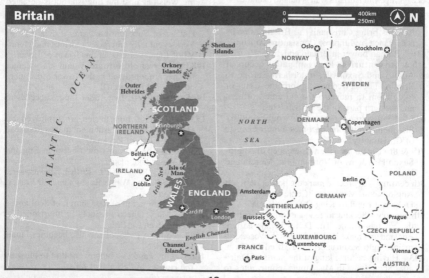

Facts about Britain

HISTORY

It must be said that perhaps the greatest thrill about cycling in Britain is the density of historical sites along the road. Occupied by humans for millennia, these lands are rich in visible signs of habitation that speak of disparate peoples' rise from prehistoric roots, through waves of invasion and internal turmoil, to industrialisation and world power. In some cases the roads themselves are slices of history, their courses first plotted by the Romans.

Historically, Britain is a rich merging of different cultures over time. The following provides a condensed outline of Britain's history before considering a more detailed look at the history of cycling in Britain.

4000 BC – Stone Age peoples arrive in Britain from mainland Europe.

3000 BC – Various ceremonial complexes such as Stonehenge and Avebury are built.

800 BC – European invasion begins with the arrive of the Celts from central Europe; Bronze Age begins.

500 BC – Scots and Picts in the north, plus Britons in the south make up the three main Celtic tribes; Iron Age begins.

43 AD – The mainland invades again, this time with the Romans.

122 – Emperor Hadrian's wall is built to exclude the Scots, who continue to resist Roman conquest.

313 – New religions enter the cultural mix as the Romans bring Christianity to Britain after its acceptance by Emperor Constantine in Rome.

410 – Roman power in Britain ends.

5th & 6th centuries – Heavy migration occurs of Angles and Saxons from northern Europe to Britain. The newcomers absorb the Celts or force them to move to the extreme northern and western parts of the British Isles.

635 – Lindisfarne monastery is established by St Aiden and it soon becomes a major centre of Christianity.

7th & 8th centuries – First emergence of Anglo-Saxon kingdoms of Northumbria, Mercia and Wessex.

8th century – In order to mark the border between Anglo-Saxon Mercia and Celtic Wales, Offa's Dyke is created by King Offa of Mercia.

9th century – Seeking to conquer northern Britain, the Vikings invade. The Danes invade eastern England and make York their capital. Wessex remains Anglo-Saxon under King Alfred the Great.

843 – Having become king of the Scots of Dalriada, Scot Kenneth MacAlpine, contributes to the decline of Pictish culture in the territory that later became known as Scotland.

9th & 10th centuries – Repeated attacks are mounted on the Welsh by Anglo-Saxon tribes.

10th century – Edward the Elder, Alfred's successor, gains control of both northern 'Danelaw' territories and southern Wessex, uniting England for the first time.

1066 – Norman Conquest of Britain is led by William the Conqueror.

1085 – Domesday Book is produced, providing a census of England's people, landowners and potential future success.

1170 – Henry II has Archbishop Thomas Becket murdered in Canterbury Cathedral.

1215 – Magna Carta is signed by King John, ending the absolute authority of the monarchy.

1272–1307 – Reign of Edward I, who establishes authority over Wales, builds the castles of Conwy, Beaumaris, Caernarfon and Harlech, and removes the Scots' coronation stone, the Stone of Destiny, from Scone to England.

1314 – Robert the Bruce, King of Scotland, defeats the English at the Battle of Bannockburn.

1337 – The Hundred Years' War between England and France begins.

1349 – The Black Death in England kills more than 1.5 million people (one-third of the population).

1380 – First English translation of the Bible.

1381 – The Peasants' Revolt during Richard II's reign is suppressed.

1387 – Chaucer's *Canterbury Tales* is first published.

1400–06 – Owain Glyndwr leads a rebellion of the Welsh against the English, but is defeated by Henry IV.

1445–85 – War of the Roses is fought between the Houses of York and Lancaster. Edward IV of York eventually emerges victorious and Henry VI of Lancaster dies in the Tower of London.

1483 – 12-year-old Edward V and his younger brother are murdered in the Tower of London, possibly by Richard III.

1485 – Henry VII, first Tudor king, succeeds to the throne.

1536–40 – The monasteries are dissolved by Henry VIII, whom Parliament makes first head of the Church of England.

1536–43 – The Acts of Union between England and Wales take place.

1558–1603 – Reign of Elizabeth I; Shakespeare, Francis Bacon, Walter Raleigh and Sir Francis Drake era.

1560 – Reformation of the Church of Scotland.

1567 – Mary Queen of Scots is imprisoned in Loch Leven Castle.

1603 – James VI of Scotland also becomes James I of England.

1605 – Guy Fawkes' Gunpowder Plot to blow up the Houses of Parliament fails.

1625 – Charles I becomes king.

1644 – The Civil War begins between the Royalists and the Parliamentarians.

1649 – Charles I is executed. The Commonwealth is established and ruled by Oliver Cromwell.

1660 – Parliament restores the Monarchy and crowns Charles II as king.

1688 – William of Orange defeats James II at the Battle of the Boyne in Ireland to take the crown of England.

1707 – The Act of Union joins the Scottish and English parliaments.

1714 – Queen Anne, the last of the Stuart monarchs, dies. The Hanoverians succeed her.

1715 – First Jacobite Rebellion attempts to restore the Stuart monarchs to the throne.

1745 – Second Jacobite Rebellion is led by Charles Stuart (Bonnie Prince Charlie), supported by the Scottish Highlanders.

1746 – Bonnie Prince Charlie flees Britain after defeat at the Battle of Culloden.

1750s – The Industrial Revolution in Britain begins; Britain begins to rise as a world power.

1776–82 – American colonies are lost in War of Independence.

1801 – Act of Union ends Irish parliamentary independence and creates United Kingdom of Great Britain and Ireland.

1803–15 – Napoleonic Wars; decisive battles of Trafalgar (1805) and Waterloo (1815) confirm British power.

1837–1901 – Reign of Queen Victoria.

1840s–1860s – The Highland Clearances sees Scottish Highlanders forced off the land to make way for sheep and deer runs.

1860s–1900 – Governments under Benjamin Disraeli and William Gladstone legalise trade unions, make education universal and extend voting rights to most men.

1914–18 – World War I.

1919–21 – Anglo-Irish War results in independence for the Republic of Ireland. Six counties in the north become Northern Ireland and remain part of the United Kingdom.

1928 – Women gain full voting equality with men.

1930s – British economy, weakened by WWI, suffers further decline during the Great Depression.

1936 – King Edward VIII abdicates to marry a US divorcee. George VI becomes king.

1939–45 – World War II.

1945 – Labour Government is elected and subsequently establishes the post-war welfare state with unemployment benefits, a national health system and nationalisation of key industries.

1952 – George VI dies.

1953 – Elizabeth II is crowned queen.

1960s – Attempts to join the European Economic Community (EEC) fail.

1973 – EEC admits Britain as a member.

1979–90 – Margaret Thatcher's Conservative Government curbs union powers and sells off national industries.

1982 – Falklands War is fought.

1990–97 – Conservative Government is led by John Major.

1997 – New Labour Government, led by Tony Blair, is elected with record parliamentary majority. Blair pledges 'modernisation' of Britain.

1998 – 'Good Friday Agreement' lays framework for peace in Northern Ireland and, possibly, a future united Ireland. Britain plays major role in NATO military intervention in Kosovo.

1999 – (January) Common currency (Euro) introduced in 11 European Union (EU) countries; Britain declines, but has option to join later. (December) Britain lifts £5 billion burden of debt owed to it by 41 Third World countries.

2000 – Northern Ireland peace process stalls due to failure to achieve de-commissioning of parliamentary arsenals.

Essential Definitions

Before you read any further, some essential definitions are required. This book covers the state of Great Britain (shortened to 'Britain' throughout), which is made up of three countries: England, Wales and Scotland. The United Kingdom (UK) consists of Great Britain, Northern Ireland and some semiautonomous off-shore islands such as the Isle of Man and the Channel Isles. The island of Ireland consists of Northern Ireland and the Republic of Ireland. The latter, also called Eire, is a completely separate country. The British Isles is a geographical term for the whole group of islands that make up the UK and the Republic of Ireland.

It is common to hear 'England' and 'Britain' used interchangeably, but you should avoid this, especially in Wales or Scotland, where it may cause slight offence. Calling a Scot 'English' is something like calling a Canadian person 'American', or a New Zealander 'Australian'. Visitors can plead ignorance and get away with an occasional mix-up, but some of the worst offenders are the English themselves, many of whom seem to think that Wales and Scotland are parts of England. This naturally angers the Scots and Welsh, understandably fuelling nationalist sentiments in some quarters. This is usually completely misunderstood by the English, who simply think their neighbours carry ancient and unreasonable grudges.

History of Cycling

Evolution of the Bicycle What marks Britain's cycling history as unique is the role of British inventors in the creation of the modern bicycle.

Two-wheeled, rider-propelled machines appeared in Europe in the early 19th century. Crude but steerable, these 'swiftwalkers' were made of wood; riders made progress by pushing their feet against the ground. Swiftwalkers were more a fad than a practical means of transportation.

In 1839, Scottish blacksmith Kirkpatrick Macmillan built what's generally acknowledged as the first self-propelled bicycle. Legend has it that Macmillan made a copy of a swiftwalker brought in for repair by a customer, tinkering for years before coming up with a system of treadles, rods and cranks that powered the rear wheel. Macmillan's bike was heavy but it could move at a brisk pace. In 1842 Macmillan rode 140mi to Glasgow and back, averaging 8mph. Whatever its advantages, Macmillan's machine never became popular and it quickly passed out of fashion.

The machine built in Paris in 1861 by Pierre Michaux and his son Ernest proved

---

Cycle Museums

Given Britain's role in bicycle development, it's no surprise that there are several fine collections of cycling artefacts and memorabilia dotted about the nation. Some are contained in museums or collections dedicated to cycling, others are part of a wider collection in a larger museum.

Specialist cycling museums and collections include (call ahead to check opening hours and prices):

British Cycling Museum (☎ 01840-212811), Camelford, Cornwall; open year-round from Sunday to Thursday; entry £2.50 for adults

Mark Hall Cycle Museum & Gardens (☎ 01279-439680), Harlow, Essex; open year-round Tuesday and Wednesday plus first and third Sunday each month; £1.50

Norfolk Cycle Collection (☎ 01603-667228), Dereham, Norfolk; open year-round, by appointment only; free

WHY RIDE
IN CONSTANT
FEAR OF
PUNCTURES?

A delightful feeling of security is enjoyed by every rider of

"SPECIAL"
DUNLOPS

Made with extra thick rubber tread and tube. These tyres are practically puncture-proof, and will out-wear two or three pairs of ordinary tyres.

See that you are supplied with genuine "Special" Dunlops, on every one of which the Dunlop trade mark and the words "Special Roadster" will be found clearly marked.

PAUL FARREN COLLECTION

The Pinkerton Cycle Collection (☎ 01213-500685), Arbury Hall, Nuneaton, Warwickshire; open Sunday and Bank holidays from Easter to late September; £4

Welsh National Cycle Museum (☎ 01597-825531), Llandrindod Wells; open year-round; £2

WH Kern Cycle Collection (☎ 0151-709 4252), Liverpool; open year-round, afternoons (evenings by appointment); free

Other museums with notable cycling collections include:

Glasgow Museum of Transport (☎ 0141-287 27280), Glasgow; open year-round (closed Tuesday); free

Museum of British Road Transport (☎ 024-7683 2425), Coventry; open year-round, daily; £3.30

Museum of Science and Industry (☎ 0151-235 1661), Birmingham; open year-round, daily; free

more enduring. Its front wheel had two cranks that were rotated by the rider's feet. It still wasn't a comfortable beast to ride – it was popularly known as the 'boneshaker' – but it caught on. The Michaux family made 142 boneshakers in 1862 and by 1865 they were cranking out 400 a year.

In England the Coventry Sewing Machine Company decided to make several hundred Michaux bicycles. James Starley, their inventive young foreman, set out to reduce the weight of the ponderous machines. In 1870 Starley made a bicycle with a large front wheel and a small rear wheel. It was called a 'high-wheeler' or 'ordinary', but these days the design is better known as the 'penny-farthing', the name it was given in 1890, when it was well past its prime.

The ordinary had a gear that allowed the wheel to be turned twice for each pedal revolution and light iron wheels with radial wire spokes. In 1874 Starley introduced eyed-and-threaded nipples to hold the spokes individually, and later used tangential spoking in order to ease sideways stress. The bike typically weighed about 50lbs, but it could be built as light as 21lbs for track racing.

From this point onwards, Britons moved rapidly to improve bicycle design. In 1874 HJ Lawson designed the first chain-driven bike. His machine, called the 'safety bicycle', was more stable and easier to mount and stop than an ordinary. But the Safety remained unpopular – one complaint was that pedalling so near to the ground left one's feet muddy – until after 1885, when the Rover Safety model was released by James Starley's nephew, John K Starley. With it came the introduction of the diamond-pattern frame. The frame was strong, compact (still the basis of most modern bike frames), lighter and more efficient (ie, riders went farther for their efforts). The safety dominated the market by 1889 and the ordinary was out of production by the early 1890s.

One of the most significant advances occurred in 1888: the introduction of pneumatic tyres by JB Dunlop, a Belfast veterinarian. These tyres made bicycles more comfortable to ride, as well as making them significantly faster. Thus, bicycles became a genuine proposition for transport, and not just a leisure plaything. This propelled the bicycle industry towards building inexpensive, practical machines.

By 1893 bicycles had evolved into the familiar diamond-pattern frame models with pedal-and-chain drive and air-filled rubber wheels. The newer models could freewheel, meaning that there was no need to pedal continuously, and also that cycling downhill didn't require the rider to dangle their feet off the pedals. The new models also had efficient, easy-to-use brakes. These two advances made a joy of the last years of cycling's golden age (generally acknowledged as 1870 to the turn of the 20th century). As well as providing an affordable transportation and leisure option for working men, the safety bicycle helped increase women's mobility. Since the 1870s female bicycle enthusiasts had been largely restricted to clunky and impractical tricycles. The safety bicycle is also credited with a role in instituting 'common sense' dressing for women – bustles and corsets were highly impractical as cycling-wear.

Rising Popularity The rise of organised cycling in Britain paralleled the machine's development. The first recorded cycling race was held in June 1868 at Hendon, Middlesex; the winner was James Moore. The next year he also won the first recorded town-to-town race, from Rouen to Paris. Road racing quickly took off in Europe, but poor road conditions in Britain made track racing more common.

Since green showed the dirt, CTC uniforms were changed to grey for 'practicality' (1885).

The National Cyclists Union (NCU), now the British Cycling Federation (BCF), was founded in 1878; it argued for the formation of International Cyclist Association (ICA), which was established in 1892. The British were thought by some to have too much influence at the ICA, and some member countries broke away and founded the Union Cycliste Internationale (UCI) in 1900. A presumably more co-operative Great Britain joined the UCI a few years later after the ICA was disbanded.

Recreational cyclists organised clubs shortly after the racers. In England, the Bicycle Touring Club was founded in 1878 (in 1883 it became the Cyclists' Touring Club, CTC). The CTC had nearly 60,000 members early in the 20th century and it continues to thrive today.

In the early 20th century British cycle racing declined somewhat as cars rose in popularity, and the uncertain legality of racing on roads resulted in the activity being banned by the NCU. This led to the advent of time-trial racing, intended both to circumvent the law and avoid the supposed dangers of massed start races on British roads.

Remarkably, there wasn't a mass-started road race in Great Britain until 1942. The Tour of Britain began in 1951 and from 1958 was run annually as the Milk Race. Professional cycling – long a feature of the cycling scene in Europe – was finally introduced in 1965 by which time British riders were already making a mark on the professional racing scene. Tom Simpson raced in the Tour de France from 1960 to 62 – wearing the yellow jersey and finished sixth in the general classification in 1962 – and again from 1964 to 67, when he tragically died on Mont Ventoux. Barry Hoban won eight Tour stages between 1967 and 1975; his successor, gritty Scot Robert Millar, won two Tour stages and, in 1984, the King of the Mountains title during a long professional career.

The best of Britain's latter-day road professionals include Sean Yates, who won a Tour time trial in 1988 and wore the yellow jersey in 1994; and Chris Boardman, who won three Tour prologues (and therefore the yellow jersey) in the 1990s. Currently, there's one Britain-based professional team in Europe, the Linda McCartney (vegetarian foods) team, which boasts a predominantly British roster. The pre-eminence of professional road racing was underlined in 1994, when two stages of the Tour de France visited Britain. Today Britain also has strong competitions in track, mountain bike and cyclo-cross racing.

Recreational cycling also declined in the early 20th century, making a comeback in the years between WWI and WWII. In the 1920s manufacturers responded to an upsurge in interest in outdoor activities by applying lightweight technologies (previously reserved for racing cycles) to touring bikes. The Great Depression was a boon for cycling; cars became unaffordable. CTC membership, which had been in decline, rose again and the club scene boomed.

Cycling's popularity remained relatively constant again until the 1950s, when the British public, cautious with their money through years of wartime austerity, went on a consumer-goods spending spree. Their primary interest was the motor car, and the number of cars on British roads tripled between 1945 and 1955. In broad terms the bicycle slump continued until the early 1970s, when the oil-price crisis led to another cycling surge, which has been sustained more or less until the present day. The rise of different forms of cycling, especially mountain biking, and increased public awareness of the health and environmental benefits of cycling has helped to sustain interest. Since 1988 at least 2 million new cycles have been sold in Britain each year.

Today there is increasing pressure from groups such as Sustrans, the CTC (current membership about 69,000), the Cycle Campaign Network and the London Cycling Campaign (LCC) for cycle-friendly cities and car-free routes (the number of vehicles on British roads has increased nearly fourfold since the late 1960s). About 2% of journeys in Britain are made by bicycle; the figure in Germany is about 10%, nearer to 20% in Denmark and approaching 30% in Holland.

GEOGRAPHY

Britain is small but its geography is extremely varied.

England covers just over 50,000 sq miles, much of it flat or low-lying. The heavily populated Midlands includes rolling country up to 200m (650ft). The English Lowlands, including populous London, cover much of England's east and south, where

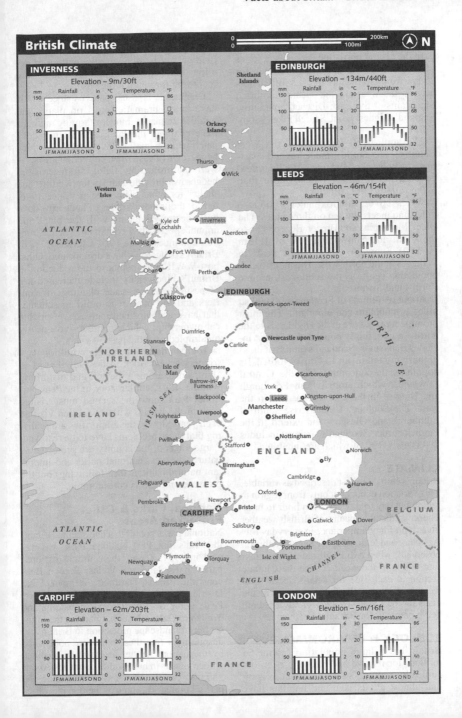

terrain rarely rises above 100m (325ft). In the south are chalk uplands called downs.

In the central north, the Pennines, a series of mountains, hills and valleys stretch for 250mi from Derbyshire to the Scottish border. To the west are the scenic Cumbrian Mountains of the Lake District, containing England's highest point, Scafell Pike (980m/3209ft).

The south-west peninsula – the West Country – has a mild climate, rugged coastline, many beaches and tracts of wild, grass-covered moor, which rise to more than 620m (2030ft) in Dartmoor.

Wales covers approximately 8000 sq miles and meets the sea on three sides. The Black Mountains and Brecon Beacons lie to the south and Snowdonia, site of 1113m (3650ft) Snowdon, the highest peak in Wales, is in the north-west. The main Welsh population centre is the south-east, around Cardiff and Swansea.

About two-thirds of Scotland's 30,000 sq miles is mountain and moorland. The most prominent ranges are in the Highlands to the north – a vast, thinly populated area that includes Ben Nevis, Scotland's (and Britain's) highest mountain at 1343m (4406ft). Its population is concentrated in the Central Lowlands, which stretch from Edinburgh and Dundee in the east to Glasgow in the west. The Southern Uplands rise south of Edinburgh and Glasgow and extend to the English border. Scotland's territory includes 790 islands, 130 of which are inhabited.

CLIMATE

Britain's climate is best described as variable. This variation occurs not only from region to region but day to day and even hour to hour. The unpredictable nature of British weather gives it profound importance in everyday life. As author and lexicographer Samuel Johnson observed: 'when two Englishmen meet their first talk is of the weather.' See the Climate section in each ride for details about local weather. See also Weather Forecasts in the Facts for the Cyclist chapter for advice about being prepared for Britain's weather.

ECOLOGY & ENVIRONMENT

Britain has a large population (about 56 million) for its size and has long been occupied by humans, so it's hardly surprising that almost all its land and habitats have been greatly altered by human interaction with the environment. Generally, Britain's biodiversity is following the pattern of decline that environmental scientists are recording throughout the world.

Changes to land-use patterns since WWII have had a dramatic effect on plants and wildlife. In places, modern farming methods have changed the landscape from a cosy patchwork of small fields separated by thick hedgerows to vast, open cultivated areas. As well as protecting fields from erosion, hedgerows provide habitat for wildlife and shelter for other plant species. Since 1946, tens of thousands of miles of hedgerow have been destroyed, along with the plant and animal species they contained. The destruction continues; since 1984 a further 23% of Britain's hedgerows have disappeared. Other post-WWII contributors to the reduction in Britain's biodiversity include increased use of pesticides, large-scale plantings of conifers and the huge road-building schemes that have accompanied increases in private car ownership; vehicle numbers have nearly quadrupled over the past 30 years.

Tourism doesn't help. Eight million day-trippers a year flock to the New Forest in Hampshire, eroding the soil and disturbing wildlife. It's a similar story in the Peak National Park, now the second most visited park in the world, with 22 million visitors each year. Slowly the authorities are realising that these problems have to be resolved. Large tracts of the country are protected as nature reserves, national parks and important natural habitats (see following) but the pressure on them is considerable.

National Parks & Other Protected Areas

National parks got off to a late start in Britain; the land's first, Peak National Park, was created in 1951. Today, there are 11 national parks in England and Wales: Brecon Beacons, the Broads, Dartmoor, Exmoor, Lake District, Northumberland, North York Moors, Peak, Pembrokeshire Coast, Snowdonia and Yorkshire Dales. 'National park' is the highest tier of landscape protection in Britain, but despite their title these parks are not owned by the nation; neither are they uninhabited wilderness, as in many other countries. About 250,000 people live and work inside the parks' boundaries, some of them in industries

National Parks

An increased appreciation of wild, uncultivated landscapes grew in 19th century Britain, and by the early 20th century, outdoor recreational activities such as walking and cycling enjoyed ever greater popularity, particularly among the middle and working classes.

Participants in these recreations became frustrated when vast tracts of moor and mountain were closed to the public by owners anxious to keep the land for activities such as grouse shooting, and popular demand for access to the moorlands and mountains grew. Eventually, a number of recreational societies were formed and campaigned for the rights of outdoor enthusiasts. The other significant development during the early 20th century was increased awareness of the need to protect Britain's open spaces from ill-conceived and unrestricted building developments. Various conservation organisations formed, the most notable being the Council for the Protection of Rural England.

The recreation and conservation bodies grew in strength and influence, and parliament finally had to start taking note. In 1929, the British prime minister agreed to set up an enquiry into the possibility of national parks in Britain (the world's first national park had been established in the USA in the 1870s). The subsequent report, published in 1931, recommended the establishment of an authority to select the areas most appropriate for designation as national parks. A change of government and the Great Depression saw these recommendations shelved.

Frustration with the lack of progress resulted in a large conference being held in London in 1935. As a direct result of this, the Standing Committee on National Parks (SCNP) was born in 1936, with the single goal of creating national parks. SCNP members represented the interests of both the conservationists and the recreationists. They published a manifesto which stated their general objective: '(a) That a sufficient number of extensive areas, carefully selected from the unspoilt wilder country of Britain, should be strictly preserved and specifically run as National Parks; (b) that the remainder of the unspoilt wilder country should be regarded as a reserve for further National Parks in the future, any developments therein being permitted only if shown to be essential in the public interest.

This formed the crux of their campaign over the following decade, which culminated in the National Parks & Access to the Countryside Act of 1949. The door was now open: between 1951 and 1957 there were 10 national parks created; the first was the Peak District, and the last the Brecon Beacons. In 1989 the Norfolk & Suffolk Broads Special Area achieved the same status as a national park, bringing the national total to 11.

that do great damage to the supposedly protected landscapes, and more than 100 million visits are made to the parks every year.

There are various other designated areas of protection in Britain, including Areas of Outstanding Natural Beauty (AONBs), National Scenic Areas (NSAs), Sites of Special Scientific Interest (SSSIs), Forest Nature Reserves (FNRs) and Countryside Stewardship Schemes (CSSs). A number of different government bodies are responsible for these areas.

Bicycle tourers will generally have no access problems in any conservation area provided that they stick to the roads. If you plan to ride off-road you should always check before proceeding; in parts of Britain thoughtless off-road riding has resulted in

considerable damage to trails, and one can imagine that cyclists' rights of access will be eroded if they aren't more responsible. For more information on rules for off-road riding see the Mountain Biking section in the Facts for the Cyclist chapter.

In addition to the institutional conservation bodies mentioned earlier, Britain has hundreds of wildlife and environmental groups that range from polite debating societies to serious activist organisations. The better known groups include the National Trust (NT; ☎ 020-7222 9251), a conservation charity of more than a century's standing that's also a major landowner, with holdings including woods, parks, coastlines, gardens and historic buildings; the Wildlife Trusts (☎ 01522-544400); the World Wide Fund for

Nature (WWF; ☎ 01483-426444); Greenpeace (☎ 020-7354 5100); and Friends of the Earth (☎ 020-7490 1555). To find out more about the environmental impact of tourism, contact Tourism Concern (☎ 020-7753 3330).

FLORA & FAUNA

Despite seemingly overwhelming odds, Britain still boasts a great diversity of plants and animals – a reflection of the range of natural habitats found here. Some of the best examples of Britain's habitats now are protected to a greater or lesser extent in national parks and other designated areas. Rides covered in the main route descriptions pass through some of the areas that contain these special habitats, but you shouldn't expect to see legions of rare and unusual plants and animals. Many of these natural treasures are obscure or furtive and you'll need to get off the bike in order to properly enjoy them.

The wonderful thing about British habitats is that there's such variety in such small

areas. On a short tour you're likely to see examples of several different habitats in a matter of days, if not hours.

Flora

Britain's natural vegetation is deciduous broad-leaved forest dominated by oak, but don't expect to see too much of it; the grassy green, hedge-crossed hills of story and fable dominate the British countryside. Large-scale deforestation since the Industrial Revolution has reduced Britain's cover of woodlands to the dismal level of about 2% today. Efforts to restore woodlands in the past century have seen large stands of fast-growing conifers planted, but it's now recognised that these probably create more environmental problems than they solve. In recent years there has been a switch to establishing new broadleaf woodlands, composed of mainly native deciduous trees such as oak, ash, sycamore, beech, hazel and lime. Areas of forest are widely scattered

The skylark is known for singing while hovering at a great height.

With its natural predator, the wolf, now extinct the Red Deer is multiplying freely in Scotland.

For hedgehogs, rolling themselves into a spikey ball is sadly no protection from cars.

Seals are common at Blakeney Point in eastern England.

and usually small, but they're invariably quite beautiful.

About 25% of Britain is occupied by moorlands and heathlands. Like the forest and pasture lands, these areas have been extensively changed by human intervention; few would be essentially in their natural state. Moors are characterised by hardy low-growing plants – true alpine species on the high points in Scotland and the more common peat moss, heather, bilberry, and thin grasses on the moors lower down. Lowland heath is usually dominated by purple-flowering common heather, bilberry or bell heather.

One area in which you're likely to see vegetation that's more or less in its natural state is the thin strip of land that abuts the coastline, an area that traditionally hasn't been affected by humans and farm animals.

Fauna

British birdlife is too extensive to detail, but birds are unquestionably the animals you are most likely to see. For more information about bird species and the best places to watch them contact the Royal Society for the Protection of Birds (RSPB) on ☎ 01767-680551.

The red deer is the largest British mammal, with herds found on Exmoor and Dartmoor in the Lake District, and in such large numbers in Scotland that culling is required. Fallow deer – smaller than red deer and distinguished by white spots on their backs – are the most common woodland deer of England and Wales. They are thought to have been introduced by the Normans in about the 12th century. Roe deer are even smaller and are native. They are most commonly found in northern England and Scotland. Britain has few other large mammals. The reindeer, beaver and auroch (wild ox) are all now extinct; the last wolf was shot in Scotland in the 17th century.

Foxes, badgers, hedgehogs and rabbits have the dubious honour of being the staple British roadkills. Originally a rural animal, the fox has adapted well to a scavenging life in country towns and even on city fringes. Badgers, now a protected species, are strictly nocturnal and rarely seen. The grey squirrel, introduced from North America, is very common and has almost entirely replaced the smaller native red squirrel. The

mink, introduced to stock fur farms, is now established in the wild and is seen mainly on river banks. The rare pine marten is again being seen in some forested regions, especially in Scotland.

The otter was in decline, but numbers are growing now that these sleek nocturnal swimmers are protected. They inhabit the banks of rivers and lakes, particularly in upland areas and on the coast in Scotland. Brown hares, with longer legs and ears than rabbits, are often seen on downland; territorial battles between males in early spring have given rise to the expression 'mad as a March hare'. Small rodents found in a variety of habitats include harvest mice, shrews and voles. These are prey for larger mammals such as weasels and stoats. Moles are rarely seen, but evidence of their digging can be found all over grasslands in the form of piles of earth or 'molehills'.

The most common aquatic mammal is the water vole, which is often seen low down on river banks. It may be confused with the brown rat, also a riverside inhabitant. Bats are widespread, and often roost in house roofs and barns. British coasts host two seal species: the larger grey seal and the common seal, which is actually less common than the grey.

Britain has just three native snakes; one of them, the adder, may be harmful. The grass snake, recognised by the pale ring on its neck, is common in England and Wales. The much-smaller smooth snake is found only in heathlands of southern England. The adder is found throughout mainland Britain in dry, open country and can be easily recognised by the dark zigzag stripe down its back. It grows to about 23in.

GOVERNMENT & POLITICS

Britain has no constitution; its law is a mixture of legislation, legal precedents ('common law') and convention. The legislative body is the Parliament at Westminster, which has three separate elements – the monarch, the House of Commons and the House of Lords. The supreme body is the House of Commons, for which elections are held a every five years (earlier in certain circumstances). The members of the Lords, Parliament's house of review, were, until 1999, all either appointed or, strange as it seems, born to the job. As a result of reforms since the Blair government was elected in 1997, only 92 hereditary peers now sit in the Lords, compared to the pre-1999 figure of around 1100 people who were qualified to sit (though not all did). The monarch is sovereign in name only, acting almost entirely on the advice of Parliament.

Real power rests with the prime minister, the leader of the majority party in the House of Commons. The prime minister appoints ministers who are responsible for government departments; 20 or so ministers make up the Cabinet, which, although answerable to parliament, meets confidentially and in effect manages the government and its policies. Since 1945 either the Conservative Party (also known as the Tory party) or the Labour Party has held power. The Conservatives draw support mainly from England's countryside and suburbia, while Labour's support comes from England's urban industrialised areas, Scotland and Wales.

Until recently, Scotland and Wales had long been governed from London, but this is changing (at least in part) thanks to the Blair New Labour Government.

Elections for the new Scottish Parliament were held in 1999 and the parliament will convene in 2000. It will sit for four-year terms and be responsible for income taxes, education, health and other domestic affairs. Westminster will still control areas like defence, foreign affairs and social security.

In 1997 the people of Wales voted to be governed by a Welsh Assembly based in Cardiff from May 1999, rather than from the House of Commons in London. The country is as resoundingly Labour in its attitudes as Scotland, no doubt because of its industrial history. The nationalist party Plaid Cymru is the largest opposition party in Wales, with four MPs at Westminster. Wales also returns four MEPs to the European Parliament.

Wales is represented in the British government by a secretary of state for Wales, who has overall responsibility for a wide range of functions including health, social services, education, local government, housing, tourism and the environment.

The likelihood of Wales emerging as a nation independent of the rest of Britain is currently small – certainly smaller than Scotland's, which has independent judicial and education systems.

ECONOMY

Britain's domination of 19th century world trade fuelled its powerful economy but when the 20th century dawned, decline was already under way, and both WWI and the Great Depression hastened it. Following WWII much industry was nationalised – railways, gas and electricity services, coal mines, steel manufacturing and shipbuilding, and later even cars. If anything, public ownership only accelerated the decline until the worldwide upheavals in manufacturing in the 1970s and 80s turned the gradual fall into a precipitous drop.

The Thatcher Government's sell-off of nationalised businesses was sometimes successful, as in the case of British Airways. But many traditional industries such as mining and engineering simply disappeared and only North Sea oil shielded Britain from a disastrous economic crash. Although manufacturing continues to play an important role (particularly in the Midlands), service industries like banking and finance have grown rapidly, particularly in London and the south-east. Elsewhere, those regions worst affected by mine and factory closures are still struggling to recover.

Towards the end of the 1990s the British economy was in better shape than many of its European neighbours'. Inflation was low and apparently steady, but interest rates were rising and the stronger pound was less favourable for exporters. Today unemployment has fallen from the grim days of the 1980s and business confidence is generally stronger.

In Scotland, unemployment is generally above the British average. Tourism is a growth industry, and Edinburgh is an important international finance centre. Some traditional industries, such as whisky distilling, continue to survive.

Wales has been devastated by mine closures; most jobs are now in tourism services. It's also been phenomenally successful in attracting foreign investment, particularly from Japanese companies, among them Sony, National Panasonic, Aiwa and Toyota. Wales has only 5% of Britain's population, but since 1986 it's succeeded in attracting more than 16% of inward investment.

POPULATION & PEOPLE

Britain has a population of around 56 million, or around 600 inhabitants per sq mile, making it one of the most crowded islands on the planet. To these figures should be added an annual influx of nearly 26 million tourists.

England's population is 48 million, with most people living in and around London, in the Midlands and in northern urban areas around Birmingham, Manchester, Liverpool, Sheffield, Leeds and Newcastle. Wales has a population of around 3 million, mostly around the cities and industrial valleys in the south. Scotland's population is about 5 million; the largest cities are Glasgow, Edinburgh, Aberdeen and Dundee. The northern Highlands region of Scotland is Britain's most sparsely populated, with an average of only 20 people per sq mile.

The Brits are a diverse bunch. Since the Industrial Revolution, England has attracted large numbers of people from Scotland, Wales and Ireland. In the 18th, 19th and 20th centuries there have also been significant influxes of refugees, most recently from troubled corners of the globe like Somalia and eastern Turkey. Since WWII there has also been significant immigration from many ex-colonies, especially the Caribbean, Pakistan and India. Outside London and the big Midlands cities, however, the population is overwhelmingly Anglo-Saxon.

ARTS

England, Scotland and Wales have all made contributions to a national artistic life that's rich and varied, with the range and quality of theatre, music, dance and visual arts considered outstanding.

Literature

Travelling in the footsteps of the great English, Scottish and Welsh writers, and their characters, is a highlight of visiting Britain.

Dating from pre-Norman times, the heroic poem *Beowulf* preserves Britain's first literary language, the Germanic Anglo-Saxon known as Old English.

The influence of the French language was apparent when Geoffrey Chaucer's *Canterbury Tales* was written in the late 14th century; Chaucer gives a vivid insight into medieval society.

Shakespeare's work is the best known of the English Renaissance (and its influence on theatre has been little diminished by the passage of time); Christopher Marlowe, Edmund Spenser and Ben Jonson are other notable writers of the era.

The works of John Milton, sometime political pamphleteer and author of *Paradise Lost*, provide an insight into the political and religious conflicts in the 17th century, while the diary of Samuel Pepys – compiled in cipher between 1660 and 1669 and decoded and published in 1825 – reveals much about London life, including accounts of the plague and Great Fire.

During the 18th century the growth of a literate middle class marked the rise of the popular novel. Pioneering efforts include Daniel Defoe's *Robinson Crusoe* and *Moll Flanders*, Samuel Richardson's *Pamela* and Henry Fielding's *Tom Jones*. In Scotland, poet Robert Burns wrote of rural life; his work is still widely available. At the dawn of the 19th century Romanticism found a voice through the poems of William Blake, William Wordsworth, John Keats and Samuel Taylor Coleridge, and the poetry and prose of perhaps the greatest romantic writer, the Scot Sir Walter Scott.

The 19th century again saw the rise of the novel, through the efforts of Jane Austen – who finally gave the game away because she couldn't find a publisher – Charles Dickens and the Scot Robert Louis Stevenson. It was also a time when writers were influenced by, and their work immutably tied to, particular regions – Wordsworth and the Lake District, the Brontë sisters and the Yorkshire moors, Thomas Hardy in Dorset, Charles Dickens in London and, into the early 20th century, DH Lawrence in the Midlands coalfields.

Twentieth century British literature includes revelations from the Empire's outposts (Rudyard Kipling); the influence of expatriates (the Americans Henry James and TS Eliot, Polish-born Joseph Conrad and Irishman George Bernard Shaw); portraits of modern life, places and manners (Muriel Spark's *The Prime of Miss Jean Brodie*, Graham Greene's *Brighton Rock*, George Orwell's *Down and Out in Paris and London)*; and glimpses into the future (Orwell's *Nineteen Eighty-Four*). The 1950s brought Dylan Thomas's evocative window on small-town Wales, *Under Milk Wood*, which is required reading for anyone heading to the author's home in Laugharne.

Popular or widely lauded contemporary works include *Trainspotting*, Irvine Welsh's tour of modern Edinburgh's seedy underworld of drugs, drink and despair; the novels of Jeanette Winterson, such as *Oranges are Not the Only Fruit*; Will Self's bizarre modern fables, such as *Cock & Bull*; and Nick Hornby's glimpses of late 20th century blokedom, including *Fever Pitch* and *About a Boy*. Isla Dewar's novels *Women Talking Dirty* and *Giving up on Ordinary* reveal small-town life in modern Scotland. Of the Welsh-language authors, one of the best selling is Kate Roberts; *Feet in Chains: A Novel* and *Living Sleep* are both available in English.

Architecture

Britain's architectural heritage reaches back more than 5000 years to remarkable Stonehenge and the village of Skara Brae in Orkney. Although the record is sometimes sparse, work survives from every period after that.

Roman and Saxon work is rare, as are complete Norman buildings, although there are still examples of 900-year-old craftsmanship in everyday use, especially in churches and cathedrals. Many medieval castles and other defensive structures – not always intact – have also survived to the present. Buildings from the 16th and 17th centuries are more common, and more ordinary domestic architecture survives alongside the grand houses that are such a distinctive feature of the countryside. Thatched cob cottages, many of which date back to the 17th century, are also a feature of rural Britain.

Since the Industrial Revolution builders have spent as little money as possible; aesthetic considerations have been for the wealthy few. Since WWII much building has shown a lack of regard for the overall fabric of the cities. Prince Charles, for one, has been an outspoken advocate of a more humanistic and aesthetically sensitive approach. Fortunately there is a strong campaign to protect Britain's architectural heritage (thanks in particular to the National Trust and English Heritage organisations).

Interesting buildings can be seen throughout Scotland, and Edinburgh has a particularly remarkable architectural heritage that spans about eight centuries. Wales is best known for the medieval castles in various states of decay that ring its coasts and the Marches (border areas). There's also an abundance of industrial architecture – great colliery towers and winding gear once regarded as eyesores and now seen through the rose-tinted glasses of nostalgia.

The standard works of reference on British architecture are the wonderfully detailed *Buildings of Britain* books by Nikolaus Pevsner.

Theatre

London is still one of the world's theatre capitals, with a historical legacy stretching back to Shakespeare and medieval times. Most regional cities have at least one world-class company and the facilities to stage major touring productions. These days there's less innovative new theatre than one would hope for – in London you're well served if revived (or long-running) old favourites are your thing.

Noted modern British dramatists include Harold Pinter, John Osborne, Tom Stoppard, Alan Ayckbourn, Alan Bennett, David Hare and Simon Gray.

Cinema

The British film industry has a small and lively output. Unfortunately, it's too often the Hollywood films of British film-makers and actors that get attention – a pity because there's a wealth of talent and tradition associated with film in Britain. Chaplin and Hitchcock are probably the best known Brits from cinema's early days; in recent times there's been work as diverse as Mike Leigh's gritty and compelling films *Naked* and *Secrets and Lies*, which won the 1996 Palme d'Or at the Cannes Film Festival; lush period pieces such as *Howards End*, from the renowned Merchant-Ivory team; successful popular films such as *Four Weddings and a Funeral* and *The Full Monty*; and the black humour of *The Crying Game* and *Lock, Stock and Two Smoking Barrels*.

Classical Music

British music lovers are well served by several symphony and many smaller orchestras. Although the big cities – especially London – get the lion's share of performances, regional Britain doesn't miss out. Until last century virtually the only truly major British composer was Henry Purcell (1659–95). Big 20th century names include Edward Elgar, Ralph Vaughan Williams, Benjamin Britten and William Walton.

John Tavener's popularity soared after his music was played at the funeral of Diana, Princess of Wales. Liverpool-born Steve Martland is among the best of the contemporary composers.

Popular Music

Since the swinging 60s – when the Beatles, the Rolling Stones, the Who and the Kinks led the charge – British popular music has been characterised by an innovative spirit. The Americans might have invented rock 'n' roll, but the Brits seem superior at *re*-inventing it.

There were the glam years of the early 70s (David Bowie, T-Rex) and the raw energy of the punk era (The Sex Pistols, The Clash). The turbulent, ever-changing music scene of the post-punk 80s produced polyglot styles and a mixture of successful bands – the Police, the Eurythmics, Wham, Simple Minds, Duran Duran, Dire Straits, UB40, Simply Red and the Smiths, to name but a few. In the early 1990s, American grunge dominated rock music. However, the late 90s brought the renaissance of the quintessentially English indie pop band with the likes of Blur, Elastica, Pulp, Suede and above all Oasis. Welsh bands Manic Street Preachers and Catatonia have also enjoyed considerable success.

Visual Arts

British artists of significance include Joshua Reynolds, William Hogarth and Thomas Gainsborough (all 18th century); William Blake, John Constable (who influenced later French impressionists), JMW Turner, John Everett Millais, William Holman Hunt, Dante Gabriel Rossetti, Edward Burne-Jones and William Morris (19th century). Morris's emphasis on good artistry has been the inspiration for generations of small, craft-based workshops in England.

In the 20th century the sculptor Henry Moore and painters Francis Bacon and David Hockney have ensured the place of British art in the international arena. The work of both Paul Nash and Graham Sutherland is noteworthy, while Richard Hamilton's 1956 photomontage *Just what is it that makes today's homes so different, so appealing?* launched the pop-art movement in England. In the 1990s a number of young artists working in a variety of media have come to prominence, including Rachel Whiteread, Damien Hirst and Tracey Emin.

Since the 19th century, Glasgow has dominated the Scottish art scene. The Glasgow School of Art has produced several outstanding artists, including Charles Rennie Mackintosh. Augustus and Gwen John are two of the few Welsh artists to have achieved real fame.

There are galleries, several with world-class collections, in the major cities and throughout regional Britain.

SOCIETY & CONDUCT
Traditional Culture

Although many things unite them, the English, Scots and Welsh have distinct cultures and national characteristics.

The English are probably the hardest to pin down. They're certainly a creative, energetic and aggressive people who have had an impact on the world that's entirely out of proportion to their numbers. They're often portrayed as reserved, inhibited and stiflingly polite, but visit a nightclub in one of the big cities, a football match, a good local pub, or a country B&B and terms such as uninhibited, passionate, sentimental, hospitable and friendly might more readily spring to mind. These days England's best-known traditions seem to be the various arcane ceremonies attached to royalty that tourists so love – guards changing, that sort of thing. In fact, so much of English culture is universally accepted that it's easy to forget it was English in the first place.

The Scots are a generous people – forget the overdone popular portrayal of them as a tight-fisted bunch. They appear reserved, but are passionate in their beliefs whether it's politics, religion or football. They generally treat visitors courteously, and the class distinctions that so bedevil England are less prevalent. The Scots take their poisons seriously, spending an average 9% of their weekly income on booze and cigarettes, the highest consumption in Britain.

It's easier to identify the tendrils of traditional culture in Scottish life. Highland Games (originally organised by clan chiefs and kings, who recruited the strongest competitors for their armies and as bodyguards) take place in summer. Some events are peculiarly Scottish, particularly those that test strength, such as tossing the caber (a tree trunk). Dancing events are accompanied by – what else? – bagpipes. The Scots still enjoy a ceilidh (pronounced 'kaylee'), originally a social gathering in the house after a day's work, now an evening of entertainment including music, song and dance. A less visible but very distinctive trait is clan loyalty. The clan system evolved in the Highlands and islands between the 11th and 16th centuries. Suppression of Highland culture after the Jacobite rebellions broke down the clan system, but the spirit of clan loyalty remains strong and extends to the 25 million Scots living abroad. Each clan still has its own chief (a figurehead) and its own tartan – another distinctively patterned Scottish tradition.

The friendly and welcoming Welsh have retained their language (see the following Language section) and the tradition of the eisteddfod. The origins of eisteddfodau are obscure, but the word means a gathering of bards, and the traditional eisteddfod was a contest involving poetry and music. The first recorded event seems to have taken place at Cardigan in 1176, but they were declining in the 17th and 18th centuries becoming less frequent and lively as the dour nonconformist sects got their claws into Wales.

All this changed in the 1860s when the National Eisteddfod Society was established to revive the old traditions. There are now three major annual eisteddfodau: the International Music Eisteddfod in purpose-built premises at Llangollen every July; the Royal National Eisteddfod, which moves between North and South Wales each August; and the newer Urdd (Youth – under-25s only) Eisteddfod, which also alternates between sites in North and South Wales each May.

Dos & Don'ts

Britain is a reasonably tolerant place. It's reasonably difficult to cause offence without meaning to. People do tend to keep to themselves, and if you need to approach a stranger in the street for help with directions do so gently and politely. It's regarded as very poor form to 'push in' to a queue. Aside from dress regulations for certain clubs and restaurants and traditional dress codes for places of worship, the Brits are pretty easygoing about what you choose to wear. Bare feet outside of the home seems to attract attention, but everyone's too polite to suggest you put your shoes on. When in Scotland and Wales, remember that the natives are Scots and Welsh – they don't like being called English.

LANGUAGE

The English language, perhaps Britain's most significant contribution to the modern world, continues to evolve, and in Britain you'll hear many English words that would not be recognised or understood in other English-speaking countries. On top of this are regional accents (some verging on dialects – most notably the Geordie of Northern England), using local words and phrases that can sometimes be virtually impenetrable for outsiders. It's OK to ask someone to repeat what they've said, but laughing at them is unlikely to go down well.

See the Glossary of British terms and abbreviations at the back of this book for explanations of some peculiarly English words, including those relating to road-use and cycling.

English is not Britain's only language. In parts of Wales (especially in the north), Welsh is the first language of many. Welsh is Celtic in origin and very different to English, making it difficult for foreigners (including those from England) to pronounce. Luckily for visitors, all Welsh speakers are also fluent in English. See the boxed text 'The Welsh Language' in the Wales chapter.

Scotland also has its own language – Gaelic – which is also Celtic in origin. It was once spoken in all of Scotland, but there are now only about 80,000 Gaelic speakers, mainly in north-western Scotland and the Hebridean islands. As in Wales, English is Scotland's *lingua franca*, but the Scots accent can make English almost unintelligible to outsiders, and there are numerous Gaelic and Lallan (Lowland Scots) words that linger in everyday English speech.

Facts for the Cyclist

HIGHLIGHTS

It cannot be denied that Britain is a crowded place, and its main roads can be uncomfortably busy, but a staggering network of minor roads and laneways make it possible to cycle just about anywhere without spending too much time in traffic. While there aren't any major mountain ranges in Britain, there are plenty of challenging riding in the Welsh and Scottish uplands. English terrain varies from the flat coastal lowlands of the east to the hilly Cotswolds, Peak District and Yorkshire Dales; in western England you'll find high and lonely moorlands and stunning coastline.

See the Table of Rides (pp4–5) for the page numbers of rides featuring these highlights:

Coastal Scenery
Isle of Mull Hard to beat in fine weather, this section on The West Coast ride serves a visual mixture of lush vegetation, white sandy beaches and reflections of mountains in the still sea lochs.

Cornish Coastline The coast of Cornwall on The South-West ride is dotted with charming seaside towns, craggy cliffs and sandy beaches.

Mountain Scenery
Isle of Skye's Cuillin Range This range on The West Coast ride varies from the smooth and rounded 'Red Cuillins', to dramatic, dark and jagged peaks.

Brecon Beacons & Snowdonia Regions For compact and accessible mountain scenery it's hard to beat these regions on the Lôn Las Cymru ride.

Top Downhills
Grampian Mountains Not for the faint-hearted, the Scottish highlands section of the Land's End to John o'Groats ride serves up a nightmarish climb with a reward of 10 glorious miles, dropping in altitude from 626.7m (2089ft) to 324.6m (1082ft).

Lake & Peak Districts, Brecon Beacons & Snowdonia Covered in the Northern England, Central England and Wales chapters, these regions provide several downhills that are a welcome relief from quite intense climbs.

Top Ascents
Glen Lyon This long, gradual rise on the Highlands Circuit passes alternately through lightly wooded fields and woodlands, eventually with mountains unfolding all around.

Talybont Reservoir to 'the Gap' This section on the Brecon Beacons Gap is challengingly long, yet fortunately also gradual (from 180m/590ft to 600m/1965ft), offering fine views and a lengthy descent.

Porlock Manor Estate Toll Road The 4.3mi climb to the A39 on The South-West ride rises from just above sea level to 410m (1345ft); the road passes through mixed woodland of great beauty before emerging into open heath and pasture, and the climbing is gradual and pleasant at every turn of the pedals.

Fitness Challenges
Perth to Grantown-on-Spey Stretching through the Grampians on the End to End ride involves eight significant climbs, four of them steep, over 97.5mi.

Lôn Las Cymru Very few parts of Wales are flat, and this ride is hilly throughout, featuring several long climbs.

Cornish Coast This leg on The South-West ride is notoriously up-and-down, although fortunately most of the climbs are short and sharp but they can be quite steep.

Remote Riding
Lairg to Betty Hill This section on the End to End ride has only an isolated inn and a small town (with a pub and one B&B) in 43.5mi.

Ardnamurchan Peninsula The unfortunate 18th-century inhabitants of this westernmost part of the British mainland fell foul of the Highland Clearances and the region, on The West Coast ride, is now home to few people and lots of sheep.

Wooler to Bellingham Travel lonely roads through the wilds of Northumberland National Park on the Northern Explorer ride.

Mountain Biking
Long Mynd This ride features great sweeping climbs and superb views in a surprisingly compact area.

Brecon Beacons This region, covered on the Brecon Beacons Gap and Lôn Las Cymru rides, is popular with off-roaders from all over Britain.

100mi South Downs Way The only National Trail on which mountain bikes are allowed for the entire length is covered on the South Downs Way & Beachy Head ride.

New Forest This ride in the Southern England chapter is the perfect introduction to off-road riding, with wide, flat, well-maintained trails and superb signposting.

Wildlife Spotting

Scotland's North This is the pick of Britain, with the first part of the Highlands Circuit ride good for forest-dwelling animals such as rabbits and squirrels. Between Dalmally and Oban on The West Coast ride there are plenty of highland cows, while the islands and far north coast is inhabited by marine mammals and seabirds.

Wales' Countryside Small herds of wild ponies roam the hillsides of the Brecon Beacons and Snowdonia, pine martens are quite common in the extensive conifer plantations of mid-Wales, and forest dwelling creatures such as rabbits, hares, foxes and grey squirrels can be seen all over.

Central & Eastern England Countryside This region is rich in pheasants in summertime, with a seal colony at Blakeney Point, on the Suffolk & Norfolk Coast ride.

Historical Touring

Scottish Borders Much evidence of the Roman invasion is on this ride, with stately homes, museums and plenty of easily accessible historical information.

Kilmartin Glen This stretch on The West Coast ride has easily visible evidence of early British peoples; known as the 'cradle of modern Scotland' it is where the Scotti tribe first came to Scotland from Ireland.

Berwick-upon-Tweed to Whitehaven This section on the Northern Explorer ride is crammed with sites connected with border warfare; Day 3 shadows Hadrian's Wall with its wealth of Roman sites, before passing Lanercost priory, from where Edward I briefly ruled the kingdom, and ends in Carlisle, with its castle and excellent Tullie House Museum.

Anglesey Evidence of Wales' earliest settlements, dating back to the Neolithic era and Bronze Age, (eg, the earth fort on Holyhead Mountain), can be seen on day seven of the Lôn Las Cymru ride.

Central England Explorer This ride travels past Domesday Book towns and villages, with evidence of Roman and Viking occupation, and various castles; also featured are the stone towns of Oundle and Stamford, the Brontë village of Haworth, and the John Bunyan town of Bedford.

South-East Coast This ride starts at England's ecclesiastical centre, Canterbury, and passes through a string of historic towns and villages en route to Portsmouth, long the seat of British naval power.

SUGGESTED ITINERARIES

For one- and two-week visits you'll get the best value by concentrating on a particular region. If you have a month or more to play with consider an extended tour or tours that will at least touch on most parts of Britain.

One Week

In Scotland, start with the Highlands Circuit (three days), then catch a train to Edinburgh for the Scottish Borders (three days).

The Northern Explorer (see the Northern England chapter; five days), A Cotswolds Triangle (see the Central England chapter; four days) and Suffolk and Norfolk Coast (see the Eastern England chapter; four days) rides all provide pleasant introductions to their respective regions. Consider supplementing any of these rides with a couple of days' riding and sightseeing in London.

The Lôn Las Cymru ride serves up seven days in Wales (see the Wales chapter); follow it with the Chepstow to Bristol section of the End to End ride, then return to London via the Across the South ride (see the Southern England chapter; three days).

In southern England, the South-East Coast and Isle of Wight rides add up to six days of cycling in Britain's warmest and driest corner. For an extra day's rest, combine the South-East Coast and either South Downs Way & Beachy Head or New Forest day rides (see the Southern England chapter).

Two Weeks

In Scotland, ride The West Coast ride (10 days), then take the train from Mallaig to Crianlarich and ride the Highlands Circuit (see the Scotland chapter).

For middle and northern England (see the Central England chapter), ride Central England Explorer (eight days), then go by train to Whitehaven for the Sea to Sea ride (see the Northern England chapter; four days).

This book provides 12 days of cycling in Wales, although a more interesting look at this part of Britain would come from completing the Lôn Las Cymru, riding from Holyhead to Chester via Conwy, then returning to Chepstow, in southern Wales, by doing the first three days of The Marches, Cheshire & Lancashire ride (see the Central England chapter) in reverse.

For a jaunt in southern England, follow the South-East Coast ride with a day in the New Forest, then take the train to Weymouth and do The South-West ride. See the Southern England chapter for more details.

One Month

With breaks from the saddle for sightseeing, the End to End ride (20 days) comfortably fills a month and showcases the entrancing diversity of Britain's landscape, people and settlements big and small. Alternatively, you could link several of the smaller regional rides. Try Westminster & the City (one day; see the London chapter), followed by the Isle of Wight ride (two days; see the Southern England chapter), Lôn Las Cymru (seven days; see the Wales chapter), Peak District (two days; see the Central England chapter), Northern Explorer (five days; see the Northern England chapter) and either The West Coast (nine days; see the Scotland chapter) or the Highlands Circuit (three days; see the Scotland chapter).

If you want an exclusively Scottish trip, do the Edinburgh Orientation and Scottish Borders rides, then catch a train to Ardrossan for The West Coast ride (nine days), followed by the Highlands Circuit (three days).

Two Months

If you've got 60 days to enjoy, we suggest a program that includes plenty of time for breaks and connecting train travel – one day off the bike for every five spent cycling.

Ease into the saddle with a day in London (any of the rides in the London chapter) and a day in the New Forest (see the Southern England chapter). Take the train to Weymouth, then ride six days of The South-West ride. At Land's End, pick up the End to End ride and stay with it for five days to Chep-

stow (see the Land's End to John o'Groats chapter). Then detour onto the Lôn Las Cymru (seven days; see the Wales chapter) and take it to Holyhead. Follow up with the Views from the Valley ride (see the Wales chapter), then pick up the last two days of The Marches, Cheshire & Lancashire ride (see the Central England chapter) to end your first month in Lancaster.

Kick off your explorations of Britain's northern half with the North York Moors & Mansions (four days) and wonderful Sea to Sea (C2C; four days) rides, both in the Northern England chapter. Follow with the Edinburgh Orientation, The West Coast ride (nine days; see the Scotland chapter) and a combination of the last section of the End to End ride and Highlands Circuit (six to seven days total; see the Land's End to John o'Groats and the Scotland chapters) to complete the journey.

PLANNING
When to Cycle

A busy mid-summer tourist season and cool, sometimes unpleasant winter weather narrow the periods during which cycling conditions are ideal in Britain. Roads are most crowded and accommodation is at a premium during the summer school holidays (August to September). The ideal time to tour is late March to late June, a period when there's lengthening daylight hours, warmer temperatures, and fewer tourists and holiday-makers about.

These cycling maps from the 19th century showed 'in a very clear manner the nature and surface of over 28,000 miles of road' and 'the position of 1700 dangerous hills'.

September or October are worth considering, as long as you keep in mind that days are becoming shorter and cooler.

Mid-winter touring in Scotland's north is out of the question given the risk of snowfall and very short days. Additionally, many services, such as ferries, run less frequently or close down between October and April, restricting the areas you can easily access. Expect wet weather whenever you ride in Scotland. May and June are the driest months. September is generally wetter, but it's after the main tourist rush.

The higher reaches of Wales and central and northern England are also subject to unfavourable winter weather. Lowland areas in these regions are rideable year-round, but to get the most cycling possible you're better off sticking to the spring-autumn window.

In the south it's possible to cycle year-round. Most areas are less crowded and no less beautiful in cooler weather, although reduced daylight hours can make longer days a bit of a rush. It's worth considering an autumn tour in the south, where fair cycling conditions extend into early November.

Maps

Britain's national mapping agency, Ordnance Survey (OS), has Britain covered at scales of 1:250,000 (Travelmaster series, £4.25 each) and 1:50,000 (Landranger series, £5.25 each). These maps are comprehensive, easy to read and regularly updated. Most of the rides in this book are on-road only. The Travelmaster series is fine for such rides. If a route includes some off-road riding, Landranger maps are superior, but each covers a smaller area, and using them for longer tours is therefore not really practical.

The OS *Outdoor Leisure* (1:25,000, £6.50) and *Explorer* (1:25,000, £5.50) series cover in great detail selected regions (for instance the New Forest); they're invaluable for off-road riding. The OS *Great Britain Route Planner* (1:625 000, £4.25) is useful for pre-trip planning.

Goldeneye produces a small (and growing) range of cycling-specific maps (£4.99) that highlight route suggestions and points of interest.

Unquestionably one of the best mapping resources is Sustrans' award-winning series of *National Cycle Network Route Map & Guides* (£5.99 each). These sheets break each stage of a long route into an individual panel, each including distance (traffic-free distance is indicated), an elevation cross-section, detailed inset maps for navigating through town centres, and useful contact numbers. There are currently 19 sheets in the series.

What to Bring

The greater your independence when touring, the greater your flexibility to adjust plans on the road. Maximum flexibility comes from carrying everything – including camping gear – on the bike. If this is the way you choose to travel, lightweight clothing and equipment is of critical importance. Fortunately the short distance between towns and villages reduces your need to carry food; generally you'll only need a day's supply at most.

The great choice of accommodation in Britain – especially B&Bs – makes touring without camping equipment a fine weight-saving option with a minimum loss of flexibility. You'll need to be slightly more organised when planning a route and – if touring in mid-summer – take more care to book accommodation in advance, but riding without a tent and sleeping bag is a great weight saver.

If you choose to join a supported tour you'll be confined to the organiser's specified route (not that this is necessarily a bad thing), but you'll probably have to carry little more than water, snacks and wet-weather gear. It's hardly independent travel, but it sure feels good on long uphill climbs.

Clothing For maximum comfort you are always better off using cycling-specific clothing, waterproofs and footwear.

Wear padded Lycra bike shorts ('knicks'), which prevent chafing, or 'shy shorts', which look like ordinary shorts and have a lightweight knick-style inner. Lightweight breathable cycling tops made from fabrics such as Coolmax or Intercool are best. Long-sleeved tops are best for cooler or very sunny conditions.

For cool or wet days you'll need to carry warm and waterproof clothing. Lycra tights or padded thermal 'longs' and breathable, waterproof overpants are essential for the cooler months in Britain. In the warmer months you can get away with just the overpants; indeed, in summer rain, many cyclists

Equipment Check List

This list is a general guide to the things you might take on a bike tour. Your list will vary depending on the kind of cycling you want to do, whether you're roughing it in a tent or planning on luxury accommodation, and on the time of year. Don't forget to take on board enough water and food to see you safely between towns.

Bike Clothing
- ☐ cycling gloves
- ☐ cycling shoes and socks
- ☐ cycling tights or leg-warmers
- ☐ helmet and visor
- ☐ long-sleeved shirt or cycling jersey
- ☐ padded cycling shorts (knicks)
- ☐ sunglasses
- ☐ thermal undershirt and arm-warmers
- ☐ T-shirt or short-sleeved cycling jersey
- ☐ visibility vest
- ☐ waterproof jacket & pants
- ☐ windproof jacket or vest

Off-Bike Clothing
- ☐ change of clothing
- ☐ spare shoes
- ☐ swimming costume
- ☐ sunhat
- ☐ fleece jacket
- ☐ thermal underwear
- ☐ underwear and spare socks
- ☐ warm hat and gloves

Equipment
- ☐ bike lights (rear and front) with spare batteries (see torch)
- ☐ elastic cords
- ☐ camera and spare film
- ☐ cycle computer
- ☐ day-pack
- ☐ medical kit* and toiletries
- ☐ sewing/mending kit (for everything)
- ☐ panniers and waterproof liners

- ☐ pocket knife (with corkscrew)
- ☐ sleeping sheet
- ☐ small handlebar bag and/or map case
- ☐ small towel/chamois travel towel
- ☐ tool kit, pump and spares*
- ☐ torch (flashlight) with spare batteries and globe – some double as (front) bike lights
- ☐ water containers
- ☐ water purification tablets, iodine or filter

Camping
- ☐ cooking, eating and drinking utensils
- ☐ clothesline
- ☐ dishwashing items
- ☐ portable stove and fuel
- ☐ insulating mat
- ☐ matches or lighter and candle
- ☐ sleeping bag
- ☐ tent
- ☐ toilet paper and toilet trowel

* see the 'First Aid Kit' boxed text in the Health & Safety chapter; 'Spares & Tool Kit' boxed text in the Your Bicycle chapter

Gosh! Lots of luggage. Where's your bike? In there... somewhere!

prefer to wear only a waterproof top and let their knicks get wet. Tops and bottoms come in a range of fabrics. Some, such as Activent or Pertex, are compact and lightweight but won't really withstand heavy rain; these are a good choice for longs. Gore-Tex is still the preferred fabric for jackets.

Choose bright colours for all your cycling gear, especially your wet-weather top. They are cooler and more visible to motorists.

Fingerless cycling gloves reduce jarring on your hands, stop sunburn and protect your palms if you fall. Full-finger gloves are a sensible addition for cycling in Britain, even in summertime. You can also get thin polypropylene 'inner' gloves – best worn under regular fingerless gloves – or longer wind- and/or rain-resistant models.

Helmets aren't compulsory in Britain but you're always wise to wear one. A cloth cover that sports both a peak to help keep sun and rain off your face, and a legionnaire-style back flap to protect your neck from sunburn is a wise addition. Sunglasses or eye wear with clear protective lenses are essential. They protect your eyes from UV radiation, insects, and from drying out in the wind.

Stiff-soled cycling shoes transfer power more efficiently from pedal stroke to pedal. Soft-soled training shoes lack the same 'drive' and using them can leave you with sore feet. Thermal socks and neoprene booties are useful for cold and/or wet days.

Off the Bike Pack as little additional clothing as you can reasonably get away with. Let the main influence on your after-cycling kit be the style of accommodation you've chosen and, to a lesser extent, the type of eating out you plan to do.

Whether you go all-casual (track pants and T-shirts) or with a tad more style (a shirt with a collar, perhaps), try not to duplicate items (socks and undies excepted). For instance, you should only take a long-sleeved T-shirt – you can always roll up the sleeves on warm nights. Choose colours that will look acceptable without washing,

and that will endure a bit of flapping around on your panniers – the unofficial (and very effective) on-the-road clothes-drying rack.

Campers need to place greater emphasis on warm clothing. Thermal underwear is warm and compact. A synthetic fleece jacket is probably best for warmth as it will also come in handy for cold days on the bike. Not quite as versatile but very compact is a lightweight down jacket in a stuff sack. Take only lightweight cotton trousers – you can wear your thermals underneath on a cold night. A lightweight folding umbrella is useful for wet nights when your wet-weather gear is already soaked.

Remember also to take a separate pair of shoes.

Bicycle For detailed information on types of bicycles and necessary additional equipment for touring see the Your Bicycle chapter.

If you're new to the cycle-touring caper and looking to buy a bike in Britain, it's best to make your purchase from a big bike shop in a city. Many stock specialist touring bikes as well as hybrids and mountain bikes, and staff can advise you on the best type and size of bike for starting out. For more information see the Buying or Hiring Locally section, later.

Camping & Outdoor Equipment If you're camping you'll obviously need to take a tent, sleeping mat and a sleeping bag

'John Piggott's Touring Outfits. Best Value in the World.'
Cycling clothing has come a long way since this ad dated 28 August 1907.

A Cycling Survivor

In many ways cycle touring is an activity that evokes memories of times past, a slower, gentler form of travel. It's nice to know then that while most cyclists these days understandably opt for the performance of high-tech frames and components, one piece of equipment, and a British one at that, has largely survived the technological onslaught and remains the choice of many touring cyclists – the Brooks saddle. In a recent issue of *Men's Journal* magazine, the Brooks B17, a touring favourite, was included in their list of '85 Perfect Things'.

Proudly handmade in Nottingham for over 130 years, few pieces of cycling kit enjoy such a loyal following. Looking oh-so retro, all leather and studded with large copper rivets, the classic designs have changed little over the years. It's easy to picture Biggles with his posterior parked on one, pedaling his rod-brake Hercules off to the aerodrome. To the unacquainted they're heavy and look painfully hard, but stop for a roadside chat with a Brooks owner and they'll set about converting you from foam and plastic with near missionary zeal. I was first introduced by an English couple on a five year around-the-world marathon tour who spoke of theirs so lovingly, you might have thought they were talking about their first born.

If you do get one however, don't throw away your padded bike shorts straight away. Achieving saddle nirvana on a Brooks can require more than a little patience. During the 'breaking in' process the leather, like a good pair of shoes, moulds to fit the contours of your rear. People have come up with all sorts of ways to speed up this sometimes lengthy process, from bashing the seat with a rolling pin to soaking it in the bathtub (neither endorsed by the manufacturer), but in reality there's no real substitute for time on the road.

They're not everyone's cup of tea but if you're looking to pick up a practical souvenir of your tour around Britain, you could do worse than a Brooks.

Ian Duckworth

and a camping stove (open fires are generally not allowed), as well as cooking and eating utensils.

Your tent needn't be expedition strength (although you should expect some fairly wild winds from time to time) but it must be lightweight and waterproof. A sleeping bag rated 0°C is fine for summer touring; a -5°C rated bag is better for winter. If you take your own stove, remember that fuel can't be carried on the aircraft.

Britain is well served with specialist outdoor equipment shops if you choose to buy camping gear or outdoor clothing on arrival.

Buying & Hiring Locally Bicycle shops and their range of goods will vary in size and quality depending on location. In major centres, most shops are well stocked with a range of cycles and accessories for all types of cycling, including specialist touring bikes.

In small towns the local sporting-goods emporium sometimes doubles as the cycle shop. Most have such essentials as standard-sized tyre tubes and puncture kits.

Currency exchange rates will influence your view of local prices. You ought to be able to buy a decent basic bike in the £250 to £400 range. Once over £550 you'll be buying better quality frame materials and components. Don't expect to pay less than £1000 for a top-class touring bike. You should be able to find a pair of rear panniers for less than £100 (quite a bit less if you opt for lesser quality) and front panniers from £60 to £50 and under.

The Cyclists' Touring Club's (CTC; see the Useful Organisations section in this chapter for more information) magazine *Cycle Touring and Campaigning* (£2.50, free to members) will be useful if you plan to buy a lot of your touring kit in Britain. It has a range of advertisements for specialist touring frame builders, equipment suppliers and shops, and its 'Small Ads' (classifieds) section has a listing for private sales of bikes and equipment. Some shops sell second-hand equipment, although prices tend to be better if you buy privately.

Hiring a bicycle is a good option, provided you're prepared (and have the know-how) to do some work and possibly spend a little extra money to personalise the set-up. Most decent hire shops have a range of cycles of varying age and quality, so take your time when choosing. Look for the basics – frame and wheels – to be in good shape, a comfortable saddle (if you haven't brought your own from home) and quality alloy components. Most hire outlets charge on a decreasing scale: probably in the range of £25 to £35 for the first week, £18 to £25 for the second week and less again for weeks thereafter. If you're hiring for an extended period, don't be afraid to haggle. The CTC's *Cycle Hire Directory* has a comprehensive list of hire outlets arranged by region. It's free to members; within Britain, send a self-addressed A5 envelope to the CTC. Check with the CTC office (see the Useful Organisations entry in this chapter) if you're mailing from outside Britain.

TOURIST OFFICES
Local Tourist Offices
Every British town (and many villages) has its own Tourist Information Centre (TIC) which have a wide range of information, particularly about the region within a 50-mile radius. Most also operate a local bed-booking system and a Book-A-Bed-Ahead (BABA) scheme. In addition there are National Park Visitor Information Centres. Local libraries are also good sources of information.

Most TICs are open from 9 am to 5 pm Monday to Friday. In popular tourist areas they generally stay open later in the evening and also open on Saturday. In real honeypots like Stratford and Bath they'll be open seven days a week throughout the year. From October to March many smaller TICs are either closed or open only for limited hours.

Some TICs have 24-hour computer databases that can be accessed even when the office is closed. Others put posters with basic information about accommodation and a town plan in the window.

The Wales Tourist Board (WTB; ☎ 029-2049 9909, ☐ www.tourism.wales.gov.uk) has its headquarters in Brunel House, 2 Fitzalan Rd, Cardiff CF2 1UY. There's a branch in the British Travel Centre (☎ 020-7808 3838), in London. The WTB has a range of comprehensive free publications, including some on cycling.

The Scottish Tourist Board (STB; ☎ 0131-472 2035, fax 315 4545, ☐ www.visitscotland.com) has its headquarters at 23 Ravelston Terrace (PO Box 705), Edinburgh EH4 3EU (STB London office ☎ 020-7930 8661).

Tourist Offices Abroad
British Tourist Authority (BTA) offices stock masses of information, much of it free. It's worth contacting the BTA before you leave home; some of the discounts they offer are only available to people who book before arriving in Britain.

Overseas, the BTA represents the tourist boards of England, Scotland and Wales. The BTA Web site (☐ www.bta.org.uk) is comprehensive, and includes the addresses of over 40 BTA offices worldwide, as well as many useful links.

Addresses of some offices are:

Australia (☎ 02-9377 4400, fax 9377 4499) Level 16, The Gateway, 1 Macquarie Place, Circular Quay, Sydney, NSW 2000
Canada (☎ 416-925 6326, fax 961 2175) Suite 450, 111 Avenue Rd, Toronto, Ontario M5R 3JD
France (☎ 01 44 51 56 20) Tourisme de Grand-Bretagne, Maison de la Grande Bretagne, 19 Rue des Mathurins, 75009 Paris (entrance in les Rues Tronchet et Auber)
Germany (☎ 069-238 0711) Taunusstrasse 52–60, 60329 Frankfurt
Ireland (☎ 01-670 8000) 18–19 College Green, Dublin 2
Netherlands (☎ 020-685 50 51) Stadhouderskade 2 (5e), 1054 ES Amsterdam
New Zealand (☎ 09-303 1446, fax 377 6965) 3rd floor, Dilworth Building, cnr Queen & Customs Sts, Auckland 1
USA (☎ 1 800 GO 2 BRITAIN) 625 N Michigan Avenue, Suite 1510, Chicago IL 60611 (personal callers only), 551 Fifth Ave, Suite 701, New York, NY 10176-0799

VISAS & DOCUMENTS
Passport & Visas
All foreign nationals entering Britain need a passport. It should be valid for the period of your visit and at least six months after.

You don't need a passport to travel between England, Scotland and Wales. If you arrive in Scotland or Wales from the Republic of Ireland or any other country, normal British customs and immigration regulations apply.

Visa regulations are always subject to change, so it's essential to check the situation with your local British embassy, high commission or consulate before leaving home. Currently, citizens of Australia, Canada, New Zealand, South Africa and the USA don't need visas to enter Britain; you're given 'leave to enter' at your place of arrival. Tourists from these countries are generally permitted to stay for up to six months, but are prohibited from working. To stay longer you need to apply for an entry clearance certificate at the high commission.

Citizens of the European Union (EU) can live and work in Britain free of immigration control. You don't need a visa to enter the country.

Visa Extensions

To extend your stay in Britain contact the Home Office (☎ 020-8686 0688), Immigration and Nationality Department, Lunar House, Wellesley Rd, Croydon CR9 2BY UK, *before* your existing permit expires. You'll need to send your passport or ID card with your application.

Onward Tickets

Although you don't need an onward ticket to be granted 'leave to enter' on arrival, this could help if there's any doubt over whether you have sufficient funds to support yourself and then purchase an onward ticket in Britain.

Travel Insurance

A travel insurance policy to cover theft, loss and medical problems is essential. Some policies offer lower and higher medical expense options – go for as much as you can afford.

Always read the small print carefully. Some policies specifically exclude 'dangerous activities' such as scuba diving, motorcycling, skiing, mountaineering and even trekking. Obviously, make sure that cycling *isn't* excluded.

In general, policies that pay doctors or hospitals directly (rather than you having to pay and claim the money back later) are better. If you have to claim later, make sure you keep all documentation. Some policies ask

you to call (reverse charges) a centre in your home country where an immediate assessment of your problem is made.

Check that your policy covers ambulance, helicopter rescue or emergency flights home. Most policies exclude cover for pre-existing illnesses, including HIV/AIDS.

Other Documents

Apart from your passport, no special documents are required for Britain, but there are a number you should consider.

Your normal driving licence is legal for 12 months from the date you last entered Britain; you can then apply for a British licence at post offices. Ask your automobile association for a Card of Introduction. This entitles you to services offered by British sister organisations (touring maps and information, help with breakdowns, technical and legal advice etc), usually free of charge.

Your local automobile association also issues a Camping Card International, which is basically a camping ground ID. They're also issued by local camping federations, and sometimes on the spot at camping grounds. They incorporate third party insurance for damage you may cause, and many camping grounds offer a small discount if you sign in with one. Some hostels and hotels also accept carnets for signing-in purposes, but won't give discounts.

Membership of the Youth Hostel Association (YHA) or Hostelling International (HI) is a must (£11 over-18-years-old, £5.50 under-18). There are around 320 hostels in Britain and members are also eligible for all sorts of discounts. See the Accommodation section later in this chapter for more information about hostelling in Britain.

An International Student Identity Card (ISIC) can yield many benefits, including discounts on many forms of transport and cheap or free admission to attractions, as well as cheap meals in some student restaurants. There's a worldwide industry in fake student cards, and many places now stipulate a maximum age for student discounts or, more simply, substitute a 'youth discount' for a 'student discount'. If you're under 26 but not a student, you can apply for a Federation of International Youth Travel Organisations (FIYTO) card or a Euro26 Card. These cards give much the same discounts. Your hostelling organisation should be able to help with this. Both types of card are issued by student unions, hostelling organisations and student travel agencies. They don't automatically entitle you to discounts, but you won't know unless you try.

Discount cards for over 60s are available for rail travel, the best option for cyclists. See the Railcards entry in the Getting Around chapter for more information.

You'll need an International Health Card & Form E111 if you're travelling onwards through parts of Asia, Africa and South America, where yellow fever is prevalent. If you're a national of another EU country, Form E111 (available from post offices) entitles you to free or reduced-cost medical treatment in Britain.

Copies

It's wise to keep photocopies of all important documents (passport, air tickets, insurance policy, travellers cheques serial numbers) in a separate place in case of theft. Stash £50 away with the photocopies just in case. Ideally, you should leave a second set of copies with someone in your home country.

EMBASSIES & CONSULATES
British Embassies & Consulates

Some British embassies abroad include:

Australia (☎ 02-6270 6666) Commonwealth Ave, Yarralumla, Canberra, ACT 2600
Canada (☎ 613-237 1530) 80 Elgin St, Ottawa K1P 5K7
France (☎ 01 42 66 38 10) 9 Ave Hoche, 8e, Paris
Germany (☎ 0228-23 40 61) Friedrich-Ebert-Allee 77, 53113 Bonn
Ireland (☎ 01-205 3742) 29 Merrion Rd, Ballsbridge, Dublin 4
Japan (☎ 03-3265 5511) 1 Ichiban-cho, Chiyoda-ku, Tokyo
Netherlands (☎ 070-427 0427) Lange Voorhout 10, 2514 ED, The Hague
New Zealand (☎ 04-472 6049) 44 Hill St, Wellington 1
South Africa (☎ 21-461 7220) 91 Parliament St, Cape Town 8001
USA (☎ 202-462 1340) 3100 Massachusetts Ave NW, Washington DC 20008

Embassies & Consulates in Britain

Countries with diplomatic representation in Britain include:

Australia (☎ 020-7465 8218) Australia House, The Strand, London WC2

Canada (☎ 020-7629 9492) Macdonald House, 1 Grosvenor Square, London W1
France (☎ 020-7838 2050) 6A Cromwell Place, London SW7
Germany (☎ 020-7824 1300) 23 Belgrave Square, London SW1
Ireland (☎ 020-7235 2171) 17 Grosvenor Place, London SW1
Japan (☎ 020-7465 6500) 101 Piccadilly, London W1
Netherlands (☎ 020-7584 5040) 38 Hyde Park Gate, London SW7
New Zealand (☎ 09069-100 100) New Zealand House, 80 Haymarket, London SW1
South Africa (☎ 020-7930 4488) Trafalgar Square, London WC2
USA (☎ 020-7499 9000) 5 Upper Grosvenor St, London W1

France, Germany, the Netherlands, Japan, Canada and the USA all have consulates in Edinburgh.

CUSTOMS

If you're entering Britain from a non-EU country (including the Canary Islands, the Channel Islands and Gibraltar) there are strict allowances for the quantity of goods you may import duty free. These are: 200 cigarettes or 250g of tobacco, 2L of still wine plus one litre of spirits or another 2L of wine (sparkling or otherwise), 60 cc of perfume, 250 cc of toilet water, and all other goods (including gifts and souvenirs) to the value of £145. If you bring in something over the £145 limit you'll have to pay charges on the full value, not just the value above £145. If you're travelling with friends, you can't 'pool' allowances for a single item worth more than the limit – you'll have to pay charges on the full value of the item.

If you have no more than these allowances and no banned or restricted goods you should go through the green 'nothing to declare' exit. If you need to declare goods, or if you're not sure, go through the red exit (or use the phone provided).

For travellers entering Britain from other EU countries there is a separate exit (usually marked with a blue sign). If you're using the blue exit, you're entitled to bring in 'guideline' quantities of tobacco and alcohol *for your own use* (800 cigarettes, 400 cigarillos, 200 cigars, 1kg of smoking tobacco, 10L of spirits, 20L of fortified wine, 90L of wine – only 60 of which may be sparkling – and 110L of beer).

Customs officials carry out spot checks at blue exits for banned and restricted goods. If you're checked and found to be carrying more alcohol or tobacco than the guidelines allow, you must be able to satisfy the official that the goods are for your own use. If you can't, the goods may be confiscated.

If you're under 17, you're not entitled to the tobacco or alcohol allowance in any circumstance.

MONEY
Currency
The British currency is the pound sterling (£), with 100 pence (p) to a pound. One and 2p coins are copper; 5p, 10p, 20p and 50p coins are silver; the £1 coin is gold-coloured; and the £2 coin gold and silver-coloured. Like its written counterpart the word pence is usually abbreviated and pronounced 'pee'.

Notes (bills) come in £5, £10, £20 and £50 denominations and vary in colour and size. You may also come across notes issued by several Scottish banks, which are legal tender on both sides of the border. If you have any problems getting them accepted in England and Wales, ask a bank to swap them for you. Wales has the same currency as England and you will find the same banks and ATMs.

Exchange Rates
The currencies in the table below, as well as many other European currencies, are all readily exchanged in Britain. Check up-to-date exchange rates (🖥 www.x-rates.com).

country	unit	euro	pound
Australia	A$1	€0.61	£0.37
Canada	C$1	€0.75	£0.45
euro	€1	–	£0.60
France	10FF	€1.50	£0.92
Germany	DM1	€0.51	£0.31
Japan	¥100	€1.00	£0.65
Netherlands	fl	€0.45	£0.27
New Zealand	NZ$1	€0.46	£0.28
USA	US$1	€1.17	£0.70

Exchanging Money
In Britain it's wise to always have some cash at hand, and to travel with a widely accepted credit card. Except for big hotels, you won't find too many places that take travellers cheques for everyday transactions.

Cash The bureaux de change at international seaports and airports are open 24 hours, charge less than most High St banks, and guarantee that you can buy up to £500 worth of most major currencies on the spot. Some airport foreign exchanges will also accept foreign coins – a rarity at banks. Bank hours vary but you'll be safe if you visit between 9.30 am and 3.30 pm, Monday to Friday.

It's difficult to open a bank account, but if you're planning to work it may be essential. Building societies tend to be more welcoming and often have better interest rates. You'll need a (semi) permanent address, and it will smooth the way considerably if you have a reference or introductory letter from your bank manager at home, as well as bank statements for the previous year. Owning credit/charge cards also helps.

Travellers Cheques Travellers cheques have an advantage when it comes to security. American Express, MasterCard, Visa and Thomas Cook travellers cheques are widely recognised and have efficient replacement policies. Remember to keep records of cheque numbers and cheques cashed separate from the cheques themselves.

Bring travellers cheques in pounds sterling to avoid changing currencies twice. Bureaux de change at international airports and seaports cash sterling travellers cheques free of charge. American Express offices are often cheapest, charging 1% commission, with no minimum charge. Banks charge commissions (usually in the 1% to 2% range) and usually have a minimum charge in the £3 to £5 range.

ATMs Known as cashpoints in Britain, ATMs are usually linked to international money systems such as Cirrus, Maestro or Plus. This allows you to use the 'cash card' you use in your home country. ATMs aren't fail-safe, especially if the card was issued outside Europe, but card-swallowing episodes are rare.

Credit Cards Credit and credit/debit cards like Visa and MasterCard (also known as Access in Britain) are widely accepted. Costs are low provided you select an account with low fees and avoid interest charges by keeping your account in credit. Carry a credit card with a PIN and you can also make withdrawals from ATMs – request a PIN from your bank and ask which ATMs abroad will accept your particular card.

If you're relying on plastic, go for two different cards – an American Express or Diners Club with a Visa or MasterCard. Better still, combine plastic and travellers cheques so you have something to fall back on if an ATM swallows your card or the local banks don't accept your card.

International Transfers It's always wise to give someone back home the authority to access your bank account in case of emergency, but these days money transfers, however they're sent, are costly. It's better and faster to have your account keeper move some cash into your credit card account. If your credit card is linked to a savings account you may even be able to transfer the money yourself with phone banking facilities.

You can also transfer money via American Express or Thomas Cook, but be sure to check the charges. Americans can also use Western Union although it has fewer offices in Britain from which to collect.

Moneychangers Be careful using bureaux de change outside of international airports and seaports. They frequently levy outrageous commissions and fees, so make sure you check in advance. You'll find bureaux de change in many TICs.

Security

Routine caution is sufficient – you can't prepare for an outbreak of bad luck. Never leave valuables in panniers or handlebar bags when you lock your bike and walk away, and be extra careful in cities and large regional centres.

Costs

Britain is an expensive place to travel. Travelling primarily by bicycle will certainly reduce some of your overheads, but you'll still have to budget carefully. Accommodation will be the biggest expense wherever you go, with the cost of a bed highest in the big cities, especially London.

Camping and camping barns (where available) are the cheapest alternative; they'll cost from £1.50 to £8 per person per night. But chances are that inclement weather will drive you gratefully indoors

from time to time. Prices in hostels vary; a bed in a basic country hostel will be between £7 and £10, while London hostels charge between £16 and £23. A night in a home-style B&B (with shared facilities) might be as little as £15 in the sticks; you'll pay a lot more in the cities if you want a central location and private facilities. Depending on location and facilities, hotel rooms range from £20 to £30 (in budget establishments with shared facilities) to much, much more than you want to pay if you're reading this book.

Even on a survival diet of fruit, dry bread, basic pasta and tap water you'll need a minimum of £4 to £7 a day. Fresh food costs roughly the same as in Australia and the USA. Pub meals aren't always wonderful but they're filling and usually among the cheapest hot meals; main course prices start at £3 to £4 in the countryside, more in cities. Restaurant food shows a wide variation in price and quality. You'll be lucky to find a pint of beer anywhere for much less than £2.

Entry fees to attractions vary considerably. Some of the very best are cheap or free; sometimes the tackiest are outrageously expensive. If you're hell-bent on seeing something in particular check the admission fee in advance and budget accordingly.

Transportation costs will prompt you to use your bicycle on all but the most inclement days. Buses are the cheapest alternative but they're not the best for bicycles (many companies don't carry bikes at all; others will insist that you dismantle your bike – a particular nuisance on short hops). Domestic air travel is more expensive than buses but similarly inconvenient. Trains, the most convenient option, are in between; discounts are available if you book ahead and as a result this is always advisable. For more information on traveling within Britain see the Getting Around chapter.

Backpacker accommodation is more readily available in Scotland than in England, so you'll be able to keep costs down. Edinburgh is more expensive than most other mainland Scottish towns, however, prices rise steeply in remote parts of the Highlands and on the Islands where supplies depend on ferries. Petrol can cost 10p to 15p a litre more on the Islands than in the central Lowlands.

Tipping & Bargaining

If you eat in a restaurant you should generally leave a tip of at least 10% unless the service was unsatisfactory. If the bill already includes a service charge of 10% to 15% you needn't add a further tip.

Taxi drivers also expect to be tipped (about 10%), especially in London. It's less usual to tip minicab drivers.

Bargaining is virtually unheard of, even at markets, although it's fine to ask if there are discounts for students, young people, or youth hostel or CTC members.

Value-Added Tax

A value-added tax (VAT) of 17.5% is levied on virtually all goods and services except food and books. Restaurant prices must by law include VAT.

POST & COMMUNICATIONS
Post

Post office hours can vary, but most are open from 9 am to 5 pm, Monday to Friday, and from 9 am to noon on Saturday.

If you don't have a permanent address, mail can be sent to poste restante in the town or city where you are staying. American Express Travel offices will also hold card-holders' mail free of charge.

An air-mail letter generally takes less than a week to get to the USA or Canada, and around a week to get to Australia or New Zealand.

Telephone

Pay phones are abundant. You'll find them in the most out-of-the-way places, and all come with reasonably clear instructions (for English readers). Local, national and international calls are charged by time. The cheapest rates are available on weekends and between 6 pm and 8 am on weekdays. It's wise to buy a phonecard if you want to avoid a pannier-pocket full of coins.

BT phonecards cost from £2 to £20 and are available at all sorts of retailers, but their rates aren't competitive, especially for international calls. Cards from any of several private phone service providers, such as Swiftlink and Alpha Telecom, offer better value. They can be used from any touch-tone phone, even a home phone. Provided you have a credit card you can top up your account over the phone.

In this guide, telephone area codes are listed at the start of the town entry. Other codes worth knowing about are:

service	code
Britain (UK) country code	☎ 44
call is free to caller	☎ 0800
call is free to caller	☎ 0808
emergency (fire, police	
or ambulance)	**☎ 999**
international direct-dial code	☎ 00
international directory assistance	☎ 153
international operator	☎ 155
local and national operator	☎ 100
local call rates apply	☎ 0845
national call rates apply	☎ 0870
national directory assistance	☎ 192
premium rates apply	☎ 090

Beware of other codes that may indicate you're calling a mobile phone. This is usually considerably more expensive than calling a conventional phone.

Fax

Many hotels, motels and many hostels have fax machines. Shops offering a fax service will probably have a sign on the door. It's generally cheaper to make a phone call or check email at a cybercafe.

Email & Internet Access

Modern hotels will be geared up for access and most big towns have at least one cybercafe. Bear in mind that, among western nations, Britain's take-up rate for Internet access is low.

INTERNET RESOURCES

Britain has plenty of Web sites to interest cyber-travellers. An increasing number of towns, attractions, organisations and B&Bs have their own Web sites. The Lonely Planet Web site (🖳 www.lonelyplanet.com.au) is the best place to find links to numerous sites of interest to travellers to Britain.

The Cyber Cyclery (🖳 www.cycling.org), is US-based but it takes a world view – it's a remarkable resource. UK sites with a good range of general links include Cycling.UK (🖳 www.cycling.uk.com), Cyclehub (🖳 www.cyclehub.co.uk), the CTC site (🖳 www.ctc.org.uk), the London Cycling Campaign site (🖳 www.lcc.org.uk), the British Cycling Federation (BCF) site (🖳 www.bcf.uk.com) and the Association of Cycle Traders site

(⌨ www.CycleSource.co.uk). The on-line hub for touring cyclists is very useful (⌨ www.hikerbiker.co.uk). It includes information about (and links to) accommodation options, route information, weather news and several other topics. Sustrans (⌨ www.sustrans.org.uk) has an on-line shop through which you can order its award-winning National Cycling Network (NCN) maps.

Full contact details for several of the organisations mentioned here, can be found in the Useful Organisations section, later in this chapter.

BOOKS

The Arts section in the Facts about Britain chapter gives an overview of Britain's rich contribution to English-language literature. When you arrive, one of your first stops should be a good bookshop such as WH Smith or Books. For travel books and maps, Stanford's in Covent Garden, London (☎ 020-7836 1915), 12-14 Long Acre, WC2, is beyond compare. YHA Adventure Shops and various other outdoor equipment retailers are also well stocked with a range of travel titles and maps.

There are numerous local guidebooks dealing with travel and life in regional England, Scotland and Wales. Many are stocked by the larger TICs and by bookshops at visitor attractions. The most useful are mentioned in text in the relevant chapters. Some of the many guides to B&Bs, restaurants, hotels, country houses, camping and caravan parks, and self-catering cottages are of questionable objectivity as the places they cover pay for inclusion. Those published by the tourist authorities are reliable (if not comprehensive) and widely available in TICs. The *Which?* books produced by the Consumers' Association are useful and accurate – plus, no money changes hands for recommendations.

Lonely Planet

For general information, *Britain* is best. *Walking in Britain* expands on country travel and out-of-the-way accommodation, as well as detailing walks for those craving a change of pace. Guides like *Scotland*, *London* and *Edinburgh* have more detailed information if you're planning extended visits to these places. *Out to Eat – London* has a good overview of London restaurants.

Cycling

The range of cycling publications is extensive, and one of the better places to begin your investigations is the Bicycling Books on-line catalogue (⌨ www.bikebook.demon.co.uk). The CTC's *Cycle A-way!* (£2 for CTC members, £4 for nonmembers; send money and A5-sized stamped, addressed envelope to CTC; see the Useful Organisations section, later in this chapter, for the address) lists cycle routes throughout Britain and Ireland and the various publications (including free information) that cover them.

Among recent publications, the *Ordnance Survey Cycle Tour* series is excellent for planning short tours in particular regions; there are 16 titles in the series, covering Britain from Scotland to Cornwall and including Wales. *Stillwell's Britain Cycleway Companion* lists places to stop and stay along 20 Sustrans and CTC routes.

In many popular cycling areas, local councils and tourist authorities produce a range of brochures and pamphlets detailing routes and the services along them, such as accommodation and repair shops. Usually available in TICs, these are often free (or, at worst, inexpensive) and provide a wealth of information.

General

For history, art and architecture, the excellent *Blue Guide* series offers a wealth of scholarly information on all the important sites, including good maps. They have separate guides to England, Scotland and Wales.

People of a literary bent might like to look at the *Oxford Literary Guide to Great Britain and Ireland*, which details the many writers who have immortalised various towns and villages. *A Traveller's History of England* by Christopher Daniell offers a quick introduction to English history. For a left-looking analysis of Britain's position at the close of the 20th century, try either *The State We're In* or *The State to Come*, both by *Observer* editor Will Hutton.

Bill Bryson's highly entertaining and perceptive *Notes from a Small Island* is a recent travelogue covering Britain. Older but still readable is John Hillaby's *Journey Through Britain* which describes a 1969 walk from Land's End to John o'Groats, great for measuring the changes that have taken place over the last 30 years. Nick Danziger's picture of late 20th century Britain in *Danziger's*

Britain (1997) is thoroughly depressing but this guy has seen the world and if this is how he says it is, then it's hard to argue with him.

Natasha Walter has written an upbeat account of the state of late 20th century feminism in Britain in *The New Feminism*. One of the striking things about the 1997 election was the arrival of 100-odd female MPs in a House of Commons previously even more dominated by men. Linda McDougall's *Westminster Women* examines what difference their presence is likely to make.

Windrush – The Irresistible Rise of Multi-Racial Britain by Mike and Trevor Phillips traces the history of black Britain and the impact of immigrants on British society.

For Scottish history, try Richard Killeen's *A Short History of Scotland*, a concise and up-to-date introduction. One of the greatest Scottish travelogues is *The Journal of a Tour to the Hebrides with Samuel Johnson* by James Boswell. *Native Stranger* (1995), by Alistair Scott, recounts the efforts of a Scot (who knew 'more about the Sandinistas') to learn about the realities of modern Scotland by travelling throughout the country. *Danziger's Britain* describes the grim reality of life for many marginalised people in the Highlands and Glasgow.

For an entertaining description of Wales and its history, look for Jan Morris's *The Matter of Wales*, a modern travel writer's account of her home country. John Davies' *A History of Wales* fills in the more prosaic facts and figures.

NEWSPAPERS & MAGAZINES
Newspapers
Britons retain an insatiable appetite for newsprint and are served widely, if not always well, by national, regional and local newspapers. Most national dailies cover European pro road-racing, with some reporting on the big events, especially the Tour de France. The best coverage comes from *The Guardian*. There's no coverage of mountain bike racing.

For general content in the national dailies, the tabloid gutter-press – represented by such institutions as *The Sun*, *The Mirror*, the *Daily Star* and *The Sport* – is great for a laugh but short on useful and objective reporting. The tabloid market includes the Conservative-leaning *Daily Mail*, the *Daily Express* and the *European*, which makes an honourable

attempt to make the British feel part of the continent. Broadsheets include some of the world's better written and edited English-language newspapers. Try the *Daily Telegraph* if your politics are Tory. *The Times*, once Britain's finest paper, has lost ground under Rupert Murdoch's ownership but remains conservative and influential. Try either *The Independent* or the mildly left-wing *The Guardian* for alternative points of view.

Scotland's home-grown dailies include the *Scotsman*, the *Herald* (formerly the *Glasgow Herald*) and the tabloid *Daily Record*. Most papers sold elsewhere in Britain are available in Scotland, some with specific for Scottish editions. In Wales, try the *Western Mail*.

Sunday papers loom large in British life and most of the national dailies have a Sunday stablemate that shares their political views. The oldest of the Sundays, *The Observer*, is the seventh day version of *The Guardian*. The *Sunday Post* is Scotland's best-selling Sunday paper. *Wales on Sunday* is the *Western Mail*'s stablemate.

Magazines
There's a range of British cycling magazines of offer, each with a calendar of events and classifieds. The general interest monthlies are *Cycling Today* and *Cycling Plus*.

Racing enthusiasts are well served. *Pro Cycling* and *Cycle Sport* cover the road scene; *Cycling Weekly* covers mostly road racing with some other disciplines, while *Mountain Biker International* is exclusively dedicated to mountain bike racing.

Mountain bike monthlies, which include club listings, are *Mountain Biking UK* and *Mountain Bike Rider*.

For tourers, the CTC magazine *Cycle Touring and Campaigning* (free to CTC members – see the Useful Organisations section later in this chapter) is aimed at a more mature audience, but it's certainly informative and includes a useful events calendar and, from time to time, contact lists for local clubs and district associations.

WEATHER FORECASTS
The best advice with Britain's weather is to come prepared for all conditions whatever season you choose to ride, to check regional climatic variations while planning rides and to stay abreast of forecasts along the way.

Telephone Weather Services

In a region known for its changeable weather conditions, it's useful to have access to up-to-date forecasts before heading out into exposed or remote areas.

Weather Check is a telephone weather service that gives seven-day national and regional forecasts.

For the national forecast, dial ☎ 0891-333 111 100. For regional forecasts, dial ☎ 0891-333 111 plus the code for the region (listed below). Calls are charged at 50p per minute. The Helpline is ☎ 08705-133 345. The regional codes are:

region	code
west Highlands & Islands	☎ 101
east Highlands	☎ 102
central & southern Scotland	☎ 103
north-east England	☎ 105
north-west England	☎ 106
Midlands	☎ 107
south-east England	☎ 108
central England	☎ 109
south-east England	☎ 110
central south coast	☎ 111
south-west England	☎ 112
Wales	☎ 113

CLIMBline, on the same number, offers additional service for mountainous regions, including details of wind speed and direction, cloud base and freezing level. The codes are:

mountainous region	code
west Highlands	☎ 198
east Highlands	☎ 197
Peak District	☎ 195
Snowdonia	☎ 199

Not surprisingly, British newspapers have uniformly good weather sections and TICs usually have the local forecast and telephone weather lines listed. But if all else fails, you can always strike up a conversation with the first person you meet each morning. Wherever you are, you're sure to find someone who'll chat about the weather.

TV & RADIO

Britain still turns out what's arguably some of the world's best TV, although the increasing competition as channels proliferate has seen a decline in standards (a notable exception to this are the films created by the BBC's peerless Natural History Unit). There are currently five regular TV channels – BBC1 and BBC2 are publicly funded by a TV licence and don't carry advertising; ITV and Channels 4 and 5 are commercial stations. They're up against competition from Rupert Murdoch's BSkyB and assorted cable channels.

Channel 4 broadcasts a 30-minute Tour de France highlights package daily during the race, but there's precious little cycling on free-to-air TV otherwise. During summer, Eurosport (a satellite channel) offers lots of road racing and the mountain bike cross-country and downhill World Cups, much of it screened live.

BBC radio caters for most tastes, covering pop music in its various guises on Radio 1 (275M/1089kHz and 285M/1053kHz MW; 98.8MHz FM), Radio 2 (88–90.2MHz FM) and Radio 3 (247M/1215kHz MW; 91.3MHz FM). Radio 4 (1500M/198kHz LW; 417M/720kHz MW; 93.5MHz FM) still appeals mainly to a more mature audience, offering a mixed bag of drama, news and current affairs. Radio 5 Live (463M/693kHz MW) intersperses sport with current affairs; it has live coverage of the Tour de France. The BBC World Service (463M/648kHz MW) offers brilliant news coverage and quirky bits and pieces from around the world.

In Scotland and Wales, TV and radio stations are linked to the national network, although there are considerable regional variations. Scottish Television (STV) carries Gaelic-speaking programs. Wales has an alternative to Channel 4, Sianel Pedwar Cymru (S4C), that broadcasts Welsh-language (but not exclusively) programs daily. BBC Radio Wales offers daily news and features on Wales, while BBC Radio Cymru transmits the same in Welsh.

PHOTOGRAPHY & VIDEO

Print film is widely available but slide film can be more elusive; if there's no specialist photographic shop around, Boots, the High St chemist chain, is the likeliest stockist. Expect to pay £4 to £5 for print film (36-exposure) and £4 to £8 to have it processed, depending on film speed. Process-inclusive slide film is usually cheapest although these will usually need to be developed in Britain.

36-exposure films cost from £7 to £11 depending on film speed. British videos are VHS PAL format (also used in Germany, Australia and China) and not compatible with NTSC (used in the USA, Canada and Japan) or SECAM (used in France).

If you opt to take film home for processing, they'll have to go through the X-ray machines at all British airports. The machines are advertised as film-safe and few travellers report problems. Feel free to lug around a lead-lined bag if you're doubtful.

Many tourist attractions either charge for taking photos or prohibit it altogether. Use of flash is frequently forbidden to protect delicate pictures and fabrics. Video cameras are often disallowed because of the inconvenience they can cause to other visitors.

TIME
London is home to GMT, so if you want to work out where you are relative to London, find out how many hours ahead or behind GMT you are.

From late March to late October, Britain adopts daylight-saving time (DST), and so is an hour ahead of GMT itself. In Britain, the international operator on ☎ 155 can tell you the exact difference.

Most British public transport timetables use the 24-hour clock.

ELECTRICITY
The standard voltage throughout Britain is 240V AC, 50Hz. Plugs have three square pins and adaptors are widely available.

WEIGHTS & MEASURES
In theory Britain has now moved to metric weights and measures although nonmetric equivalents are still used by much of the population. Distances continue to be given in miles except on some Scottish islands where hostel locations are indicated in kilometres. Most liquids other than milk and beer are sold in litres. This book uses miles (mi) as its primary distance indicator. For conversion tables see the inside back cover.

LAUNDRY
Most High Streets (main streets) have a laundrette and there are laundry facilities at many camping or caravan parks and hostels. In a laundrette, expect to pay £1.50 to £2 for a single load of washing, and around £1 or more

for drying. Bring soap powder with you; it can be expensive if bought in a laundrette.

WOMEN CYCLISTS
On the whole, Britain is a safe country for women travellers and there's no need to consider more than the ordinary cautionary measures, such as not camping in or cycling through isolated areas, especially in the larger towns and cities. Solo women cyclists are a common sight on British roads and few report problems other than with the traffic.

There are no women's touring clubs, but the women's mountain bike organisation, Women on Wheels (WOW), puts on a few all-women mountain bike teaching/fun weekends each year around the country. WOW has BCF backing (see Useful Organisations later in this chapter). To find out more, contact the BCF for details.

The venerable Women's Cycle Racing Association (WCRA), which organises the women's road-racing calendar, dates back to the days when women who rode for Britain weren't allowed to wear the British jersey. Contact the WCRA on ☎ 01480-392957, 38 Bedford St, St Neots, Cambs.

Most big towns have a Well Woman Clinic that can advise on general health issues. Find the address in the local phone book or ask in the library. Should the worst come to the worst, Rape Crisis Centres can offer support after an attack.

If you'd like to stay with women while you're travelling it's worth joining Women Welcome Women, an organisation that puts women travellers in touch with potential hostesses. It's at 88 Easton St, High Wycombe, Bucks HP11 1LT (☎/fax 01494-465441).

GAY & LESBIAN CYCLISTS
In general, Britain is tolerant of homosexuality. Certainly it's possible for people to acknowledge their homosexuality in a way that would have been unthinkable 20 years ago; there are several openly gay MPs in the present parliament, which recently voted to reduce the age of homosexual consent from 18 to 16. That said, there remain pockets of out-and-out hostility, and overt displays of affection are not necessarily wise away from acknowledged 'gay' venues and districts.

A good source of information is the 24-hour Lesbian & Gay Switchboard (☎ 020-7837 7324) that can help with most general inquiries. London Lesbian Line (☎ 020-7251 6911) offers similar help but only from 2 to 10 pm, Monday and Friday and from 7 to 10 pm on Tuesday and Thursday.

CYCLISTS WITH A DISABILITY

Britain is a mixed bag for disabled travellers. These days few buildings go up that are not accessible to wheelchair users; large, new hotels and modern tourist attractions are therefore usually fine. However, most B&Bs and guesthouses are in hard-to-adapt older buildings. This means that travellers with mobility problems may end up paying more for accommodation than their more able-bodied fellows.

The 1995 Disability Discrimination Act makes it illegal to discriminate against people with disabilities in employment or the provision of services. Over the next decade barriers to access will have to be removed

and the situation for wheelchair users should slowly improve.

Many ticket offices, banks etc are fitted with hearing loops to assist the hearing impaired; look for the symbol of a large ear. Some tourist attractions have Braille guides or scented gardens for the visually impaired.

If you have a physical disability, get in touch with your national support organisation and ask for information about the countries you plan to visit. They often have complete libraries devoted to travel, and can put you in touch with travel agents who specialise in tours for the disabled.

The Royal Association for Disability and Rehabilitation (RADAR) publishes a useful guide titled *Holidays and Travel Abroad: A Guide for Disabled People*, which gives a good overview of facilities available in Europe. Its *Access in London* is required reading. Contact RADAR (☎ 020-7250 3222)

Bicycle Touring with Children

Children can travel by bicycle from the time they can support their head and a helmet, at around eight months. There are some small, lightweight, cute-looking helmets around, such as the L'il Bell Shell.

To carry an infant or toddler requires a child seat or trailer. Child seats are more common for everyday riding and have advantages of being cheaper, easier to move as a unit with the bike and letting you touch and talk to your child while moving.

Disadvantages, especially over long distances, can include exposure to weather, the tendency of a sleeping child to loll, and losing luggage capacity at the rear. The best makes, such as the Rhode Gear Limo, include extra moulding to protect the child in case of a fall, have footrests and restraints, recline to let the child sleep and fit very securely and conveniently onto a rack on the bike.

With a capacity of up to 50kg (versus around 18kg for a child seat), trailers can accommodate two bigger children and luggage. They give better, though not always total, protection from sun and rain and let children sleep comfortably. Look for a trailer that is lightweight, foldable, conspicuous (brightly coloured, with flag) and that tracks and handles well. It's also handy to be able to swap the trailer between bikes so adults can alternate towing and riding beside the trailer. Child trailers tend to be preferred for serious touring, but may be illegal in some places, and you should check with local traffic authorities before setting out. Trailers or seats are treated as additional luggage items when flying.

Be sure that the bike to which you attach a child seat or trailer is sturdy and low-geared, to withstand – and help *you* withstand – the extra weight and stresses.

IS THAT DOG STILL FOLLOWING US?

Unit 12, City Forum, 250 City Rd, London EC1V 8AF.

The Holiday Care Service (☎ 01293-774535), 2nd Floor, Imperial Buildings, Victoria Rd, Horley, Surrey RH6 7PZ, publishes the *Guide to Accessible Accommodation and Travel* for Britain and can offer general advice.

SENIOR CYCLISTS

Senior citizens are entitled to discounts on things like public transport, museum admission fees etc, provided they show proof of their age. Sometimes you will need a special pass. The minimum qualifying age is generally 60 to 65 for men, 55 to 65 for women.

Two groups are aimed specifically at senior cyclists: the Fellowship of Cycling Old-Timers (contact Jim Shaw, ☎ 01628-483 325, 2 Westwood Rd, Marlow, Bucks SL7 2AT) and the Forty Plus Cycling Club (contact

Trevor Blake, ☎ 01277-228071, 58 Woodway, Hutton, Brentwood, Essex CM13 2JR).

CYCLING WITH CHILDREN

If you're travelling with youngsters, the welcome you get will vary from region to region. England is notorious as a country whose residents prefer animals to children but, generally, children seem accepted in a much wider variety of public venues – pubs, restaurants and so on – than they were 10 or 15 years ago. Still, anyone travelling with children should be prepared for hotels that won't accept their offspring and the odd frosty stares if they bring them into restaurants.

Some of Britain's traffic-free cycle paths – such as the Bristol & Bath Railway Path and the Tarka Trail in Devon – offer cycling for children that's as safe and easy as you'll find. But check your route carefully before leading younger riders on a road tour. Some

Bicycle Touring with Children

From the age of about four, children can move on to a 'trailer-bike' (effectively a child's bike minus a front wheel which hitches to an adult's bike) or to a tandem (initially on the 'stoker', as the back seat is called, with 'kiddy cranks') – this lets them assist with the pedalling effort. The tandem can be a long-term solution, keeping you and your child together and letting you compensate if the child tires.

Be careful of children rushing into touring on a solo bike before they can sustain the effort and concentration required. Once they are ready and keen to ride solo, at about age 10 to 12, they will need a good quality touring bike, properly fitted (A$300, US$200, UK£130 up).

The British publication *Encycleopedia*, by Alan Davidson et al, is a good guide to quality trailers, trailer-bikes and tandems available from manufacturers around the world.

Bike touring with children requires a new attitude as well as new equipment. Be sensitive to their needs – especially when they're too young to communicate them fully. In a seat or trailer, they're not expending energy and need to be dressed accordingly. Take care to keep them dry, at the right temperature and protected from the sun.

Keep their energy and interest up. When you stop, a child travelling in a seat or trailer will be ready for action, so always reserve some energy for parenting. This means more stops, including at places like playgrounds. Older children will have their own interests and should be involved in planning a tour.

Before setting off on a major journey, try some day trips to check your set-up and introduce your child to cycling.

Children need to be taken into account in deciding each day's route – traffic and distances need to be moderate and facilities and points of interest adequate. Given the extra weight of children and their daily needs, you may find it easier to leave behind the camping gear and opt for indoor accommodation or day trips from a base or series of bases. The very fit and adventurous may not need to compromise to ride with children, but those who do will still find it worthwhile.

As with other activities, children bring a new perspective and pleasure to cycle touring. They tend to love it.

Alethea Morison

minor roads and lanes, even though they may see few cars, can be narrow, with vision ahead obscured by hedges.

For more information, see Lonely Planet's *Travel with Children* by Maureen Wheeler.

It has been assumed that most touring cyclists are in their late teens or older, so admission and accommodation costs for children are not included in this book.

MOUNTAIN BIKING

Britain hosts a lively mountain bike scene, with tens of thousands of recreational riders and 2000 registered racers. According to the CTC (see Useful Organisations in this chapter), Britain has more than 100,000mi of paths and unsealed tracks. The CTC and BCF are the best central contacts for off-roaders. The BCF annual handbook contains a race calendar and club listing. CTC Off-road helps members with information on good mountain biking areas, routes and contacts – another reason you might consider joining the CTC.

Since the Countryside Act of 1968, mountain bikers in England and Wales have been allowed to use the bridleway network, which accounts for 90% of the off-road trails around the country. Bridleways are marked clearly on OS *Landranger* maps (see Maps, earlier in this chapter) as dashed lines and, as the name would suggest, they're shared with horse riders. Mountain bikers can also use two minority types of track – Roads Used as Public Paths (RUPPs), and Byways Open to All Traffic (BOATs). These occur only in certain parts of the country and are also marked on OS maps. Unclassified country roads (UCRs) are also legal for mountain bike riding. Country parks, of which there are any number around the country, will often have dedicated tracks and signboards showing where you can ride. Remember that cyclists are not legally permitted to ride on footpaths (and many are unsuitable anyway).

If you're planning to do a lot of off-road riding, it is best to choose your area and buy the appropriate map, or link up with a local mountain bike club for inside knowledge.

In Scotland there's no law of trespass like there is in England and Wales. Cyclists can only be prosecuted if they cause damage or nuisance. On private land, you can ride on legally recognised rights of way. In open country there is generally open access that assumes you will ride responsibly and observe seasonal restrictions regarding hunting, game and wildlife.

USEFUL ORGANISATIONS
National Cycling Organisations

The Cyclists' Touring Club (CTC; ☎ 01483-417 217, fax 426 994, ⓔ cycling@ctc.org.uk; Cotterell House), 69 Meadrow, Godalming, Surrey GU7 3HS, is Britain's national cyclists' association and is without doubt the most useful contact point for touring cyclists; the £25 annual fee is well worth it. CTC members receive the invaluable *Cyclists Handbook*, which – among other things – lists cycle-friendly accommodation and repair shops throughout Britain.

The British Cycling Federation (BCF; ☎ 0161-230 2301, fax 231 0591), National Cycling Centre, Stuart St, Manchester M11 4DQ, is the governing body of road, track and mountain bike racing. The Welsh Cycling Union (☎ 01745-888754), 15 Palmeria Gardens, Prestatyn, Denbighshire L19 9NS, does the same job in Wales. The equivalent Scottish organisation is the Scottish Cyclists' Union (SCU; ☎ 0131-652 0187), the Velodrome, London Rd, Edinburgh EH7 6AD.

Bristol-based Sustrans (☎ 0117-929 0888, fax 929 4173, ⌨ www.sustrans.co.uk), 35 King St, Bristol BS1 4DZ, is, as its name suggests, concerned with sustainable transport. This dynamic charity works on practical projects to encourage walking and cycling, so as to reduce motor traffic and its adverse effects. Its flagship project is the National Cycling Network (NCN), which in June 2000 saw the opening of 5000mi of routes on traffic-free paths and traffic-calmed and minor roads, reaching all parts of Britain.

The Bicycle Association of Great Britain (☎ 024-7655 3838, fax 7622 8366), Starley House, Eaton Rd, Coventry CV1 2FH, is the peak body for British bicycle manufacturers and importers.

There are also national bodies for several other cycling organisations:

The British Cyclo-Cross Association (☎/fax 01325-482052) 14 Deneside Rd, Darlington, Co Durham Dl3 9HZ

The Tandem Club (⌨ www.tandem-club.org.uk) 25 Hendred Way, Abingdon, Oxfordshire OX14 2AN

Vintage-Veteran Cycle Club (☎ 01923-774026) 31 Yorke Road, Croxley Green, Rickmansworth, Herts WD3 3DW

Sustrans & the NCN

In 1978, when the civil engineering charity Sustrans (Sustainable Transport) first announced its objective of creating a network of cycle paths and traffic-calmed roads throughout Britain, it was barely taken seriously. In the years since, matters such as greenhouse-gas emissions, global warming and increasingly congested roads made the public reconsider the exalted place of the car in modern Britain, and in June 2000 Sustrans' flagship project, the National Cycle Network (NCN), was officially launched (see the map of the network opposite p112).

Sustrans
NATIONAL CYCLE NETWORK

The NCN features 5000mi of routes. Its bike-friendly tentacles reach into every corner of Britain, passing through major cities, villages and across national park lands. Half of it is traffic-free thanks to the revitalisation of disused railways and careful negotiation to allow cyclists on canal towpaths. Many parts of the NCN opened pre-2000, and are already popular with cyclists. Among these, the Bristol & Bath Railway Path, Lôn Las Cymru (the Welsh National Cycle Route) and Sea to Sea (C2C) route, in northern England, appear in this book in their entirety. Substantial portions of others, such as the West Country Way, are used in other tours. Without exception, the authors came to revere the trusty NCN route markers throughout Britain.

While Sustrans receives funding from many sources, it was a £43.5 million grant from the Millennium Commission – the money drawn from National Lottery funds – that really pushed the network ahead in the years leading up to 2000. But the turn of the century has not signalled the end of Sustrans' work. The charity continues to develop the NCN, and to assist and promote projects that provide safe walking and cycling routes to schools and to train stations.

For information on how to contact Sustrans, see Useful Organisations in this chapter.

Touring Clubs

The CTC has about 200 affiliate District Associations (DAs) and 'sections' – or local clubs – spread around Britain. The *CTC Handbook* (only available to members) also has contacts for regional touring advisers.

Audax UK (AUK) promotes noncompetitive long-distance cycling and runs events from 120mi to 370mi; it's also the body through which British riders qualify for the 1200km Paris-Brest-Paris, held every four years. Audax riders visiting Britain can contact Noel Simpson via email (@ quackers@globalnet.co.uk) or the post: Meadowview Cottage, Far Bank Lane, Fishlake, Doncaster DN7 5LW. The AUK ride calendar is available on the organisation's Web site (💻 www.audax.uk.com) or from 43 Marriot Grove, Scandal, Wakefield WF2 6RP.

Other Organisations

Membership of English Heritage (EH; ☎ 020-7973 3434, 💻 www.english-heritage.org.uk) and the National Trust (NT; ☎ 020-8315 1111, 💻 www.nationaltrust.org.uk) is worth considering if you're going to be in Britain for a while and are particularly interested in historical sites. Both are nonprofit organisations dedicated to the preservation of the environment, and both care for hundreds of spectacular sites. A Great British Heritage Pass will give you access to NT and EH properties and some of the expensive private properties. There are seven-day and 15-day and one-month passes available, costing from £30 to about £60.

The NT (which covers England, Wales and Northern Ireland) has reciprocal arrangements with National Trust organisations in Scotland (NTS; ☎ 0131-226 5922), Edinburgh; Australia; New Zealand; Canada; and the USA (the Royal Oak Foundation); all of which are cheaper to join. A year's membership of the NTS (£25) provides access to all NTS and NT properties. Short-term membership (touring ticket) costs £16 for one week and £24 for two weeks. YHA members and student-card holders get half-price entry to NTS properties.

Historic Scotland (HS; ☎ 0131-668 8800), in Edinburgh, manages more than 330 historic sites, including attractions such as the

Edinburgh and Stirling castles. A year's membership (£22) gives free entry to HS sites and half-price entry to EH properties in England and Cadw properties in Wales. It also offers short-term 'Explorer' membership – seven or 14 days.

Cadw (☎ 029-2050 0200), the Welsh Historic Monuments agency, looks after most of the ruined abbeys and castles in Wales. A one-year membership (£20) gives admission to all Cadw sites. Cadw members are also eligible for half-price admission to EH and HS sites (free from the second year of Cadw membership onwards). Three/seven-day Explorer Passes are also available for £9/15.

The London Walkabout Club (☎ 020-7938 3001), Deckers London Club (☎ 020-7244 8641) and Drifters (☎ 020-7402 9171) all offer back-up services like mail holding, local information, discounts on film processing, freight forwarding and equipment purchase, and cheap tours. They're mainly aimed at Aussies and Kiwis, but anyone is welcome. Membership is around £15.

For details of the benefits of membership with the YHA (Hostelling International) see the Accommodation section later in this chapter.

LEGAL MATTERS

Traffic laws most likely to catch out visitors relate to speeding in, and parking of, cars. The current speed limits are 30mph in built-up areas (indicated by the presence of street lighting), 60mph elsewhere and 70mph on motorways and dual carriageways. Other speed limits will be indicated by signs.

Parking a car in the wrong place, or failing to pay carpark charges, can cost you a lot of money. If your car is clamped and you have to pay to retrieve it from a pound you won't see much change from £100.

On-the-spot fines are rare. The two main exceptions are on trains (including London Underground trains) and buses, where people who can't produce a valid ticket on demand for an inspector can be fined there and then; at least £5 on the buses, £10 on the trains. No excuses are accepted (as Prime Minister Blair's wife Cherie learnt early in 2000).

Although even possession of cannabis is still illegal, drugs of every description are widely available. Much of Britain's crime is associated with drug dealing. Don't even think of getting caught up in it, and remem-

ber that the dodgiest areas of the cities are usually those associated with dealing.

BUSINESS HOURS

Offices are generally open 9 am to 5 pm, Monday to Friday. Shops may be open longer hours, and most are open on Saturday from 9 am to 5 pm. An increasing number of shops also opens on Sunday, perhaps from 10 am to 4 pm. Late-night shopping (more likely in cities) is usually on Thursday or Friday. In country towns, particularly in Scotland and Wales, shops may have an early-closing day – usually Tuesday, Wednesday or Thursday – and they're less likely to be open on Sunday. In the Scottish Highlands and Islands many pubs have the infuriating habit of closing for two hours mid-afternoon (usually 2 to 4 pm).

Seven-day, late-night convenience stores are more and more common, but don't assume you'll find one in isolated areas or villages. Outside of the major towns and cities, it's safest *never* to assume that bike shops will be open on Sundays. During winter, many tourist attractions are open limited hours or not at all. If you're touring in the off-season you should always phone ahead to check.

Opening hours for TICs, post offices and banks are mentioned in the appropriate place in this chapter. Throughout the book, opening hours are indicated only if they differ considerably from the norm.

PUBLIC HOLIDAYS & SPECIAL EVENTS
Public Holidays

Most banks, businesses and some museums and other places of interest are closed for the following public holidays:

New Year's Day 1 January (2 January Bank Holiday in Scotland)
Good Friday the Friday before Easter Sunday
Easter Monday the Monday after Easter Sunday (not in Scotland)
May Day Bank Holiday first Monday in May
Spring Bank Holiday last Monday in May
Summer Bank Holiday first Monday in August (Scotland), last Monday in August (outside Scotland)
Christmas Day 25 December
Boxing Day 26 December

Scottish towns normally have a spring and autumn holiday; dates vary not only from year to year but also from town to town.

Museums and other attractions may well observe the Christmas Day and Boxing Day holidays but generally stay open for the other holidays. Exceptions are those that normally close on Sunday; they're quite likely to close on bank holidays too. Some smaller museums close on Monday and/or Tuesday, and others, including the British Museum, close on Sunday morning.

Special Events

Countless events are held around Britain all year. Even small villages have weekly markets, and many still re-enact traditional customs and ceremonies, some dating back hundreds of years. Useful BTA publications include *Forthcoming Events* and *Arts Festivals*; these list a selection of the year's events and festivals with their dates.

January
Hogmanay A huge street party held in Edinburgh and Glasgow to celebrate the New Year.

March
Cheltenham Gold Cup The famous horse race meeting at Cheltenham is held mid-month.

April
Grand National The famous horse racing meeting held at Aintree (Liverpool) on the first Saturday in April.

May
Brighton Festival An arts festival that runs for three weeks from the start of the month.
FA Cup Final The deciding match in the English football league is traditionally held at Wembley (London) in early May.
Scottish Cup Final The deciding match in the Scottish football league is traditionally held at Hampden Park (Glasgow) in early May.
Chelsea Flower Show Premier flower show held at Royal Hospital (London) during the last week of the month.

June
Derby Week Horse racing and people watching at Epsom (Surrey) in the first week.
Royal Ascot More horses and hats at Ascot (Berkshire) mid-month.
Trooping the Colour The Queen's birthday parade with its spectacular pageantry from Whitehall (London) is held mid-month.
Glastonbury Festival Huge open-air festival and hippy happening at Pilton (Somerset); late June.
Henley Royal Regatta Rowing and social event at Henley-on-Thames (Oxfordshire); late June.
London Pride Europe's biggest gay and lesbian march and festival; late June.

Cycling Events

If a get-together of cyclists is your idea of a good time, Britain's the place for you. Each year there's a staggering range of organised rides at local, regional or national level, many in support of charities.

The best sources of information on the hundreds of other organised rides are the CTC's *Cycle Events Guide*, distributed with *Cycle Touring and Campaigning* magazine, and *Bike Events* magazine, available from Bike Events (☎ 01225-480130), PO Box 75, Bath, BA1 5BX.

The British Heart Foundation's (BHF) annual **London to Brighton Bike Ride**, held each June, is one of the best-known events. More than 25,000 people make the journey each year; for entry forms ☎ 0891-616077.

The CTC's **York Cycle Rally** at Knavesmire racecourse, also in June, is the country's biggest annual bicycle get-together. About 35,000 cyclists gather each year for rides and many other cycling-related events; contact the CTC for details (☎ 01438-417217, @ events@ctc.org.uk).

Charities with extensive cycling events lists include:

Action Research (☎ 01403-210406), Sports Unit, Action Research, Vincent House, Horsham, West Sussex, RH12 2DP
Barnardo's (☎ 0345-697967) Biking for Barnardo's, Tanner's Lane, Barkingside, Essex IG6 1QG
BHF (BHF Bike Rides) 14 Fitzhardinge St, London W1H 4DH
Marie Curie Cancer Care (☎ 020-7201 2359, fax 7201 2386), National Promotions Office, Marie Curie Cancer Care, 28 Belgrave Square, London SW1X 8QG

Royal Highland Show Scotland's national agricultural show, which is held in Edinburgh in late June.
Lawn Tennis Championships Strawberries, cream and two weeks of Grand Slam tennis at Wimbledon (London) in late June.

July
Royal Welsh Show Welsh national agricultural show held at Llanelwedd (Builth Wells) in early July.
Cowes Week A yachting extravaganza held off the Isle of Wight in late July.

August

Edinburgh Military Tattoo Three weeks of military pageantry at Edinburgh castle.

Royal National Eisteddfod of Wales Gaelic cultural festival (alternates between sites in North and South Wales) held in early August.

Edinburgh International and Fringe Festivals Premier international arts festivals that runs for three weeks from mid-August.

Notting Hill Carnival Huge Caribbean carnival in Notting Hill (London) in late August.

Reading Festival Outdoor rock and roll for three days in Reading (Berkshire) in late August.

September

Braemar Royal Highland Gathering Kilts and cabers in Braemar (Scotland) held early in the month.

November

Guy Fawkes Day Commemorates an attempted Catholic coup with bonfires and fireworks on 5 November.

CYCLING ROUTES
Route Descriptions

This guide covers what its authors consider to be the best on-road cycle touring routes in England, Scotland and Wales. It also details a 20-day route from Land's End, England, to John o'Groats, Scotland – Britain's best-known long-distance journey. To select the routes, authors researched material from several sources, including existing routes suggested by the CTC, Sustrans and local cycling authorities. In some cases, part or all of a route in this book follows one of these existing routes, many of which are of undoubted quality.

The routes described range from one to several days and, in most cases, can be linked to create longer tours. Transport options – including cycling – for getting to and from each route are discussed. Each day's riding includes information on accommodation options, places to buy food and points of interest.

Ride Difficulty

Each ride is graded according to its difficulty in terms of distance, terrain, road surface and navigation. The grade appears both in the Table of Rides at the beginning of the book and the facts box in each ride's introduction.

Grading is unavoidably subjective and is intended as a guide only. Britain has an intricate network of roads, and 'easy' navigation

here might be considered quite complex in, say, Australia or New Zealand. The rides have been graded in optimum weather conditions and, broadly, foul weather makes any day's riding less pleasant and usually harder.

Easy These are rides of only a few hours' duration, over *mostly* flat terrain on good road surfaces. Navigation is simple.

Moderate These present a moderate challenge to someone of average fitness. They are up to several hours long, are likely to include hills and some poor road surfaces, and may require more detailed navigation.

Hard These are suited to fit and experienced cyclists. They may include long daily distances and/or challenging climbs, traverse some poor road surfaces and require complex navigation.

Times & Distances

Riding days in the book vary in distance from 8mi to 69mi; the average distance over the days covered is 40mi to 45mi. The distance per day has been chosen by individual authors – some of whom are younger and fitter than others – on largely subjective criteria; some shorter days include outstanding attractions or more strenuous climbs.

A suggested riding time is given for each day, but because individual riding speed varies these should be used only as a guide.

Ride Profiles

Each day's riding includes a 'cue sheet' (usually found on the map) with concise directions given according to distance marks. You should expect slight variation on distance marks; even if cycle computers are properly calibrated, different riders choose slightly different lines.

Many riding days include an elevation chart. It's worth remembering that while much of Britain lacks mountains, it has a great many hills, so any riding day without an elevation chart isn't necessarily a flat day.

ACTIVITIES

There's no escaping the fact that Britain is an expensive place to travel, but if you've saved a few quid by cycling from place to place you should definitely consider having a go at one of the many activities on offer.

Most activities are well organised and have clubs and associations that can give visitors invaluable information and, sometimes, substantial discounts. Many of these organisations have national or international affiliations, so check with local clubs before leaving home. The BTA has brochures on most activities, which can provide a starting point for further research.

Walking

The infrastructure for walkers is excellent. Every TIC has details (free or for a nominal charge) of suggested walks that take in local points of interest. Hundreds of books are available and describe walks ranging from half-hour strolls to multi-day expeditions.

Every village and town is surrounded by footpaths, so consider taking breaks from the bike in interesting spots with a view to exploring the surrounding countryside.

As far as longer walks are concerned civilisation is never far away (with the exception of parts of Scotland), so it's easy to put together walks that connect with public transport and link hostels and villages. In most cases a tent and cooking equipment aren't necessary. Warm and waterproof clothing, sturdy footwear, lunch and some high-energy food for emergencies, a water bottle with purification tablets, a first-aid kit, a whistle, a torch (flashlight), a map and a compass are all you need.

Lonely Planet's *Walking in Britain* covers not only all the main long-distance walks but also has a good selection of day hikes. Those intent on tackling a serious walk should contact the Ramblers' Association (RA; ☎ 020-7339 8500), 1 Wandsworth Rd, London SW8 2XX. The RA Web site (💻 www.ramblers .org.uk) has numerous links and information on many walks.

Golf

Britain, particularly Scotland, is the home of golf. There are, in fact, more courses per capita in Scotland than in any other country in the world. The game has been played here for centuries and there are currently over 1900 courses in Britain, both private and public. Most are playable all year round. Some of the private clubs only admit members, friends of members, or golfers who have a handicap certificate or a letter of introduction from their club, but the majority welcome visitors.

Note that most clubs give members priority in booking tee-off times; it's always advisable to book in advance. It should be easier to book a tee-off time on a public course, but weekends on all courses are usually busy. Given that most cyclists pack light, it's wise to check whether the club you've targeted has a dress code, and, of course, whether it has golf clubs for hire (not all do).

Tourist boards have information leaflets; the BTA has a useful *Golfing Holidays* booklet giving lists of hotels and golfing events. *Golf in Scotland* is a free brochure listing 400 courses and clubs with details of where to stay. Contact the Scottish Tourist Board (☎ 0131-332 2433), 23 Ravelston Terrace, Edinburgh EH4 3EU, for a copy. The Golf Club of Great Britain (☎ 020-8390 3113) is based at 3 Sage Yard, Douglas Rd, Surbiton, Surrey KT6 7TS.

Tracing your Ancestors

Many visitors to Britain have ancestors who once lived in this country. Your trip would be a good chance to find out more about them and their lives; you may even discover relatives you never knew about. Records for England and Wales are kept in London. Scottish records are kept in Edinburgh.

The best place to start a search for your ancestors is the Public Record Office Web site, 💻 www.pro.gov.uk, which has comprehensive information for genealogists and a list of useful publications.

For records of births, marriages and deaths in England & Wales since 1 July 1837 contact the Family Records Centre (☎ 020-8392 5300), 1 Myddelton St, Islington, London EC1R 1UW. The Public Record Office (PRO; ☎ 020-8876 3444) has records from 1086 (the Domesday Book) to the present day. It is based at Ruskin Ave, Kew, Richmond, Surrey TW9 4DU. The PRO publication *The Current Guide* will help you to find your way around the records, but it is quite a complex task nonetheless. If you'd like someone to complete the search for you (for a fee), the PRO, and the Association of Genealogists & Record Agents (1 Woodside Close, Stanstead Rd, Caterham, Surrey CR3 6AU) can send you a list of professional record agents and researchers. The association can also supply the name of an agent who will search for living relatives.

If your ancestors were Scottish you should first go to the General Register Office (GRO; ☎ 0131-314 4433), New Register House, 3 West Register St, Edinburgh EH1 3YT. This office holds birth, marriage and death records since 1855, as well as the census records and old parochial registers. The office opens Monday to Friday from 9 am to 4.30 pm. Staff will answer simple inquiries by correspondence if precise details are given. If you want further research to be carried out for you (perhaps before you come) the office can send you a list of professional searchers. All correspondence should be addressed to The Keeper of the Records of Scotland, Scottish Record Office, and sent to the earlier address.

Never Been Here Before by Jane Cox and Stella Colwell is a useful guide to the Family Records Centre. *Tracing Your Scottish Ancestors* by Cecil Sinclair is also useful.

Surfing & Swimming

Most overseas visitors do not think of Britain as a place to go for a beach holiday – with good reason. Climate and water temperature dictate that you need to be hardy or equipped with a wetsuit to do anything more than take a quick dip. But Britain has some truly magnificent coastline and some wonderful sandy beaches. And the British have been taking holidays by the seaside since the 18th century, so there is a fascinating, sometimes bizarre tradition to explore.

Visiting a British seaside resort should be high on the list of priorities for anyone wishing to gain an insight into British society. The resorts vary from quiet retirement enclaves like Eastbourne to vibrant cultural centres like Brighton and cheerful family resorts like Hastings. And then there's Blackpool, which pretty much defies categorisation. One thing remains common to them all, however, and that is that the fun happens on shore and it's done fully clothed.

The best beaches with the best chance of sun and sand are in Cornwall and Devon. Newquay, on the west Cornish coast (see The South-West ride in the Southern England chapter) is the capital of the British surf scene, and it has a plethora of decent-priced surf shops. Good breaks around Newquay include Fistral Beach, England's premier surfing beach and home to the main surfing contests. There are similar conditions on the Gower Peninsula and the

south-west corner of Wales from Tenby to Fishguard.

Northern Scotland has Britain's biggest and best surf, particularly around Thurso, which has a large surfing community, thanks to several famous breaks. Reef, in front of the harbour wall, has lefts and rights. Thurso East (Castle Reef) is the big one – a huge right that works up to almost 4.5m (15ft).

Fishing

Fishing is enormously popular but also highly regulated. Many prime stretches of river are privately owned, and fishing there can be expensive.

To fish anywhere in England and Wales you must have the correct licence and the permission of the owner or tenants of the fishing rights. For more information contact the Environment Agency (☎ 01454-624400), Rio House, Waterside Drive, Aztec West, Almondsbury, Bristol BS12 4UD. Rod licences are available from every post office in England and Wales, bankside agents and Environment Agency regional offices. Licence costs vary, but don't expect to pay less than £2 for a day or more than £20 for a week.

Dates for closed seasons vary according to the region and need to be checked in advance – the Environment Agency will be able to advise you.

Fishing in Scotland, where there is a dense thicket of regulations on salmon fishing, is amazingly expensive. Purchasing a 'time-share' right to fish a river in Scotland costs about £6000 per year.

Horse Riding & Pony Trekking

Riding schools cater to all levels of proficiency, many of them in national park areas.

If you're an experienced rider there are numerous riding schools with horses to rent – TICs have details. For more information contact the British Horse Society (☎ 01926-707795).

Canal & Waterway Travel

Britain's surprisingly extensive network of canals and waterways spread rapidly across the country at the same time as the Industrial Revolution transformed the nation. As a method of transporting freight (passengers were always secondary) they were a short-lived wonder, trimmed back by railways and killed off by modern roads. Today, however, the canals are once again booming, this time as part of the leisure industry.

Narrowboats can be rented from numerous operators around Britain and for a family or a group they can provide surprisingly economical transport and accommodation. Canals lead you to a Britain of idyllic villages, pretty countryside, and convenient and colourful waterside pubs.

As narrowboats usually come so well equipped for everyday living, food supplies are all you need to worry about and there are plenty of places to shop along the waterways. Alternatively, careful planning can see you moored at a riverside pub or restaurant for most meals. Boats can accommodate from two or three people up to 10 or 12.

The canals are not restricted to narrowboat users. Canal towpaths have become popular routes for walkers and cyclists who can enjoy the same hidden perspective as people actually out on the waterways. There are more than 3000mi of navigable canals and rivers in Britain, so there's plenty to explore.

More information on the canal system is available from the Inland Waterways Association (☎ 020-7586 2510), 114 Regent's Park Rd, London NW1 8UQ. It publishes *The Inland Waterways Guide*, a general guide to holiday hire with route descriptions. Approximately two-thirds of the waterways in Britain are operated by the British Waterways Board (☎ 01923-226422), Willow Grange, Church Rd, Watford, Hertfordshire WD1 3QA. It publishes *The Waterways Code for Boaters*, a free booklet packed with useful information and advice. Also available is a complete list of hire-boat and hotel-boat companies.

Skiing

Many people are surprised to learn that there are ski resorts in Britain. There are actually five, all in Scotland, but the slopes are far less extensive and the weather considerably less reliable than anything you'll find in the Alps. On a sunny day, however, and with good snow, it can be very pleasant. The hard part will be riding a bicycle this far north in winter.

Scotland offers both alpine (downhill) and nordic (cross-country) skiing as well as other snow-related sports. The high season is from January to April, but it's sometimes possible to ski from as early as November to as late as May. Package holidays are available but with all kinds of accommodation on offer in and around the ski centres, it's very easy to make your own arrangements.

The biggest centres are Glenshee and Cairngorm. Glenshee offers the largest network of lifts and selection of runs in Scotland and has snow machines for periods when the real thing doesn't appear. Cairngorm has almost 30 runs spread over an extensive area; its service town is Aviemore, from which there's a bus service to the slopes. The other centres are Glencoe, The Nevis Range and The Lecht.

Contact the Scottish Tourist Board (STB; ☎ 0131-332 2433) for its detailed *Ski Scotland* brochure and accommodation list.

Steam Trains

There are now nearly 500 private railways in Britain, many of them narrow gauge, using steam or diesel locomotives from all over the world. A useful guide to private steam railways is *Railways Restored* (Ian Allan). The guide is published annually and lists the major preserved railways, museums and preservation centres in the British Isles. It also gives details of opening times and includes a locomotive stock list for most centres.

Spectator Sports

The Brits love their games. They play and watch them with fierce, competitive dedication. They've been responsible for inventing or codifying many of the world's most popular spectator sports: cricket, tennis, football (soccer) and rugby; and the Scots can claim golf. To this list add billiards and snooker, lawn bowls, boxing, darts, hockey, squash and table tennis.

The country also hosts premier events for a number of sports: Wimbledon (tennis), the FA Cup Final (football), the British Open (golf), test cricket, Badminton Horse Trials (equestrian), the British Grand Prix (motor racing), the Isle of Man TT (motorcycle racing), the Derby and the Grand National (horse racing), the Henley Regatta (rowing), the Six Nations Tournament (rugby union), the Super League Final (rugby league) and the Admirals Cup (yachting).

Keep an eye on the national media for fixtures, times, venues and ticket prices of major sporting events.

Shopping

London has some of the world's greatest department stores (Harrods, Fortnum & Mason, Harvey Nichols, Liberty, Marks & Spencer), some of the best bookshops (Borders, Waterstones, Blackwells, Foyles), some of the best fashion (Camden Market, Kensington Market, Covent Garden, Oxford St, Kensington), some of the best music shops (HMV, Virgin, Tower) and specialist shops of every description.

Making things to sell to tourists is big business in Scotland, and almost every visitor attraction seems to have been redesigned to funnel you through the gift shop. Among the tourist kitsch are some good-value, high-quality goods.

If you're interested in visiting mills, factories and craft shops, pick up a copy of the STB publication *See Scotland at Work*. Popular items include Scottish textiles (particularly tartans and knitwear), jewellery & glassware, Scottish shortbread and, of course, whisky – although you're probably better off buying it duty-free at the airport than in High Street shops.

Wales has plentiful shopping fodder for visitors with a yen for pottery, knitwear and lovespoons. Indeed, there can be hardly a visitor attraction left that doesn't have its shop selling commemorative T-shirts, pencils, stationery, books and souvenir fudge. Even the industrial sites have got in on the act, hawking repro miner's lamps, coal sculptures and similar artefacts. Prices are often high and quality is variable, but among the furry red dragons there are some classy items on offer.

ACCOMMODATION

This will almost certainly be your single greatest expense. Even camping can be expensive at official sites. Cyclists will particularly be on the lookout for accommodation providers who welcome bicycles and, preferably, who have secure undercover storage for bikes. Fulfilling the first of these desires isn't difficult; cycle use is widespread and widely accepted in Britain and in the experience of this book's authors, few accommodation providers will be reluctant to welcome a cyclist. Finding a place to secure your bike is usually no problem; however, securing it undercover is sometimes more difficult.

There are three main options for travel on the cheap: camping grounds, YHA hostels and bed & breakfasts (B&Bs), although over the past few years several independent backpackers' hostels have opened and the number is growing, particularly in popular hiking regions.

In the middle range, superior B&Bs are often in beautiful old buildings and some rooms will have private bathrooms with showers or baths. Guesthouses and smaller hotels are more likely to have private bathrooms, but they also tend to be less personal. If money's no object, there are also some superb hotels, the most interesting of which are built inside converted castles and mansions.

All these options are promoted by local TICs. Many charge a nominal fee – usually £1 – for local bookings within the next two nights, although you may also have to pay a 10% deposit (which is subtracted from the nightly price). Most TICs also participate in the Book-A-Bed-Ahead (BABA) scheme that allows you to book accommodation for the next two nights anywhere in Britain. Most charge around £3 and take a 10% deposit. Outside opening hours, most TICs put a notice and map in their window showing which local places have unoccupied beds. If you choose to tour during the peak summer season you *must* book ahead to secure accommodation. YHA hostels, especially, are often booked out weeks in advance.

In this guide, accommodation prices (except for tent pitches) are given as per person per night, unless otherwise stated.

Camping

Free camping is rarely possible, except in Scotland. Pitches (camp sites) vary widely in quality although most have reasonable facilities. The headache is that they're sometimes distant from nearest town. The RAC's *Camping & Caravanning in Britain* has extensive lists and local TICs also have details.

The cost of a tent pitch varies; expect to pay somewhere in the £3 to £9 range. As a rule, you'll save money if you're travelling with a partner, although some sites charge per person, not per site.

If you're planning to camp extensively, consider joining the Camping & Caravanning Club (☎ 024-7669 4995, 🖳 www .campingandcaravanningclub.co.uk), Greenfields House, Westwood Way, Coventry CV4

8JH. The club runs many British sites. Many are open to nonmembers, but some are not, and nonmembers must pay higher fees. Overseas visitors can buy a temporary membership for £10. If you hold a Camping Card International, you can access all club sites, including members-only sites, at members' rates.

The National Trust has many camp sites; for a list of addresses send a stamped, addressed envelope to the Membership Dept, PO Box 39, Bromley, Kent BR1 3XL (☎ 020-8315 1111, 🖳 www.nationaltrust.org.uk). You can also camp in several Forestry Commission forest parks and in the New Forest; contact the Forestry Commission (☎ 0131-334 0303, 🖳 www.forestry.gov.uk), Corstophine Rd, Edinburgh EH12 7AT for details.

In Scotland, you can camp free on public land (unless it's specifically protected). Commercial camping grounds are geared to caravans and vary widely in quality. A tent site costs around £6.50. *Scotland: Camping & Caravan Parks*, available from most TICs, will prove useful for planning. Camping and caravan parks are graded by the STB, reflecting the level and quality of facilities.

In Wales, camping grounds are concentrated in the national parks and along the coast. The TICs have a free *Wales Touring Caravan & Camping* leaflet with sites graded for facilities and quality by the Wales Tourist Board.

Camping Barns, Bunkhouses & Bothies

A camping barn – usually a converted farm building – provides basic accommodation for £3 to £7 per night. To use them, you must bring everything you'd need to camp except a tent. Many camping barns are privately run by farmers. YHA (see the following YHA Hostels entry) has a large network in England; their camping barns brochure is available from YHA customer services (☎ 01727-845047).

Bunkhouses are a grade or two up from camping barns. They have stoves for heating and cooking and may supply utensils. They may have mattresses, but you'll still need a sleeping bag. Most charge around £6.50.

Bothies are simple shelters in Scotland, often in remote places. They're not locked, there's no charge and you can't book. Take your own cooking equipment, sleeping bag

and mat. Users should stay one night only and leave it as they find it.

YHA Hostels

Membership of your national Youth Hostel Association (YHA) and possession of a Hostelling International (HI) card gives you access to the network of hostels throughout England, Wales and Scotland; you don't have to be young or single to use them. For cycle touring, YHA (England/Wales) and SYHA (Scotland) hostels should be towards the top of your list of accommodation options. They're the most likely place to meet other cyclists. Most have secure cycle storage. All hostels have facilities for self-catering and an increasing number provide cheap meals.

Booking policies vary: most hostels accept phone bookings and payment with Visa or Access (MasterCard) cards; some will accept same-day bookings, although they will usually only hold a bed until a set time; some participate in the Book-A-Bed-Ahead scheme; some work on a first come, first served basis.

The YHA and SYHA both publish their own accommodation guides. If you plan to use hostels extensively it's wise to get hold of these as they include the often complicated opening times, as well as exact details of how to reach each place. In England and Wales overnight tariffs (full price for adults) range from £6.10 in rustic backcountry hostels to more than £20 in flash models in London. Scottish hostels are generally cheaper and often better than those in England; overnight tariffs range from £4.65 in the sticks to £11.50 in big cities.

For England and Wales the head office is 8 St Stephen's Hill, St Albans, Herts AL1 2DY (☎ 01727-855215, 🖳 www.yha.org.uk). The accommodation guide and membership information are also available at YHA Adventure Shop branches all around the country, or you can join in your home country. The SYHA head office is at 7 Glebe Crescent, Stirling FK8 2JA (☎ 01786-891400).

Independent Hostels

There's a growing network of independent hostels around Britain but their facilities vary tremendously. Some are among the worst dosshouses (flophouses) you're likely to find, others are wonderful. Prices range from £9 to £12 per night for bunkroom accommodation.

The *Independent Hostel Guide* (£3.95), which lists the indie's addresses and contact details, is available from Backpackers Press (☎ 01629-580427), 2 Rockview Cottages, Matlock Bath, Derbyshire DE4 3PG For a brochure listing the 80 or so indies in Scotland, send a stamped, addressed envelope to Pete Thomas, Croft Bunkhouses & Bothies, 7 Portnalong, Isle of Skye IV47 8SL.

University Accommodation
Many British universities rent student accommodation to visitors during the holidays; usually for three weeks over Easter and Christmas and from late June to late September. Bed and breakfast normally costs £18 to £25 per person. Check ahead for cycle storage facilities.

For more information contact British Universities Accommodation Consortium (BUAC; ☎ 0115-950 4571, fax 942 2505), Box No 1562E, University Park, Nottingham NG7 2RD.

B&Bs & Guesthouses
B&Bs are a great British institution and the cheapest private accommodation around. At the bottom end (£12 to £18 per person) you get a bedroom in a private house, a shared bathroom and an enormous cooked breakfast. In small B&Bs you really feel like a guest of the family – they may not even have a sign. If you're travelling alone, you're sure to grow somewhat weary of the lack of single rooms in B&Bs (and when you do get one, it's often the worst room in the house). The best you can do is phone ahead to check.

More upmarket B&Bs have private bathrooms and TVs in each room. Traditionally the British have preferred baths to showers, but showers are increasingly common.

Guesthouses, which are often just large converted houses with half a dozen rooms, are an extension of the B&B concept. They range from £12 to £50 a night, depending on the quality of the food and accommodation. In general they're less personal than B&Bs, and more like small budget hotels.

Scottish B&Bs and guesthouses tend to be cheaper than their English counterparts; budget travellers are unlikely to have to pay more than £18 per person. In Wales, outside Cardiff, Swansea and Newport, you're unlikely to have to pay more than £16 a head, even in high season.

Hotels
The term hotel covers everything from local pubs to the grand playgrounds of the hyper-wealthy. Pubs usually have a bar or two and a lounge where cheap meals are served; sometimes they'll also have a more upmarket restaurant.

In the countryside hotels also offer comfortable mid-range accommodation, but they can vary widely in quality. Staying in a pub can be good fun since it places you in the hub of the community, but they can be noisy and are not always ideal for lone women travellers. There are often big, old-style, residential hotels in tourist towns. The cheapest are sometimes entirely occupied by long-term residents, so it's wise to stick with tourist-board-approved places except in rural areas.

Prices vary. In the English countryside it's not unusual to get bed & breakfast for under £20; in larger centres it's more likely to cost around £30. On the whole hotel owners don't object to bicycles but they're not always set up to store them.

Short-Term Rentals
There has been an upsurge in the number of houses and cottages available for short-term rent, although as rents are usually for three days' minimum these will only interest cyclists keen to explore a particular area on a series of day rides.

You may be able to book rental properties through TICs in England, but there are also excellent agencies who supply brochures to help the decision-making. Most have agents in North America and Australasia. Among them, Country Holidays (☎ 01282-445566), Spring Mill, Earby, Colne, Lancashire BB8 6RN, comes highly recommended.

The National Trust also rents out over 240 cottages that tend to be above average in charm, location and price. For a brochure write to the Holiday Booking Office, PO Box 536, Melksham, Wiltshire SN12 8SX (☎ 01225-791133), enclosing £2 towards postage.

There's plenty of self-catering accommodation in Scotland and Wales but, in summer at least, the minimum stay is usually one week. Details are in the accommodation guides available from TICs, the STB's *Scotland: Self-Catering Accommodation* and the WTB's *Wales Self-Catering*.

FOOD
Local Food
This is the land that brought us bangers and mash, mushy peas, stodgy Yorkshire pudding and various types of prepared offal, a cuisine so undesirable that there's no English equivalent for the French phrase *bon appétit*.

Fortunately, especially in the south, in recent years the supply of fresh fruit and vegetables has improved immeasurably and in the main towns and cities a cosmopolitan range of cuisines is available. You should be able to get a reasonable meal almost anywhere. Meat dishes are popular, despite the bad press British beef has copped in recent years. There's good seafood in coastal towns, especially in Scotland. Various regional specialties are worth a try; you'll have plenty of opportunities to sample a pasty in Cornwall, rarebit in Wales or haggis in Scotland.

As usual, non-meat-eaters will have a harder time finding places to eat; buy *The Vegetarian Travel Guide*, published annually by the UK Vegetarian Society, which covers hundreds of places to eat and stay. Most restaurants have at least a token vegetarian dish, although, as is the case almost anywhere, vegans will find the going tough. Indian restaurants offer a welcome choice. Incidentally, curries have overtaken fish and chips as Britain's most popular takeaways; it's widely said, with a trace of irony, that the national cuisine is Indian food.

Where to Eat
Takeaways, Cafes & Pubs All the usual suspects (McDonald's, KFC, Pizza Hut, and the home-grown Wimpy) are available. The best of the worst is Burger King, which even serves a vegetarian beanburger.

In the bigger towns you'll also find cafes, referred to as 'caffs' or 'greasy spoons'. Despite their appearance, they are usually warm and friendly and serve cheap cooked breakfasts, morning tea/coffee (don't bank on the coffee being too flash) and plain but filling lunches. Prices are often attractive – a big breakfast might be £3 to £4.

If you're watching pennies, you'll prabably eat in the odd pub, and it's here that you'll find the last stronghold of traditional British cuisine like roast beef and Yorkshire pud or steak-and-kidney pie. You'll find an increasing number of pubs (especially in tourist towns) serving varied and genuinely tasty meals, often at great prices.

It's worth knowing that many supermarkets and department stores have reasonable cafes; these have the same opening hours as the host store.

Restaurants Like anywhere else in the world, Britain has good and bad restaurants; broadly, you need to save up for the former and avoid the latter. The listings magazines in cities will help you find a good restaurant; when you're in the countryside seek a local recommendation.

Self-Catering
The cheapest way to eat in Britain is to cook for yourself, and the density of towns ensures that you rarely have to carry more than a day's food. As well as stocking all the necessary ingredients for make-your-own meals, supermarkets have an ever-wider range of pre-cooked meals. Much as it's nice to support local grocers (where they still exist), supermarkets are also the cheapest place to stock up on fruit, food bars and energy drinks for the road.

Large supermarket chains include Tesco, Safeway, Sainsbury and Somerfield. Smaller 'convenience store' chains such as Alldays are often seen in mid-sized towns. Many villages that might once have had a corner store of some kind are now shop-less (indeed, some of them no longer have a pub), so be sure to check ahead if you're deliberately avoiding the larger population centres.

DRINKS
See Hydration in the Health & Safety chapter for advice about replenishing fluids.

Nonalcoholic Drinks
There's no problem drinking water from the cold tap in towns and cities. At country camp sites water is sometimes piped straight from a spring without treatment, but there's usually a sign telling you whether the local rain is safe or not. It's easiest to fill your water bottles at pubs or cafes along the route.

The British national drink is undoubtedly tea, although coffee is now just as popular. It's easy to get a cappuccino or espresso in southern towns, but coffee lovers should be aware that in the countryside a lot of smaller places still serve instant.

You can almost measure your geographical position by the strength of the tea in cafes. From a point somewhere around Birmingham the tea gets progressively stronger (and more orange) – the sort of brew you can stand your teaspoon up in, or so idiom would have it. Farther south you're as likely to be offered Earl Grey or a herbal tea as a traditional Indian or Sri Lankan brew.

Alcoholic Drinks

Pubs may open for any 12 hours a day Monday to Saturday. Most maintain the traditional 11 am to 11 pm hours; the bell for last orders rings at about 10.45 pm. On Sunday most open from noon to 3 pm and from 7 to 10.30 pm, though some stay open all day.

The wide choice of beers ranges from very light (almost like lager) to extremely strong and treacly. They're usually served at room temperature, which may come as a shock if you've been raised on lager. But if you think of these 'beers' as something completely new, you'll discover subtle flavours that a cold, chemical lager can't match. Ales and bitters are similar; it's more a regional name difference than anything else. The best are actually hand-pumped from the cask, not carbonated and drawn under pressure. Stout is a dark, rich, foamy drink. Beers are usually served in pints (from £1.80 to £2.50 and more), but you can also ask for 'a half' (a half pint). Ask at the bar if there's a local brew to try; you might attempt the aptly-named Skullsplitter in Scotland's Orkneys, and don't leave Cardiff without downing a pint of Brains, the local brew.

Good wine is widely available in off-licences (liquor stores) and is very reasonably priced (except in pubs and restaurants). In supermarkets an ordinary but drinkable bottle can still be found for around £4, and choice can be huge – it's not unusual to find wines from throughout Europe, Australia, California and South America.

First distilled in Scotland in the 15th century, whisky (spelt without an 'e' if it's Scottish) is Scotland's best-known product and biggest export; over 2000 brands are now produced. There are two kinds of whisky: single malt, made from malted barley, and blended whisky, distilled from unmalted grain (maize) and blended with selected malts. Single malts are rarer (there are only about 100 brands) and more expensive than blended whiskies. When out drinking, Scots may order a dram (measure) of whisky as a chaser to a pint of beer. Only tourists ask for 'Scotch' – what else would you be served in Scotland?

British Beer

What the British call beer is technically 'ale' – usually brown in colour, and more often called 'bitter'. What most people from the 'New World' know as beer (usually yellow) is called 'lager' in Britain. There are some British lagers, but imported brand names (including Fosters and Budweiser) have infiltrated in a big way. However, when in Britain you should at least try some good British beer.

If you've been raised on amber nectar, a traditional British bitter is something of a shock – a warm, flat and expensive shock. Part of this is to do with the climate (beer here does not need to be chilled) and the way it's often served (hand pumped, not pressurised). Pubs that serve good beer are recommended by the

Campaign for Real Ale (CAMRA) organisation. Look for their endorsement sticker on pub windows. Once you've got used to British beer, you can start experimenting with some of the hundreds of different regional types, all with varying subtle flavours and strengths. Look out for 'special brews' or 'winter warmers', but beware – some are almost as strong as wine. Another popular drink is Guinness, a dark, rich, foamy 'stout'. There are many other similar brews.

Health & Safety

Keeping healthy on your travels depends on your predeparture preparations, your daily health care and diet while on the road, and how you handle any medical problem that develops. Few touring cyclists experience anything more than a bit of soreness, fatigue and chafing, although there is potential for more serious problems. The sections that follow are not intended to alarm, but they are worth a skim before you go.

Before You Go

HEALTH INSURANCE
Make sure that you have adequate health insurance. For details, see Travel Insurance in the Visas & Documents section in the Facts for the Cyclist chapter.

IMMUNISATIONS
You don't need any vaccinations to visit Britain. However, it's always wise to keep up-to-date with routine vaccinations such as diphtheria, polio and tetanus – boosters are necessary every 10 years and protection is highly recommended.

FIRST AID
It's a good idea at any time to know the appropriate responses in the event of a major accident or illness, and it's especially important if you are intending to ride off-road in a remote area. Consider learning basic first aid through a recognised course before you go, and carrying a first aid manual and small medical kit.

Although detailed first aid instruction is outside the scope of this guidebook, some basic points are listed in the section on Traumatic Injuries later in this chapter. Undoubtedly the best advice is to avoid an accident in the first place. The Safety on the Ride section at the end of this chapter contains tips for safe on-road and off-road riding, as well as information on how to summon help should a major accident or illness occur.

PHYSICAL FITNESS
Most of the rides in this book are designed for someone with a moderate degree of cycling

---

First Aid Kit

A possible kit could include:

First Aid Supplies
- ☐ sticking plasters (Band Aids)
- ☐ bandages & safety pins
- ☐ elastic support bandage for knees, ankles etc
- ☐ gauze swabs
- ☐ nonadhesive dressings
- ☐ small pair of scissors
- ☐ sterile alcohol wipes
- ☐ butterfly closure strips
- ☐ latex gloves
- ☐ syringes & needles – for removing gravel from road-rash wounds
- ☐ thermometer (note that mercury thermometers are prohibited by airlines)
- ☐ tweezers

Medications
- ☐ antidiarrhoea, antinausea drugs and oral rehydration salts
- ☐ antifungal cream or powder – for fungal skin infections and thrush
- ☐ antihistamines – for allergies, eg, hay fever; to ease the itch from insect bites or stings; and to prevent motion sickness
- ☐ antiseptic powder or solution (such as povidone-iodine) and antiseptic wipes for cuts and grazes
- ☐ nappy rash cream
- ☐ calamine lotion, sting relief spray or aloe vera – to ease irritation from sunburn and insect bites or stings
- ☐ cold and flu tablets, throat lozenges and nasal decongestant
- ☐ painkillers (eg, aspirin or paracetamol/cetaminophen in the USA) – for pain and fever
- ☐ laxatives

Miscellaneous
- ☐ insect repellent, sunscreen, lip balm and eye drops
- ☐ water purification tablets or iodine

Getting Fit for Touring

Ideally, a training program should be tailored to your objectives, specific needs, fitness level and health. However, if you have no idea how to prepare for your cycling holiday these guidelines will help you get the fitness you need to enjoy it more. Things to think about include:

Foundation You will need general kilometres in your legs before you start to expose them to any intensive cycling. Always start out with easy rides – even a few kilometres to the shops – and give yourself plenty of time to build towards your objective.

Tailoring Once you have the general condition to start preparing for your trip, work out how to tailor your training rides to the type of tour you are planning. Someone preparing for a three-week ride will require a different approach to someone building fitness for a one-day or weekend ride. Some aspects to think about are the ride length (distance and days), terrain, climate and weight to be carried in panniers. If your trip involves carrying 20kg in panniers, incorporate this weight into some training rides, especially some of the longer ones. If you are going to be touring in mountainous areas, choose a hilly training route.

Recovery You usually adapt to a training program during recovery time, so it's important to do the right things between rides. Recovery can take many forms, but the simple ones are best. These include getting quality sleep, eating an adequate diet to refuel the system, doing recovery rides between hard days (using low gears to avoid pushing yourself), stretching and enjoying a relaxing bath. Other forms include recovery massage, spas and yoga.

If you have no cycling background this program will help you get fit for your cycling holiday. If you are doing an easy ride (each ride in this book is rated; see Cycling Routes in the Facts for the Cyclist chapter), aim to at least complete Week 4; for moderate rides, complete Week 6; and complete the program if you are doing a hard ride. Experienced cycle tourists could start at Week 3, while those who regularly ride up to four days a week could start at Week 5.

Don't treat this as a punishing training schedule: try cycling to work or to the shops, join a local touring club or get a group of friends together to turn weekend rides into social events.

	Monday	Tuesday	Wednesday	Thursday	Friday	Saturday	Sunday
Week 1	10km*	–	10km*	–	10km*	–	10km*
Week 2	–	15km*	–	15km*	–	20km*	–
Week 3	20km*	–	20km*	25km*	–	25km*	20km†
Week 4	–	30km*	–	35km*	30km†	30km*	–
Week 5	30km*	–	40km†	–	35km*	–	40km†
Week 6	30km*	–	40km†	–	–	60km*	40km†
Week 7	30km*	–	40km†	–	30km†	70km*	30km*
Week 8	–	60km*	30km†	–	40km†	–	90km*

* steady pace (allows you to carry out a conversation without losing your breath) on flat or undulating terrain
† solid pace (allows you to talk in short sentences only) on undulating roads with some longer hills

The training program shown here is only a guide. Ultimately it is important to listen to your body and slow down if the ride is getting too hard. Take extra recovery days and cut back distances when you feel this way. Don't panic if you don't complete every ride, every week; the most important thing is to ride regularly and gradually increase the length of your rides as you get fitter.

For those with no exercise background, be sure to see your doctor and get a clearance to begin exercising at these rates. This is especially important for those over 35 years of age with no exercise history and those with a cardiac or respiratory condition of any nature.

Kevin Tabotta

fitness. As a general rule, however, the fitter you are, the more you'll enjoy riding. It pays to spend time preparing yourself physically before you set out, rather than let a sore backside and aching muscles draw your attention from some of the world's finest cycle touring countryside.

Depending on your existing level of fitness, you should start training a couple of months before your trip. Try to ride at least three times a week, starting with easy rides (even 5km to work, if you're not already cycling regularly) and gradually building up to longer distances. Once you have a good base of regular riding behind you, include hills in your training (you'll appreciate hill fitness in parts of Britain) and familiarise yourself with the gearing on your bike. Before you go you should have done at least one 60km to 70km ride with loaded panniers.

As you train, you'll discover the bike adjustments needed to increase your comfort – as well as any mechanical problems.

Staying Healthy

The best way to have a completely lousy holiday (especially if you are relying on self-propulsion) is to become ill. Heed the following simple advice and the only thing you're likely to suffer from is that rewarding tiredness at the end of a full day.

Reduce the chances of contracting an illness by washing your hands frequently, particularly after working on your bike and before handling or eating food.

HYDRATION
You may not notice how much water you're losing as you ride, because it evaporates in the breeze. However, don't underestimate the amount of fluid you need to replace – particularly in warmer weather. The magic figure is supposedly 1L per hour, though many cyclists have trouble consuming this much – remembering to drink enough can be harder than it sounds. Sipping little and often is the key; try to drink a mouthful every 10 minutes or so and don't wait until you get thirsty. Water 'backpacks' can be great for fluid regulation since virtually no physical or mental effort is required to drink. Keep drinking before and after the day's ride to replenish fluid.

Use the colour of your urine as a rough guide to whether you are drinking enough. Small amounts of dark urine suggest you need to increase your fluid intake. Passing reasonable quantities of light yellow urine indicates that you've got the balance about right. Other signs of dehydration include headache and fatigue. For more information on the effects of dehydration, see Dehydration & Heat Exhaustion later in this chapter.

Water
While tap water is always safe to drink in Britain unless there is a sign to the contrary (eg, on trains), the intestinal parasite *Giardia lamblia* has been found in water from lakes, rivers and streams. Giardia is not common but, to be certain, water from these sources should be purified before drinking. For more information on giardiasis, see Infectious Diseases later in this chapter.

The simplest way of purifying water is to boil it thoroughly. Vigorous boiling for five minutes should do the job.

Simple filtering will not remove all dangerous organisms, so if you can't boil water treat it chemically. Chlorine tablets will kill many pathogens, but not giardia. Iodine is very effective in purifying water and is available in tablet and liquid form, but follow the directions carefully and remember that too much iodine can be harmful. Flavoured powder will disguise the taste of treated water and is a good thing to carry if you are spending time away from town water supplies.

Sports Drinks
Commercial sports drinks such as Gatorade and PowerAde are an excellent way to satisfy your hydration needs, electrolyte replacement and energy demands in one. On endurance rides especially, it can be difficult to keep eating solid fuels day in, day out, but sports drinks can supplement these energy demands and allow you to vary your solid fuel intake a little for variety. The bonus is that those all-important body salts lost through perspiration get re-stocked. Make sure you drink plenty of water as well; if you have two water bottles on your bike (and you should), it's a good idea to fill one with sports drink and the other with plain water.

If using a powdered sports drink, don't mix it too strong (follow the instructions) because, in addition to being too sweet, too many carbohydrates can actually impair your body's ability to absorb the water and carbohydrates properly.

NUTRITION

One of the great things about bike touring is that it requires a lot of energy, which means you can eat more. Depending on your activity levels, it's not hard to put away huge servings of food and be hungry a few hours after.

Because you're putting such demands on your body, it's important to eat well – not just lots. As usual, you should eat a balanced diet from a wide variety of foods. This is increasingly easy in Britain, with fresh food now more widely available (see Food in the Facts for the Cyclist chapter).

The main part of your diet should be carbohydrates rather than proteins or fats. While some protein (for tissue maintenance and repair) and fat (for vitamins, long-term energy and warmth) is essential, carbohydrates provide the most efficient fuel. They are easily digested into simple sugars, which are then used in energy production. Less-refined foods like pasta, rice, bread, fruits and vegetables are all high in carbohydrates.

Eating simple carbohydrates (sugars, such as lollies or sweets) gives you almost immediate energy – great for when you need a top-up (see the boxed text 'Avoiding the Bonk'); however, because they are quickly metabolised, you may get a sugar 'high' then a 'low'. For cycling it is far better to base

Avoiding the Bonk

The bonk, in a cycling context, is not a pleasant experience; it's that light-headed, can't-put-power-to-the-pedals, weak feeling that engulfs you (usually quite quickly) when your body runs out of fuel.

If you experience it the best move is to stop and refuel immediately. It can be quite serious and risky to your health if it's not addressed as soon as symptoms occur. It won't take long before you are ready to get going again (although most likely at a slower pace), but you'll also be more tired the next day so try to avoid it.

The best way to do this is to maintain your fuel intake while riding. Cycling for hours burns considerable body energy, and replacing it is something that needs to be tailored to each individual's tastes. The touring cyclist needs to target foods that have a high carbohydrate source. Foods that contain some fat are not a problem occasionally, as cycling at low intensity (when you're able to ride and talk without losing your breath) will usually trigger the body to draw on fat stores before stored carbohydrates.

Good on-bike cycling foods include:

- bananas (in particular) and other fruits
- bread with jam or honey
- breakfast and muesli bars
- rice-based snacks
- prepackaged high carbohydrate sports bars (eg, PowerBar)
- sports drinks

During lunch stops (or for breakfast) you can try such things as spaghetti, cereal, pancakes, baked beans, sandwiches and rolls.

It's important not to get uptight about the food you eat. As a rule of thumb, base all your meals around carbohydrates of some sort, but don't be afraid to also indulge in local culinary delights.

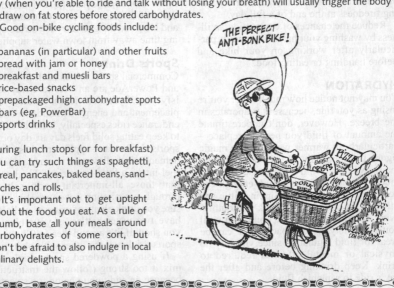

THE PERFECT ANTI-BONK BIKE!

your diet around complex carbohydrates, which take longer to process and provide 'slow-release' energy over a longer period. (But don't miss the opportunity to indulge guiltlessly in scones with jam and cream every now and then.)

Cycle Food: a Guide to Satisfying Your Inner Tube, by Lauren Hefferon, is a handy reference for nutrition and health advice with practical recipes.

Day-to-Day Needs

Eat a substantial breakfast – wholegrain cereal or bread is best – and fruit or juice for vitamins. If you like a cooked breakfast, include carbohydrates (such as porridge, toast or potatoes). Try to avoid foods high in fat, which take longer to digest.

Bread is the easiest food for lunch, topped with ingredients like cheese, peanut butter, salami and fresh salad vegetables. If you're in a town, filled rolls make for a satisfying meal (chips or pizza, with their high fat content, will feel like a lump in your stomach if you continue straight away).

Keep topping up your energy during the ride. See the boxed text 'Avoiding the Bonk' for tips.

Try to eat a high carbohydrate meal in the evening. If you're eating out, Mexican, Vegetarian, Italian or Asian restaurants tend to offer more carbohydrate-based meals.

Rice, pasta and potatoes are good staples if you're self-catering. Team them with fresh vegetables and ingredients such as instant soup, canned beans, fish or bacon. Remember that even though you're limited in terms of what you can carry on a bike, it's possible – with some imagination and preparation – to eat camp meals that are both delicious and nutritious.

AVOIDING CYCLING AILMENTS
Saddle Sores & Blisters

While you're more likely to get a sore bum if you're out of condition, riding long distances does take its toll on your behind. To minimise the impact, always wear clean, preferably padded bike shorts (also known as 'knicks'). Brief, unfitted shorts can chafe, as can underwear (see Clothing under What to Bring in the Facts for the Cyclist chapter). Shower as soon as you stop and put on clean, preferably nonsynthetic, clothes. Moisturising or emollient creams or baby nappy rash cream also help guard against chafing – apply liberally around the crotch area before riding. For information on correctly adjusting your bike seat, see the Your Bicycle chapter.

If you do suffer from chafing, wash and dry the area and carefully apply a barrier (moisturising) cream.

You probably won't get blisters unless you do a very long ride with no physical preparation. Wearing gloves and correctly fitted shoes will reduce the likelihood of blisters on your hands and feet. If you know you're susceptible to blisters in a particular spot, cover the area with medical adhesive tape before riding.

Knee Pain

Knee pain is common among cyclists who pedal in too high a gear. While it may *seem* faster to turn the pedals slowly in a high gear, it's actually more efficient (and better for your knees) to 'spin' the pedals – that is, use a low enough gear so you can pedal quickly with little resistance. For touring, the ideal cadence (the number of pedal strokes per minute) ranges from 70 to 90. Try to maintain this cadence even when you're climbing.

It's a good idea to stretch before and after riding, and to go easy when you first start each day. This reduces your chances of injury and helps your muscles to work more efficiently.

You can also get sore knees if your saddle is too low, or if your shoe cleats (for use with clipless pedals) are incorrectly positioned. Both are discussed in greater detail in the Your Bicycle chapter.

Numbness & Backache

Pain in the hands, neck and shoulders is a common complaint, particularly on longer riding days. It is generally caused by leaning too much on your hands. Apart from discomfort, you can temporarily damage the nerves and experience numbness or mild paralysis of the hands. This can be prevented by wearing padded gloves, cycling with less weight on your hands and changing your hand position frequently (if you have flat handlebars, fit bar ends to provide more hand positions).

When seated your weight should be fairly evenly distributed through your hands and seat. If you're carrying too much weight on your hands there are two ways of adjusting

Stretching

Stretching is important when stepping up your exercise levels: it improves muscle flexibility, which allows freer movement in the joints; and prevents the rigidity developing in muscles that occurs through prolonged cycling activity.

Ideally, you should stretch for 10 minutes before and after riding and for longer periods (15 to 30 minutes) every second day. Stretching prepares muscles for the task ahead, and limits the stress on muscles and joints during exercise. It can reduce post-exercise stiffness (decreasing the recovery time between rides) and reduce the chance of injury during cycling.

You should follow a few basic guidelines:

- Before stretching, warm up for five to 10 minutes by going for a gentle bike ride, jog or brisk walk.
- Ensure you follow correct technique for each stretch.
- Hold a stretch for 15 to 30 seconds.
- Stretch to the point of discomfort, not pain.
- Breathe freely (ie, don't hold your breath) and try to relax your body whenever you are stretching.
- Don't 'bounce' the stretch; gradually ease into a full stretch.
- Repeat each stretch three times (on both sides, when required).

Do not stretch when you have an injury to a muscle, ligament or tendon (allow it to heal fully), as it can lead to further injury and/or hinder recovery. Warming up the muscles increases blood flow to the area, making it easier to stretch and reducing the likelihood of injury.

The main muscle groups for the cyclist to stretch are: quadriceps, calves, hamstrings, lower back and neck. Use the following stretches as a starting point, adding extra stretches that are already part of your routine or if you feel 'tight' in other areas (eg, add shoulder rolls if your shoulders feel sore after a day's cycling).

Quadriceps

Facing a wall with your feet slightly apart, grip one foot with your hand and pull it towards the buttocks. Ensure the back and hips are square. To get a better stretch, push the hip forward. You should never feel pain at the knee joint. Hold the stretch, before lowering the leg and repeating the stretch with the other leg.

Calf

Stand facing a wall, placing one foot about 30cm in front of the other. Keep the heels flat on the ground and bend the front leg slowly toward the wall – the stretch should be in the upper-calf area of the back leg. Keep the back straight and bend your elbows to allow your body to move forward during the stretch. Hold the stretch; relax and repeat the stretch with the other leg.

Hamstrings

Sit with one leg extended and the other leg bent with the bottom of the foot against the inside of the extended leg. Slide your arms down the extended leg – bending from the waist – until you feel a pull in the hamstring area. Hold it for 15 seconds, before returning to the start position. Keep the toes pointed up; avoid hunching the back.

Lower-Back Roll

Lie on your back (on a towel or sleeping mat) and bring both knees up towards the shoulders until you feel a stretch in the lower back. Hold the stretch for 30 seconds; relax.

'Cat Stretch' Hunch

Another stretch for the lower back. Move to the ground on all fours (hands shoulder-width apart; legs slightly apart), lift the hips and lower back towards the sky until you feel a stretch. Hold it for 15 seconds; return to start position.

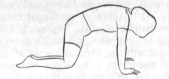

'Cat Stretch' Arch

One more stretch for the lower back. With hands and knees in the same position as for the Cat Stretch above, roll the hips and lower back toward the ground until you feel a stretch. Hold it for 15 seconds; return to start position.

Neck

Gently and smoothly stretch your neck each of the four ways: forward, back and side to side. Do each stretch separately. (Do not rotate the head in a full circle.) For the side stretches, use your hand to pull the head very gently in the direction of the stretch.

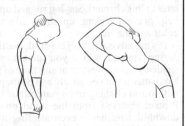

your bike to rectify this: either by raising the height of your handlebars or, if you are stretched out too much, fitting a smaller stem (talk to your local bike shop). For more guidance, see the Your Bicycle chapter.

Fungal Infections

Warm, sweaty bodies are ideal environments for fungal growth, and physical activity, combined with inadequate washing of your body and/or clothes, can lead to fungal infections. The most common are athlete's foot (tinea) between the toes or fingers, and infections on the scalp, in the groin or on the body (ringworm). You can get ringworm (which is a fungal infection, not a worm) from infected animals or other people.

To prevent fungal infections, wash frequently and dry yourself carefully. Change out of sweaty bike clothes as soon as possible.

If you do get an infection, wash the infected area at least daily with a disinfectant or medicated soap and water, and rinse and dry well. Apply an antifungal cream or powder like tolnaftate. Expose the infected area to air or sunlight as much as possible, avoid artificial fibres and wash all towels and underwear in hot water, change them often and let them dry in the sun.

Staying Warm

Except on extremely hot days, put on another layer of clothing when you stop cycling – even if it's just for a quick break. Staying warm when cycling is as important as keeping up your water and food intake. Particularly in wet or sweaty clothing, your body cools down quickly after you stop working. Muscle strains occur more easily when your body is chilled and hypothermia can result from prolonged exposure (for prevention and treatment, see Hypothermia later in this chapter). Staying rugged up will help prevent picking up chest infections, colds and the flu.

It's not advisable to cycle at high altitude during winter; however, you *can* get caught suddenly in bad weather at any time of year. No matter when you go, always be prepared with warm clothing and a waterproof layer. Protect yourself from the wind on long downhill stretches – even stuffing a few sheets of newspaper under your shirt cuts the chill considerably.

Medical Problems & Treatment

ENVIRONMENTAL HAZARDS

Whatever the season, cyclists in Britain should be prepared for difficult conditions. For suggestions on appropriate clothing and equipment, see also Planning in the Facts for the Cyclist chapter.

Cold

Cold-weather cycling can be a joy if you're prepared and experienced; if not, it can be both unpleasant and hazardous. The physical exertion of pedalling is a great way to stay warm in low temperatures, but on the coldest days it's essential to dress appropriately to ward off wind chill and stay dry, and to ensure that you have enough to eat.

Beware of frosty roads on cold mornings. Cycling during a snowfall is quite a novelty and always dangerous. Avoid setting out if snow is forecast. If there's snow overnight, don't continue your tour until roads are cleared and ice-free. If you're caught out in a severe snowstorm, seek shelter at the first opportunity – don't try to push on.

Hypothermia This is a real danger in Britain because of the changeable weather.

Hypothermia occurs when the body loses heat faster than it can produce it and the core temperature of the body falls. It is surprisingly easy to progress from very cold to dangerously cold due to a combination of wind, wet clothing, fatigue and hunger, even if the air temperature is above freezing.

Symptoms of hypothermia are exhaustion, numb skin (particularly toes and fingers), shivering, slurred speech, irrational or violent behaviour, lethargy, stumbling, dizzy spells, muscle cramps and powerful bursts of energy. Irrationality may take the form of sufferers claiming they are warm and trying to take off their clothes.

To prevent hypothermia, dress in layers (see Clothing under What to Bring in the Facts for the Cyclist chapter). A strong, waterproof outer layer is essential. Protect yourself against wind, particularly for long descents. Eat plenty of high-energy food when it's cold; it's important to keep drinking too – even though you may not feel like it.

To treat mild hypothermia, first get victims out of the wind and/or rain, remove wet clothing and replace it with dry, warm clothing. Give them hot liquids – not alcohol – and some high-kilojoule, easily digestible food. Do not rub victims: instead, allow them to slowly warm themselves. This should be enough to treat the early stages of hypothermia; however, medical treatment should still be sought urgently if the hypothermia is severe. Early recognition and treatment of mild hypothermia is the only way to prevent severe hypothermia, which is a critical condition and potentially fatal.

Sun

Even in temperate Britain, and even when there's cloud cover, it's possible to get sunburnt surprisingly quickly. Take sun protection seriously – unless you want to be fried and increase your chances of heatstroke and skin cancer:

- Cover yourself wherever possible: wear a long-sleeved top with a collar, and a peaked helmet cover – you may want to go the extra step and add a 'legionnaire's flap' to your helmet to protect the back of your neck and ears. Make sure your shirt is sunproof: very thin or loosely woven fabrics still let sun through. Some fabrics are designed to offer high sun protection.
- Use high protection sunscreen (30+ or higher). Choose a water-resistant 'sports' sunscreen and reapply every few hours as you sweat it off. Don't forget to protect your neck, ears, hands, and feet if wearing sandals. Zinc cream is good for sensitive noses, lips and ears.
- Wear good sunglasses; they will also protect you from wind, dust and insects and are essential protection against sticks and flying objects if you're mountain biking.
- Sit in the shade during rest breaks.
- Wear a wide-brimmed hat when off the bike.

Mild sunburn can be treated with calamine lotion, aloe vera or sting-relief spray.

Heat

Extreme heat is rare in Britain. If heatwave conditions are forecast, consider staying off the bike through the middle part of the day. Generally, if you cycle through the cool of the morning and during the long midsummer evenings you'll have plenty of time to stay on schedule.

Dehydration & Heat Exhaustion Dehydration is a potentially dangerous and generally preventable condition caused by excessive fluid loss. Sweating and inadequate fluid intake are common causes of dehydration in cyclists, but others include diarrhoea, vomiting and high fever – see Diarrhoea later in this chapter for details on appropriate treatment in these circumstances.

The first symptoms are weakness, thirst and passing small amounts of very concentrated urine. This may progress to drowsiness, dizziness or fainting when standing up and, finally, coma.

It's easy to forget how much fluid you are losing via perspiration while you are cycling, particularly if a strong breeze is drying your skin quickly. Make sure you drink sufficient liquids (see Hydration earlier in this chapter). Refrain from drinking too many caffeinated drinks such as coffee, tea and some soft drinks (which act as a diuretic, causing your body to lose water through urination) throughout the day; don't use them as a water replacement.

Dehydration and salt deficiency can cause heat exhaustion. Salt deficiency is characterised by fatigue, lethargy, headaches, giddiness and muscle cramps; salt tablets may help, but adding extra salt to your food is probably sufficient.

If one of your party suffers from heat exhaustion, lie the casualty down in a shady spot and encourage them to drink slowly but frequently. If possible, seek medical advice.

Heatstroke This serious and occasionally fatal condition can occur if the body's heat-regulating mechanism breaks down and the body temperature rises to dangerous levels. Continuous periods of exposure to high temperatures and insufficient fluids can leave you vulnerable to heatstroke.

The symptoms are feeling unwell, not sweating very much (or at all) and a high body temperature (39°C to 41°C or 102°F to 106°F). Where sweating has ceased, the skin becomes flushed and red. Severe, throbbing headaches and lack of coordination will also occur, and the sufferer may be confused or aggressive. Eventually the victim will become delirious or convulse.

Hospitalisation is essential, but in the interim get the casualty out of the sun, remove their clothing, cover them with a wet sheet or towel and then fan continuously. Give them plenty of fluids (cool water) if conscious.

Hay Fever

Hay fever sufferers should ensure they have the appropriate medicine. Spring, as usual, is the worst time.

INFECTIOUS DISEASES
Diarrhoea

Simple things like a change of water, food or climate can cause a mild bout of diarrhoea, but a few rushed toilet trips with no other symptoms are not indicative of a major problem. More serious diarrhoea is caused by infectious agents transmitted by faecal contamination of food or water, by using contaminated utensils, or directly from one person's hand to another. Paying particular attention to personal hygiene, drinking purified water and taking care of what you eat are important measures to take to avoid getting diarrhoea while touring.

Dehydration is the main danger with any diarrhoea, particularly in children or the elderly, as it can occur quickly. Under all circumstances, the most important thing is to replace fluids (at least equal to the volume being lost). Urine is the best guide to this – if you have small amounts of dark-coloured urine, you need to drink more. Weak black tea with a little sugar, soda water, or soft drinks allowed to go flat and diluted 50% with clean water are all good. With severe diarrhoea it's better to use a rehydrating solution to replace lost minerals and salts. Commercially available oral rehydration salts should be added to boiled or bottled water. In an emergency, make a solution of six teaspoons of sugar and a half teaspoon of salt in a litre of boiled or bottled water. Keep drinking small amounts often. Stick to a bland diet as you recover.

Gut-paralysing drugs such as diphenoxylate or loperamide can be used to bring relief from the symptoms, although they do not actually cure the problem. Only use these drugs if you do not have access to toilets, that is, if you *must* travel. These drugs are not recommended for children under 12 years of age, or if you have a high fever or are severely dehydrated.

Seek medical advice if you pass blood or mucus, are feverish or suffer persistent or severe diarrhoea.

Another cause of persistent diarrhoea in travellers is giardiasis.

Giardiasis

This intestinal disorder is contracted by drinking water contaminated with the Giardia parasite. The symptoms are stomach cramps, nausea, a bloated stomach, watery and foul-smelling diarrhoea, and frequent gas. Giardiasis can appear several weeks after you have been exposed to the parasite. The symptoms may disappear for a few days and then return; this can go on for several weeks. Seek medical advice if you think you have giardiasis but where this is not possible, tinidazole or metronidazole are the recommended drugs. Treatment is a 2g single dose of tinidazole or 250mg of metronidazole three times daily for five to 10 days.

Tetanus

This disease is caused by a germ that lives in soil and in the faeces of horses and other animals. It enters the body via breaks in the skin. The first symptom may be discomfort in swallowing, or stiffening of the jaw and neck; this is followed by painful convulsions of the jaw and whole body. The disease can be fatal. It can be prevented by vaccination.

BITES & STINGS
Bees & Wasps

These are usually painful rather than dangerous. However, anyone allergic to these can suffer severe breathing difficulties and will need urgent medical care.

Calamine lotion or a commercial sting-relief spray will ease discomfort, and ice packs will reduce the pain and swelling. Antihistamines can also help.

Midges

Midges – small blood-sucking flies – can be a major problem in the Scottish Highlands and Islands from June through September. They're at their worst in the evening, or in still and shady conditions.

To avoid being bitten, cover yourself up with light-coloured clothing and use repellent containing DEET or DMP (note that prolonged overuse of DEET may be harmful, especially to children). Treat bites with antihistamine.

WOMEN'S HEALTH

Cycle touring is not hazardous to your health, but women's health issues are relevant wherever you go, and can be a bit more tricky to cope with when you are on the road.

If you experience low energy and/or abdominal or back pain during menstruation, it may be best to undertake less strenuous rides or schedule a rest day or two at this time.

Gynaecological Problems

If you have a vaginal discharge that is not normal for you with or without any other symptoms, you probably have an infection.

- If you've had thrush before and think you have it again, it's worth self-treating for this (see the following section).
- If not, get medical advice, as you may need a laboratory test and an appropriate course of treatment.
- It's best not to self-medicate with antibiotics because there are many causes of vaginal discharge, which can only be differentiated with a laboratory test.

Thrush (Vaginal Candidiasis) Symptoms of this common yeast infection are itching and discomfort in the genital area, often in association with thick white vaginal discharge (said to resemble cottage cheese). Many factors, including diet, pregnancy, medications and hot climatic conditions can trigger this infection.

You can help prevent thrush by wearing cotton underwear off the bike and loose-fitting bicycle shorts; maintaining good personal hygiene is particularly important when wearing cycling knicks. It's a good idea to wash regularly, but don't use soap, which can increase the chance of thrush occurring. Washing gently with a solution of 1tspn salt dissolved in 1L warm water can relieve the itching. If you have thrush a single dose of an antifungal pessary (vaginal tablet), such as 500mg of clotrimazole is an effective treatment. Alternatively, you can use an antifungal cream inserted high in the vagina (on a tampon). A vaginal acidifying gel may help prevent recurrences.

If you're stuck in a remote area without medication, you could use natural yoghurt (applied directly to the vulva or on a tampon and inserted in the vagina) to soothe and help restore the normal balance of organisms in the vagina.

Avoid yeasty products such as bread and beer, and eat yoghurt made with acidophilus culture to balance the bacteria in your gut.

Urinary Tract Infection

Cystitis, or inflammation of the bladder, is a common condition in women. Symptoms include burning when urinating and having to urinate urgently and frequently. Blood can sometimes be passed in urine.

If you think you have cystitis:

- Drink plenty of fluids to help flush the infection out; citrus fruit juice or cranberry juice can help relieve symptoms.
- Take a nonprescription cystitis remedy to help relieve the discomfort. Alternatively, add a teaspoon of bicarbonate of soda to one glass of water when symptoms first appear.
- If there's no improvement after 24 hours despite these measures, seek medical advice as a course of antibiotics may be needed.

TRAUMATIC INJURIES

Although we give guidance on basic first aid procedures here remember that, unless you're an experienced first aider and confident in what you're doing, it's possible to do more harm than good. Always seek medical help if it is available, but if you are far from any help, follow these guidelines.

Cuts & Other Wounds

Here's what to do if you suffer a fall while riding and end up with road-rash (grazing) and a few minor cuts. If you intend continuing on your way, there's likely to be a high risk of infection, so the wound needs to be cleaned and dressed. Carry a few antiseptic wipes in your first-aid kit to use as an immediate measure, especially if no clean water is available. Small wounds can be cleaned with an antiseptic wipe (only wipe across the wound once with each). Deep or dirty wounds need to be cleaned thoroughly:

- Clean your hands before you start.
- Wear gloves if you are cleaning somebody else's wound.
- Use bottled or boiled water (allowed to cool) or an antiseptic solution like povidone-iodine.
- Use plenty of water – pour it on the wound from a container.
- Embedded dirt and other particles can be removed with tweezers or flushed out using a syringe to squirt water (you can get more pressure if you use a needle as well) – this is especially effective for removing gravel.
- Dry wounds heal best, so avoid using antiseptic creams that keep the wound moist; instead apply antiseptic powder or spray.

• Dry the wound with clean gauze before applying a dressing – alternatively, any clean material will do as long as it's not fluffy (avoid cotton wool), because it will stick.

Any break in the skin makes you vulnerable to tetanus infection – if you didn't have a tetanus injection before you left, get one now.

A dressing will protect the wound from dirt, dust and flies. Alternatively, if the wound is small and you are confident you can keep it clean, leave it uncovered. Change the dressing regularly (once a day to start with), especially if the wound is oozing, and watch for signs of infection.

If you have any swelling around the wound, raising the affected limb can help the swelling settle and the wound to heal.

It's best to seek medical advice for any wound that fails to heal after a week or so.

Bleeding Wounds

Most cuts will stop bleeding on their own, but if a blood vessel of any size has been cut it may continue bleeding for some time. Wounds to the head, hands and at joint creases tend to be particularly bloody.

To stop bleeding from a wound:

• Wear gloves if you are dealing with a wound on another person.
• Lie the casualty down if possible.
• Raise the injured limb above the level of the casualty's heart.
• Use your fingers or the palm of your hand to apply direct pressure to the wound, preferably over a sterile dressing or clean pad.
• Apply steady pressure for at least five minutes before looking to see if the bleeding has stopped.
• Put a sterile dressing over the original pad (don't move this) and bandage it in place.
• Check the bandage regularly in case bleeding restarts.

Never use a tourniquet to stop bleeding as this may cause gangrene – the only situation in which this may be appropriate is if the limb has been amputated.

Major Accident

Crashing or being hit by an inattentive driver in a motor vehicle is always a possibility when cycling. When a major accident does occur what you do is determined to some extent by the circumstances you are in and how readily available medical care is. However, remember that emergency services may be different from what you're used to at home.

And, as anywhere, if you are outside a major town they may be much slower at responding to a call, so you need to be prepared to do at least an initial assessment and to ensure that the casualty comes to no further harm. First of all, check for danger to yourself. If the casualty is on the road ensure oncoming traffic is stopped or diverted around you. A basic plan of action is:

• Keep calm and think through what you need to do and when.
• Get medical help urgently; send someone to phone ☎ 999.
• Carefully look over the casualty in the position in which you found them (unless this is hazardous for some reason, eg, on a cliff edge).
• Call to the casualty to see if there's any response.
• Check for pulse (at the wrist or on the side of the neck), breathing and major blood loss.
• If necessary (ie, no breathing or no pulse), and you know how, start resuscitation.
• Check the casualty for injuries, moving them as little as possible; ask them where they have pain if they are conscious.
• Don't move the casualty if a spinal injury is possible.
• Take immediate steps to control any obvious bleeding by applying direct pressure to the wound.
• Make the casualty as comfortable as possible and reassure them.
• Keep the casualty warm by insulating them from cold or wet ground (use whatever you have to hand, such as a sleeping bag).

Safety on the Ride

ROAD RULES

In Britain, traffic travels on the left side of the road. Unless signs indicate otherwise, you're allowed to cycle on any road except a motorway. If riding a bicycle on a public road, you must obey all traffic signs and signals and use appropriate hand signals to indicate your intention to turn or change lanes. You're not allowed to use a bus lane unless signs indicate it's okay (the signs will include a cycle symbol).

You're not entitled to ride on a road-side footpath (pavement) unless signs indicate it's allowed. If you're riding on a cycle track (away from the road) that's shared with pedestrians, you must keep to the part of the track allocated to cyclists. Where cycle tracks cross roads, you must dismount and walk your bike across unless the signals indicate a bicycle crossing (but only when the green cycle symbol is showing).

Various regulations govern British bicycle specifications. They're mostly common sense requirements and strictly don't apply to bicycles brought into Britain for use on a tour or holiday. But you'd be awfully silly to ride a bicycle that, for instance, didn't have properly functioning brakes and gears. If you decide to ride at night, you must have working front and rear lights and a rear red reflector.

It's illegal to cycle under the influence of drugs and alcohol. While you don't often hear of cyclists being stopped for drink-riding, the laws against drink-driving are treated very seriously. Currently you're allowed to have a blood-alcohol level of 35mg/100ml, but the safest approach is not to drink anything at all if you're planning to ride or drive.

You're not allowed to carry a passenger unless your bike has been specially built or adapted for the purpose.

The Stationery Office's publication The Highway Code (99p) is widely available and worth reading.

Rider Safety

Helmets are not compulsory for cyclists but they are strongly recommended by British health, cycling and traffic authorities. Make sure it fits properly: it should sit squarely on your head with the front low on your brow to protect your forehead. It should be snug, but not tight, once it has been fastened, and there should be no slack in the straps. If it has been in a crash, replace it.

Whether it is day or night, it is always a good idea to wear brightly coloured clothing, and at night garments with reflective strips are safer.

Do not hesitate to use your bell or voice to make your presence known.

RIDING OFF-ROAD

Some mountain bike rides are suggested in Things to See & Do sections under town headings throughout the book. Although most rides are not far from civilisation, you should always remember one of the first rules about mountain bike riding: never go alone. It's not uncommon for people to go missing, either through injury or after losing their way. It's best, if possible, to go in a small group – four is usually considered the minimum number. This way, if someone in the group has an accident or is taken ill, one person can stay with the casualty and the others can go for help.

Always tell someone where you are going and when you intend to be back – and make sure they know that you're back! Take warm clothing, matches and enough food and water in case of emergency. Carry enough tools with you so that you can undertake any emergency bicycle repairs (see the Your Bicycle chapter for advice on a basic tool kit).

Carry a map and take note of your surroundings as you ride (terrain, landmarks, intersections and so on) so if you do get lost, you're more likely to find your way again. If you get really lost, stay calm and stop. Try to work out where you are or how to retrace your route. If you can't, or it's getting dark, find a nearby open area, put on warm clothes and find or make a shelter. Light a fire for warmth and assist searchers by making as many obvious signs as you can (such as creating smoke, displaying brightly coloured items, or making symbols out of wood or rocks).

EMERGENCY PROCEDURE

If you or one of your group has an accident (even a minor one), or falls ill during your travels, you'll need to decide on the best

---

Medical Emergencies

Dial ☎ 999 (free call) for an ambulance or police. Dial ☎ 0800-665544 for the address of the nearest doctor or hospital. Not all hospitals have an accident and emergency department; look for red signs with an 'H', followed by 'A&E' (Accident & Emergency).

Pharmacies should have a notice in the window, advising where you'll find the nearest late-night branch.

Tips for Better Cycling

These tips on riding technique are designed to help you ride more safely, comfortably and efficiently:

- Ride in bike lanes if they exist.
- Ride about 1m from the edge of the kerb or from parked cars; riding too close to the road edge makes you less visible and more vulnerable to rough surfaces or car doors being opened without warning.
- Stay alert: especially on busy, narrow, winding and hilly roads it's essential to constantly scan ahead and anticipate the movements of other vehicles, cyclists, pedestrians or animals. Keep an eye out for potholes and other hazard as well.
- Keep your upper body relaxed, even when you are climbing.
- Ride a straight line and don't weave across the road when you reach for your water bottle or when climbing.
- To negotiate rough surfaces and bumps, take your weight off the saddle and let your legs absorb the shock, with the pedals level (in the three and nine o'clock positions).

At Night
- Only ride at night if your bike is equipped with a front and rear light; consider also using a reflective vest and/or reflective ankle bands.

Britain's fantastic network of bikepaths enable safer, more-enjoyable riding.

Braking
- Apply front and rear brakes evenly.
- When your bike is fully loaded you'll find that you can apply the front brake quite hard and the extra weight will prevent you doing an 'endo' (flipping over the handlebars).
- In wet weather gently apply the brakes occasionally to dry the brake pads.

Climbing
- When climbing out of the saddle, keep the bike steady; rock the handlebars from side to side as little as possible.
- Change down to your low gears to keep your legs 'spinning'.

Cornering
- Loaded bikes are prone to sliding on corners; approach corners slowly and don't lean into the corner as hard as you normally would.
- If traffic permits, take a straight path across corners; hit the corner wide, cut across the apex and ride out of it wide – but never cross the dividing line on the road.
- Apply the brakes before the corner, not while cornering (especially if it's wet).

Descending
- Stay relaxed, don't cramp up and letyour body go with the bike.
- A loaded bike is more likely to wobble and be harder to control at speed, so take it easy.

Tips for Better Cycling

- Pump the brakes to shed speed rather than applying constant pressure; this avoids overheating the rims, which can cause your tyre to blow.

Gravel Roads
- Avoid patches of deep gravel (often on the road's edge); if you can't, ride hard, as you do if driving a car through mud.
- Look ahead to plan your course; avoid sudden turning and take it slowly on descents.
- Brake in a straight line using your rear brake and place your weight over the front wheel if you need to use that brake.
- On loose gravel, loosen your toe- clip straps or clipless pedals so you can put your foot down quickly.

Group Riding
- If you're riding in a group, keep your actions predictable and let others know, with a hand signal or shout, before you brake, turn, dodge potholes etc.
- Ride beside, in front or behind fellow cyclists. Don't overlap wheels; if either of you moves sideways suddenly it's likely both of you will fall.
- Ride in single file on busy, narrow or winding roads.

In Traffic
- Obey the rules of the road, and signal if you are turning.
- Look at the wheels to see if a car at a T-junction or joining the road is actually moving or not.
- Scan for trouble: look inside the back windows of parked cars for movement – that person inside may open the door on you.
- Look drivers in the eye; make sure they've seen you.
- Learn to bunny-hop your bike (yes, it can be done with a fully loaded touring bike; just not as well) – it'll save you hitting potholes and other hazards.

SO THAT'S WHY IT'S CALLED A 'BUNNYHOP'!

In the Wet
- Be aware that you'll take longer to slow down with wet rims; exercise appropriate caution.
- When descending apply the brakes lightly to keep the rims free of grit/water etc and allow for quicker stopping.
- Don't climb out of the saddle (unless you want a change); shift down a gear or two and climb seated.

On Bikepaths
- Use a bell or call out to warn others of your approach on bikepaths.

course of action, which isn't always easy. Obviously, you will need to consider your individual circumstances, including where you are and whether you have some means of direct communication with emergency services, such as a mobile phone (cell phone). Some basic guidelines are:

- Use your first aid knowledge and experience, as well as the information in this guide if necessary, to make an assessment of the situation.
- For groups of several people, leave one person with the casualty, leaving as much equipment, food and water as you can sensibly spare. Have the rest of the group go for help.
- If there are only two of you, the situation is more tricky, and you will have to make an individual judgement as to the best course of action.

- If you leave someone, mark their position carefully on the map (take it with you); you should also make sure they can be easily found by marking the position with something conspicuous, such as bright clothing or a large stone cross on the ground. Leave the person with warm clothes, shelter, food, water, matches and a torch (flashlight).
- Try attracting attention by using a whistle or torch, lighting a smoky fire (use damp wood or green leaves) or waving bright clothing; shouting is tiring and not very effective.

The uncertainties associated with emergency rescue in remote wilderness areas should make it clear how important careful planning and safety precautions are, especially if you are travelling in a small group.

YOUR
BICYCLE

Fundamental to any cycle tour you plan is the bicycle. In this chapter we look at choosing a bicycle and accessories, setting it up for your needs, learning basic maintenance, and loading and carrying your gear. In short, everything you need to gear up and get going.

CHOOSING & SETTING UP A BICYCLE

The ideal bike for cycle touring is (strangely enough) a touring bike. These bikes look similar to road bikes but generally have relaxed frame geometry for comfort and predictable steering; fittings (eyelets and brazed-on bosses) to mount panniers and mudguards; wider rims and tyres; strong wheels (at least 36 spokes) to carry the extra load; and gearing capable of riding up a wall (triple chainrings and a wide-range freewheel to match). If you want to buy a touring bike, most tend to be custom-built these days, but Cannondale (🖥 www.cannondale.com) and Trek (🖥 www.trekbikes.com) both offer a range of models.

Of course you can tour on any bike you choose, but few will match the advantages of the workhorse touring bike.

Mountain bikes are a slight compromise by comparison, but are very popular for touring. A mountain bike already has the gearing needed for touring and offers a more upright, comfortable position on the bike. And with a change of tyres (to those with semi-slick tread) you'll be able to reduce the rolling resistance and travel at higher speeds with less effort.

Hybrid, or cross, bikes are similar to mountain bikes (and therefore offer similar advantages and disadvantages), although they typically already come equipped with semi-slick tyres.

Racing bikes are less appropriate: their tighter frame geometry is less comfortable on rough roads and long rides. It is also difficult to fit wider tyres, mudguards, racks and panniers to a road bike. Perhaps more significantly, most racing bikes have a distinct lack of low gears.

Tyres Unless you know you'll be on good, sealed roads the whole time, it's probably safest to choose a tyre with some tread. If you have 700c or 27-inch wheels, opt for a tyre that's 28–35mm wide. If touring on a mountain bike, the first thing to do is get rid of the knobby tyres – too much rolling resistance. Instead, fit 1–1½ inch semi-slick tyres or, if riding unpaved roads or off-road occasionally, a combination pattern tyre (slick centre and knobs on the outside).

To protect your tubes, consider buying tyres reinforced with Kevlar, a tightly woven synthetic fibre very resistant to sharp objects. Although more expensive, Kevlar-belted tyres are worth it.

Pedals Cycling efficiency is vastly improved by using toe clips, and even more so with clipless pedals and cleated shoes. Mountain bike or touring shoes are best – the cleats are recessed and the soles are flexible enough to comfortably walk in.

 Fold & Go Bikes

Another option is a folding bike. Manufacturers include: Brompton (🖥 www.phoenixcycles.com), Bike Friday (🖥 www.bikefriday.com), Slingshot (🖥 www.slingshotbikes.com), Birdie (🖥 www.whooper.demon.co.uk) and Moulton (🖥 www.alexmoulton.co.uk). All make high-quality touring bikes that fold up to allow hassle-free train, plane or bus transfers. The Moulton, Birdie, Brompton and Slingshot come with suspension and the Bike Friday's case doubles as a trailer for your luggage when touring.

Touring Bike

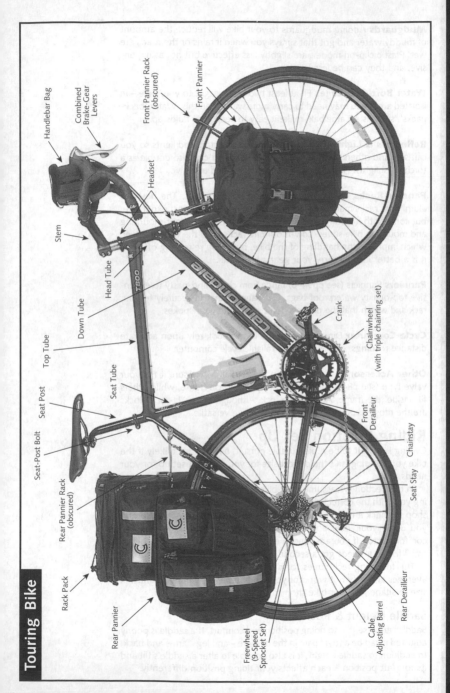

Handlebar Bag

Combined Brake-Gear Levers

Front Pannier Rack (obscured)

Front Pannier

Stem

Headset

Head Tube

Down Tube

Top Tube

Seat Tube

Seat Post

Seat-Post Bolt

Rear Pannier Rack (obscured)

Rack Pack

Rear Pannier

Freewheel (9-Speed Sprocket Set)

Cable Adjusting Barrel

Rear Derailleur

Chainstay

Seat Stay

Front Derailleur

Chainwheel (with triple chainring set)

Crank

Mudguards Adding mudguards to your bike will reduce the amount of muddy water and grit that sprays you when it rains or the roads are wet. Plastic clip-on models are slightly less effective but not as expensive, and they can be less hassle.

Water Bottles & Cages Fit at least two bottle cages to your bike – in isolated areas you may need to carry more water than this. Water 'backpacks', such as a Camelbak, make it easy to keep your fluids up.

Reflectors & Lights If riding at night, add reflectors and lights so you can see, and others can see you. A small headlight can also double as a torch (flashlight). Flashing tail-lights are cheap and effective.

Pannier Racks It's worth buying good pannier racks. The best are aluminium racks made by Blackburn. They're also the most expensive, but come with a lifetime guarantee. Front racks come in low-mounting and mountain bike styles. Low-mounting racks carry the weight lower, which improves the handling of the bike, but if you're touring off-road it is a better idea to carry your gear a bit higher.

Panniers Panniers (see pp94–6) range from cheap-and-nasty to expensive top-quality waterproof bags. Get panniers that fit securely to your rack and watch that the pockets don't swing into your spokes.

Cycle Computer Directions for rides in this book rely upon accurate distance readings, so you'll need a reliable cycle computer.

Other Accessories A good pump is essential. Make sure it fits your valve type (see p84). Some clip on to your bicycle frame, while others fit 'inside' the frame. Also carry a lock. Although heavy, U- or D-locks are the most secure; cable locks can be more versatile.

Riding Position Set Up

Cycling is meant to be a pleasurable pursuit, but that isn't likely if the bike you're riding isn't the correct size for you and isn't set up for your needs.

In this section we assume your bike shop did a good job of providing you with the correct size bike (if you're borrowing a bike get a bike shop to check it is the correct size for you) and concentrate on setting you up in your ideal position and showing you how to tweak the comfort factor. If you are concerned that your bike frame is too big or small for your needs get a second opinion from another bike shop.

The following techniques for determining correct fit are based on averages and may not work for your body type. If you are an unusual size or shape get your bike shop to create your riding position.

Saddle Height & Position

Saddles are essential to riding position and comfort. If a saddle is poorly adjusted it can be a royal pain in the derriere – and legs, arms and back. In addition to saddle height, it is also possible to alter a saddle's tilt and its fore/aft position – each affects your riding position differently.

Saddle Tilt Saddles are designed to be level to the ground, taking most of the weight off your arms and back. However, since triathletes started dropping the nose of their saddles in the mid-1980s many other cyclists have followed suit without knowing why. For some body types, a slight tilt of the nose might be necessary. Be aware, however, that forward tilt will place extra strain on your arms and back. If it is tilted too far forward, chances are your saddle is too high.

Fore/Aft Position The default setting for fore/aft saddle position will allow you to run a plumb bob from the centre of your forward pedal axle to the protrusion of your knee (that bit of bone just under your knee cap).

Fore/Aft Position: To check it, sit on your bike with the pedals in the three and nine o'clock positions. Check the alignment with a plumb bob (a weight on the end of a piece of string).

Saddle Height The simplest method of roughly determining the correct saddle height is the straight leg method. Sit on your bike wearing your cycling shoes. Line one crank up with the seat-tube and place your heel on the pedal. Adjust the saddle height until your leg is almost straight, but not straining. When you've fixed the height of your saddle pedal the cranks backwards (do it next to a wall so you can balance yourself). If you are rocking from side to side, lower the saddle slightly. Otherwise keep raising the saddle (slightly) until on the verge of rocking.

The most accurate way of determining saddle height is the Hodges Method. Developed by US cycling coach Mark Hodges after studying the position of dozens of racing cyclists, the method is also applicable to touring cyclists.

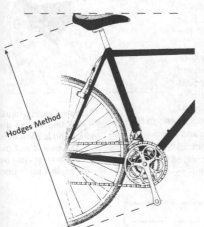

Hodges Method

Standing barefoot with your back against a wall and your feet 15cm apart, get a friend to measure from the greater trochanter (the bump of your hip) to the floor passing over your knee and ankle joints. Measure each leg (in mm) three times and average the figure. Multiply the average figure by 0.96.

Now add the thickness of your shoe sole and your cleats (if they aren't recessed). This total is the distance you need from the centre of your pedal axle to the top of your saddle. It is the optimum position for your body to pedal efficiently and should not be exceeded; however, people with small feet for their size should lower the saddle height slightly. The inverse applies for people with disproportionately large feet.

If you need to raise your saddle significantly do it over a few weeks so your muscles can adapt gradually. (Never raise your saddle above the maximum extension line marked on your seat post.)

Handlebars & Brake Levers

Racing cyclists lower their handlebars to cheat the wind and get a better aerodynamic position. While this might be tempting on windy days it doesn't make for comfortable touring. Ideally, the bars should be no higher than the saddle (even on mountain bikes) and certainly no lower than 75mm below it.

Pedals

For comfort and the best transference of power, the ball of your foot should be aligned over the centre of the pedal axle (see right).

If using clipless pedals consider the amount of lateral movement available. Our feet have a natural angle that they prefer when we walk, run or cycle. If they are unable to achieve this position the knee joint's alignment will be affected and serious injury may result. Most clipless pedal systems now have some rotational freedom (called 'float') built in to allow for this, but it is still important to adjust the cleats to each foot's natural angle.

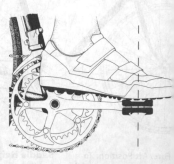

Pedal Alignment: Th ball of your foot shoul be over the centre o the pedal axle fo comfort and the bes transfer of powe

Comfort Considerations

Now that you have your optimum position on the bike, there are several components that you can adjust to increase the comfort factor.

Handlebars come in a variety of types and sizes. People with small hands may find shallow drop bars more comfortable. Handlebars also come in a variety of widths, so if they're too wide or narrow change them.

With mountain bike handlebars you really only have one main position, so add a pair of bar-ends. On drop bars the ends should be parallel to the ground. If they're pointed up it probably means you need a longer stem; pointed down probably means you need a shorter stem.

On mountain bikes the **brake levers** should be adjusted to ensure your wrist is straight – it's the position your hand naturally sits in. For drop bars the bottom of the lever should end on the same line as the end section.

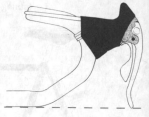

Brake Levers: Adjus your drop bars so th end section is parallel t the ground and th brake lever ends o this same line

Getting the right **saddle** for you is one of the key considerations for enjoyable cycling. Everybody's sit bones are shaped and spaced differently, meaning a saddle that suits your best friend might be agony for you. A good bike shop will allow you to keep changing a new (undamaged) saddle until you get one that's perfect. Women's saddles tend to have a shorter nose and a wider seat, and men's are long and narrow.

If you feel too stretched out or cramped when riding, chances are you need a different length **stem** – the problem isn't solved by moving your saddle forward/aft. Get a bike shop to assess this for you.

Record Your Position

When you've created your ideal position, mark each part's position (scratch a line with a sharp tool like a scribe or use tape) and record it, so you can recreate it if hiring a bike or when reassembling your bike after travel. The inside back cover of this book has a place to record all this vital data.

MAINTAINING YOUR BICYCLE

If you're new to cycling or haven't previously maintained your bike, this section is for you. It won't teach you how to be a top-notch mechanic, but it will help you maintain your bike in good working order and show you how to fix the most common touring problems.

If you go mountain biking it is crucial you carry spares and a tool kit and know how to maintain your bike, because if anything goes wrong it's likely you'll be miles from anywhere when trouble strikes and face a long walk home.

If you want to know more about maintaining your bike there are dozens of books available (*Richard's Bicycle Book*, by Richard Ballantine, is a classic; if you want to know absolutely everything get *Barnett's Manual for Bicycle Maintenance* or *Sutherland's Handbook*) or inquire at your bike shop about courses in your area.

Predeparture & Daily Inspections

Before heading off on tour get your bike serviced by a bike shop or do it yourself. On tour, check over your bike every day or so (see the boxed text 'Pre-Departure & Post-Ride Checks' on p87).

Spares & Tool Kit

Touring cyclists need to be self-sufficient and should carry some spares and, at least, a basic tool kit. How many spares/tools you will need depends on the country you are touring in – in Britain, bike shops are common and the towns are not too spread out so you should get by with the following.

Multi-tools (see right) are very handy and a great way to save space and weight, and there are dozens of different ones on the market. Before you buy a multi-tool though, check each of the tools is usable – a chain breaker, for example, needs to have a good handle for leverage otherwise it is useless.

Adjustable spanners are often handy, but the trade-off is that they can easily burr bolts if not used correctly – be careful when using them.

The bare minimum:

☐ pump – ensure it has the correct valve fitting for your tyres
☐ water bottles (2)
☐ spare tubes (2)
☐ tyre levers (2)
☐ chain lube and a rag
☐ puncture repair kit (check the glue is OK)
☐ Allen keys to fit your bike
☐ small Phillips screwdriver
☐ small flat screwdriver
☐ spare brake pads
☐ spare screws and bolts (for pannier racks, seat post etc) and chain links (2)

For those who know what they're doing:

☐ spoke key
☐ spare spokes and nipples (8)
☐ tools to remove freewheel
☐ chain breaker
☐ pliers
☐ spare chain links (HyperGlide chain rivet if you have a Shimano chain)
☐ spare rear brake and rear gear cables

Always handy to take along:

☐ roll of electrical/gaffer tape
☐ nylon ties (10) – various lengths/sizes
☐ hand cleaner (store it in a film canister)

Fixing a Flat

Flats happen. And if you're a believer in Murphy's Law then the likely scenario is that you'll suffer a flat just as you're rushing to the next town to catch a train or beat the setting sun.

Don't worry – this isn't a big drama. If you're prepared and know what you're doing you can be up and on your way in five minutes flat.

Being prepared means carrying a spare tube, a pump and at least two tyre levers. If you're not carrying a spare tube, of course, you can stop and fix the puncture then and there, but it's unlikely you'll catch that train and you could end up doing all this in the dark. There will be days when you have the time to fix a puncture on the side of the road, but not always. Carry at least two spare tubes.

1 Take the wheel off the bike. Remove the valve cap and unscrew the locknut (hex nut at base; see Valve Types) on Presta valves. Deflate the tyre completely, if it isn't already.

2 Make sure the tyre and tube are loose on the rim – moisture and the pressure of the inflated tube often makes the tyre and tube fuse with the rim.

3 If the tyre is really loose you should be able to remove it with your hands. Otherwise you'll need to lift one side of the tyre over the rim with the tyre levers. Pushing the tyre away from the lever as you insert it should ensure you don't pinch the tube and puncture it again.

4 When you have one side of the tyre off, you'll be able to remove the tube. Before inserting the replacement tube, carefully inspect the tyre (inside and out); you're looking for what caused the puncture. If you find anything embedded in the tyre, remove it. Also check that the rim tape is still in

---

 Valve Types

The two most common valve types are Presta (sometimes called French) and Schraeder (American). To inflate a Presta valve, first unscrew the round nut at the top (and do it up again after you're done); depress it to deflate. To deflate Schraeder valves depress the pin (inside the top). Ensure your pump is set up for the valve type on your bike.

Unscrew

Locknut

Presta   Schraeder

place and no spoke nipples (see pp92–3) protrude through it.

5 Time to put the new tube in. Start by partially pumping up the tube (this helps prevent it twisting or being pinched) and insert the valve in the hole in the rim. Tuck the rest of the tube in under the tyre, making sure you don't twist it. Make sure the valve is straight – most Presta valves come with a locknut to help achieve this.

6 Work the tyre back onto the rim with your fingers. If this isn't possible, and again, according to Murphy's Law, it frequently isn't, you might need to use your tyre levers for the last 20–30cm. If you need to use the levers, make sure you don't pinch the new tube, otherwise it's back to Step 1. All you need to do now is pump up the tyre and put the wheel back on the bike. Don't forget to fix the pucture that night.

Fixing the Puncture

To fix the puncture you'll need a repair kit, which usually comes with glue, patches, sandpaper and, sometimes, chalk. (Always check the glue in your puncture repair kit hasn't dried up before heading off on tour.) The only other thing you'll need is clean hands.

1. The first step is to find the puncture. Inflate the tube and hold it up to your ear. If you can hear the puncture, mark it with the chalk; otherwise immerse it in water and watch for air bubbles. Once you find the puncture, mark it, cover it with your finger and continue looking – just in case there are more.

2. Dry the tube and lightly roughen the area around the hole with the sandpaper. Sand an area larger than the patch.

3. Follow the instructions for the glue you have. Generally you spread an even layer of glue over the area of the tube to be patched and allow it to dry until it is tacky.

4. Patches also come with their own instructions – some will be just a piece of rubber and others will come lined with foil (remove the foil on the underside but don't touch the exposed area). Press the patch firmly onto the area over the hole and hold it for 2–3 minutes. If you want, remove the excess glue from around the patch or dust it with chalk or simply let it dry.

5. Leave the glue to set for 10–20 minutes. Inflate the tube and check the patch has worked.

Chains

Chains are dirty, greasy and all too often the most neglected piece of equipment on a bike. There are about 120 or so links in a chain and each has a simple but precise arrangement of bushes, bearings and plates. Over time all chains stretch, but if dirt gets between the bushes and bearings this 'ageing' will happen prematurely and will likely damage the teeth of your chainrings, sprockets and derailleur guide pulleys.

To prevent this, chains should be cleaned and lubed frequently (see your bike shop for the best products to use).

No matter how well you look after a chain it should be replaced regularly – about every 5000–8000km. Seek the advice of a bike shop to ensure you are buying the correct type for your drivetrain (the moving parts that combine to drive the bicycle: chain, freewheel, derailleurs, chainwheel and bottom bracket).

If you do enough cycling you'll need to replace a chain (or fix a broken chain), so here's how to use that funky-looking tool, the chain breaker.

1 Remove the chain from the chainrings – it'll make the whole process easier. Place the chain in the chain breaker (on the outer slots; it braces the link plates as the rivet is driven out) and line the pin of the chain breaker up with the rivet.

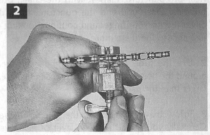

2 Wind the handle until the rivet is clear of the inner link but still held by the outer link plate.

3 Flex the chain to 'break' it. If it won't, you'll need to push the rivet out some more, but not completely – if you push it all the way out, you'll have to remove two links and replace them with two spare links. If you're removing links, you'll need to remove a male and female link (ie, two links).

4 Rejoining the chain is the reverse. If you turn the chain around when putting it on you will still have the rivet facing you. Otherwise it will be facing away from you and you'll need to change to the other side of the bike and work through the spokes.

Join the chain up by hand and place it in the breaker. Now drive the rivet in firmly, making sure it is properly lined up with the hole of the outer link plate. Stop when the rivet is almost in place.

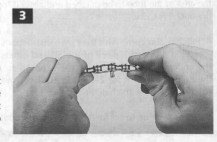

5 Move the chain to the spreaders (inner slots) of the chain breaker. Finish by winding the rivet into position carefully (check that the head of the rivet is raised the same distance above the link plate as the rivets beside it). If you've managed to get it in perfectly and the link isn't 'stiff', well done!

Otherwise, move the chain to the spreaders on the chain breaker and gently work the chain laterally until the link is no longer stiff.

If this doesn't work (and with some chain breakers it won't), take the chain out of the tool and place a screwdriver or Allen key between the outer plates of the stiff link and carefully lever the plates both ways. If you're too forceful you'll really break the chain, but if you're subtle it will free the link up and you'll be on your way.

 Chain Options

Check your chain; if you have a Shimano HyperGlide chain you'll need a special Hyper-Glide chain rivet to rejoin the chain. This will be supplied with your new chain, but carry a spare.

Another option is to fit a universal link to your chain. This link uses a special clip to join the chain – like the chains of old. You'll still need a chain breaker to fix a broken chain or take out spare links.

Pre-Departure & Post-Ride Checks

Each day before you get on your bike and each evening after you've stopped riding, give your bike a quick once-over. Following these checks will ensure you're properly maintaining your bike and will help identify any problems before they become disasters. Go to the nearest bike shop if you don't know how to fix any problem.

Pre-Departure Check List
☐ brakes – are they stopping you? If not, adjust them.
☐ chain – if it was squeaking yesterday, it needs lube.
☐ panniers – are they all secured and fastened?
☐ cycle computer – reset your trip distance at the start.
☐ gears – are they changing properly? If not, adjust them.
☐ tyres – check your tyre pressure is correct (see the tyre's side wall for the maximum psi); inflate, if necessary.

Post-Ride Check List
☐ pannier racks – check all bolts/screws are tightened; do a visual check of each rack (the welds, in particular) looking for small cracks.
☐ headset – when stationary, apply the front brake and rock the bike gently; if there is any movement or noise, chances are the headset is loose.
☐ wheels – visually check the tyres for sidewall cuts/wear and any embedded objects; check the wheels are still true and no spokes are broken.
☐ wrench test – wrench (pull) on the saddle (if it moves, tighten the seat-post bolt and/or the seat-clamp bolt, underneath); wrench laterally on a crank (if it moves, check the bottom bracket).

Brakes

Adjusting the brakes of your bike is not complicated and even though your bike shop will use several tools to do the job, all you really need is a pair of pliers, a spanner or Allen key, and (sometimes) a friend.

Check three things before you start: the wheels are true (not buckled), the braking surface of the rims is smooth (no dirt, dents or rough patches) and the cables are not frayed.

Begin by checking that the pads strike the rim correctly: flush on the braking surface of the rim (see right and p89) and parallel to the ground.

Calliper Brakes

It's likely that you'll be able to make any minor adjustments to calliper brakes by winding the cable adjusting barrel out. If it doesn't allow enough movement you'll need to adjust the cable anchor bolt:

1 Undo the cable anchor bolt – not completely, just so the cable is free to move – and turn the cable adjusting barrel all the way in.

2 Get your friend to hold the callipers in the desired position, about 2–3mm away from the rim. Using a pair of pliers, pull the cable through until it is taut.

3 Before you tighten the cable anchor bolt again, check to see if the brake lever is in its normal position (not slack as if somebody was applying it) – sometimes they jam open. Also, ensure the brake quick-release (use it when you're removing your wheel or in an emergency to open the callipers if your wheel is badly buckled) is closed.

4 Tighten the cable anchor bolt again. Make any fine-tuning to the brakes by winding the cable adjusting barrel out.

 Brake Cables

If your brakes are particularly hard to apply, you may need to replace the cables. Moisture can cause the cable and housing (outer casing) to bond or stick. If this happens it's often possible to prolong the life of a cable by removing it from the housing and applying a coating of grease (or chain lube) to it.

If you do need to replace the cable, take your bike to a bike shop and get the staff to fit and/or supply the new cable. Cables come in two sizes – rear (long) and front (short) – various thicknesses and with different types of nipples.

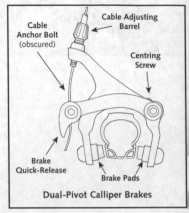

Cable Anchor Bolt (obscured)

Cable Adjusting Barrel

Centring Screw

Brake Quick-Release

Brake Pads

Dual-Pivot Calliper Brakes

Cantilever Brakes

These days most touring bikes have cantilever rather than calliper brakes. The newest generation of cantilever brakes (V-brakes) are more powerful and better suited to stopping bikes with heavy loads.

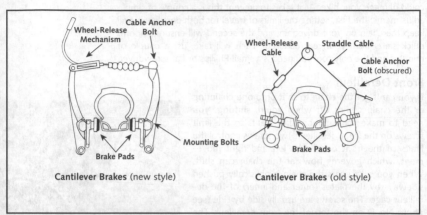

Cantilever Brakes (new style)

Cantilever Brakes (old style)

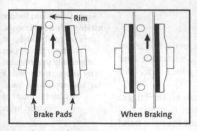

Cantilever Brake Toe-In: This is how the brake pads should strike the rim (from above) with correct toe-in.

On cantilever brakes ensure the leading edge of the brake pad hits the rim first (see left). This is called toe-in; it makes the brakes more efficient and prevents squealing. To adjust the toe-in on cantilever brakes, loosen the brake pad's mounting bolt (using a 10mm spanner and 5mm Allen key). Wiggle the brake pad into position and tighten the bolt again.

If you only need to make a minor adjustment to the distance of the pads from the rim, chances are you will be able to do it by winding the cable adjusting barrel out (located near the brake lever on mountain bikes and hybrids). If this won't do you'll need to adjust the cable anchor bolt:

1 Undo the cable anchor bolt (not completely, just so the cable is free to move) and turn the cable adjusting barrel all the way in. Depending on the style of your brakes, you may need a 10mm spanner (older bikes) or a 5mm Allen key.

2 Hold the cantilevers in the desired position (get assistance from a friend if you need to), positioning the brake pads 2–3mm away from the rim. Using a pair of pliers, pull the cable through until it is taut.

3 Before you tighten the cable anchor bolt again, check to see if the brake lever is in its normal position (not slack as if somebody was applying it) – sometimes they jam open.

4 Tighten the cable anchor bolt again. Make any fine-tuning to the brakes by winding the cable adjusting barrel out.

Gears

If the gears on your bike start playing up – the chain falls off the chainrings, it shifts slowly or not at all – it's bound to cause frustration and could damage your bike. All it takes to prevent this is a couple of simple adjustments: the first, setting the limits of travel for both derailleurs, will keep the chain on your drivetrain, and the second will ensure smooth, quick shifts from your rear derailleur. Each will take just a couple of minutes and the only tool you need is a small Phillips or flat screwdriver.

Front Derailleur

If you can't get the chain to shift onto one chainring or the chain comes off when you're shifting, you need to make some minor adjustments to the limit screws on the front derailleur. Two screws control the limits of the front derailleur's left and right movement, which governs how far the chain can shift. When you shift gears the chain is physically pushed sideways by the plates (outer and inner) of the derailleur cage. The screws are usually side by side (see photo No 1) on the top of the front derailleur. The left-hand screw (as you sit on the bike) adjusts the inside limit and the one on the right adjusts the outside limit.

Screws

Cage Plates

Front Derailleur: Before making any adjustments, remove any build-up of grit from the screws (especially underneath) by wiping them with a rag and applying a quick spray (or drop) of chain lube.

After you make each of the following adjustments, pedal the drivetrain with your hand and change gears to ensure you've set the limit correctly. If you're satisfied, test it under strain by going for a short ride.

Outer Limits Change the gears to position the chain on the largest chainring and the smallest rear sprocket. Set the outer cage plate as close to the chain as you can without it touching. Adjust the right-hand limit screw to achieve this.

Inner Limits Position the chain on the smallest chainring and the largest rear sprocket. For chainwheels with three chainrings, position the inner cage plate between 1–2mm from the chain. If you have a chainwheel with two chainrings, position the inner cage plate as close to the chain as you can without it touching.

Rear Derailleur

If the limit screws aren't set correctly on the rear derailleur the consequences can be dire. If the chain slips off the largest sprocket it can jam between the sprocket and the spokes and could then snap the chain, break or damage spokes or even break the frame.

The limit screws are located at the back of the derailleur (see photo No 2). The top screw (marked 'H' on the derailleur) sets the derailleur's limit of travel on the smallest sprocket's (the highest gear) side of the freewheel. The bottom screw ('L') adjusts the derailleur's travel towards the largest sprocket (lowest gear).

Outer Limits Position the chain on the smallest sprocket and largest chainring (see photo No 3). The derailleur's top guide pulley (the one

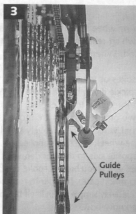

Guide
Pulleys

closest to the sprockets) should be in line with the smallest sprocket; adjust the top screw ('H') to ensure it is.

Inner Limits Position the chain on the largest rear sprocket and the smallest chainring (see photo No 4). This time the guide pulley needs to be lined up with the largest sprocket; do this by adjusting the bottom screw ('L'). Make sure the chain can't move any further towards the wheel than the largest sprocket.

Cable Adjusting Barrel

If your gears are bouncing up and down your freewheel in a constant click and chatter, you need to adjust the tension of the cable to the rear derailleur. This can be achieved in a variety of ways, depending on your gear system.

The main cable adjusting barrel is on your rear derailleur (see photo No 5). Secondary cable adjusting barrels can also be found near the gear levers (newer Shimano combined brake-gear STI levers) or on the downtube of your frame (older Shimano STI levers and Campagnolo Ergopower gear systems) of some bikes. Intended for racing cyclists, they allow for fine tuning of the gears' operation while on the move.

Raise the rear wheel off the ground – have a friend hold it up by the saddle, hang it from a tree or turn the bike upside down – so you can pedal the drivetrain with your hand.

To reset your derailleur, shift gears to position the chain on the second smallest sprocket and middle chainring (see photo No 6). As you turn the crank with your hand, tighten the cable by winding the rear derailleur's cable adjusting barrel anti-clockwise. Just before the chain starts to make a noise as if to shift onto the third sprocket, stop winding.

Now pedal the drivetrain and change the gears up and down the freewheel. If things still aren't right you may find that you need to tweak the cable tension slightly: turn the cable adjusting barrel anti-clockwise if shifts to larger sprockets are slow, and clockwise if shifts to smaller sprockets hesitate.

Replacing a Spoke

Even the best purpose-made touring wheels occasionally break spokes. When this happens the wheel, which relies on the even pull of each spoke, is likely to become buckled. When it is not buckled, it is considered true.

If you've forgotten to pack spokes or you grabbed the wrong size, you can still get yourself out of a pickle if you have a spoke key. Wheels are very flexible and you can get it roughly true – enough to take you to the next bike shop – even if two or three spokes are broken.

If you break a spoke on the front wheel it is a relatively simple thing to replace the spoke and retrue the wheel. The same applies if a broken spoke is on the non-drive side (opposite side to the rear derailleur) of the rear wheel. The complication comes when you break a spoke on the drive side of the rear wheel (the most common case). In order to replace it you need to remove the freewheel, a relatively simple job in itself but one that requires a few more tools and the know-how.

If you don't have that know-how fear not, because it is possible to retrue the wheel without replacing that spoke *and* without damaging the wheel – see Truing a Wheel (below).

1 Remove the wheel from the bike. It's probably a good idea to remove the tyre and tube as well (though not essential), just to make sure the nipple is seated properly in the rim and not likely to cause a puncture.

2 Remove the broken spoke but leave the nipple in the rim (if it's not damaged; otherwise replace it). Now you need to thread the new spoke. Start by threading it through the vacant hole on the hub flange. Next lace the new spoke through the other spokes. Spokes are offset on the rim; every second one is on the same side and, generally, every fourth is laced through the other spokes the same way.

3 With the spoke key, tighten the nipple until the spoke is about as taut as the other spokes on this side of the rim. Spoke nipples have four flat sides – to adjust them you'll need the correct size spoke key. Spoke keys come in two types: those made to fit one spoke gauge or several. If you have the latter, trial each size on a nipple until you find the perfect fit.

Truing a Wheel

Truing a wheel is an art form and, like all art forms, it is not something mastered overnight. If you can, practise with an old wheel before leaving home. If that's not possible – and you're on the side of the road as you read this – following these guidelines will get you back in the saddle until you can get to the next bike shop.

1 Start by turning the bike upside-down, so the wheels can turn freely. Check the tension of all the spokes on the wheel: do this by

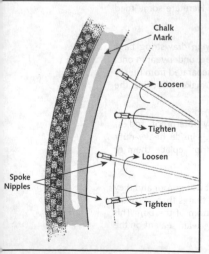

squeezing each pair of spokes on each side. Tighten those spokes that seem loose and loosen those that seem too tight. Note, though, the spokes on the drive side of the rear wheel (on the same side as the freewheel) are deliberately tighter than the non-drive side.

2 Rotate the wheel a couple of times to get an idea of the job at hand. If the wheel won't rotate, let the brakes off (see pp88–9).

3 Using the chalk from your puncture repair kit, mark all the 'bumps'. Keep the chalk in the same position (brace the chalk against the pannier rack or bike's frame) and let the bumps in the wheel 'hit' the chalk.

4 In order to get the bumps out you'll need a constant point of reference – to gauge if the bumps are being removed. Often, if it is not a severe buckle, you can use a brake pad. Position the brake pad about 2–3mm from the rim (on the side with the biggest buckle).

5 With your spoke key, loosen those spokes on the same side as the bump within the longest chalked area, and tighten those on the opposite side of the rim. The spokes at the start and the finish of the chalked area should only be tightened/loosened by a quarter-turn; apply a half-turn to those in between.

6 Rotate the wheel again; if you're doing it correctly the buckle should not be as great. Continue this process of tightening and loosening spokes until the bump is as near to gone as you can get it – as the bump is removed turn the nipples less (one-eighth of a turn on the ends and a quarter-turn in between). Experienced exponents can remove buckles entirely, but if you can get it almost out (1mm here or there) you've done well.

7 If the wheel has more than one bump, move onto the second-longest chalk mark next. As each bump is removed you might find it affects the previous bump slightly. In this case, remove the previous chalk mark and repeat Steps 4–6. Continue to do this until all the buckles are removed.

Don't forget to readjust the brakes.

If you've trued the wheel without replacing the broken spokes, have them replaced at the next bike shop.

Chalk Mark

Loosen

Tighten

Loosen

Spoke Nipples

Tighten

LOADING YOUR BICYCLE

If you've ever been to Asia and seen a bike loaded with boxes piled 2m high or carrying four, five or six people, plus a chicken or two, you'll realise that there are more ways to carry your gear than would otherwise seem. More realistic options for you come from a combination of front and rear panniers, a handlebar bag or trailer.

'Credit-card tourists', who are intent on travelling lighter, further and faster and who are happy to stay in hotels or hostels, can get by with a handlebar bag and/or rear panniers (see top right). The downside to this configuration is poor bike-handling; the steering feels particularly 'airy'. It's possible to adopt the 'lighter, further, faster' principle and still camp, but it means frugal packing.

If you want to be more self-sufficient or you're carrying 20kg or more, you'll probably find it easier (and your bike will handle better) with front and rear panniers. The tried-and-tested configuration that works best for a touring bike is to use four panniers: two low-mounting front panniers with two high-mounting rear panniers (see bottom right). The only other thing you might want to add is a small handlebar bag for this book, snacks, sunblock, money, camera etc.

Pannier configurations the four-pannier system is the best way of carrying your gear and having a bike that handles well; packing light saves weight but the compromise can be poor bike handling

This combination, with a few light but bulky items on the rear rack (eg, tent, sleeping mat etc), allows you to carry a large load and still have predictable and manageable bike-handling.

If you're riding a mountain bike and riding off-road you'll probably want high-mounting front panniers to give you more clearance.

Packing Your Gear

It's frequently said that, in packing for a cycle tour, you should lay out everything you need to take and then leave half of it behind. The skill is in knowing which half to leave behind. Almost as much skill is needed in organising the gear in your panniers. Here are some tried and tested tips.

Compartmentalise Pack similar items into nylon drawstring bags (stuff sacks), to make them easier to find again (eg, underwear in one, cycling clothes in another, and even dinner food separated from breakfast food). Using different coloured stuff sacks makes choosing the right one easier.

Waterproof Even if your panniers are completely waterproof, and especially if they're not, it pays to put everything inside heavy-duty plastic bags. Check bags for holes during the trip; replace them or patch the holes with tape.

Reduce Flood Damage If your panniers are not waterproof and they pool water, you can reduce problems by putting things that are unaffected by water, say a pair of thongs, at the bottom of the bag. This keeps the other stuff above 'flood level'. Try using seam sealant on the bags' seams beforehand, too.

Load Consistently Put things in the same place each time you pack to avoid having to unpack every bag just to find one item.

Balance the Load Distribute weight evenly – generally around 60% in the rear and 40% in the front panniers – and keep it as low as possible by using low-mounting front panniers and packing heavy items first. Side-to-side balancing is just as critical.

Group Gear Pack things used at the same time in the same pannier. Night/camp things like your mat, sleeping bag and pyjamas, which you don't need during the day, could all be in the bag most difficult to access – likely to be on the same side as the side of the road you are riding on, since you will probably lean that side of the bike against a tree, pole or roadside barrier.

Put all clothing in one pannier, if possible, sorted into separate bags of cycling clothes, 'civilian' clothes, underwear, wet weather gear and dirty clothes. Keep a windproof jacket handy on top for descents.

In the Front Food and eating utensils are convenient to have in a front pannier along with a camping stove. Toiletry items, towel, first-aid kit, reading material, torch and sundry items can go in the other front bag.

In the Pockets or Bar Bag Easily accessible pockets on panniers or on your cycling shirt are useful for items likely to be needed frequently or urgently during the day, such as snacks, tool kit, sun hat or sunscreen. A handlebar bag is good for these items if your panniers don't have pockets, but remember that weight on the handlebars upsets a bike's handling.

Keep Space Spare Remember to leave some spare space for food and, if using a camping stove, for the fuel canister. Be mindful when

Another Option – Trailers

Luggage trailers are gaining in popularity and some innovative designs are now on the market. By spreading the load onto more wheels they relieve the bike and can improve rolling resistance. Their extra capacity is a boon for travelling on a tandem or with a young family. They can be combined with racks and panniers, but the hitch (point it connects with the bike) of some trailers may interfere with your panniers, so check first.

PETER HINES

Two-wheeled trailers are free standing and can take very heavy loads, including babies and toddlers. Often brightly coloured, they give a strong signal to car drivers who tend to give you a wide berth. However, their relatively wide track can catch a lot of wind and makes them ungainly on rough, narrow roads or trails.

Single-wheeled trailers such as the BOB Yak share the load with the bike's rear wheel. They track well and can be used on very rough trails and may be the easiest option for full-suspension bikes. The load capacity of these units is somewhere between that of a bike with a rear rack only and a fully loaded (four panniers plus rack-top luggage) touring bike.

packing foods that are squashable or sensitive to heat and protect or insulate them – unless you're working on a gourmet pasta sauce recipe that includes socks.

Prevent 'Internal Bleeding' Act on the premise that anything that can spill will, and transfer it to a reliable container, preferably within a watertight bag. Take care, too, in packing hard or sharp objects (tools, utensils or anything with hooks) that could rub or puncture other items, including the panniers. Knives or tools with folding working parts are desirable.

Fragile Goods Valuables and delicate equipment such as cameras are best carried in a handlebar bag, which can be easily removed when you stop. Alternatively, carry these items in a 'bum bag', which will accompany you automatically.

Rack Top Strap your tent lengthways on top of the rear rack with elastic cord looped diagonally across from front to rear and back again, and maybe across to anchor the rear end. Be sure the cord is well-tensioned and secure – deny its kamikaze impulses to plunge into the back wheel, jamming the freewheel mechanism, or worse.

What to Look for in Panniers

Panniers remain the popular choice for touring luggage. They offer flexibility, in that one, two or four can be used depending on the load to be carried and they allow luggage to be arranged for easy access.

Many people initially buy just a rear rack and panniers, and it is wise to buy the best quality you can afford at this stage. These bags will accompany you on all of your tours as well as for day-to-day shopping and commuting trips for years to come.

The attachment system should be secure, but simple to operate. That big bump you hit at 50km/h can launch a poorly designed pannier and your precious luggage.

The stiffness of the pannier backing is another concern – if it can flex far enough to reach the spokes of the wheel the result can be catastrophic. Good rack design can also help avoid this.

The fabric of the panniers should be strong and abrasion- and water-resistant. You can now buy roll-top panniers, made from laminated fabrics, that are completely waterproof. Bear in mind that these bags are only waterproof until they develop even the smallest hole, so be prepared to check them and apply patches occasionally. Canvas bags shed water well, but should be used in conjunction with a liner bag to keep things dry. Cordura is a heavy nylon fabric with excellent abrasion resistance. The fabric itself is initially waterproof, but water tends to find the seams, so using a liner bag is a good idea once again.

Pockets and compartments can help to organise your load, but the multitude of seams increase the challenge of keeping the contents dry in the wet. A couple of exterior pockets are great for sunscreen, snacks and loose change that you need throughout the day. Carrying front panniers as well as rear ones allows more opportunities to divide and organise gear.

When fitting rear panniers check for heel strike. Long feet, long cranks and short chainstays will all make it harder to get the bags and your body to fit.

Getting There & Away

AIR
Airports & Airlines

In Britain the main airports are Heathrow, Gatwick, Stansted and Luton (all near London); plus Manchester, Newcastle, Edinburgh and Glasgow. Most long-haul flights arrive at Heathrow and generally, cheaper flights will take you to one of the other London airports.

There are direct air services from several European cities (including London) to Edinburgh, Glasgow, Dundee, Aberdeen, Inverness or Kirkwall, and from North America to Glasgow. If flying from farther afield to Scotland, you will probably have to change planes at a London or European airport.

At Cardiff, the international airport is mainly used for holiday charter flights, although there are some scheduled flights to Aberdeen, Amsterdam, Belfast, Brussels, the Channel Islands, Dublin, Edinburgh, Glasgow, the Isle of Man, Manchester and Paris.

Buying Tickets

Various travel agencies are competing for your money and it's always worth researching the current state of the market. Start early – some of the cheapest tickets have to be bought months in advance, and some popular flights sell out early. Return (or round-the-world) tickets usually work out cheaper than buying two one-ways.

Especially when you're looking for bargain air fares, go to a travel agency rather than directly to the airline. From time to time airlines do have promotional fares and special offers, but generally they only sell fares at the official listed price. One exception to this rule is the expanding number of 'no-frills' carriers operating in the USA and north-western Europe, which mostly sell direct to travellers. Unlike the 'full service' airlines, no-frills carriers often make one-way tickets available at around half the return fare, meaning that it is easy to put together a return ticket when you fly to one place but leave from another.

Seriously consider booking on the Internet. Many airlines, both full-service and no-frills, offer some excellent fares to Web surfersand many travel agencies around the world have Web sites. On-line ticket sales work well if you are doing a simple one-way

or return trip on specified dates. However, there's no substitute for a travel agent who knows all about special deals, has strategies for avoiding stopovers and can offer advice on everything from which airline is the most relaxed about carrying bicycles to the best travel insurance to bundle with your ticket.

Examine your options carefully. If you purchase a ticket and later want to make changes to your route or get a refund, you need to contact the original travel agency. Airlines only issue refunds to the purchaser of a ticket – usually the travel agency who bought the ticket on your behalf.

Student & Youth Fares Even though full-time students and people under 26 have access to better deals than other travellers, this may not always mean cheaper fares. It can, however, include more flexibility to change flights or routes. You have to show a document proving your date of birth or a valid International Student Identity Card (ISIC) when buying your ticket and boarding the plane.

Frequent Flier Programs Nowadays, most airlines offer frequent flier deals that can earn you free air tickets or other goodies. Generally, you must pay a fee and then accumulate sufficient mileage with the same airline or airline alliance. The drawback of frequent flier programs is that they lock you into one airline, which may not always have the cheapest fares or most convenient flight

Packing for Air Travel

We've all heard the horror stories about smashed/lost luggage when flying, but a more real threat to cycle tourists is arriving in a country for a two-week tour and finding their bike with broken wheels or in little bits spread out around the baggage carousel. Fixing a damaged bike could take days, and the delay and frustration could ruin your holiday.

How do you avoid this? Err on the side of caution and box your bike. Trust airline baggage handlers if you want (we're told some people actually do) and give your bike to them 'as is' – turn the handlebars 90°, remove the pedals, cover the chain with a rag or bag (to protect other people's baggage) and deflate your tyres (partially, not all the way) – but is it worth the risk? If you want to take that sort of a risk do it on your homeward flight, when you can get your favourite bike shop to fix any damage any time.

Some airlines sell bike boxes at the airport, but most bike shops give them away. Fitting your bike into a box requires a few simple steps and only takes about 15 minutes:

1 Loosen the stem bolt and turn the handlebars 90°; loosen the clamp bolt(s) and twist the handlebars as pictured.

2 Remove the pedals (use a 15mm spanner, turning each the opposite way to how you pedal), wheels and seat post and saddle (don't forget to mark its height before removing it).

3 Undo the rear derailleur bolt and tape it to the inside of the chainstay. There's no need to undo the derailleur cable. You can

remove the chain (it will make reassembly easier) but it isn't necessary.

4 Cut up some spare cardboard and tape it beneath the chainwheel to prevent the teeth from penetrating the floor of the box and being damaged.

5 Remove the quick-release skewers from the wheels and wrap a rag (or two) around the cluster so it won't get damaged or damage anything else.

If you run your tyres at very high pressure (above 100psi), you should partially deflate them – on most bikes this won't be necessary.

6 Place the frame in the box, so it rests on the chainwheel and forks – you might want to place another couple of layers of cardboard underneath the forks.

Most boxes will be too short to allow the front pannier racks to remain on the bike; if so, remove them. The rear rack should fit while still on the bike, but may require the seat stay bolts to be undone and pushed forward.

Packing for Air Travel

Side View

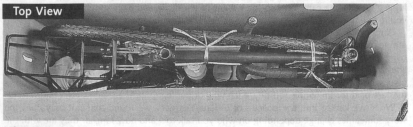

7 Place the wheels beside the frame, on the side opposite the chainwheel. Keep the wheels and frame separate by inserting a piece of cardboard between them and tying the wheels to the frame (to stop them moving around and scratching the frame).

8 Slot the saddle and seatpost, your helmet, tools and any other bits and pieces (eg, tent, sleeping bag) into the vacant areas. Wrap the skewers, chain and other loose bike bits in newspaper and place them in the box. Add cardboard or newspaper packing to any areas where metal is resting on metal.

9 Seal the box with tape and write your name, address and flight details on several sides.

Now all you need to do is strap your panniers together and either take them with you as carry-on luggage or check them in.

Top View

Bike Bags

If you're planning on travelling between regions via train, plane or bus then consider taking a bike bag. The simplest form of zippered bike bag has no padding built into it, is made of Cordura or nylon, and can be rolled up and put on your rear pannier rack and unfurled when you need to travel again.

Some of the smaller ones require you to remove both wheels, the front pannier racks, pedals and seatpost to fit inside the bag. However, these make for (relatively) easy and inconspicuous train, plane or bus transfers so the extra effort is worthwhile.

schedule, although the various airline alliances are making this less of a problem.

Cyclists with Special Needs

Help is available for people with special needs – most airlines can cater for travellers with disabilities or people with young children, for instance.

Special dietary preferences (vegetarian, kosher etc) can be catered for if you provide advance notice. If you are travelling in a wheelchair most international airports can provide an escort from check-in desk to plane where needed, and ramps, lifts, toilets and phones are generally available.

Departure Tax

Flying from Britain incurs an Air Passenger Duty (built into the price of an air ticket). Those flying to countries in the European Union pay £10; those flying beyond pay £20.

Round-the-World Tickets

If you are looking for a cheap ticket alternative, Round-the-World (RTW) tickets can also be great bargains, sometimes cheaper than an ordinary return ticket. RTW prices start at about UK£900, A$2000 or US$1900 depending on the season.

Standard practice is usually for official RTW tickets to be put together by two or more airlines, which permits you to fly anywhere on their route systems so long as you don't backtrack. There may be restrictions on how many stops you are permitted, and on the length of time the ticket remains valid.

The USA & Canada

Having to make sense of the flight options from the North Atlantic (the world's busiest long-haul air corridor) can be bewildering. If you're flying from New York to London, you should be able to find a return fare for under US$600; New York to Glasgow is generally a bit more expensive. There are direct flights from the US and Canadian west coasts to London.

Discount travel agencies in the USA are known as consolidators (although you won't see a sign on the door saying Consolidator). San Francisco is the ticket consolidator capital of America, although some good deals can be found in Los Angeles, New York and other big cities. Consolidators can be found through the *Yellow Pages* or the major daily newspapers. The *New York Times*, *Los Angeles Times*, *Chicago Tribune*, *San Francisco Chronicle* and *San Francisco Examiner* all

---

Cycle-Friendly Airlines

Not too many airlines will carry a bike free of charge these days – at least according to their official policy. Most airlines regard the bike as part of your checked luggage. Carriers working the routes to Britain through Europe, Asia and Australia usually allow 20kg of checked luggage (excluding carry-on), so the weight of your bike and bags shouldn't exceed this. If you're over the limit, technically you're liable for excess-baggage charges.

Carriers flying routes to Britain through North America use a different system. Passengers are generally allowed two pieces of luggage, each of which must not exceed 32kg. Excess baggage fees are charged for additional pieces, rather than for excess weight. On some airlines a bike may be counted as one of your two pieces; others charge a set fee for carrying a bike, which may then be carried in addition to your two other pieces. Check whether these fees are paid for the whole journey, each way or per leg.

When we looked into the policies of different carriers, we found that not only does the story sometimes change depending on who you talk to – and how familiar they are with the company's policy – but the official line is not necessarily adhered to at the check-in counter. If a company representative or agent reassures you that your bike travels for free, ask them to annotate your passenger file to that effect. If your flight is not too crowded, the check-in staff are often lenient with the excess charges, particularly with items such as bikes.

The times when you are most likely to incur excess baggage charges are on full flights and, of course, if you inconvenience the check-in staff. If you suspect you may be over the limit, increase your chances of avoiding charges by checking in early, being well organised and being friendly and polite – a smile and a 'thank you' can go a long way!

have travel sections in which you'll find any number of travel agencies' ads.

Council Travel, America's largest student travel organisation, has around 60 offices in the USA; its head office (☎ 800-226 8624, 🖳 www.ciee.org) is at 205 E 42 St, New York, NY 10017. STA Travel (☎ 800-777 0112, 🖳 www.statravel.com) has offices in Boston, Chicago, Miami, New York, Philadelphia, San Francisco and other major cities. Call for office locations.

Canadian discount air ticket sellers are also known as consolidators and their air fares tend to be about 10% higher than those sold in the USA. Scan the budget travel agencies' ads in the *Globe & Mail*, the *Toronto Star*, the *Montreal Gazette* and *Vancouver Sun*. Travel CUTS (☎ 800-667 2887, 🖳 www.travelcuts.com) is Canada's national student travel agency and has offices in all major cities.

Australia & New Zealand

Cheap flights from Australia to Europe generally go via South-East Asian capitals, involving stopovers at Kuala Lumpur, Bangkok or Singapore. If a long stopover between connections is necessary, check whether transit accommodation is included.

Since Australia is pretty much on the other side of the world from Europe, it can sometimes work out cheaper to go round the world than do a U-turn on a return ticket. RTW tickets that go east from Australia (ie, via the USA first) are one way that you can defeat the weight rules for checked baggage for flights to Britain via Asia (see the boxed text 'Cycle-Friendly Airlines'). The cheapest fares to Britain from New Zealand mostly take the eastbound route via the USA, so weight is less of a problem, but a RTW ticket may still sometimes be cheaper than a return.

The Saturday travel sections of the *Sydney Morning Herald* and Melbourne's *The Age* newspapers have ads offering cheap fares to London, but they're often low-season fares on obscure airlines with conditions attached, so don't be surprised if you end up paying more. Discounted return fares on mainstream airlines through a reputable agency usually cost between A$1800 (low season) and A$3000 (high season).

Two well-known agencies for cheap fares are STA Travel and Flight Centre. STA Travel (☎ 03-9349 2411) has its main office at 224

Faraday St, Carlton, Vic 3053, and offices in all major cities and on many university campuses. Call 131 776 Australia-wide for the location of your nearest branch or visit its Web site (🖳 www.statravel.com.au). Flight Centre (☎ 131 600 Australia-wide, 🖳 www.fligh tcentre.com.au) has a central office at 82 Elizabeth St, Sydney, and there are dozens of offices throughout Australia. Sydney-based travel.com.au (☎ 02-9249 5444, 🖳 www .travel.com.au) is a good place to try for specials, especially via its Web site.

The *New Zealand Herald* has a travel section in which travel agencies advertise fares. Flight Centre (☎ 09-309 6171) has a large central office in Auckland at National Bank Towers (corner Queen and Darby Sts) and many branches throughout the country. STA Travel (☎ 09-309 0458) has its main office at 10 High St, Auckland, and has other offices in Auckland as well as in Hamilton, Palmerston North, Wellington, Christchurch and Dunedin.

Continental Europe

You can fly to London and other points in Britain from most major European cities. The variety of carriers and special fares is staggering; indeed, it's rare for anyone to pay as much as an airline's ordinary economy fare. 'Airport fares' – bought, as the name suggests, at an airport – are often the cheapest.

Excellent discount charter flights are often available to full-time students aged under 30 and all young travellers aged under 26 (you need an ISIC card or an official youth card) and are available through the large student travel agencies. France has a network of student travel agencies that can supply discount tickets to travellers of all ages. Belgium, Switzerland, the Netherlands and Greece are also good places for buying discount tickets.

Across Europe many travel agencies have ties with STA Travel, where cheap tickets can be purchased and STA-issued tickets can be altered (usually for a US$25 fee). Outlets in major cities include:

ISYTS (☎ 01-322 1267) 11 Nikis St, Upper Floor, Syntagma Square, Athens
Passaggi (☎ 06-474 0923) Stazione Termini FS, Gelleria Di Tesla, Rome
STA Travel (☎ 030-311 0950) Goethestrasse 73, 10625 Berlin
Voyages Wasteels (☎ 08-03 88 70 04) 11 rue Dupuytren, 756006 Paris

South Africa

STA Travel, in Johannesburg (☎ 011-447 5551) and Cape Town (☎ 021-418 6570), is primarily aimed at students and has discounted youth fares to London. It's also worth checking the South African Student's Travel Services (☎ 011-716 3045), which has an office at the University of the Witwatersrand, in Johannesburg. The Africa Travel Centre (☎ 021-235 555) on the corner of Military Rd and New Church St, Tamboerskloof, Cape Town, also has good prices.

Nairobi, Kenya, is probably the best place in Africa to buy tickets to Britain, thanks to the many bucket shops and the strong competition between them.

Asia

Although you'll now find fairly competitive air fare deals in most Asian countries, Bangkok, Singapore and Hong Kong are still the best places to shop around for discount tickets. Hong Kong's travel market can be unpredictable, but some excellent bargains are available if you are lucky.

Bangkok has a number of excellent travel agencies but there are also some suspect ones; STA Travel (☎ 02-236 0262), 33 Surawong Rd, is a good and reliable place to start.

Singapore, like Bangkok, has hundreds of travel agencies, so you can compare prices of flights. Chinatown Point shopping centre on New Bridge Rd has a good selection of travel agencies. STA Travel (☎ 737 7188) in the Orchard Parade Hotel, 1 Tanglin Rd, offers competitive discount fares.

Hong Kong has a number of excellent, reliable travel agencies. Many travellers use the Hong Kong Student Travel Bureau (☎ 2730 3269), 8th floor, Star House, Tsimshatsui. You could also try Phoenix Services (☎ 2722 7378), 7th floor, Milton Mansion, 96 Nathan Rd, Tsimshatsui.

In India, you can get cheap tickets in Mumbai (Bombay), Kolkata (Calcutta) and particularly Delhi. STIC Travels (☎ 011-332 5559), an agent for STA Travel, has an office in Delhi in Room 6 at the Hotel Imperial in Janpath. In Mumbai, STIC Travels (☎ 022-218 1431) is located at 6 Maker Arcade, Cuffe Parade.

TRAIN

The Channel Tunnel links Britain with Europe and two train services operate through it.

Eurotunnel runs a rail shuttle service for motorbikes, cars, buses and freight vehicles between terminals at Folkestone in Britain and Coquelles, near Calais in France. At the time of writing you could only take a cycle on Eurotunnel by either having it in or on a car or by taking the cycle mini-bus, which collects you at a designated point near the terminal; your bike travels on a trailer. The return fare for cyclists is £30. You must make a reservation (☎ 0870-535 3535).

British, French and Belgian railway companies jointly operate Eurostar (☎ 0870-518 6186), a high-speed passenger service that connects London to Paris, Lille and Brussels. Bikes are only accepted on Eurostar if they're in a bag that fits in the luggage racks; maximum bag size is 120cm x 80cm x 50cm. Eurostar also has an arrangement with the Esprit parcel company (☎ 0870-585 0850) to forward bikes; it costs £20 per bike and you need a Eurostar ticket to book.

There's no departure tax if you leave Britain by the Channel Tunnel.

BUS

Eurolines, the main bus operator from Britain to Europe, won't take bikes, not even folding bikes.

The best option is European Bike Express (EBE; ☎ 01642-251440/750077, fax 01642-232209, ℮ bolero@bolero.demon.co.uk), located at 31 Baker St, Middlesbrough TS1 2LF, a joint venture between Bolero International Holidays and the CTC (Cyclists' Touring Club). The EBE runs from May to October; there are 15 pick-up/drop-off points in England (stretching from Middlesbrough to Dover) and 30 in Europe. The service can carry a total of 52 cycles towed in a covered cycle trailer behind a luxury coach (handlebars need to be turned 90 degrees before a bike is loaded), which crosses the Channel by ferry. Depending on pick-up/drop-off point, fares range from £149 to £169 (CTC members get a £10 discount). There is no departure tax if you travel by bus.

SEA

There's no departure tax if you leave Britain by sea.

Passenger Ships

Regular long-distance passenger ships disappeared with the advent of cheap air travel.

They have been replaced by a small number of luxury cruise ships.

It's also possible to join some freighters as a paying passenger; with a bit of homework you'll be able to find passage to Britain from just about anywhere else in the world. Passenger freighters typically carry six to 12 passengers (more than 12 would require a doctor on board) and give you a real taste of life at sea.

Whether by cruise ship or passenger freighter, passage by sea is expensive. The standard reference for passenger ships is the *ABC Cruise & Ferry Guide* published by the OAG Worldwide (☎ 01582-600111), Church St, Dunstable, Bedfordshire LU5 4HB. This guide is also a good source of information about passenger freighters.

Ferries to/from Europe

The main alternatives for sea travel to Britain come primarily from mainland Europe. Services offered are comprehensive but complicated. The same ferry company often has a host of different prices for the same route, depending upon the time of day or year and the validity of the ticket. It's worth planning (and booking) ahead where possible as there may be special reductions on off-peak crossings.

While most ferry companies will transport cycles, some do so for free, but others levy a charge, which is sometimes reduced in winter. Examples of fares and charges are included here, but always check in advance.

France The shortest ferry links between Britain and Europe are from Dover and Folkestone to Calais and Boulogne. Dover is the most convenient port for cyclists who are travelling on to their starting point in Britain by train. Between Dover and Calais, return ferry passage with P&O Stena Line (☎ 0870-600 0600) costs from £48 (£24 for five-day return); bikes travel free.

There are also good rail links to elsewhere in Britain from Portsmouth. P&O European Ferries (☎ 0870-242 4999, 🖳 www.poef .com) operates Portsmouth-Cherbourg and Portsmouth–Le Havre services. Return passage costs £64 plus £10 for the bike in summer; £36, with bike free, in winter.

Brittany Ferries (☎ 0870-901 2400) has at least one voyage each day Portsmouth to/from Caen and St Malo. Portsmouth-Caen

passenger fares are roughly the same as the P&O routes; the Portsmouth–St Malo route costs a little more. Cycles travel free on these routes from October to March and cost £5 at other times. Brittany also has a ferry from Plymouth to Roscoff; charges for cycles are as per the Portsmouth services.

Spain P&O European Ferries operates a Portsmouth-Bilbao service. Return passage is £160 plus £20 for the bike in summer; £95 plus £15 for the bike in winter.

Brittany Ferries operates services between Plymouth and Santander (on Spain's north coast). A single is in the £50 to £90 range, with bikes costing £7.50 and rising to £10 in peak season.

Belgium, the Netherlands & Germany DFDS Seaways (formerly Scandinavian Seaways; ☎ 0870-533 3000) runs ferries between Harwich and Hamburg (Germany); return fares in a four-berth couchette (sleeping seat) start at £118, bikes are free. The Newcastle-Amsterdam service also takes bikes; return fares in a four-berth couchette start at £71.

Stena Line (☎ 0870-570 7070, 🖳 www .stenaline.com) runs services between Harwich and the Hook of Holland (the Netherlands). Single fares in July and August are £29 plus £5 for the bike; £24 plus £3 for the bike at other times.

Scandinavia DFDS Seaways runs ferries between Harwich and Esbjerg (Denmark); return fares in a four-berth couchette start at £121 (bikes free). In summer, DFDS also has a Newcastle-Gothenburg (Sweden) service; return fares in a four-berth couchette start at £141 and bikes are free.

Norway's Color Line (☎ 0191-296 1313) operates ferries year-round between Newcastle, and Stavanger, Haugesund and Bergen in Norway.

An adventurous possibility for Scotland-bound cyclists is the summer-only link between Shetland, Norway, the Faroe Islands and Iceland. The operator is Smyril Line but the agent is P&O Scottish Ferries (☎ 01244-572615). P&O Scottish have a regular ferry service from Aberdeen in Scotland to Lerwick (Shetland).

Ireland There's a great variety of ferry services linking Britain to Ireland. Bicycles are free on many services (always check ahead) and there are often special deals worth investigating. Services and operators include:

Swansea to Cork – mid-March to early January only; Swansea Cork Ferries (☎ 01792-456116)
Fishguard/Pembroke to Rosslare – year-round
Fishguard-Rosslare: Stena Line (☎ 01233-647047)
Pembroke-Rosslare: Irish Ferries (☎ 0990-171717).
Holyhead to Dublin/Dun Laoghaire – year-round; contact Stena Line for Holyhead-Dun Laoghaire, and Irish Ferries for Holyhead-Dublin (see previous listing)
Liverpool to Belfast – year-round; Norse Irish Ferries (☎ 0151-944 1010)
Stranraer to Belfast – year-round (high-speed catamaran); SeaCat (☎ 0845-752 3523)
Stranraer/Cairnryan to Larne (Northern Ireland) – year-round; contact Stena Line for Stranraer-Larne and P&O (☎ 01581-200276) for Cairnryan-Larne
Liverpool/Heysham via Douglas (Isle of Man) to Dublin – year-round; Isle of Man Steam Packet Company (☎ 01624-661661/645645)
Campbeltown to Ballycastle – year-round; Argyll & Antrim Steam Packet Company (☎ 0845-752 3523)

ORGANISED TOURS

Scores of companies around the world offer cycling tours in Britain. The best places to begin searching for a tour company include the British Tourist Authority (BTA) or their representatives in other countries (see Tourist Offices in the Facts for the Cyclist chapter); travel agencies that specialise in adventure travel; and the Internet.

Sites for both Action Trips (⌨ www.actiontrips.com) and the Adventure Cycling Association (⌨ adv-cycling.org) provide a wealth of information and links; they're both included in the directory of touring companies and links in the huge Cyber Cyclery site (⌨ www.cycling.org).

As a rule, the best-informed tour guides are those that work for British cycle-touring companies. There's quite a range of companies offering bicycle tours of various sorts throughout Britain. Most are for small groups covering a set route with vehicle support and accommodation in B&Bs. Many will customise tours; almost all offer bikes for hire.

Costs vary depending on the location, type and length of tour. Usually there'll be additional charges if you hire a bike and if you're travelling alone. A seven-day self-guided itinerary would usually start in the £300 to £400 range. Fully supported and with superior accommodation, a seven-day tour may run to over £1000.

The CTC has one of the most varied tour programs with truly national scope. In 1999 the CTC offered about 30 rides in Britain, some of which included vehicle support. You must be a CTC member to join a tour, but they're competitively priced – some tours of six to eight days' duration are under £200.

Tour companies worth contacting include:

England
Acorn Activities (☎ 08707-405055, ⌨ www.acornactivities.co.uk) – active holiday specialist with a good range of supported cycling on offer, from weekend jaunts to two-week tours.
Country Lanes (☎ 01425-655022, ⓔ bicycling@countrylanes.co.uk, ⌨ dspace.dial.pipex.com/countrylanes) – one of the larger English tour companies, offering both supported and self-guided tours in Hampshire and the New Forest, the Cotswolds and the Lake District.
London Bicycle Tour Company (☎ 020-7928 6838, ⓔ london.bicycle@btinternet.com) – good if you'd like some company while exploring London or south-eastern England.
Rough Tracks (☎ 07000-560749, ⌨ www.rough-tracks.co.uk) – supported tours off-road in England or Wales

Scotland
Bespoke Highland Tours (☎ 0141-334 9017, ⌨ www.scotland-info.co.uk/tours) – highlands and islands specialist
Scottish Cycle Safaris (☎ 0131-556 5560, ⌨ www.cyclescotland.co.uk)
Scottish Cycling Holidays (☎ 01250-876100, ⌨ www.scotcycle.co.uk)
Singletrack Scotland (☎ 01224-626360) – off-road tours in Scotland

Wales
Beics Eryri Cycle Tours (☎ 01286-676637, ⌨ www.beicseryri.clara.net) – Welsh specialist, especially good for northern Wales.
Bicycle Beano (☎ 01982-560471, ⌨ www.bicyclebeano.co.uk) – tours in Wales and the Welsh borders area with a vegetarian cuisine theme.
Rough Tracks (☎ 07000-560749, ⌨ www.rough-tracks.co.uk) – supported tours off-road in England or Wales

Getting Around

In Britain, a cyclist's off-the-bike travel options are notionally wide open. Trains, some bus services and most domestic planes and ferries will all carry bikes, and hire cars are plentiful. However, if you weigh up the variables – cost, convenience and areas served – there's little doubt that train travel remains the best alternative.

AIR

Having taken into account Britain's relatively small size and comprehensive rail network, the location of airports and the hassles (and possible costs) associated with packing a bike and gear for air travel, it soon becomes obvious that travelling within Britain by air is not a cyclist's best option. Unless you're going from southern England to northern Scotland, planes are only marginally quicker than trains if you include the time it takes to get to/from airports and to prepare your bike for travel.

Domestic Air Services

Air Services are offered by many companies, but the main carriers are British Airways (☎ 0845-773 3377, ▣ www.british-airways.com), British Midland (☎ 0870-607 0555, ▣ www.iflybritishmidland.com) and KLM UK (☎ 0870-507 4074, ▣ www.klmuk.com). There are several other smaller companies, including easyJet (☎ 08706-000000, ▣ www.easyjet.com) and the new British Airways no-frills offshoot, Go (☎ 0845-605 4321, ▣ www.go-fly.com).

All the domestic airlines are now set up to take bookings via their Web sites, and some actively encourage Web bookings with special deals.

Cost

Various tickets are offered by British airlines, including full fare (very expensive but flexible), Apex (for which you must book at least 14 days in advance) and various special offers on some services. There are also youth fares (for under 25s), but Apex and special-offer fares are usually cheaper. Prices vary enormously. For example, if you're flying from London to Edinburgh return on British Airways you'd be unlucky to pay more than £100, and it's likely you'll find a seat (with conditions attached) for much less. The full-fare cost is more than £260.

Shop around not only on the basis of price, but also taking into account the most convenient airports for departure and arrival. Some of the cheapest flights may not service the most convenient airports.

Carrying Your Bicycle

Some flights, especially those where smaller aircraft are used, will place a restriction on the total number of bikes allowed on the flight *in addition* to a weight restriction. Cycles are not permitted at all on some smaller aircraft. *Always* check with the airlines before making a reservation.

Examples of domestic carriers' policies for bicycles can be found in the boxed text 'Cycle-Friendly Airlines' in the Getting There & Away chapter.

Domestic Departure Tax

Every ticket should have a £10 airport departure tax added to the price of tickets – check that this is included in the price you're quoted.

BUS

In general, bus travel is cheaper than train travel and therefore worth investigating if you're on a tight budget.

Not the most effective option for long distance (most city-to-city) travel, buses are provided by various private companies. National Express (☎ 0870-580 8080), which runs the largest national network and completely dominates the market, will carry only folding bikes; rigid-framed bikes are excluded even with wheels detached. Strictly speaking, you should be able to take a boxed bike on a National Express bus, but you'd be wise to check before booking the journey.

While many bus companies in regional Britain will carry bikes, often the areas they cover would be better enjoyed from a cycle. Terms and conditions vary: some will take a bike free, although most charge a small fee; sometimes bikes are carried and fees are levied at the driver's discretion. Tourist Information Centres (TICs) are generally the best places to ask questions about the local buses.

There are some excellent bus services run for cyclists. The privately run Yorkshire Bikeliner (☎/fax 01482-222122, ✉ simon@bikeliner.karoo.co.uk, 🖥 www.bikeliner.karoo.net) offers services between England (Yorkshire) and Scotland. The Devon Bike Bus (☎ 01392-382800/383223) is organised by the Devon County Council Environment Department; it services points on National Cycle Network route No 27, the 'Devon Coast to Coast', during summer.

The Cyclists' Touring Club (CTC) touring department produces the information sheet *Taking A Cycle By Bus & Coach* is available to members; this is very useful if you plan to use buses extensively.

TRAIN

For the past 20 years British government policy has favoured car ownership. Correspondingly, some local rail services have been reduced, but the British railway network is still a marvel. There are very few parts of Britain more than a day's ride (about 50 miles) from a train station.

The way the railways are run isn't quite as marvellous. Following privatisation, services began to be provided by various operators, and these days 25 train operating companies (TOCs) look after the actual trains. A separate company, Railtrack, owns and maintains the track and the stations. For the sake of convenience the British Rail logo and name are still used on direction signs and there's a central telephone inquiry service – you don't have to travel with the contact details for the separate TOCs.

Whatever you think of the privatised railways, there's no doubt that trains remain the most convenient and often fastest way for cyclists to transport bikes and gear to and from tours.

Train Passes

No matter how popular the BritRail and Rail Rover passes are with general travellers, their high cost will probably only suit cyclists planning to spend every second day on the train. Contact the British Tourist Authority (BTA; see 🖥 www.bta.org.uk) in your country for the best deals.

Railcards

You can get discounts of up to 33% on most off-peak fares (except Apex and SuperApex – see Tickets, following) if you're aged 16 to 25, over 60, studying full-time or disabled, but you must first buy the appropriate railcard. Cards are valid for one year and most are available from major stations. You'll need two passport photos and proof of age (birth certificate or passport) or student status.

There's also a Family Railcard, very useful if your touring party includes children. With a Family Railcard holder in your group, adults get discounted fares (usually 33%) and children pay a flat fare of £2 each.

If you're planning a lot of travel in a particular region, check with the TOCs to see if there's an annual regional discount card available. For instance, if you intend to travel and cycle mostly in south-eastern England (ie, if you're basing yourself in London), a Network South-East card (about £20 per year) will deliver a 33% discount on most train journeys.

Tickets

Provided you've checked in advance that there's space for your bike, you can just roll up to a station and buy a standard single or return ticket valid for the journey at any time on the day specified, but these are relatively expensive. Cheap Day Return tickets are valid for the journey on the day specified, but they're usually only available for short journeys, there are time restrictions (you're not usually allowed to travel on a train that leaves before 9.30 am) and the savings often aren't great.

Open Return tickets are probably best for cyclists; they're valid for outward travel on a stated day and return on any day within a month. SuperSaver tickets are the cheapest available without advance purchase (return journey must be within one calendar month), but they're not available in south-eastern England and can't be used on Fridays and Saturdays in July and August or in London before 9.30 am, or between 4 and 6 pm. Saver and SuperAdvance tickets cost more than SuperSaver, but can be used any day and there are fewer time restrictions (SuperAdvance tickets must be bought before 2 pm on the day before travel and both outward and return journey times must be specified).

Apex and SuperApex tickets are both cheap but must be booked well in advance – a minimum of seven days prior to travelling is required.

Children under five travel free; aged between five and 15 they pay half-price for most tickets and full fare for Apex/Super-Apex tickets. If you're travelling with children it's almost always worth buying a Family Railcard (see the Railcards entry, earlier in this section).

Classes

There are two classes of rail travel: 1st, and what is now officially referred to as standard (although in class-conscious Britain this will always be called 2nd class). First class costs 30% to 50% more than 2nd and, except on very crowded trains, isn't really worth the extra money.

Reservations

To make a booking, first phone the 24-hour national rail inquiry line (☎ 0845-748 4950) to get the time of your train and the ticket price. You'll then be given the relevant TOC's number for credit-card bookings. You can also check train times and get TOC numbers at 💻 www.railtrack.co.uk.

Bookings can be paid for with MasterCard (Access), Visa, American Express, Diners Club and Switch. Tickets must be ordered at least five days in advance and are then sent by post. Booking lines for some companies are open Monday to Friday from 9 am to 5 pm but others (particularly InterCity) are open daily from 8 am to 10 pm.

Costs

The advantage of cycle touring is flexibility, so by definition cyclists are less likely to plan far enough ahead to take advantage of discounted fares. However, there are considerable savings available if you plan ahead. For instance, a standard single from London to Edinburgh is £69; the Apex fare is £36.

The following examples are all standard one-way fares:

from	to	one way
Carlisle	Leeds	£25.80
Chepstow	Cardiff	£5.00
London	Canterbury	£14.70
London	Manchester	£47.20
London	Newcastle	£72.00
London	Peterborough	£14.90
London	St Albans	£7.00
London	Weymouth	£38.50
Newcastle	Edinburgh	£29.50
Newcastle	York	£10.50

Carrying Your Bicycle

There are now 25 TOCs and 25 variations on policy regarding taking cycles by train. Some TOCs require reservations, some charge a fee and many have time restrictions. It should be noted that the policies aren't all bad news. At least one TOC – Anglia Train Services, which services an area including Norfolk, Suffolk and parts of Essex and Cambridgeshire – has a 'cycle rescue scheme', whereby cyclists left stranded through illness, breakdown or theft can call a number and arrange transport to the nearest train station!

To make matters more interesting, the situation is far from stable. TOCs with less-enlightened policies are under pressure from any number of national, regional and local lobby groups, and policies are changing. *Always* call the 24-hour national rail inquiry line (☎ 0845-7484950) before travelling; operators are generally up-to-date with each TOC's policy and will inform you of any restrictions and/or charges. If there's any doubt, the operator will give you the number of the TOC with whom you'll be travelling.

CAR

A rental car could be useful if you're pushed for time, although you should bear in mind that busy roads can render cars a slower option than trains. While trains usually deposit you near the centre of a town or city, rental cars often have to be returned to out-of-the-way parts.

Rental cars are expensive in Britain and parking is difficult in town and city centres. In fact, it's increasingly rare to find free parking, and you can end a day's car sightseeing several quid poorer from parking fees alone. Then there's fuel costs – at 70p or more per litre, petrol is expensive by American or Australian standards; diesel is only a few pence cheaper. Fortunately, distances aren't great. There's often a penalty if you want to return the car to a destination other than where you started, although this might be a one-off fee that's easily absorbed over several days. Generally, any car rental will make better financial sense if you have the car for a longer period.

For all their negatives, cars remain attractive because they offer flexibility and independence. If you think you'll be renting a car in Britain, consider making arrangements in your home country before departure to take advantage of any package deals on offer.

The main rental companies include Avis (☎ 0870-590 0500), British Car Rental (☎ 024-7671 6166), Budget (☎ 0800-181181), Europcar (☎ 0845-222525), National Car Rental (☎ 01895-233300), Hertz (☎ 0870-599 6699) and Thrifty Car Rental (☎ 01494-751500). For cheap operators check the ads in *TNT Magazine,* available from pavement bins in London and elsewhere. TICs usually have lists of local car-hire companies. Generally, the operator will provide information on British road rules.

Remember that small cars (Ford Fiestas, Peugeot 106s etc) are unlikely to fit more than two riders with bikes and gear. If you're doing a few days' sightseeing by car it's best not to leave valuables (bike included) in the car if you park it in an isolated area.

FERRY

Intra-Britain ferry travel is restricted to small hops across rivers and lakes and longer island services, such as to the Isle of Wight, Isle of Man and, more notably, the Scottish Hebrides, Orkney and Shetland Islands. Cycles are generally allowed on ferries free or for a small charge. Cost and conditions of ferries used on routes in this book are discussed in the relevant rides. If you're planning your own route and it involves a ferry crossing, make sure you check in advance for the ferry operator's rules on carrying bicycles.

ORGANISED RIDES

For information about the range of companies offering bicycle tours in Britain, see Organised Tours in the Getting There & Away chapter.

London

☎ 020

To have no interest in visiting London, you would have to have somehow missed hearing about the past 2000 or so years of European history.

This is the city that the Roman Empire began, in which Edward the Confessor built an abbey at Westminster, that plague and fire nearly destroyed, and that Christopher Wren helped to restore. From it, an empire was created and managed, and enemies defied. Its buildings, streets and parklands form a wondrous tapestry of princely wealth and desperate poverty; of brilliant democracy and gross privilege; of deep-fried cod and all the spices of India. Nineteenth century prime minister Benjamin Disraeli described it as 'a nation, not a city'.

London's blessed with mostly flat terrain, and the variety of cycling experiences available – street, off-road path, mountain bike – is unexpected. Less surprising is the fact that it's possible to create some very long rides in what is a vast (more than 770 sq miles) urban region.

HISTORY

The Romans, London's first developers, built a wooden bridge across the Thames in about AD 43 and, some 200 years later, a defensive wall enclosing the square mile now known as the City of London. The Romans left c. 410, and little is known of London between then and the last years of Edward the Confessor's reign, when Westminster Abbey and palace were first established.

After 1066, following Edward's lead, the Normans chose Westminster as their place of residence and government, while the City remained the centre of commerce and trade.

By the 14th century, London had grown into a vibrant city of about 80,000 people; its food-supply arteries extended up to 100km into the surrounding countryside and air pollution was becoming a problem. The Black Death, which struck 1348–49, slowed the city's development – for a time.

The maze of streets that characterises much of central London – and proves such a navigational challenge to visiting cyclists –

In Summary

Terrain
Mostly flat; some small rises.

Special Events
Wimbledon, the FA Cup, New Year's Parade and Notting Hill Carnival: big and not-so-big events are a constant in London. Check out the tourist board's bimonthly *Events in London* or its *Annual Events* pamphlet.

Cycling Events
• **London to Brighton Bike Ride** (June)

Tourist Information
• **British Travel Centre: ☎ 8846 9000**

• **London Tourist Board:**
  ⌨ **www.londontown.com**

• **Victoria TIC: ☎ 7730 3488**

began to grow beyond the immediate surrounds of the City and Westminster in the 16th century, during Elizabeth I's reign. At one point Elizabeth banned further building, but neither her decree nor a similar one from Charles I, almost a century later, could deter London's spread.

An outbreak of the plague in 1664–65 killed about 70,000 and was immediately followed by the 1666 Great Fire, which burnt about 80% of the City. Rapid rebuilding didn't allow for a new street plan, although the old streets were widened and straightened. Development continued unevenly until the 19th century, during which time London acquired many of the characteristics of a modern city – street lighting, a police force, water and sanitation works, and public transport (first buses, in the late 1820s, then railways).

The 20th century saw a gradual rise in the use of private transport and increasing congestion on London's streets, which even the greater emphasis on planning that followed

WWII has largely failed to quell. Today, Greater London is home to between seven and 12 million people (depending on where you draw the boundary).

CLIMATE

London's climate is about as good as it gets for Britain. Summer temperatures range from an average low of 12°C to a top of 21°C during the day, while winter averages hover below 10°C (but usually above 0°C). Generally, you should expect cooler temperatures in London from late October to April or May. Average annual rainfall is 585mm and it's fairly evenly distributed throughout the year, with July to August, and October to November usually wettest. On average, London has 200 dry days each year. Snow is rare, usually falling January to March, and it rarely settles.

INFORMATION

For more-detailed information on London, see Lonely Planet's *London* (£9.99). *Time Out* magazine, published weekly, is a staggeringly detailed listing of London entertain-ment, attractions, art and much besides. There are many free listing/classifieds magazines; *TNT* is the best known (call ☎ 7373 3377 for the nearest distribution point) .

The British Travel Centre (☎ 8846 9000) at Piccadilly Circus offers information; accommodation, transport and theatre bookings; and has a map and guidebook shop. There are Tourist Information Centres (TICs) at Heathrow, Gatwick, Luton and Stansted airports, at Waterloo International Terminal, Victoria Station and Liverpool St Underground station. The Victoria TIC (☎ 7730 3488), the main centre, gets very busy.

Maps

Lonely Planet's *London City Map* (£3.99) is waterproof, lightweight and handy for leaving heavy guidebooks at home. The Westminster & the City ride in this chapter can be traced directly onto the map.

The London Cycling Campaign (LCC) has released three (of a planned nine) cycle-route maps covering Greater London – *Central*, *West* and *North West*. These show both signposted and planned London Cycle Network (LCN) routes, as well as traffic-free

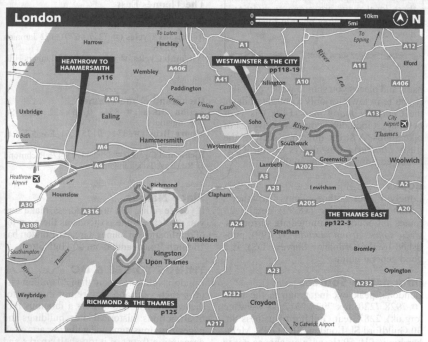

Warning

Expect traffic to be heavy – but drivers usually well mannered – whenever you're on major roads. Always wear a helmet. They're not compulsory, but London isn't the place to get sentimental about the breeze in your hair.

Wherever you are, *always* lock your bike securely. If leaving the bike locked and unattended for an extended period take everything with you – computer, lights, bottles and toolkit.

The Clean Air Acts of 1956 and 1968 – which outlawed coal burning, among other measures – and London's changeable weather combine to stymie the development of pea-soup smog. But a rancid cocktail of traffic fumes and other pollutants can build up, causing eye irritation and increasing the incidence of asthma and respiratory complaints. Face masks are a common sight on regular London cyclists.

The blue London Cycle Network (LCN) signs are invaluable, reducing the need to reach for a map, but note that here and there local wags are prone to twisting them on poles so they point in the wrong direction.

---

paths and places you should walk your bike. If you're in town for only a couple of days, the *Central London* map (£4.95) is your best buy; it includes a comprehensive list of bike shops. A street directory such as the trusty *London A-Z* is always useful. Ring-bound editions are about £6.00.

Books
Lonely Planet author Nicky Crowther's *London Cycle Guide* (£8.99) details 25 routes in London and immediate surrounds. *Cycle tours: Around London* (£9.99), published by the Ordnance Survey (OS), is a good general guide.

Information Sources
London's peak cycling group is the LCC (☎ 7928 7220, fax 7928 2312, ⌨ www.lcc .org.uk), 228 Great Guildford Business Sq, 30 Guildford St, London, SE1 OHS. Membership is £19.50 (less if you choose not to

get the LCC magazine). The LCC's handbook *On Your Bike* contains useful tips on local traffic and cycling laws, bike security and safe city riding. The handbook is usually sold in a package with the LCC's superb *Central London* route map (see the Maps section, earlier).

The LCC's bi-monthly magazine *London Cyclist* comes with LCC membership or is available from bike shops; it includes a calendar of organised local rides.

Bike Shops
Following is a list of London bike shops on or near the rides described in this chapter.

Riding to/from Heathrow Airport
Action Bikes (☎ 8994 1485), 176 Chiswick High Rd, W4
Richmond Cycles (☎ 8741 0115), 155 King St, W6

Westminster & the City
Bikepark (☎ 7430 0083), Stukeley St, WC2
Covent Garden Cycles (☎ 7836 1752), 2 Nottingham Court, Shorts Gardens, WC2

The Thames East
The Magic Bicycle Company (☎ 7375 2993), 187 Whitechapel Rd, E1
Robinsons Cycles (☎ 7237 4679), 172 Jamaica Rd, SE16
Witcomb Cycles (☎ 8692 1734), 25 Tanners Hill, SE8

Richmond & the Thames
Action Bikes (☎ 8547 0775), 22 Eden St, Kingston
Moore Bros (☎ 8744 0175), 61 London Rd, Twickenham
Richmond Cycles (☎ 8892 4372), 425 Richmond Rd, East Twickenham

Place Names
If you're riding to a street address, make sure you're clear on the postcode as there's a lot of duplication of names. Greater London has 18 High Roads and about 50 High Streets.

THINGS TO SEE & DO
London welcomes more than 20 million visitors each year and they're not in town for the weather. London offers a fabulous mix of attractions: historical sites, buildings and pageantry; museums and galleries; arts of all description (most of it top-shelf); parks and

The National Cycle Network routes open June 2000

Shetland Islands

Orkney Islands

Irish Sea

North Sea

English Channel

sustrans
ROUTES FOR PEOPLE

www.nationalcyclenetwork.org.uk

Issue 5
May 2000

See London by bike – start at the Tower Bridge and head off along the River Thames...

... or take in the tour boats at Westminster and try to out-pedal the buskers at Covent Garden...

...there's time for a quick call home, but slow down or even walk to negotiate busy Trafalgar Square.

gardens; various events, festivals and carnivals; food; shopping – just about anything a visitor's heart desires.

The Westminster & the City and The Thames East rides in this chapter are dedicated to sight-seeing around London's best-known attractions for which enquiry numbers are also given. For a starting point to learn more about London attractions, see the Information section in this chapter.

PLACES TO STAY

Accommodation in London is expensive and in demand. The peak tourist months (summer) are the busiest; definitely book ahead if you plan to visit during these times.

Having a bicycle with you will add to the fun. Generally, it seems to be less trouble parking your bike if you stay at the cheapest accommodation (a camping ground or some hostels) or the most expensive – top hotels such as The Savoy or The Ritz could probably arrange helicopter parking if required. In between are a vast pantheon of cheap hotels and B&Bs, for which you should always check on cycle parking or storage facilities before making a firm booking.

Several organisations arrange B&B accommodation in Londoners' homes, which can be a bit more pleasant than a cheap hotel. Contact *At Home in London* (☎ 8748 1943, fax 8748 2701, ⓔ athomeinlondon@compuserve.com, 🖳 www.athomeinlondon.co.uk) or *London Bed & Breakfast Agency* (☎ 7586 2768, fax 7586 6567) for more information.

In the following entries, prices are per person per night unless otherwise stated, and the cheapest rates at B&Bs are usually based on sharing a room. 'Train' refers to overground train stations and 'tube' to the London Underground.

Camping

As you'd expect, there are no camping grounds in central London, but campers don't have to go to the very fringe of the Greater City.

Tent City Acton (☎ 8743 5708; Old Oak Common Lane, W3; tube: East Acton) is open June to September; accommodation in dorm-style tents and tent pitches is £6. *Tent City Hackney* (☎ 8985 7656; Millfields Rd, E5; train: Clapton) is open July to August. It has the same accommodation as TC Acton for £5.

The *Crystal Palace Caravan Club Site* (☎ 8778 7155; Crystal Place Parade, SE19; train: Crystal Palace) is open year-round; tent pitches for cyclists start at £4.90.

Lea Valley Leisure Centre Camping & Caravan Park (☎ 8803 6900; Meridian Way, N9; train: Edmonton Green) is open year-round. The cost of a tent pitch for two people is £5.20.

Hostels

London has seven Youth Hostel Association (YHA) hostels, three of which have secure cycle storage.

The venerable *Earl's Court* (☎ 7373 7083; 38 Bolton Gardens, SW5; ⓔ earlscourt@yha.org.uk; tube: Earl's Court) is in a reasonably lively part of town. Most of the 154 beds are in 10-bed dorms. The charge (including breakfast) is £19.45.

The shiny and new *St Pancras International* (☎ 7388 9998; 79–81 Euston Rd, NW1; ⓔ stpancras@yha.org.uk; train/tube: Kings Cross, St Pancras or Euston) is handy to the West End and popular Camden Town. Its 150 beds are in mostly 5- and 4-bed rooms. Beds cost £22.15 (including breakfast).

For the same rates, the huge *Rotherhithe* (☎ 7232 2114; 20 Salter Rd, SE16; ⓔ rotherhithe@yha.org.uk; tube: Rotherhithe) is in a quiet part of town just south of the River Thames. Its 320 beds are in mostly 2-, 4- and 6-bed rooms.

Independent hostels are scattered about, especially in west and south-west London, and at most the cheapest beds are in the £12 to £20 range. Earl's Court has the biggest selection. Try *Curzon House Hotel* (☎ 7581 2116; 58 Courtfield Gardens, SW5; tube: Gloucester Rd) or *Windsor House* (☎ 7373 9087; 12 Penywern Rd, SW5; tube: Earl's Court).

The *Palace Hotel* (☎ 7221 5628; 31 Palace Court, W2; tube: Notting Hill Gate) is handily located in groovy Notting Hill; dorm beds are £15 to £18.

The Generator (☎ 7388 7666; Compton Place, WC1, ⓔ generator@lhdr.demon.co.uk31; tube: Russell Square) is a converted police barracks with more than 800 beds, shared dining and social areas, and a licensed bar open until 2 am. Singles are in the £30 to £40 range but rates fall dramatically in shared rooms.

B&Bs

London's most convenient B&B or budget hotel enclaves are Bayswater, Bloomsbury and the Pimlico-Victoria area; Earl's Court is a little farther out. The choice is massive, and outside the high season it's usually possible to negotiate a better rate if you're staying for more than a couple of nights.

In Bayswater try the *Garden Court Hotel* (☎ *7229 2553; 30 Kensington Gardens Square, W2; tube: Bayswater)*. Expect to pay in the £20 to £30 range at the minimum. You'll pay a bit more at *Parkwood* (☎ *7402 2241, fax 7402 1574; 4 Stanhope Place, W2; tube: Marble Arch)* but the location is brilliant – opposite Hyde Park and a short walk from the West End. Rates start from £30 to £40.

In Bloomsbury, the *Repton Hotel* (☎ *7436 4922; 31 Bedford Place, WC1; tube: Russell Square)* offers room beds from about £35 a night. A limited number of dorm beds go for less then £20. The pleasant *Jenkins Hotel* (☎ *7387 2067, fax 7383 3139; 45 Cartwright Gardens, WC1,* @ *reservations@jenkinshotel.demon.co.uk; train: Euston; tube: Russell Square, Euston)* has rates in the £30 to £40 range.

Luna & Simone Hotels (☎ *7834 5897, 47 Belgrave Rd SW1; train/tube: Victoria)* are handy to Buckingham Palace and Westminster; prices start in the £20 to £30 range. At *Woodville & Morgan Houses* (☎ *7730 1048/2384, fax 7730 2574/8442; 107 & 120 Ebury St, SW1; train/tube: Victoria)* rates start at about £20 (for quad share); singles are £42.

Convenient for the Richmond & the Thames ride, the *Riverside Hotel* (☎*/fax 8940 1339; 23 Petersham Rd, TW10; train/tube: Richmond)* overlooks the Thames at Richmond, Surrey. From here you can ride alongside the Thames either way – to Hampton Court Palace, to the west, or Putney Bridge, east. Prices start in the £25 to £35 range.

Hotels

At the upper reaches of the price range are many outstanding hotels, all in convenient locations.

Wilbraham (☎ *7730 8296, fax 7730 6815; 1 Wilbraham Place, SW1; tube: Sloane Square)* is handy to Kings Rd, Chelsea; expect to pay £50 or more. *Hazlitt's* (☎ *7434 1771, fax 7439 1524; 6 Frith St, W1; tube: Tottenham Court Rd)* occupies three linked Georgian houses smack in the middle of Soho. You'll pay a jot less than £100 per person in a double room.

Prices are more reasonable in chain hotels. Try *Travel Inn* (☎ *7902 1600, fax 7902 1619; County Hall, Belvedere Rd, SE1;* ▢ *www.travelinn.co.uk; train/tube: Waterloo)*, where double room prices start at around £60.

Step up to such institutions as *The Ritz* (☎ *7493 8181, fax 7493 2687; 150 Piccadilly, W1;* @ *enquiries@theritzhotel.co.uk; tube: Green Park)* and *The Savoy* (☎ *7836 4343, fax 7240 6040; Strand, WC1;* @ *info@thesavoy.co.uk; train/tube: Charing Cross)* and you enter the realm of genuine luxury, with prices to match. Expect to pay £260 for a double room at the minimum.

PLACES TO EAT

If it's 10 years or more since you've visited London you'll be pleasantly surprised at both the increased variety of restaurants and cafes and the quality of food served. And as the choice grows, recommendations become less relevant – by definition, you need to read the latest reviews in newspapers and *Time Out* to have any hope of staying abreast of the latest and choicest. Among the regularly updated local food guides, Lonely Planet's *Out to Eat – London* is worth a look.

For self-caterers, there are plenty of supermarkets (Sainsbury, Safeway, Somerfield and Tesco have about 150 London branches between them), markets and grocery shops to choose from. Compulsory is at least one visit (with intent to buy) to the food halls at *Harrods* (☎ *7730 1234; 87 Brompton Rd, SW1)* or *Selfridges* (☎ *7629 1234; 400 Oxford St, W1)*.

Although it's still easy to find 'traditional' British fare (check the nearest pub first), it's the range of cuisines on offer that really tempts the tastebuds. Indian food – often referred to as 'the national cuisine' – is most common. But your taste buds can now pretty much travel the world in a restaurant centre like Soho, and there's reasonable variety on many High Sts.

If you're trolling for a decent meal, the West End is the still best place to head. You'll find plenty of choice wandering the streets of Soho and nearby Covent Garden (try Neal's Yard, off Monmouth St for vegetarian cuisine). Farther out, the Bayswater/

Notting Hill area and Camden Town are both worth visiting.

It's pretty rare these days to find a pub that *doesn't* serve food, and many have made the leap to incorporate genuinely fine fare in their offerings to punters. A meal will cost more in one of these enlightened boozers (and, at some, the pints seem a few pence more). If you're eating on a budget, there's still plenty of pub grub about.

GETTING THERE & AWAY

See the Getting There & Away and Getting Around chapters for advice about getting to/from London.

GETTING AROUND

London is serviced by both surface and underground railways, an extensive bus network, and taxis and mini-cabs. For more information about taking your bike on a London train, see the boxed text 'Train Your Bike?'.

Generally, bikes are not accepted on London buses. Black cabs can certainly fit a bike – sometimes two – and most mini-cab companies have larger vehicles that you may be able to pre-book for transporting cycles.

To/From the Airport

See the boxed text 'Riding to/from Heathrow Airport' for a route description of the ride into London from Heathrow. The straight-line distances from central London to Gatwick, Luton and Stansted airports are all more than double the distance from Heathrow. Gatwick is about 26mi south, Luton 27mi north and Stansted about 30mi north-east. Using the most direct routes possible – all heavily trafficked A-roads – the road distance to London exceeds 30mi in each case.

Unless you're keen to begin your explorations of Britain with a sustained ride amid traffic noise and fumes, you're better off taking a train into town.

Airport Trains Bicycles are carried free on train services from Heathrow and Gatwick airports to central London. On the Heathrow Express (☎ 8745 0578, 🖳 www.heathrowe xpress.co.uk), which runs between Heathrow and London (Paddington), there's a limit of three bikes per train at busy times. All Gatwick Express services (☎ 0870-530 1530, 🖳 www.gatwickexpress.co.uk), from Gatwick to London (Victoria), have a roomy luggage van.

Train Your Bike?

Bikes are allowed – it would be stretching it to say they're welcome – on all London overground and some Underground rail services.

The Underground's 'shallow' routes – Circle, District, Hammersmith & City, and Metropolitan lines – allow bikes on all sections outside of peak hours (7.30 to 10 am and 4 to 7 pm) Monday to Friday and all day on weekends. Bikes can't be taken on the Victoria line or the 'deep' sections of the Bakerloo, Central, Jubilee, Northern and Piccadilly lines, which account for most central London Underground stations. Bikes travel free on the Underground; for information call ☎ 020-7222 1234.

Several different companies control London's overground railway lines, some of which don't permit bikes during peak hours. Bikes usually travel free, but check with the train operating company (TOC) before travelling: National Rail Enquiries (☎ 0845-748 4950).

Riding to/from Heathrow Airport

1:100,000

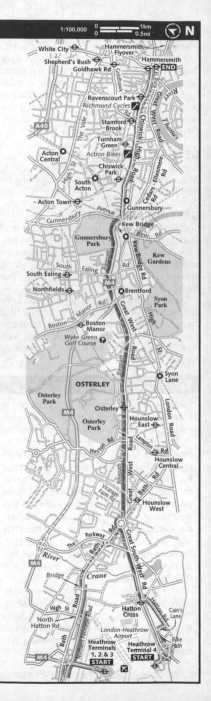

On the assumption that most people leaving airports are primarily interested in a shower and a bed, this route is the most direct from both Heathrow's terminal 4 and terminals 1, 2 and 3 to central London. It's around 11mi and takes cyclists to Hammersmith (1–1½ hours), about 5mi west of central London, where there are connections for Underground lines.

Planning

Pick up the London Cycling Campaign's (LCC's) *Central* and *West London* cycling maps at the airport or buy them before departure (see the Information Sources section (pp112) for LCC contact details). They provide the option of a longer scenic route into town and the means to navigate past Hammersmith.

The Ride

Heathrow terminal 4 and terminals 1, 2 and 3 are about 0.8mi apart and serviced by different traffic arteries. Negotiating the airport-nightmare tangle of roads surrounding the terminals requires a bit of concentration. But the astonishingly busy airport is eventually left behind via paths next to busy roads. It isn't pretty, but it's pretty direct.

Leaving Heathrow terminals 1, 2 and 3, head north on the vehicle tunnel. Take the west ramp at 0.5mi, before looping around onto the Northern Perimeter Rd.

Leaving terminal 4, go south-east on Swinton Rd, then turn right onto Snowdon Rd (0.1mi). At 0.2mi, turn left at the roundabout onto Shrewsby-Swansea Rd. The bikepath (right at 0.5mi) leads to Cain's Lane.

The routes join at the intersection of Bath, Great West and Great South-West Rds, then continue, by traffic-free path, beside the Great West Rd. In the Great West Rd/M4 overpass section there's some twisting and road-crossing before the route veers left onto Chiswick High Rd and joins the traffic. Chiswick High Rd becomes King St at Goldhawk Rd and continues direct to Hammersmith. The last section requires some walking – King St becomes one-way against you, and there are usually far too many people around for footpath riding.

At time of writing, bicycles were not permitted on the fast Stansted Airport Skytrain, but they were allowed on a slower hourly service to Stansted. For information call West Anglia Great Northern trains (☎ 0845-781 8919).

Westminster & the City

Duration	.................................1–3½ hours
Distance	....8.5mi
Difficulty	....easy
Start/End	...........Duke of Wellington Place

You'll feel a right git if you don't cycle to some of London's best-known sights. This ride links Westminster and the City, combining a look at some of the great buildings of Church, State and commerce with visits to the theatre district, Covent Garden and every visiting cyclist's least-favourite meeting place, Trafalgar Square. Points of interest along the way are highlighted, with phone numbers for you to follow up on those you want to spend time seeing.

PLANNING
When to Ride
This ride is tailored to Sunday, when Constitution Hill and The Mall, near Buckingham Palace, are closed to traffic and the City is dead. Expect dense pedestrian crowds, especially in summer.

Maps & Books
Lonely Planet's *London City Map* (£3.99) covers most of the route on this ride. Trace the route onto the map and leave your guidebook at home.

Otherwise, the LCC's *Central London* route map is good; parts of the ride follow marked LCN routes. The City Information Centre (☎ 7332 1456), open April to September on the south side of St Paul's Churchyard, has maps and guides to sights and events in the Square Mile.

What to Bring
Cleated shoes are not recommended. This route takes in packed tourist precincts and one-way streets, so expect to be regularly dismounting and walking. Bring along a bike lock so you can stop at the many attractions on the route.

THE RIDE
Provided it's undertaken on a Sunday, the ride starts with one of London cycling's truly blissful experiences. On Sundays, Constitution Hill and The Mall are closed to traffic, enabling a cruise from Hyde Park Corner; past peaceful **Green Park**; around the **Queen Victoria Memorial**, carved from a single block of white marble; and on up past **St James's Park**; towards **Admiralty Arch**, erected in honour of Queen Victoria. On the way the route passes **Buckingham Palace** (0.4mi; ☎ 7930 4832), the royal family's London home since 1837. The open roads are a serious ray of hope on summer Sundays, when inner London crowds are at their most intense.

Time your ride to catch some free entertainment, such as the **Changing of the Guard**, at 11.30 am at Buckingham Palace, or at 10 am (11 am on weekdays) at Horse Guards, up The Mall in Whitehall. Be early if you're serious about seeing something.

Traffic isn't an issue until you leave Horse Guards Rd and head up Storey's Gate towards **Westminster Abbey** (1.5mi; ☎ 7222 5152). Dismount to cross The Sanctuary, then take your time walking past the Abbey, where all but two English monarchs since 1066 have been crowned. Resist the temptation to visit on this occasion. Cycle parking is banned in this area – your bike will be removed if you lock it and leave it.

The neogothic-style **Houses of Parliament** (☎ 7219 4272/3107) face you as you exit the Abbey precinct next to historic **St Margaret's Westminster** (☎ 7222 5152), where John Milton worshipped. Cross the road at St Margaret's St or Old Palace Yard and drift down to Victoria Tower Gardens, where a **statue of suffragist Emmeline Pankhurst** occupies a leafy corner near Parliament, which granted women full voting equality with men a month after Pankhurst's death, in 1928.

From Lambeth Bridge to Blackfriars Bridge you're in a shared pedestrian-and-cycle precinct; be watchful for pedestrians, particularly children. Along this section you pass a wealth of sights including: old County Hall, now home to the **London Aquarium** (☎ 7967 8000); the **Millennium Wheel**, billed as the world's biggest Ferris wheel; **markets** under the Waterloo Bridge and at Gabriel's Wharf; **Royal Festival** and

LONDON

Westminster & the City

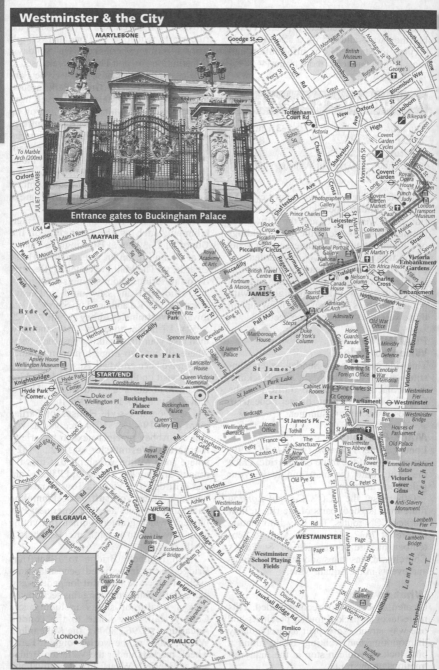

Entrance gates to Buckingham Palace

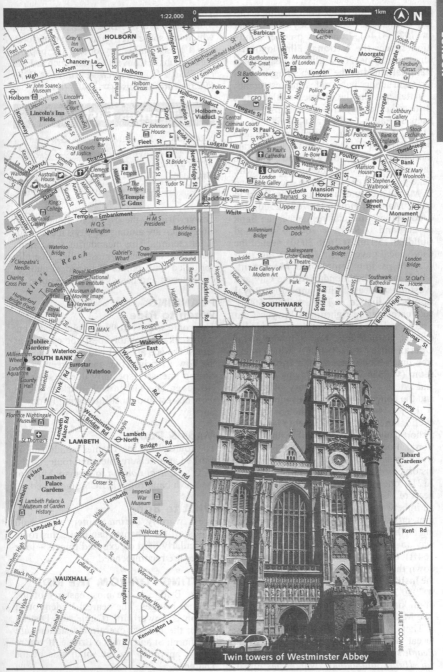

1:22,000

0   0.5mi   1km   N

HOLBORN

Red Lion Sq

Bedford Row

Gray's Inn Court

Chancery La

Greville St

Hatton Garden

Charterhouse St

Smithfield Market

Barbican

Barbican Centre

Aldersgate St

Museum of London

Fore St

Moorgate

South Pl

Finsbury Circus

High Holborn

Brooke St

Furnival St

W Smithfield

St Bartholomew-the-Great

St Bartholomew's

King Edward St

London Wall

Aldermanbury

Moorgate

Coleman St

Lothbury Gallery

Stock Exchange

Sir John Soane's Museum

Holborn

Lincoln's Inn

Lincoln's Inn Fields

Kingsway

Serle St

Chancery La

Holborn Circus

Shoe La

Holborn Viaduct

Police

GPO

Newgate St

Gresham St

Guildhall

Police

St Martin's le Grand

Noble St

Foster La

Wood St

Lothbury St

Bank of England

Police

Prince's St

Threadneedle

Dr Johnson's House

Fetter La

Fleet St

Old Bailey

Central Criminal Court/ Old Bailey

St Paul's

St Paul's Churchyard

Cheapside

St Mary-le-Bow

Poultry

CITY

Bank

St Mary Woolnoth

Royal Courts of Justice

Temple Bar

Strand

Bouverie St

Bride's St

New Bridge St

Ludgate Hill

St Paul's Cathedral

St Paul's Churchyard

London Bible Galley

Watling St

Mansion House

St Stephen Walbrook

Aldwych

Clement's Inn

Australia House

St Clement Danes

Arundel St

Norfolk St

Surrey St

Temple

The Temple

Temple Gdns

Tudor St

Temple Av

Blackfriars

Queen Victoria St

Castle Baynard St

Queen

Cannon

Mansion House

Cannon Street

Monument

Waldorf

Catherine St

India House

King's College

Courtauld Gallery

Savoy Pl

Victoria Embankment

Temple

H Q S Wellington

Blackfriars Bridge

White Lion

Upper Thames

Cousin La

St

Cleopatra's Needle

Charing Cross Pier

King's Reach

Gabriel's Wharf

Oxo Tower

Upper Ground

Millennium Bridge

Queenhithe Dock

Southwark Bridge

London Bridge

Hungerford Bridge (foot)

Royal National Theatre, National Film Institute

Museum of the Moving Image

Hayward Gallery

Queen Elizabeth Hall

Royal Festival Hall

Stamford St

Upper Ground

Cornwall

Rennie St

Hopton St

Holland St

Bankside

Tate Gallery of Modern Art

Shakespeare Globe Centre & Theatre

Park St

Southwark Bridge Rd

Park St

Stoney

Southwark Cathedral

St Olaf's House

IMAX

Roupell St

Blackfriars Rd

Southwark

Sumner St

SOUTHWARK

Borough High St

Jubilee Gardens

Waterloo

Eurostar

Waterloo

Waterloo East

The Cut

Long La

SOUTH BANK

Millennium Wheel

London Aquarium

County Hall

Belvedere Rd

York Rd

Waterloo Rd

Westminster Bridge Rd

Baylis Rd

Lambeth North

Lambeth Rd

LAMBETH

Lambeth Bridge

St George's Rd

Kennington Rd

Imperial War Museum

Tabard Gardens

Kent Rd

Florence Nightingale Museum

St Thomas's

Hercules Rd

Cosser St

Brook Dr

Walcott Sq

Lambeth Palace Gardens

Lambeth Palace & Museum of Garden History

Lambeth Rd

Lambeth Walk

Walnut Tree Walk

Kennington Rd

Fitzalan

Wincott St

Black Prince Rd

Lambeth High St

VAUXHALL

Lollard St

Kennington

Chester Way

Kennington La

Vauxhall Walk

Vauxhall St

Tyers

Newburn St

Cardigan Rd

Cleaver St

JULIET COOMBE

Twin towers of Westminster Abbey

Queen Elizabeth Halls, both hosting a variety of music recitals; the Hayward Gallery (☎ 7928 3144), London's premier exhibition space; the National Film Institute, screening some 2000 films a year; Royal National Theatre, the nation's flagship theatre; and sundry pubs, cafes and restaurants.

After crossing the Thames at Blackfriars Bridge the Sunday crowds diminish. Apart from St Paul's Cathedral (4.4mi; ☎ 7236 4128), Christopher Wren's masterpiece built 1675–1710, there's not a lot to draw tourists to the City on weekends, and you can explore the sights pretty much at will. Take your time exploring the streets around St Mary-Le-Bow church, built by Wren in 1680; Mansion House (☎ 7626 2500), the Lord Mayor's official residence; the Bank of England (4.9mi; ☎ 7601 5545); and Guildhall (5.1mi; ☎ 7606 3030), seat of the City's local government for 800 years.

After passing Temple Bar Monument, which marks the boundary of the City and Westminster, and the imposing Royal Courts of Justice (6.1mi; ☎ 7936 6000), take care veering right into Aldwych from The Strand. Expect to dismount often in the Covent Garden area, home of: the Royal Opera House (☎ 7240 1200), which offers free lunch-time concerts; the Theatre Museum (☎ 7836 7891), displaying costumes and artefacts from the history of theatre; and the London Transport Museum (6.7mi; ☎ 7379 6344), interesting though light on cycling artefacts. From Covent Garden it's a short haul back to The Mall, with the National Portrait Gallery (☎ 7306 0055), which puts faces to the names of British history; the National Gallery (7.2mi; ☎ 7839 3321), one of the world's finest; and the heart of visitor's London, Trafalgar Square, all in between. This section is best done on foot, crossing St Martin's Place, then walking on the footpath to Pall Mall. It's the best way to properly check out 50m-high (or 164ft) Nelson's Column. After a bump down the stairs (7.5mi), it's worth visiting the Institute for Contemporary Arts (7.5mi; ☎ 7930 3647), said to be on the cutting edge of all kinds of arts, where the route rejoins The Mall.

There is a mass of pubs and other places to eat along the route. For lunch, try The People's Palace (☎ 7928 9999; Royal Festival Hall, Southbank), which has great

Thames views; or The Place Below (☎ 7329 0789), at St Mary-le-Bow church in the City, which has some pretty fair vegetarian food. For a lively dinner, try one of the popular bars or pubs at Convent Garden, such as Fuel (☎ 7836 2137), Punch & Judy (☎ 7379 0923) or Roadhouse (☎ 7240 6001).

The Thames East

Duration	2–5 hours
Distance	9.5mi
Difficulty	easy
Start	Tower Bridge
End	Tower of London

Tower Bridge, the Tower of London and Greenwich are among the city's most popular attractions. This meandering route along the River Thames is mostly flat, liberally sprinkled with points of historical and social interest and passes many fine pubs.

PLANNING
When to Ride
The route mostly follows quiet roads, but mid-week is probably best for cycling as tourist crowds at either end of the route – in the Tower Bridge area, and at Greenwich – can be intense, especially during summer. However, the Greenwich markets are at their busiest and most interesting Friday to Sunday.

Maps & Books
The route along the Thames' south bank is marked as a 'leisure, pleasant' route, on the LCC's Central London route map. Much of the north bank route is LCN signposted.

What to Bring
Dress warmly during winter, when cold winds off the Thames can make this route particularly hard on exposed fingers – long gloves are recommended.

GETTING TO/FROM THE RIDE
Tower Bridge is the most easterly of the Thames bridges. The nearest Underground station is Tower Hill (Circle and District lines); the nearest overground stations are Fenchurch St and London Bridge. If you're riding, approach on the south side of the Thames.

THE RIDE

This mostly flat and traffic-free route follows either the Thames Path (marked by a brown sign with acorn symbol) or an LCN route. Signs are rarely out of sight, limiting your need to consult a map. The Thames meanders through London and this route wanders with it, providing changing perspectives of both the river and London's east and south-east.

There are some great pubs en route. On the south side of the Thames, *The Angel* (☎ 7237 3608; 101 Bermondsey Wall East, SE16), the *Mayflower* (☎l 7237 4088; 117 Rotherhithe St, SE16) and the *Dog & Bell* (☎ 8692 5664; 116 Prince St, SE8) are all worth a stop. The *Gipsy Moth* (☎ 8858 0786, 60 Greenwich Church St) near Greenwich Pier is perfect for lunch – it's at the midpoint of the ride. On the north side, it's hard to pass up a pint at the venerable *Prospect of Whitby* (☎ 7481 1095; 57 Wapping Wall, E1).

The route starts at William Curtis Park and passes first through old docklands. Cobblestones on Shad Thames and overhead walkways above it give the flavour of the area's mercantile past, although rather expensive-looking shops and eateries now predominate. Just before St Saviour's Dock, featured in Dicken's *Oliver Twist*, you'll pass the **Design Museum** (0.2mi; ☎ 7403 6933), which shows the fascinating evolution of product design.

Through Bermondsey, many of the old riverside warehouses have been developed as groovy apartments, but charming examples of old London remain. On Bermondsey Wall East, **The Angel** (0.8mi) pub has survived the changing city and hosted a few famous names – James Cook reputedly among them. Opposite The Angel is all that's left of **Edward III's moated manor house**, built in the mid-14th century. Farther east, **The Mayflower** pub was named for the Pilgrim Fathers' vessel, which moored near this site before the voyage to America in 1620.

Watch your directions in the Bonding Yard Walk area. A little farther along on the **Dockside Heritage walk**, interpretive signs remind you that the Thames was busy with trading vessels as little as 40 to 50 years ago. Until the rise last century of public road and rail transport, the Thames was also London's main passenger artery, with about 20 million people each year travelling on paddle steamers. The riverfront here is also inextricably linked to the Royal Navy. Fighting ships were built, repaired and supplied at the historic Deptford Victualling Yards for five centuries.

Be very watchful of pedestrians in the **Greenwich Pier** area (4.9mi), in fact it's safer to dismount on busy days. This is the site of the magnificently restored **Cutty Sark** (the world's only surviving tea clipper, built 1869) and **Gipsy Moth IV**, the vessel of Francis Chichester during his 1966–67 circumnavigation of the world.

The route's second half includes some trickier navigating and a few walking sections. The first walk is the 400yd long Greenwich Foot Tunnel under the Thames (5.0mi), where cycling is prohibited (although you'll invariably see a number of people riding as you push your bike along).

Traffic is busy at Westferry Circus (6.9mi) – take particular care here. It's worth stopping at **Limehouse Basin**, where the Grand Union Canal meets the Thames.

Go straight ahead where Narrow Street veers right up to the busy Highway, dismount and follow the Thames Path past Stone Stairs and Free Trade Wharf to King Edward Memorial Park. Once you remount on Glamis Rd, it's an easy ride along relatively quiet streets. Take care on the cobblestone sections through Wapping, where fashionable pubs, cafes and shops now line the waterfront. It's best to walk through the **St Katherine's Dock** area, weaving around St Katherine's Lock, past The Tower Hotel and under **Tower Bridge** to the Tower of London. It's worth spending some time here; dating from 1078, the **Tower of London** (☎ 7709 0765) is a World Heritage site, famous as a prison for the likes of Sir Thomas More and Henry VIII's wives.

Side Trip: Greenwich Park
30 minutes, 1.6mi

It's definitely worth the short ride past **Greenwich markets** and other nearby historic attractions to the **Royal Observatory** (☎ 8858 4422), where you can straddle the eastern and western hemispheres, in lovely **Greenwich Park** (☎ 8858 2608). Here, a lookout provides expansive views of Greenwich's historic buildings, the Isle of Dogs and, in the distance to the west, the City.

LONDON

The Thames East

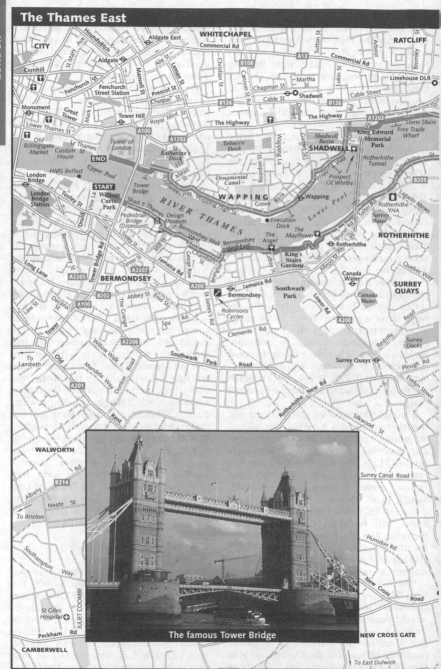

The famous Tower Bridge

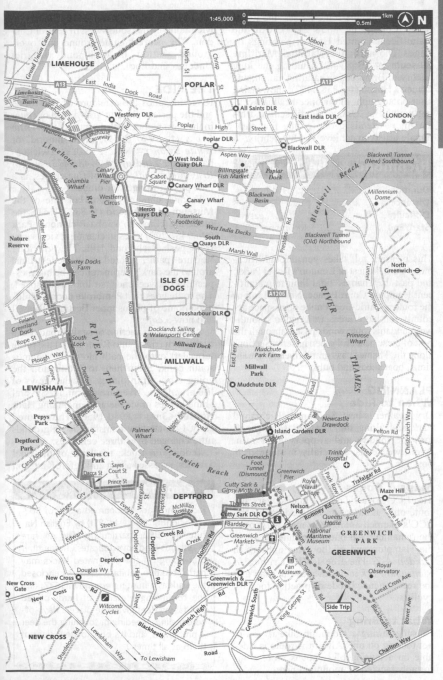

On the way, the route passes: the **Royal Naval College** (☎ 8858 2154), with the magnificent Painted Hall of paintings by James Thornhill; the **National Maritime Museum** (☎ 8858 4422), telling the long history of Britain as a seafaring nation; and **Queen's House** (☎ 8858 4422), showcasing laser photographs of the once-beautiful ceiling painted by Orazio Gentileschi and his daughter Artemisia, one of the few early female artists to achieve much celebrity.

Richmond & the Thames

Duration	3–4 hours
Distance	24.0mi
Difficulty	easy
Start/End	Richmond TIC

This pleasant roll takes you through Richmond Park, largest of London's Royal Parks, and past the Thames' tidal limit to magnificent Hampton Court Palace. Nearly 15mi of the route is traffic-free. Public open space accounts for large areas in London's south-west, and this route winds past or through the best of these peaceful green havens. Sections along the Thames pass grand riverfront mansions, boat sheds and pubs.

PLANNING
When to Ride
Dry weather is best. Sections in Richmond Park and along the Thames' south bank may be muddy and slippery after rain. Avoid weekends, especially in summer, if possible.

Maps & Books
The LCC's *West London* map covers the route only as far south as Teddington; the LCC's planned *South West* map will cover the remainder. All but a one-mile elbow at the Hampton end of the route appears in *London A-Z*. The free leaflet *Cycling in Richmond Park* includes a useful map and the recommended code of practice for park cyclists.

What to Bring
Consider hiring a mountain bike if you're not touring on one. All of the route is rideable on a touring bike, but is more comfortably tackled by mountain bike.

GETTING TO/FROM THE RIDE
Richmond is 9mi south-west of central London. The nearest Underground and overground station is Richmond (District Underground line).

THE RIDE
Riverside pubs are a feature of this route, and the perfect place to grab a feed or (later in the day) recline with a pint. Try the *White Cross* (☎ 8940 0959), at Richmond, or *White Swan* (☎ 8892 2166), at Twickenham. *Chez Lindsay* (☎ 8948 7473; 11 Hill Rise, Richmond), home of fine crepes, is a nice place to linger for dinner.

From Richmond Town Hall, site of the **Museum of Richmond** (☎ 8332 1141), the moderate climb to 955ha **Richmond Park** (☎ 8948 3209) takes in charming views east from posh Richmond Hill. The 7mi long 'leisure path', shared with pedestrians, around the park's perimeter can be busy, especially on weekends, so limit your speed. The route goes past **Pembroke Lodge**, childhood home of philosopher Bertrand Russell and now a *cafe*.

After a short section of sealed road and a tricky turn (right, into River Lane) the route turns left onto the path along the Thames south bank. From here to Teddington the going is rough in places, but the views of life around the river are charming. Several grand homes grace the area, including **Ham House** (9.3mi; ☎ 8940 1950). The restored early 17th-century mansion sits in grounds little changed over three centuries.

Teddington Lock, the limit of the tidal Thames, is passed about 2mi before Kingston

Richmond Park

Richmond Park was named a Site of Special Scientific Interest (SSSI) by English Nature in 1992, particularly for its rare grasslands and invertebrates. Remember that riding off the designated tracks may harm sensitive habitats. Charles I enclosed the park as a hunting ground in 1637, and the continuing presence of herds of red and fallow deer gives the place a days-of-yore feeling. (Feeding or touching the deer is prohibited, and it's best to steer clear of them at all times.)

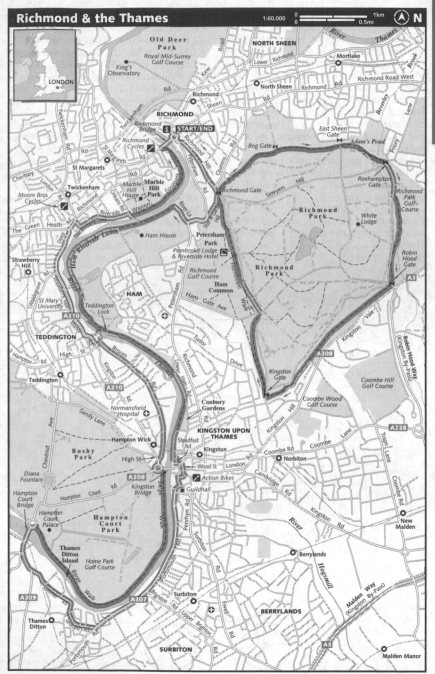

Richmond & the Thames

1:60,000

0 — 1km
0 — 0.5mi

N

upon Thames. These mostly residential areas have long histories, largely because the Thames was affordable hereabouts. Teddington (Tudinton in earlier times) dates to 969. **Kingston**, which tradition holds as the coronation place of several 9th- and 10th-century Anglo-Saxon kings, was recorded as early as 838, as Cyningestun (King's Estate). Today Kingston is one of outer London's main retail centres; crowds of shoppers can make navigation tricky through the town centre. Follow the 'All Routes' LCN signs and you can't go wrong; you'll know you're on the right track when you pass the Guildhall, resting place of the Anglo-Saxon kings' Coronation Stone.

Traffic is bearable along the short Portsmouth Rd (A307) section, and it thins after the right turn onto St Leonard's Rd. The section on the A309 can be busy, and caution's required.

On the return route to Richmond, first follow Barge Walk path and pass the splendid **Hampton Court Palace** (16.5mi; ☎ 8781 9500). It was built by Cardinal Wolsey and enlarged by Henry VIII in the 16th century, with renovations and additions by Wren in the 1690s. From Kingston Bridge, the route follows roads – including the busy A310, which fortunately has fine cycle lanes – back to pleasant Twickenham before turning back to the Thames. The final section passes several beckoning riverside pubs – a well-earned stop if you're thirsty. North of the Warren Footpath, the historic **Marble Hill House** (☎ 8892 5115) is encircled by a lovely verdant park. The Palladian villa was whacked up for Henrietta Howard, George II's mistress, and was later home to Mrs Fitzherbert, George IV's secret wife. It has been beautifully restored and is adorned with Georgian furniture.

Southern England

For cyclists – or any visitor – England's south presents a number of advantages, including climate (this is the warmest part of Britain) and proximity to both London (the regional and national transport hub) and to Europe (ferries leave for France or Spain from several southern ports). Throughout the south you'll find innumerable points of historical interest, splendid coastline and, at Dartmoor and Exmoor, relatively wild national parks.

There are marked differences between the south-east and south-west. The south-eastern counties – Berkshire, Surrey, Kent, East and West Sussex and Hampshire – have arguably more points of interest per mile than any other part of Britain. However, they're densely populated, crowded with cars and – especially in summer – swarming with visitors. London's wealth and appetite for labour sees the capital's toilers spread around the south-east's towns and villages. Surrounding rural districts are dotted with homes that only city stockbrokers and sundry moneyed types could afford. The south-east's defining characteristic is London's inexorable pull.

The south-west is more diverse. The parts nearer London – counties Dorset, Wiltshire, Avon and eastern Somerset – have agricultural, manufacturing and service industries. Farther west, Cornwall and Devon are poorer and rely increasingly on tourism for jobs, not surprising given their beautiful coastlines. Cornwall has the added interest of being England's last Celtic stronghold – the Celtic language was spoken there until the 18th century.

HISTORY

The south has been under human influence a long time. It contains examples of Neolithic camps and Iron age hill forts. Later, it was a source of grain and iron ore for the Romans. Since Roman times, invaders and the threat of invasion have shaped the region, which harbours relics of early continental invaders, such as the Celts; the Romans, who tamed locals in modern-day Kent in AD 43; Jutes and Saxons; and the Normans, who in 1066 were the last of the

In Summary

Terrain

Some low-lying areas in Kent, Sussex and Somerset, otherwise mostly undulating; Cornwall has some hilly sections; longer climbs and descents in Exmoor National Park.

Special Events

- **Bath International Festival** (May)
- **Brighton Festival** (May)
- **Glastonbury Festival** (June), Pilton (8mi from Glastonbury)
- **Guy Fawkes** (5 November), Lewes especially but also throughout England
- **Henley-on-Thames Rowing Regatta** (July)
- **Padstow 'Obby 'Orse** (1 May)

Cycling Events

- **London to Brighton Bike Ride** (June)

Food & Drink Specialities

- cider in Somerset
- cream teas in Devon
- Cornish pasties
- seafood

Tourist Information

British Travel Centre: ☎ 020-8846 9000

invaders. The Normans rebuilt Canterbury Cathedral (although little remains of their work) and erected many castles, including the majestic keep still seen at Dover.

In subsequent centuries the threat of invasion, although never realised, continued to shape the region, especially along the coastline. In the 16th and early 19th centuries, fear of French or Spanish aggression led to the development of coastal fortifications and naval dockyards. Invasion fears peaked in Napoleonic times and again in 1940, when a German invasion was expected.

NATURAL HISTORY

The region is best described as undulating. Higher terrain includes the North and South Downs and North Dorset Downs; the White Horse Hills; and particularly Dartmoor, Exmoor and Bodmin Moor in the west. Along the south-eastern coast there are some large areas of dead flat – often reclaimed – land, such as Romney Marsh, in Kent. The region has been settled for millennia and, away from the major centres, farmland dominates. Well-known 'natural' areas include the New Forest and Dartmoor and Exmoor National Parks.

The coastline throughout is striking. In the extreme south-west at Land's End the sea meets ancient granite. As you travel eastwards you'll see coastal landforms that include different types of sandstone, limestone and finally the white chalk cliffs that extend intermittently from the Isle of Wight to Dover.

Rivers such as **the** Arun, Avon, Exe, Ouse, Stour, Tamar and Test all drain into the English Channel, forming charming valleys where they twist through moors and chalk downs.

CLIMATE

Southern England's climate resembles London's. Generally it's wetter and windier the farther west you go, but western parts such as Cornwall are among Britain's warmest regions. Snow is reasonably rare along the coast, but you should always check forecasts carefully before heading to higher

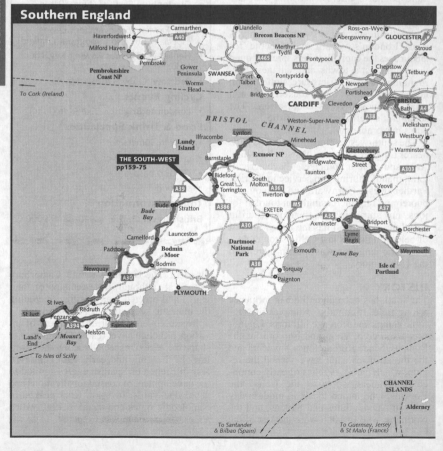

Why 'Downs' When They're Up?

Rounded, grass-covered hills – typically composed of chalk – are a feature of Southern England. Such hills will have you shifting gears in Berkshire, Hampshire, Kent, East and West Sussex, Surrey and Wiltshire.

Their apparently contradictory name is a wonderful example of the polyglot origins of the modern English language: it's a leftover from the Germanic Anglo-Saxon language known as Old English. 'Down' comes from the Old English 'dun', meaning hill, which in turn stems from the Old Saxon 'duna'. Chalk hills of a comparable type found in Lincolnshire and Yorkshire are called wolds, a word with lineage from Old English, Old Saxon, Old High German and Old Norse.

parts – such as Dartmoor – in mid-winter (see Weather Forecasts in the Facts for the Cyclist chapter). Seasonal variations of daylight hours are an important consideration for touring cyclists. In mid-summer you'll see 16 or so hours of light on a sunny day; an equally clear day in mid-winter will yield eight hours at a squeeze.

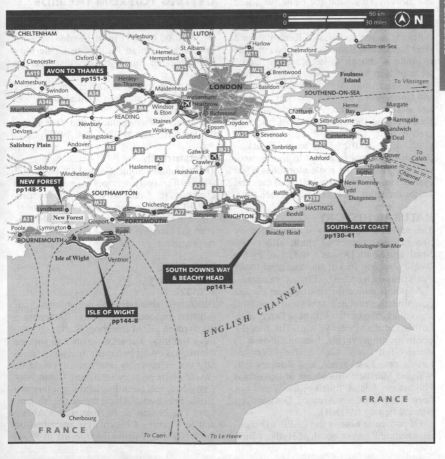

GATEWAY CITIES
London
See the London chapter for information about accommodation, other services and getting to/from London.

South-East Coast

Duration	4 days
Distance	193.8mi
Difficulty	moderate
Start	Canterbury
End	Portsmouth

This comfortable four-day journey heads from England's primary ecclesiastical centre of Canterbury, past the chalk cliffs at Dover and Beachy Head and the beautiful South Downs, to Portsmouth, long the main port for the Royal Navy.

Taking in the counties of Kent, East and West Sussex and Hampshire, the countryside en route is enough to keep a rider happy; areas of Kent and East Sussex are particularly lovely. Almost without exception, cities and towns along the way are neat, friendly and easily navigated. Accommodation is abundant and there are plenty of places to grab a feed. The only disappointment is likely to be traffic. This region contains Britain's principal gateways to Europe and, with no point on the route more than 65mi from central London, the density of cars and lorries on major roads is a sight to behold.

NATURAL HISTORY
The region's topography is dominated by two rounded ranges of chalk hills – the North and South Downs – separated by the Weald, a rolling area of clay and sandy soils that's heavily wooded by English standards.

At points where the downs meet the sea you find the region's spectacular coastal formations, the chalk cliffs near Dover and, farther south, at Beachy Head. The Weald's ocean frontage varies, but much of it is marshy flat lands, such as the Pevensey Levels near Eastbourne, and Romney and Walland Marshes, south-west of Dover and Folkestone. Inland, much of the Weald has been designated an Area of Outstanding Natural Beauty (AONB).

Of particular note is the RSPB's Dungeness Nature Reserve, south of Hythe, which protects an important sea bird breeding habitat. An exposed shingle spit, Dungeness is a bleak place for a cyclist on a damp, windy day, but it has a desolate beauty that's enhanced by the abundant bird life.

PLANNING
When to Ride
Late spring to early summer, or early autumn, is best; avoid summer school holidays.

Maps
The ride is covered by OS Travelmaster map No 9 (1:250,000) *South East England*. The OS *Cycle Tours: Kent, Surrey & Sussex* could be useful if you plan to explore off the route.

GETTING TO/FROM THE RIDE
Canterbury
Train Catch a Connex South Eastern train (☎ 0870-603 0405) from London Victoria or London Bridge stations to Canterbury (£14.70); the journey takes just over an hour.

The train trip from Dover Priory (ferry port to/from France) to Canterbury is less than 30 minutes.

For all train timetable and fare information telephone ☎ 0845-748 4950.

Portsmouth
Train Connex South Central (☎ 0870-603 0405) offers daily services from Portsmouth Harbour to London Waterloo. It costs £19.70 for the journey of 1½ to two hours. There's also trains from Portsmouth Harbour to Dover Priory and Folkestone, which run regularly.

THE RIDE
Canterbury
☎ 01227
Beautiful Canterbury has drawn crowds of pilgrims and tourists since the 12th century martyrdom of Archbishop Becket. These days the city, a market town and service centre, has about two million visitors annually but, remarkably, manages to retain its character. Its primary attraction, Canterbury Cathedral, has been England's primary ecclesiastical centre since the early 7th century. The cathedral, St Augustine's Abbey and St Martin's Church were inscribed on the UNESCO World Heritage list in 1988.

Information Canterbury TIC (☎ 766567, e canterburyvisitorinformation@compuserve.com) is at 34 Margaret's St (closed Sunday during winter); it has a bureau de change (☎ 780063) and will make accommodation bookings.

The post office is on the corner of High and Stour Sts; all the big banks and building societies are represented in the High St area. Canterbury Cycle Mart (☎ 761488), on Lower Bridge St, is handy to the city centre and has a good range of spares and accessories. There's a laundrette on St Peter's St.

Things to See & Do Although the crowds can be distracting, **Canterbury Cathedral** (☎ 762862) will keep you occupied for hours; a visit during choral evensong (5.30 pm weekdays, 3.15 pm weekends) is particularly moving. The city's other UNESCO World Heritage sites – **St Augustine's Abbey** (☎ 767345), on Longport, and **St Martin's Church** (☎ 459482), on North Holmes Rd – are high on informed visitors' lists. The **Canterbury Heritage**, **Roman** and **West Gate museums**, all near the city centre, shed light on Canterbury's 2000-year history. **The Canterbury Tales** (☎ 479227), on St Margaret's St, provides a quirky and odorous introduction to Geoffrey Chaucer's classic yarns about medieval Canterbury visitors. A short section of the **city walls** near the Dane John Gardens is open to walkers.

Places to Stay Less than 2mi east of the city, the *Canterbury Camping & Caravanning Club Site (☎ 463216, Bekesbourne Lane)* is off the A257. Tent sites cost about £14. *Ashfield Farm (☎ 700624, Petham)*, about 4.5mi south, also has sites.

With a nightly charge of £10.15, the *YHA hostel (☎ 462911, e canterbury@yha.org.uk, 54 Dover Rd)* has a cycle storeroom, self-catering kitchen, drying room and serves breakfast and dinner. It's closed in January. Dorm beds cost about £10 at the independent hostel *Kipps (☎ 786121, 40 Nunnery Fields)*.

Castle Court Guest House (☎ 463441, 8 Castle St) and *Tudor House (☎ 765650, 6 Best Lane)* both offer B&B close to the city centre at about £18 per person. A bit farther out (bear in mind that Canterbury's not a big place), you'll find B&Bs clustered on London Rd to the north-west and pricier hotels on New Dover Rd, south-east.

Places to Eat The High St and St Peter's St strip has the widest choice. *Goodchilds Bakery (Butchery Lane)*, near the cathedral, opens at 8.15 am daily in summer for rolls, pastries and 50p takeaway coffees. The *Old Weavers House (☎ 464 660, 2 Kings Bridge)*, next to the River Stour, is a fun place for coffee or a big breakfast (£3 to £4); nearby are *Frankie & Johnnie's* where you'll get a decent pasta for £5 to £6, and the chain eateries *Cafe Rouge (☎ 763 833; Cogan House, 53 St Peters St)* and *Caffe Uno (☎ 479 777, 49a St Peters St)*.

Farther east, *Queen Elizabeth's Restaurant (High St)* offers £5 to £7 main courses in an ancient setting – the room where Elizabeth I is reputed to have interviewed a potential suitor, the Duke of Alencon, in 1573. For an outdoor beer, the *Franklin & Firkin* pub, with tables opposite the cathedral's Christ Church Gate, is hard to beat.

Day 1: Canterbury to Hythe
5–7 hours, 44.4mi

Charming Kent countryside, coastal towns and castles are the stars of this meandering day. Road surfaces are fair throughout and traffic is manageable – it can be busy on weekends on the A257 out of Canterbury and around the coastal towns.

The rolling country east of Canterbury leads to pretty **Sandwich**, reputedly one of England's most complete medieval towns. Until the 17th century, English Channel tides came far enough up the River Stour estuary to make Sandwich a Cinque Port; get the full story at the Sandwich TIC (☎ 01304-613565). Leave Sandwich on the bikepath beside the Stour, which joins St George's Rd.

Cyclists pay no toll at the entrance to Sandwich Bay Private Estate. On the Ancient Highway, which crosses the estate, you'll be entertained by birdsong and the sight of golfers duffing their shots on the area's famous links courses.

The route is flat all the way from Sandwich to Kingsdown. En route, you'll pass **Deal** (where, it's claimed, Julius Caesar landed in 55 BC) and **Walmer**, both of which have fine castles – built by Henry VIII as protection against possible French invasion. Now EH properties, they are open

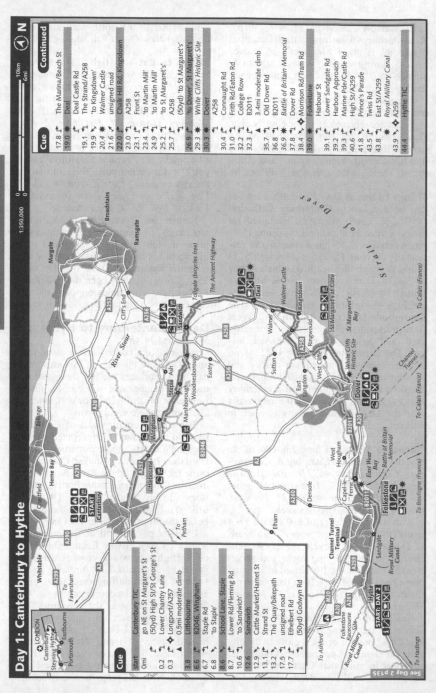

Day 1: Canterbury to Hythe

1:350,000

N

Cue		
start		Canterbury TIC
0mi		go NE on St Margaret's St
		(50yd) High St/St George's St
0.2		Lower Chantry Lane
0.3		Longport/A257
		0.5mi moderate climb
3.8		Littlebourne
6.6		B2046, Wingham
6.7		Staple Rd
6.8		'to Staple'
8.6		School Lane, Staple
8.7		Lower Rd/Fleming Rd
10.6		'to Sandwich'
12.6		Sandwich
12.9		Cattle Market/Harnet St
13.1		Strand St
13.2		The Quay/bikepath
		unsigned road
17.5		Ethelbert Rd
17.7		(50yd) Godwyn Rd

Cue		Continued
17.8		The Marina/Beach St
19.0		Deal
		Deal Castle Rd
19.1		The Strand/A258
19.9		'to Kingsdown'
20.4		Walmer Castle
21.6		unsigned road
22.0		Chalk Hill Rd, Kingsdown
23.0		A258
23.1		Front St
23.4		'to Martin Mill'
24.9		'to Martin Mill'
25.2		'to St Margaret's'
25.7		A258
		(50yd) 'to St Margaret's'
26.9		'to Dover, St Margaret's'
29.3		White Cliffs Historic Site
30.3		Dover
		A258
30.4		Connaught Rd
31.0		Frith Rd/Eaton Rd
32.2		College Row
32.3		B2011
		3.4mi moderate climb
35.7		Old Dover Rd
36.8		B2011
36.9		Battle of Britain Memorial
37.8		Dover Rd
38.4		Morrison Rd/Tram Rd
39.0		Folkestone
39.1		Harbour St
39.2		Lower Sandgate Rd
		Harbour Approach
39.3		Marine Pde/Castle Rd
40.6		High St/A259
41.8		Prince's Parade
43.5		Twiss Rd
43.8		East St/A259
43.9		Royal Military Canal
44.4		Hythe TIC

See Day 2 p135

to the public; ☎ 01304 225229 for information. From Kingsdown, short climbs and descents punctuate the few miles to Dover. There's no charge for cyclists to enter the **White Cliffs** historic site (29.3mi), where you'll get the best views of Dover's bustling, 600 acre port. The route passes near **Dover Castle**, standing a proud 375ft above the sea, and avoids the town centre.

The day's longest climb leads you out of town on the B2011. It's steady rather than steep, and the **Battle of Britain Memorial** at its top is a good place to catch your breath. The evocative monument – under skies that, in 1940, witnessed the most hectic aerial battles in Britain's defence – was opened in 1993. Downhill from the memorial, Folkestone has an interesting **Museum and Gallery** (☎ 01303-850123) and the **Russian submarine** (☎ 01303-240400). The day ends just after you cross another memorial of sorts to a potential invasion – the **Royal Military Canal**, built as a defensive moat when Napoleon was Europe's main man.

Hythe
☎ 01303

The ancient Cinque Port of Hythe is a pleasant seaside resort these days. It's an engaging place, with period houses lining the old streets and lanes that tumble down Quarry Hill to High St. The Norman tower on St Leonard's Church, which dates from 1080, is the dominant feature.

Information The TIC (☎ 267799, 🖥 www .hythe.co.uk), Red Lion Square, is open from Easter to September, Monday to Saturday (closed from 1 to 2 pm).

Hythe post office is on High St, where most of the big banks are represented. There's a bicycle shop (☎ 262100) with basic spares attached to Swains Garage, 19 Seabrook Rd. You can check email at Tec Know Cafe (☎ 237842), inside the World of Entertainment, 61 High St.

Things to See & Do Hythe's best-known attractions are the **Romney, Hythe & Dymchurch Railway** (☎ 01797-362353), 'the world's smallest public railway', which runs from Hythe to Dungeness; and the crypt of **St Leonard's Church**, which contains 2000 skulls and 8000 thigh bones gathered between AD 800–900 and the early 16th cen-

How the Cinques were Sunk

The medieval Cinque Ports confederation was formed to supply ships and men for the king's service; the vessels and seamen they supplied were effectively a forerunner of the Royal Navy. The original five 'Head Ports' – Dover, Hastings, Hythe, Romney and Sandwich – were probably first allied during Edward the Confessor's reign (1042-66). In 1278 Edward I recognised the towns' cooperative arrangement by granting various privileges in exchange for their services. The towns of Winchelsea and Rye were later added as Head Ports, and at times up to 30 smaller 'limb' towns in Kent and Sussex were also associated.

The Cinque cartel lost its exclusive rights after the 14th century. The towns still kept chipping in for the navy, but their contribution was irrelevant by 1588, when the Spanish Armada threatened invasion. In decline, one of the confederation's greatest enemies was erosion. Here and there the sea attacked the coastline, toppling cliffs and shifting shingle banks. Elsewhere, siltation elbowed tidal river waters downstream, leaving towns such as Sandwich and Rye miles inland.

Most of the Cinque Ports' liberties were abolished in 1855; only some arcane rights under Admiralty law have endured.

tury. The **Hythe Local History Room** (☎ 267 111), on Stade St, is worth a look.

Places to Stay There's no camping ground or hostel-style accommodation in Hythe – the nearest camping ground is the *Folkestone Racecourse Site* (☎ 261761) near Westenhanger, 3.4mi north-west.

Hotels and B&Bs are plentiful. *Moyle Cottage* (☎ 262106, The Fairway), off South Rd, does B&B from £16 to £20 per person. Nearby *Hill View* (☎ 269783, 4 South Rd) is in the same price range. At *Seabrook House* (☎ 269282, 81 Seabrook Rd) you'll pay up to £26 if you're on your own, but facilities are good.

Places to Eat There's plenty of variety on High St. For cakes and rolls, try the *Old*

SOUTHERN ENGLAND

Traditional Bakery (100a High St). The *Old Willow* (☎ 265626, 40 High St) does a full breakfast for £2.50 and serves 80p coffees (refills cost 45p). Try the *Capri Italian* (☎ 269898, 30–34 High St) for pizza or pasta (£4 to £7), or the *Royal Bengal Tandoori* (☎ 267372, 9 High St) for Indian vegetarian dishes (£2 to £3). *Betty's* (☎ 262034, 78 High St) has a carbo-lover's ravioli and bread roll for £4.

Day 2: Hythe to Eastbourne
6–8 hours, 59.1mi

This longish ride is made easier by being as good as completely flat for the first 25mi and having no significant climbs. Road surfaces throughout are fair or better; expect to encounter heavier traffic around Rye and Eastbourne.

Just 2.8mi from Hythe TIC, a glorious 5.5mi off-road section starts on the seafront promenade. This leads down to Littlestone-on-Sea. From here, it's flat all the way to Dungeness on the Coast Drive. Consider visiting the 143ft **Old Lighthouse** at Dungeness; with good weather you'll get spectacular views north to the white cliffs and east to France. The road to Lydd-on-Sea has fast-moving traffic and can be trying, but the bird life in the **Royal Society for the Protection of Birds (RSPB) Denge Reserve** and its watchers will keep you entertained. The rest of the journey to Rye twists through fairly stark terrain broken by such delights as quarries and electricity stanchions. Distant hills hold the promise of nicer surrounds.

Lovely **Rye** is so Olde Englishe it's almost twee and, not surprisingly, tourists crowd its cream-tea and antique shoppes. The route passes Rye TIC (☎ 01797-226696) on Strand Quay, the best place to begin explorations.

The B2089 out of Rye can get busy with traffic, but for the next 20-or-so miles it provides a taste of **Weald** woodlands. Forest tracts, rolling farmlands and attractive villages make it a memorable section. There's a short stretch on the A21 just after Sedlescombe, then more quiet pedalling up to the short side trip to **Battle Abbey** (TIC ☎ 01424 -773721), site of William of Normandy's clash with King Harold II in 1066 (go right at 46.1mi).

Apart from the turns around Catsfield and Ninfield (the signs can confuse) it's a

The 1066 Country Walk

Upon reaching Eastbourne on the South-East Coast ride, consider taking a couple of days off the bike to enjoy the 1066 Country Walk, which opened in late 1997. The 31mi path is an excellent way to put the rich history of East Sussex – the area where foreign forces last successfully invaded Britain – into perspective.

The 1066 path runs between Pevensey Castle and Rye, passing Herstmonceux Castle, Battle and Winchelsea en route. There's also a side route down to Hastings, William the Conqueror's landing site.

It's a short train journey from Eastbourne back to Rye, and the walk can be completed in two days at a comfortable pace. TICs in the area stock a free leaflet showing the route and listing places to stay along the way.

fairly straightforward run to Eastbourne. The route passes Ninfield and **Pevensey Castle**, William's first stronghold on English soil – parts of the old Roman fort walls still stand. **St Mary the Virgin church** in nearby Westham was the first Norman church in England, built in 1080.

The route chosen into Eastbourne is less trying for traffic (you can opt for a bikepath on the Cross Levels Way section), but for a more direct route, peel left at the roundabout before the Langney shopping centre, then right onto the A259. Either way, once into the town centre, follow signs to the TIC.

Eastbourne
☎ 01323

While it may lack Brighton's mad sparkle, Eastbourne is a quintessentially, do-like-to-be-beside-the-seaside English coastal resort. Beyond the inevitable fun pier and legion fish and chip joints, it's a dignified place, renowned for its gardens, theatres and grass court tennis centre, site of the annual women's tournament that's a traditional Wimbledon lead-up.

Information Eastbourne TIC (☎ 411400) is on Cornfield Rd. You can check theatre listings and there's an accommodation booking service (charges apply).

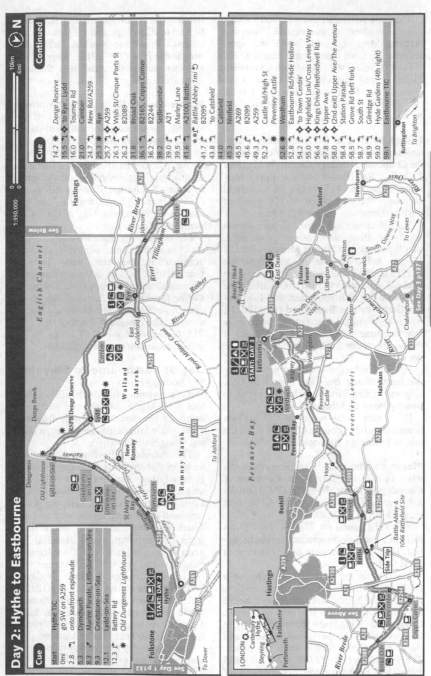

Day 2: Hythe to Eastbourne

Cue	
start	Hythe TIC
0mi	go SW on A259
2.8	onto seafront esplanade
5.3	Dymchurch
8.3	Marine Parade, Littlestone-on-Sea
9.3	Greatstone-on-Sea
12.1	Lydd-on-Sea
12.3	Battery Rd
	Old Dungeness Lighthouse

Cue	Continued
14.2	Denge Reserve
15.5	'to Rye', Lydd
16.0	Tourney Rd
21.0	Camber
24.7	New Rd/A259
25.3	Rye
25.7	A259
26.1	Wish St/Cinque Ports St
26.2	B2089
31.8	Broad Oak
36.1	B2165, Cripps Corner
36.2	B2244
38.2	Sedlescombe
39.0	A21
39.5	Marley Lane
41.6	A2100, Battle
	Battle Abbey 1mi
41.7	B2095
43.8	'to Catsfield'
44.0	Catsfield
45.3	Ninfield
45.5	A269
45.6	B2095
49.3	A259
52.2	Castle Rd/High St
	Pevensey Castle
52.6	Westham
52.8	Eastbourne Rd/Hide Hollow
54.2	'to Town Centre'
55.0	Highfield Link/Cross Levels Way
56.4	Kings Drive/Bedfordwell Rd
57.8	Upper Ave
58.0	(2nd exit) Upper Ave/The Avenue
58.4	Station Parade
58.5	South St
58.7	Gilredge Rd
58.9	Hyde Gardens (4th night)
59.0	
59.1	Eastbourne TIC

The main post office is on Station Parade; there's another in the central shopping precinct. Most of the big banks are represented in the town centre, many near the TIC.

Heath Cycles (☎ 733404), 106 Cavendish Place, is well appointed and close to the town centre. Farther out, Phoenix Cycles (☎ 729060), 217–219 Seaside, is good for repairs.

Things to See & Do The past two centuries of Eastbourne history are covered at the **Eastbourne Heritage Centre** (☎ 411189), 2 Carlisle Rd. Both it and the quirky **Museum of Shops** (☎ 737143), 20 Cornfield Terrace – 'keeping place' of 150 years of trash and treasure – are worth a look.

For a slice of Eastbourne life, take a stroll north-east along the seafront promenade. You'll pass the fun **Puppet Museum** (☎ 417 7760) – home of what are said to be the world's largest Punch and Judy puppets – the **Lifeboat Museum** (☎ 730717), charting the exploits of local lifeboatmen, and Edwardian **Grand Parade Bandstand** (☎ 410611), which hosts military band music twice daily from late June to September. Hit the beach if the weather's good; deck chair hire is £1.20 per day.

For a nice longer walk, go south along the seafront and over the downs to Cow Gap and **Falling Sands** beach, with views to **Beachy Head Lighthouse**.

It's a nice cycle north on the **eastern promenade** for a couple of miles from the pier to **Sovereign Harbour**.

Places to Stay About 3.5mi north of the town centre, the *Bay View Caravan & Camping Park* (☎ 768688; Old Martello Rd, Pevensey Bay) is just off the A259. Tent sites are £7.70 to £8.40.

The *YHA hostel* (☎ 721081, East Dean Rd) has a cycle storeroom and serves breakfast. The nightly charge is £8.35 (more with breakfast).

The TIC is the best place to choose a B&B or hotel, of which there are endless choices. The larger, more expensive hotels are spread along the seafront on Royal, Grand and King Edward parades. The smaller (and cheaper) guesthouses and B&Bs are usually further from the beach. The *Afton Hotel* (☎ 733162, 1–8 Cavendish Place) and *Ellesmere Hotel* (☎ 731463, 11

Wilmington Square) both offer B&B in the £17.50 to £26 range and are just a block or so back from the seaside. B&B at the *Alexandra Hotel* (☎ 720131, King Edwards Parade)*, across the road from the beach, starts from £20.

Places to Eat Restaurants and cafes are strewn around the town centre and down towards the seaside. For rolls and pastries, try the *Cavendish Bakery* (Terminus, Trinity Trees) or the *Saffron Patisserie* (51 Grove Rd)*. Coffee drinkers will find a mass of groovier establishments on Bolton Rd, including *Exchange* (7 Bolton Rd)*, *Isobel's* (1–5 Bolton Rd) and *Darton's*. You'll also snare a decent cap or latte at *Cafe Continental* (18 Grove Rd)*.

For burgers, try *Rumblebelly* (5 Seaside Rd)*. The widest choice of food is available on Terminus Rd between Trinity Trees and Grand Parade. Closer to the seafront on Terminus, fish and chips shops rule. Try *Macaris Coffee Lounge* (246 Terminus Rd)*, an early opener, for £2 to £4 breakfasts and big basic dinners. *The Spaghetti Factory* (☎ 727282, 215 Terminus Rd) has £4 to £6.50 pasta dishes, including several vegetarian.

Day 3: Eastbourne to Steyning
5–7 hours, 45.9mi

With fair weather, this day is likely to be the tour's highlight. Mostly, the route skirts north of the beautiful **South Downs** on quiet, sealed roads, passing through charming villages and towns.

The route out of Eastbourne on the A259 includes one of the day's longer climbs and is usually busy with traffic, which evaporates once you've turned right towards Litlington (6.6mi). From here, the going is easy and undulating all the way to Lewes. There are some tricky turns around the villages of Chalvington and beautiful Ripe; keep following the signs to Ripe and Laughton and you won't go wrong.

The side trip (at 22.2mi) to **Glyndebourne Opera House** (☎ 01273-812321) is a treat for opera and garden enthusiasts. The world-renowned opera house was built in 1924 and revamped in the early 1990s. Performances are held May to October.

Lewes, roughly the halfway mark, is a fascinating place to explore. The TIC (☎ 01273-483448) is at 187 High St. The remains of

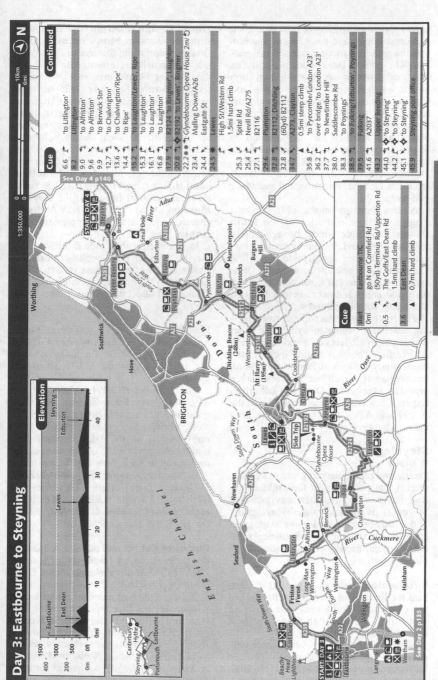

Day 3: Eastbourne to Steyning

Elevation

| Eastbourne | East Dean | Lewes | Edburton | Steyning |

1500
1000
500
0ft
400
200
0m

0m   10   20   30   40   0mi

SOUTHERN ENGLAND

Cue — Continued

6.6	↰	'to Litlington'
8.2		Litlington
9.0	↰	'to Alfriston'
9.6	↰	'to Alfriston'
9.9	↰	'to Berwick Stn'
12.7	↰	'to Chalvington'
13.6	↰	'to Chalvington/Ripe'
14.4	↰	'to Ripe'
15.2	↱	'to Laughton/Lewes'; Ripe
15.3	↰	'to Laughton'
16.1	↰	'to Laughton'
16.8	↱	'to Laughton'
17.9	↱	B2124 'to Ringmer', Laughton
20.8	↱	B2192 'to Lewes'; Ringmer
22.2	●●◆	Glyndebourne Opera House 2mi
23.4	↰	Malling Down/A26
24.4	↱	Eastgate St
24.5		Lewes
25.3	◀	High St/Western Rd
25.4		1.5mi hard climb
25.4	↱	Spital Rd
27.1	↰	Nevill Rd/A275
29.6		B2116
32.8	↰	Plumpton
32.8	↱	B2112, Ditchling
34.7		(60yd) B2112
		A273, Clayton
35.8		0.5mi steep climb
		'to Pyecombe/London A23'
36.2	↰	over bridge 'to London A23'
37.7	↰	'to Newtimber Hill'
38.0	↰	Saddlescombe Rd
38.3		'to Poynings'
38.5	↱	'to Fulking/Edburton', Poynings
39.5		Fulking
41.6	↱	A2037
43.2		Upper Beeding
44.0	↰	'to Steyning'
44.2	↰	'to Steyning'
45.1	◆	'to Steyning'
45.9		Steyning post office

Cue

start			Eastbourne TIC
			go N on Cornfield Rd
0mi	↱		(50yd) Terminus Rd/Upperton Rd
0.5	↱	▲	The Goffs/East Dean Rd
			1.5mi hard climb
3.6		▲	East Dean
			0.7mi hard climb

See Day 4 p140

START - DAY 4
Steyning

See Day 2 p135

START - DAY 3
Eastbourne

Side Trip
Glyndebourne
Opera House

1:350 000

0   10km
0   6mi

N

Lewes Castle (☎ 01273-486290) date back to Norman times and the adjacent museum puts the region's various masters in perspective. The narrow lanes (known locally as 'twittens') that drop steeply south from High St are worth a look; Walwers Lane and Church Twitten are probably the most arresting. Lewes is also known for it's impressive festivities on Guy Fawkes Night (5 November). The first part of the climb up High St is very steep and you may find it easier to walk, if your bike is heavily laden. Lewes Cycles (☎ 01273-483399), 28 Western Rd, is the place for spares and assistance mid-route.

After a short run on the A275 comes a magical section in the lee of the **South Downs**. The route winds through lovely tracts of woodland, broken by broad views north over Sussex countryside. Ditchling (32.8mi) is a nice spot for a break. Here, cyclists on the annual London to Brighton bike ride enjoy a descent before the stiff climb past **Ditchling Beacon**.

The route takes a steep climb and relieving descent en route to Pyecombe, near which a bikepath lets you avoid the roaring A23 traffic. The next section includes the quiet, pretty villages of **Poynings**, **Fulking** (on weekends, watch out for cars parked near The Shepherd & Dog) and **Edburton**. Expect a few miles of heavier traffic on the A2037 and A283, but things quieten after the turn to Steyning.

Steyning
☎ 01903

Serene and pretty, Steyning was a thriving market and port town in the middle ages (the River Adur was then navigable to Steyning). It's a quiet place where many Tudor and Stuart houses survive to the present, enlivened by interesting historical footnotes, several friendly pubs and some good places to eat.

Information There are information signs near the library and museum, both reached via Church St. The library and Steyning post office, both on High St, are the best sources of local information.

Most of the big banks have branches with ATMs on High St. There's no bike shop but Steyning Motor Spares (☎ 812219), 116 High St, carries some spares and can do repairs.

Things to See & Do On High St, notable structures such as **Penn's House** – where Quaker theorist and founder of Pennsylvania, William Penn, often preached – and the **Market House** mix easily with the lesser-known of Steyning's 125 heritage-listed buildings. At the corner of High and Church Sts is the house where Irish nationalist Charles Stewart Parnell married his love, Kitty O'Shea, shortly before his death in 1891. On Church St you'll pass several beautifully preserved Tudor and Stuart buildings, including the **Brotherhood Hall**, a school for the past 400 years. Bone up on local history at the **Steyning Museum** (☎ 813333), near **St Andrew's church**, which has a rather impressive 12th-century nave.

In Bramber, a short ride from Steyning, are the ruins of the Norman-era **Bramber Castle** and **St Mary's House** (☎ 816205), a fine medieval inn that's said to be the best example of late-15th-century timber framing in Sussex.

Places to Stay Pitch a tent at the *Farmhouse Caravan & Camping Site* (☎ 01273-493157; Tottington Dr, Small Dole), to the east of Steyning off the A2037, about 5mi by road.

The *Truleigh Hill YHA Hostel* (☎ 813 419; Tottington Barn, Truleigh Hill) has great facilities but is tricky to find. It's 2mi along a bridleway from near the Rising Sun pub (44.0mi on the Day 3 route). The nightly charge is £9.15. The hostel is closed on Sunday in April, May and September.

In Steyning, *Jennifer Morrow* (☎ 812286, 5 Coxham Lane) offers nice home-style B&B for £15 a night. B&B rates start at £30 at the pleasant *Springwell Hotel* (☎ 812446, cnr High St & Dog Lane).

Places to Eat For nice pastries, scones and 80p cappuccinos, try *Truffles* (☎ 816140, 66 High St). The *Model Bakery* (Church Lane) is also worth a look.

Pubs are the best place to get bulk on a budget. Try the *Star Inn* or *Chequer Inn*, both on High St. Also on High St, *Saxons* (☎ 813533, 76 High St) and *Milestones* (High St) restaurants have higher prices and food quality to match. *Steyning Wine Bar & Ristorante* (High St) has pizzas for up to £6.50 and various pasta dishes from £5.95.

Day 4: Steyning to Portsmouth
5–7 hours, 44.4mi

This day is a ride in two parts, both of them characterised by some of the tour's busier roads and heaviest traffic.

The undulating first part of the route continues along the picturesque northern flank of the South Downs. About 10mi into the day, the route passes the **Amberley Museum** (☎ 01798-831370), open from March to October. This is well worth a visit if traditional crafts and trades interest you – working exhibits include blacksmith, clay-pipe maker, wheelwright and wood-turner shops. There's a solid climb of 1.5mi over the downs after **Houghton** village, followed by a howling, 2mi downhill.

The route's second part, from about Nyton onwards, is mostly on level, straight roads, broken only by a mid-route visit to busy **Chichester**, which has a TIC (☎ 01243-775888) at 29A South St. It's easy navigating in and out of the town centre, but take care in surrounding traffic. Dismount in the busy shopping precinct. A rest on the lawns surrounding 900-year-old **Chichester Cathedral** (☎ 01243-782595) is a must. Just outside Chichester, at Fishbourne, consider a short side trip to the fascinating **Roman Palace and Museum** – turn right at Salthill Rd (26.9mi), then right into Roman Way.

From Chichester to Portsmouth the route is flat and – easy cycling aside – the outlook somewhat drab after a few days in the Sussex countryside. The A259 traffic isn't so noticeable; the road only occasionally narrows, and you can opt for roadside bikepaths here and there. There's a pedestrian precinct to negotiate in Havant, where you'll pass Bikehut, a brilliant bike shop.

The final miles into Portsmouth are surprisingly pleasant (apart from a few moments close to, but not endangered by, fast-moving traffic). More than half of the route's last 6mi are on bikepaths or roadside cycle lanes, and there are fine views of the **Farlington Marshes**, a bird reserve, and **Langstone Harbour**.

Portsmouth
☎ 023

Trashed in parts by WWII bombing, Portsmouth isn't the prettiest place at first glance, but its long association with the Royal Navy lends it a certain gritty aura.

The city's points of interest, not surprisingly, are mostly associated with maritime and coastal defences.

Information There are TICs at The Hard (☎ 9282 6722, 🖳 www.portsmouthcc.gov .uk/visitor), near the Naval Heritage Area, and in the central shopping precinct (☎ 9283 8382) on Station St; they offer an accommodation reservation service.

Most banks are represented in the city centre and, nearer Southsea, at Palmerston Rd shopping precincts.

A dozen or so bike shops are spread around Portsmouth. Closest to the centre is Rock 'n' Road Cycles (☎ 9229 4770), at 10 Lord Montgomery Way. If you're staying at Southsea, a closer option is Portsmouth Cycle Exchange (☎ 9281 5918), 4–8 Gothic Buildings, Victoria Rd.

Things to See & Do A visit to the Naval Heritage Area **Flagship Portsmouth** (☎ 9286 1512) is a must: it's home of the remnant hull of the Tudor warship *Mary Rose* and some artefacts from it; Nelson's lovingly preserved *Victory*; and the Victorian-era HMS *Warrior*.

The **City Museum** (☎ 9282 7261), on Museum Rd, is halfway between Flagship Portsmouth and Southsea, where you'll find Henry VIII's **Southsea Castle** (☎ 9282 7261) and the **D-Day Museum** (☎ 9282 7261), near the seafront. Views from here to the Isle of Wight, broken by the castle-island Solent forts and constant maritime traffic, are an evocative reminder of Portsmouth's – and England's – long history as a seafaring power.

Places to Stay The closest place to pitch a tent is the *Harbour Side Site* (☎ 9266 3867); it's on the route into town, at about the 40mi mark. About 4mi north of the city centre, *Portsmouth YHA Hostel* (☎ 9237 5661; Old Wymering Lane, Cosham) has a cycle storeroom, drying room and serves breakfast and dinner. The nightly charge is £8.35; check ahead for the opening nights in winter. The independent *Portsmouth & Southsea Backpackers Lodge* (☎ 9283 2495; 4 Florence Rd, Southsea) is closer to the action; it's £9 a night.

There are plenty of B&Bs and guesthouses, especially in Southsea. Try *Victoria Court* (☎ 9282 0305, 29 Victoria Rd); prices

SOUTHERN ENGLAND

SOUTHERN ENGLAND

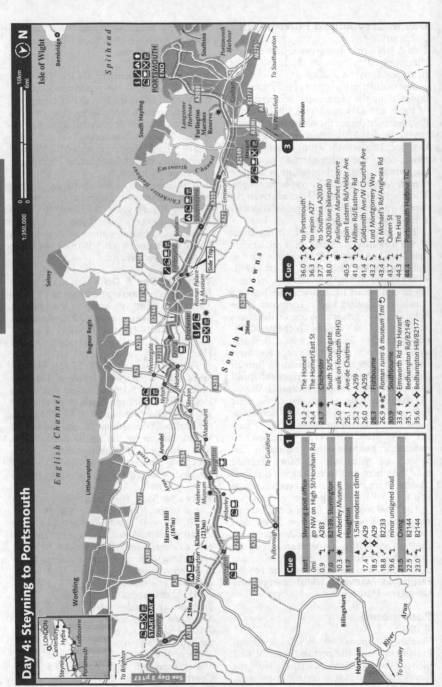

Day 4: Steyning to Portsmouth

1:350,000

N

10km
6mi

Isle of Wight

Bembridge

Spithead

Southsea

PORTSMOUTH END

Portsmouth Harbour

South Hayling

Langstone Harbour

Cosham

A3(M)

Farlington Marshes Reserve

To Southampton

Horndean

To Petersfield

A3

A2030

M275

M27

A2177

Havant

Emsworth Channel

Chichester Harbour

Emsworth

B2149

Southbourne

Fishbourne

Bosham

Roman Palace & Museum

Side Trip

Selsey

Bognor Regis

Westergate

B2145

B2144

B3165

A259

B2233

Oving

Nyton

Slindon

Chichester

A27

Arundel

A29

Madehurst

Houghton

Amberley Museum

Amberley

Harrow Hill (167m)

Kithurst Hill (213m)

Washington

Storrington

238m

START DAY 4
Steyning

Worthing

English Channel

Littlehampton

A259

A29

A284

A283

B2139

A24

A280

A283

B2135

To Guildford

To Crawley

River Arun

Arun

Billingshurst

To Horsham

To Brighton

South Downs

206m

B2146

Norton

See Day 3 p137

London
Canterbury
Steyning Hythe
Eastbourne
Portsmouth

See Day 3 p137

Cue 1

start		Steyning post office
0mi	↰	go NW on High St/Horsham Rd
0.9	↱	A283
7.0	↱	B2139, Storrington
10.3	✳	Amberley Museum
11.7	◢	Houghton
		1.5mi moderate climb
17.4	◆↱	A29
18.5	◆↰	A29
18.8	↱	B2233
19.6	↱	minor unsigned road
21.5		Oving
22.5	↰	B2144
23.0	↱	B2144

Cue 2

24.2	↰	The Hornet
24.4	↱	The Hornet/East St
24.7	✳	Chichester
	↱	South St/Southgate
25.0	◢	walk on footpath (RHS)
25.1	↱	Ave de Chartres
25.2	↰	A259
26.0	◆↰	A259
26.3		Fishbourne
26.9	●↰	Roman ruins & museum 1mi ↻
30.9		Southbourne
33.6	↰	Emsworth Rd 'to Havant'
35.1	↱	Bedhampton Rd/B2149
35.6	◆↰	Bedhampton Hill/B2177

Cue 3

36.0	◆↱	'to Portsmouth'
36.3	◆↱	'to rejoin A27'
37.7	↰	'to Southsea A2030'
38.0	↱	A2030 (use bikepath)
		Farlington Marshes Reserve
40.5	✳	rejoin Eastern Rd/Velder Ave
41.0	↰	Milton Rd/Eastney Rd
41.4	◆↱	Goldsmith Ave/W Churchill Ave
43.2	↰	Lord Montgomery Way
43.4	↱	St Michael's Rd/Anglesea Rd
43.7	↰	Queen St
44.3	↱	The Hard
44.4		Portsmouth Harbour TIC

range from £17.50 to £28 per night. *Hamilton House (☎ 9282 3502, ⓔ sandra@hamiltonhouse.co.uk, 95 Victoria Rd North)* costs £18 to £23. The *University of Portsmouth (☎ 9284 3178, ⓔ reservations@port.ac.uk, Southsea Terrace)* offers B&B at their halls of residence, overlooking Southsea Common, from £16.75 (in summer only).

Places to Eat Palmerston Rd shopping precinct, near Southsea, is the place to angle for food, with a mix of cuisines and prices to suit most tastes. Go to *Snookies (82 Osborne Rd)* for coffee, pastries and bread; try *Oysters Wine & Tapas Bar* for main courses for about £5. *Chez Choi (☎ 9282 6900, 46 Osborne Rd)* noodle bar and *Sonargaon Tandoori Indian Restaurant (☎ 9287 6090, 38a Osborne Rd)* are both worth a look; *Jewel in the Crown (☎ 9282 7787, 60 Osborne Rd)* also serves Indian food. Pubs, cafes and all manner of takeaway places are spread around the city.

South Downs Way & Beachy Head

MOUNTAIN BIKE RIDE

Duration	4–5 hours
Distance	24.8mi
Difficulty	moderate
Start/End	Eastbourne

A short spin on the off-road South Downs Way (SDW) is the highlight of this cruisy day, which also takes in Seven Sisters Country Park and Beachy Head. Lovely views over Eastbourne are a feature.

The 100mi SDW national trail is the only one of England's classic long-distance walks that's also a bridleway for its entire length, and therefore open to cyclists. The SDW follows the downs from Winchester to Alfriston, roughly 6mi west of Eastbourne, from where it splits into a separate walking path following the spectacular coastline, and a bridleway that loops inland offering lush views.

NATURAL HISTORY

Features such as burial mounds, burial barrows and hill forts mark the passing of the downs' various ancient inhabitants. The route of the South Downs Way was probably a Bronze age trading route.

Cycling the South Downs Way

Unique among Britain's National Trails, the SDW is designated as a bridleway for its entire length: this allows cyclists – and horses – to share the 100mi route with walkers. The only exception is the stage between Alfriston and Eastbourne, where cyclists take the bridleway across Windover Hill (see the South Downs Way & Beachy Head ride), while the walkers' trail hugs the coastal cliffs.

Cycling the SDW takes as long or as short as you like. It's been done in a single day, but such haste would rob you of the opportunity to enjoy some of southern Britain's finest vistas and prettiest villages. Tackling it on a bike gives you considerable flexibility to wander off the route to coastal resorts (such as Brighton) and interesting towns (for instance Chichester). If you aim to cover 20mi to 30mi a day you'll complete the route in four days and have energy for off-track detours. Be prepared for regular dismounts to open and close gates – there are more than 80 along the route.

You *could* tackle the SDW on a touring bike, but a lot of the terrain really merits a mountain bike. Tracks, particularly up on the ridge line, are often strewn with flints and sharp stones; the rough going makes for some challenging climbs and descents. Make sure your touring tool kit is up to scratch before departure, and carry spare brake blocks and a couple of inner tubes in addition to your puncture repair kit. As with any off-road cycling, you shouldn't ride alone.

Although you're never too far from help, major repairs in the middle of the trail will prompt a detour north or south to a cycle shop in a major town. Shops at either end of the SDW are good sources of advice about the ride and trail conditions. In Winchester, try Peter Hargreaves Cycles (☎ 019 62-860005), 26 Jewry St, or Peter Hansford Cycles (☎ 01962-877555), 91 Oliver's Battery Rd. In Eastbourne, there's Heath Cycles (☎ 01323-733404), 106 Cavendish Place, and Phoenix Cycles (☎ 01323-729060), 217/219 Seaside; both are easy to find.

Through the centuries, grazing practices and agriculture co-existed on the downs and quietly moulded their green and rolling appearance. But changes this century have been more dramatic. Parts of the downs have been cultivated for food production, resulting in the disappearance in places of the hedges and fences that harbour wildlife and provide the downs' patchwork charm. The SDW crosses protected landscapes – the East Hampshire and Sussex Downs Areas of Outstanding Natural Beauty (AONB) – for its entire length, and these days farmers are being encouraged to sow pastures and graze sheep rather than cultivate crops.

PLANNING
When to Ride
The downs are in England's warmer, drier south, and the route reaches a high point of only 195m (650ft), so it's possible to ride year-round. Remember that upland sections are exposed and can become very bleak in winter.

Maps & Books
The OS Landranger sheet No 199 *Eastbourne, Hastings & Surrounding Area* is recommended. Collect a town map from the Eastbourne TIC, which also has a range of South Downs Way publications; the best is *The South Downs Way* official guide by Paul Millmore (£10.99).

What to Bring
Less than one-third of the route is truly off-road, and all but a few sections are manageable on a touring bike. A mountain bike is more comfortable, so consider hiring one from Cuckmere Haven (☎ 01323-870310) at Seven Sisters Country Park.

GETTING TO/FROM THE RIDE
Eastbourne
Train Connex South Central trains (☎ 0870-603 0405) runs services between London and Eastbourne. It costs £16.90 for the 1½-hour journey.

Bicycle Eastbourne is the second night stop on the South-East Coast ride, described earlier in this chapter. It's an easy day's ride from several south-coast centres, including Brighton, and from Gatwick airport.

THE RIDE
Eastbourne
See Eastbourne (pp134–6) in the South-East Coast ride for information about accommodation and other services.

South Downs Way & Beachy Head
4–5 hours, 24.8mi
This route follows the SDW bridleway out of Eastbourne and onto the Downs and returns via lanes and roads that reveal the sights of the SDW Alfriston–Eastbourne walking section.

Start by going south (towards the seaside) on Cornfield Rd and Cornfield Terrace. Follow through Compton St, Carlisle Rd, Meads Rd and Paradise Drive to the start of the first dirt section, a left off Paradise Drive at 1.3mi. A tricky climb follows; watch for the acorn symbol signposts (which mark the SDW as a National Trail) and follow the chalky path and you won't go wrong. Cross the fast-moving A259 (at 2.5mi) near Eastbourne Downs Golf Club; there are spectacular views of Eastbourne at various points along the section to Willingdon Hill (at 4.2mi).

Take care on the bumpy 1mi downhill into Jevington. Go right at 5.3mi then left 50yd up the road into Church Lane. The route is almost immediately back onto dirt and climbing and the going is bumpy. Go right at the trail junction at 6.0mi then follow the trail for 2.1mi. Given good weather, this section (on Windover Hill) will be a highlight; one of the Downs' best-known chalk figures – the **Long Man of Wilmington** – is just over the ridge from the point where the descent begins (at about 7.2mi). The trail surface is mostly grassy, at least until the downhill. Go left and back onto sealed road at 8.1mi and follow, through Litlington, for 3mi to the A259.

Dogleg carefully across the A road, then follow the sealed bike/wheelchair path through **Seven Sisters Country Park** out to **Cuckmere Haven**. This is another highlight; the path is nice and flat, and fine views of Seven Sisters cliffs await. Return via the same path to the A259, and go right (at 14.1mi). There's a 2mi moderate climb to negotiate next, and the A259 to East Dean can be busy with traffic. It's quieter on the rambling road that comes after the right into

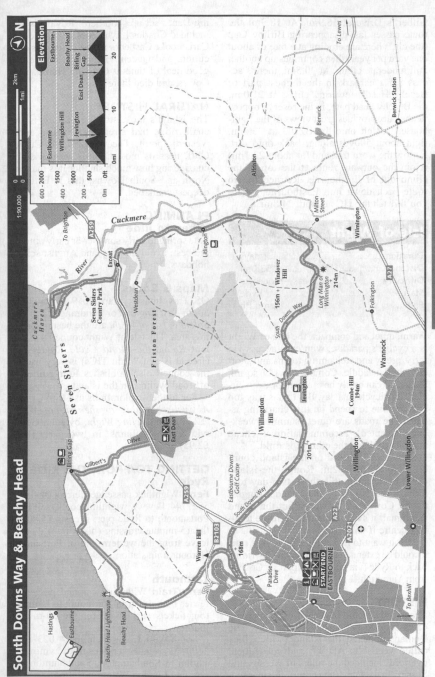

South Downs Way & Beachy Head

Gilbert's Drive at 16.9mi. At 18.3mi the route passes fast-disappearing Birling Gap (the cliffs here are eroding at a rate of about one yard per year) then continues up another 2mi moderate climb. At 20.5mi, there's access via a carpark to the highest part of Beachy Head's towering cliffs; at 21.0mi, the Beachy head path, in the reserve opposite the pub, provides great views of the lighthouse. Go left onto the B2103 at 22.2mi, right about 500yds along, back onto dirt. Follow the worn trail and (at about 22.7mi) rejoin the outward route at the top of the climb out of Eastbourne. Retrace the to route back down into Eastbourne, where you'll reach the TIC at about 24.8mi.

Isle of Wight

Duration	2 days
Distance	53.0mi
Difficulty	easy–moderate
Start	Ryde
End	Yarmouth

Warm, quiet and compact, the Isle of Wight is a cyclist's paradise, with easy access via ferry, pretty and welcoming towns and short days in the saddle. Compact at 147 sq mi, the island can easily be crossed, or even circled, by bicycle in a day. But this is way too short a time to spend on this charming island. The roads are quiet (summer weekends excepted), accommodation is cheap and plentiful and the climate is mild.

Substantially based on the island council's wonderful, 62mi Round-the-Island (RTI) cycle route, this short, two-day tour (56mi) avoids two of the island's biggest towns, Cowes and Newport, but the island is so small it's no problem to re-route to either centre if you wish.

If you want to make this a three-day ride, it could be extended by another day by riding back to Ryde (via either Newport or Cowes) from Yarmouth.

HISTORY

The island's record of prehistoric settlement dates back to before the Bronze age. The Romans annexed the island (which they called Vectis) in AD 43, and subsequent overlords included the rulers of Wessex and Sussex. In the late-10th century the maraud-ing Danes set up shop here. Royal visitors included Charles I, who cooled his heels in Carisbrooke Castle for a time before his execution, and Queen Victoria, who spent a good deal of time at Osborne House, near Cowes, and died there.

NATURAL HISTORY

The island's most striking feature is the chalk ridge that stretches from its most westerly point, The Needles, to Culver Cliff, near its most easterly. Remarkably, considering how much smaller it is than the North and South Downs, this is Britain's deepest chalk bed.

PLANNING
When to Ride

Late spring to early summer or early autumn are best; avoid the July and August school holidays.

Maps & Books

OS Travelmaster map No 9 (1:250,000) *South East England* or Landranger 196 *The Solent & Isle of Wight* are the best maps for this area. The Isle of Wight council's excellent *Round-the-Island Cycle Route* map (free at Isle of Wight TICs) is very useful; the council also publishes four guides to off-road cycling on the island.

For further explorations use Ron Crick's *A Cyclist's Guide to the Isle of Wight* (£2.70) and *Cycling Wight*, by John Goodwin & Ian Williams, in two parts (both £2.95).

GETTING TO/FROM THE RIDE
Ryde

Ferry Wightlink passenger ferries (☎ 0870-5827744, 🖳 www.wightlink.co.uk) sail from Portsmouth to Ryde pier; it costs £5.80 for the 15-minute crossing (bikes free). Ferries leave from the western end of Portsmouth Harbour train station.

Yarmouth

Ferry/Train Wightlink car and passenger ferries both sail from Yarmouth to Lymington; tickets cost £6.60 for the 30-minute journey.

South West Trains (helpline ☎ 023-8021 3600) has regular services from Lymington station to Southampton, Southampton airport and London Waterloo station.

Loading up at the Street YHA near Glastonbury, south-west England.

It's cyclists and walkers only on southern England's Tarka Trail.

Spoilt for choice in Somerset.

Cornwall's Bodmin Moor is actually some of the highest terrain in southern England.

Explore the Old Harbour in lively, historic Weymouth, southern England.

The London to Brighton ride.

Weymouth's Old Harbour is lined with attractive old buildings.

Pass through moorland, heath, oak and pine in the New Forest, near Lyndhurst, southern England.

THE RIDE
Ryde
☎ 01983

The Isle of Wight's largest town, Ryde has pleasant beaches, a range of services and is close to the mainland.

Information The TIC (☎ 562905, 💻 www.isleofwight.gov.uk/tourism.htm) is on Western Esplanade. The post office is halfway up Union St. Most of the big banks are represented on High St and Union St and St Thomas Square. The nearest bike shops are in Cowes and Newport.

Things to See & Do Cruising along the seafront is lovely; the promenade passes parks, gardens and sandy beaches, with views over The Solent towards Southsea and Portsmouth. The town, with Georgian and Victorian buildings a feature, is a friendly place for coffee or something stronger. The

Cycling the Green Gullies

Ah, the romance of trundling a bicycle along an English country lane...no traffic, birds twittering, hedges blocking the cross winds. The charming English countryside of your dreams hasn't disappeared, but do take a swig from the reality bottle before cycling along its renowned lanes.

It *is* rare to encounter motor vehicles in narrow lanes, but you're in for a shock when it happens. A larger vehicle will sometimes occupy the *whole* lane, from hedge to hedge: it goes without saying that you should *always* resist the temptation to go flat-out downhill. You must also stay well away from laneside detritus. In spring and summer, hedge trimmings are usually left where they fall, and given that most decent hedges contain a couple of thorny plant species, these leafy leftovers are a prime source of punctures.

But you'll learn to love hedges; at least, you'd better, because cycling along hedge-lined lanes can be like exploring the land via a series of green gullies. You know there's a lovely landscape out there – you catch flashes of it on hill crests and at gates – but for much of the time the view is limited to a green-walled, narrow strip of tar.

Commodore Cinema (☎ 56 5609) is on Star St and the **Ryde Theatre** (☎ 568099) is on Lind St.

Places to Stay & Eat The nearest camping ground, less than 2mi east, is the *Pondwell Camping Holiday* (☎ 612330) at Seaview; tent pitches cost £4 to £7. There's a wide choice of B&Bs; the Isle of Wight accommodation hotline (☎ 813813) is the place to begin inquiries. Try *Seaward Guest House* (☎ 563168, 14/16 George St), where B&B costs £14 to £18.

The town's reliance on tourism ensures a good choice of cafes and pubs, and Union and High Sts are the best places to start. *Grace's Bakery (High St)* has a fine selection of breads and sticky buns, which you can wash down with a 70p coffee. *Dolly's Tea Room (Cross St)* is nice for lunch-time sandwiches and baguettes. The *Coffee Pot* (☎ 56 5457, 10 Union St) has an all-day £2.55 breakfast; *The Redan* pub (☎ 56 2466, 76 Union St) has pasta or curries for £3.95.

Day 1: Ryde to Ventnor
3–4 hours, 27.0mi

The route meanders to and from the coast throughout; traffic is rarely a problem (but watch for cars on the narrow lanes) and road surfaces are good. The views are wonderful, especially the ocean vistas, although here and there you'll see nothing but the high hedges lining the lanes – you'll encounter some very deep, narrow lanes. While you're able to travel most of the day by following the RTI route signs, here and there are unsigned turns, and the route wanders about so much that you occasionally become disoriented.

It's a busy start to the day, with traffic in Ryde and on the A3054 to contend with. The ruins of **Quarr Abbey** (2.2mi) are worth a look, but generally the quicker you get onto quiet roads (after 3.1mi) the happier you'll be.

At 12.3mi you'll pass the island's only surviving windmill, **Bembridge Windmill**, complete with its creaky-looking wooden machinery. It's open from March to October and is a National Trust monument. Farther along, **Appuldurcombe House**, an English Heritage building, and the **Owl & Falconry Centre** (23.3mi; ☎ 852484) are both worth a look.

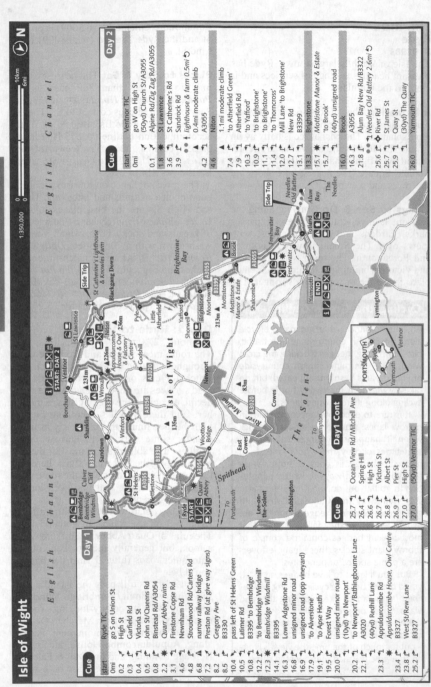

Take care on the steep roads leading into Ventnor; they wind down the southern face of the National Trust-managed Ventnor Downs, which rise abruptly from the seaside to one of the island's highest points, 231m (770ft) St Boniface Down.

Ventnor
☎ 01983

A pretty town with an often-mentioned 'Mediterranean feel', Ventnor enjoys a sheltered southerly aspect and is reputedly one of the sunniest spots on the island. This quiet, Victorian-era spa town has a lovely beach and some nice pubs overlooking the sea. The town is compact and, given the hills, it's a fair idea to walk around rather than ride once you've settled into accommodation.

Information Ventnor TIC (☎ 853625) is at 34 High St. Midlands and Lloyds banks have branches with ATMs on High St; the post office is on Church St. Extreme Cycles (☎ 852232) is angled towards mountain bikers but it carries a fair range of spares. There's a laundrette on the corner of High St and Spring Hill.

Things to See & Do Take a stroll down Shore Hill past the tumbledown **Cascades** gardens, then along The Esplanade to a seafront table (and a few pints) at the **Spyglass Inn**. From near the pub, the **Coastal Path** leads west into **Ventnor Park**, which has charming gardens with wonderful ocean views, and on to the **Ventnor Botanic Garden** (☎ 855397). Just east of Ventnor is chic **Bonchurch**, where Charles Dickens pounded out six chapters of *David Copperfield* in a hotel. The tiny **Old Church of St Boniface** in Bonchurch was built by Benedictine monks in 1070; it's said to be one of the oldest churches in southern England.

Places to Stay There are a couple of camping grounds in Shanklin, 2.5mi northeast of Ventnor. At *Landguard Camping Park* (☎ 867028; *Landguard Manor Rd, Shanklin*), tent pitches (for two people) cost £11 in the high season.

There are plenty of B&Bs in Ventnor. Try *Glen Islay House* (☎ 854095, *St Boniface Rd*), where the owners have a bent for walking and cycling. B&B costs from £20. You'll pay the same at nearby *Hillside*

Hotel (☎ 852271, 151 Mitchell Ave), renowned for its vegetarian food.

Places to Eat For coffee and scones (£1.20), try *Raffles Tea Rooms (High St)*. If you're watching pennies there are some *takeaway* shops on The Esplanade, but it's hard to go past the seafood at the *Spyglass Inn* (☎ 855338, *Esplanade*), where most main courses are in the £5 to £10 range. *Tillys* (☎ 852284, 28 Pier St) has some interesting vegetarian options, most under £4. The *Thistle Cafe* (☎ 852681, 30 Pier St) does a vegetarian breakfast for £3.95. *Shanghai Lil's (Church St)* has an interesting mix of Thai and Chinese dishes.

Day 2: Ventnor to Yarmouth
3–4 hours, 26.0mi

This is another cruisy day, again mostly following the RTI cycle route signs, with wonderful ocean views most of the way. There can be some traffic along the first section on the A3055 but it's worth putting up with. The road rises and falls on its way past lovely homes and through lush stands of woodland; the ocean stretches south from the steep shoreline, which is on your left.

In the day's first 2mi you'll pass the **Ventnor Botanic Garden**; the **Smuggling Museum** (☎ 853677), open daily from April to September; and the **Rare Breeds & Waterfowl Park** (☎ 852582), open year-round.

It's worth making the short climb, on the side trip at 3.9mi, to the 1840s **St Catherine's Lighthouse**; and National Trust-listed **Knowles Farm**, which has fields divided by stone walls rather than hedges. Guglielmo Marconi, inventor of the first successful wire telegraph, lived at Knowles for a time and conducted some of his earliest experiments in wireless here.

There are several places to grab a bite in Niton before completing the climb up **Blackgang Down**, from which you'll get what's probably the island's best outlook, the sweeping view north-west towards the chalk cliffs of West Wight.

Mottistone Manor and Estate (☎ 741020; NT), at 15.1mi, has a magnificent garden while the historic fortification at **Needles Old Battery** (☎ 754772; NT) – side trip at 21.8mi – provides fine views of the island's best-known natural feature, the weather-beaten chalk rocks called **The Needles**.

Yarmouth
☎ 01983

Compact Yarmouth is a busy ferry port and it's also worth a look around. The west Wight towns – Yarmouth, Totland and Freshwater – are close to one another (a couple of miles at most), opening up accommodation options beyond Yarmouth.

Information Yarmouth TIC (☎ 760015) is on The Quay. There's a Lloyds Bank with ATMs on The Square in Yarmouth; NatWest and Midland banks have branches with ATMs on Avenue Rd, Freshwater. The post office is on Quay St.

There's no bike shop in Yarmouth but Isle Cycle Hire (☎ 760219), on The Square, might be able to help with emergency spares.

Things to See & Do Completed in 1547, **Yarmouth Castle** (☎ 760678; EH) was Henry VIII's last addition to his network of coastal defences. It includes displays about Old Yarmouth and the Isle of Wight. In Freshwater, **Dimbola Lodge** (☎ 756814), former home of Victorian-era photographer Julia Margaret Cameron, is now a gallery with work by Cameron and other photographers.

There are lovely walks in this area – the Tennyson Trail, Coastal Path and Freshwater Way are all worthwhile. A lovely, flat bikepath links Yarmouth and Freshwater; it's the best route to take if your accommodation is in Freshwater or Totland, and is worth a ride in its own right.

Places to Stay High-season tent pitches cost £7 at both **Heathfield Farm Camping Site** (☎ 756756; Heathfield Rd, Freshwater) and **Stoats Farm** (☎ 755258; Weston Lane, Totland). With 72 beds, **Totland Bay YHA** (☎ 752165, Hurst Hill) has a cycle storage room and drying room and serves breakfast and dinner; a bed costs £10.15.

There's any number of B&Bs; most easily found through the Isle of Wight accommodation hotline (☎ 813813). The **Royal Standard Hotel** (☎ 753227, School Green Rd), is pleasant and charges from £21 for B&B. Prices start at £18 at **Sandpipers Hotel** (☎ 753634, Coastguard Lane), overlooking Freshwater Bay.

Places to Eat In Yarmouth, a lovely place for coffee (80p) is **Gossips Cafe**, on the waterfront. **Salty's** restaurant (☎ 761550, Quay St) has tasty seafood but most main courses top £12.

In Freshwater, School Green Rd is the place to search for food. Try **The Bakery at Freshwater** (19 School Green Rd) for scones and bread. The **Royal Standard Hotel** restaurant has mains including pastas and curries in the £4.50 to £8 range, while **Fatima Indian Cuisine** (☎ 755121, 46 School Green Rd) has several vegetarian dishes for under £6.

In Totland, look on The Broadway for places to eat.

New Forest

MOUNTAIN BIKE RIDE

Duration	4–6 hours
Distance	39.2mi
Difficulty	easy
Start/End	Lyndhurst

The 148 sq mi New Forest is Europe's largest surviving area of ancient pasture woodland. It's not a national park; day-to-day management is mainly in the hands of the Forestry Commission (FC), but New Forest lands are actually governed by arcane (and charming) traditions and laws that date back to William the Conqueror's time.

This ride can be done on either a mountain or touring bike; savour the flat, wide trails and easy navigation.

HISTORY

William gave the New Forest its name when setting it aside as a royal deer-hunting preserve in 1079. William introduced Forest Law, which allowed commoners (land users) to graze livestock but not to fence. The early, fairly draconian, laws were replaced by the more relaxed Charter of the Forest in 1217. This 'Forest Magna Carta' established the Court of the Verderers, which still sits today in Lyndhurst (although these days it's more administrative than judicial). The New Forest's traditional 'police' – the Agisters – still oversee the drift, or round-up, of commoners' livestock prior to branding, tail-marking and worming.

NATURAL HISTORY

Free-roaming, grazing animals nibbled new tree shoots keeping the forest as mostly

Know Your New Forest Rights

Reckon present-day New Forest commoners have some cool land-use rights? Perhaps, but think of the ancient rights of common they've either lost, or no longer exercise.

The forest was a chillier place in the old days – winters are said to be nowhere near as severe nowadays – and, with winter approaching, you'd surely find time to exercise your Common of Turbary (the right to cut turf for fuel) or Common of Estovers (the right to collect firewood). But the real fun would come in warmer months. Given half a chance, who could resist the exercise of their Common of Pannage – better known as a licence to allow one's pig to forage for acorns and beechnuts.

heath, grass and moor lands from William's time until the late 15th century. The increased demand for boat-building timber saw the first Inclosure Act passed in 1482. New Forest timber was first recorded as being used for naval ships in 1611. A 1698 Act allowed the Crown use of a maximum of 6000 acres of woodland, and the navy needed it – a large wooden warship consumed up to 60 acres of timber.

The New Forest's biggest threat today is tourists (some 25 million annually) and the Forestry Commission is kept busy with forest track maintenance and erosion repairs, removal of alien and pest plant species, and the restoration of the forest's rare lowland valley mires (75% of Europe's remaining lowland valley mires are in the New Forest).

PLANNING
When to Ride
It's possible to ride all year. The forest is beautiful in the greenery of spring and summer but the crowds are intense. The forest in winter can appear stark but there are fewer people about.

Maps & Books
The Forestry Commission's *Cycling in the New Forest: The Network Map* is basic but does the job. The OS Outdoor Leisure map (1:25,000) *New Forest* is best for detail, or the OS Landranger series (1:50,000) has

two maps that cover the area – No 195, *Bournemouth & Purbeck;* and No 196, *The Solent & Isle of Wight.* Hancock & Tom's *MTB Guide to Hampshire and New Forest* (£4.95) is useful if you're planning an extended stay.

GETTING TO/FROM THE RIDE
Don't even think of driving a car here, especially in summer.

Lyndhurst
Train Stations at Ashurst, Brockenhurst and Beaulieu Road provide immediate access to the forest and are a short ride (less than 5mi) from the New Forest's main centre, Lyndhurst. Trains to/from London Waterloo run regularly with Connex South Central, South West and Virgin TOCs; call ☎ 0845-748 4950 for timetable and fare details. The standard return fare is £23.90 (to Ashurst), £24.20 (Beaulieu Road) and £25.20 (Brockenhurst) for the 1½-hour journey. Outside peak times you should find a service on which bikes are carried for free; otherwise, a £3 reservation fee may apply. Lyndhurst is also on the train line to Weymouth, the start of The South-West ride, detailed later in this chapter.

THE RIDE
Lyndhurst
☎ 023
The New Forest's 'capital' is pretty but very, very busy, especially in mid-summer. The bodies that play the greatest role in forest management, the Forestry Commission and Verderers Court, are based in Lyndhurst and the New Forest District Council is also represented there.

Information The New Forest TIC (☎ 8028 2269) fronts the main car park, off High Street. It has an extensive range of maps, books and brochures and can help with accommodation; it's also the place to bone up on the New Forest Cycle Code – nine rules, all common sense, for cycling in the New Forest.

Lyndhurst post office is on High St, as are the major banks and their ATMs. AA Bike Hire (☎ 8028 3349) is next to the TIC; the area's main bike shop is New Forest Cycle Experience (☎ 01590-624204), next to the A337 at Brockenhurst.

SOUTHERN ENGLAND

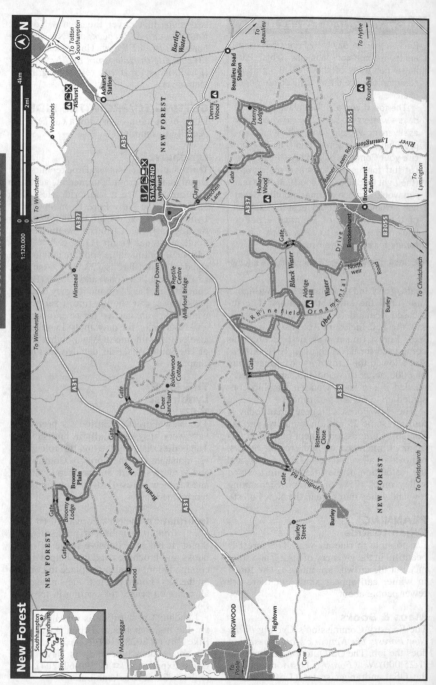

Things to See & Do In the same building as the TIC, the **New Forest Museum** (☎ 8028 3914), is a good place to start learning about the forest's history and ecosystems. At nearby Beaulieu (pronounced 'bew-lee'), the **Palace House & Abbey ruins** (☎ 01590-612123) are interesting, as is **Buckler's Hard** (☎ 01590-616203), a little farther south-east, where 19th-century warships were built.

Places to Stay The Forestry Commission has 10 camping grounds in the New Forest. Advance bookings are advisable (☎ 0131-314 6505) through Forest Holidays, 231 Corstorphine Rd, Edinburgh, EH12 7AT. The closest sites to Lyndhurst are *Ashurst*, off the A35, *Hollands Wood*, off the A337 near Brockenhurst, and *Roundhill*, off the B3055. All open from late March to late September. Pitches during high season at weekends for four people cost £10.60 at Ashurst, £11 at Hollands Wood and £9.70 at Roundhill.

There's a wide variety of B&Bs and hotels; look in the *New Forest Where to Stay* guide, available from the TIC. There are some lovely home-style B&Bs in the area. Just north of Lyndhurst, try *Acres Down Farm* (☎ 8081 3693, Minstead), with rates from £17.50. Just outside Ashurst, *Kingswood Cottage* (☎ 8029 2582, 10 Woodlands Rd) is a comfy house in a beautiful setting; the rate for singles is £19. For a little more luxury, you could try *Ormonde House Hotel* (☎ 8028 2806; Southampton Rd, Lyndhurst)*, where B&B costs £32 to £39 at weekends; it's cheaper midweek.

Places to Eat For bread and cakes, or a hot beverage, stop at *Tasty Pastries (16a High St, Lyndhurst)*. There's a wide choice of pub food throughout the area; *The Happy Cheese*, at Ashurst, is a big, cheerful pub with decent food. In Lyndhurst, *Hunters* (with £6.50 pasta), *The Fox & Hounds*, *The Stag* and *The Mailmans Arms* are all worth a look. *The Lyndhurst Rooms* licensed restaurant (☎ 8028 2656, 26 High St) has an interesting menu, as does *Il Cervo* (☎ 8028 2106, High St), an Italian place. Restaurant bookings are advisable on summer weekends.

New Forest
4–6 hours, 39.2mi
Cycling in the New Forest provides a wonderful break from the road, and the best part of this route is that its 25 miles of off-road tracks are well-signposted, invariably smooth and mostly very flat. A mountain bike is best for the ride, but you'll manage it easily on a touring bike.

There's something of interest at just about every stage. Most noticeable are the ubiquitous ponies for which the New Forest is renowned (remember: no feeding), but expect to see all manner of livestock. The changing habitats are fascinating. You'll pass through moorland, heath and magnificent, whispering oak and pine forest and, remarkably in this part of the England, enjoy spells of genuinely peaceful solitude.

In spring, the **Rhinefield Ornamental Drive** section (22mi to 24mi) will be ablaze with rhododendron blossoms. Unfortunately, these densely flowering evergreens are a pest, and they're eradicated when they spread into the surrounding forest.

The only thing you may find tiresome are gates; there are 21 on the route, plus several cattle grids. Be especially careful around Lyndhurst if you're touring on a summer weekend – the traffic can be intense.

From Lyndhurst TIC, go north to High St then circle around with the one-way traffic on Gosport Lane and Chapel Lane to the A35 (at 1mi). On leaving the A35 (1.2mi), the change of tempo is almost immediate: deciduous trees soar overhead, casting cool shadows, and cows wander freely.

From Burley Rd in Brockenhurst, go right at The Rise (30.4mi), left at Sway Rd (the B3055; 30.6mi) and left onto Lyndhurst Rd (the A337; 31.0mi). After just 400yd on the A road, go right at Balmer Lawn Rd (the B3055) then veer left ('to Beaulieu') at 31.6mi; the route is back on dirt for the last time, for the day's longest off-road section (of 6.6mi).

Avon to Thames

Duration	3 days
Distance	139.6mi
Difficulty	moderate–hard
Start	Bristol
End	Richmond (London)

This 140mi jaunt heads from the heart of Bristol, south-western England's largest city, to leafy Richmond, in south-western

London. Highlights are the Bristol & Bath Railway Path (B&BRP), Sustrans' flagship traffic-free path; beautiful Bath; the Wiltshire Downs around Marlborough and Avebury; and Royal Windsor.

HISTORY

The historical sites in this part of England cover almost the entire period of documented history. West Kennett Long Barrow dates from about 3500 BC and the prehistoric complex around Avebury was established from about 2600–2100 BC. Bath was first developed by the Romans as a spa town but it wasn't until the Georgian era that the city's distinctive appearance was established. Windsor Castle's association with British royalty extends back 900 years.

PLANNING
When to Ride

Summer is very pleasant although crowds can slow progress in centres such as Bristol, Bath and Windsor. Winter riding is fine; the route's high point is about 240m (720ft).

Maps & Books

The route is entirely covered by two OS Travelmaster maps (1:250,000): No 8, *South West England & South Wales;* and No 9, *South East England.* Parts of the route follow NCN 4, and Sustrans' *Severn & Thames* route map (1:100,000) is useful, especially for the B&BRP section. The OS's Cycle Tours books *Avon, Somerset & Wiltshire* and *Berks, Bucks & Oxfordshire* (both £10) could be useful if you plan further explorations.

Wiltshire is one of the better organised counties when it comes to cycling. Look in TICs for the free brochures *Cycling in the Wiltshire Downs* and *Wiltshire Cycleway.*

GETTING TO/FROM THE RIDE
Bristol

Train Bristol is the south-west's major rail hub, and trains leave regularly for London, the Midlands as well as Somerset/Cornwall/ Devon. The service from London Paddington to Bristol (£32) takes 1½ hours; there's a £3 reservation fee for bicycles (£1 if booked at least two hours in advance).

Bicycle Bristol is passed through on Day 5 (from Glastonbury to Chepstow) of the

Land's End to John o'Groats ride (see the chapter of the same name).

Richmond

Richmond is 9mi south-west of central London. Richmond has an Underground station on the District line and an above ground station (see the boxed text 'Train Your Bike?' in the London chapter for more information).

If you're continuing into central London by bike, take the wonderful riverside bikepath, which will keep you out of the traffic as far as Putney Bridge.

THE RIDE
Bristol
☎ 0117

Some people think busy Bristol is the best little city in Britain. It's certainly a lively and entertaining place with plenty to see, nice places to eat and a wide choice of accommodation. It's also a good place to cycle – perhaps not surprising given that Sustrans is headquartered here – with well-signposted routes around town and the Bristol & Bath Railway Path (B&BRP) leading away.

Information The Bristol TIC (☎ 926 0767, 🖳 www.visitbristol.co.uk) is in Anchor Rd at The Annexe, Wildscreen Walk, Harbourside. The fortnightly listings magazine *Venue* is useful if you're in town for a while. There's any number of ATMs and post offices around the city.

Bike shops nearest the town centre are Bristol Bicycle Workshop (☎ 926 8961), 84 Colston St, and Bike-Tech (☎ 929 7368), 12–14 Park St.

Things to See & Do A ride from the city centre alongside the River Avon on the **Ashton & Pill Path** is a must. The path, part of NCN4 (the Severn & Thames route) follows the Avon for about 6mi to Pill, passing directly under the renowned **Clifton Suspension Bridge.** The bridge, completed in 1864, is one of the best-known works of brilliant engineer Isambard Kingdom Brunel. Another of his designs, the **SS *Great Britain*** (☎ 926 0680), off City Dock, was (in 1836) the world's first ocean-going iron ship. It's been under restoration in the dry dock, where it was built, since its return to Bristol (in 1970); enter it via the **Maritime**

Heritage Centre. Other popular attractions include **Bristol Cathedral** (☎ 926 4879), founded in 1140, and the **City Museum & Art Gallery** (☎ 922 3571), on Park St.

Places to Stay Tent pitches at the centrally-located *Baltic Wharf Caravan Club (☎ 926 8030, Cumberland Rd)* cost £10.50 for two people. Advance bookings are essential at weekends and advisable at other times.

The swish *Bristol YHA (☎ 922 1659, 14 Narrow Quay St)* is in a brilliant central location and it fills up fast at busy times. The nightly charge is £12.15; breakfast and dinner are available and there's a cycle storeroom and laundry.

There are B&Bs and hotels spread around the city, the cheaper ones are usually some distance from the centre. There's a number to choose from in Southville, just across the River Avon from the city centre. Try *Alpha Guest House (☎ 966 3215, 36 Coronation Rd)*, *Glanville Guest House (☎ 963 1634, 122 Coronation Rd)* or *Raglan Guest House (☎ 966 2129, 132 Coronation Rd)*. Farther out, the *Rockdale Hotel (☎ 971 2831; 512–514 Bath Rd, Brislington)* charges £30. A double room at the modern *Town & Country Lodge (☎ 01275-392441, Bridgewater Rd/A38)*, on the city's fringe, costs £44 with breakfast.

Some of the centrally located hotels are pricey during the week but worth a look on weekends. You should get B&B at the weekend for under £50 at the *Thistle Bristol Hotel (☎ 929 1645, Broad St)* but it's more than £100 weekdays. Weekend rates are also worth checking at the *Avon Gorge Hotel (☎ 973 8955; Sion Hill, Clifton)*.

Places to Eat There are cafes and restaurants spread around town, with the main concentrations in the city centre and inner-city suburbs including Clifton, Kingsdown and Redland.

In central Bristol, there's a lot to choose from in Corn St: try *St Nicholas Market* for the cheapest eats – you should find sandwiches from around £1.50; chain restaurants include *All Bar One* and *Via Vita*. *San Carlo* is good for pizza and pasta – a filling feed costs from about £5 – and *Markwicks* is worth a look.

Nice for food or a relaxing bevvy are the cafe bars in the *Arnolfini* and the *Water-shed Centre*, which are on either side of St Augustine's Reach. Fast, simple fare here is in the £5 to £6 range. For a bit of fun, try the *Belgo Bristol (☎ 905 8000, Queen Charlotte St)*, in the Old Granary, Welsh Back, where the waiting staff turn out in Trappist monk gear. Belgian fare is the house specialty; there's a £5 lunch menu, while you should expect to pay £15 to £20 for a three-course dinner.

Over the river but just south-east of the city centre, try *Glasnost (☎ 972 0938, 1 William St, Totterdown)* for vegetarian food.

Heading north-west from the city centre, there's a stack of reasonably-priced cafes and restaurants on Park St and, a bit farther out, on Whiteladies Rd. You might try *Pastificio (☎ 949 9884, 39 Park St)* or *Vincenzo's (☎ 926 0908, 71a Park St)* for pizza; *Bella Pasta (☎ 973 8887, 96a Whiteladies Rd)* is ideal for carbo-loading and *Thai Classic (☎ 973 8930, 87 Whiteladies Rd)* is good for tasty Thai.

Day 1: Bristol to Marlborough
5–7 hours, 51.3mi

This day is cruisy and interesting at either end and has a few sections of busier road, with less to see, in the middle.

The ride begins from St Nicholas church in St Nicholas St, site of the Bristol TIC at the time of research. Ask for directions to the church at the new TIC in Anchor Rd.

The B&BRP to Bath is remarkable and, depending on the day and the weather, sometimes remarkably busy. It may be free of motor traffic, but the assortment of cyclists, walkers, runners and, of course, dogs can make for slow progress. In the early sections, especially, there are a lot of feeder paths joining the route and you need to stay alert.

Bath (16.1mi) defies superlatives – except if you're discussing the number of tourists gadding about the place in summer; it's history stretches back to Roman times and its wonderful Georgian architecture has seen it described on the World Heritage List. Outside of central London, this is about as intensely busy as it gets. The visiting hordes and maze of streets make Bath city centre a sensible place to walk the bike, and – to encourage a meandering course hereabouts – the route is intentionally not prescribed in the section between Green Park Rd and George St (roughly half a mile).

SOUTHERN ENGLAND

SOUTHERN ENGLAND

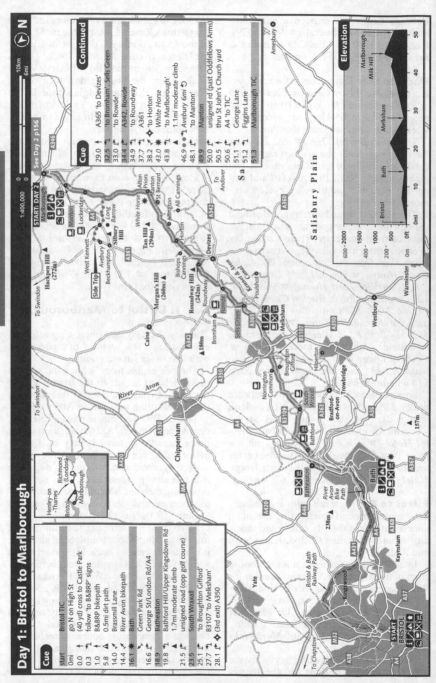

Day 1: Bristol to Marlborough

Cue

start	Bristol TIC
0mi	go N on High St
0.0 ↰	(40 yd) cross to Castle Park
0.3 ↱	follow 'to B&BRP' signs
1.0	B&BRP bikepath
5.8	0.5mi dirt path
14.0 ↱	Brassmill Lane
14.4 ↰	River Avon bikepath
16.1	Bath
16.6 ↱	Green Park Rd
17.7 ↱	George St/London Rd/A4
18.9	Batheaston
19.8 ↰	Bathford Hill/Upper Kingsdown Rd
	1.7mi moderate climb
21.5 ↱	unsigned road (opp golf course)
23.5	South Wraxall
25.1 ↰	'to Broughton Gifford'
27.7 ↱	B3107 'to Melksham'
28.1 ↰◇	(3rd exit) A350

Cue — Continued

29.0 ↰	A365 'to Devizes'
32.5 ↱	'to Bromham', Sells Green
33.0 ↰	'to Rowde'
34.4 ↱	A342, Rowde
34.9 ↱	'to Roundway'
37.7 ↰	A361
38.2 ◇↱	'to Horton'
43.0 ✳	White Horse
43.8 ↰	'to Marlborough'
	1.1mi moderate climb
46.9 ↩	Avebury 6mi ↻
48.1 ↱	'to Manton'
49.9	Manton
50.0 ↱	unsigned rd (past Oddfellows Arms)
50.5	thru St John's Church yard
50.6 ↱	A4 'to TIC'
51.1 ↱	George Lane
51.2 ↱	Figgins Lane
51.3	Marlborough TIC

Elevation

Plan ahead (Bath TIC ☎ 01225-462831), if you're serious about seeing more than a glimpse of Bath. **City Cycles** (☎ 01225-311595), 6 Monmouth Place, is in the town centre.

From around 28.1mi, near Melksham, to Horton (39.2mi), the route wanders onto A-roads and you should be careful of traffic. The remaining section across the downlands of central Wiltshire is quiet and the scenery beautiful. Look for mysterious **'crop circles'** in the fields (try to imagine how pleased the farmers are to see tourists trampling paths through perfectly good grain crops to reach the circles). Near Stanton St Bernard, you'll pass a striking **White Horse** just before commencing the climb up **Pewsey Down**. Once up, it's a pleasant roll to Marlborough.

Side Trip: Avebury
1–1½ hours, 6.0mi
A left (signposted to East Kennett and West Overton) at 46.9mi will take you towards fascinating **Avebury** and nearby **Silbury Hill** (one of the largest artificial hills in Europe built from 2500 BC) and **West Kennett Long Barrow** (a burial ground dating from 3500 BC). Along with Stonehenge, these are the best-known sites of prehistoric Britain. The Avebury TIC (☎ 01672-539425) is the place to begin inquiries. Relics from the Avebury stone circle are displayed at the **Alexander Keiller Museum** (☎ 01672-539250), named for the philanthropic marmalade magnate who bought most of Avebury to preserve its archaeological treasures.

Marlborough
☎ 01672
This former market town dates back to Saxon times. The town's name is derived from 'Merle Barrow', a mound now in the grounds of Marlborough College that was said to be the burial place of Merlin, King Arthur's legendary magician.

Information The TIC (☎ 513989) is open daily in summer and Monday to Saturday from October to March. Most of the big banks (with ATMs) and the post office are on High St.

Things to See & Do Marlborough's most striking feature is its ultra-wide **High St**, reputedly one of the widest in Europe; it's easy to imagine a bustling market day here in the days before motor vehicles. Stroll around the High St into the various lanes and alleys and you'll find some medieval timber-framed houses that survived the Marlborough 'Great Fire' of 1653. The fire is supposed to have started on the site of present-day No 8 High St. The **Merchant's House** (☎ 511291), built in 1656, contains some fine decorative work. There are several interesting churches dotted about town and some fine pubs, mostly on High St. Just outside town is **Savernake Forest**, a Site of Special Scientific Interest (SSSI) with charming woodlands and a small herd of roe and fallow deer.

Places to Stay The Forestry Commission's *Postern Hill* camping ground (☎ 515195) is a couple of miles east of town off the A4. It's open from spring to October and bookings are advised for peak times (summer weekends and school holidays).

The TIC is the best place to begin inquiries for B&Bs and hotels – there's an excellent choice. Try *Mrs Waite's* (☎ 513296; 5 Reeds Ground, London Rd) with B&B from £17. The *Fisherman's House* (☎ 515390, Mildenhall) does B&B for £30/25. The *Vines Guest House* (High St) has singles/doubles from £35/55, while its upmarket stablemate across the road, the *Ivy House Hotel* (☎ 515333, 43 High St), is £65 for a single with a to-die-for breakfast included.

Places to Eat A nice place for coffee is *Stone's of Marlborough* (Old Hughenden Yard); go to *Charlotte's Patisserie* (High St) to stock up on pastries. Both the *Sun Inn* and *Bear Inn*, at opposite ends of High St, do reasonable bar food in the £5 to £7 range. The *Merlin Hotel* (High St) and *Ivy House Hotel* (High St) have restaurants if you've some more money to spend. Try *Rajinas* behind the town hall for Indian food; most mains cost from £5 to £8 with rice and *naan* (Indian bread) under £2.

Day 2: Marlborough to Henley-on-Thames
5–6 hours, 45.2mi
After a gentle enough start surrounded by more sights, sounds and smells of rural England, this is the day that you begin to feel London's inexorable pull.

SOUTHERN ENGLAND

Day 2: Marlborough to Henley-on-Thames

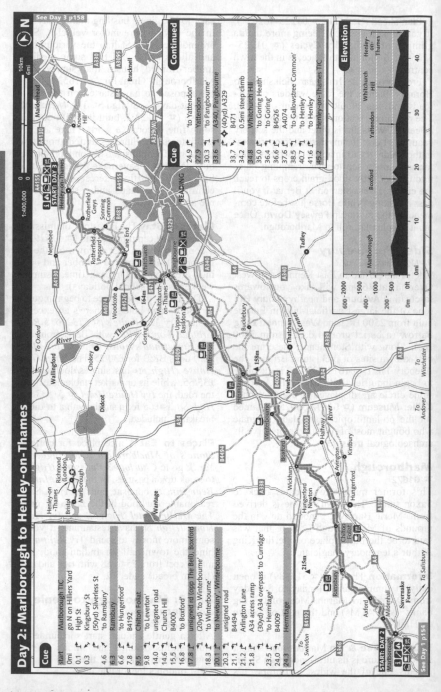

See Day 3 p158

N

1:400,000

| | 0 | 6mi |
| 0 | 10km |

See Day 3 p158

START: DAY 3
Henley-on-Thames

Maidenhead

Bracknell

A330
A3095
A404(M)
A4130
A329(M)
A4155

Knowl Hill

Rotherfield Greys
Sonning Common
Lane End
Nettlebed
Rotherfield Peppard
A4130
Woodcote
A4074
B481
Whitchurch Hill

READING

Whitchurch-on-Thames
164m
Goring
Upper Basildon
Pangbourne
A340
A4
Tadley
B471

To Oxford
Wallingford
River Thames
Cholsey
Didcot
Wantage
B4009
Yattendon
158m
Hermitage
Bucklebury
Thatcham
Newbury
Kennet
River
A339
A34
A4

To Winchester
To Andover

Boxford
Winterbourne
Halfway
Kintbury
Hungerford
Hungerford Newton
Wickham
A338
Avington
B4000
B4494

215m
Chilton Foliat
Ramsbury
B4192
Axford
Mildenhall
Savernake Forest
START: DAY 2
Marlborough
See Day 1 p154

To Swindon
To Salisbury
A346

Henley-on-Thames
Richmond (London)
Bristol
Marlborough

Cue

start	Marlborough TIC
0mi	go N on Hilliers Yard
0.1	High St
0.3	Kingsbury St
4.6	(50yd) Silverless St
6.3	'to Ramsbury'
6.6	Ramsbury
7.8	'to Hungerford'
9.5	B4192
9.8	Chilton Foliat
14.0	'to Leverton'
14.6	unsigned road
15.5	Church Hill
16.8	'to Boxford'
17.8	unsigned rd (opp The Bell), Boxford
18.3	(20yd) 'to Winterbourne'
20.1	'to Winterbourne'
20.3	'to Newbury', Winterbourne
21.1	unsigned road
21.2	B4494
21.2	Arlington Lane
21.8	A34 access ramp
	(30yd) A34 overpass 'to Curridge'
23.5	'to Hermitage'
24.0	B4009
24.3	Hermitage

Cue Continued

24.9	'to Yattendon'
27.9	Yattendon
30.3	'to Pangbourne'
33.6	A340, Pangbourne
	(40yd) A329
33.7	B471
34.2	0.5mi steep climb
34.8	Whitchurch Hill
35.0	'to Goring Heath'
36.4	'to Goring'
36.6	B4526
37.6	A4074
38.5	'to Gallowstree Common'
40.7	'to Henley'
41.6	'to Henley'
45.2	Henley-on-Thames TIC

Elevation

| 0m | 10 | 20 | 30 | 40 |
| 0mi | | | | |

Marlborough
Boxford
Yattendon
Whitchurch Hill
Henley-on-Thames

600 – 2000
400 – 1500
1000
200 – 500
0m – 0ft

For most of the morning the route winds through the rolling hills between the two great roads that lead west from the capital, the M4 and A4, but you'll only occasionally catch glimpses of these fume-oozing monstrosities. You finally cross the M4 – mercifully, on an overpass – at about 26mi. From Yattendon to Pangbourne you need to watch the navigation; it's quite a maze of minor roads and there are some tricky twists.

After crossing the River Thames at the toll bridge (bikes are free) outside Pangbourne, you face the day's only real climb, to **Whitchurch Hill** (34.2mi). It's a solid incline, but fortunately only short. Navigating becomes trickier in the following section, through Rotherfield Peppard and Rotherfield Greys. Be particularly careful on the steep uphill pinch around 40.8mi to 40.9mi; if you're heavily laden and slow it may be better to dismount and walk on the footpath on the left-hand side of the road.

By now you'll have a sense of the greater level of traffic about (Henley is only 40mi from London) and you need to be watchful on the hill into Henley. Dismount when you reach the one-way town centre road system (pull over into the car parking spaces outside The Victoria pub) and walk the last few yards to the TIC.

Henley-on-Thames
☎ 01491

Henley lies in a splendid setting alongside the River Thames; it's hard to imagine a nicer way to spend an afternoon than sitting and sipping at one of the riverside pubs. Henley's best known for its rowing regatta, a long-standing annual opportunity for grown men to wear boaters.

Information Henley TIC (☎ 578034) is downstairs in the town hall, which faces Market Place, Hart St and, in the distance, the Thames. The big banks have branches in the Market Place/Bell St/Hart St shopping area; the post office is on the corner of Bell and Hart Sts.

Things to See & Do Unless you fancy big crowds it's probably best to avoid the **Henley Royal Regatta**, which is held in the first week of July. Oddly, given that the many 'spectators' seem to pay it little attention, the rowing is keenly contested and an exciting spectacle.

At other times you can get a fix of scull and oar by visiting the **River & Rowing Museum** (☎ 415600), Mill Meadows, where the collection covers the history of Henley, the Thames and rowing. Alternatively, wander down to the river and row your own (hired) boat. Be sure to grab a pint at **The Red Lion** or **The Angel on the Bridge**, the coaching inns that face the Thames at Henley Bridge.

Places to Stay & Eat Just north of Henley, the *Swiss Farm International Camping* (☎ 573419, Marlow Rd) opens March to October; a tent pitch costs less than £10.

At *Mrs Watson's* B&B (☎ 574081, 72 Reading Rd) prices start at £18. *No 4 Riverside* (☎ 571133, 4 River Terrace) is more expensive but rooms with a river view are worth it. *Avalon* (☎ 577829, 36 Queen St) is one street back from the river and in the £20 to £25 range.

Foodwise, there's a lot to choose from on Hart St and Market Place. Try the *Henley Delicatessen* (36 Hart St) for sandwiches and the *Old Rope Walk* (22 Hart St) or *Crispins Tea Rooms* (52 Hart St) for coffee. If you favour the tried and true, there are branches of *Pizza Express* (☎ 411448, 35 Market Place), *Cafe Rouge* (☎ 411733, 37 Hart St) and *Caffe Uno* (☎ 412227, 8 Hart St). *Thai Orchid*, next to Barclays Bank, has mains mostly from £6 to £7. Around the corner, *Francesco's Cafe Bar* (☎ 573706, 8 Bell St) offers more pasta, pizza and pastries.

Day 3: Henley-on-Thames to Richmond
5–6 hours, 43.1mi

The Day 3 ride moves from pockets of what could reasonably be described as 'country', to what is inescapably city. The A321, which takes you away from Henley, can be busy, but it's followed by a longish stretch of rural and semi-rural roads. However, once the B3024 takes a right towards Windsor (13.6mi) you'll be in and out of traffic for the rest of the day.

Try to go through Windsor on a weekday. **Windsor Castle** (☎ 01753-831118) is fascinating and well worth a visit, but it's one of the most popular attractions in Britain and practically sinks under the weight of tourists on summer weekends. Just across the river, snobbish **Eton College** (☎ 671177), school of umpteen British prime ministers, is open

SOUTHERN ENGLAND

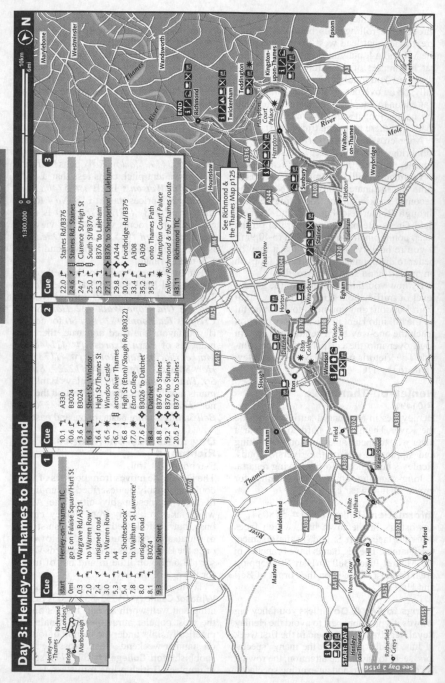

Day 3: Henley-on-Thames to Richmond

Cue 1

start	Henley-on-Thames TIC
0mi	go E on Falaise Square/Hart St
0.3	Wargrave Rd/A321
2.0	'to Warren Row'
2.4	unsigned road
3.0	'to Warren Row'
5.3	A4
5.4	'to Shottesbrook'
7.8	'to Waltham St Lawrence'
8.0	unsigned road
8.1	B3024
9.3	Paley Street

Cue 2

10.1	A330
10.6	B3024
13.6	B3024
16.3	Sheet St, Windsor
16.4	High St/Thames St
16.5	Windsor Castle
16.7	across River Thames
16.8	High St (Eton)/Slough Rd (B0322)
17.0	Eton College
17.6	B3026 to Datchet'
18.4	Datchet
18.8	B376 'to Staines'
19.2	B376 'to Staines'
20.5	B376 'to Staines'

Cue 3

22.0	Staines Rd/B376
24.6	Staines Rd, Staines
24.7	Clarence St/High St
25.0	South St/B376
25.3	B376 'to Laleham'
27.1	B376 to Shepperton', Laleham
29.8	A244
30.2	Fordbridge Rd/B375
33.4	A308
35.2	A309
35.3	onto Thames Path
	follow Richmond & the Thames route
	Hampton Court Palace
43.11	Richmond TIC

See Richmond &
the Thames Map p125

END — Richmond

START – DAY 3
Henley-on-Thames

See Day 3 p156

from Easter to the end of summer (afternoons only during school terms). It's an interesting place with several historic buildings; the seemingly endless green, green playing fields are a revelation.

From Eton the going is flat and fast and you need to be on the watch for traffic, especially through busy Staines. At **Hampton Court Palace** (☎ 020-8781 9500) you leave the road for a glorious riverside path for a few miles.

The **Guildhall** in Kingston-upon-Thames contains the resting place of the Anglo-Saxon kings' Coronation Stone. From Kingston, the route follows London Cycle Network routes or lanes past Teddington (**Teddington Lock** marks the limit of the tidal Thames) to Twickenham. From there, you hug the river on the Warren Footpath into Richmond. See the Richmond & the Thames ride in the London chapter for route detail.

Richmond (London)

Richmond is 9mi south-west of central London. See the London chapter for information about accommodation and other services.

The South-West

Duration	7 days
Distance	350.4mi
Difficulty	moderate-hard
Start	Weymouth
End	Falmouth

England's south-west is *the* place to cycle. Here you'll find lush countryside; historic towns, cities and castles; the stark heights of Bodmin Moor, Exmoor and Dartmoor (the latter two enshrined as national parks); and, particularly in Cornwall, truly enticing sandy beaches (although you may change your mind about swimming after checking the water temperature). This longer tour for fit riders features plenty of ups and downs as it follows mainly back country lanes through the counties of Dorset, Somerset, Devon and Cornwall.

HISTORY

Like much of the south, the west country contains abundant evidence of past cultures and kingdoms. Cornwall, in particular, retains a flavour of its Celtic past. Along with

tangible history, throw in a tangy dash of legend and mysticism. Glastonbury Abbey, reached on the route's second day, is said to be the burial place of King Arthur; Tintagel, off-route on Day 5, is supposedly where Arthur was born. In more recent times, Dorset has become indelibly associated with writer Thomas Hardy, who was born and died in the county and based many of his novels in it.

NATURAL HISTORY

Like most of Britain, the south-west has a long history of human settlement and has few, if any, truly 'wild' areas. The highlights in the region are Exmoor and Dartmoor National Parks. Wild ponies, horned sheep and England's last wild red deer make a living in Exmoor, which has dramatic sea cliffs to the north. Dartmoor's distinctive tors (granite outcrops) somehow give it a more isolated, bleak feel, even though its highest point, High Willhays (713m/2037ft), is just over 100m higher than Exmoor's peak, Dunkery Beacon. The limestone cliffs near Lyme Regis, on the south Dorset coast, have yielded a wealth of Jurassic-era fossils.

PLANNING
When to Ride

This is one of the warmest parts of Britain and the route can be tackled year-round, but April to June and September to November are best. In mid-summer, seaside resorts (and the roads leading to them) get particularly crowded, especially in Cornwall. In mid-winter, the higher parts of the route in Exmoor can be gloomy and disheartening in poor weather.

Maps & Books

The route is entirely covered by OS Travelmaster map No 8 (1:250,000) *South West England & South Wales*. Parts of the route follow NCN 3 and Sustrans' (1:100,000) *West Country Way* route map, which is very useful, especially for the Tarka and Camel trail sections. The OS's Cycle Tours books *Dorset, Hampshire and Isle of Wight; Avon, Somerset and Wiltshire;* and *Cornwall and Devon* (all £10) are useful for planning day rides off the route. Look in TICs for free brochures; many of them are very useful.

GETTING TO/FROM THE RIDE
Weymouth
Train Weymouth is linked by rail to Bristol, Southampton and London. All trains carry a 'limited' number of cycles except those arriving in or leaving London during peak times. The journey from London takes 2½ to three hours and the standard one-way fare is £38.50; bikes travel free.

Bicycle Weymouth is about 50mi from Lyndhurst, where the New Forest ride starts/ends.

Ferry Ferries run to Weymouth from Cherbourg in France, and also from the Channel Islands.

Falmouth
Train Trains run from Falmouth through Plymouth and Exeter to Bristol and London. Most long-distance trains from the south-west carry only two bicycles; there's a £3 reservation fee (£1 if booked at least two hours in advance). The journey to London takes 5½ to six hours and the standard one-way fare is £63.

THE RIDE
Weymouth
☎ 01305

In spite of its slightly worn appearance, Weymouth is a lively place and a pleasant starting point for a longer tour. George III's dip in Weymouth waters in 1789 sealed the town's destiny as a tourist drawcard; a somewhat cross-eyed statue of 'Farmer George' on Royal Terrace proclaims his affection in the hearts of Weymouth people.

Information The TIC (☎ 785747), on The Esplanade, takes accommodation bookings and has a bureau de change. Most banks and the main post office are on St Thomas St. Try Westham Cycles (☎ 776977), about 1mi from the seafront on the B3157, for spares and repairs; there's also a bike shop in Tilley's Auto Centre, on Frederick Place in the town centre.

Things to See & Do As in all seaside resorts, there are far worse things to do than cruise along **The Esplanade**. Watch the Punch & Judy show, tuck into some whelks and jellied eel, or hire a deck chair and veg out in the sun. Just north of town are walking trails and observation hides at the RSPB's **Lodmoor Nature Reserve** (☎ 773519). The RSPB **Radipole Lake Nature Reserve** (☎ 778313), near the train station, includes a swannery. Go west on St Thomas St and across the town bridge to explore the lovely **Old Harbour** and **Hope Square**. **Brewer's Quay** includes the **Timewalk** (☎ 777622), a 'journey' through Weymouth history; nearby **Tudor House** (☎ 812341) provides a look at Tudor living. Farther east, the Nothe Fort (☎ 787243) houses the **Museum of Coastal Defence**.

Places to Stay You'll have no trouble finding accommodation in Weymouth except in the busiest times; start by calling the accommodation bookings line (☎ 0800-765223).

Camping grounds are dotted about. *Bagwell Farm Touring Park* (☎ 782575, Chickwell) is on the route out of Weymouth; a high-season tent pitch is £10.50.

Shop around for B&Bs – there's an abundance in the £15 to £20 range. Try the *Pebbles Guest House* (☎ 784331, 18 Kirtleton Ave)* or *Oakdale Guest House* (☎ 774179, 14 Kirtleton Ave), both under £20 a night. You'll generally pay a bit more to stay in decent digs near the seafront or Old Harbour; there's a row of possibilities at the southern end of The Esplanade.

Places to Eat There's a wide choice of pubs, cafes and restaurants. *The House on Pooh Corner* (50 Mary St) does nicely for coffee and cakes; stock up on pastries at *Ye Olde Sally Lunne Bakery* (St Alban St). You're home and hosed if you like fish and chips, of which you'll get takeaways for £3 to £5. For this traditional seaside fare, try *Fish n Fritz* (9 Market St) or the *Waterfront* (14 Trinity Rd), facing the harbour. *Sorrento Restaurant Al Italia* (☎ 789406, 43 Maiden St) has pastas for £6 to £9 as well as pizzas. Try *Cafe 21* (☎ 767848, 21 East St) for vegetarian food. Pubs worth a look include *Finn M'Coul's* (☎ 778098, 26 Westham Rd) and *The Hogshead* (Frederick Place).

Day 1: Weymouth to Lyme Regis
4–5 hours, 37.6mi
Primarily a sweep through rolling Dorset farm country, this is an up-and-down day that includes some intense short climbs. The

SOUTHERN ENGLAND

Day 1: Weymouth to Lyme Regis

1:375,000

N

Cue		
start		Weymouth TIC
0mi	↑	go W on Esplanade
0.1	↑↓	King St
0.3	◊↑	Swannery Bridge/Abbotsbury Rd
1.3	↑↓	Chickerell Rd/B3157
7.3	↑	Portesham
7.5	↓	'to Hardy Monument'
	▲	0.8mi steep climb
8.7	● ↑ ↑	'Hardy Monument 1.5mi' ↻
9.1	↑	'to Littlebredy'
10.0	↑	'to Littlebredy'
10.5		Littlebredy
12.0		Long Bredy
12.1	↑	'to Litton Cheney'
13.5	↑	Litton Cheney
17.9	↑	B3157
18.1		Burton Bradstock
20.1	✳	Bridport
21.5	↑	West St
21.7	↑	Dottery Rd/B3162
23.2	↓	'to Broadoak'
24.3		Broadoak
27.5	↑	'to Marshwood'
	▲	1.5mi hard climb
29.2	↑↑	B3165, Marshwood
34.0	↑	A35
35.7		(20yd) Lyme Rd/B3165
37.4		Broad St/Church St
37.6		Lyme Regis TIC

Elevation

day begins on the sometimes busy B3157, slowly moving inland from the sweep of 10mi-long Chesil Beach and the seabird haven of Fleet Lagoon.

The day's first difficult climb, up Black Down, is a beauty: a 0.8mi rise at an average gradient of 17%. It's worth the strain. From **Hardy Monument** (side trip at 8.7mi) you'll get grand views – weather permitting – of Weymouth, the Dorset countryside, Chesil Beach and Fleet Lagoon and, of course, of the moody English Channel. The run from here to Bridport starts with the roller-coaster downhill to the village of Littlebredy and passes through charming Long Bredy and Litton Cheney.

There's evidence of Bridport's past as a rope-making centre in the town's narrow **rope walks**; the TIC (☎ 01308-424901, 32 South St) can tell you more. Consider dropping in to Wheels N' Deals Cycle Warehouse (☎ 01308-420586, 37 St Michaels Trading Estate); it's the last proper bike shop you'll pass for more than a day.

The winding lanes in Marshwood Vale, between the B3162 and B3165, lead through classic rural Dorset (remember, cowpat bespattered roads are very slippery in the wet) and the views make up for the steep climb into Marshwood village.

Lyme Regis
☎ 01297

It would take a lot to dull the appeal of this lovely seaside town, its harbour and historic stone jetty, The Cobb. There's a calm assurance about the place and its people; the streets and lanes lead steeply down to a town centre delightfully free of modern development. East and west of Lyme is heritage coastline with the limestone cliffs that yielded Britain's first dinosaur fossils.

Information The TIC (☎ 442138) is in Guildhall Cottage on Church St; it's closed Sunday from September to May. There are several banks with ATMs on Broad St; the post office (with a bureau de change) is at 37 Broad St. There's a laundrette on Lym Close.

Things to See & Do Exploring the town centre will pass many hours. Various shops, pubs and places to eat line **Broad, Bridge and Church Sts**, and there are some delightful nooks and crannies around Coombe

St and Mill Lane, where the River Lim tumbles through town to the ocean. Displays at the **Philpot Museum** (☎ 443370), on Bridge St, reveal local history and fossils. Farther up Coombe St, you'll find more fossils at **Dinosaurland** (☎ 443541). A walk along Marine Parade to **The Cobb** is essential. Wander out to the end of the serpentine, 183m-long breakwater and pretend you're Sarah from *The French Lieutenant's Woman* (the work of renowned local author John Fowles). Learn a bit about local ocean life at the **Marine Aquarium** (☎ 443678), on Lyme's compact harbour.

Places to Stay The *Uplyme Touring Park* (☎ 442801; Hook Farm, Uplyme) is the closest place to camp; a tent pitch in summer for two people is less than £10. There's a wide choice of B&Bs, guesthouses and hotels. Many are excellent value and the TIC will make bookings. A bed at *Harbour View* (☎ 443910, Cobb Rd) with views of The Cobb is a bargain at £14.50 (no breakfast). A night at *Southernhaye* (☎ 443077, Pound Rd), a bit farther out of town but also with a fine outlook, will cost £16 to £18. *Coverdale* (☎ 442882, Woodmead Rd) charges £16 to £22. For a bit more luxury, try the *Buena Vista Hotel* (☎ 442494, Pound St) at £36 to £52 a night.

Places to Eat With great views of Lyme Bay, *Bell Cliff* (5–6 Broad St) is nice for morning or afternoon coffee; and *Village Bakery (Pitt House, Broad St)* has good coffee and pastries. *Cafe Sol* (☎ 443404, 1a Coombe St) does continental breakfasts for £1.95.

It's nice to have dinner near The Cobb; try either the *Cobb Arms* or *Royal Standard* for pub food, or the *Polly Victoria* restaurant, with mains in the £7 to £9.50 range; all three are on Marine Parade. In the town centre, the *Pilot Boat*, *Volunteer Inn* and *Royal Lion* pubs all do decent food. *Antonio Trattoria* (☎ 442352, 7 Church St) has pastas for around £6, while the *Millside Coffee Shop & Wine Bar (Mill Lane)* is the place to blow some money on good wines and food.

Day 2: Lyme Regis to Glastonbury
4–5 hours, 39.8mi
There is some solid up-hill-and-down-dale action to open the day. The climb out of

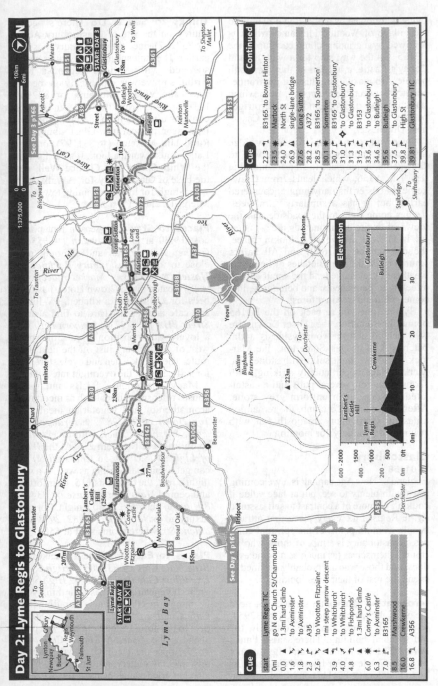

Day 2: Lyme Regis to Glastonbury

1:375,000

Cue		
start	Lyme Regis TIC	
0mi	go N on Church St/Charmouth Rd	
0.0	1.3mi hard climb	◄
1.6	'to Axminster'	⤙
1.8	'to Axminster'	⤛
2.3	A35	⤙
2.6	'to Wootton Fitzpaine'	◄
3.9	1mi steep narrow descent	⤛
4.0	'to Whitchurch'	⤙
4.8	'to Whitchurch'	⤛
6.0	'to Fishponds'	⤙
6.3	Coney's Castle	✳
7.0	1.3mi hard climb	⤙
8.5	'to Axminster'	
	B3165	
16.8	Marshwood	⤙
	Crewkerne	
	A356	

Cue		Continued
22.3	B3165 'to Bower Hinton'	
23.5	Martock	✳
24.0	North St	
26.9	single-lane bridge	⚠
27.6	Long Sutton	
28.2	A372	
28.5	B3165 'to Somerton'	⤙
30.1	Somerton	
30.7	B3165 'to Glastonbury'	⤛
31.0	'to Glastonbury'	⤙
31.3	'to Glastonbury'	⤛
31.5	B3153	
33.6	'to Glastonbury'	⤙
34.6	'to Butleigh'	⤛
35.6	Butleigh	
37.5	'to Glastonbury'	⤙
39.8	High St	⤛
39.81	Glastonbury TIC	

Elevation

SOUTHERN ENGLAND

Lyme is followed by a plunging downhill to the village of Wootton Fitzpaine, which is followed by a grinding climb back up to the B3165. On the way, stop for a walk around **Coney's Castle**, a hill fort of the Dumnonii people. Around 500 BC, this was the frontier country between the Dumnonii, from which 'Devon' was derived, and the Durotriges people, who were based at Maiden Castle, near Dorchester.

Once you're on the B3165, follow ridge tops, rising and descending all the way to **Crewkerne**, a fair place to stop for morning tea. The A356, which leads from Crewkerne, is busier than anything encountered earlier but it has a similarly rural feel; hedges come right to the roadside and the views of encircling farmlands are wonderful. In Martock, a solid, stony looking place, the **old school** (c. 1660) and **All Saints Church** catch the eye. Blotches of lichen on weathered grey stone lend the small church a feeling of permanence and belonging, like some grand old tree in a forest.

By the time you're back on the B3165 bound for Somerton, the Dorset Downs are well behind and the countryside is a flat patchwork of hedges. Somerton, like Martock, is a town built solid with stone. The **Market Place** is particularly striking, with shops, a church, several pubs and a castellated rotunda all in uniform grey stone. After a descent and a climb, the remaining miles into Glastonbury are mostly flat, with striking **Glastonbury Tor** looming.

Glastonbury
☎ 01458

England's 'New Age capital' is a welcoming town with plenty to see, but at face value it couldn't be more of a contrast to self-assured Lyme Regis. Like every place that attracts people from all points of the spiritual compass, Glastonbury is a mix of those who've 'found' themselves (as much as anyone ever does) and those who are probably destined to spend the rest of their lives looking.

Information Many of the services you need are on High St, including the TIC (☎ 832954, ⓔ glastonbury.tic@ukonline.co.uk) in the old tribunal building. There's also banks (with ATMs), a laundrette and the Internet (at Cafe Galatea). For bike bits and repairs go to Pedalers (☎ 831117) on Magdalene St.

Things to See & Do There's been a church on the site of **Glastonbury Abbey** (☎ 832267) since the 7th century, possibly earlier. The atmospheric abbey ruins are associated with various legends; King Arthur's grave was supposedly on the site. The **Lake Village Museum** (☎ 832949; EH), upstairs from the TIC on High St, contains artefacts from the prehistoric village near present-day Glastonbury. The **Rural Life Museum** (☎ 831197), on Bere Lane, is also worth a look. It's not far from the **White Spring** and **Chalice Well**, near the base of **Glastonbury Tor**. A walk up the 160m-high Tor to the remaining tower of St Michael's church is a must.

Places to Stay High-season tent pitches cost £9.60 at *Isle of Avalon* (☎ *833618, Godney Rd)* caravan and camping park, close to town. *Glastonbury Backpackers Hostel* (☎ *833353, 4 Market Place)*, centrally located in the Crown Hotel, has dorm beds for £10; there's a kitchen, TV lounge and cafe and it's not hard to find a drink. *Street YHA* (☎ *442738, Ivythorn Hill)* is in a lovely, quiet position about 3mi southwest of Glastonbury just off the next day's route. There's a kitchen and cycle storeroom for self-caterers; the overnight rate is £8.35.

Many Glastonbury B&Bs and guesthouses offer specialities such as meditation, aromatherapy and vegetarian meals. Try *Tor Down* (☎ *832287,* ⓔ *torangel@aol .com, 5 Ashwell Lane)*, with lovely views south from the Tor, from £15. At the *Wheel of Light* (☎ *831970, 56 Chilkwell St)* you can get a spiritual reading as well as a good night's rest; the bed costs £15. Comfortable and central *Hangman's House* (☎ *834163, 8 High St)* charges £17.50 a night. For more luxury go to *No 3 Hotel* (☎ *832129, 3 Magdalene St)*, where rooms start at £50.

Places to Eat For coffee and cakes, the *Blue Note Cafe* (☎ *832907, 4 High St)* and *Excalibur Cafe* (☎ *834521, 52 High St)* are great. If vegetarian food is your thing you'll be happy in Glastonbury. For dinner try *Cafe Galatea* (☎ *834284, 5A High St)*; expect to pay from £6 for a main. If you phone ahead to the *Assembly Rooms Cafe* (☎ *83 4677)*, opposite the TIC, it will cater for any special dietary requirements. You'll also get good-value meals at the *Mitre Inn*

(☎ 831203, 27 Benedict St) and the **Rifle-man's Arms** (☎ 831023, 4 Chilkwell St).

Day 3: Glastonbury to Lynton & Lynmouth
6–8 hours, 60.4mi
This big day starts in traffic on the A39 and A361, which is fortunately soon behind you. After this comes an interlude on the strange, almost eerie Somerset moorlands. The low-lying farmlands here are sometimes divided by canals, not hedges; if you're cycling through here on a wet day it feel's like the entire precinct is about to go under.

Getting through Bridgwater can be a bit of a trial, but by once you reach the big round-abouts near Cannington the worst is past. You'll have pedalled towards the **Quantock Hills** throughout the morning. At about the 22mi mark, veer off the A39 and shortly after climb up the hills' steep eastern face to **Dead Woman's Ditch** (25.3mi). The Quantocks' shallow acid soils and the practice of swaling (burning off heather to encourage green shoots for livestock feed) discourages forest growth, so the hills have a stark appearance.

The next 10mi are very up and down and care is needed on some steep descents. **Cleeve Abbey** (35mi) contains some inter-esting relics, including 13th-century pave-ment tiles. It was founded in the 12th century and dissolved in 1536. There are good views of **Dunster** from the route; pretty Dunster village is just off the route and a nice place for a tea stop. Beautiful vil-lages feature farther on, too. **Selworthy** is a 2mi side trip and well worth a visit. Farther on, the route leaves the A39 at **Allerford** and winds into **Porlock**, both charming villages.

The longest climb of the day – and the chapter – follows: the 4.3mi spin up the toll road through **Porlock Manor Estate**. It's a gradual climb through woodland groves and fields with stunning views most of the way; definitely a highlight. The return to the A39 brings some more traffic but the stretch into Lynmouth is fast and the outlook – the Bris-tol Channel and Wales to the north and Ex-moor's stark plateaus and plunging valleys to the south – is engrossing. The day ends with the screaming ride down **Countisbury Hill** into Lynmouth; road signs suggest you consider walking and the soaring cliffs to the right certainly give cause to keep a firm grip on the brakes.

Lynton & Lynmouth
☎ 01598
Only the particularly hard-hearted would find nothing to like about the twin villages of Lynmouth, at the mouth of the River West Lyn, and Lynton, perched about 210m above. It's the perfect place to stop to ex-plore the Exmoor coastline on foot for a few days.

Information Day 3 ends at the Exmoor National Park TIC (☎ 752509) on the seafront at Lynmouth; this is the place for walks information. Lynton TIC is up the hill, in the Town Hall on Lee Rd. There's no bike shop; banks with ATMs and the post office are on Lee Rd.

Things to See & Do To save your legs and savour the view, make sure you travel between Lynton and Lynmouth on the **cliff railway**, an ingenious piece of 19th-century engineering that relies on the cost-effective forces of water and gravity for energy. The 2mi walk along the riverside trail to **Watersmeet** is a must; take tea, coffee or snacks at the trail's end under spreading trees around the NT tea rooms. Near Lyn-mouth, the rebuilt river banks are evidence of the tragic 1952 flood that claimed 34 lives and destroyed nearly 100 houses; learn more about the disaster at the **Lyn & Exmoor Museum** (☎ 752317), on Lynton's Market St.

Places to Stay Camp at the *Channel View Caravan Park* (☎ 753349; *Manor Farm, Barbrook*), a couple of miles from Lynton; it's open from Easter to October with tent pitches from £7 to £8.50. The wonderful *Lynton YHA* (☎ 753237) is about 1mi out of town in Lynbridge (turn off Lynbridge Rd at Ye Olde Cottage inn). The 34-bed hostel has a cycle storeroom, laundry and serves breakfast and dinner; the nightly charge is £9.15.

To avoid riding (or pushing) up the hill upon arrival, try *Oakleigh* (☎ 752220; *4 Tors Rd, Lynmouth*) for B&B at £19 a night. Up the hill in Lynton, there's *The Retreat* (☎ 753526; *1 Park Gardens, Lydiate Lane*), charging £15, and *South View* (☎ 752289, 23 Lee Rd) charging £15 to £19. For more creature comforts try the *Lynton Cottage Hotel* (☎ 752342, North Walk), with B&B from £41 to £75.

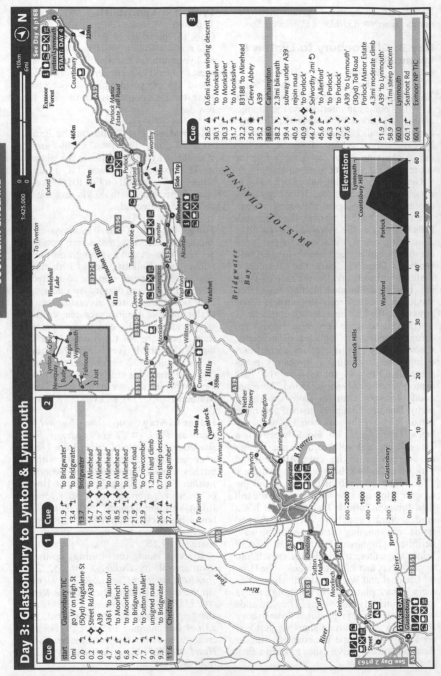

Day 3: Glastonbury to Lynton & Lynmouth

1

Cue		
start		Glastonbury TIC
0mi		go W on High St
0.0	⌐	(50yd) Magdalene St
0.2	⌐	Street Rd/A39
0.8	◇	A39
4.7	⌐	A361 'to Taunton'
6.6	⌐	'to Moorlinch'
6.8	⌐	'to Moorlinch'
7.4	⌐	'to Bridgwater'
7.7	⌐	'to Sutton Mallet'
9.0		unsigned road
9.3	⌐	'to Bridgwater'
11.6		Chedzoy

2

Cue		
11.9	⌐	'to Bridgwater'
13.4	⌐	'to Bridgwater'
13.7		Bridgwater
14.7	◇	'to Minehead'
15.7	◇	'to Minehead'
16.4	◇	'to Minehead'
18.5	⌐	'to Minehead'
19.2	⌐	'to Minehead'
21.9	⌐	unsigned road
23.9	⌐	'to Crowcombe'
		1.2mi hard climb
26.4	◀	0.7mi steep descent
27.1	⌐	'to Stogumber'

3

Cue		
28.5	◀	0.6mi steep winding descent
30.1	⌐	'to Monksilver'
30.3	⌐	'to Monksilver'
31.7	⌐	'to Monksilver'
32.2	⌐	B3188 'to Minehead'
35.0	✳	Cleeve Abbey
35.2	⌐	A39
38.0		Carhampton
38.2		2.3mi bikepath
39.4		subway under A39
40.5	⌐	rejoin road
40.9	⌐	'to Porlock'
44.7	↻	Selworthy 2mi
45.6	⌐	'to Allerford'
46.3	⌐	'to Porlock'
47.2	⌐	'to Porlock'
47.6	⌐	A39 'to Lynmouth'
		(30yd) Toll Road
		Porlock Manor Estate
		4.3mi moderate climb
51.9	⌐	A39 'to Lynmouth'
58.9	◀	1.1mi steep descent
60.0		Lynmouth
60.1	⌐	Seafront Rd
60.4		Exmoor NP TIC

See Day 4 p168
See Day 2 p163

Places to Eat You're spoiled for choice in Lynton and Lynmouth, both have a staggering number of restaurants and tea rooms. Collect your daily bread at *Greenhouse Bakery (Lee Rd, Lynton)*; try *Lovejoys Tea Rooms (Lee Rd, Lynton)* for morning or afternoon tea or coffee. Most of the pubs serve food, although it's hard to go past *The Rising Sun (☎ 753223; Harbourside, Lynmouth)*, facing the ocean, for dinner. The *Greenhouse Restaurant (Lee Rd, Lynton)* and *Upstairs Downstairs (☎ 752484; 9 Watersmeet Rd, Lynmouth)* both have interesting menus.

Day 4: Lynton & Lynmouth to Bude

6–8 hours, 60.8mi

Morning traffic and some steady climbs persist only as far as Blackmoor Gate, where you return to quiet lanes for the run to the village of Loxhore. The last section into Loxhore features a narrow, twisting downhill where care is needed. From here, the road runs near the lovely River Yeo for much of the way into Barnstaple.

A largish and lively place, **Barnstaple** has some decent bike shops if you're in need of repairs; Cyril Webber (☎ 01271-343277), on Bear St, and the Bike Shed (☎ 01271-328628), on The Square, are both close to the route. The somewhat fiddly navigating to get through Barnstaple is rewarded when you join the **Tarka Trail** (19.6mi) – for the next 18mi the going is traffic-free and mostly flat, with wonderful views over the Rivers Taw and Torridge. The trail surface is mostly dirt or fine gravel but it's well kept and presents no problem for touring bikes. As tempting as it is to really wind up some speed, remember that walkers have right of way on the trail. The **Bideford Tarka Trail Centre** (28.9mi), at the old Bideford train station, is a great place to stop for information and refreshments.

The day's last third will take you from Devon into Cornwall. The roads are mostly very quiet (with the exception of a short section on the A388 around the 48mi mark) although navigating is confusing at times. You'll certainly learn (if you didn't already know) that back-road cycling in this part of England provides an interconnected series of climbs and descents. You'll also notice that the road surfaces are generally in a poorer state as you get farther west (al-

though there are none so terrible that they must be avoided).

After the tricky descent into Stratton, there's a short climb and a few more turns before a sweeping downhill into Bude.

Bude

☎ 01288

One of Cornwall's seemingly innumerable coastal resort towns, Bude has pleasant beaches and a relaxed family air, especially on Summerleaze Beach, the sandpatch nearest town. It's also very popular with surfers, lending the pubs quite a groovy-tanned-and-tattoos feeling.

Information The TIC (☎ 354240, @ bude.tic@ukonline.co.uk, ☐ www.bude.co.uk) is on the Crescent, facing the car park. The town (and region) is well organised to cater for cyclists riding the NCN West Country Way route – there's even a specific email address (@ cycle@bude.co.uk) for inquiries. You'll finds banks with ATMs in the town centre on Landsdown Rd and Belle Vue. The post office is on Belle Vue and there's a laundrette at 2 Bramble Hill. For spares and repairs go to Tracks (☎ 356689, 20 Queen St).

Things to See & Do A stroll out to the headland overlooking **Summerleaze Beach** is a great way to unwind after the day's ride; in mid-summer, it's not unusual to see surfers in the water well after 9 pm. The **Bude-Stratton Museum** (☎ 353576) is on Lower Wharf. Its exhibits cover local history, particularly the Bude Canal and shipwrecks along this stretch of coast. The **Bude Canal** runs through town to the harbour; it was built in 1823 to transport sand from the coast to farmlands and its unusual sea lock is still used.

Places to Stay The *Upper Lynstone Camping & Caravan Park (☎ 352017, Lynstone Rd)* is on the Day 5 route just south of town; it's open from Easter to September and tent pitches cost £7 to £10.50. For B&B try *Hampton Villa (☎ 352665, 65 Valley Rd)* or *Laundry Cottage (☎ 353560, Higher Wharf)*, both charge £16; *Clovelly House (☎ 352761, Burn View)* charges from £21 (packed lunches available from £2.50). Prices start at £22 at the *Meva-Gwin Hotel (☎ 352347, Upton)*, just outside town on the Day 5 route.

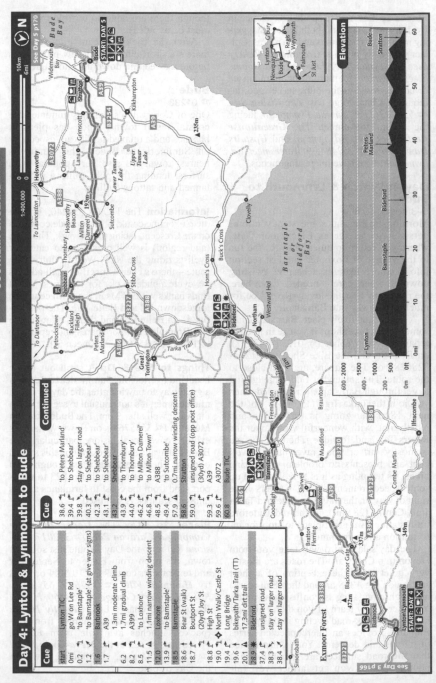

See Day 5 p170

Day 4: Lynton & Lynmouth to Bude

Cue

start		Lynton TIC
0mi	↰ ↱	go W on Lee Rd
0.2	↱	'to Barnstaple'
1.2	↱	'to Barnstaple' (at give way signs)
1.6		Barbrook
1.7	◀ ↰	A39
		1.3mi moderate climb
6.2	◀ ↱	A399
		1.7mi gradual climb
8.2	↰	A399
8.5	↱	'to Loxhore'
		1.1mi narrow winding descent
11.5	↱	'to Loxhore'
12.0		Loxhore
13.9	↰	'to Barnstaple'
18.5		Barnstaple
18.6	↱	Bear St (walk)
18.7	↰	Boutport St
18.8	↱	(20yd) Joy St
18.9		High St
19.0	↰	North Walk/Castle St
19.4	◈	Long Bridge
19.6		bikepath/Tarka Trail (TT)
20.1	▲	17.3mi dirt trail
28.9	✳	Bideford
37.4	↱	unsigned road
38.3	↰	stay on larger road
38.4	↱	stay on larger road

Cue **Continued**

38.6	↰	'to Peters Marland'
39.4	↱	'to Shebbear'
39.8		stay on larger road
40.3	↰	'to Shebbear'
42.3	↱	'to Shebbear'
43.1	↰	'to Shebbear'
43.2		Shebbear
43.9	↰	'to Thornbury'
44.0	↱	'to Thornbury'
46.2	↰	'to Milton Damerel'
46.8	↱	'to Milton Town'
48.5		A388
49.4	↰	'to Sutcombe'
57.9	▲	0.7mi narrow winding descent
58.6		Stratton
59.0	↰	unsigned road (opp post office) (30yd) A3072
59.3	↰	A39
59.6	↱	A3072
60.8		Bude TIC

Elevation

600 - 2000	
400 - 1500	
1000	
200 - 500	
0m - 0ft	
	0mi 10 20 30 40 50 60

Lynton · Barnstaple · Bideford · Peters Marland · Stratton · Bude

See Day 3 p166

SOUTHERN ENGLAND

Places to Eat You'll find 80p cappuccinos at *The Coffee Shop (32 Landsdown Rd)*. The *Bakery (12 Queen St)* is also good for hot bevvies – it's one of several decent bakeries in town; the *Landsdowne bakery (Landsdown Rd)* is also worth a look.

There are several pubs where you can grab a meal; the *Bencoolen Inn (☎ 354694, Bencoolen Rd)* has meals in the £5 to £6 range and a cruisy family atmosphere, while the *Carriers Inn (☎ 352459, The Strand)* seems popular with the surfing set. Seafood is the flavour at the *Villa Restaurant (☎ 354799, 16 The Strand)*, while *Boater's (Belle Vue)* has a pasta of the day at £8 to £10. *Belinda's (Princes St)* has a £3.45 vegetarian breakfast and a decent dinner menu.

The Padstow 'Obby 'Orse

Every year on 1 May the residents of Padstow re-enact a curious ritual with its origins in medieval fertility rites. A man dressed up as a horse in a tent-like costume parades through town preceded by a masked 'teaser'. Women are occasionally dragged under the horse costume and pinched. Eventually the 'obby 'orse is ritually killed, only to spring to life again the next year – a reminder of days when the village leader may have been killed and his blood sprinkled on the ground to ensure fertility for another year.

Day 5: Bude to Newquay
6–8 hours, 60.9mi

This tour's longest day (by a whisker) includes some fascinatingly steep – although fortunately short – climbs and descents, magnificent coastal and rural scenery and another extended stretch on a traffic-free path.

The best of the hills keep your eyes on the road during the first six miles out of Bude. The sandy beaches and craggy cliffs along here are stunning but you'll work hard for the view; gradients near Millook reach 30%, unrideable uphill and requiring extreme caution on descents (you may want to dismount for some downhills). Thankfully, things level out approaching Wainhouse Corner, and the hills around interesting **Boscastle** are long and gradual rather than plunging and rearing.

About 5mi past Boscastle, the **British Cycling Museum** (☎ 01840-212811) has more than 400 bikes as well as books and exhibits covering cycling since the early 19th century; it's open Sunday to Thursday year-round.

The first section of the **Camel Trail**, from 32.3mi to 40.4mi, is a bit rougher under the tyres than the Tarka Trail, but is still quite manageable on a touring bike. Through Dunmere Wood the trail hugs the River Camel and the shady outlook with burbling water nearby is particularly pleasant. There's a bit of traffic to contend with through Wadebridge but the cycle lanes are well signposted and navigation isn't a problem. The final miles on the trail to Padstow feature magnificent views across the wide, tidal part of the River Camel.

The day's last section is classic up-and-down Cornwall coastal terrain and the final few hills are tiresome, but again the views are a good distraction.

Newquay
☎ 01637

Brash? Crass? It's hard to know how to describe Newquay, Britain's surfing capital. Its strength is lovely beaches and the fact that, like most resort towns, it has plenty of places to stay and eat. The downside is its apparent lack of soul; it's as if the entire place (including, sadly, the young people that flock here to surf and work) is being slowly sucked into a vortex of consumerist idiocy.

Information The TIC (☎ 871345) is on Marcus Hill; it makes accommodation bookings. All the big banks (with ATMs) are represented in the Bank and East Sts area; the main post office is on East St. Cycle Xtreme (☎ 874888, 3a Beachfield Ave) is centrally located.

Things to See & Do There's a lot of touristy stuff and not a whole lot of substance (especially if you don't like surfing or golf of any sort). North of Towan Beach, the Huer's House was once the lookout for the local pilchard fishing fleet – someone literally watched the water for signs of pilchard schools. East of town near Porth Beach you'll find **Trevelgue Cliff Castle**, a Bronze age site including two burial mounds. Among Newquay's pay-for-pleasures are several pitch-and-putt golf courses, a waterslide park and a miniature railway. If

SOUTHERN ENGLAND

Day 5: Bude to Newquay

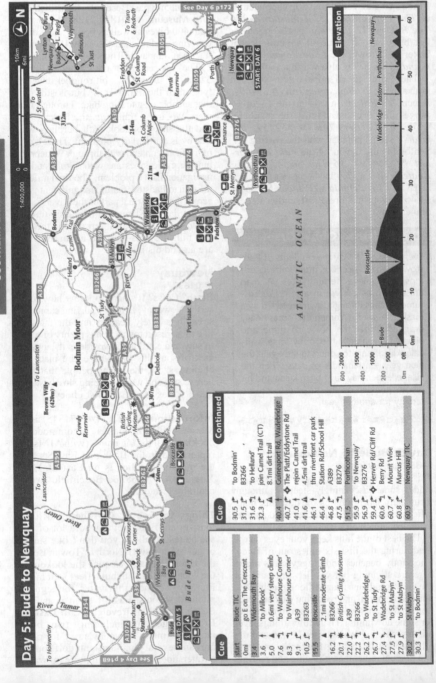

Cue		
start		Bude TIC
0mi	↰	go E on The Crescent
3.4		Widemouth Bay
3.6	↑	'to Milook'
5.0	◀	0.6mi very steep climb
7.6	↰	'to Wainhouse Corner'
8.3	↰	'to Wainhouse Corner'
9.1	↰	A39
10.5	↰	B3263
15.5		2.1mi moderate climb
	◀	Boscastle
16.2	↰	B3266
20.1	✳	British Cycling Museum
22.0	↰	A39
22.2	↰	B3266
26.2	↰	'to Wadebridge'
26.7	↘	'to St Tudy'
27.4	↘	Wadebridge Rd
27.5	↰	'to St Mabyn'
27.9	↰	'to St Mabyn'
30.2		St Mabyn
30.3	↰	'to Bodmin'

Cue		Continued
30.5	↰	'to Bodmin'
31.5	↰	B3266
31.6	↰	'to Helland'
32.3	↰	join Camel Trail (CT)
		8.1mi dirt trail
40.4		Guineaport Rd, Wadebridge
40.7	↰◆	The Platt/Eddystone Rd
41.0		rejoin Camel Trail
41.6	◀	4.5mi dirt trail
46.1	↑	thru riverfront car park
46.4	↘	Station Rd/School Hill
46.8	↰	A389
47.5	↰	B3276
51.5		Porthcothan
55.9	↰	'to Newquay'
56.9	↰	B3276
59.4	↰◆	Henver Rd/Cliff Rd
60.6	↘	Berry Rd
60.7	↘	Mount Wise
60.8	↰	Marcus Hill
60.9		Newquay TIC

When did Cornish Die?

A Celtic language akin to Welsh, Cornish was spoken west of the River Tamar until the 19th century. Written evidence indicates it was still widely spoken at the time of the Reformation, but was suppressed after a Cornish rising against the English in 1548. By the 17th century only a few people living in the peninsula's remote western reaches still spoke nothing but Cornish.

Towards the end of the 18th century linguistic scholars foresaw the death of Cornish and fanned out around the peninsula in search of people who still spoke it. One such scholar, Daines Barrington, visited Mousehole in 1768 and recorded an elderly woman named Dolly Pentreath abusing him in Cornish for presuming she couldn't speak her own language.

Dolly died in 1769 and has gone down in history as the last native speaker of Cornish. However, Barrington knew of other people who continued to speak it into the 1790s, and an 1891 tombstone in Zennor commemorates one John Davey as 'the last to possess any traditional considerable knowledge of the Cornish language'.

Recently efforts have been made to revive the language. Unfortunately there are now three conflicting varieties of 'Cornish' – Unified, Phonemic and Traditional – and no sign that it can regain its former importance.

---

you can surf or are at least interested in giving it a whirl, most of the surf shops in town rent boards and wetsuits.

Places to Stay There are several camping grounds in the area. *Newquay Holiday Park* (☎ 871111, @ enquiries@newquay-hol-park .demon.co.uk) is about 2mi from town off the A3059. It's open from May to September; tent pitches cost £7.25 to £12.35. Of the several independent hostels dotted about town, *Newquay International Backpackers* (☎ 879366, 🖥 www.backpackers.co.uk, 69– 73 Tower Rd) is probably the best for cyclists; the nightly tariff is £6 to £10.

The sheer volume of B&Bs and price variation depending on the season makes recommendations just about pointless; the

TIC is the place to begin inquiries; bookings are essential in July and August. *Alicia* (☎ 874328, 136 Henver Rd) does B&B from £14. The *White House Hotel* (☎ 87 3030, Headland Rd) is in a great spot overlooking Fistral Beach; B&B is £18 to £23 (with dinner £23.50 to £29). The *Windsor Hotel* (☎ 875188, Mount Wise) is set farther back from the ocean but closer to shops and restaurants; you'll pay £16.50 to £34 for B&B. Right in the centre of town, the *Hotel Victoria* (☎ 872255, East St) offers dinner, bed and breakfast from £30 to £70, depending on the season.

Places to Eat With such a wide choice it's best to hit the street and check menus and prices as you go. Get pastries from the *Leslie Nile Bakery* (Bank St). There are plenty of *fish and chip* joints around, while *Oasis American Bar & Diner* (☎ 851426, 24 Fore St) stays open late and is good for burgers and fries. The *Maharajah* (☎ 877 377 39 Cliff Rd) and *Rani's Balti & Tandoori Indian Restaurant* (☎ 850666, 49 Fore St) both do takeaways and have good ranges of vegetarian dishes. Try the *Mexican Cantina* (☎ 851700, 38 Cliff Rd) or nearby *Senõr Dick's* (☎ 851601, East St) for Mexican. The *Upper Deck* restaurant (☎ 851426, 26 Fore St) has great ocean views and a fair selection of meals.

Day 6: Newquay to St Just
5–7 hours, 47.5mi

This (mercifully) shorter day features some striking coastal terrain, especially past St Ives on the stretch towards St Just and Land's End. It's another day with quite a few climbs and descents – fortunately, none as steep as those encountered out of Bude.

The A3075 out of Newquay can be busy with traffic, but you're soon off it and following back roads to Perranporth, which you enter after a pacey downhill, and exit climbing. There is some tricky navigation after you turn off the B3285, with a particularly high number of unsigned roads. After Mawla there's a pleasant flat stretch of around 3mi on the old **Portreath Tramroad**. Built in the early 19th century, this tram ran between Portreath Harbour and copper mines inland.

After the climb out of Portreath the ocean and cliff views are spectacular, especially from lookouts around the 22.5mi

SOUTHERN ENGLAND

SOUTHERN ENGLAND

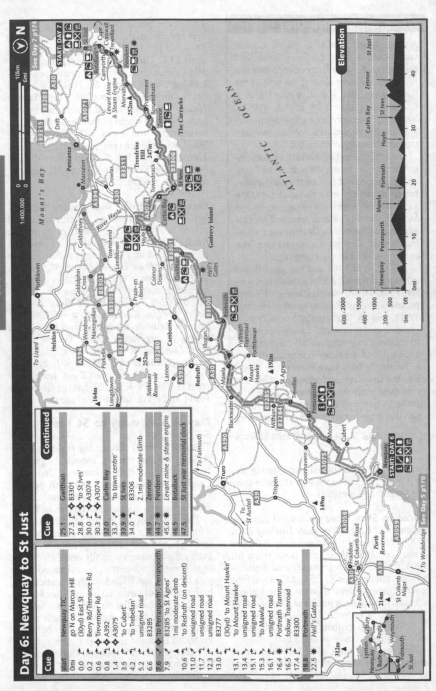

Day 6: Newquay to St Just

Cue

start		Newquay TIC
0mi		go N on Marcus Hill
0.0	↰	(30yd) East St
0.2	↱	Berry Rd/Trenance Rd
0.6	↱	Trevemper Rd
0.8	↱	A392
1.4	↱	A3075
3.5	↰	'to Cubert'
4.2	↰	'to Trebellan'
5.2	↱	unsigned road
6.6	↱	B3285
7.6	↗	'to Perranporth' Perranporth
7.9	↖	B3285 'to St Agnes'
		1mi moderate climb
10.6	↰	'to Redruth' (on descent)
11.0	↱	unsigned road
11.7	↰	unsigned road
12.3	↱	unsigned road
13.0	↱	B3277
		(30yd) 'to Mount Hawke'
13.1	↰	'to Mount Hawke'
13.4	↱	unsigned road
15.1	↱	unsigned road
15.3	↘	'to Mawla'
16.1	↱	unsigned road
16.4	✳	Portreath Tramroad
16.5	↰	follow Tramroad
17.4	↱	B3300
		Portreath
18.8	✳	Hell's Gates
22.5	✳	

Cue — Continued

25.1		Gwithian
27.3	↰◇	B3301
28.8	↱◇	'to St Ives'
30.0	↰◇	A3074
30.3	↱◇	A3074
32.0		Carbis Bay
33.7	↱	'to town centre'
33.9	✳	St Ives
34.0	◀	B3306
		2.1mi moderate climb
38.9		Pendeen
44.7	✳	Zennor
45.6	✳	Levant mine & steam engine
46.5		Botallack
47.5		St Just war memorial clock

mark, from which you'll see the craggy coastal formations known as **Hell's Gates**. A few miles farther down the road, Hayle Cycles (☎ 01736- 753825), on Penpol Terrace in Hayle, is the last bike shop for quite a few miles.

Beautiful St Ives (33.9mi) is the day's highlight town. If you're short of time, taking in the view of the town centre and harbour from **Malakoff Gardens** will suffice, but if possible, take a break and visit the wonderful **St Ives Tate Gallery** (☎ 01736- 796226), which overlooks Porthmeor Beach.

The day's longest hill – the 2.1mi grind out of St Ives on the B3306 – follows, rewarded by stunning views north-east across St Ives Bay. The next section is a joy, winding along the coastal hills and passing through several isolated settlements including **Zennor**, where DH Lawrence wrote part of *Women in Love*.

The **Geevor Tin Mine** (☎ 788662; NT) in Pendeen closed in 1990 but preserves the region's mining past; it's open daily in July and August, closed Saturday at other times between March and October. The nearby **Levant Beam Engine** (☎ 786156; NT), Cornwall's oldest steam beam engine, has been restored to working order.

Although the day 'officially' ends at St Just, there's accommodation spread from here to Sennen, an easy 4mi ride south and the nearest village to Land's End.

St Just
☎ 01736

Inland from Cape Cornwall, isolated St Just-in-Penwith is a friendly village, the community of artists and writers hereabouts lending the place a pleasant, easy-going air.

There's a tourist noticeboard near the St Just war memorial clock but no TIC. The nearest bike shops are in Hayle (Day 6) and Penzance (Day 7), so plan ahead if you're having problems.

In Cornwall's days as a wealthy mining county, St Just was a centre for tin and copper mining. The isolated 19th-century mine chimney and fishing cove at **Cape Cornwall** is evocative and worth a look. Consider planning ahead so you can take in a performance at the **Minack Theatre** (see Side Trip on Day 7), which is about 3mi from Land's End.

Places to Stay & Eat St Just and the surrounding villages provide accommodation for visitors to Land's End, and places to stay are strung out from St Just to Sennen.

Pitch a tent for £6 at *Kelynack Caravan & Camping Park* (☎ 787633), just off the B3306, about 1mi south of St Just; there's also a bunk barn with beds at the same price. *Land's End (St Just) YHA* (☎ 788437) is nearby and has the advantage of serving dinner; the 43-bed hostel has a cycle storeroom and charges £9.15 a night. *Whitesands Lodge* (☎ 871776, Sennen), on the A30 on the town's outskirts, is a quality independent hostel with a bar and restaurant (excellent food); a dorm bed with breakfast costs £14 while B&B in a standard room is £18.50.

Cyclists are welcome at the *Sunnybank Hotel* (☎ 871278; Seaview Hill, Sennen), where B&B costs £15 per person. Also in Sennen, the *Old Manor Hotel* (☎ 871280) charges £18 for singles.

To really celebrate reaching Land's End, the *Land's End Hotel* (☎ 871844) is right on the spot, with very comfortable rooms (many with ocean views) and fine food; about £50 is the least you'll pay.

There's a small supermarket and a few pubs and cafes in St Just, and Sennen has a convenience store and the *First and Last Inn*. But it's wise in this part of Britain to consider accommodation in a place that can also provide dinner.

Day 7: St Just to Falmouth
5–6 hours, 43.4mi

After all the hard work, this day is a simple spin around Cornwall's – and England's – extreme south-west. There's no major traffic worries, no big hills and plenty of time to take in some lovely sights.

Land's End is the day's best-known waypoint, and one that fails to live up to its wild, end-of-island reputation. The *Land's End Hotel* and a theme park (☎ 01736-871501) sully the cliff above an otherwise rugged coast; even the famed signpost (6.2mi) is a let-down, with the resident photographic concession extracting £5 for a picture.

The section from Land's End to Penzance is more pleasant, the roads are generally quiet and the views of rural West Cornwall are refreshing. At 9.2mi detour right to visit Minack Theatre (see Side Trip). There are several prehistoric sites hereabouts; one, the

SOUTHERN ENGLAND

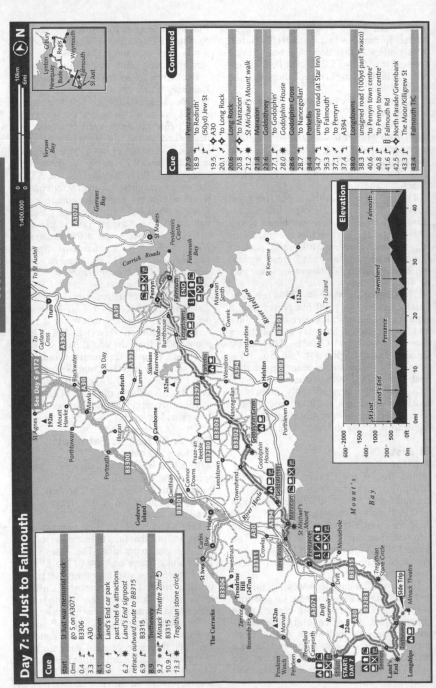

Day 7: St Just to Falmouth

Cue

start	St Just war memorial clock
0mi	go S on A3071
0.4	B3306
3.3	A30
4.1	Sennen
6.0	Land's End car park
	past hotel & attractions
6.2	Land's End signpost
	retrace outward route to BB315
6.9	B3315
8.9	Trethewey
9.2	Minack Theatre 2mi
10.9	B3315
13.3	Tregithian stone circle

Cue

17.9	Penzance
18.9	'to Redruth'
	(50yd) Jew St
19.5	A30
20.1	'to Long Rock'
20.6	Long Rock
20.8	'to Marazion'
21.2	St Michael's Mount walk
21.8	Marazion
23.6	Goldsithney
27.1	'to Godolphin'
28.0	Godolphin House
28.6	Godolphin Cross
28.7	'to Nancegollan'
34.4	Porkellis
34.7	unsigned road (at Star Inn)
35.3	'to Falmouth'
37.1	'to Penryn'
37.4	A394
38.0	Longdowns
38.3	unsigned road (100yd past Texaco)
40.6	'to Penryn town centre'
40.8	'to Penryn town centre'
41.6	Falmouth Rd
42.5	North Parade/Greenbank
43.3	The Moor/Killigrew St
93.4	Falmouth TIC

Elevation

Tregithian stone circle, is on the route and easily accessible (and free). The run downhill to Penzance is a pleasure, bringing with it the first sight of Mount's Bay.

There's some traffic to contend with through and beyond Penzance, but the reward is worth it. **St Michael's Mount** (☎ 01736-710265; NT), a 14th-century castle, rises above a rocky island just offshore from pretty Marazion; you can walk across a causeway (at 21.2mi) at low tide (there's a ferry for high-tide access) to the mount, which is open from April to October.

Most of the remaining miles pass through quiet countryside. **Godolphin House** (28mi; ☎ 01736-762409), a grand 15th-century home, is worth a look. It's open limited hours; Thursday in May and June, and Tuesday and Thursday in July and August.

Expect some heavier traffic after the left turn onto the A394 (37.4mi); the final run through Penryn and into Falmouth is mostly downhill, with delightful views.

Side Trip: Minack Theatre
1 hour, 2mi

Perched on a cliff top, the 750-seat Minack (Cornish for 'rocky place') is one of the world's most remarkable open-air theatres. It's largely the work of Rowena Cade, who first provided the space for a local production of *The Tempest* in 1932, and continued to develop it until her death in 1983. There are shows most evenings (and some matinees) from late May to late September; it's wise to book (☎ 01736-810181). The theatre's exhibition centre is open year-round (entry £2); it's worth a look even if you don't see actors treading the, er, rocks.

Falmouth
☎ 01326

It's not Cornwall's most vibrant town, but Falmouth has more ambience than, say, Newquay. The town and beaches are easy on the eye and some of the nearby villages on the Lizard Peninsula are quite charming.

The TIC (☎ 312300) is on Killigrew St. All the big banks (with ATMs) are in the central shopping precinct; the main post office is on The Moor.

Things to See & Do An important defensive weapon since Tudor times, **Pendennis Castle** (☎ 316594; EH) is south-east of the town centre, on Castle Drive. There are great views from the castle ramparts and you can learn about coastal fortifications and weapons at the museum and discovery centre. The **Cornwall Maritime Museum** (☎ 240670), just off Market St, has some fine models and interesting port records. A stroll at sunset along the promenade above **Castle Beach** is very pleasant; in summer you'll often hear music wafting from **Princess Pavilion** (☎ 211 222) in Gyllyngdune Gardens.

Places to Stay The *Penance Mill Farm* (☎ 317431) is about 2mi from Falmouth, near Maenporth Beach. It's open from March to December; tent pitches cost £7.50 to £9. *Pendennis Castle YHA* (☎ 311435, ✉ pendennis@yha.org.uk, Castle Dr) is a Victorian-era army barracks in the castle. The 76-bed hostel is open seven nights from mid-February to early October and five nights (closed Sunday and Monday) until late November. There's a cycle storeroom and laundry and dinners are available; the nightly charge is £9.15.

There are stacks of B&Bs along Melvill and Avenue Rds and big hotels facing Castle Beach on Cliff Rd. Try the *Cotswold House Hotel* (☎ 312077, 49 Melvill Rd) from £22 a night or the *Trevelyan* (☎ 311545, 6 Avenue Rd) at £16 to £19. You'll pay £22 at the *Grove Hotel* (☎ 319577, Grove Place), which fronts the harbour and is closer to town centre pubs and restaurants. Set in magnificent gardens, the *Gyllyngdune Manor Hotel* (☎ 312978, Melvill Rd) is a fair place for a splurge; low-season prices start at £25.

Places to Eat The cafe upstairs from *WC Rowe Hot Bread Shop* is good for coffee; you'll find more bread and pastries at the *Oggy Oggy Pastry Co & Bakery*, which has shops on Church and Arwenack Sts. *Lizzie's Cafe (Lower High St)* has a £2.50 all-day big breakfast and £2.95 vegie burgers. There are many pubs on the Market, Church and Arwenack Sts strip, including the *Grapes Inn* (☎ 314704, 64 Church St) and *The Chain Locker*, which has tables overlooking the harbour. Farther along, *The Pirate Inn (Bank Place)* has live music most nights. *Maz's Bistro* (☎ 318229, 2 Quay Hill) does a mean mushroom stroganoff for £7 and *Casablanca (Grove Place)* has a big variety of pastas and pizzas at £4.95.

SOUTHERN ENGLAND

Eastern England

In the counties of Essex, Cambridgeshire, Suffolk and Norfolk you'll find pretty low-lying lands, as well as towns that are less populated than the rest of the country. The riding is rarely taxing, as the highest point of the four counties is 144m (482ft) in Essex, while the landscape is surprisingly varied, including heath, farmland and woodland. Except for Cambridge, most counties have been overlooked, or at least are yet to be swamped, by tourists. These factors together make for excellent cycle touring.

Here, the countryside is dissected by a system of rivers, lakes and former marshes. Bridges, ferries and crossings can be few and far between – which is deceptive, since you'd think a flat land would be easily accessible. The web of country roads is dense and gives ample opportunity for exploring a hidden side of England. The coast is peppered with holiday resorts that cater for varying tastes and make travelling in the region easy, with plentiful camp sites and hostelries.

NATURAL HISTORY

A lot of Eastern England is at sea level or, in the case of the sinking fens (reclaimed marshlands), below it, and is therefore vulnerable to flooding from inland waters and rising sea levels. Livestock farming is abundant, as are bird and small-mammal populations. The lack of good building stone in the north has meant that flint is an important material.

CLIMATE

Very little rain falls in East Anglia – it is one of the driest parts of the country. It can suffer drought in isolation from the rest of the land because much of the prevailing rains that blow in from the Atlantic fall on Wales and the Midlands before they reach the eastern shores. Balancing that, however, is the region's exposure to the colder North Sea and to chilly north-easterlies from the Continent and Siberia.

INFORMATION
Maps & Books

The OS Travelmaster map No 6 (1:250,000), *East Midlands & East Anglia,* is the best

In Summary

Terrain
Picturesque low-lying country throughout with the pancake-flat fenlands to the north around The Wash. A lot of the region is at sea level – the Fens are below – and is therefore vulnerable to flooding.

Special Events
- **Mildenhall Air Fete** (May)
- **Great Annual Re-Creation of Tudor Life** (June/July), Long Melford
- **Cambridge Folk Festival** (July), Cherry Hinton
- **Ely Folk Festival** (July)
- **World Music Festival** (July), Clare

Food & Drink Specialities
- specially cured Suffolk ham
- Yarmouth herrings, Southend shellfish, Sheringham lobsters, Cromer crabs, and fish and chips
- real ale from local brewers Adnams, Tolly Cobbold and Elgoods

Tourist Information
East of England Tourist Board:
☎ 01473-822922; Toppesfield Hall, Hadleigh, IP7 5DN

choice for the region. *East Anglia north* and *East Anglia south* are two OS Cycle Tours books featuring one-day road and mountain bike rides.

GATEWAY CITIES
London

East Anglia is readily accessible from England's capital city. See the London chapter for information about accommodation, other services and getting to/from eastern England.

EASTERN ENGLAND

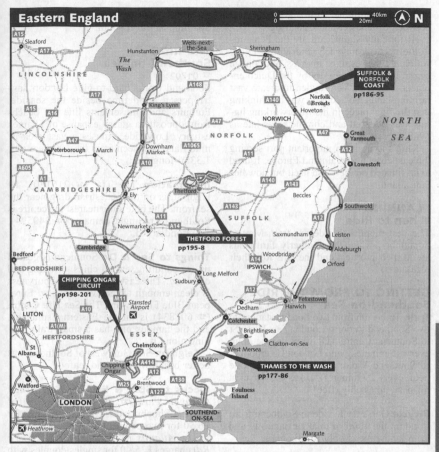

SUFFOLK & NORFOLK COAST pp186-95

THETFORD FOREST pp195-8

CHIPPING ONGAR CIRCUIT pp198-201

THAMES TO THE WASH pp177-86

EASTERN ENGLAND

Thames to the Wash

Duration	3 days
Distance	158.3mi
Difficulty	easy-moderate
Start	Southend-on-Sea
End	King's Lynn

This region of East Anglia is full of beauty, history and variety, from holiday resorts, to fishing ports, nature reserves and inland waterways. From a cyclist's point of view the region can hardly be beaten: the riding is easy, the views are long and the pubs are frequent.

Home to an intricate network of back roads, the charms of East Anglia remain undiminished by the passing of time. The gentle landscape is peppered with old villages of pink-washed houses and medieval churches. The south is full of tidal estuaries, and the north is flat, fascinating fens. The historically significant towns of Colchester, Cambridge, Ely and King's Lynn are linked by this ride.

Few, if any, hills can be found in this part of the country, although Cambridgeshire is more rolling than you might expect.

If you only have two days, ride from Colchester to King's Lynn to explore the more picturesque parts of the region.

NATURAL HISTORY

South Essex's coastal plain is cut into deeply by the Rivers Crouch (near South Woodham Ferrers) and Blackwater (near

Maldon), with higher farmland to the west between Colchester and Cambridge.

Historically significant are the Fenlands to the north around Ely and King's Lynn, which are the result of impressive drainage begun in the 17th century by the Dutch engineer Cornelius Vermuyden to create vast farming lands. So accurate was his thinking that the final piece in his waterworking jigsaw was adopted and completed as late as 1968.

King's Lynn is an important port serving the east coast and mainland Europe. It used to be situated on the Wash itself but now lies 5mi inland.

PLANNING
When to Ride
The best months to ride are from May to September, when the southerly farmlands are at their prettiest and the fens lose their bleakness.

GETTING TO/FROM THE RIDE
Southend-on-Sea
Train Trains run from two London stations to two Southend stations: London Fenchurch St to Southend Central (£8 off-peak, one hour, every 15 minutes); and London Liverpool St to Southend Victoria (£9.20 off-peak, one hour, every 20 minutes). Bikes can travel at off-peak times only (free).

Bicycle Don't try to ride to Southend from London; the 40mi of dual carriageway and grim landscape is only for die-hards.

King's Lynn
Train Trains originate at King's Lynn for Cambridge (£6.90 off-peak, 30 minutes, every half hour) and London (£20.90 off-peak, 1¼ hours, every half hour). Bikes travel free, but can only be carried on trains arriving in London off-peak.

Bicycle King's Lynn is the start of the Suffolk & Norfolk Coast ride later in this chapter.

The town is also on the 369mi Eastern Heritage Cycle Route (NCN 1) from Hull to Harwich (in practice it's now Felixstowe); a Sustrans route.

To pick up the Central England Explorer ride (see the Central England chapter) and travel north, follow the NCN 1 westwards

for 50mi to Boston; turn off at Holbeach for Spalding to travel south.

THE RIDE
Southend-on-Sea
☎ 01702
Southend works hard to give London daytrippers a good time beside the seaside. Funfairs and amusements line the beachfront opposite a glassy expanse of Thames estuary. Low tide exposes a vast area of mud flats, best seen from the 100-year-old, 1.33mi-long pier.

Information The TIC (☎ 215120), 19 High St, is on the pedestrian drag near the seafront. The bike shop nearest the centre is Southend Trading Company (☎ 349594), 190 London Rd.

Things to See & Do Southend is geared up for paddling, eating chips, drinking and clubbing. The **East Beach** at Shoeburyness is clean enough to receive a coveted European Blue Flag award. **The Sea Life Centre** (☎ 601834) is on the Eastern Esplanade, and the famous pier has a small **train** running along it.

Leigh-on-Sea, 3mi west of Southend, has better beach walking and seafood.

Places to Stay & Eat The *East Beach Caravan Park* (☎ 292466), 4mi east of town at Shoeburyness, has tent pitches for £6.50 for two people and a tent.

The *Atlantis* (☎ 332538, 63 Alexandra Rd) charges £25/40 for singles/doubles with shared facilities and £30/50 with en suite. The *Haven House Hotel* (☎ 585212, 47 Heygate Ave) has rooms for £20/35.

Clifftown Hotel (☎ 339483, 12 Clifftown Parade) charges about £35 for a single. The eye-catching Victorian clifftop *Westcliff Hotel* (☎ 345247; Westcliff Parade, Westcliff-on-Sea) costs £70/85.

People who take eating seriously will find it hard to get excited in Southend, although the local shellfish, harvested by traditional cockle boats, is worth a try. One good restaurant to try is *Fleur de Provence* (☎ 352987, 52 Alexandra St), where the exceptional main courses include imaginative fish dishes from the surrounding region starting from £15. Desserts include delicious home-made ice cream.

Day 1: Southend-on-Sea to Colchester

3–5 hours, 44.8mi

After Southend, the route travels into true East Anglian countryside with its many river estuaries, quiet back roads and the distinctive plasterwork on many houses.

The first place to pause is Battlesbridge on an inlet of the River Crouch. Old **Battlesbridge Mill** (13.3mi), with a *cafe*, is on a picturesque spot on one of the river's inlets.

Soon after, beyond South Woodham Ferrers, the traffic thins and the lanes turn pastoral on the approach to **Maldon**. This pleasant old town is a good place to halt. The picturesque quayside of the River Blackwater has old barge moorings and friendly mariners pubs. Crystals from the saltyards are sold worldwide.

Along the B-road to Colchester lies **Abberton Reservoir nature reserve** (40.5mi), popular with bird-watchers and another good place to break.

The day's traffic blackspot is the A130 roundabout (13.8mi) near South Woodham Ferrers. If there's traffic, it's best to walk your bike here, heading anticlockwise to the fourth and last exit.

Colchester

☎ 01206

Colchester, Britain's oldest recorded town, has a rich history. Before London's rise to prominence, it was the capital of Roman Britain and these days it's home to a handful of important sites, including a fine castle.

It's quite a vibrant town, with nearby Essex University and the influx of tourists in summer.

The Colchester Cycling Campaign is active and has worked with the council to put in urban bikepaths and to extend the traffic-free Wivenhoe Trail east beside the River Colne.

Information The TIC (☎ 282920) is at 1 Queen St. Colchester Cycle Stores (☎ 56 3890) is at 50 St Johns St, on the south side of the centre.

Things to See & Do Guided walks are conducted daily from the TIC. The tour includes the **Norman castle**, which has a larger keep than the Tower of London and is built on the foundations of the Roman fort sacked by Boudicca, queen of the Iceni tribe, in AD

60. The **museum** at the castle contains Roman mosaics and statues. Remains of sections of the original town wall and the largest Roman gateway can still be seen.

The **Dutch Quarter**, just north of High St, was established in the 16th century by Protestant refugee weavers from the Netherlands.

Places to Stay & Eat About 1.5mi west along the Lexden Rd bikepath is *Colchester Camping* (☎ 545551; Cymbeline Way, Lexden). Bike and tent together cost £3, plus £3.90 per person.

The *Scheregate Hotel* (☎ 573034, Osborne St), in the centre of town, charges from £22/37 a single/double for B&B. Rooms at the friendly and pleasantly situated *Old Manse* (☎ 545154, 15 Roman Rd), part of the Roman wall beside Castle Park, start from £30/42.

One of the town's top historic hotels is the *Rose & Crown* (☎ 866677, East St), where all the rooms are doubles with bathrooms, priced from £65 to £99, which includes breakfast on the weekends. Franco, the Rose & Crown's chef, is renowned for his meat and seafood dishes. Set lunch is £14 and dinner is £19; seared smoked ham with sliced king scallop is £15.95.

A *Halfords* store, handy for small supplies, is on East St at the bottom of East Hill.

Traditional English tea is served at *The George Hotel* (High St), while coffee and bagels go down well at *Vagabonds* (51 St John's St). For a 'traditional' Essex curry there's the *Simla Balti House* (26 North Hill). Pizza and pasta are available at a handful of establishments around the centre. For modern British cuisine on the terrace, *The Lemon Tree* (☎ 767337, 48 St Johns St) does imaginative dishes such as vegetable strudel topped with goat's cheese for £7.50, and duck with ginger and lime sauce for £10.95.

Day 2: Colchester to Cambridge

3½–5½ hours, 53.7mi

The Stour valley and the plateau to the west show off Essex and Suffolk well. Cows graze in water meadows and pink-washed flint houses line the quiet roads.

The town of Sudbury (15.5mi), on the banks of the River Stour, was the birthplace of Thomas Gainsborough, the 18th-century

EASTERN ENGLAND

EASTERN ENGLAND

Day 1: Southend-on-Sea to Colchester

1:350,000

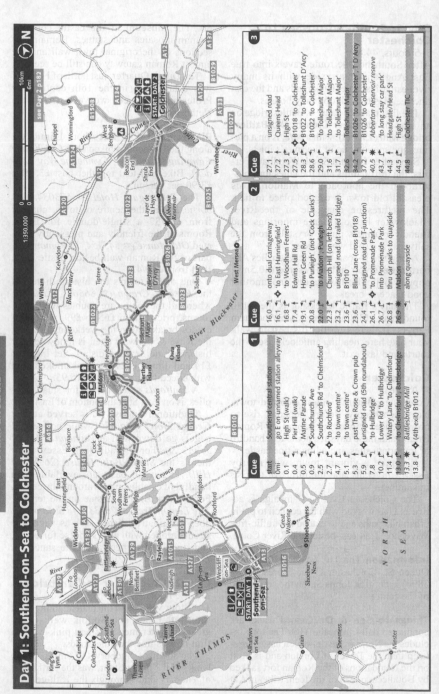

Cue 1

start	0mi	Southend central station
0.1		go E on unnamed station alleyway
0.4		High St (walk)
0.5		Pier Hill (walk)
0.9		Marine Parade
2.5		Southchurch Ave
2.7		Southchurch Rd 'to Chelmsford'
4.7		'to Rochford'
5.1		'to town centre'
5.3		'to town centre'
5.9		past The Rose & Crown pub
7.8		unsigned road (5th roundabout)
10.2		'to Hullbridge'
11.4		Lower Rd 'to Hullbridge'
13.0		Watery Lane 'to Chelmsford'
13.3		'to Chelmsford', Battlesbridge
13.8		Battlesbridge Mill
13.8		(4th exit) B1012

Cue 2

16.0	onto dual carriageway
16.1	'to East Hanningfield'
16.8	'to Woodham Ferrers'
17.4	Edwins Hall Rd
19.1	Howe Green Rd
20.8	'to Purleigh' (not 'Cock Clarks')
22.0	'to Maldon', Purleigh
22.3	Church Hill (on left bend)
23.2	unsigned road (at railed bridge)
23.6	B1010
23.6	Blind Lane (cross B1018)
24.4	unsigned road (at T-junction)
26.1	into Promenade Park
26.7	into Promenade Park
26.8	thru car parks to quayside
26.9	Maldon
	along quayside

Cue 3

27.1	unsigned road
27.2	Queens Head
27.3	High St
27.5	B1018 'to Colchester'
28.3	B1022 'to Tolleshunt D'Arcy'
28.6	B1022 'to Colchester'
29.0	'to Tolleshunt Major'
31.6	'to Tolleshunt Major'
31.7	'to Tolleshunt Major'
32.6	Tolleshunt Major
34.2	B1026 'to Colchester', T D'Arcy
37.2	B1026 'to Colchester'
40.5	Abberton Reservoir reserve
43.7	'to long stay car park'
44.3	Headgate/Head St
44.5	High St
44.8	Colchester TIC

landscape and portrait painter, who is commemorated at **Gainsborough's House**, 46 Gainsborough St.

The area is also involved in the world of antiques, with lovely villages like **Clare** and **Cavendish** centres for buying and selling collectibles. The BBC TV series *Lovejoy* was filmed at nearby Long Melford.

Cambridge
☎ 01223

Cambridge, home to one of the world's leading universities and dozens of beautiful historic buildings, is also a city of bicycles; about 25% of commuter journeys are made by bike. The train station's bike parking facility is a sea of used and abused bikes.

The city is a busy place, packed for much of the year with residents, students and tourists. However, its human scale, watermeadows and breathtaking colleges earn Cambridge top marks from most visitors.

Information The TIC (☎ 322640) is tucked away in the pedestrianised centre at the Old Library, on Wheeler St.

Accessible bike shops include Haywards (☎ 352294), on Trumpingtons St, and Howes (☎ 350350), on Regent St. From Monday to Thursday a stall in Market Square does repairs and stocks a range of small parts.

On Saturday, the Cambridge Cycling Campaign (☎ 5040950) staffs a stall outside the guildhall. From 10 am until 4 pm the pedestrian streets are closed to cycling, but the approach routes are nearly all bike-calmed and well-used in response.

Things to See & Do Cambridge has over 30 individual colleges, the majority of them planned around 'courts'. The first, Peterhouse, was established in 1284 with tutors and students living together like monks. The idea developed into the collegiate system that is unique to Oxford and Cambridge.

To see the colleges, take a guided walking or cycle tour. Geoff of **Geoff's Cycle Tours** (☎ 365629) is a Cambridge graduate who does 2½-hour tours for £6.50 (£9.50 with bike hire). **Walking tours** leave the TIC daily, and private guides are advertised there too.

Two must-sees are the interior of **King's College Chapel**, one of the finest examples of Gothic architecture in England, and the Great Court at **Trinity College**, founded by

How to Punt

1. Standing at the end of the punt, lift the pole out of the water at the side.

2. Let the pole slide through your hands to touch the shallow bottom of the river.

3. Tilt the pole forward (in the direction of travel) and push down to propel the punt forward.

4. Twist the pole to free the end from the mud at the bottom of the river, and let it float up and trail behind the punt. You can then use it to steer as with a rudder.

5. If you've not yet fallen in, raise the pole out of the water and into the vertical position to begin again.

The art of punting: you'll need quite a bit of muscle and a lot of balance.

JON DAVISON

Henry VIII. Other colleges of particular interest include **Gonville & Caius**, **Trinity Hall**, **Christ's**, **Jesus**, **Magdalene**, **Queens'**, **Peterhouse** and **Emmanuel**. Further buildings to visit are **Great St Mary's Church**, **Senate House** and the church of **Corpus Christi**.

For light relief, there's little to match **punting along the Backs**, the stretch of River Cam by the lawns of the central colleges. The waters get crowded when the sun is shining. You can hire boats from Trinity

EASTERN ENGLAND

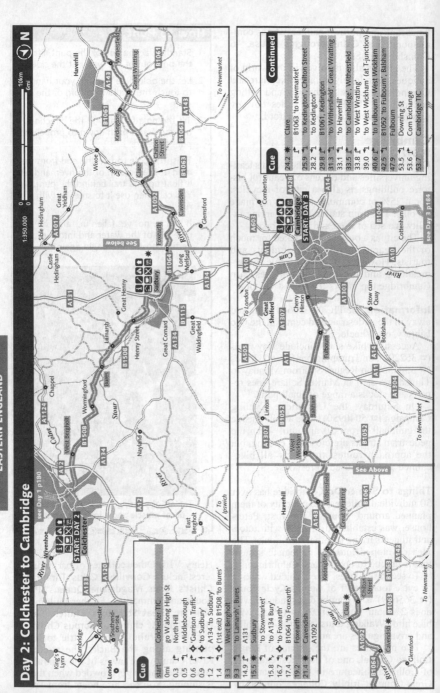

Day 2: Colchester to Cambridge

Cue

start	Colchester TIC
0mi	go W along High St
0.3	North Hill
0.5	Middleborough
0.6	◇⬥ 'Garrison Traffic'
0.9	◇⬥ 'to Sudbury'
1.2	◇⬥ A134 'to Sudbury'
1.4	A134 '1st exit B1508 'to Bures''
3.3	West Bergholt
9.3	'to Lamarsh', Bures
14.9	A131
15.5	Sudbury
15.8	'to Stowmarket'
16.7	'to A134 Bury'
17.4	B1064 'to Foxearth'
19.2	Foxearth
21.4	Cavendish
	A1092

Cue — Continued

24.2	Clare
25.9	✳ B1063 'to Newmarket'
28.2	B1063 'to Kedington, Chilton Street
29.8	'to Kedington'
31.3	B1061, Kedington
33.1	'to Withersfield', Great Wratting
33.5	'to Haverhill'
33.8	'to Cambridge', Withersfield
39.0	'to West Wratting'
40.6	'to West Wickham' (at T-junction)
42.5	B1052 'to Fulbourn', West Wickham
47.9	B1052 'to Fulbourn, Balsham
53.5	Fulbourn
53.6	Downing St
53.7	Corn Exchange
	Cambridge TIC

Punts behind Trinity College, beside the Granta pub, Newnham Rd, or down by Silver St. Charges rise from £6 plus a £25 deposit at Trinity. Give *Choices Cafe (☎ 360 211, Newnham Rd)* a day's notice and they'll make you up a picnic punting hamper from £2.50 to £12.50 per head.

Places to Stay Four miles south-west of the city in the town of Comberton, there's *Highfield Farm Camping (☎ 262308, Long Rd)*, which charges £8.25 per tent and two people.

Denver Sluice & the Fens

Flat and fertile, the Fenland Plain lies in a massive arc around the Wash and makes up nearly all the prime farming land in England. The region was hard-won and remains under threat from flooding and rising sea levels. The relationship between water and land is so finely balanced that it is constantly measured in inches, with a great percentage of the area below sea level.

Although the Fens are bleak and inhospitable in grim weather, things are much more secure than 400 years ago, when upland rivers and gale-driven tides pushed and pulled the water freely over large areas. Much of the land was little more than marsh. Summertime pastures were often drowned during the winter.

The great drainage works, a series of cuts, drains and sluices, of which the Denver Sluice is a critical part, were begun in the 16th century. The work continues today as engineers attempt to predict and control the effect of global warming and rising sea levels, which complicate the effects of wind, rain and tide.

The original Denver sluice (the first the route passes over) was built by Dutch engineer Sir Cornelius Vermuyden, the key engineer in the vast project. It was rebuilt in 1835 and enlarged in 1923. The second sluice the route crosses, the AG Wright sluice, was constructed after the disastrous flooding of 1947, when almost 40,000 acres of fenland went under water after unusually heavy winter snowfalls melted. It was one of the last pieces in Vermuyden's watery jigsaw and made the area secure – for now.

Cambridge Youth Hostel (☎ 354601), around the corner from the train station, is very popular, so book early. Adults costs £11.15 per night.

Directly outside the train station, *Sleeperz Hotel (☎ 304050, Station Rd)* is an attractive converted granary with quality B&B and en suite single room rates from £25, twins from £38 and doubles at £47.

B&Bs are everywhere, but it is advised that you book ahead. The *Six Steps Guest House (☎ 353968, 93 Tenison Rd)* has a bar on the premises and is commended for its bread. Prices start from £25 per person. Nearer the centre is *Linwood House (☎ 500 776, 217 Chesterton Rd)*, where prices start from £22/45 for singles/doubles. North of the city is *Benson House (☎ 311594, 24 Huntingdon Rd)*, which charges from £40 for a nice double room.

Near the Fitzwilliam Museum is the *Lensfield Hotel (☎ 355017, 53 Lensfield Rd)*, where singles are £40 (£50 with an en suite) and £75 for a double. One good place in town is the *Garden House Hotel (☎ 259 988, Mill Lane)*, boasting pastoral riverside views and charges £120/150 per room, without breakfast. Its weekend deals are a little cheaper.

Places to Eat A variety of good-value food is available in Cambridge and many establishments give student discounts.

A good vegetarian cafe over the road from King's College is *Rainbow (☎ 321 551, 9 King's Parade)*. In an old cricket pavilion, *Hobbs' Pavilion (☎ 67480, Park Terrace)* specialises in filled pancakes. *Sticky Fingers (Regent St)* is owned by Bill Wyman and he is often on the premises, but even if he isn't the place is plastered with Stones memorabilia. If you want an Internet cafe, there's *CB1 (☎ 576306, Mill Rd)*, with nine terminals, coffee and cake.

Heading upmarket, try *Browns (☎ 461 655, 23 Trumpington St)*, which serves a la carte fresh fish and vegetables from a starting price of about £10 per main course. You can also find gourmet dishes at *Twenty-two (☎ 351880, 22 Chesterton Rd)*, from around £24 for the set dinner. At *Midsummer House (☎ 369299)*, overlooking the river at Midsummer Common, choose from superb cuisine and a comprehensive wine list; book ahead.

EASTERN ENGLAND

EASTERN ENGLAND

Day 3: Cambridge to King's Lynn

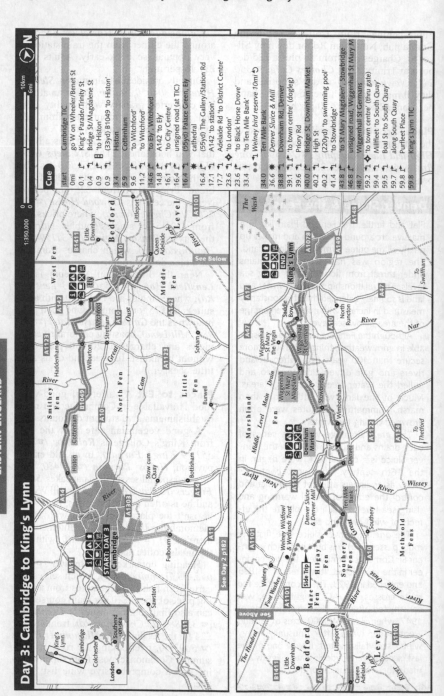

Cue		
start	0mi	Cambridge TIC
		go W on Wheeler/Benet St
0.1		King's Parade/Trinity St
0.4		Bridge St/Magdalene St
0.9		(33yd) B1049 'to Histon'
0.9		'to Histon'
3.4		Histon
5.9		Cottenham
9.6		'to Witchford'
11.2		'to Witchford'
14.6		'to Ely', Witchford
14.8		A142 'to Ely'
16.1		'to City Centre'
16.4		unsigned road (at TIC)
16.4		(55yd) Palace Green, Ely cathedral
16.4		(55yd) The Gallery/Station Rd
17.1		A142 'to station'
17.7		Adelaide Rd 'to District Centre'
23.6		'to London'
23.6		'to Black Horse Drove'
33.4		'to Ten Mile Bank'
16.4		Welney bird reserve 10mi ↻
34.0		Ten Mile Bank
36.6		Denver Sluice & Mill
38.8		Downham Rd, Denver
39.1		'to town centre' (dogleg)
39.6		Priory Rd
40.0		Bridge St, Downham Market
40.2		High St
40.2		(220yd) 'to swimming pool'
41.4		'to Stowbridge'
43.8		'to St Mary Magdalen', Stowbridge
46.8		unsigned road, Wiggenhall St Mary M
48.7		Wiggenhall St Germans
59.2		'to town centre' (thru gate)
59.4		Millfleet 'to South Quay'
59.5		Boal St 'to South Quay'
59.7		along South Quay
59.8		Purfleet Place
59.8		King's Lynn TIC

Day 3: Cambridge to King's Lynn
4–6 hours, 59.8mi

There's lots to see after leaving Cambridge as the route heads into the flat and atmospheric fenlands towards King's Lynn. After Cottenham the traffic evaporates and the fens stretch out towards the tower of Ely cathedral.

Ely (16.6mi; pronounced 'ee-lee') used to be an island in the marshes and is named after the eels that swam around it. Its bike shop, City Cycle Centre (☎ 01353-663131) is in Market St.

The Norman Romanesque **cathedral** is one of England's finest, with a sublime view from inside the main west door. The octagon and lantern, constructed in 1322 after the original central tower collapsed, are superb.

The town was home to Oliver Cromwell, the Protestant military leader of the victorious parliamentarian forces in the Civil War, who subsequently made himself lord protector of the country. He lived for 10 years at **Oliver Cromwell's House**, which now houses the TIC (near the cathedral).

Down the hill from the Georgian town is the pretty **waterfront** of the River Great Ouse (pronounced 'ooze'), its pub and cafes good places from which to watch for birds and boats.

The ride continues through the fens along the embankment of the Great Ouse into Norfolk. About 4mi west of Ten Mile Bank is a side trip to **Welney Wildfowl & Wetlands Trust** bird reserve (☎ 01353-860711), a treasure-trove of migrating and roosting fowl observable from hides. Thousands of swans winter here from about October to February, peaking during January.

Denver Sluice (36.6mi) is one of the main gates of the vast fen drainage system and flood defences. **Denver Mill** (37.8mi), a little farther on, is being restored to working order and will soon be open to the public (see the boxed text, earlier).

King's Lynn
☎ 01553

Once sited on the Wash itself, King's Lynn now lies 5mi inland. The fishing industry operates from new docks, while the town centre and old quayside are full of history. Merchants' houses, and port and civic buildings line the streets. Seafood and samphire, a seaweed delicacy, can be bought from the market barrows on Tuesday.

Information Occupying the former Custom House, the TIC (☎ 763044) is on Purfleet Quay, originally the town's main dock. Richardsons Cycles (☎ 767014), 120 London Rd, and Cranks Cycles (☎ 660363), in Tower Place, are minutes away.

Things to See & Do A stroll along the **South Quay** beside the Great Ouse sets the mood for a look around the medieval town centre. Nelson St, which runs off it, has a series of fine 17th- and 18th-century facades. **Tuesday Market Place**, a large traditional square towards the north end of town, is edged with old buildings, including the **Corn Hall** and the **Duke's Head Hotel**. **St George's Guildhall**, in King St, is the largest surviving 15th-century guildhall in the country and now houses the Art Centre.

An unusual exhibition at the **Tales of Old Gaol House** tells the story of witches, murderers and highwaymen via a series of tableaux and sound effects.

Places to Stay & Eat The nearest camping ground is *King's Lynn Caravan & Camping Park (☎ 840004, New Road)*, 3mi south-east on the A47 (Norwich Rd); tent pitches start at £3.50.

King's Lynn is blessed with a perfectly sited *Youth Hostel (☎ 772461, College Lane)*, in 500-year-old Chantry College, virtually over the road from the TIC. It costs £8.35 per adult, but is only open every day during July and August.

The B&Bs are reasonable. The cycle-friendly *Maranatha Guest House (☎ 774 596, 115 Gaywood Rd)* has displayed a CTC 'place-to-stay' sign for 25 years. Run by Mrs Bastone, it lies a short mile east of the centre of town. Singles/doubles start from £20/28. Next door at the *Havana Guest House (☎ 772331, 117 Gaywood Rd)* rooms start from £18/32.

At *Fairlight Lodge (☎ 762234, 79 Goodwins Rd)*, 1mi south-east of centre, rooms cost £16/34; £25/40 with en suite.

For a well-priced luxury two-night stay, go to the *Duke's Head (☎ 774996)*, in the grand Tuesday Market Square, where the B&B weekend price is £42/52 with dinner. During the week there is a supplement for singles of £30.

For cheap and cheerful eats, *Littlewoods* restaurant *(High St)* has plates of fish and

EASTERN ENGLAND

chips for £3.75. *Archer's Cafe-Bar*, in Purfleet near the TIC, has jacket potatoes, sandwiches and salads for a few pounds.

Pub grub at the **Tudor Rose Hotel** *(St Nicholas St)* and the **Lattice House** *(cnr Chapel St & Market Lane)* is good; the latter also has a Thai restaurant.

One of the nicest restaurants in town is the **Riverside** *(☎ 773134)*, on the riverfront behind the guildhall, which serves samphire (in season) as a dinnertime starter for £3.95, and has a wide choice of fish dishes from £12. At *Rococo (Saturday Market Place)*, a two-course dinner of lasagna with Swiss chard and haloumi is £24.50.

Suffolk & Norfolk Coast

Duration	4 days
Distance	175.3mi
Difficulty	easy-moderate
Start	Felixstowe
End	King's Lynn

The East Anglian coastline is ideal for cycling. The pace is slow, the views are lovely and the sights and pretty villages are a constant diversion. Both the Suffolk and Norfolk shores are infused with a fine quality of light and sense of remoteness. These regions remain a secret to the majority of Britons, whose common belief is that they are flat, ergo dull, although the image has no basis in fact.

This is not a trip concerned with dodging A-roads, but a tour through a well-to-do region with a low population and bordered by the ocean on two sides. On this tour it's an advantage to like fish, especially served the battered British way.

NATURAL HISTORY
The low shoreline of East Anglia is made up of dunes, marshes and cliffs with nature reserves rich in flora and fauna. These include the reserves at Minsmere in Suffolk and Blakeney Point in Norfolk, with its 400-strong seal colony.

Coastal erosion has virtually eradicated the old clifftop town of Dunwich in Suffolk, while towns along the North Norfolk shore, such as Wells-next-the-Sea, lie inland of brackish marshes, where once they were open to the North Sea.

Inland, the scene is rural, with reclaimed lands around the Norfolk Broads. The old water-filled peat-diggings form an important protected habitat for bird and water life, and are one of Britain's most popular destinations for boating holidays.

North Norfolk disproves the popular conception that East Anglia is all flat, with hills that rise to nearly 100m (330ft) a few miles in from the sea.

PLANNING
When to Ride
East Anglia is good for cycling all year round. From Easter to October, Suffolk and Norfolk are in full bloom and the resorts are crammed with the English at play. Accommodation must be booked ahead. Out of season, the charm of the little towns is just as evident, if not more so.

East Anglia is one of the driest parts of the country, but during the winter it can get the full force of the Continental winds.

The ferry at Bawdsey runs only on occasional weekends in the winter (ring Felixstowe TIC for details), and the detour is long. The ferry at Walberswick (Southwold TIC) runs in the summertime and school holidays, but the road route alternative is fine, if busy.

What to Bring
This is a feasible camping tour, with plentiful sites throughout the region. The major towns have bike shops, but the smaller ones don't always have specialist stockists. Food and accommodation are never far away.

GETTING TO/FROM THE RIDE
Felixstowe
Train Felixstowe is accessible by train from London via Ipswich (£23 one way, 1¾ hours, hourly). A bike reservation (☎ 01603-764776) costs £1 between Ipswich and Felixstowe, and £3 between Ipswich and London.

Bicycle Sudbury and Colchester, on the Thames to the Wash ride (see earlier in this chapter) are about 30mi from Felixstowe – making it possible to turn this into a five or six-day ride, if you were to start at Southend-on-Sea.

Felixstowe lies on the Suffolk Coastal Cycle Route, a 75mi signposted circuit around Orford, Framlingham and Woodbridge.

Since the closure of the local passenger ferry to Harwich, the town has also become the southern terminus of the 369mi Eastern Heritage Cycle Route (NCN 1), from Hull; a Sustrans route.

King's Lynn

See the Thames to the Wash ride (p178) for information on getting to and from King's Lynn.

THE RIDE
Felixstowe
☎ 01394

Felixstowe cargo port, on the mouth of the River Orwell, handles a third of Britain's freight. Around the corner, the pleasant, flower-bedecked Edwardian town faces the open sea and is a popular holiday resort with pier, promenade and pavilion.

Suffolk is a favourite cycling destination for Dutch and German tourers, as well as Britons, so hosts in the area are familiar with bikes and cyclists.

Information The TIC (☎ 276770) is next to the pier on the seafront. Bike supplies are available at two bike shops positioned opposite each other in the centre of town: Alfords (☎ 284719) and the chain-store Halfords (☎ 279738).

Things to See & Do The main activity in Felixstowe is soaking up the sea air and amusements along the town's 4mi beachfront. You can also visit the local history **museum** at the Landguard fortifications built on the point in 1774. Next door is an active **nature reserve** (☎ 673782) with a bird-watching observatory and events.

Felixstowe's most unusual offering is shipwatching. From the new John Bradfield Viewing Area, inland of the Landguard, you can get an impressive view of cargo ships piled high with containers setting sail from **Felixstowe port** for any of 370 harbours in over 100 countries. The port first opened in 1886 and was recently redeveloped by its Hong Kong owners.

Places to Stay & Eat There are two camping grounds, *Peewit Caravan Park (☎ 284 511, Walton Ave)* and *Suffolk Sands Holiday Park (☎ 273434, Carr Rd)*, both are open from April to October. The nearest hostel, just

off the route at *Blaxhall (☎ 01728-688206)*, is £8.35 per night.

Situated 1.5mi out of town, near Old Felixstowe and the ferry, is *Primrose Gate (☎ 271 699, 263 Ferry Rd)*, a pleasant B&B with singles/doubles for £18/33. At the dock end of the main town is the reasonable *Dolphin Hotel (☎ 282261, 41 Beach Station Rd)*, where rooms start from £18/32. In the town centre, the Victorian *Orwell Hotel (☎ 285 511, Hamilton Rd)* has a restaurant and bars; the rooms are £45/55, with breakfast included.

Seafood is Felixstowe's culinary mainstay, from fish and chips on the beach to the traditional offerings at *The Regal (☎ 282678, Sea Rd)* near the TIC. In the mix is the fresh modern menu at the *Lobster Pot (Undercliff Rd)*, on the seafront.

For steaks and poultry dishes try *The Buregate (☎ 273755, Sea Rd)*, or get yourself a tasty slice at *Perfect Pizza (☎ 671521, High Rd West)*.

Day 1: Felixstowe to Southwold
2½–4½ hours, 41.4mi

The Suffolk coast is indented with tidal river estuaries and speckled with otherworldly towns. Leave plenty of time to enjoy this day, which starts and finishes with ferry crossings and features four side trips (not including signposted nature reserves). At times you cross paths with the signposted Suffolk Coastal Cycle Route.

Leaving Felixstowe behind, the roads become rural beyond the **Bawdsey (Old Felixstowe) ferry** across the River Deben. Wave the bat, and the harbourmaster in the white cap fetches you and your bike for £2 (daily from April to October, some weekends only from November to March).

From Alderton (5.7mi), there's a 12mi (return) side trip along the B1083 to **Woodbridge**, the site of a historic tidal mill, and **Sutton Hoo**, the fabulous 7th-century Anglo-Saxon royal burial ground, from which a complete longship has been excavated. Digging continues at this enormous site.

At the town of Butley, an 8mi side trip south (13.2mi) gets you to the town of Orford, home to a fine **Norman castle** and a pleasant seashore.

Back on the route the ride through peaceful lanes brings you to **Snape Maltings**, on the picturesque River Alde. The old buildings

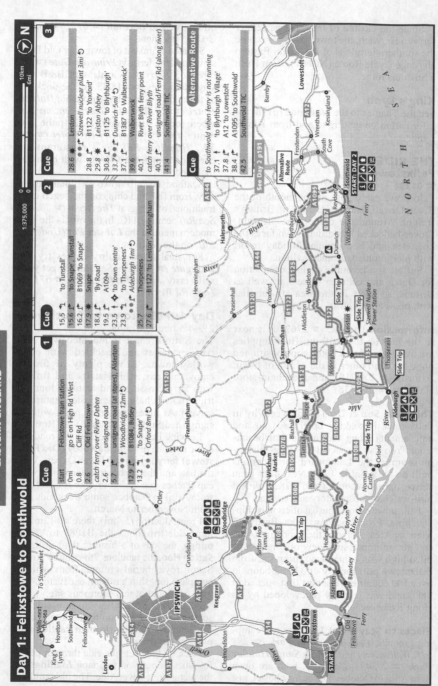

Day 1: Felixstowe to Southwold

EASTERN ENGLAND

1:375,000

⊕ N

10km
6mi

Cue 1

start	Felixstowe train station
0mi	go E on High Rd West
0.8 ←	Cliff Rd
2.6	Old Felixstowe
	catch ferry over River Deben
2.6 ↑	unsigned road
5.7	unsigned road (at stores), Alderton
	●●● 'Woodbridge 12mi' ↺
12.9 ↑	B1084, Butley
13.2 ↑	'to Snape'
	● ↑ 'Orford 8mi' ↺

Cue 2

15.5 ←	'to Tunstall'
15.6 ←	'to Snape', Tunstall
16.2 ←	B1069 to Snape'
17.9 ✳	'By Road'
18.4 ←	Snape
19.5 ←	A1094
23.5	'to town centre'
23.9 ←	'to Thorpeness'
	◇ 'Aldeburgh 1mi' ↺
25.7	Thorpeness
27.6 ←	B1122 'to Leiston', Aldringham

Cue 3

28.6	Leiston
	●●● 'Sizewell nuclear plant 3mi' ↺
28.8 ←	B1122 'to Yoxford'
29.8 ←	Leiston Abbey
30.8 ←	B1125 'to Blythburgh'
	●● 'Dunwich 5mi' ↺
33.7 ←	B1387 'to Walberswick'
37.1 ←	Walberswick
39.6	River Blyth ferry point
	catch ferry over River Blyth
40.1 ←	unsigned road/Ferry Rd (along river)
41.4	Southwold TIC

Alternative Route

Cue	to Southwold when ferry is not running
37.1 ↑	'to Blythburgh Village'
37.8 ←	A12 'to Lowestoft'
38.4 ←	A1095 'to Southwold'
42.5	Southwold TIC

See Day 2 p191

START: DAY 2

Alternative Route

NORTH SEA

have been converted to a concert venue (with cafe and shops) that every June play host to the Aldeburgh Music Festival (box office ☎ 01728-453543), which was founded in 1948 by composer Benjamin Britten.

On a quick detour, arty **Aldeburgh** is one of the best towns on the Suffolk coast. Its long, old high street parallels the shore and sees nightly queues for fish fry-ups.

Follow the signs around Leiston (28.6mi) past the ruins of **Leiston Abbey** to get to the **nuclear power plant** at Sizewell, where the visitor centre's educational wing (☎ 01728-642139) is renowned for its enthusiastic use of the word 'safety'. The power station is open daily from 10 am to 4 pm, and there is no cost to enter.

At Westleton, turn right (33.7mi) to get to the half-village of **Dunwich**, which has disappeared under the waves over the past thousand years (see the boxed text below). Close by are nature reserves and some interesting off-road riding can be had on Dunwich heath.

The route runs to Walberswick (39.6mi) for the **rowboat ferry** (cyclists 60p), which takes you across the narrow River Blyth to Southwold. The ferry runs from 9 am to 12.30 pm and 2 to 5.30 pm every school holiday, daily over the Easter holidays, daily from June to September and weekends during October. More trips are available, weather permitting.

An alternative A-road route is detailed on the map for those times when the ferry is not running.

Southwold
☎ 01502

Much has been written about this unique Suffolk seaside town. It has resisted development without drowning in snobbery and it handles thousands of holiday-makers a year without losing its own identity. True, Volvo families from London load and unload all around, and properties go for ludicrous sums of money, but its nine greens, old lighthouse, beach huts and happy residents give Southwold an air of lively dignity that makes a visit worthwhile regardless of weather or season.

Information The TIC (☎ 724729) is in the middle of town in Market Place. There are bike hire centres, but no bike shops. For help, try Station Cycle Hire (☎ 723140), Station Rd, or Southwold Cycle Hire (☎ 724280), Blyth Rd. The nearest shop, Cedar Cycles, is at Wrentham, 3mi north.

Things to See & Do The main activity in Southwold is enjoying the town and beach, although mention should be made of the

---

Dunwich – the Disappearing Town

The purpose of going to Dunwich is to marvel at something you can't see any more. The first recorded advance by the sea was made in the 11th century, and since the 13th century the waves have swallowed up six of the former town's eight churches and its town walls (entirely). Only the western fringes of what was once an important harbour settlement remain. Dunwich has been reduced to a hamlet of a few hundred souls.

The place had its heyday as a gated town and port in the time of King John, but the sea had been encroaching for centuries before then. The Domesday Book of 1086 records that between 1066 and 1086 a Norman manor lost 120 acres of land to the waves. In the 13th century, when the town was at its peak, St Felix was the first church to succumb, followed by St Leonard's around 1300. In 1328, great storms choked the harbour with shingle and the river jumped course miles northwards to Walberswick. St Bartholomew's and St Michael's went in 1331, followed shortly by St Martin's and St Nicholas'; St John's was dismantled in time to save the materials. In 1350, 400 houses with shops and windmills disappeared under the continual encroachment of the sea. In 1570, the Gilden and South Gates were both swallowed and St Peter's was saved the same fate by human demolition. It would have been under the sea by the time the town's first history was written in 1754.

The ocean's progress has persisted in the modern era, when the last medieval parish church, All Saints, was eaten up. The town's western gate disappeared in 1968. These days Dunwich is a shadow of its former self with a 19th-century church and the old leper hospital the only reminders of the thriving town it once was.

Sailors Reading Room, on East Cliff, which has items of maritime interest.

For architectural sites, Southwold's **lighthouse** is well worth a look, having been built in 1890. The local **church** is also of note, with its 30m (99ft) spire and flint features. The town is also home to Adnam's brewery, which offers no tours, just plenty of pints in the local hostelries.

Places to Stay & Eat The *Harbour Caravan & Camping (☎ 722486, Ferry Rd)* is on the Southwold side of the ferry, and charges £6.20 per one-person tent.

The B&B at *Church Farmhouse (☎ 578 532, Uggeshall)* is 6mi west of Southwold. Charges start from £22 per person in a restored farmhouse full of flowers.

Northcliffe (☎ 724074, 20 North Parade) is one of several B&Bs along the seafront road at the north end of town. It charges from £22 to £30 per person. *Saxon House (☎ 723651, 86 Pier Ave)*, around the corner, charges a little more: from £25 to £35 per

person. The most elegant hotel, *The Swan (☎ 722186, Market Place)*, lies in the focal point of town with rooms from £46 to £85.

Places to eat are limited and illustrate Southwold's desire to remain true to itself. In the absence of chain restaurants, local fish and seafood is everywhere, from the pub menus at the *Red Lion (South Green)* and the *Sole Bay (East Green)* to the recommended *Sutherland House (☎ 722260, 56 High St)*, specialising in Sutherland Smokies' (haddock in a very strong cheese sauce with mussels) for £10. A good menu can also be found at the *Crown Hotel (☎ 722275, High St)*.

Day 2: Southwold to Hoveton
2½–4½ hours, 41.0mi

Turning inland to avoid the bigger towns and remoter reaches of the coastline, this day starts by exploring the farmland that extends to the charming riverside town of **Beccles** (14.7mi). Follow the brown signs north from the town centre for a taste of tranquility and refreshments on the **quayside**.

After Beccles the route heads over the marshes to the **Reedham ferry** (open 364 days a year; cyclists 50p), a contender for the shortest car ferry trip in the land; it has a conveniently placed lunchtime pub. This is the only way over the River Yare between Norwich and Lowestoft.

This area forms the skirts of the pretty **Norfolk Broads** (see the boxed text), famous for its 200km of safe navigable lakes and waterways. The prettiest cycling miles lie in between South Walsham and Wroxham and touch **Malthouse Broad** at Ranworth (34.7mi).

The day finishes at the twin towns of Wroxham and Hoveton on the River Bure.

Wroxham & Hoveton
☎ 01603

Wroxham and Hoveton, on the south and north banks of the River Bure are known collectively as 'the Gateway to the Broads'. More than a dozen boatyards line the banks of the river and in summer the little place teems with people starting their boating holidays.

Trading in the town is dominated by Roys of Wroxham, a local family business that began at the turn of the century when the brothers first brought groceries in from London for the new holiday trade.

The Origin of the Broads

For many years the origin of the Norfolk Broads was unclear. The rivers were undoubtedly natural and many thought the lakes were too – it's hard to believe they're not when you see them – but no one could explain how they could have formed.

The mystery was solved when records were discovered in the remains of St Brenet's Abbey on the River Bure. They showed that from the 12th century certain parts of land in Hoveton Parish were used for peat digging. The area had little woodland and the only source of fuel was peat. Since East Anglia was well populated and prosperous, peat digging became a major industry.

Over a period of about 200 years, approximately 25,000 acres were dug up. However, water gradually seeped through, causing marshes and, later, lakes to develop. The first broad to be mentioned in records is Ranworth Broad (in 1275). Eventually the amount of water made it extremely difficult for the diggers and the peat-cutting industry died out. In no other area of Britain has human effort changed the natural landscape so dramatically.

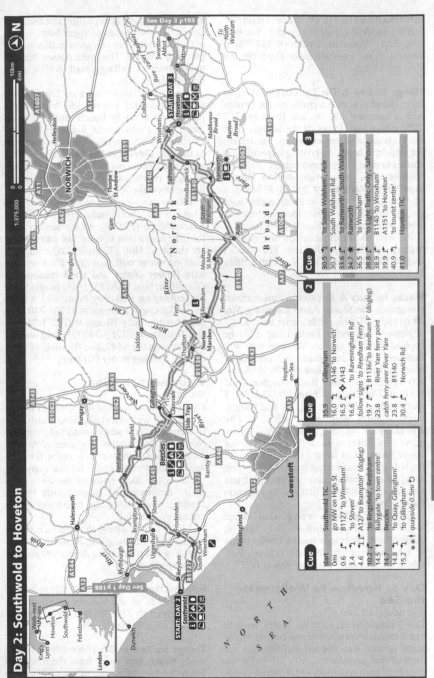

Day 2: Southwold to Hoveton

EASTERN ENGLAND

See Day 3 p193

START: DAY 3
Hoveton

Malthouse Broad
Barton Broad

NORWICH

Norfolk

Broads

River Yare

River Chet

River Waveney

Beccles

Side Trip

Lowestoft

NORTH SEA

START: DAY 2
Southwold

See Day 1 p188

1:375,000

0   10km
0   6mi

N

Kings Lynn • Wells-next-the-Sea
Hoveton
Southwold
London • Felixstowe

Cue		
start		Southwold TIC
0mi	↖	go NW on High St
0.6	↱	B1127 'to Wrentham'
3.4	↱	'to Stoven'
4.6	↱	A12/'to Brampton' (dogleg)
10.2	↱	'to Ringsfield', Redisham
14.5		Ballygate 'to town centre'
14.7		Beccles
14.8	↱	'to Quay, Gillingham'
15.2	↱	'to Gillingham'
	•●↑	quayside 0.5mi ↻

Cue		
15.9		Gillingham
16.0	↱	A146 'to Norwich'
16.5	↱	◈ A143
16.6	↱	'to Raveningham Rd'
		follow signs 'to Reedham Ferry'
19.7	↑ ↱	B1136/'to Reedham F' (dogleg)
23.8		River Yare ferry point
		catch ferry over River Yare
23.8	↱	B1140
30.4	↱	Norwich Rd

Cue		
30.5	↱	'to South Walsham', Acle
30.7	↱	South Walsham Rd
33.6	↱	'to Ranworth', South Walsham
34.7	✳	Ranworth
36.5	↰	'to Wroxham'
38.8		'to Light Traffic Only', Salhouse
38.9	↱	B1140 'to Wroxham'
39.9	↱	A1151 'to Hoveton'
40.9	↱	'to tourist centre'
41.0		Hoveton TIC

Information The TIC (☎ 782281) is on Station Rd beside the river in Hoveton. The best bike shop is Wroxham Cycles (☎ 784188), 6 Broad Centre, while Camelot Craft (☎ 783 096) hires bikes.

Things to See & Do The obvious thing to do in Hoveton is take a **cruise** on the Broads with a company like Broads Tours (☎ 782 207), whose yard is beside the bridge. Trips last 1½ hours, and cost around £6. It also hires out self-drive boats; no boating experience is needed to pilot one of these babies.

Hoveton is the starting station for the **Bure Valley Railway** (☎ 01263-733858), a 15-inch gauge steam locomotive that runs the 9mi to Aylsham. Train rides can be combined with boat trips from Broads Tours.

As well as information on the **natural history** of the Broads, the TIC stocks leaflets detailing long and short **bike rides** in the region.

Places to Stay & Eat About 5mi north of Hoveton is the *Sloley Farm Camping Site* (☎ *01692-636281)*; pitches cost from £5.

Accommodation is limited and must be booked ahead in season. You can stay in a thatched waterside cottage and eat home-made bread at *South Bank* (☎ *78640, Beech Rd)* for £20 per person B&B. Another good B&B is *The Dragon Flies* (☎ *783822, 5 The Avenue)*, 500yd south of the bridge, where singles/doubles are £25/38. *The Wroxham* (☎ *782061; The Bridge, Wroxham)* is a hotel with a riverside terrace where rooms start from £35/60. This hotel has a big and varied bar menu all day and evening; an evening carvery from £5.45 and an a la carte restaurant that serves a scampi flambe for £11.95.

Eating during the day is somewhat limited to pubs and fish and chip shops of varying quality. In the evenings try the Italian menu at *La Carrozza* (☎ *783939, Station Rd)*, where the speciality chicken dish is £8.75.

Day 3: Hoveton to Wells-next-the-Sea

3–5 hours, 48.2mi
Day 3's route heads on to the North Norfolk coast through rural countryside and handsome estates. The houses and villages are built of flint and the majority are at least a couple of hundred years old. Church spires and towers, many also of flint, dot the horizon in between fields of sugar beet.

Grand estates are common in this cut-off part of the world. The route passes through the grounds of **Felbrigg Hall**, which is not open to the public.

The seaside resort area of **Sheringham** (24.6mi), a 1mi return side trip (to the right), has a sandy beach and is a good lunch stop. Farther west, **Blakeney** is a fascinating town on marshes that was once part of the sea. **Cley-next-the-Sea** has a bird reserve and is also worth a look. To get there, go right (north) at Wiveton (37.1mi) and then east on the A149.

The remainder of the route is graced with a load of attractions, including: the **castle** at Baconsthorpe (29.9mi), a 15th-century part-fortified house now in ruins; the **antique** and **art shops** of Holt (32.8mi); Letheringsett's working **water mill**, just after the town; the **wild flower centre** and **shell museum** at Glandford; boat trips (£5; 1–1½ hours) to the **seal colony** on Blakeney Point, which leave from Blakeney (Bishops ☎ 01263-740753), and Morston quay (Beans ☎ 01263-740038 and Temples ☎ 01263-740791) 1mi west of Blakeney on the A149; and the ruins of 12th-century **Binham priory** (40.6mi).

Wells-next-the-Sea
☎ 01328
Day 3 comes to a satisfying close at the little town of Wells-next-the-Sea, which, like Blakeney, is nowadays protected from the North Sea by marshes and creeks. An impressive tide brings in new crabs for holidaying children to catch on the quayside, which is the focal point of the town. It is easily distinguished in postcards by the soaring, dodgy-looking overhang of its grainstore building.

A little farther along, the marina is full of boats and boatmen going about their business. The town was once dependent on fishing for its living.

Information The TIC (☎ 710885) is near the quayside at the bottom of Staithe St. Walsingham (☎ 710438) bike shop is opposite the TIC at 78 Staithe St.

Things to See & Do The waves roll up a sandy **beach** 1mi away from the town and linked to it by road, miniature railway and

Day 3: Hoveton to Wells-next-the-Sea

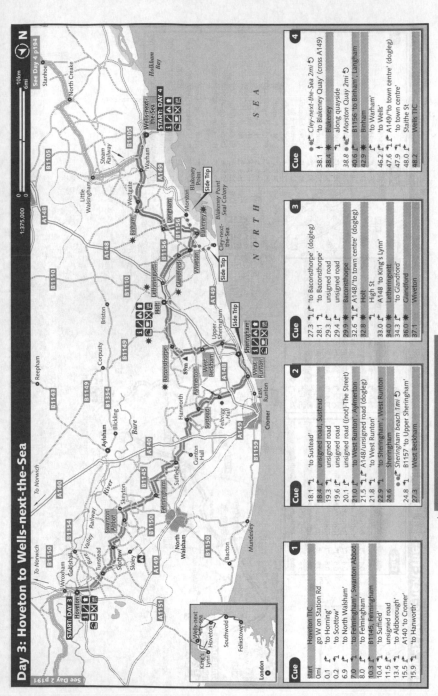

See Day 2 p191

See Day 4 p194

N

1,375,000

0   10km
0   6mi

NORTH SEA

START: DAY 3

START: DAY 4

EASTERN ENGLAND

Cue ❶

start		Hoveton TIC
0mi		go W on Station Rd
0.1	↰	'to Horning'
0.2	↱	'to Scottow'
6.9	↱	'to North Walsham'
7.0	↱	'to Felmingham', Swanton Abbot
8.0	↱	'to Felmingham'
10.3	↰	B1145, Felmingham
10.4	↱	'to West Runton'
11.5	↰	'to Suffield'
13.4	↱	unsigned road
		'to Aldborough'
15.5	↰	A140 'to Cromer'
15.9	↱	'to Hanworth'

Cue ❷

18.1	↰	'to Sustead'
18.4	↱	unsigned road, Sustead
19.3	↱	unsigned road
19.6	↰	unsigned road
20.1	↱	unsigned road ((not) The Street
21.0		'to West Runton', Aylmerton
21.5	↱↰	A148/unsigned road (dogleg)
21.8	↱	'to West Runton'
22.9	↱	'to Sheringham', West Runton
24.6		Sheringham
	● ⊶↰	Sheringham beach 1mi ⟲
24.8	↱	B1157 'to Upper Sheringham'
27.3		West Beckham

Cue ❸

27.3	↱↰	'to Baconsthorpe' (dogleg)
28.1	↰	'to Baconsthorpe'
29.3	↰	unsigned road
29.4	↱	unsigned road
29.9		Baconsthorpe
32.6	↰↱	A148/'to town centre' (dogleg)
32.8		Holt
33.0		High St
33.0	↰	A148 'to King's Lynn'
34.0		Letheringsett
34.3	↱	'to Glandford'
36.0		Glandford
37.1		Wiveton

Cue ❹

	● ⊶↰	Cley-next-the-Sea 2mi ⟲
38.1		'to Blakeney Quay' (cross A149)
38.4	✦	Blakeney
	↰	along quayside
38.8	● ⊶↱	Moreston Quay 2mi ⟲
40.6	↱	B1156 'to Binham', Langham
42.9		Binham
	↰	'to Warham'
46.2	↱	'to Wells'
47.6	↰↱	A149/'to town centre' (dogleg)
47.9	↱	'to town centre'
48.0		Staithe St
48.2		Wells TIC

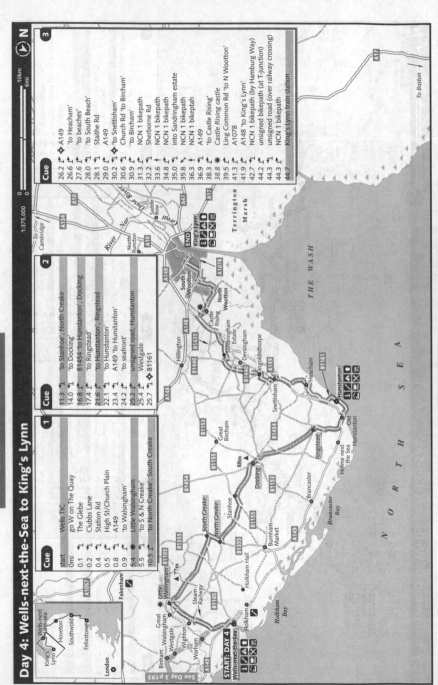

Day 4: Wells-next-the-Sea to King's Lynn

EASTERN ENGLAND

N

1:375,000

0   10km
0   6mi

Cue (1)

start		Wells TIC
0mi		go W on The Quay
0.1		The Glebe
0.2		Clubbs Lane
0.4		Station Rd
0.5		High St/Church Plain
0.8		A149
0.9		'to Walsingham'
5.4		Little Walsingham
5.5		'to S & N Creake'
10.5		'to North Creake', South Creake

Cue (2)

11.3		'to Stanhoe', North Creake
14.0		'to Docking'
16.8		B1454 'to Hunstanton', Docking
17.4		'to Ringstead'
21.6		'to Hunstanton', Ringstead
22.1		'to Hunstanton'
23.4		A149 'to Hunstanton'
24.2		'to seafront'
25.2		unsigned road, Hunstanton
25.4		Westgate
25.7		B1161

Cue (3)

26.2		A149
26.6		'to Heacham'
27.6		'to beaches'
28.0		'to South Beach'
28.1		Staithe Rd
29.0		A149
30.2		'to Snettisham'
30.4		Church Rd 'to Bircham'
30.6		'to Bircham'
30.9		NCN 1 bikepath
31.3		Sherborne Rd
32.2		NCN 1 bikepath
33.6		NCN 1 bikepath
34.8		into Sandringham estate
35.0		NCN 1 bikepath
35.8		NCN 1 bikepath
36.3		NCN 1 bikepath
36.9		A149
38.3		'to Castle Rising'
38.8		Castle Rising castle
39.5		Ling Common Rd 'to N Wootton'
41.3		A1078
41.9		A148 'to King's Lynn'
42.7		NCN 1 bikepath (by Hamburg Way)
44.2		unsigned bikepath (at T-junction)
44.3		unsigned road (over railway crossing)
44.3		NCN 1 bikepath
44.7		King's Lynn train station

To Boston

To Cambridge

Great Ouse River

A134

A10

A47

A10

A17

Saddle Bow

North Runcton

River Nar

Terrington Marsh

THE WASH

END King's Lynn

South Wootton

North Wootton

Castle Rising

Sandringham Estate

Dersingham

Ingoldisthorpe

A149

A148

B1440

B1439

Hillington

A148

B1153

Snettisham

Heacham

B1161

Hunstanton

Old Hunstanton

Holme next the Sea

Ringstead

B1454

Great Bircham

B1155

B1153

Docking

88m

Brancaster

Burnham Market

Brancaster Bay

A149

Stanhoe

B1355

South Creake

North Creake

B1355

Holkham Hall

B1105

NORTH SEA

Little Walsingham

77m

Great Walsingham

Steam Railway

Westgate

Wighton

Warham

A149

Holkham

Holkham Bay

START: DAY 4 Wells-next-the-Sea

See Day 3 p193

Fakenham

A1067

Binham

Wells-next-the-sea

Hoveton

Southwold

Felixstowe

King's Lynn

London

See Day 3 p193

a grassy-sea defence. It's possible to cycle along a path that runs beside the beach; if you can't hire a mountain bike, at least choose a bike with thick tyres.

The town itself is quite pretty, with streets of **Georgian houses** set away from the sea.

Nearby **Holkham Hall** (☎ 710227), 2mi from Wells, is a Palladian Mansion where you can cycle in the extensive grounds, part of which was designed by Capability Brown, the father of English landscape design.

Places to Stay & Eat The *Pinewoods Camping Park (☎ 710439)* is out at the beach and charges £7.50 per pitch.

B&Bs in the town start from around £18 per head. *Eastdene (☎ 710381, Northfield Lane)*, a two-minute walk from the TIC, charges from £18 per person. *Ilex House (☎ 710556, Bases Lane)*, sitting on its own grounds in the lanes west of the quayside, charges from £20 per person. *Machrimore (☎ 711653, Burnt St)*, in a converted barn also on its own grounds, charges from £22.

Luxury lodgings are found at *The Crown (☎ 710209, The Buttlands)* for £60 to £70 per person (breakfast included), in a hotel that has hosted travellers for 400 years.

The smell of chips permeates the air in Wells. But in addition to eating from the wrapper perched on the quayside, there is a sound basic menu upstairs at the *Golden Fleece*, on the roadside, where cod and chips and three-cheese bake costs around £5.25.

The *Robert Catesby (☎ 711459, Staithe St)* is a new wine bar and restaurant serving dressed crab at lunch for £4.95 and braised rabbit for £9.95. The best restaurant in town is *The Moorings (☎ 710949, Freeman St)*, at the western end of the quay. A four-course dinner will sting you £25 and the menu includes offerings like haloumi and samphire.

Day 4: Wells-next-the-Sea to King's Lynn

3–5 hours, 44.7mi
Inshore hills debunk the myth that Norfolk is all flat. Out from Wells, the gradient steepens past **Little Walsingham** (5.4mi), a renowned religious centre and destination of pilgrims. Don't forget to check out the Anglican Shrine of Our Lady of Walsingham built in 1061.

The route crosses through the higher farmland and then descends to the coast and the big resort of Hunstanton (25.2mi), overlooking the Wash to Lincolnshire. Hunstanton has all the facilities, but absolutely none of the charm of the previous seaside towns. Heacham, to the south, is much smaller but continues the theme of less-than-attractive sand flats and caravan parks.

NCN 1 points the way through the little villages on the eastern side of A149, and bisects the Queen's estate at **Sandringham** (35.0mi), which has extensive off-road riding. The interesting castle at **Castle Rising** (38.8mi) was used as a location for the BBC *Blackadder* series, which starred Rowan Atkinson.

The ride finishes on a rail trail leading to the train station at King's Lynn.

King's Lynn

See King's Lynn (pp185–86) in the Thames to the Wash ride for information about accommodation and other services.

Thetford Forest

MOUNTAIN BIKE RIDE

Duration	2–3 hours
Distance	25.0mi
Difficulty	easy-moderate
Start/End	Thetford Forest

Thetford Forest is East Anglia's most mountain bike–friendly area. You can ride wherever you want – as long as you don't stray onto army land – on and off the forest tracks, which vary from vehicle doubletracks to single file paths. This sample ride includes a section of Peddars Way long distance path.

Thetford is Britain's largest lowland pine forest and as such is an important commercial timber resource that also provides a habitat for a host of birds, animals and insects. The sandy soil drains readily after rain, making it an all-weather biking venue.

HISTORY

Thetford Forest is beloved among British mountain bike racers, even those sceptical of getting a good ride in a flat region, as the venue of highly successful rounds of the national series. Ever since one former organiser

EASTERN ENGLAND

of this race ran the course virtually through his backyard in the early 1990s, the site has been a firm fixture in the competitive psyche.

PLANNING
When to Ride
This ride is an all-weather ride, and can be done at all times of the year.

Maps
The OS Landranger map No 144 (1:50,000), *Thetford and Diss,* is a good source for this area.

Two signposted 6mi-long family mountain bike routes start from the High Lodge Forest Centre, but Thetford's real glory lies in its miles of singletrack. A single-track map is likely to be available in the future to supplement the *Cycling in the Forest* double-track map (50p), available at the High Lodge Forest Centre.

GETTING TO/FROM THE RIDE
High Lodge Forest Centre
Train Catch the train to Thetford from Ely (£5.90, 25 minutes, hourly), or from Norwich (£5, 30 minutes, hourly). Direct services from London run from King's Cross (£16.20, 1 hour, hourly).

After you've made it to Thetford you'll need to ride out to the High Lodge Forest Centre; the driveway is 3mi north-west of Thetford on the B1107.

Bicycle The Peddars Way long distance path starts nearby and runs up the eastern side of the forest on its way to the North Norfolk coast.

THE RIDE
Thetford
☎ 01842
Thetford, a little flint town on the confluence of the Rivers Little Ouse and Thet, has quite a heritage. An important settlement since the Iron Age, it features ancient monuments and curious little museums. Surrounded by tracts of forest, the town continues to retain a remote feel today.

Information The Thetford TIC is housed in the Ancient House Museum (☎ 752599), in White Hart St. The town bike shop, Mutton Brothers (☎ 753743), can be found at 27 Guildhall St.

In Thetford Forest, the High Lodge Forest Centre (☎ 810271) is geared up for visitors with a cafe and shop to browse in after a hard day in the saddle.

Forest Cycles (☎ 01842-815078 or ☎ 0589-100831), next door to High Lodge, hires mountain bikes for £4 per hour or £11 per day, offers guided riding tours and is the best place to find out about local cycling events.

Things to See & Do Thomas Paine, revolutionary writer and author of *Common Sense,* a book that argued for American independence, was born here in 1737 and is commemorated with a gilt **statue** outside the church. The Charles Burrell **steam engine museum** is full of fine old crocks, while on the outskirts is East Anglia's largest **Iron Age mound**, which became a Norman mottle and bailey castle. A ruined **priory** dates back to 1104, a time when it was the third largest in the region.

Places to Stay & Eat There's camping at *The Dower House Touring Park (☎ 01953-717313, East Harling),* 6mi east of town on a lane that forks north off the A1066. Tent pitches are £7.15.

There's no budget accommodation in town and the friendly *Wereham Guesthouse (☎ 761956, 24 White Hart St)* is one of the only B&Bs. It charges £45/57.50 for singles/doubles. It also has a restaurant with a broad menu including ostrich and five vegetarian dishes; the average dinner price is £18.

The two-star *Thomas Paine Hotel (☎ 755 631, White Hart St)* has a weekend rate of £47/58. The best hotel is the 500-year-old *Bell (☎ 754455, King St),* opposite the church, whose rooms cost £70/85. Its set dinner is £17.95 with such offerings as collops (slices) of pork with Stilton cheese crumble, and an a la carte menu with gravlax (dry-cured salmon) for £4.95.

Daytime refreshment can be found at *Julie's Diner,* beside the church. Evening dining is confined to hotel restaurants and the obligatory Indian and Chinese, although *The Hungry Horse,* on the crossroads on the way into town, has a regular burger-in-a-basket menu.

For something more exotic, travel to Ashill, where *The White Hart (☎ 01760-440217)* serves not-so-local game like alligator and kangaroo as well as vegetarian fare.

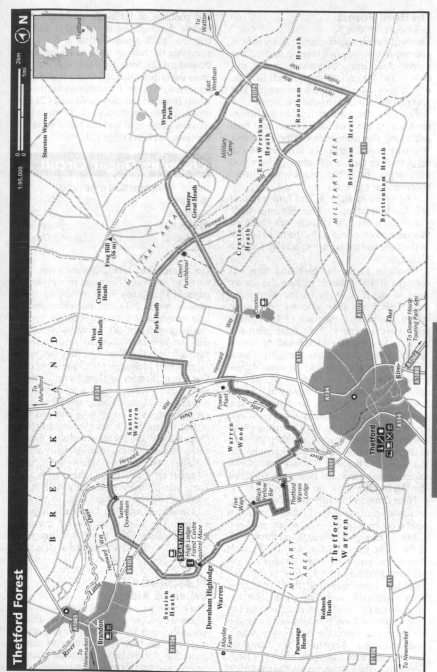

Thetford Forest

2–3 hours, 25.0mi

Thetford Forest's open-access policy means you are free to go anywhere on and off the myriad doubletrack. Anywhere, that is, except on the extensive military lands like the rifle ranges. All restricted areas are marked and you are advised to heed the signs.

From the forest centre, head to the Squirrel Maze in the south-east corner and turn left along the main track. After 1mi, at a five-way corner (area 81), turn left on the main track as far as the roadway, where you turn right past the black-and-yellow-coloured bar (area 28).

At 1.9mi turn right; at 2mi turn left; and at 2.2mi turn left again. This sequence leads you to the ruin of the 15th-century **Thetford Warren Lodge**, occupied by the head keeper of the time and today maintained by English Heritage.

Continue to the car park and turn left onto the B1107; after 55yd take the grassy track to the right (between the wire fencing). This leads shortly to an open area, where you pick up the track (3.1mi) going right. On the corner (3.3mi), dogleg left and right on to a smaller track beside a stream full of rushes that leads to the Little Ouse. Cross over at the weir and turn left downstream. Keep to the bank for a while, then follow the arrows that lead away at first but keep you parallel with the river. At the power plant (which burns chicken waste and wood chips), turn right (5.1mi), go over the railway level crossing and then turn left at the A134. After about 70yd turn right into the woods at the sign 'Crown Estate' and take the main track, the Hereward Way, not the black-and-yellow bar.

Near **Croxton** (6.7mi), continue in a similar direction on the B-road. After 1.5mi, turn right onto the Hereward Way again, and keep going for another 3.5mi, crossing the A1075, as far as the track junction with the Peddars Way, where you turn left northwards. Follow the long distance path for 1.5mi to the road. Turn left, cross back over the A1075, and keep going past the military camp for another 4.5mi (17.5mi). Turn right, still on tarmac – past the **Devil's Punchbowl** (a glacial ice hollow in which the water mysteriously rises and falls) – keep going for 2.2mi and turn left onto a broad forestry track (19.8mi). Continue to the bottom, follow the track right

and continue as far as the A134 (20.8mi). Follow that right for about 100yd and turn left onto track again. Follow it for 1.5mi, alongside the railway track as far as **Santon Downham** (22.3mi). Turn left on to the road, cross the railway line and the river and go up through the village. Turn right on the road towards Brandon and after half a mile (23.3mi) turn left onto forest track. Half a mile later, cross over the road into the forest drive and continue to High Lodge (25.0mi).

Chipping Ongar Circuit

MOUNTAIN BIKE RIDE

Duration ....2–4 hrs
Distance 12.0mi
Difficulty ....moderate
Start/End ....Chipping Ongar

Going mountain biking in Essex requires a nerve of its own. The tracks in well-known parts of the county such as Epping Forest may be worn and clear, but elsewhere the bridleways can present plenty of unexpected challenges. They get overgrown because they are little used, they can seem to start in people's back gardens, and they get waterlogged after prolonged rain. Ploughing occasionally obliterates legal tracks across fields, which can force you to pick your own way around the edge of fields, sometimes even requiring that you get off your bike and push.

But do not be put off. Around Chipping Ongar there are pretty woodland pockets full of tracks, idyllic little streams, and the villages are well stocked with pubs. Chances are you'll be on your own too. The route is half bridleway and half road, but the road sections are over quickly.

The fertile agrarian landscape is gently rolling. The route runs around the upper reaches of the little River Roding, which empties into the River Thames at Barking in east London.

PLANNING
When to Ride

The main elemental hazard is rainwater. After a period of wet weather in this region, this ride is hardly worth the bother. Wear long sleeves and leggings from mid-summer to autumn, especially for the more neglected tracks, to protect you from brambles and nettles.

Maps

Because the tracks become obscure in places, getting lost is quite likely so take the OS Landranger map No 167 (1:50,000), *Chelmsford, Harlow & Bishop's Stortford,* along.

GETTING TO/FROM THE RIDE
Train

The southern end of the circuit is 5mi from Brentwood, which has fast, frequent connections to London Liverpool St (£5.50 offpeak, 30 minutes, every 10 minutes).

The London Underground station at Ongar was shut in the mid-1990s.

Car

Parking in the long-term car park on the eastern side of the High St in Chipping Ongar costs 60p for four hours. The town is about 30mi north-east of London, along the M11.

THE RIDE
Chipping Ongar
☎ 01277

With its old high road layout and warm brickwork buildings, Chipping Ongar is a typical little Essex country town. A plaque commemorates the African explorer David Livingstone, who resided here for a while during the 19th century in one of the dwellings on High St.

The Chipping Ongar Library (☎ 362616), on High St, is the only source of local information. Behind the library is an ancient earthwork that may hold your interest for a few minutes.

Places to Stay & Eat The only accommodation to be found is the *Travelodge (Harlow East)* (☎ 0800-050950, *A414 Tylers Green),* which has doubles for £49.95. For a standard pub meal with a post-ride beer try *The Cock (High St)* or grab a freshly made bite at *Conor's Deli (High St).*

Chipping Ongar Circuit
2–4 hours, 12mi

From the long-term car park on the eastern side of Chipping Ongar High St, go south (along High St) and turn left on the outskirts onto the A128 to Brentwood. After almost a mile, just over the Langford Bridge, turn left on to the bridleway farm track beside 'The Lodge'. Round the corner take the grassy doubletrack to the right, which joins up soon with a bigger farm track coming in from the left.

Stay on the bridleway through open fields with the stream on your left, then hug the bushes by the stream where the fields are ploughed. When a bushy ditch crosses your path, continue – you may have to scramble over a plough, probably placed there to keep motorbikes at bay. A little farther round the edge of this field is a clear track left into Pole's Wood, which you take.

The wood has myriad tracks, making it tricky but fun trying to follow the course of the bridleway. Keep the stream on your left and try to exit the woods on the track that emerges in a continuous direction to **Kelvedon Hatch**. Otherwise, exit the woods up to the high right-hand side, and take the track at the edge of the field to the A128, then turn left in Kelvedon Hatch.

Turn left, eastwards, along this road, continue straight through the wooded bikepath and again back on the road. About 2mi farther on go left on the track before the yellow house, curve round the back and continue. Pass between two houses (signposted footpath), to come face to face with a field, which, despite the fact that the bridleway goes through the middle, may be ploughed. If so, skirt the left-hand edge (probably pushing), regain the road and turn right to **Paslow Wood Common** (6.5mi). Otherwise, emerge on the road through the village. Take the signposted bridleway opposite, left and westward (it's hidden in the bush corridor behind the right-hand house). This is overgrown in places, but satisfying. Follow it in the same direction for 1mi to the farm buildings at Paslow Hall.

Make your way round the buildings and head to the right to the road. Turn left to the A414, and turn right carefully onto it, heading east. After 0.3mi turn left on the signposted bridleway at **Chevers Hall** and watch for the track going off to the right before the first barn. Follow this over the fields to the flint church at **Norton Mandeville**. Go left at the church and through the wooden gate, signed 'Private Rd, bridleway only'. Follow it around to the right, and continue. Bear right through the metal gate signed 'Private Road', then straight on where the main track bears left. You'll emerge at a track T-junction

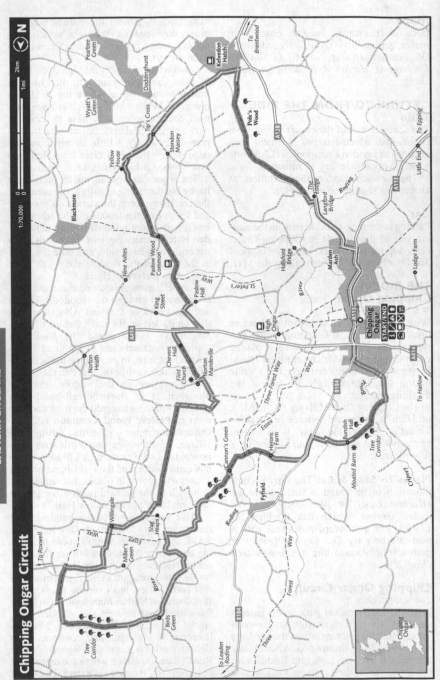

Chipping Ongar Circuit

next to open fields. Go left and follow the signposted bridleway through the middle of the open fields – it may be bumpy. After 1mi, go right through the slag heaps and left on the concrete track to the road.

Turn right to **Willingale**, and left in the village centre to Roxwell. About 1mi later turn left before the white house onto the Essex Way and follow it to the road. Go left and immediately right on the tarmac, and at the top of the field, turn left onto the bridleway through the tree corridor (which may be overgrown). Emerge at the houses and continue to the road, then turn left. Continue on this road, signed 'to Fyfield and Ongar', then turn left at **Birds Green**, signed 'to Fyfield', and left again after 0.5mi towards **Miller's Green**. Follow the signposted right to Fyfield, and after a short mile, take the next bridleway left on a right-hand bend at **Witney Green**, through another tree corridor. This may force you up right to the edge of a field, but keep going in the same direction to the village of **Cannon's Green**. The signposted bridleway

continues a little farther through the village. This is good singletrack. Keep right at the fork and stay with the track to the River Roding. Cross on the bridge and hug the right-hand edge of the field ahead towards the farm. (The Essex Way is more clearly marked left along the stream).

Go through **Herons Farm**, turn left on to the road and continue to the B184, where you turn left. After about 200yd turn right on a concrete track through fields towards houses. Just beyond is Bundish Hall with its **moated barns**. Continue on the bridleway and keep going straight ahead through another tree corridor where the bigger track turns right. At the bottom, go over a stile and turn left through the field with the river on your right (there may be cows and horses grazing). Cross the river by the bridges at the end and see the bridleway exit up the field on the left. Rejoin the road, turn left and continue to the B184. Turn right once you're on it, to the A414 roundabout. Continue straight over to complete the circuit at Chipping Ongar.

Central England

Stretching from Wales in the west as far as the fens in the east, and from the outskirts of the capital, to above the northern cities, central England is a fascinating and disparate area with regions of great beauty nestling against grim working lands.

The cycling highlights occur in the Marches, the Cotswolds, the Pennines and anywhere away from the cities and main towns in the rest of the region. The rides in this chapter seek out the beauty spots and uplands by threading their way around the centres of population and industry.

Historic cities en route include Oxford, Lincoln, York, Shrewsbury, Chester, with other gems such as Oundle and Stratford-upon-Avon also on the agenda.

NATURAL HISTORY
The Pennine hills begins in the middle of England and bisects it as it heads northwards, providing the highest land in the region. Out in the west, the foothills of the Marches rise out of fertile valleys without the harshness of their Welsh mountain cousins. Elsewhere, central England is undulating, green and largely rural, from the Thames Valley in the south to the Yorkshire Dales in the north.

CLIMATE
The temperature drop slightly as you travel northward, and it is considerably cooler as soon as you hit high land. The weather in the Pennines is changeable and can be very cold and wet, so always ride prepared.

INFORMATION
Maps
Three OS Travelmaster maps (1:250,000) pretty much cover the region: No 5, *Northern England*; No 7, *Wales and the West Midlands*; and No 6, *East Midlands and East Anglia*.

Books
OS Cycle Tours publishes regional guides with one-day mountain bike and road routes; they include *Gloucestershire and Hereford & Worcester* and *Berks, Bucks & Oxfordshire*. There are numerous books on activities in the Peak District and the Cotswolds, which are major hiking and cycling areas.

In Summary

Terrain
Generally undulating, charming countryside with the Pennines as a backbone; much of the east lies at sea level, while the west offers tougher tests such as the Cotswold Hills rising from the east and the foothills of the Marches.

Special Events
- **Sea Shanty Singers Festival** (April), Lancaster
- **Hay Festival of Literature** (June), Hay-on-Wye
- **Streetbands Festival** (July), Lancaster
- **Buxton Festival** (late July/early August)
- **Flower Show** (August), Southport

Cycling Events
- **York Cycle Rally** (June)
- **Lancaster Cycle Fest** (every second August)
- **Tour of the Peak** (September), Peak District – annual pro-am road race
- **Lincoln Grand Prix** (May) – annual pro-am road race

Food & Drink Specialities
- Morecambe Bay shrimps
- Lincolnshire sausages
- Yorkshire Pudding
- Bakewell tart

Tourist Information
- **English Tourism Council: ☎** 020 8846 9000, 🖳 www.englishtourism.org.uk or 🖳 www.visitbritain.com

GATEWAY CITIES
London
See the London chapter for information about accommodation and other services, and getting to/from the city.

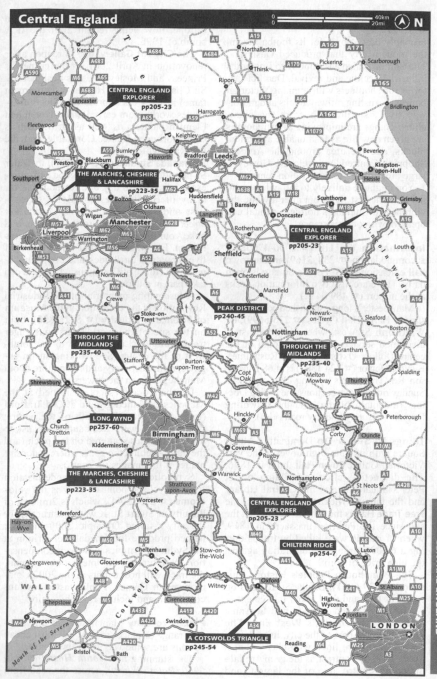

Central England

0 40km
0 20mi

N

CENTRAL ENGLAND EXPLORER
pp205-23

THE MARCHES, CHESHIRE & LANCASHIRE
pp223-35

CENTRAL ENGLAND EXPLORER
pp205-23

PEAK DISTRICT
pp240-45

THROUGH THE MIDLANDS
pp235-40

THROUGH THE MIDLANDS
pp235-40

LONG MYND
pp257-60

THE MARCHES, CHESHIRE & LANCASHIRE
pp223-35

CENTRAL ENGLAND EXPLORER
pp205-23

CHILTERN RIDGE
pp254-7

A COTSWOLDS TRIANGLE
pp245-54

CENTRAL ENGLAND

Manchester

☎ 01727

Probably best known for its football team, the modern city that produced Oasis and The Smiths is also a testimony to England's industrial decline and revival. Derelict factories rub shoulders with stunning Victorian buildings, rusting railway tracks and motorway flyovers with flashy bars and nightclubs. Things are improving as warehouses are given new life as fashionable apartment blocks, and the area around the Arndale Shopping Centre is redeveloped. However, large areas of urban deprivation remain.

You might be unlikely to fall in love with the place at first sight, but after a while the vibrancy of England's northern capital can break down your resistance.

Information The TIC (☎ 0906-4700847, accommodation ☎ 234 3169) in the town hall extension off St Peter's Square is open daily. There are also two information desks at the airport (☎ 489 6412).

Manchester's long-established central bike shop is Harry Hall Cycles (☎ 236 5699), 67 Whitworth St West, where informed staff give good service. About 2mi south of the centre (follow Oxford St/Rd to Rusholme), Bicycle Doctor (☎ 224 1303) is at 68 Dickinson Rd. The shop's cycling club organises Sunday rides in two sections, the Flying Doctors (mountain biking) and the Dawdling Doctors (leisurely country road rides).

Things to See & Do Dominating Albert Square with its 85m-high tower is the vast Victorian Gothic **Town Hall**, built in 1876. The distinctive circular building on St Peter's Square houses the **Central Library** and the **Library Theatre**. On Peter St, the **Free Trade Hall** is the third to be built on the site since the Peterloo massacre in 1819, when 11 people were killed by troops during a 60,000-strong demonstration against the high price of corn.

The **Pumphouse People's History Museum** (☎ 839 6061), Bridge St, focuses on social history and the Labour movement.

The area around King St and St Ann's Square is Manchester's **West End**. The most attractive part of the city, its pedestrianised streets are lined with classy shops. To the east, by contrast, is the grim **Arndale Shopping Centre**, one of the largest (and surely ugliest) covered shopping areas in Europe, now being rebuilt after the IRA bomb of 1996.

The **City Art Gallery**, due to reopen after renovation in April 2001 on the corner of Princess and Mosley Sts, was designed by Sir Charles Barry (of Houses of Parliament fame) in 1824. Its impressive collection includes works from early Italian, Dutch and Flemish painters as well as British artists Gainsborough, Blake, Constable and the Pre-Raphaelites.

Granada Studios (☎ 832 4999), in Water St, provides an unexpectedly good and quintessentially British day out. Responsible for many of Britain's best-loved TV series – first and foremost the soap *Coronation Street* – you can walk around the sets and poke your nose into the famous pub **Rovers Return**. Elsewhere, the tour offers a mix of live shows and thrill rides, and even a mock-up of the House of Commons where you can take part in a debate.

A fascinating memorial of the Industrial Revolution is the collection in the **Museum of Science & Industry** (☎ 832 1830), built on the site of the world's first passenger train station in Liverpool Rd to the southwest of the centre. See working steam engines, mill machinery and learn more about Manchester from the sewers upwards.

Football craziness is enshrined at the Manchester United ground at **Old Trafford** (tours ☎ 868 8631), south of the centre, where almost every week supporters ask to have their ashes scattered on the pitch (and they are – behind the goals where it doesn't matter if it damages the grass).

Symbolic of Manchester's modernisation from a cyclists' point of view is the **velodrome** (☎ 223 2244), which is 2mi east of the city at Stuart St. It was constructed for the city's failed Olympic 2000 bid, but helped produce four medals for Britain at the Sydney Olympics by way of compensation. A fixture on the international circuit, the track will host events of the 2002 Commonwealth Games. Public taster sessions cost £6.50 and include track bike hire.

Places to Stay Manchester has a reasonable range of places to stay, but most cheap options are some way from the centre.

The stunning new *Youth Hostel* (☎ 839 9960, Potato Wharf), across the road from the Museum of Science & Industry in the Castlefield area, has comfortable four-bed dorms from £17.40 including breakfast.

About 2mi south of the centre, Stretford has two private hostels. Tiny **Peppers** (☎ 848 9770, 17 Greatstone Rd) has beds from £10, and the **International Backpackers Hostel & Guest House** (☎ 872 3499, 10 Hornby Rd) charges £11.

The **Commercial Hotel** (☎ 834 3504; 125 Liverpool Rd, Castlefield) is a traditional pub close to the museum, charging £25/40 for singles/doubles. Rather pricier is the modern **Castlefield Hotel** (☎ 832 7073, Liverpool Rd), with rooms for £49/59 at weekends, including use of its pool and sauna.

Didsbury, 3mi south of the centre has many hotels in converted Victorian houses. The pleasant **Baron Hotel** (☎ 434 3688; 116 Palatine Rd, West Didsbury) is typical, with en suite rooms from £25/35. The comfortable **Elm Grange Hotel** (☎ 445 3336, 561 Wilmslow Rd) has rooms from £32/52.

Across the road from Piccadilly station is the luxurious **Malmaison** (☎ 278 1000) with rooms for a flat-rate £110 and a French brasserie.

Places to Eat The most distinctive restaurant zones are Chinatown in the city centre and Rusholme, the 'Curry Mile Quarter', to the south. Chinatown has many restaurants that are not Chinese, and most aren't particularly cheap. The most acclaimed is the **Little Yang Sing** (☎ 228 7722, 17 George St), specialising in Cantonese cuisine. The daytime set menu is £8.95 plus service, but expect to pay twice that in the evening. Readers also rate **Pearl City** (☎ 228 7683, 23 George St), where dim sum Sunday lunch costs £10.

Rusholme, on Wilmslow Rd, the extension of Oxford St/Rd has numerous cheap, excellent Indian and Pakistani places. Try the **Sanam Sweet House & Restaurant** (☎ 224 8824, 145 Wilmslow Rd) for Karachi chicken for £6 as well as an array of mouthwatering sweets.

Smart cafe bars have taken off in a big way. The originals, **Dry 201** (☎ 236 9840, 28 Oldham St) and **Manto** (☎ 236 2667, 46 Canal St), are still among the best. Another is **Grinch** (☎ 907 3210, Chapel Walk), which serves salmon fishcakes for £6.95 in arty surroundings.

Albert Square is gradually filling up with places to eat. Try **Tampopo** (☎ 819 1966), a minimalist noodle bar where mee goreng costs £6.25. More unusual is the basement **Armenian Taverna** (☎ 834 9025, 3–5 Princess St) serving Tbilisi kebab for £7.95.

In a class of its own is the four-storey **Mash & Air** (☎ 661 1111, 40 Chorlton St). This super-trendy place has a cafe bar with its own brewery on the ground floor and a much posher restaurant upstairs.

Getting There & Away Manchester is about 180mi from London, 210mi from Glasgow, 65mi from York and 50mi from Lancaster.

Air Manchester airport (☎ 489 3000) is 7mi south of the city centre and is the largest in the UK outside London. A train to the airport costs £2.70 and bicycles are carried free without booking, but can be refused if the train is crowded.

To ride from the airport to the city centre, begin by heading for Wythenshawe. Continue to Northenden, where you should pick up Palatine Rd and stay on that for 6mi to the centre.

Train Piccadilly is Manchester's main station (2.5 hours to London).

Use the national rail inquiry line (☎ 0845-7484950) for times and the numbers of the different operators for telephone bookings. There is usually a small charge for bike carriage on inter-city trains, and booking is essential although this can be made when you buy a ticket for immediate travel.

Central England Explorer

Duration	8 days
Distance	385.6mi
Difficulty	moderate-hard
Start	St Albans (London)
End	Lancaster

Rural back roads link a chain of historic towns on this long trip across the north-south divide of England.

The landscape rolls away from London for three days as far as Northampton Shire, then flattens into the Lincolnshire Fens and rises to the Lincolnshire Wolds to the broad

Humber estuary. The route turns westward, where the Pennine hills form a dramatic finale. The home strait is through the Trough of Bowland road almost to the north-west coast to Lancaster.

On the way, the cathedral cities of St Albans, Lincoln and York deserve a good look, with handsome towns like Oundle, Stamford, Boston and Wetherby providing stone-built tradition on the way. The push over the Pennines stops overnight in steep-sided Haworth, the home of the Brontë sisters.

Three days of the trip, from Boston to the Humber, follow the NCN 1 route. Every mile has been chosen for its peacefulness and often its beauty. The signposting makes navigation child's play.

NATURAL HISTORY
England's geography changes markedly as the ride progresses, from the softer southern landscapes to the harsher northern slopes, with their rich mineral deposits, harsher climate and an economic history of heavy industry and mining.

PLANNING
When to Ride
Bad weather in the Pennines is a serious matter, and many high roads are closed by snowfall in the winter. The best time to ride is between May and September.

Maps
Recommended maps are OS Travelmaster (1:250,000) No 6, *East Midlands & East Anglia*, and No 5, *Northern England*.

Parts of the route are also covered by the Sustrans maps *Hull to Fakenham* and *The White Rose Route*.

What to Bring
In this well-populated part of England you are never far from shops and pubs, but carry a minimum of fluid, snacks and bike repair items just in case. Bike shops feature in virtually all the starting and finishing towns.

Camp sites are thin on the ground, so it is necessary to stay in lodgings every other night.

GETTING TO/FROM THE RIDE
St Albans (London)
Train It's a 30-minute journey from London Kings Cross to St Albans on the Thameslink

line; after 9.30 am, trains leave up to four times hourly. A single is £7 and bikes are free, but cannot be carried weekday evenings from 4.30 to 6.30 pm.

Bicycle The route from central London to St Albans amounts to little more than 20mi of unedifying urban sprawl and is only for purists. Take the A5 Edgware Rd from Marble Arch in the centre as far as the M1 motorway, then the A5083.

Lancaster
Train Good connections run southwards to London Euston (£45.50 return, three hours, twice hourly), northwards to Glasgow (£29.90 return, 2½ hours, every two hours) and eastwards to Leeds (£18.50 return, two hours, four daily).

Bicycle Lancaster is on the End to End ride (see the Land's End to John o'Groats chapter) and is the final destination for the Marches, Cheshire & Lancashire ride later in this chapter.

THE RIDE
St Albans
☎ 01727
St Albans is a well-to-do little town dating back 2000 years to Roman times, when the settlement of Verulamium lay at the bottom of the hill upon which the magnificent cathedral and abbey church now stand. Alban, whose shrine lies there, was the first Christian martyr in England, a Roman soldier beheaded in AD 209 for his beliefs.

Information The TIC (☎ 864511) is easy to find – in the cream-coloured town hall at the end of Market Place. If you arrive after 5.30 pm an accommodation list is stuck on the window.

For bike bits, try the Halfords superstore (down Holywell Hill, left at the bottom and left into the shopping complex) or St Albans Cycles, about half a mile east of the TIC along Victoria St.

Things to See & Do The heavy exterior of the Norman **cathedral** and **abbey church** contrasts with its interior, which reveals a light and lofty place of ancient worship. The broad nave has columns decorated with 13th- and 14th-century murals and the shrine of St Alban remains a destination for pilgrims today.

Down the hill in **Verulamium Park** lies the foundations of a Roman town house dating from AD 200 and its **hypocaust**, a form of underfloor heating designed to soften the blow of the English winter.

The **Verulamium Museum** (☎ 819339), on St Michael's St, has one of the finest displays of Roman mosaic pavements and murals in the country.

Places to Stay There is no camp site or youth hostel in St Albans.

Cheaper B&Bs near the train station include *Mrs Jameson's* (☎ 865498, 7 Marlborough Gate), which charges £16/32 for singles/doubles with shared bathroom. *Mrs Matheson-Titt's* (☎ 766764, 3 Upper Lattimore Rd) has a garden where bikes can be secured; charges are £35/50. On the pretty west side of town is the comfortable *Black Lion Inn* (☎ 861785, 190 Fishpool St), with a tariff of £50/52 for room only; breakfast costs £3.75.

Places to Eat Between the TIC and the cathedral are numerous places to eat. The *Pasta Bowl* (☎ 812683, 5 High St) serves a filling calzone calabrese for £6.95. There is a wide choice of sandwiches at *Palmers* a few doors along.

A traditional bakery where you can buy buns for the ride is *Harringtons (Market Place)*. For lunch for around £5.50, try the *Abbey Refectory* in the cathedral Chapter House, open until 4.30 pm Monday to Saturday and 5 pm Sunday. For sheer Englishness you can't beat the inn, *Ye Olde Fighting Cocks* (☎ 869152) is in a converted 15th-century pigeon house below the abbey beside the park. It has a large menu of quality meat and veg pub grub from £5 for a main course.

Day 1: St Albans to Bedford
2½–4 hours, 39.1mi
The peaceful ride through exquisite villages and rolling farmland leads through Hertfordshire and Bedfordshire to the county town of Bedford. The climbs and descents give views over handsome landscape.

Take care for the 0.9mi along the narrow A507 beyond Upper Gravenhurst, and crossing the A6 near Haynes West End at the 31mi mark.

A nice place for a breather is the market town of Hitchin (16.5mi), where the small streets and cobbled **Market Place** date back to Saxon times and are sprinkled with *cafes*.

From the high land before Houghton Conquest (31.7mi) see the Great Stour Valley, the chimney stacks of Stewartby **brickworks** to the west and the gargantuan **airship hangars** to the east, about 2.5mi east of Cardington. These defunct hangars were built in the 1920s to house the historic airships R100 and R101. One of them may in the future house an airship and balloon museum.

Bedford
☎ 01234
Bedford straddles the River Great Ouse, has a handful of historic honey-coloured buildings and a decent shopping precinct.

Bedford's most famous son was John Bunyan (1628–88), the radical Anglican preacher and author of *Pilgrim's Progress*, the allegorical tale of a Christian's journey to paradise via the Slough of Despond and Hill of Difficulty, both inspired by places nearby. Bunyan wrote the work in 1678 while detained 'at his majesty's pleasure' in the town jail for his nonconformist views.

During WWII the BBC broadcast from here after its evacuation from London, as did American big band leader Glenn Miller, before he made his last fateful flight from RAF Twinwoods, nearby.

Information The TIC (☎ 215226), 10 St Paul's Square, stocks *John Bunyan's Bedford*, a free guide to places with a Bunyan connection.

For a bike shop go to Michael's Cycles (☎ 352937), 54 Midland Rd, only 0.3mi west from the TIC, or Cycle King (☎ 351 525), 40 Greyfriars, past the bus station.

Things to See & Do Two Bunyan attractions worth visiting are the **Bunyan Meeting Free Church** (Mill St), with its commemorative stained-glass window, and the **Bunyan Museum**. There are pleasant islands in the river at **Mill Meadows**; access from the 1888 suspension bridge on the Embankment. The **Cecil Higgins Art Gallery** (☎ 211222), at Castle Close, has an award-winning display of ceramics, glass and watercolours.

Day 1: St Albans to Bedford

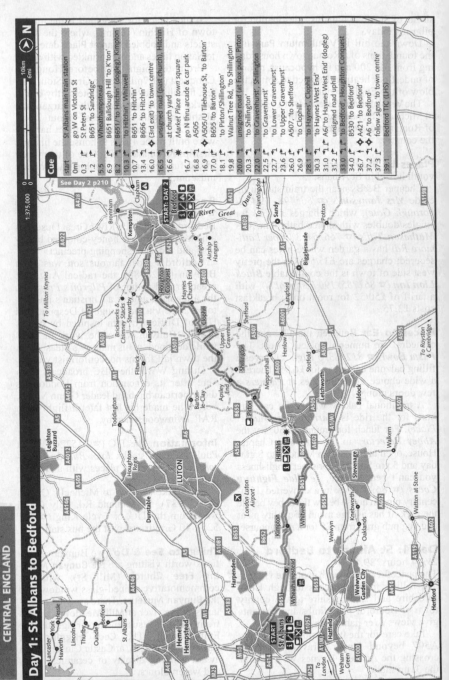

The Duke's Head Hotel, one of King's Lynn's many old beauties.

Ely Cathedral, eastern England.

King's College Chapel, Cambridge.

Wells-next-the-Sea is a fishing port and popular holiday town.

The pancake-flat terrain of eastern England at Walberswick National Nature Reserve.

JON DAVISON

In central England, retrace the Pilgrim Fathers' steps at Boston...

ELLIOT DANIEL

...marvel at St Albans Cathedral...

CHRIS IVIN

...feel Fotheringhay's history...

CHRIS MELLOR

...explore Lincoln Castle...

CHRIS MELLOR

...get all steamy in York...

NEIL SETCHFIELD

...stock up at the York markets, or just enjoy the bike-friendly city and its glorious medieval Minster.

Places to Stay & Eat For the nearest camp site head 3mi north-west along the busy A6 to *Woodlands Park (☎ 259584; Bedford Rd, Clapham)*, where a tent pitch is £3.50 per night for two, £1 per extra person. There is no hostel.

A number of well-priced B&Bs lie close to the town centre. The owners of *Park View (☎ 341376, 11 Shaftesbury Ave)* are tandem cyclists who charge £17.50/34 for singles/doubles. Find them 1mi east along the river. *Stonelodge (☎ 267666, 75 Goldington Ave)*, 0.6mi north-east of the centre, has rooms for £17/32. Just north of the city centre is the *Hertford House Hotel (☎ 350007, 57 De Pary's Ave)*, where rooms cost £25/45.

During the day *Green Cuisine (St Cuthbert St)* serves snacks with vegan options. Spinach and fetta goujons are £3.50 and veg chilli £5.10. *Cafe Bliss (Silver St)* in the pedestrian area has seating outside and does a dish of the day from around £5, and tea and cake for £1.69. The town is well served with Italian restaurants, as the owners' forefathers came to work in the Stewartby brickworks in the 1930s. Along the Bunyan Meeting Free Church is *Pizzeria Santaniello (☎ 353742, Newnham St)* with pizzas from £3.90. *Pitchers Sports Bar & Diner (☎ 350766, High St)* has an American flavour, with burgers and Coca-Cola served to a pumping beat.

Day 2: Bedford to Oundle
2½–4 hours, 38.0mi
This ride is truly pretty, particularly in the summer months when the hedgerows are in full bloom. The traffic is mostly light, although crossing the A6 (14.0mi) near Sharnbrook needs care. There are no hills to look forward to.

Meander northwards from Bedfordshire to Northamptonshire through lovely villages off the beaten track. Highlights are the old bridge crossing of the River Great Ouse water meadows (flood plains) at **Odell** (where the country park has a good tearoom), and riding along the **River Nene** beyond Raunds. **Wadenhoe** is a particularly well-preserved old village on a side trip 4mi before the charming town of Oundle.

Oundle
☎ 01832
One of the best examples of a honey-coloured sandstone Northamptonshire town, Oundle rises above the water meadows of the River Nene. It pays little heed to the modern era until the weekends when the local youth appears out of nowhere to flood the pubs.

Information The TIC (☎ 274333), 14 West St, has a £1 town guide that includes a 1½-hour walking trail around the town. Basic bike supplies are available at Owen & Hartley (☎ 272591) on North St.

Things to See & Do Despite being petite, the town has a sizeable 13th-century **church**, an old **public school** around which much town life revolves, a **theatre**, a weekend **museum** and a fistful of handsome 17th- and 18th-century buildings.

Every July the **Oundle International Festival** (tickets ☎ 272026) of classical and jazz music takes place in and around the town.

Places to Stay & Eat Accommodation is limited and gets booked out when a school function or the music festival is on.

The nearest camp site is at *Castle Farm (☎ 226326)* at Fotheringhay, 4mi to the north (follow Day 3 directions; turn right beyond the bridge). A tent pitch for two people is £3. There are no toilets.

In Oundle, the only B&B is *Ashworth House (☎ 275312, 75 West St)* with prices from £25 for a single. The *Ship Inn (☎ 273 918, 18 West St)* has a comfy living room and rooms for £25/50 for singles/doubles. The classy old town hotel, *The Talbot (☎ 273 621, New St)* has rooms for £70/85. It also has a *restaurant*. Its staircase came from the demolished Fotheringhay castle, and Mary Queen of Scots is supposed to have descended it on her day of execution in 1587.

Buy local sausages at *Trendall's (22 Market Place)* butchers, while a hearty selection of sandwiches and cakes is to be found at the *Oundle Bakery (2 Market Place)*, nearby.

Hunting down dinner is easy. Try a filling Indian takeaway from *Eastern Spices (☎ 272 662, West St)* starts from £2.75, or there's a sit-down Indian option at *Onkar (☎ 274312, West St)*. Mid-priced pizzas are on offer at *San Giorgio (☎ 272720, 74 West St)*.

Day 3: Oundle to Thurlby
2½–4 hours, 40.6mi
Northamptonshire, Rutland (England's smallest county) and Lincolnshire are rich

CENTRAL ENGLAND

Day 2: Bedford to Oundle

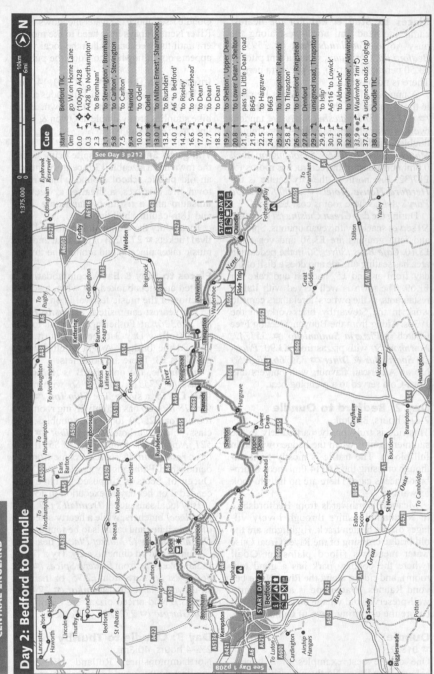

Cue		
start		Bedford TIC
0mi		go W on Home Lane
0.0	◇�??↓	(100yd) A428
0.3	◇↑↓	A428 'to Northampton'
2.3	↓	'to Bromham'
3.1	↓↑	'to Stevington', Bromham
5.8	↑↓	'to Carlton', Stevington
7.5	↑↓	'to Carlton'
9.4		Harrold
10.0	↑↓	'to Odell'
11.0	✳	Odell
13.0	↓	'to Milton Ernest', Sharnbrook
13.5	↓	'to Rushden'
14.0	↓	A6 'to Bedford'
14.2	↓	'to Riseley'
16.6	↓	'to Swineshead'
17.0	↓	'to Dean'
17.7	↓	'to Dean'
18.2	↓	'to Dean'
19.5	↓	'to Shelton', Upper Dean
20.8	↓	'to Lower Dean', Shelton
21.3		pass 'to Little Dean road
21.9	↓	'to Hargrave'
22.5	↓	B645
24.3	↓	B663
25.2	↓	'to Thrapston', Raunds
25.8	↓	'to Thrapston'
26.7	↓	'to Denford', Ringstead
27.8		Denford
29.2	↓	unsigned road, Thrapston
29.5	↓	'to Islip'
30.3	↓	A6116 'to Lowick'
30.5	↓	'to Aldwincle'
32.8	↓	'to Wadenhoe', Aldwincle
33.9	●↓↩	Wadenhoe 1mi ↩
37.6	↓↩	unsigned roads (dogleg)
38.0		Oundle TIC

See Day 3 p212

in royal, industrial and social history, with plenty of pretty lanes.

Heavy traffic raises its ugly head crossing the A47 before Morcott and on the broad A606 into Stamford.

First feature of the day is the village of **Fotheringhay**, where Mary Queen of Scots lost her head in 1587 after outstaying her welcome as a 'guest' of Queen Elizabeth I. The castle has long since been demolished, but the site is pretty and historically quite evocative.

A few miles later the route passes beneath the 82 arches of the massive **Seaton Viaduct**, stretching out over ancient preserved hay meadows beside the River Welland.

Beyond the day's lone hill (16.9mi), on the far side of the valley, lies the great reservoir of **Rutland Water**, with a picnic area, views, *cafe* and *restaurant*. Continue around the popular perimeter bikepath – it's rough but rideable on narrow tyres – and over the dam.

The fine-stone town of Stamford is a good final destination for the day and has plentiful accommodation and facilities, though it will make the next day's ride more challenging at 78.5mi. The day officially ends at the village of Thurlby, 10mi farther on, at the youth hostel, where camping is also an option.

Thurlby & Stamford
☎ 01780

Thurlby is a tiny village offering little more than a hostel, hotel and some eateries. Anyone after a faster pace should choose to stay in Stamford.

Stamford is a pretty and friendly little town straddling the River Welland beneath a skyline of spires. Its renown lies in its architecture – it was declared a conservation area in 1967 – with its collection of 600 listed buildings, the majority being of yellow stone that glows in sunshine. In Elizabethan times the Cecil family constructed the magnificent mansion and grounds of Burghley House, nearby. The architectural boom came in the Georgian period, when the town developed into the handsome monument to stone architecture it is today. The structure spanning St Martin's on High St, on the south bank, is the old gallows, built to deter nefarious travellers. The official line nowadays is that the

silhouette is a symbol of welcome. Still, it's best not to jump any red lights.

Information The Stamford TIC (☎ 755611), 27 St Mary's St, lies in the heart of town, next to St George's Square, well known to Britons as the period setting for the BBC production of George Eliot's novel *Middlemarch*.

Get bikes sorted at Just Wheels (☎ 480 455), 7 North St, or Stamford Cycle Centre (☎ 755605), on Star Lane.

Things to See & Do If the weather is good, Stamford is best discovered on foot. The town's main church is the 600-year-old **St Mary's** on St Mary's Hill. **St Martin's** on High St is a late-15th-century perpendicular work and the last place of rest of the Cecil family. The Georgian theatre at the **Arts Centre**, built in 1766, has been restored and continues to show work today. Beside the river at the bottom of town lie the **Meadows**, where residents snooze on the lawns and fishing hot-spots are reserved for people with disabilities.

Paying a visit to the grand **Burghley House** (☎ 52451, £6.10, open 11 am to 4.30 pm April to September), 1mi south of town, is a must. Renowned among the equine fraternity for the annual trials held here in September, the Tudor palace is set amid extensive gardens and vast grounds and is still home to the Cecil family's descendants.

Places to Stay & Eat The day's ride finishes at *Thurlby YHA (☎ 01778-425588, 16 High St)*, a relative outpost 10mi on from Stamford. Camping is also available here. Dining out in Thurlby is best at *The Horseshoe (☎ 01778-421576)* pub, where a full menu includes vegetarian options from about £8 for dinner.

Stamford has shelter for all budgets. Two minutes from the town centre a single room at *Mr Curtis' (☎ 765946, 2 North St)* costs £14, with twins for £30. *Mrs Jones' (☎ 753 999)* central B&B charges from £18 for a single; ring for details. *St George's (☎ 482 099, 16 St George's Square)* sits in one of Stamford's finest squares and offers rooms with a 6ft-long bath to soak in from £25/45 for singles/doubles. A historic pub is the *Bull & Swan (☎ 763558; High St, St Martin's)* where booking is advisable; singles/doubles cost £35/45.

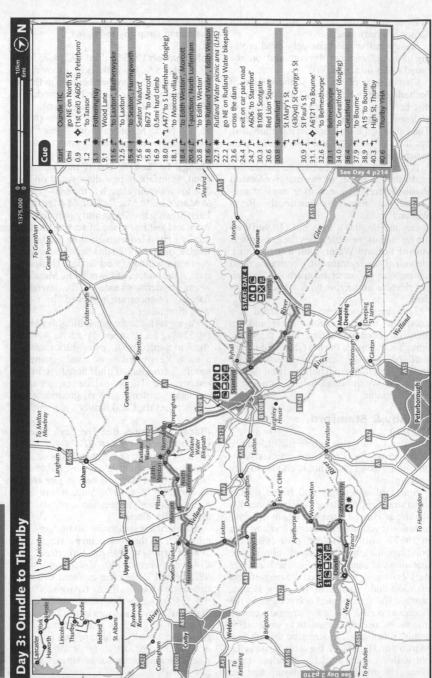

Day 3: Oundle to Thurlby

CENTRAL ENGLAND

Cue

start		Oundle TIC
0mi	↑	go NE on North St
0.9	◇	(1st exit) A605 'to Peterboro'
1.2	↓	'to Tansor'
3.1	✳	Fotheringhay
9.1	↓	Wood Lane
11.6	↓	'to Laxton', Blatherwycke
12.5	↓	'to Laxton'
15.4	↓	'to Seaton', Harringworth
15.6	✳	Seaton Viaduct
15.8	↓	B672 'to Morcott'
16.9	↓	0.5mi hard climb
18.0	↱	A47/'to S Luffenham' (dogleg)
18.1	↓	'to Morcott village'
18.4	↓	'to Edith Weston', Morcott
20.4	↓	T-junction, North Luffenham
20.8	↓	'to Edith Weston'
21.6	↓	'to Rutland Water', Edith Weston
22.1	✳	Rutland Water picnic area (LHS)
22.2	↓	go NE on Rutland Water bikepath
23.6		cross the dam
24.4	↓	exit on car park road
24.7	↓	A606 'to Stamford'
30.3	↓	B1081 Scotgate
30.6	↓	Red Lion Square
30.8	✳	Stamford
30.9	↓	St Mary's St
		(430yd) St George's St
31.1	↓	St Paul's St
31.6	↓	'to Bourne'
32.6	↓	'to Belmesthorpe'
33.1		Belmesthorpe
34.0	◇	'to Greatford' (dogleg)
36.4		Greatford
37.9	↓	'to Bourne'
38.9	↓	A15 'to Bourne', Thurlby
40.3	↓	High St, Thurlby
40.6		Thurlby YHA

See Day 4 p214

See Day 2 p310

Self-caterers can buy Lincolnshire sausages and pies at *Nelson's* or *Trendall's* butchers in the centre; don't hold your breath for veg versions.

Get refreshed al fresco at the *Sugar Bowl (High St)* or take cream tea (afternoon tea) in the ivy leaf-covered courtyard at the *George Hotel (☎ 750750; High St, St Martin's)* for a reasonable £2.75. Mexican and Mediterranean dinners can be found at *El Hombre Gordo (☎ 762868, North St)* with burritos and chimichangas from £6.55. *Fratelli's (☎ 7543333, St Mary's Hill)* does good-value Italian dishes, although the drinks are pricey.

Day 4: Thurlby to Lincoln
4½–7½ hours, 68.7mi

Crossing the Lincolnshire fens is an unforgettable experience. Flat the land may be, but boring? Never – especially for the philosophical cyclist caught up in a summer tailwind with the fields bursting with vegetation and ducks swimming in the canals.

A vast area of marshland, the fens were reclaimed in the 17th century using an impressive system of drains and rivers. Constituting much of eastern England, pancake-flat lands such as these produce a considerable proportion of the nation's harvest.

There is little shelter from sun or storm in the fens, but many roads have no traffic and the experience is rewarding for its feeling of other-worldliness.

At Boston, the route joins NCN 1, and this is the route for two more days as far as York. (Hessle to York is NCN 65, the White Rose Route.) Signs make navigating a breeze.

A lunch stop at **Boston** (27.3mi) is just right. A major wool port in the Middle Ages, it was from here that the founding fathers of America made their first attempt to escape religious persecution. The **tower** of the church of St Botolph's, 'the Stump', is visible for miles around. The TIC (☎ 01205-356656), which is closed Sunday, and a bike shop are both found in the central Market Place. A good little cafe-restaurant is *Churches Coffee House (Church Lane)*, near the church, where they celebrate Sunday with a very good value £2.75 roast platter.

Another highlight of the day is the tranquil ride along the top of the embanked **River Witham** from Dogdyke to Woodhall Spa. About 20mi from Lincoln the great towers of the cathedral beckon you in, as they have other travellers and pilgrims for 900 years.

Lincoln
☎ 01522

The hill-top city of Lincoln has held strategic importance for 2000 years. It is dominated by the wonderful cathedral, the third largest in Britain, which looms over the medieval city centre as it falls away down steep cobbled streets to the river below.

The small scale of the place makes it easy to master. There are modern chain stores at the bottom, trendy drinking holes halfway up, and individual book, candle and wine stores huddling below the castle and cathedral at the top.

Information The TIC (☎ 873213), 9 Castle Hill, is at the top of the hill between the cathedral and the castle.

The first bike shop stop is F&J Cycles (☎ 545311), Hungate, down an alley on another steep hillside street. Lincoln Cycle Centre (☎ 525803), 69 Camwick Rd), is on the way from the centre to the YHA.

Things to See & Do The sights of Lincoln fall within a square mile. From **Brayford Pool**, where you can take a boat trip along the waterways, pitch yourself against the steepening incline of High St, **The Strait** and **Steep Hill** with their quaint shops. At the top of the hill the streets around the cathedral open out and are well worth a nose.

The **cathedral** is a mix of architectural majesty, and both community and spiritual activity. The soaring limestone and marble nave seats 2000 people. Rare original medieval stained-glass windows throw shafts of coloured light on to the flagstones. The Lincoln imp, the city's symbol, can be spied high up in the crook of a column above the angel choir – he got caught chatting up an angel and was turned to stone. On the exterior, the setting sun illuminates the magnificent 12th-century West Front with the force of floodlights. A £3 donation is requested.

The **Usher Gallery**, a little way down the hill, houses the city's art collection. Lincoln's copy of the Magna Carta, the charter signed by King John in 1215 recognising the rights of the barons and freemen, lives inside the Norman **castle** (☎ 511068), where the old prison is the most interesting feature.

CENTRAL ENGLAND

Day 4: Thurlby to Lincoln

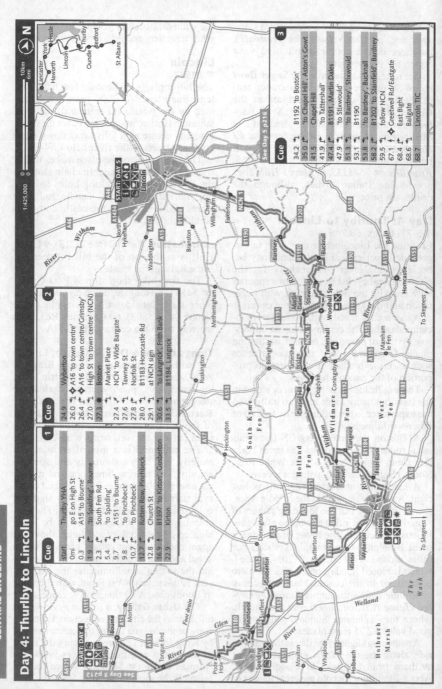

Cue 1

start	Thurlby YHA
0mi	go E on High St
0.3 ↱	A15 'to Bourne'
1.9 ↱	to Spalding, Bourne
2.3	South Fen Rd
5.4 ↱	'to Spalding'
9.7 ↱	A151 'to Bourne'
9.8 ↱	'to Pinchbeck'
10.7 ↱	'to Pinchbeck'
12.7	Rotten Row, Pinchbeck
12.8 ↱	Church St
16.9 ↰	B1397 'to Kirton', Gosberton
22.9	Kirton

Cue 2

24.9	Wyberton
26.0 ↱	A16 'to town centre'
26.4 ⬦ ⬦	A16 'to town centre/Grimsby'
27.0 ↱	High St 'to town centre' (NCN)
27.3 ✳	Boston
	Market Place
27.4 ↰	NCN 'to Wide Bargate'
27.6 ↱	Tawney St
27.8 ↱	Norfolk St
28.0 ↱	B1183 Horncastle Rd
29.1	'to Langrick', Frith Bank
	at NCN sign
30.6 ↱	B1184, Langrick
33.5 ↰	

Cue 3

34.2 ↰	B1192 'to Boston'
35.0 ↰	'to Chapel Hill', Aston's Gowt
41.5	Chapel Hill
41.9 ↱	'to Tattershall'
47.4 ↱	B1191, Martin Dales
47.9 ↱	'to Stixwould'
51.3 ↱	'to Bardney', Stixwould
53.1 ↱	B1190
53.8 ↱	'to Bardney', Bucknall
58.2 ↱	B1202 'to Stainfield', Bardney
59.5 ↱	follow NCN
67.1 ↰	Greetwell Rd/Eastgate
68.4 ↱	East Bight
68.6	Balgate
68.7	Lincoln TIC

See Day 5 p216

See Day 3 p212

START: DAY 5   Lincoln

START: DAY 4   Thurlby

Hardened road-racing cyclists blanch at the mention of the city's name; it's hard to forget the killer circuits up and down the steepest cobbled streets in the annual **Lincoln Grand Prix** in May.

Places to Stay & Eat The Lincoln *YHA (☎ 522076, 77 South Park)* is 1mi south of the old town (South Park is opposite the cemetery, not the B1190 as in the YHA book). The nearest camping is at *Hartsholme Country Park (☎ 686264, Skellingthorpe Rd)*, 2mi south-west. It's open March to October with sites costing £5.30.

A historic guesthouse is the former residence of the bishops of Lincoln next to the cathedral. *Edward King House (☎ 528778; The Old Palace, Minster Yard)* charges just £19/37 for singles/twins. The best hotel in town is the 15th-century *White Hart (☎ 526 222, Bailgate)*, around the corner from the cathedral, where weekend B&Bs start from £54/90 for singles/doubles.

Good Lincolnshire meat sausages and pies can be purchased at *Elite Meats (Bailgate)* at the top of town.

During warm weather the *Cathedral Coffee Shop* extends out to the cloisters for snacks and teas until 4.30 pm. For a traditional meal sample the menu at the *Wig & Mitre (☎ 535190, 29 Steep Hill)*, an inn at the top of town. Its near neighbours *Brown's Pie Shop (☎ 527330, 33 Steep Hill)* serves speciality Lincolnshire pies.

The best restaurant in town is the *Jew's House (☎ 524851, 15 The Strait)*, of historic interest in its own right, where a reservation is de rigueur but the set lunch a mere £12.95. Nearby is *Mylos Greek Taverna (☎ 575550, 376 High St)*, while *Tequilas (☎ 529991, 77 High St)* Mexican restaurant sits at the top of Bailgate.

High St is the place Lincoln's youth heads for beats and lagers at *O'Neill's*, *Walkabout* and *Edwards*.

Day 5: Lincoln to Hessle
4–6 hours, 55.6mi

Road traffic evaporates on the 500ft-ridge of the rural Lincolnshire Wolds. The only sounds are those of sheep, birdsong and the occasional buzz of light aircraft from Humberside airport. The views are long and fine, both westwards into the Lincolnshire Fens, and eastwards to the sea ports and resorts.

Two pieces of off-road bridleway are rideable on narrow tyres if you take care. The first, north of Lincoln (2.2mi), is almost 1mi with some flints, the second (39.9mi) is longer, over 2mi and OK in the dry. North of Lincoln, the NCN 1 is still in development so watch out for the thundering lorries.

The climb out of Walesby (21.6mi) up the Wolds is the biggest of the day, and passes the **Ramblers Church**, which was adopted by the national walking group in 1914 as their church. On high, the route undulates through quiet villages to the River Humber.

Dropping down off the ridge, the **Humber bridge** piers come into view. When it was built in 1981 the bridge's 1mi central span was the longest in the world. It has since been overtaken by structures in Denmark and Japan. The Hunter Bridge TIC (☎ 01482-640852) and services are on the north bank. On the bridge, cyclists use the separated pedestrian track, which gives you space to enjoy the view.

At Hessle, NCN 1 turns east to finish at Hull, 6mi on – follow the signs. (This route turns west on the NCN 65). Overnighting in Hessle avoids retracing your pedalstrokes, unless the call of Hull, with its docks, seafood and city life, is irresistible.

Hessle & Hull
☎ 01482

Hessle dates from Anglo-Saxon times, and is an ordinary little town with a limited choice of accommodation and eating-out options.

Hull (Kingston-upon-Hull) is a major port with a population of 250,000, many employed in the docks handling freight and passengers on the ferries to the Dutch ports of Rotterdam and Zeebrugge. Hull is safely off the tourist trail, but has an old town and marina with a certain charm, and features quirky trails by which to plot two community mainstays – fish and ale.

Information The Hull TIC (☎ 223559), 1 Paragon St, at the north end of the main shopping centre, has leaflets for the fish and ale trails. For bikes shops try Blazing Saddles (☎ 620806), 6 Savile St, where you can also park your bike (£1 per day), or Freetown Sports (☎ 589066), 70–80 Prospect St. Both are north of the TIC.

CENTRAL ENGLAND

Day 5: Lincoln to Hessle

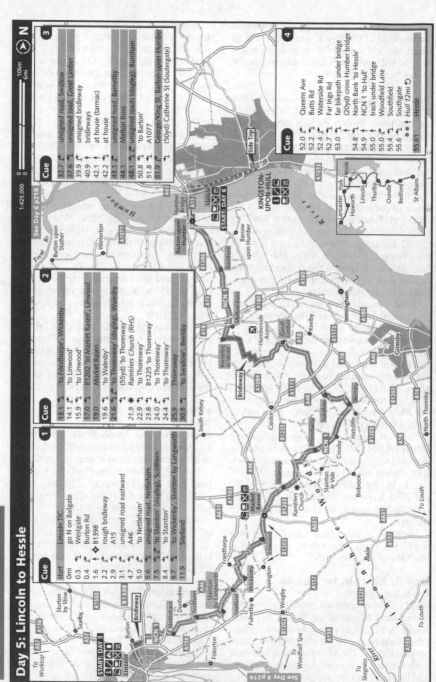

1:425,000

N

0   5mi
0   10km

See Day 6 p218

Cue

start		Lincoln TIC
0mi	↑	go N on Bailgate
0.3	↑↖	Westgate
0.4	↑	Burton Rd
1.6	↖	B1398
2.2	↖	rough bridleway
2.9	↑	A15
3.1	↗	unsigned road eastward
4.7	↖	A46
5.0	↗	'to Nettleham'
5.6	↗	unsigned road, Nettleham
7.5	↑↗	'to Stainton' (dogleg), Scothern
8.4	↖	'to Stainton'
9.7	↖	to Wickenby', Stainton by Langworth
11.9	↖	Snelland

Cue

13.1	↗	'to Friesthorpe', Wickenby
14.1	↖	'to Linwood'
15.9	↖	'to Linwood'
17.0	↗	B1202 'to Market Rasen', Linwood
19.0	↑	Market Rasen
19.6	↖	'to Walesby'
21.6	↑↖	'to Thoresway' (dogleg), Walesby
21.9	✱	(55yd) 'to Thoresway' Ramblers Church (RHS)
22.9	↖	'to Thoresway'
23.8	↗	B1225 'to Thoresway'
24.0	↗	'to Thoresway'
24.4	↖	'to Thoresway'
25.9		Thoresway
30.5	↖	'to Swallow', Beelsby

Cue

32.7	↖	unsigned road, Swallow
37.6	↖	unsigned road, Great Limber
39.9	↗	unsigned bridleway
40.9	↖	bridleway
42.1	←	at house (tarmac)
42.2	↗	at house
43.1	↖	unsigned road, Barnetby
44.1		Melton Ross
48.1	↗	unsigned roads (dogleg), Burnham
50.8	↖	'to Barton'
51.8		A1077
51.9	↖	George/King St, Barton-upon-Humber (50yd) Catherine St (Soutergate)

Cue

52.0	←	Queens Ave
52.2	↖	Butts Rd
52.4	←	Waterside Rd
52.7	↑	Far Ings Rd
53.0	↗	far bikepath under bridge (20yd) cross Humber bridge North Bank 'to Hessle'
54.8	↗	NCN 1 'to Hull'
54.9	↑	track under bridge
55.0	↖	Woodfield Lane
55.4	←	Southfield
55.6	↖	Southgate
55.61	⊙	Hessle

Hull 12mi →

START: DAY 6
KINGSTON-UPON-HULL

START: DAY 5
Lincoln

See Day 4 p214

Bridleway

Humber Bridge
Hessle
Barton-upon-Humber
Burnham
Barrow upon Humber

Humber R.
Trent R.
Burton upon Stather
Winterton

Humberside Airport
Great Limber
Melton Ross
Keelby
Immingham
Grimsby
North Thoresby

Barnetby le Wold
Swallow
Thoresway
Hatcliffe
Beelsby
Croxby
Caistor
Binbrook

Market Rasen
Ramblers Church
Walesby
Linwood
Lissington
Wickenby
Friesthorpe
Snelland
Wragby

Stainton by Langworth
Scothern
Durnholme
Nettleham
Fiskerton

Sturton by Stow
Saxilby
Burton
Lincoln
To Worksop
To Woodhall Spa
To Skegness
To Louth

Lancaster York Hessle
Haworth Thurlby
Lincoln
Oundle
Bedford
St Albans

Things to See & Do The **Fish Pavement Trail** starts from the TIC and follows depictions of marine creatures inlaid into the pavements, walls and decking around the centre and the marina. If you've got the stamina for a serious pub crawl, the **Ale Trail** links 35 varied historic pubs serving beers from local breweries like Cameron's and the Old Mill. Other guided walks take in Hull's award-winning Victorian and mid-war public conveniences with polished brass, glass cisterns and hanging flower baskets.

In the 1930s Hull was known as the 'Bicycle City' because so many people owned and rode bikes. The **Streetlife Transport Museum** in Hull houses a permanent exhibition of historic bicycles from the penny farthing to cycles of the present day.

Places to Stay & Eat With neither a camp site nor a youth hostel in the area, accommodation is limited to guesthouses.

In Hessle, turn left at Southgate for *Sandford B&B (☎ 648655, 79 Ferriby Rd)* where singles/doubles are £18/36. Visible from the bridge bikepath is the *Country Park Lodge (☎ 640526)*, where rooms cost £39/49. Standard bar fare here starts at £4 and the *restaurant* serves fresh fish dishes from around £10. Standard Oriental fare is served at the *Mandarin Chinese*, which lies off Hull Rd in Hessle's centre.

Hull has a choice of well-priced guesthouses. The *Clyde House Hotel (☎ 343276, 13 John St)*, 0.5mi north of the TIC near the New Theatre, has basic rooms from £22/38. The *Old English Gentleman (☎ 324659, 22 Worship St)*, north of George St, is listed on the Ale Trail. B&B singles/twins are £25/38. One of Hull's high-quality hotels is the modern *Portland (☎ 326462, Paragon St)*, in the same street as the TIC, where a weekend in the en suite double is £70 per night.

In Hull, seafood specialities can be sampled at *Cerutti's (☎ 328501, 10 Nelson St)* near the pier. The *Minerva Hotel (☎ 326909, Nelson St)*, nearby, does speciality veg, and bread and butter pudding. Dotted elsewhere throughout the town are *Indian*, *Italian* and *mixed-cuisine restaurants*.

Day 6: Hessle to York
3–5 hours, 49.0mi

After six days of heading north, the route swings west towards the wild Yorkshire landscapes. But before things get hilly, there is more pleasant fenland to cross in the East Riding into North Yorkshire after Selby, the route follows an old railway line (34.1mi), then takes bikepaths into the heart of York.

Outside the towns there is only nominal traffic. Watch your navigation when the NCN signs peter out around Hemingbrough.

York
☎ 01904

Sightseeing in York should not be overlooked in a hurry to get on to the Pennines. The cathedral and university city is the historic capital of the north, with evidence of power and prosperity from different periods in the buildings, streets and town walls. It suffers from a high number of tourists – book your accommodation ahead – but a rather un-English air of liveliness and contentment suffuses the place.

To its further credit, York likes bikes. About 10% of people cycle to work along miles of effective cycle lanes.

Information The TIC is in the De Grey Rooms (☎ 621756), Exhibition Square. There's other branches at the train station (☎ 621756), on Station Rd, and 20 George Hudson St (☎ 554455).

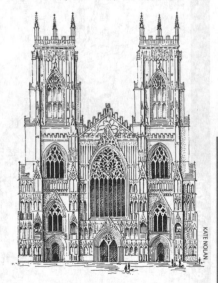

KATE NOLAN

Exploring the spectacular York Minster could easily take the best part of a day.

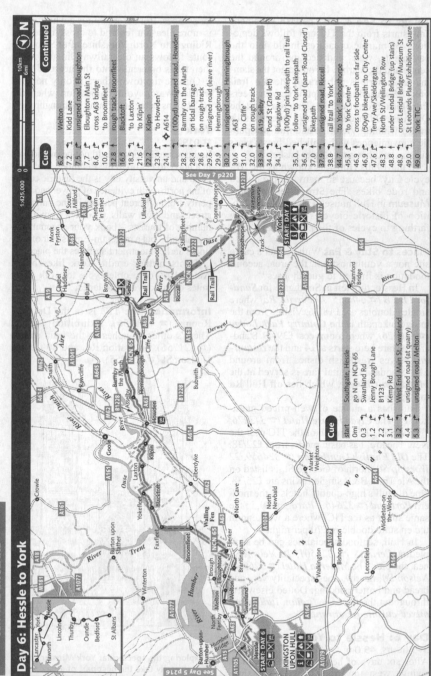

CENTRAL ENGLAND

Day 6: Hessle to York

Cue (Continued)

6.2	Welton
7.2	Kidd Lane
7.5	unsigned road, Elloughton
7.7	Elloughton Main St
8.6	cross A63 bridge
10.6	'to Broomfleet'
12.8	rough track, Broomfleet
16.5	Blacktoft
18.5	'to Laxton'
21.6	'to Kilpin'
22.2	Kilpin
23.4	'to Howden'
24.1	A614
	(100yd) unsigned road, Howden
28.2	Barmby on the Marsh
28.4	on tidal barrage
28.6	unsigned road (leave river)
29.6	on rough track
29.9	Hemingbrough
30.2	unsigned road, Hemingbrough
30.6	A63
31.0	'to Cliffe'
32.0	on rough track
33.9	A19, Selby
34.0	Pond St (2nd left)
34.1	Bungalow Rd
	(100yd) join bikepath to rail trail
35.0	follow 'to York' bikepath
36.5	unsigned road (past 'Road Closed')
37.0	bikepath
37.9	unsigned road, Riccall
38.8	rail trail 'to York'
44.7	'to York Centre'
45.3	cross to footpath on far side
46.9	(50yd) bikepath 'to City Centre'
46.9	Terry Ave/Skeldergate
47.6	North St/Wellington Row
48.3	under Lendal Bridge (up stairs)
48.9	cross Lendal Bridge/Museum St
49.0	St Leonards Place/Exhibition Square
49.0	York TIC

Cue

start	Southgate, Hessle
0mi	go N on NCN 65
0.3	Swanland Rd
1.2	Jenny Brough Lane
2.2	Kemp Rd
3.1	B1231
3.2	West End Main St, Swanland
4.4	unsigned road (at quarry)
5.3	unsigned road, Melton

1:425,000

See Day 7 p220

See Day 5 p216

START DAY 6

KINGSTON UPON HULL

Bike shops include the York Cycleworks (☎ 626664), 16 Lawrence St, and Cycle Heaven (☎ 636578), 2 Bishopthorpe Rd.

Things to See & Do York's centrepiece is its glorious **Minster**, which was the largest medieval structure in the kingdom. The seat of the Archbishop of York, the deputy head of the Church of England, it is famous for 128 medieval stained-glass windows and a high, wide nave. A £2 donation is requested from adults.

Another highlight is a walk around the medieval **town wall**, with its sections of older, preserved Roman fortifications. For train buffs, there's the **National Railway Museum** (☎ 621261), on Leeman Rd beside the train station, full of original engines and carriages from the golden age of steam.

The **York Cycle Rally**, the country's biggest annual bicycle get-together, takes place around the third weekend in June at Knavesmire racecourse (en route), when 40,000 members of the Cyclists' Touring Club (CTC) and the public gather to view antique bikes, enjoy racing and gossip about gear ratios.

Places to Stay Beside the river 1mi south from the centre, *Rowntree Park Caravan Site* (☎ 658997) has pitches for £2 per tent and £4 per person. Take the 'to City Centre' bikepath.

Cheap accommodation is plentiful but fills up fast in summer. *York YHA* (☎ 653 147; *Water End, Clifton*) is open all year. The nightly cost is £15.25, including breakfast. It lies 1mi north of the centre: from the TIC turn left into Bootham, which becomes Clifton (the A19), then left into Water End; or take the riverside footpath from the train station. The *York Youth Hotel* (☎ 625904, 11 *Bishophill Senior*) is central. Prices range from £9 to £14 per night for an adult; breakfast and sheet hire are extra. Turn left from Skeldergate along Buckingham St. The *York Backpackers Hostel* (☎ 627720, 88–90 *Micklegate*) is also central. Prices start from £9 for dormitories to £13 for a shared room. Turn left off the route at Micklegate instead of continuing into North St.

B&Bs and hotels number well over 100. Around the corner from the TIC is the *Bootham Bar Hotel* (☎ 658516, 4 High Petergate), where singles/doubles start from £22/44 in summer. Claremont Terrace, beyond the northern walls, has several guesthouses, including the *Claremont* (☎ 625 158, 18 Claremont Terrace), where doubles with bath start from £28. For a quiet night beside the river try the *Riverside Walk* (☎ 620769, 9 Earlsborough Terrace), 0.25mi along from Lendal Bridge, where rooms start from £30/40.

Places to Eat Many of York's real ale pubs serve roast dinners with Yorkshire pudding, a delicious savoury puff drowned in gravy. The *Blake Head Vegetarian Cafe* (☎ 623767, 104 Micklegate) is open during the day with filling dishes from £4.95 (it also has a bookshop). Chain eateries are easy to find.

A restaurant with unique character is *St William's* (☎ 634830, 5 College St), which also feeds the Dean of the Minster. All dishes are cooked from fresh local ingredients and there's no freezer on the premises. A two-course dinner from a varied menu starts from £12.95.

The *Rubicon* (☎ 676076, 5 Little Stonegate) is a veg and vegan restaurant with starters at around £3 and filling mains from £6 to £9 (moussaka is £6.50). Near Bootham Bar, *Plunket's* (☎ 637722, 9 High Petergate) does mainly American and New Mexican dishes such as burgers from £6, and, typically, sea bass with tangerine hot and sour sauce for £11.45.

Day 7: York to Haworth
3–5hours, 47.6mi
This route hits the hills of Yorkshire hard and finishes at the high village of Haworth.

After Wetherby the landscape changes dramatically. The first sighting of the **Pennines**, the 'backbone of England', is from Kearby Cliff along Wharfedale (21.9mi). After Otley (32.5mi) the route turns drastically upwards on the direct route over Rombalds Moor to

> ### Warning
> Heavy lorries frequent the road between Healaugh and Wetherby. Prepare for a battering over Rombalds Moor during bad weather or a headwind because cyclists are fully exposed. Stock up on supplies, money and bike parts at Keighley, as Haworth is only a little place.

CENTRAL ENGLAND

Day 7: York to Haworth

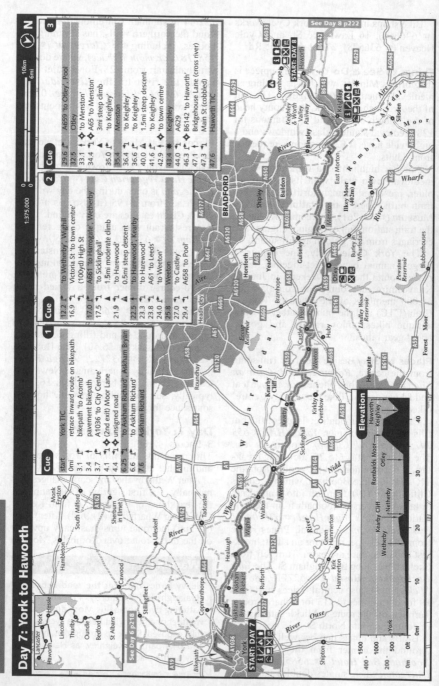

Elevation

Cue

start	York TIC
0mi	retrace inward route on bikepath
3.1	bikepath 'to Acomb'
3.4	pavement bikepath
3.7	A1036 'to City Centre'
4.1	(2nd exit) Moor Lane
4.4	unsigned road
6.25	'to Askham Richard', Askham Bryan
6.6	'to Askham Richard'
7.6	Askham Richard

Cue

12.2	'to Wetherby', Wighill
16.9	Victoria St 'to town centre'
	(100yd) High St
17.0	A661 'to Harrogate', Wetherby
17.5	'to Sicklinghall'
21.9	1.5mi moderate climb
	0.5mi steep descent
22.5	'to Harewood', Keatby
23.3	'to Harewood'
23.8	A61 'to Leeds'
24.0	'to Weeton'
25.8	Weeton
27.0	to Castley'
29.4	A658 'to Pool'

Cue

29.6	A659 'to Otley', Pool
32.5	Otley
33.1	'to Menston'
34.4	A65 'to Menston'
	3mi steep climb
35.0	'to Keighley
35.4	Menston
36.4	'to Keighley'
36.6	'to Keighley'
40.0	1.5mi steep descent
41.6	'to Keighley'
42.9	'to town centre'
43.4	Keighley
44.0	A629
46.3	B6142 'to Haworth'
47.1	Bridgehouse Lane (cross river)
47.3	Main St (cobbled)
47.6	Haworth TIC

See Day 8 p222

See Day 6 p218

Keighley (pronounced 'keith-ley'). Striking views of Yorkshire valleys and hilltops and the steep descent make the climb worthwhile, so grit your teeth for some fast driving on the tops of the bars.

Once in Keighley, a highly recommended seasonal alternative to climbing the narrow and busy A629 to Haworth is to let a steam train take the strain. A 20-minute ride on the quaint vintage **Keighley & Worth Valley Railway** costs £2.50 for adults; bikes are free. Trains run every 45 minutes on weekends throughout the year and every day from mid-June to the end of August.

Once at Haworth train station, cross the footbridge and continue 350yd up Butt Lane. At the top, turn left into Rowdon Rd. After 175yd, turn right at cobbled Main Rd; the TIC is at the top after 530yd.

Haworth
☎ 01535

Haworth, originally a weaving village, is a picturesque hamlet perched on the sides of a steep valley below wild moorland. Home of the Brontë sisters, it is second on the literary trail to Stratford-upon-Avon and at the height of the season can be overrun by tourists and English-language students clutching copies of Emily's *Wuthering Heights* or Charlotte's *Jane Eyre*.

The steep Main St is paved with stone setts (similar to cobblestones) and lined with little shops and cafes. The stone houses have withstood years of weathering and the majority are still ingrained with soot from the days of domestic coal burning. There is one grocery and a handful of restaurants and pubs, but little else.

Information The TIC (☎ 642329), 2–4 West Lane, sells the Brontë books as well as providing all the pamphlets on walks and history.

Things to See & Do The **Brontë Parsonage**, with its incorporated museum (☎ 642 323), was home to the family from 1820 to 1861, and it was here that Emily, Charlotte and Anne wrote in secret. Family relics are displayed in fondly preserved rooms, and, with the exception of Anne, all are buried in the family vault in Haworth Parish church nearby.

Walks in the moorland can be wonderful in reasonable weather. **Top Withens** (6mi return), a homestead high on the moors, may have been the inspiration for *Wuthering Heights*. Other walks are detailed in a leaflet from the TIC.

Places to Stay & Eat Haworth has a large selection of lodgings, but book ahead in the high season. The nearest camp site is *Marsh Top Farm* (☎ 642184, *Marsh Lane*) at Oxenhope, the next town 1mi up the valley. Open April to November, a tent pitch costs £5; there are no showers. Turn right up Sun St at the bottom of Main St and continue.

Haworth YHA (☎ 642234; *Longlands Dr, Lees Lane*) is on the opposite side of the valley from Main St, off the B6142 coming in from Keighley. Adults pay £9.15 per night.

B&B options are plentiful in Main St and, above it, West Lane. *Ye Sleeping House* (☎ 645992 or ☎ 644102, *8 Main St)* has a single room for £15, and a twin for £30. The *Apothecary* (☎ 643642, *86 Main St)* has a breakfast room with a view over the valley; singles/doubles start from £19/38 with bathroom. The *Old White Lion Inn* (☎ 642313, *West Lane)* was a coaching inn and has rooms from £44/60. At *Ashmount* (☎ 645 726, *Mytholmes Lane)*, a two-minute ride from the TIC, rooms with views are £25/39.

During the day there is no shortage of cafes. In the evening, though, dining out is restricted mainly to pub meals in Main St and Indian, Chinese, chippies and pizzas at the bottom of town. However, that's also where to find *Weavers Restaurant* (☎ 64 3822, 15 *West Lane)*. It has a more interesting menu, including a parsnip and cashew loaf for £9.95 and meat and potato pie for £7.95.

Day 8: Haworth to Lancaster
3–5 hours, 47.0mi

This long tour reaches a veritable climax today, as we finish the Pennine crossing. It's not a ride to be tackled in bad weather, although there are towns and villages in the valleys along the way where you can shelter. Windy conditions on the hilltops is a real danger.

This is the toughest day of the tour with five major climbs in a bleak, moorland setting. The first (0.0mi), over Haworth Moor into Lancashire, is a steady taster; the second (9.8mi) and steepest of the whole trip is above Blacko beside Pendle Hill; the third (30.7mi), the long but not so high pass – the

CENTRAL ENGLAND

Day 8: Haworth to Lancaster

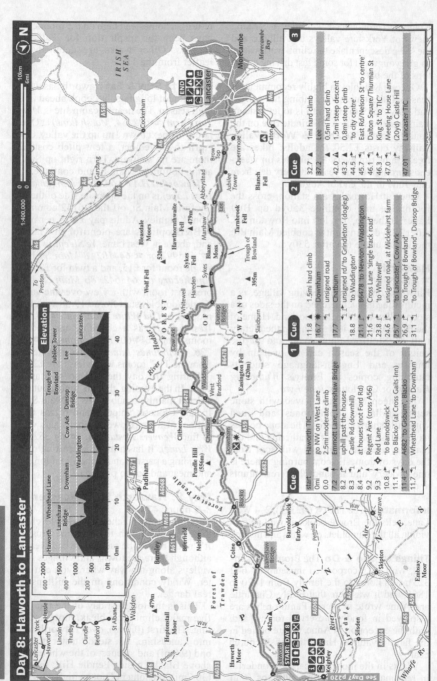

Elevation

Cue		
start	Haworth TIC	
0mi	go NW on West Lane	
0.0	2.5mi moderate climb	◀
7.2	Emmott Lane, Laneshaw Bridge	◀
8.2	uphill past the houses	
8.3	Castle Rd (downhill)	◀
8.4	at houses (not Ford Rd)	
9.2	Regent Ave (cross A56)	◀
9.3	Red Lane	◇
10.8	'to Barnoldswick'	◀
11.1	'to Blacko' (at Cross Gaits Inn)	◀
11.4	A682 'to Gisburn' Blacko	⌐
11.7	Wheathead Lane 'to Downham'	⌐

Cue		
11.8	1.5mi hard climb	▲
16.7	Downham	✳
17.7	unsigned road	◀
17.7	unsigned rd/'to Grindleton' (dogleg)	⌐
18.8	'to Waddington'	◀
21.1	B6478 'to Newton', Waddington	⌐
21.6	Cross Lane 'single track road'	⌐
23.8	'to Whitewell'	◀
24.6	unsigned road, at Micklehurst farm	◀
25.7	'to Lancaster', Cow Ark	◀
26.9	'to Trough of Bowland'	⌐
31.1	'to Trough of Bowland', Dunsop Bridge	⌐

Cue		
32.7	1mi hard climb	▲
37.2	Lee	◀
42.0	0.5mi hard climb	▲
43.2	1.5mi steep descent	◀
44.5	0.8mi steep climb	⌐
45.7	East Rd/Nelson St 'to centre'	⌐
46.1	Dalton Square/Thurman St	⌐
46.3	King St 'to TIC'	⌐
47.0	Meeting House Lane	⌐
	(20yd) Castle Hill	
47.01	Lancaster TIC	

Trough of Bowland – is rewarded with a long run towards Lancaster; the fourth (35.3mi) is up to Jubilee Tower; and the short-but-steep fifth (42.3mi) is the sting in the tail on the outskirts of Lancaster.

A good lunch-time menu is on offer at the *Assheton Arms* in **Downham** (14.7mi), a preserved stone village, on the far side of Pendle Hill, where 21st-century items like satellite dishes and dormer windows have been banned.

Lancaster
☎ 01524

This university city dates back to Roman times and has a fine castle that is still administered by the monarchy. The seaside resort of Morecambe is just a rail trail away, and the Lune Valley, a popular subject for the painter Turner, is to the north-east, with the Lake District to the north.

Despite city status, Lancaster has a nice small town atmosphere, with a calendar of folkie events such as April's gathering of sea shanty singers and July's street bands festival.

Information The large and friendly TIC (☎ 32878) is below the castle entrance at 29 Castle Hill. It's chock-a-block with information on the surrounding area as well as the town. Bike shops closest to the centre include Lancaster Cycles (☎ 844398), 103 Perry St, and MTB Sports (☎ 842273), 98 St Leonards Gate.

Things to See & Do There are guided tours of the **castle**, part of which is still used as a prison, and the neighbouring **priory church**, which dates back to 1091. **St George's Quay**, down on the banks of the Lune, is an uncluttered old waterfront of converted warehouse housing and small pubs. It is also the location of the **Maritime Museum**, which recalls the days when Lancaster was a flourishing port.

The **Assembly Rooms**, in King St, host an antique market Tuesday to Saturday and the fruit and vegetable market is on Wednesday and Saturday in Church St.

The **Lancaster Cycle Fest** is a biennial get-together featuring recumbents and other cycle alternatives as well as regular bikes. It takes place in St Martin's College, usually in August. Contact the TIC for details.

Places to Stay & Eat The nearest camp site is *New Parkside Farm (☎ 770723; Caton Rd, Denny Beck)* in the Lune Valley at Caton. It's accessible by rail trail from Lancaster, or turn north off the route 3mi before Lancaster at Quernmore.

During Easter and summer vacations, campus lodging is available 1mi south of the city centre at *St Martin's College (☎ 384460, Bowerham Rd)* at a cost of £18.92/31.61 for singles/doubles, including breakfast. At the castle is the newly refurbished *Castle Hill B&B (☎ 849137, 27 St Mary's Parade)*, where you pay £18.50/20. Near the station is the *Station House (☎ 381060, 25 Meeting House Lane)* where a single is £20 and a double or twin is £17 per person.

A lively central pub is the *John O'Gaunt (Market St)*, with live folk, jazz and blues nights and excellent food including Potts Pie Floaters (meat and potato pies) for £1.75. A good Italian place is *Il Bistro Morini (☎ 846 252, Sun St)*, where fresh pasta dishes start from £5.45, and the chef's speciality *taglialini meri al succo di mare* (seafood pasta) is £8.25. One director is connected with the Moto Morini Club, a group of enthusiasts dedicated to a defunct Italian motorbike manufacturer, hence the decor.

For a pot of the local speciality, Morecambe Bay shrimps, chow down at *Rigging Loft (☎ 66898, Market Square)*, above the Blue Anchor.

The Marches, Cheshire & Lancashire

Duration	5 days
Distance	258.9mi
Difficulty	moderate
Start	Chepstow
End	Lancaster

Travel the length of the Welsh-English border through the beautiful Marches, the Long Mynd and the Cheshire Plain, continuing on northwards to Merseyside and Lancashire. Once fiercely fought over, the Marches (from the Old English *mearc*, meaning border or frontier) are now one of the most peaceful parts of the country.

Highlights include the ferry crossing over the Mersey to the Liverpool waterfront, the rail trail from the Liverpool suburbs to Southport and the final riverside rail trail into Lancaster.

Towns of note along the way include Hay-on-Wye, which is renowned for its literary bent, Shrewsbury with its Tudor buildings, Chester with its complete town wall and Liverpool, home to the Beatles, the docks and interesting nightlife.

This ride also links with the Through the Midlands ride, later in this chapter, which starts at Shrewsbury (Day 2).

NATURAL HISTORY

The England-Wales border follows a north-south course up the outlying areas of the Welsh mountain ranges. After Shrewsbury (Day 3) the altitude drops to sea level, with the mosses and meres (lakes) around Ellesmere formed during the Ice age. The Wirral Peninsula (Day 4) is a half-rural and half-industrial promontory separated by the mighty River Mersey from Liverpool.

PLANNING
When to Ride

The summer months are warmest, but carry good waterproofs and windproofs as the Marches are prone to heavy rainfall and Merseyside and Lancashire are exposed to south-westerlies from the Irish Sea. The landscape is almost entirely rural, so riding among the spring flowers and autumn colours is especially rewarding.

Maps

OS Travelmaster maps (1:250,000) No 7, *Wales and West Midlands*; and No 5, *Northern England* are recommended.

What to Bring

All the featured towns have bike shops, but carry spares and snacks for the remote stretches between Chepstow, Hay-on-Wye and Shrewsbury.

GETTING TO/FROM THE RIDE
Chepstow

Train Chepstow is on a direct line between Cardiff (£5 single, 45 minutes, every two hours) and Birmingham (£15.80 single, 90 minutes, every two hours) stopping also at Gloucester and Cheltenham (all with links to London). Reserve a bicycle space, which costs £1, as trains take only two bikes at a

time, although there is a good chance of getting on if you just turn up.

Bicycle Chepstow lies on the End to End ride (see the Land's End to John o'Groats chapter). It also lies on NCN 4, the Celtic Trail, which runs westwards along the south coast of Wales to Fishguard and eastwards to London.

Lancaster

See the Central England Explorer ride (p206) for details on getting to and from Lancaster.

THE RIDE
Chepstow
☎ 01291

Lying on the Welsh side of the steep-sided River Wye, Chepstow is a small and pretty town with an impressive 1000-year-old castle. It originally prospered on water-borne trade from the nearby Severn estuary, and later as a typical market town. The name comes from the Old English *chepe* and *stowe* meaning marketplace.

Information The TIC (☎ 623772) is at the bottom of town in the castle car park on Bridge St. Chepstow Cycles (☎ 626126), in the middle of town at 1 St Mary St, is open Tuesday to Sunday.

Things to See & Do The town is easy to find your way around, as its buildings are set on the steep hill that rises up from the river behind the castle.

The **castle** sits dramatically on a cliff above the Wye, and is best seen in all its glory from the opposite bank. It is one of the earliest stone castles in England, work commenced a year after the Norman invasion in 1067 with extensive fortifications added during the 12th century.

Other historic monuments include the 13th-century **Port Wall** and the **museum**, which is in an 18th-century town house near the TIC and has displays of the history of Chepstow as a port.

Places to Stay & Eat The nearest camp site is *St Pierre Caravan Park* (☎ 425114), in Portskewett, 4mi west of Chepstow between the two Severn motorway bridges. It charges £8/10 for one/two people in a tent.

Chepstow fills up in summer, when three weeks ahead is supposed to be the safe booking period. *Cobweb Cottage* (☎ *626 643, Belle Vue Place*) is a B&B off Steep St run by keen cycling hosts. It has singles/ doubles from £20/36. Rooms at the *Coach & Horses* (☎ *622626, Welsh St*), close to the castle, are also £20/36. All the town hotels have character, while the *Afon Gwy* (☎ *620 158, 28 Bridge St*) has rooms with a river view for £35/47.

Dining in Chepstow offers the regular choice of pubs and hotels, Chinese and Indian. A simple steak dinner at the *Coach & Horses* (☎ *622626*) costs around £8 to £10. The *Afon Gwy* (☎ *620158*) serves good set meals and a la carte for £15 to £20. The *St Mary's Tea Rooms* (*5 St Mary St*) serves good-value food during the day.

Day 1: Chepstow to Hay-on-Wye

3½–6 hours, 54.7mi
Explore beautiful undulating farmland that hints at wilder country to the west as it dips occasionally into Wales.

Traffic is busy passing through Coleford (12.6mi), at the A40 before Pencraig (19.5mi; where you could use the footpath), and crossing the A465 at Pontrilas.

A big climb out of Chepstow leads to Coleford and beyond to **Symonds Yat**, a dramatic viewing point overlooking the River Wye and a good place to pause for refreshments.

The day's best riding, however, lies beyond Garway, where the landscape opens out over the eastern skirts of the Black Mountains and you cruise a few miles along the Golden Valley to Hay-on-Wye. Don't fall off the bike passing the London Underground coach in the garden at Broad Oak. It's worth taking a look around the beautifully situated 12th-century Cistercian priory at the town of **Abbey Dore** if you have the time. *Tan House Farm* (☎ 01981-240204, Abbey Dore), next to the priory, is a highly recommended farmhouse B&B with friendly hosts and great breakfasts. A single/double costs £18/38.

Hay-on-Wye

☎ 01497
Nestled just inside Wales on the northern slopes of the Black Mountains, Hay-on-Wye is an eccentric little place known as 'Town of Books' because of its 39 bookshops and popular annual literary festival.

In 1977 a call for 'Home Rule for Hay' was led by leading bookseller Richard Booth, who styled himself the 'King of Hay'. The demand was based on his belief in the independent local economy and the idea that the town actually lies *between* England and Wales.

Information The TIC (☎ 820144) is en route on B4348 (Oxford Rd) as you come into town. Bike supplies and a repair service is offered at Paddles & Pedals (☎ 820 604) in the town centre on Castle St. The shop also hires out bikes as well as kayaks for trips on the Wye.

Things to See & Do Browsing in the **bookshops** and supping at **cafes** are top of the list of things to do in Hay. Since Booth first promoted bookselling here in 1961, more tomes are supposed to have come to Hay than are found in all the nation's universities and libraries. Millions of words await discovery in a unique collection of independent and specialist stores. Boz Books has a big stock of Dickens, Blinking Images has volumes on photography and Outcast Books sells volumes on humanism and psychotherapy. Booksearch operates on a no-find-no-fee basis for out-of-print and rare publications.

Meanwhile Richard Booth's Bookshop is the largest second-hand stockist in the world. He and his wife bought Hay Castle in 1971 and have opened a second shop there. The **castle** itself has existed in various forms since 1200 and the mansion inside dates back to Jacobean times.

The Hay **Festival of Literature** (☎ 821299; self-addressed envelope to Box Office, Hay-on-Wye, HR3 5BX) takes place every June and features performances by comedians and musicians as well as readings by prominent authors and poets.

Hay is also a starting point for **walking** and **cycling** in the Black Mountains, to the south. For a River Wye **kayak trip**, go to Paddles & Pedals.

Places to Stay & Eat Around Hay, it is necessary to book ahead during festival month.

Down on the river two minutes' ride north-west of the centre on the Clyro road lies *Radnors End Camping* (☎ 820780), which charges £3 for a pitch.

CENTRAL ENGLAND

Day 1: Chepstow to Hay-on-Wye

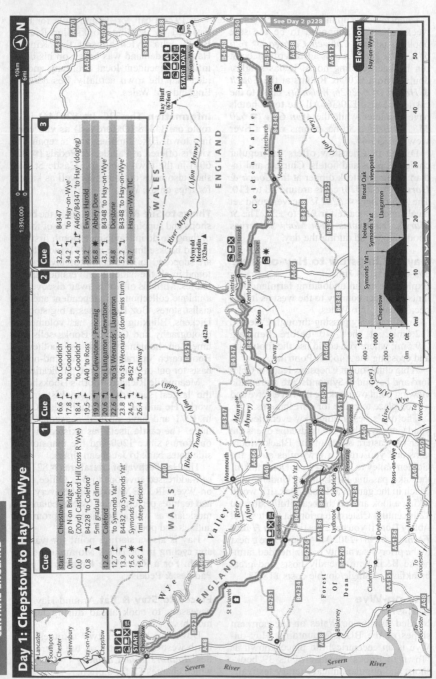

1:350,000

Cue		
start		Chepstow TIC
0mi		go N on Bridge St
0.0	↰	(20yd) Castleford Hill (cross R Wye)
0.8	↱	B4228 'to Coleford'
	▲	5mi gradual climb
12.6		Coleford
12.7	↱	'to Symonds Yat'
13.9	↱	B4432 'to Symonds Yat'
15.6	▲	Symonds Yat
15.6	▲	1mi steep descent

Cue		
16.6	↱	'to Goodrich'
17.8	↱	'to Goodrich'
18.4	↱	'to Goodrich'
19.5	↱	A40 'to Ross'
19.9	↱	'to Glewstone', Pencraig
20.6	↰	'to Llangarron', Glewstone
22.6	↱	'to St Weonards', Llangarron
23.8	↰	⚠ 'to St Weonards' (don't miss turn)
24.5	↱	B4521
26.4	↰	'to Garway'

Cue		
32.6	↱	B4347
34.2	↱	'to Hay-on-Wye'
34.4	↱	A465/B4347 'to Hay' (dogleg)
35.2		Ewyas Harold
36.8	✳	Abbey Dore
43.1	↱	B4348 'to Hay-on-Wye'
44.8		Dorstone
52.2	↰	B4348 'to Hay-on-Wye'
54.7		Hay-on-Wye TIC

Elevation

Westbrook Manor (☎ 831431) is a farmhouse en route 4mi before Hay at Dorstone, where Libby Jones charges from £16/40 for singles/doubles.

In Hay, the *Seven Stars (☎ 820886, Broad St)* has rooms from £16.50/35, including use of the swimming pool and sauna. *Clifton House (☎ 821618, 1 Belmont Rd)* costs from £20 a single for B&B, and offers guided cycling in the surrounding hills. Clyro also is the location of the *Baskerville Hall Hotel (☎ 820033, Clyro Court)*, which has a swimming pool and sauna and caters for all pockets: prices start at £15 for a dormitory bed, to £37.50 for executive rooms.

Hay has plenty of places to eat that are used to catering for regular influxes of unusually literate visitors. *Granary (☎ 821 787, Broad St)* does good veg meals. The selection of good pub restaurants is broad, try the *Blue Boar (Castle St)* and the *Old Black Lion (Lion St)*.

Day 2: Hay-on-Wye to Shrewsbury

4–6½ hours, 61.6mi
From the quaint 5p toll bridge outside Hay to the swoop down off the Long Mynd, the route proceeds through a delightful jumbled landscape of green hills where peace rules.

Any towns of size lie off the route and one of the prettiest villages is **Staunton-on-Arrow** (17.8mi). There's a little adventurous section beyond Byton (20.5mi), where the trees create a canopy over the broken road before a short, steep descent. But it is the **Long Mynd**, south of Shrewsbury, that creates the main memories of the day.

This rolling barrel of upland is crossed via a long valley climb and a hacking descent off the northern slopes. Halfway along in a steep valley lies the little village of Bridges, where, one minute off the route, the YHA offers an alternative place to stay to the centre of Shrewsbury. For a mountain bike route close by, see the Long Mynd ride later in this chapter.

Shrewsbury
☎ 01743
This county town of Shropshire, sited on a strategic bluff in a 340 degree loop in the River Severn, is famous for its half-timbered Tudor buildings and winding streets. The lack of a major monument, armaments factory or port saved Shrewsbury from WWII bombs, and from drowning by tourism. Many of the central streets are lined with chain stores and the main drag is smoky with bus fumes, but it's a comfortable place with a typical English air.

Shrewsbury's most famous son, Charles Darwin, the father of evolution theory, was born here in 1809 and educated at the renowned public school.

The Through the Midlands ride, later in this chapter, also starts at Shrewsbury.

Information The TIC (☎ 281200) is in the Music Hall (built in 1839) in the central square at the top of town. There are two bike shops: Dave Mellor Cycles (☎ 366662) at 9 New St, owned by the manager of the national mountain bike squad, and Stan Jones Cycles (☎ 343775) at 17a Hills Lane.

Things to See & Do A guided 1½-hour **walk** leaves from the TIC at 2.30 pm Monday to Saturday and 11 am on Sunday. A town map shows the location of many buildings of interest, including the **castle**,

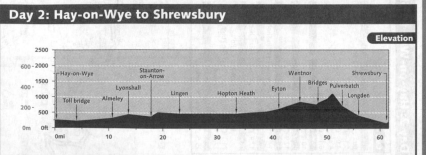

Day 2: Hay-on-Wye to Shrewsbury

CENTRAL ENGLAND

CENTRAL ENGLAND

Day 2: Hay-on-Wye to Shrewsbury

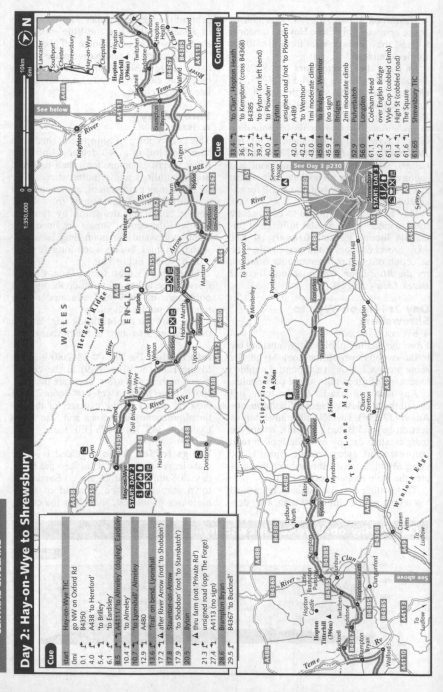

Cue

Start	Hay-on-Wye TIC
0mi	go NW on Oxford Rd
0.1	B4350
4.0	A438 'to Hereford'
5.4	'to Brilley'
6.1	'to Eardisley'
8.5	A4111/'to Almeley' (dogleg), Eardisley
10.4	'to Almeley'
10.7	'to Lyonshall', Almeley
12.9	A480
13.6	Trail' on bend, Lyonshall
17.2	after River Arrow (not 'to Shobdon')
17.8	Staunton-on-Arrow
17.9	'to Shobdon' (not 'to Stansbatch')
20.5	Byton
21.3	thru farm (not 'Private Rd')
27.4	unsigned road (opp The Forge)
28.6	A4113 (no sign)
29.5	Brampton Bryan
	B4367 'to Bucknell'

Cue

33.4	'to Clun', 'Hopton Heath'
36.1	'to Kempton' (cross B4368)
37.5	B4385
39.7	'to Eyton' (on left bend)
40.0	'to Plowden'
41.1	Eyton
	unsigned road (not 'to Plowden')
42.0	A489
42.5	'to Wentnor'
43.0	1mi moderate climb
45.0	'to Bridges', Wentnor
45.9	(no sign)
	Bridges
48.3	2mi moderate climb
52.9	Pulverbatch
56.0	Longden
61.1	Coleham Head
	over English Bridge
61.2	Wyle Cop (cobbled climb)
61.3	High St (cobbled road)
61.4	The Square
61.6	
61.65	Shrewsbury TIC

Continued

See Day 3 p230

1:350,000

10km
6mi

See below

See above

magnificent **churches**, the **abbey** and the half-timbered **houses**, several of which have been turned into **museums**.

At the **Shrewsbury Quest** (☎ 243324), on the site of old abbey buildings, visitors look for clues to solve a medieval murder, as inspired by the stories of Ellis Peters' detective monk *Brother Cadfael*.

Places to Stay About 4mi north-west along the B4380, the old ring road lies the nearest camp site, on the river at *Severn House (☎ 850229)*. Charges are £5 per tent.

Shrewsbury YHA (☎ 360170, Abbey Foregate) lies 1mi east of the English Bridge (en route on the way into town). Adults pay £8.35 per night and it's completely open from February to October.

B&Bs are abundant in Shrewsbury. At *Berwyn House (☎ 354858, 14 Holywell St)*, singles/doubles start from £17/40. The quaint *Tudor House (☎ 351735, 2 Fish St)*, on a medieval street that dates from 1460, has rooms from £26/40.

The old central coaching inn, the *Lion Hotel (☎ 353107, Wyle Cop)* once hosted Charles Dickens, and offers fine rooms for a straight £69/89.

Places to Eat Cheap cafe and restaurant eats abound during the day, with decent modern British restaurants coming to life at night.

The *Good Life Wholefood Restaurant (☎ 350455, Barracks Passage)*, just off Wyle Cop, serves well-priced, filling lunches and teas, but closes at 4.30 pm. Opposite, is the *Old Lion Tap (☎ 270330)* with a brasserie and restaurant. The *Cornhouse (☎ 231991, Wyle Cop)*, next to the English Bridge, serves imaginative main courses from around £6.

Day 3: Shrewsbury to Chester
3–4½ hours, 43.7mi
From Shrewsbury, the route drops nearer to sea level and uses quiet, countrified roads to bypass populated areas. It is a gentler landscape that leads over the Shropshire plain through a finger of Wales into Cheshire to the superbly preserved town of Chester.

Near Ellesmere (19.6mi), a short side trip off the route will take you to a **mere** (lake) in what is known as Shropshire's lake district. Five other glacial meres and several 'mosses' lie to the east (there are no hills), all linked by the Llangollen canal. The TIC

display explains their prehistoric formation, which is interesting but not essential information if you just want to picnic here.

Another pleasant place for repast is the *Queens Arms* pub at Threapwood (28.7mi), opposite an old mill.

The sights and smells of cattle farming never retreat far – watch out for crud on the road. The approach to Chester along the B5130 has high-speed traffic.

Chester
☎ 01244
Chester is famous for its complete red-sandstone walls, which encircle a handsome town centre based on an ancient cross pattern. Radiating out from this are the half-timbered, double-level Rows galleries.

Prosperous and picturesque, the town nurtures cliches about the quaintness of Olde Englande while slipping plenty of consumerism into the equation. The first tourist guide to the city was produced in 1781!

Information Chester has two TICs, one en route (☎ 402111) at Vicar's Lane, and another in the centre in the town hall (☎ 40211).

Dave Miller's bike shop is at 14 Frodsham St, north of the east-west Foregate St, and Claud Crime's (☎ 371341) is north of the city walls in Delamere St.

Things to See & Do A tour of the 2mi-long **city walls** is a treat. Originally constructed by the Romans, they were rebuilt as a fashionable promenade in the mid-17th century after being damaged in the Civil War, when the town was besieged for 18 months. Starting from the Eastgate Clock at Eastgate, and running clockwise, you pass Roman ruins, towers and gates, and the flight of four locks on the Shropshire Union canal, which was once a moat.

The existing **cathedral** was built between 1250 and 1540, and features many Victorian alterations.

Then there's the shopping, particularly staring in windows at the famous black-and-white **Rows**, which date back to the post-Roman period in various forms, and give Chester its immediate identity.

Places to Stay Despite the number of lodgings, you must book ahead during the tourist season.

CENTRAL ENGLAND

Day 3: Shrewsbury to Chester

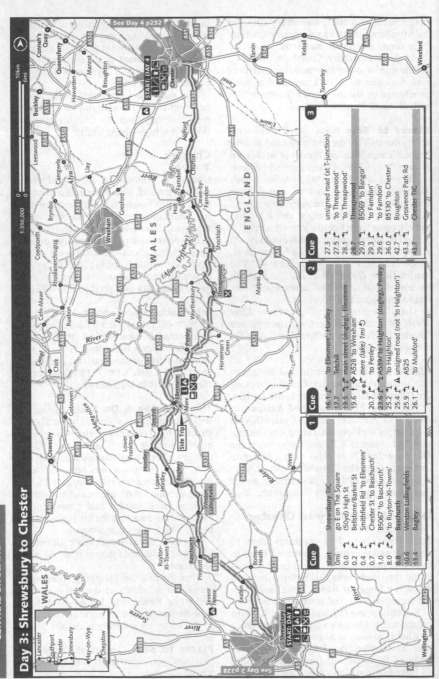

Cue			
start	Shrewsbury TIC		
0mi	go E on The Square		
0.0	(50yd) High St		
0.2	Bellstone/Barker St		
0.4	Smithfield Rd 'to Ellesmere'		
0.7	Chester St 'to Baschurch'		
1.0	B5067 'to Baschurch'		
8.0	✧ 'to Ruyton-XI-Towns'		
8.8	Baschurch		
10.6	Weston Lullingfields		
13.4	Bagley		

Cue			
16.1	'to Ellesmere'; Hordley		
17.7	Tetchill		
19.5	main street (dogleg); Ellesmere		
19.6	✧ A528 'to Wrexham'		
	● mere (lake) 1mi ⤴		
20.7	'to Penley'		
23.6	A539/'to Halghton' (dogleg), Penley		
25.2	'to Halghton'		
25.4	unsigned road (not 'to Halghton')		
25.9	A525		
26.1	'to Mulsford'		

Cue			
27.3	unsigned road (at T-junction)		
27.5	'to Threapwood'		
28.1	'to Threapwood'		
28.7	Threapwood		
29.0	B5069 'to Bangor'		
29.3	'to Farndon'		
29.6	'to Farndon'		
36.0	B5130 'to Chester'		
42.7	Boughton		
43.3	Grosvenor Park Rd		
43.7	Chester TIC		

About 3mi south along the A483 lies the *Chester Southerly Caravan Park (☎ 0976 743888; Balderton Lane, Marlton-cum-Lache)* where two adults pay £9.75 for a tent site.

Chester YHA (☎ 680056, 40 Hough Green) is a comfortable former hotel with a canteen, costing £10.15 per adult. It lies 1.5mi south-west of the centre on the A5104. The *City Road Apartments (☎ 813125, 18 City Rd)* cost from £10 to £12 per person depending on the room – bikes go in with you.

Just north-east of the centre, the *Aplas Guest House (☎ 312401, 106 Brook St)* charges £17.50/26 for singles/doubles. The *Ship Inn (☎ 671033)*, on the river at Handbridge, charges a flat rate of £18 per person.

Built in 1680, the *Chester Town House (☎ 350021, 23 King St)* lies in the north-east corner of the walled area, and charges £35/50 for singles/doubles. The finest address in town, however, is the *Chester Grosvenor Hotel (☎ 324024, Eastgate St)*, where weekend nights start from £80 per person in a double room.

Places to Eat Italian and Mexican restaurants, fast-food places and trendy drinking holes have burgeoned within the city walls. For cocktails before dinner try trendy *Via Vita (☎ 347878, 39 Watergate St)*. For a bevvy in Chester's oldest crypt, try *Watergates (13 Watergate St)*.

The choice of independent restaurants includes *Vito's (☎ 317330, 25 Bridge St)*, a family-run Italian place that does a prawn and crabmeat pasta for £7. The *Blue Bell Restaurant (☎ 317758, 65 Northgate St)* has elaborate dinner dishes in the region of £13, while *Elliot's (☎ 329932)*, which concentrates on fresh local ingredients, typically offers a veg leek mousse with local Ravensoak cheese topping for £8.50.

Day 4: Chester to Southport

3–5½ hours, 52.0mi

Today is all about Liverpool; reaching it, crossing it and making good your escape. The ride's perhaps unlikely attraction lies in arriving on the Mersey ferry and following bike routes and rail trails all the way from the city centre to the outskirts and away. With a rural start and finish, it is a unique way to visit this great and grim city.

From Chester travel along the Wirral into Birkenhead and catch the ferry across the Mersey from Woodside terminal to Pier Head terminal (hourly; £1.75, bikes free; 10–20 minutes), to get an uninterrupted view of the famous waterfront. This includes the **Cunard Building** and the **Royal Liver Building** (pronounced like *alive*) crowned by the famous 5.5m copper Liver Birds, which symbolise Liverpool.

Immediately south of the terminal lies the redeveloped **Albert Dock**, now a colonnaded walkway of cafes, shops and museums, also housing the Liverpool **Tate Gallery** and the **Beatles Story**. The TIC (☎ 0151-708 8854), in the far corner of Albert Dock, has information on history, sights and nightlife. The hip Liverpool Cycle Centre (☎ 0151-708 8819), 9 Berry St, 1mi south-east of Pier Head, has a cafe called the *Hub*, and sells the *Liverpool Cycle Map* (£3).

A riverfront cycle route continues from Albert Dock alongside the docks southward as far as Festival Park (6.6mi return). Please note that it is only available during daylight hours. The riverfront ride links up a mile later in Sefton Park with the main route.

The first part of the urban ride from the ferry terminal follows 7.1mi of bikepaths signposted NCN 56 the Trans Pennine Trail in Liverpool. Passing the huge 20th-century neogothic **Anglican cathedral** (20.1mi), it runs along backroads, through parks and even a short piece of Penny Lane (22.6mi), immortalised by the Beatles, to connect at

Warning – Alternative Route

The Liverpool Loop Line rail trail runs through urban embankments and a tunnel and is safest ridden in company during daylight hours. Women soloists in particular should consider the A59 alternative route.

Using this alternative from Liverpool city centre out to Aintree is much shorter (5.5mi) than the bikepaths and rail trails (15.7mi). However, the road carries heavy traffic. To take this alternative from the ferry terminal, take James St and then turn left into Derby St (18.8mi), right into Cook St (18.9mi) – which becomes Victoria St – to the roundabout (19.5mi). Take the A59 'to Ormskirk' and follow for it for 5mi. Rejoin the main route at A59 Warbreck Moor (34.4mi).

CENTRAL ENGLAND

Day 4: Chester to Southport

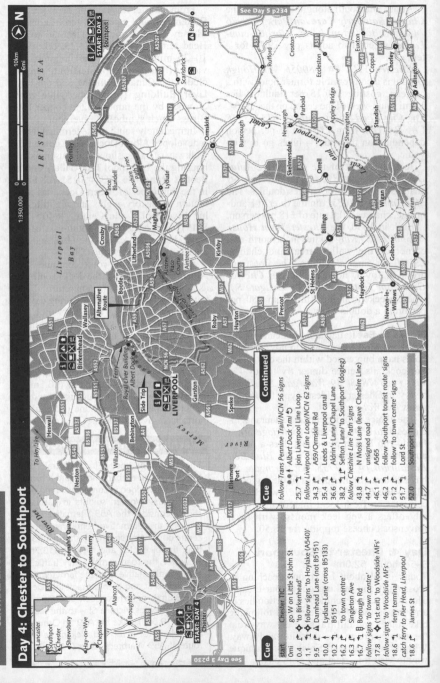

Cue

start	Chester TIC
0mi	go W on Little St John St
0.4	⟲ 'to Birkenhead'
1.1	⟲ follow signs 'to Hoylake (A540)'
9.5	⟲ Damhead Lane (not B5151)
10.0	⟲ Lydiate Lane (cross B5133)
10.2	⟳ B5151
16.2	⟲ 'to town centre'
16.3	⟲ Singleton Ave
16.7	⟲ Borough Rd
	follow signs 'to town centre'
17.8	⟲ (1st exit) 'to Woodside MFs'
	follow signs 'to Woodside MFs'
18.6	⟲ ferry terminal
	catch ferry to Pier Head, Liverpool
18.6	⟲ James St

Cue   **Continued**

	follow Trans Pennine Trail/NCN 56 signs
	● ● Albert Dock 1mi ⟲
25.7	⟲ join Liverpool Line Loop
	follow Liverpool Line Loop/NCN 62 signs
34.3	⟲ A59/Ormskird Rd
35.4	⟲ Leeds & Liverpool canal
36.6	⟲ Aldrin's Lane/Chapel Lane
38.2	⟲ Sefton Lane/'to Southport' (dogleg)
	follow Cheshire Line Path signs
43.8	⟲ N Moss Lane (leave Cheshire Line)
44.7	unsigned road
46.1	A565
46.2	follow 'Southport tourist route' signs
51.2	follow 'to town centre' signs
51.7	Lord St
52.0	Southport TIC

Childwall with the second part of the urban route, the Liverpool Loop Line rail trail (25.7mi).

The Loop Line, part of the coast-to-coast Trans Pennine Trail (NCN 62) was abandoned in 1964 and fell derelict before conversion work began in 1988. Via cuttings, embankments and bridges, the trail leads northwards around the city outskirts for 8.6mi as far as the A59 Warbreck Moor (34.3mi) at Aintree.

Here, the route passes **Aintree horse racecourse**, the venue of the Grand National every April (on which it seems nearly everyone in the land has a flutter). A mile after joining the road, the route reaches the **Leeds & Liverpool Canal** (35.3mi) and turns west along the towpath for a mile. Across fields to Maghull it finally picks up the Cheshire Lines Path (38mi), a rural rail trail that leads across drained farmland towards the coast. The route continues to track the course of the old railway along the sand-dune lined coastal road to Southport, using fine new bikepaths.

Southport
☎ 01704
Southport is a pleasant holiday town with little of the tackiness of many English resorts. A Victorian boulevard lined with well-kept gardens runs parallel to a beachfront with plenty of seaside entertainments. Miles of sand dunes and woodland support rare plants and animals, as well as British sunseekers.

Information The TIC (☎ 533333) is outside the town hall at 112 Lord St. The nearest bike shop, Southport Cycles (☎ 532265), is east of the town centre at 119 East Bank.

Things to See & Do Southport revolves around the natural and artificial attractions of its vast sandy **coastline**. The dunes to the south have walking and biking paths, the open area to the north to the Ribble estuary is popular with birdwatchers.

In town, the Marine Lake operates **water sports**. The Pleasureland **theme park** is great if you like to travel fast upside-down.

Southport's best-known annual event is the **Flower Show** (☎ 547147) which takes place in August and attracts people from all over the country.

Places to Stay Tent pitches are available at two sites near the village of Banks, 3mi north of town: the **Brooklyn Country Club** (☎ 228 534, Gravel Lane) and **Riverside Caravan Club** (☎ 228886, Southport New Rd).

There are no hostels in Southport, but there are reasonable B&Bs. The **Garden Court Hotel** (☎ 530219, 22 Bank Square) charges £14/31 for singles/doubles, and the **Tudor Court Guesthouse** (☎ 530687, 33 Talbot St) charges £14/28. **Sandy Brook Farm** (☎ 880337, Wyke Cop Rd) is a farmhouse B&B 3.5mi east of town at Scarisbrick; a room costs £19/34.

On the Promenade, the four-crown **Royal Clifton Hotel** (☎ 533771) does a reasonable summer saver of £47 in a double, including dinner.

Places to Eat Eating out is easy in Southport day and night. Numerous cafes and pubs do food and the **Arden Cafe** (☎ 546094, 75 Eastbank St) also offers well-priced veg dishes, like vegetable crumble with salad and garlic bread for £3. International cuisine includes Lebanese at **Alamir** (☎ 544615, 93 Eastbank St) and Japanese at **Samsi Yakitori** (☎ 544583, 56 Eastbank St), as well as Italian, Chinese, Indian and French. The restaurant at the **Royal Clifton Hotel** is one of the best in town. A grilled green lip mussel starter costs £5.50 and chicken stuffed with crabmeat with a lobster sauce is £9.25.

At the **Forge Brasserie** (☎ 500522, Queen Anne St), flamboyant staff serve a la carte and a daily special that you choose from the fresh fish counter. This includes exotica from around the world such as blackspotted grouper. At lunch times, fish and chips in shandy batter is £5.95.

Day 5: Southport to Lancaster
3–5 hours, 46.9mi
Lancashire's green lowlands and the Fylde plain contrast with fells rising sharply to the east on this route.

From Southport, the A565 coastal road has views over the Ribble estuary to Lytham St Anne's. It leads to the A59, which has a bikepath most of the way to **Preston**. A short detour (18.3mi), takes you to the riverside dock and marina, now a shopper's dream. It's a great place for a half-time break, either at the *chip stall* beside the marina or the *pub*. A more rural option is 10mi on at *Owd*

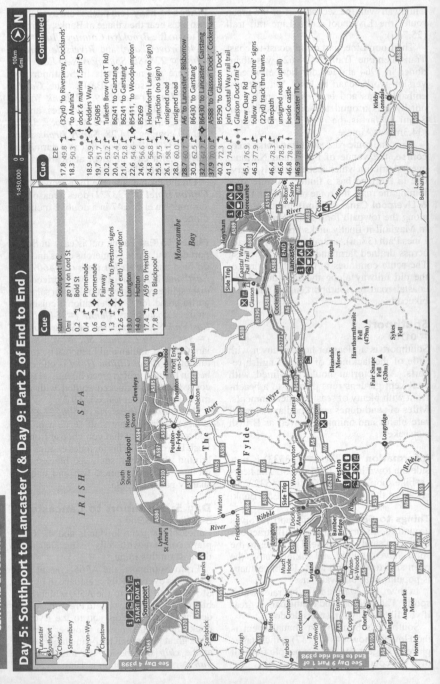

Day 5: Southport to Lancaster (& Day 9: Part 2 of End to End)

CENTRAL ENGLAND

⊙ N
10km
0
6mi
0
1:450,000

Cue | Continued
E2E
17.8 49.8 ◆ (32yd) 'to Riversway, Docklands'
18.3 50.3 ◆ 'to Marina'
        ● dock & marina 1.5mi ⟲
18.9 50.9 ↱ Pedders Way
19.7 51.7 ↰ A5085
20.2 52.2 ↱ Tulketh Brow (not T Rd)
20.4 52.4 ↱ B6241 'to Garstang'
21.4 52.8 ↱ B6241 'to Garstang'
22.6 54.6 ◆ B5411, 'to Woodplumpton'
24.6 56.6 ↰ B5269
24.8 56.8 ▲ Hollowforth Lane (no sign)
25.5 57.5 ↱ T-junction (no sign)
26.1 58.1 ↲ unsigned road
28.0 60.0 ↱ unsigned road
28.7 60.7 ↲ A6 'to Lancaster', Blisborrow
30.5 62.5 ↱ B6430 'to Garstang'
32.7 64.7 ◆ B6430 'to Lancaster', Garstang
37.9 70.0 ↱ A588 'to Glasson Dock', Cockerham
40.2 72.3 ↱ B5290 'to Glasson Dock'
        ● join Coastal Way rail trail
41.9 74.0 ⟲ Glasson Dock 1mi ⟲
45.1 76.9 ↱ New Quay Rd
46.3 77.9 ↱ follow 'to City Centre' signs
        ● (22yd) track thru lawns
46.4 78.3 ↰ bikepath
46.6 78.5 ↲ unsigned road (uphill)
46.8 78.7 ● beside castle
46.9 78.8 ■ Lancaster TIC

Cue
start   Southport TIC
0mi   go N on Lord St
0.2 ↱↰ Bold St
0.4 ↱   Promenade
0.6 ↰   Promenade
1.0 ↱   Fairway
1.3 ↱   follow 'to Preston' signs
12.6 ↰   (2nd exit) 'to Longton'
13.0   Longton
14.0   Hutton
17.4 ↰   A59 'to Preston'
17.8 ↱   'to Blackpool'

I R I S H   S E A

Morecambe Bay

Heysham
Morecambe
Bolton-le-Sands
Caton
River Lune
Low Bentham
Kirkby Lonsdale

Side Trip
Coastal Way Rail Trail
Glasson
Cockerham
Lancaster
END

Clougha
Bleasdale Moors
Hawthornthwaite Fell (479m)
Fair Snape Fell (520m)
Sykes Fell

Knott End-on-Sea
Fleetwood
Preesall
Cleveleys
Thornton
Hambleton
North Shore
Blackpool
South Shore
Poulton-le-Fylde
Kirkham
Warton
Lytham St Anne's
Freckleton

The Fylde

River Wyre
Catterall
Garstang
Bilsborrow
Longridge

Side Trip
Preston
Bamber Bridge

Dock & Marina
Longton
Hutton
Much Hoole
Banks
Leyland
Clayton-le-Woods
Euxton
Chorley
Anglezarke Moor
Horwich
Adlington
Coppull
Croston
Eccleston
Rufford
Parbold
Burscough
Scarisbrick
Southport
START: DAY 5
Southport
See Day 4 p399

River Ribble

To Northwich

See Day 9 Part 1 of End to End ride p398

Lancaster
Southport
Chester
Shrewsbury
Hay-on-Wye
Chepstow

Nell's Tavern on the canalside before the A6 turn at **Bilsborrow** (28.7mi). A big menu and open-air seating attract the hordes on sunny weekends.

An short interlude on the thundering A6 is compensated by a quick side trip to **Glasson**, a little harbour town on the mouth of the River Lune. The tranquil Lancashire Coastal Way rail trail leads to Lancaster's St George's Quay and the town centre.

Lancaster
See the Central England Explorer ride (p206) for details on getting to/from Lancaster.

Through the Midlands

Duration	3 days
Distance	152.1mi
Difficulty	moderate
Start	Shrewsbury
End	Oundle

This ride explores the historic and gentle side of England's heartland, considered, unfairly, to be wholly industrial and dull. The traditional industries have declined, however most areas are recovering. The prosperous pockets have never lost their charm and the countryside remains as lovely as it ever was.

As the route proceeds from Shropshire through Staffordshire, Leicestershire and Rutland to Northamptonshire, it weaves a path that comes within striking distance of numerous cities. It follows valleys defended by castles, visits pleasant old towns and villages and explores areas of unexpected wilderness.

Highlights include the run along the River Severn to Ironbridge, the forests of Cannock Chase and Charnwood, the quiet backwaters of Staffordshire and the beautiful landscape east of Leicester.

There are numerous drags rather than significant hills, although the roads are never flat for long. Be prepared for the contrast between the quiet lanes and the occasional thundering A-road, which you should negotiate with care.

This ride can also be linked with the Peak District ride, later in this chapter, which starts at Uttoxeter, and the Central England Explorer ride, earlier, at Oundle.

PLANNING
When to Ride
This is a lowland, largely sheltered ride that can be done at any time of year, although the summer months are best.

Maps
The OS Travelmaster maps (1:250,000) No 7, *Wales and West Midlands*; and No 6, *East Midlands & East Anglia* are good maps to use for this area.

What to Bring
The little towns and villages en route have all necessary supplies. Camping grounds can be found at each overnight stop as well as in between stops.

GETTING TO/FROM THE RIDE
Shrewsbury
Train Shrewsbury has good connections with Birmingham (£5.30, one hour, two services an hour) and Manchester (£15.50, 75 minutes, hourly). Bikes are carried off-peak.

Bicycle Shrewsbury is on the Marches, Cheshire & Lancashire ride earlier in this chapter.

Oundle
Train The nearest train station to Oundle is Peterborough, 11mi away on the A605, with fast frequent connections to London (£14.90, 65 minutes, every 10 minutes) and Leicester (£6, 55 minutes, hourly).

Bicycle Oundle links up with Day 3 of the Central England Explorer ride earlier in this chapter.

THE RIDE
Shrewsbury
See Shrewsbury (pp227–9) in the Marches, Cheshire & Lancashire ride for information about accommodation and other services.

Day 1: Shrewsbury to Uttoxeter
4–6½ hours, 59.5mi
A gentle day of riding runs through pleasant countryside, and which turns a little wilder at Cannock Chase.

The elevated road to **Ironbridge** has fine views of the meandering River Severn and the Welsh hills. The picturesque town is considered the birthplace of the Industrial

CENTRAL ENGLAND

CENTRAL ENGLAND

Day 1: Shrewsbury to Uttoxeter

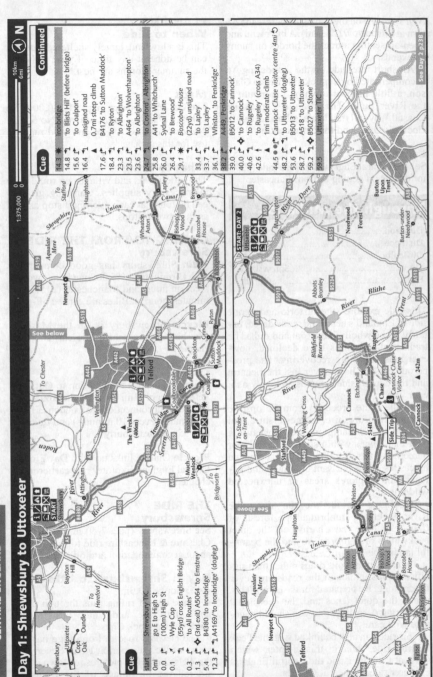

N

1:375,000

See Day 2 p238

Cue (Continued)

14.3	✳	Ironbridge
14.8	↰	'to Blists Hill' (before bridge)
15.6	↱	'to Coalport'
16.4	◀	unsigned road
		0.7mi steep climb
17.6	↱	B4176 'to Sutton Maddock'
18.4	↰	'to Ryton'
23.3	↱	'to Albrighton'
23.5	↰	A464 'to Wolverhampton'
23.6	↱	'to Albrighton'
24.7	↰	'to Cosford', Albrighton
25.8	↱	A41 'to Whitchurch'
26.0	↰	Sydnal Lane
26.4	↱	'to Brewood'
29.1	✳	Boscobel House
		(22yd) unsigned road
33.4	↱	'to Lapley'
33.7	↰	'to Lapley'
36.1	↱	Whiston 'to Penkridge'
38.2	↰	A449, Penkridge
39.0	↱	B5012 'to Cannock'
40.0	◇	'to Cannock'
40.6	↱	'to Rugeley'
42.6	←	'to Rugeley' (cross A34)
		1mi moderate climb
44.5	● ↺	Cannock Chase visitor centre 4mi
48.2	↱↰	'to Uttoxeter' (dogleg)
53.6	↱	B5013 'to Uttoxeter'
58.7	↰	A518 'to Uttoxeter'
59.2	◇	B5027 'to Stone'
59.5	◇	Uttoxeter TIC

Cue

start	0mi	Shrewsbury TIC
0.0	↱	go E to High St
0.1	↰	(100m) High St
	↱ ✳ ↰	(55yd) cross English Bridge
0.3	↱	(3rd exit) A5064 'to Emstrey'
1.3	↰	A5064 'to All Routes'
5.4	↰	B4380 'to Ironbridge'
12.3	↱↰	A4169/'to Ironbridge' (dogleg)

START
Shrewsbury

See below

Telford
Ironbridge
Gorge
Coalport
Ironbridge

The Wrekin (400m)

Much
Wenlock

Wellington
Coalbrookdale

To Chester

To Hereford

To Bridgnorth

Bayston
Hill

Attingham

River Severn
River Roden

A5
A49
A458
A488
A442
A518
A5223
A442
A4169
A4380
B4380

Brockton
Grindle
Ryton
Sutton
Maddock

Newport
Haughton

To Stafford

Aqualate
Mere

Union Shropshire
Canal

Wheaton
Aston
Bishops
Wood

Boscobel
House

Lapley
Brewood
Albrighton

See above

START: DAY 2
Uttoxeter

Nacthington
River Dove

Abbots
Bromley

River Blithe

Burton
Upon
Trent

Needwood
Forest

Barton-under-
Needwood

Blithfield
Reservoir

Rugeley
Etchinghill

Cannock
Chase
Visitor
Centre

▲ 242m

Side Trip
▲ 514m

Cannock

Penkridge

Whiston
Lapley

Union
Canal

Bishop's
Wood

Boscobel
House

Aqualate
Mere

Newport

Telford

Grindle
Ryton
Albrighton

Stafford
Weeping Cross

To Stoke-
on-Trent

River Trent

A515
A50
A511
A513
A38
A518
A449
A34
A51
A5013
A460
A500
A520
A518
B5012
B5013
B5014

Shrewsbury
Uttoxeter
Copt
Oak
Oundle

Revolution and features the **world's first iron bridge**. The End to End ride (see the Land's End to John o'Groats chapter) crosses the route here; see Ironbridge (pp393–5) for information about the **Ironbridge Gorge Museum** and its many attractions.

Country lanes lead through Albrighton to **Boscobel House** (29.1mi; ☎ 01902-850244; EH), a romantic 17th-century hunting lodge where Charles II successfully hid from his Parliamentarian enemies in the nearby 'Royal Oak' in 1651. Beyond Penkridge (38.2mi), you climb into the forests of Cannock Chase. Its **visitor centre**, a short side trip off the route, serves minimal refreshments and hopes a cafe may open soon. There is a 9mi mountain bike ride around the forest. Note that the nearby camping ground is not for tourists.

Uttoxeter
☎ 01889

This small market town in East Staffordshire has a name that has been spelt 78 different ways throughout its history. It is home to a nationally known racecourse and the headquarters of JCB, manufacturer of the famous yellow earth-diggers.

The Peak District ride, later in this chapter, also starts at Uttoxeter.

The TIC (☎ 567176) is in Carter St, round the corner from the Market Place. Uttoxeter Cycle Centre (☎ 567608), 34 Market Place, is a few doors along.

Places to Stay & Eat In the centre of the racecourse oval 0.5mi east of town, *Uttoxeter Caravan Site (*☎ *564172 or *☎ *562561)* has pitches for £4.60, but ring first as they close for race days once or twice a month. About 9mi north, near Alton Towers theme park is the *Star Caravan & Camping Club (*☎ *01538-702256; Star Rd, Cotton),* where a pitch is £6 per adult.

The *Oldroyd Guest House (*☎ *562763, 18 Bridge St),* below Market Place, does singles/doubles with en suite for £25/45.

The 16th-century coaching inn, the *White Hart (*☎ *562437, Carter St),* near the TIC, does doubles for £49 plus breakfast for £6. It also serves a varied dinner menu with main dishes from £6.

The *Bel Paese (*☎ *565676, High St)* is an Italian restaurant with a full menu, including the chef's special of *pollo sofia* (stuffed chicken breast) for £10.

A speciality widely available in the cafes in these parts are oatcakes, which are tasty filled savoury pancakes.

Day 2: Uttoxeter to Copt Oak
2½–4½ hours, 41.1mi

Historic buildings and beauty spots crop up again and again in an area where redundant open-cast coalmines have been recycled into the National Forest.

A few miles from Uttoxeter the ruined turrets of **Tutbury Castle** (9.9mi) overlook the River Dove. Run by the Duchy of Lancaster, it's open April to September.

At Ticknall is the entrance to **Calke Abbey** (22.1mi; ☎ 01332-863822; NT), which is not an abbey, but a remarkable baroque mansion known as 'the house time forgot'. Collections and furnishings were kept under dust sheets for centuries by an eccentric family before the NT recently took over.

A little further on, the reservoirs of **Foremark** (where there's a *cafe*) and **Staunton Harold** (where there's a picnic site en route at 25.7mi) are pleasant places for a break.

In Ashby de la Zouch (30.7mi; pronounced 'zoosh') the **castle** has a distinct tower and secret passages. It was partly dismantled after yielding to siege by the Parliamentary forces during the Civil War.

Much of the route runs through the new **National Forest**, a land-regeneration project due to mature later this century. Woodland and country parks have been planted for people and wildlife over a rectangular area of 20mi by 10mi, stretching from Burton on Trent to Charnwood Forest.

The day finishes at the YHA on the edge of Charnwood Forest, a piece of high forest land with rocky outcrops that was barely inhabited until the 19th century. The nearby town of Coalville has all facilities.

Copt Oak & Coalville
☎ 01530

Copt Oak is a quiet hamlet on the edge of Charnwood Forest, with only a YHA and a pub. For more accommodation and eating options, head to nearby Coalville (4mi in total – take the Whitwick road from the crossroads and turn left after 2mi).

In 150 years, Coalville grew from nothing to a sizable mining town, only to fall into rapid decline after WWII and see its last pit close in 1986. Efforts have been

Day 2: Uttoxeter to Copt Oak

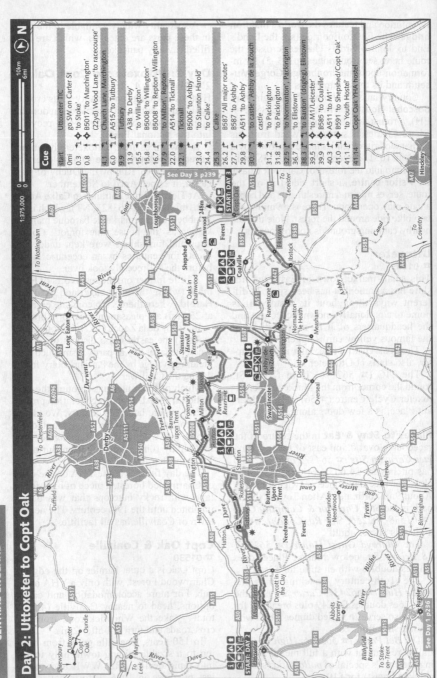

Cue		
start	Uttoxeter TIC	
0mi	go SW on Carter St	
0.3	'to Stoke'	
0.8	B5017 'to Marchington'	
	(22yd) Wood Lane 'to racecourse'	
4.1	Church Lane, Marchington	
6.0	A515/'to Tutbury'	
9.9	Tutbury	
13.9	A38 'to Derby'	
15.5	'to Willington'	
15.8	B5008 'to Willington'	
16.7	B5008 'to Repton', Willington	
17.9	'to Milton', Repton	
22.0	A514 'to Ticknall'	
22.1	Ticknall	
23.0	B5006 'to Ashby'	
	'to Staunton Harold'	
24.4	'to Calke'	
25.3	Calke	
26.2	B587 'All major routes'	
27.7	B587 'to Ashby'	
29.8	A511 'to Ashby'	
30.7	'to castle', Ashby de la Zouch	
	castle	
31.2	'to Packington'	
31.8	'to Packington'	
32.5	'to Normanton', Packington	
36.7	'to Ellistown'	
38.3	'to Bardon' (dogleg), Ellistown	
39.5	'to M1/Leicester'	
39.9	B585 'to Coalville'	
40.3	A511 'to M1'	
41.0	B591 'to Shepshed/Copt Oak'	
41.1	'to Youth Hostel'	
41.14	Copt Oak YHA hostel	

See Day 3 p239

START DAY 3

START DAY 2

Day 3: Copt Oak to Oundle

Continued

Cue	
8.2	to Cossington, Rothley
10.3	A607 'to Queniborough'
16.7	'to Baggrave Hall'
18.3	'to Cold Newton'
19.2	'to Cold Newton'
20.6	0.5mi hard climb
22.0	B6047 'to Tilton'
22.4	'to Loddington', Tilton on the Hill
22.8	'to Loddington'
26.5	'to Launde'
26.7	'to Belton'
28.8	A47 'to Uppingham'
29.2	'to Allexton'
29.3	'to Stockerston'
31.3	'to Stockerston'
31.9	B664 'to Stoke Dry'
34.3	'to Great Easton'
36.4	A6003 'to Corby'
37.1	Rockingham
38.0	0.5mi steep climb
	A6116 'to Corby'
	Rockingham Castle 0.6mi
38.1	'to Stamford'
39.0	'to Deene, Kirby Hall'
40.9	'to Kirby Hall'
41.6	Kirby Hall 0.5mi
42.8	'to Deene'
43.7	A43 'to Corby'
43.9	'to Benefield'
44.3	'to Benefield', Deenethorpe
46.7	'to Oundle'
49.5	'to Oundle'
51.5	West St (at cross)
51.52	Oundle TIC

Cue

Cue	
start	Copt Oak YHA hostel
0mi	go N on previous day's route
0.0	(44yd) B591 'to Woodhouse Eaves'
0.5	'to Woodhouse Eaves'
0.8	1.4mi moderate climb
3.5	'to Swithland'
4.6	'to Swithland'
7.7	'to Cossington'

See Day 2 p238

made with some success to regenerate it, with the arrival of new light industry and the creation of Snibston Discovery Park.

Information The TIC (☎ 81 3608) is in the Snibston Discovery Park. Coalville Cycles (☎ 832179), 28 Belvoir Rd, is in the town centre.

Things to See & Do For some informative entertainment, head to Coalville. **Snibston Discovery Park** (☎ 510851 or ☎ 813256) is a praised science and industry museum with indoor and outdoor exhibits covering a huge site formerly occupied by the No 2 Colliery (coal mine). The old coal mine buildings form part of the museum.

Places to Stay In Copt Oak, the small, simple *Copt Oak YHA* (☎ 242661), a converted schoolhouse, charges £6.80 per night. The nearest camping ground is extremely basic, at *Mill Farm* (☎ 01509-412164; Chaveney Rd, Quorn), 5mi away in the direction of the Day 3 route (continue at Woodhouse Eaves). A pitch is £1, but all you get is a chemical toilet. For full facilities, continue another mile or so on to Barrow upon Soar and *Meadow Farm Marina* (☎ 01509-816035, Houston Close), where a pitch is £6.50 per night.

Coalville has a few more upmarket options sprinkled around. *Saint Joseph's* (☎ 01509-503943, Oaks in Charnwood), 3mi north-east of town, is an old country house charging £18/36 for singles/doubles. In the centre is *Broadlawns Guest House* (☎ 836724, 98 London Rd), where prices start from £20/35. The best hotel in town is the *Hermitage Park* (☎ 814202, Whitwick Rd), with doubles from £69.50.

Well worth ringing is *Church Lane Farm* (☎ 810536), 2mi west of Coalville in the village of Ravenstone, where a night among antique furnishings, with dinner and use of a bar, is well priced at £23/38/40 for a single/twin/double. Moreover, Mrs Thorne will cook superb meals by prior arrangement for around £20.

Places to Eat Next to the YHA in Copt Oak is the *Copt Oak*, which serves decent pub fare till 10 pm (9.30 pm on Sunday). Main dishes include steak-and-mushroom pudding for £5.15, as well as some veg options. Sandwiches and baguettes cost £3 to £4.

In Coalville, you are not spoiled for choice. The *Hermitage Park Hotel* (☎ 814 814, Whitwick Rd) has a carvery for £12. The *Wise Plaice (Hotel St)* is a sit-down fish and chip shop that also serves kebabs and burgers, and there's the *Monsoon Tandoori* (☎ 510449, High St), if you fancy a bite of the new national dish.

Day 3: Copt Oak to Oundle
3½–5½ hours, 51.5mi
This picturesque ride begins with a climb through Charnwood Forest, passes the well-to-do outlying villages of Leicester and explores fine countryside to Tilton.

There are numerous short (0.5mi) climbs and descents en route, and a couple of heavy traffic sections. At Rockingham village (36.4mi) hill and traffic combine, unfortunately at odds with the historic backdrop. Walk your bike if you don't want to struggle uphill with the lorries.

Don't miss the side trip to **Rockingham Castle** (38.0mi; ☎ 01536-770240) for living history and cream teas – go right at the roundabout at the top of the hill above Rockingham and the entrance is 100yd farther on the right. The handsome, imposing fortification has guarded the Welland Valley above Rockingham for 900 years. In Tudor times Henry VIII granted it to the ancestor of the family that still lives there today.

A few miles along is **Kirby Hall** (41.6mi; ☎ 01536-203230; EH), a fine Elizabethan mansion that also serves refreshments.

The sandstone in Northamptonshire's fine buildings is from a continuation of the same rock seam as the lovely Cotswold villages.

Oundle
See Day 2 (p209) of the Central England Explorer ride for details about Oundle.

Peak District

Duration	2 days
Distance	83.4mi
Difficulty	moderate-hard
Start	Uttoxeter
End	Langsett

This is a hearty introduction to some of England's wildest and most beautiful upland areas. Although not for the unfit or

Shrewsbury, the birthplace of Charles Darwin.

Liverpool's looming Cunard Building.

Ironbridge, the 'Silicon Valley' of the 18th century.

A handy coffee stand in the heart of Oxford.

In Edale, grab a quick ale as you pass through.

High St in Burford is lined with stone cottages.

Stay off Hadrian's Wall, please.

Enjoy a dream run along Sustrans' popular C2C route.

Making hay while the sun shines near Pickering, northern England.

Row, row, row your boat across Derwent Water, Keswick.

Cycleway art near Whitehaven.

faint-hearted, the wild scenery, stone villages and easy sections of rail trail complement and relieve the very hilly riding.

HISTORY
As well as being a playground for cycle tourists and mountain bikers, the Peak District is the nursery of many a pro British racer. Roadies are often spotted on climbs they know like the back of their hand and in local cafes where they are regular faces.

The Tour of the Peak is an annual pro-am road race, and several steep climbs in the area are venues in the autumn hill climb season. Rounds of the national mountain bike series have been held beside Redmires reservoir near Sheffield.

NATURAL HISTORY
The Peak National Park is an area of high land riven by deep dales. The conurbations of Manchester and Sheffield run hard against its flanks. It divides into distinct geological halves: the southern limestone White Peak dominated by grazing and quarrying, and the northern gritstone Dark Peak, a glowering high moorland.

PLANNING
When to Ride
Providing you wear good weatherproof gear, the skies and frosts of the autumn and winter months can be thrilling. In spring and summer, things are more mellow but a spot of rain in the valleys can be a storm on the tops. Always be prepared for bad weather and seek shelter in a dale village if in doubt.

Weekends are busy with visitors from the cities, but during the summer weeks the Peaks are quieter than the coastal resorts and major tourist towns.

Maps
Recommended maps include: the OS Travelmaster maps (1:250,000) No 5, *Northern England;* No 6, *East Midlands & East Anglia;* and No 7, *Wales and West Midlands.* Also useful is the OS Outdoor Leisure (1:25 000) No 1, *The White Peak;* and No 24, *The Dark Peak;* as well as the Goldeneye Cycling map, *The Peak District* (1:126,720).

What to Bring
In good weather carry waterproofs, water and snacks (pubs and village shops get a little thin

on the ground). In winter, the Peaks can get snowed in, so in bad weather carry emergency clothing and rations.

GETTING TO/FROM THE RIDE
Uttoxeter
Train Trains run regularly to Uttoxeter from Derby (£4.10, 22 minutes, hourly) and from Crewe (£6.60, 45 minutes, hourly except Sunday), which connect to other major cities. Trains carry up to two bikes for a £3 fee.

Bicycle Uttoxeter is the start of Day 2 on the Through the Midlands ride, earlier in this chapter.

Langsett/Penistone
Penistone (4.5mi away) is the nearest town with rail connections to Langsett.

To get to Langsett take the A628 towards Crowden and Manchester. After 3.5mi on this busy road, go left to Langsett on the minor road where the A628 bears hard-right; the town is 1mi on.

Train Trains run from Penistone to Sheffield (£3, 47 minutes, hourly) and Huddersfield (£2.40, 30 minutes, hourly) for connections all over the country. Bikes are free with two to three spaces available on each train.

Bicycle To link with the Central England Explorer ride (earlier this chapter), continue from Langsett for a farther (very strenuous) 40mi northwards through the Pennines.

THE RIDE
Uttoxeter
See Day 1 (p237) of the Through the Midlands ride for details about Uttoxeter.

Day 1: Uttoxeter to Buxton
2½–4 hours, 39.8mi
Stunning scenery, fascinating rail trails, hilly and pretty villages are revealed on this route in the southern Peak District.

The roads undulate increasingly and the hills require a sturdy push on the pedals. Take care on the short sections of A-roads, particularly at the A523 at the right turn into the Manifold Way (if you choose to ride on the road). For the quarry lorries and cars, it's just another day racing the clock.

Warm up on the roads north of Uttoxeter for the trip's first challenge, the short but

Day 1: Uttoxeter to Buxton

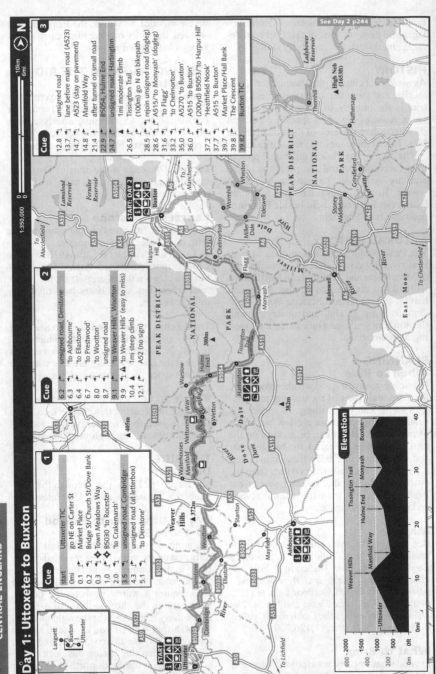

Cue

start	Uttoxeter TIC
0mi	go NE on Carter St
0.1	Market Place
0.2	Bridge St/Church St/Dove Bank
0.3	Town Meadows Way
1.0	B5030 'to Rocester'
2.0	'to Crakemarsh'
3.5	unsigned road, Combridge
4.3	unsigned road (at letterbox)
5.1	'to Denstone'

Cue

6.2	unsigned road, Denstone
6.3	'to Ashbourne'
6.4	'to Ellastone'
6.7	'to Prestwood'
8.0	'to Wootton'
8.7	unsigned road
9.1	'to Weaver Hills' Wootton
9.9	'to Weaver Hills' (easy to miss)
10.4	1mi steep climb
12.1	A52 (no sign)

Cue

12.8	unsigned road
13.7	lane before main road (A523)
14.7	A523 (stay on pavement)
14.8	Manifold Way
21.4	after tunnel on small road
22.9	B5054, Hulme End
24.7	unsigned road, Hartington
	1mi moderate climb
26.5	Tissington Trail
	(100m) go N on bikepath
28.5	rejoin unsigned road (dogleg)
28.6	A515/'to Monyash' (dogleg)
31.6	'to Flagg'
33.2	'to Chelmorton'
35.0	A5270 'to Buxton'
36.0	A515 'to Buxton'
37.2	(200yd) B5053/'to Harpur Hill'
37.7	'Heathfield Nook'
37.7	A515 'to Buxton'
39.7	Market Place/Hall Bank
39.8	The Crescent
39.82	Buxton TIC

Elevation

1:350,000

See Day 2 p244

steep ascent of Weaver Hills. A few miles farther on, turn on to the scenic 8mi **Manifold Way** at Waterhouses, a rail trail that runs through steep-sided Manifold Valley, one of the first disused lines to be converted in the 1930s. There's a *cafe* near the start, and at Wettonmill.

There's a steady climb after pretty Hartington to the final open stretch of the **Tissington Trail**, another disused railway line, which runs to Ashbourne. This is true White Peak country, a landscape of green fields, dry-stone walls and ever-changing skies.

Buxton
☎ 01298

The former spa town of Buxton in Derbyshire has a peaceful central knot of handsome Georgian buildings that contrasts with heavy quarrying on the outskirts and the thundering A6 that runs near the centre.

Information The TIC (☎ 25106) is beside the newly restored Crescent. Cycle parts, repairs and mountain bike hire (£15, plus VAT) can be found at Mark Anthony's Cycles (☎ 72114) at the far end of the pedestrianised shopping street (Spring Gardens) and over the roundabout.

Things to See & Do Buxton boomed in the 19th century, when taking the waters was all the rage among the privileged classes. A turn around the spa area includes the **Pump**

Room in the Crescent, which dispensed mineral water for nearly a century, the spa exhibition in the former **Natural Mineral Baths** (home to the TIC), the **Opera House** and the glasshouse **Pavillion**. The pedestrian shopping street, **Spring Gardens**, is east of the Crescent.

Poole's Cavern (☎ 26978), 1mi southwest, is a stalactite-rich cave with guided tours operating from March to October.

The opera house, built in 1903, is the focus of the annual **Buxton Festival**, which takes places late July to early August.

Places to Stay & Eat About 1mi south of the centre along the A515 is *Lime Tree Park* (☎ 22988, Dukes Drive) camping ground. *Buxton YHA* (☎ 22287, Harpur Hill Rd), just off the A515 on the southern outskirts of town, is £7.50 per night. It's closed on Sunday, but not on bank holiday weekends.

Cheaper B&Bs can be found just south of the centre in Compton Rd, west of London Rd. The *Griff Guest House* (☎ 23628, 2 Compton Rd) does singles for £17 per person. *Compton House* (☎ 26926, 4 Compton Rd) does singles/doubles from £20/18.50 per person. Smart guesthouses cluster on Broadwalk near the opera house.

The Grosvenor House Hotel (☎ 72 439, 1 Broadwalk) costs from £25/45 per person. One of the finest hotels in town is the nearby *Old Hall Hotel* (☎ 22841, The Crescent),

---

Mam Tor – 'Shivering Mountain'

On Mam Tor (514m/1695ft) you can scramble over a battlefield where man has been defeated by nature. Below the mountain's eastern face, to the right of the route, is the collapsed road – the twisted and broken remnants of what once was the A625, its craggy steps striking evidence of landslips which have earned the peak its other name, 'Shivering Mountain'.

The road was originally built in 1817 as an alternative to the 20% gradient of Winnats Pass, which climbs out of the Hope Valley nearby. But the weathering of the mountain is a continual process, and after countless repairs the boys from the black stuff gave up in 1979 and the road was left to its fate.

The landslides are caused by the unstable combination of Edale Shales at the base of the cliff and Millstone Grits above, which can be seen protruding from the face. In the wet, the shales revert to their original muddy form and unseat the sandstones and gritstones. This mix was also responsible for the great crash that exposed Mam Tor's face way back in geological time. The debris can be seen in the uneven land that spreads out over half a mile from the cliff base.

The ramparts of the breezy but impregnable 5th-century BC Iron Age Hillfort on the summit have also been damaged by slippage. The site commands one of the best views of the Peak District, and humanity's job there is to maintain the path against hiking boots as much as rolling rock.

CENTRAL ENGLAND

Day 2: Buxton to Langsett

1:350,000

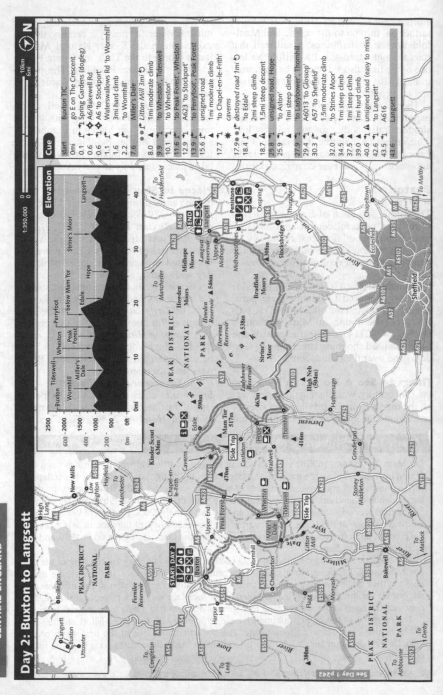

Cue

start	Buxton TIC
0mi	go E on The Crescent
0.1	Spring Gardens (dogleg)
0.6	A6/Bakewell Rd
0.6	A6 'to Stockport'
1.1	Waterswallows Rd 'to Wormhill'
1.6	3mi hard climb
2.2	'to Wormhill'
7.6	Miller's Dale
	Litton Mill 3mi
8.0	1mi moderate climb
9.9	'to Wheston', Tideswell
10.1	'to Wheston'
11.6	'to Peak Forest', Wheston
12.9	A623 'to Stockport'
13.9	'to Perryfoot', Peak Forest
15.6	unsigned road
17.7	1mi moderate climb
	'to Chapel-en-le-Frith' caverns
17.9	destroyed road 1mi
18.4	'to Edale'
18.7	2mi steep climb
25.8	1.5mi steep descent
25.9	unsigned road, Hope
	'to Aston'
27.9	1mi steep climb
29.4	A6013 'to Glossop'
30.3	A57 'to Sheffield'
	1.5mi moderate climb
32.0	'to Strines Moor'
34.5	1mi steep climb
37.5	1mi steep climb
39.0	1mi hard climb
40.6	unsigned road (easy to miss)
42.6	'to Langsett'
43.5	A616
43.6	Langsett

which charges £60/85. The bar menu is varied and affordable, considering the establishment, with mains from £7.

Eating out is easy in Buxton. The cheapest roast dinner in town is at the *Bryant Arcade cafe*, off Eagle Parade, at £3.95. Vegetarians can head to *Wild Carrot* (☎ 22843, *5 Bridge St*), with tasty mains from £5. For Italian, try *Michaelangelo's Ristorante* (☎ 26640, *Market Place*) and *Firenze* (☎ 72203, *Market Place*). *Columbine* (☎ 78752, *Hall Bank*) serves traditional English fare.

Day 2: Buxton to Langsett
3–4½ hours, 43.6mi
Beyond any doubt, this is an adventurous day, with a lot of strenuous climbing rewarded by great descents and views. The major climbs come out of Buxton, Miller's Dale, up to Mam Tor and along the glorious Strine's Moor road. 'Strines' is hallowed in local cycling lore – it has three steep sections and saves the biggest for last. Major descents include the 183m (600ft) drop from Mam Tor and hell-for-leather losses on Strines.

With all that climbing, take the day steady; the distance is not great and there are cafes and pubs aplenty – these come in the first half of the day at Tideswell, Edale and Hope.

A 3mi side trip takes in the beautiful surrounds of Miller's Dale and eventually leads to Litton Mill; follow the signs at 7.6mi.

Below Mam Tor, tour one of the spectacular **caverns** – the Blue John (☎ 01433-620512), the Treak Cliff (☎ 01433-620571) or the Speedwell (☎ 01433-620638). Just after Mam Tor is the side trip to the destroyed road (see the boxed text). Take care entering Langsett – you're on the main road between Manchester and Sheffield.

Langsett
☎ 01226
Langsett is a hamlet on the A616 above Langsett Reservoir. It has a shop doubling as a cafe, a hostel and a good pub with lodging. Penistone (4.5mi away) has more facilities.

Places to Stay & Eat The simple *Langsett YHA* (☎ 761548) is beside the cafe. A bed is £6.80. The hotel is fully open from 17 July to 30 August. The pub *Waggon & Horses* (☎ 763147) has en suite singles/doubles from £35/45 with home-cooked bar food, real ale and views over the reservoir.

In Penistone, *The Rose & Crown* (☎ 763 609) has singles starting from £18. *The Old Vicarage* (☎ 370607, *Shrewsbury Rd*) has single rooms from £25.

About 1.5mi from Langsett, south of Penistone over the steep little road from Midhopestones, lies *Cubley Hall* (☎ 766086, *Mortimer Rd*) where weekend prices are from £50/60.

A Cotswolds Triangle

Duration	4 days
Distance	195.0mi
Difficulty	moderate
Start	Jordans
End	Oxford

Ducks dabbling in the village ford and old cottages glowing in the afternoon sun, cream teas in every town and 4WDs on the school run – the Cotswolds is England at its most persistently quaint and subtly well-to-do, an ancient hilly area with honey-coloured limestone villages unspoiled by modern developments that can literally take your breath away.

Starting on a lovely 'branch line' just outside London in Buckinghamshire, the route crosses the ridges of the Chilterns and drops to the university town of Oxford. Thereafter, it becomes a triangle, exploring the countryside and towns to Cirencester and Stratford-upon-Avon and returning through Oxfordshire. In an alternatively gentle and wild landscape lie some of the sweetest villages imaginable, the majority proudly cared for and now preserved in law.

The farming roads are muddy and cruddy, so take care after rain.

NATURAL HISTORY
The Cotswold Hills form a wedge of upland that slopes up from the east in Oxfordshire to peak at 300m (1000ft) in the west at an escarpment above Cheltenham in Gloucestershire. As the land rises, countless little river valleys cut deeper shafts into the Jurassic limestone and sandstone from which the honey-coloured villages are built.

The area became prosperous in the Middle Ages when wool from Cotswolds sheep was renowned throughout Europe. Many of the most charming cottages were originally for weavers, who diverted streams to run past their doorways for rinsing cloth. Wool production in the area continues today, although it is under great economic pressure.

The Chiltern Hills of Day 1 are a chalk ridge cloaked in magnificent beech woods, which can also be enjoyed by walkers on the long-distance Ridgeway Path.

PLANNING
When to Ride
The saying 'Stow-on-the-Wold, where the wind blows cold' says it all – in winter the high Cotswolds are exposed. Riding any time of year here is enjoyable, but spring and summer are best, when the countryside and villages are at their most charming.

Maps
The OS Travelmaster map No 9, *South East England* (1:250,000) and the Goldeneye Cycling Map, *The Cotswolds,* (1: 126,720) cover this route.

What to Bring
Carry waterproofs and some spares, although there are bike shops in all the overnight towns. There is camping at every halt, so this is ideal for a self-sufficient trip, although Days 1 & 3 are hilly.

GETTING TO/FROM THE RIDE
Jordans/High Wycombe
By starting from Jordans you get to explore the pleasant wooded Chiltern Hills and the winding River Thames before starting on the Cotswolds. It is possible to start the ride at High Wycombe (8mi from Jordans), which has more transport connections and lodgings. To pick up the route (3.5mi away), take the A404 from High Wycombe south towards Marlow. At the A40 motorway roundabout take the A4010 Aylesbury road that exits the High Wycombe side of the motorway and follow that past John Lewis store. Go left at the next mini-roundabout and continue, crossing over the motorway to the B482. Pick up the route there (next cue 16.9mi).

Train Seer Green station is 1mi away on the London Marylebone line (£6.50, 30 minutes, half-hourly). Go east (right) from the station for 0.75mi and then left at the junction into Jordans.

To reach High Wycombe, trains to and from London (Marylebone) are fast and frequent (£7.20, 30–40 minutes, half-hourly). Bikes are carried free in the passenger carriages during off-peak periods.

Bicycle To ride the 25mi from central London follow the A4020 (Marble Arch, Notting Hill, Shepherds Bush, Ealing, Southall, Hayes, Hillingdon, Uxbridge) to Denham, then join the A40, continue to Gerrards Cross, and turn right 2.5mi beyond to Jordans.

Oxford
Train Oxford is on the London Paddington-Worcester line (£14.10/18 single/return, 1–1½ hours, hourly). There are other direct and connecting services. Bikes travel free in the passenger carriages in off-peak periods.

Bicycle Oxford lies on several county cycle routes, including the Oxfordshire Cycle Way. Details are available from Oxford TIC (see Oxford after Day 1 of this ride).

THE RIDE
Jordans
☎ 01494
Jordans has a village store and post office but no bike shop, and the nearest TIC is in High Wycombe (☎ 421892).

There's a cluster of old red-brick buildings in the pretty village that played a role in English Quaker history and are still in use today. Meetings for worship were first held regularly at **Jordans Farm** (now the Old Jordans guesthouse) from 1659. Attendees included such luminaries as William Penn (founder of Pennsylvania), George Fox (founder of Quakerism) and James Naylor (one of the first Quaker preachers). Meetings were often broken up by the local justices and the worshippers were thrown in jail.

In 1688 the Friends were allowed to build their own **Meeting House** next door. Penn, his two wives and children were eventually laid to rest in these grounds. The **Mayflower Barn** next to the farmhouse is the original barn, and may have been built of timbers from the famous vessel *Mayflower*.

Nearby in Chalfont St Giles, **Milton's Cottage** (now a museum) is where the poet, liberal pamphleteer and author of *Paradise Lost* went to live to escape the London plague in 1665.

See also High Wycombe (p257) in the Chiltern Ridge ride for information about accommodation and other services.

Places to Stay & Eat Camping is available at the simple *Jordans YHA (☎ 873135, Welders Lane)* up the hill behind the Meeting House. The overnight charge is £7.50, and it is only open daily during July and August.

Old Jordans (☎ 874586), in the old farmhouse, is a Quaker guesthouse 'in no way limited to members of the Society of Friends'. Check availability in advance, however, as wedding parties using the Mayflower Barn take priority. Room rates start from £29/46 for singles/doubles, rising to £36/58 for rooms with a bathroom.

Day 1: Jordans to Oxford
3–5 hours, 45.3mi
Head out through a handsome wooded landscape over the hills into Oxfordshire and the county town of Oxford. Be prepared for steep ups and downs, and even the odd hairpin bend as you traverse the Chiltern Ridge, climbing and descending to cross the twisting Thames at pretty Cookham (8.5mi) and at Marlow with its flamboyant bridge. The final effort ascends from Turville to an altitude of 240m (800ft) at Christmas Common. Following a cruise downhill, it's Oxfordshire Plain sailing from then on.

On the scarp above the River Thames, the route skirts the stately National Trust property **Cliveden** (☎ 01628-605069), the country pile of the wealthy political Anglo-American Astor family. The grounds are open, and there is a famous topiary garden.

Stanley Spencer, the 20th-century English painter renowned for his works on the world wars, has a **gallery** (☎ 01628-471885) en route at Cookham, where he was born and lived.

Oxford
☎ 01865
Oxford's handsome old centre belies the fact that this famous university town is also an industrial city with a sizable population. It sits on lands at the confluence of the Rivers Thames and Cherwell, both good for punting, and boasts the smallest cathedral in the country.

The university was established in the 12th century, when the Anglo-Normans were refused permission to study at the Sorbonne in Paris, which was then the centre of European scholarship. The first three colleges Balliol (pronounced 'bay-liol'), Merton and University were founded during the 13th century; others have been established at a rate of about three a century since then. Today, 36 colleges cater for 14,500 undergraduates.

The exquisite architecture and the town's riverside setting attract hordes of tourists in the high season, and the brains of Britain and the world year round.

Information The TIC (☎ 726871) is in the same square as the bus station in Gloucester Green, slightly west of the centre.

There are several bike shops, including Walton St Cycles (☎ 311610), 78 Walton St; and Bikezone (☎ 728788), 6 Lincoln House, Market St. The city council recently introduced electric buses to tackle the bad pollution problem, and bike lanes from the outskirts to the city centre are in place.

Things to See & Do The TIC stocks *Welcome to Oxford*, which has suggested walks and details of the increasingly restrictive college opening times. **Guided walks** start from the TIC. Any tour is principally of the college premises, although it takes more than a day to do them justice. If your time is limited, visit at least Christ Church, Merton College and Magdalen College (pronounced 'maudlin').

Christ Church is the grandest of them all, with the Tom Tower, the Cathedral, and Tom Quad, where Methodist Church founder John Wesley and poet WH Auden were students. **Merton** boasts the Mob Quad, the first of the college quadrangles, and the oldest medieval library still in use. **Magdalen** has beautiful grounds and lists Oscar Wilde among its alumni. Comedian Rowan Atkinson (Mr Bean) studied at **Queen's** (which can only be visited on an official tour), where students are still summoned to meals by a trumpet blast.

Unique museums include the **Ashmolean** (☎ 278000), England's oldest, with its collection of European art. Dinosaur skeletons and dodo relics are found in **University Museum**, and the glass cabinets in **Pitt Rivers** (☎ 270949) overflow with curious artefacts such as shrunken heads. The **Bodleian Library** is Britain's second most important copyright library. Tours (☎ 277000) of the 15th-century collection fill up fast.

CENTRAL ENGLAND

CENTRAL ENGLAND

Day 1: Jordans to Oxford

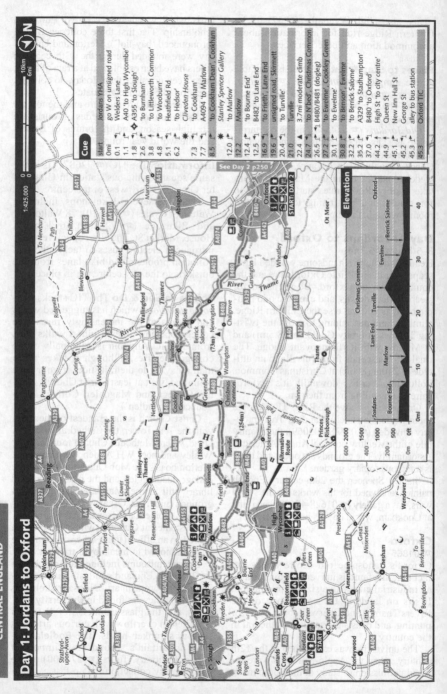

Cue		
start		Jordans YHA
0mi	↑	go W on unsigned road
0.1	↰	Welders Lane
1.1	↱	A40 'to High Wycombe'
1.8	◇	A355 'to Slough'
2.6	↑	'to Burnham'
3.8	↰	'to Littleworth Common'
4.8	↱	'to Wooburn'
5.1	↱	Heathfield Rd
6.2	↰	'to Hedsor'
	✳	Cliveden House
7.3	↱	'to Cookham'
7.7	↰	A4094 'to Marlow'
8.5		'to Cookham Dean', Cookham
	✳	Stanley Spencer Gallery
12.0	↰	'to Marlow'
12.2		Marlow
12.4	↱	'to Bourne End'
12.5	↱	B482 'to Lane End'
16.9	↱	'to Frieth', Lane End
19.6	↱	unsigned road, Skirmett
20.4	↰	'to Turville'
21.0		Turville
22.4	▲	3.7mi moderate climb
24.7	↱	'to N'bed', Christmas Common
26.5	↱	B480/B481 (dogleg)
27.2		'to Ewelme', Cookley Green
30.1	↱	'to Ewelme'
30.8	↱	'to Benson', Ewelme
32.2	↰	'to Berrick Salome'
35.2	↱	A329 'to Stadhampton'
37.0	↰	B480 'to Oxford'
44.2		High St 'to city centre'
44.9	↱	Queen St
45.1	↱	New Inn Hall St
45.2	↰	George St
45.3		alley to bus station
45.3		Oxford TIC

Places to Stay Oxford fills to bursting in the summer. Plan ahead, or queue at the TIC and pay £2.75 for help.

The large *YHA* (☎ *762997, 32 Jack Straw's Lane*) lies 2.5mi from the centre. The nightly charge is £10.15 and you can camp in the grounds. The most convenient hostel is *Oxford Backpackers* (☎ *721761, 9a Hythe Bridge St*). It's close to the TIC and with good cooking facilities. Beds in dorms cost £11 plus £5 deposit.

The *Isis Guest House* (☎ *248894, 45 Iffley Rd*), the summertime incarnation of St Edmunds Hall, offers student digs as a superior B&B for £22/44 for singles/doubles.

The cheaper B&Bs are outside the city centre. To the south just off Abingdon Rd, *Whitehouse View* (☎ *721626, 9 Whitehouse Rd*) charges £25/45. Twin rooms are £38. To the north is the comfortable *Cotswold House* (☎ *310558, 63 Banbury Rd*), with a tariff of £41/65.

It costs a few dollars more to stay at *Burlington House* (☎ *513513, 374 Banbury Rd*); rooms are £39/60. At Folly Bridge over the Thames is the pub *Head of the River* (☎ *721600, St Aldates*), where lodgings start from £75 for doubles only.

Places to Eat Due to its student population, Oxford is good for cheap, cheerful chow. Get sandwiches and bagels at the *Alternative Tuck Shop* (*Holywell St*) and *St Giles' Cafe* (☎ *552110, 52 St Giles'*), while the *Nosebag Restaurant* (☎ *721033, 6 St Michael's St*) has cooked dishes from £4.

Brown's Restaurant (☎ *511995, 5 Woodstock St*) does tasty meals with starters from £2 and main courses from £7. A recommended Indian restaurant is the *Taj Mahal* (☎ *243783, 16 Turl St*), with main dishes from £6. Enjoy a Thai set dinner from £15.50 for two at the *Bangkok House* (☎ *200705, 42a Hythe Bridge St*).

Haute cuisine menus are found at the top hotels, the *Bath Place* (☎ *791812, 4 Bath Place*) and the *Old Parsonage* (☎ *310210, 1 Banbury Rd*), where a bistro dinner will set you back a mere £25.

Day 2: Oxford to Cirencester
3–4½ hours, 43.4mi
This ride has all the elements for a quintessential day out in the Cotswolds. While any ups and downs in the road are over quite quickly. Be prepared for fast overtaking traffic on minor roads, and don't underestimate the speed of oncoming traffic when crossing the A40 at Burford and approaching the finish at Cirencester.

The hills will suddenly envelope you beyond Witney in the valley of the River Windrush. The roads become narrow and views of the exposed downs, dry-stone walls and farmland contrast with the cosy buildings nestling in the dips. Here is the exquisite village of **Minster Lovell**, with its impressive 15th-century manor house ruins.

The handsome High St of **Burford** is a natural midday halt, with antique shops, a tourist centre, a little museum and lots of *cafes* and *pubs*. From there head through peaceful farmland to the perfect hamlet of Eastleach Turville (a short side trip off the route) and Eastleach Martin, linked by clapper bridge across the River Leach. The villages of Fyfield and Southrop are additional pieces in the jigsaw of Cotswolds idyll. A stretch along the Roman road of Akeman St, leads to the Roman town of Cirencester.

Cirencester
☎ 01285
By today's standards Cirencester is a small town, but for a time, thanks to the wool trade, it was one of the most important in northwestern Europe. The old Market Place is overlooked by a fine abbey church and several buildings and hotels dating back to those great days. The town was called Corinium by the Romans, who founded it at the crossroads of Akeman St, Fosse Way and Ermin Way.

Information The TIC (☎ 654180) is dead central in the Corn Hall, Market Place. Pedal Power (☎ 640505), 5 Ashcroft Rd, is the most central bike shop.

Things to See & Do The gorgeous abbey church of St John is one of the largest in the country, with a perpendicular-style tower and three-storey south porch.

Fans of things Roman will be interested in the grassy **amphitheatre**, built back when Cirencester was the second biggest Roman town outside Londonium. There's also the **Corinium Museum** (☎ 655611), with its impressive mosaics and a section of Roman wall in the abbey grounds.

CENTRAL ENGLAND

Day 2: Oxford to Cirencester

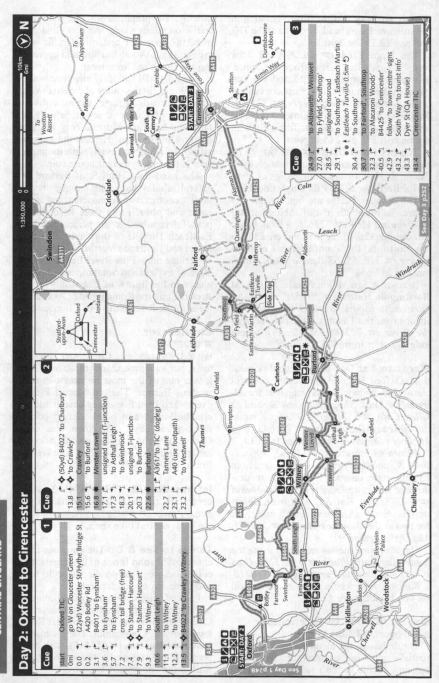

Cue (1)

start		Oxford TIC
0mi	←↑↑←↑	go W on Gloucester Green
0.0		(22yd) Worcester St/Hythe Bridge St
0.2	←↑↑	A420 Botley Rd
3.1	↑↑	B4017 'to Eynsham'
3.6	←↑	'to Eynsham'
5.7	↑↑	'to Eynsham'
7.2	✧	cross toll bridge (free)
7.4	↑↑↑	'to Stanton Harcourt'
7.9	↑↑↑	'to Stanton Harcourt'
9.3	↑↑	'to Witney'
10.6		South Leigh
11.1	←↑	'to Witney'
12.2	↑↑	'to Witney'
13.5	←↑	B4022 'to Crawley, Witney'

Cue (2)

13.8	✧↑	(50yd) B4022 'to Charlbury'
15.1	✧↑	'to Crawley'
15.6	↑↑	Crawley
16.8	☀	Minster Lovell
17.1	↑↑	unsigned road (T-junction)
17.3	←↑	'to Asthall Leigh'
18.3	↑↑	'to Swinbrook'
20.1	↑↑	unsigned T-junction
20.3	←↑	'to Burford'
22.6		Burford
22.7	↑↑↑	A361 'to TIC' (dogleg)
23.1	↑↑	Tanners Lane
23.2	←↑	A40 (use footpath)
		'to Westwell'

Cue (3)

24.9	↑→	'to Aldsworth, Westwell'
27.0	←↑	'to Fyfield, Southrop'
28.5	↑↑	unsigned crossroad
29.1	●●●	*Eastleach Turville 0.5mi* ↻
30.4	←↑	'to Southrop', Eastleach Martin
30.7	↑→	'to Fairford', Southrop
32.3	↑→	'to Macaroni Woods'
40.5	↑←	B4425 'to Cirencester'
42.9		follow 'to town centre' signs
43.2	↑↑	South Way to tourist info'
43.3		Dyer St (QA House)
43.4		Cirencester TIC

About 5mi south lies the huge **Cotswold Water Park**, with over 100 water-filled former gravel pits (interlaced with cycling routes) that are now dedicated to leisure pursuits and nature reserves.

Places to Stay The *Cotswold Hoburne Caravan & Camping Park (☎ 860216; Broadway Lane, South Cerney)* is in the Cotswold Water Park. A tent pitch here costs a pricey £23/10.50 in/out of season. About 2mi north of town is *Mayfield Touring Park (☎ 831301; Cheltenham Rd, Perrots Brook)* where a tent pitch costs £7.

Near the town centre, *Abbeymead Guest House (☎ 653740, 39a Victoria Rd)* charges £30/40 for singles/doubles. The 18th-century inn *Golden Cross (☎ 652137, Black Jack St)* has rooms for £20/30; it may also do evening meals on request. The restored, stately *Cripps House (☎ 653164, 51 Coxwell St)* is central and has doubles for £60.

Places to Eat Cirencester may be small, but *Somewhere Else (☎ 643199, Castle St)* with its £2.50 tapas menu is as trendy as they come. During the day, the *Willow Secret Garden Cafe (22 Castle St)* uses organic ingredients in its tasty mixed salad buffet (from around £4). For dinner, *Gianni's (☎ 643133, Castle St)* is a popular family-owned Italian restaurant. The *Polo Canteen (☎ 650977, 29 Sheep St)* serves poached fish for £12 and Thai herb chicken for £10.50. The traditional restaurant at the *Stratton House Hotel (☎ 651761, Gloucester Rd)* does a set menu for £18.75.

Day 3: Cirencester to Stratford-upon-Avon

3½–5½ hours, 51.4mi

Riding north along the fat end of the Cotswolds wedge means numerous steep climbs and descents across valleys that shelter sleepy villages, several of which can be visited on short side trips.

Watch out for high-speed traffic on the A40 (13.2mi) and a very rough surface on the road down to the River Windrush (20.3mi).

The village of **Upper Slaughter** is extremely pretty, and **Lower Slaughter** has a perfectly preserved line of stone cottages with a babbling stream outside the doorways. There is a pricey *pub-restaurant* there, but little else.

Other popular Cotswolds towns like quaint **Bourton-on-the-Water** and sizable **Stow-on-the-Wold** are also marked as short side trips. **Chipping Campden** combines the two qualities and is a good place to pause, although it comes towards the end of the day. Its long High St is one of the best in the area.

From there it's a steady run around the base of prominent Meon Hill (41.7mi) to Stratford-upon-Avon. As you cross the River Avon into Stratford, glimpse the water frontage of the Royal Shakespeare Theatre on the left, where performances of the Bard's plays take place most days of the week.

Stratford-upon-Avon
☎ 01789

Stratford is a thriving town and one of the busiest on the tourist trail, courtesy of its Tudor houses associated with Shakespeare's life, and theatres devoted to his work. The willow-lined river with swans is attractive, although, with the number of visitors, there's not a great feeling of intimate discovery here.

Information The main TIC (☎ 293127) is easy to find on the town side of the fine Clopton Bridge. The Pashley Store (☎ 205 057) on the town's main street, Guild St, is a general bike shop owned by the traditional supplier of bikes to the post office.

Things to See & Do Too bad Shakespeare predates the bicycle, otherwise, no doubt, we would have some sterling quotes on the comedy and tragedy of cycling.

Nevertheless, his life and works have been the focus of Stratford for centuries. The **house** of his birth in 1564 on Henley St is one of five fine Tudor buildings with family connections that can be visited on one ticket (see the TIC). The Shakespeare family home, New Place, to which he retired and where he died in 1616, was demolished more than 200 years ago by its exasperated owner, who was already fed up with being pestered by visitors!

Lying close to each other on the river is the trio of theatres – the **Royal Shakespeare**, the **Swan** and **The Other Place** (box office for all three ☎ 403403) – that forms the base of the Royal Shakespeare Company. While the Bard's works comprise most of the program, plays by Christopher Marlowe, Anton Chekhov and others also feature.

CENTRAL ENGLAND

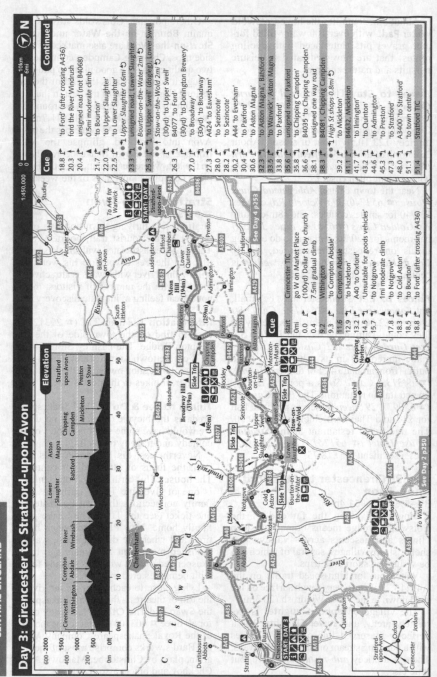

Day 3: Cirencester to Stratford-upon-Avon

Cue

start	Cirencester TIC
0mi	go W on Market Place
0.0	(100yd) Dollar St (by church)
0.4	7.5mi gradual climb
9.2	Withington
9.3	'to Compton Abdale'
11.6	Compton Abdale
12.9	'to Hazleton'
13.2	A40 'to Oxford'
14.5	'Unsuitable for goods vehicles'
15.7	'to Notgrove'
17.8	1mi moderate climb
17.8	'to Notgrove'
18.3	'to Cold Aston'
18.5	'to Bourton'
18.8	'to Ford' (after crossing A436)

Cue — Continued

18.8	'to Ford' (after crossing A436)
20.3	ford the River Windrush
20.4	unsigned road (not B4068)
	0.5mi moderate climb
21.7	'to Bourton'
22.0	'to Upper Slaughter'
22.5	'to Lower Slaughter'
	Upper Slaughter 0.6mi
23.3	unsigned road, Lower Slaughter
	Bourton-on-the-Water 2mi
25.3	'to Upper Swell (dogleg), Lower Swell'
	Stow-on-the-Wold 2mi
26.3	(30yd) 'to Donington Brewery'
	B4077 'to Ford'
27.0	'to Broadway'
	(30yd) 'to Broadway'
27.3	A424 'to Eavesham'
28.0	'to Sezincote'
28.2	'to Sezincote'
30.2	A44 'to Evesham'
30.4	'to Paxford'
30.6	'to Aston Magna'
32.3	'to Aston Magna', Batsford
33.5	'to Warwick', Aston Magna
33.8	'to Paxford'
35.6	unsigned road, Paxford
35.8	'to Chipping Campden'
36.6	B4035 'to Chipping Campden'
38.1	unsigned one way road
38.3	B4081, Chipping Campden
	High St shops 0.8mi
39.2	'to Mickleton'
41.1	B4632, Mickleton
41.7	'to Ilmington'
43.2	'to Quinton'
44.6	'to Admington'
45.3	'to Preston'
47.3	'to Stratford'
48.0	A3400 'to Stratford'
51.1	'to town centre'
51.4	Stratford TIC

N

1:450,000

0 — 10km
0 — 6mi

Elevation

Cirencester · Withington · Compton Abdale · River Windrush · Lower Slaughter · Batsford · Aston Magna · Chipping Campden · Mickleton · Preston on Stour · Stratford upon Avon

600–2000 · 400–1500 · 1000 · 200–500 · 0ft

0mi · 10 · 20 · 30 · 40 · 50

START DAY 3

See Day 2 p250

See Day 4 p253

START DAY 4

To A46 for Warwick

Side Trip

Day 4: Stratford-upon-Avon to Oxford

Cue	
start	Stratford TIC
0mi	go E 'to Tiddington'
0.1	B4086 'to Tiddington'
1.2	'to Wellesbourne', Tiddington
4.7	A429 'to Stow'
5.0	'to Walton'
5.3	'to Walton'
5.4	'to Walton'
6.8	unsigned road, Walton
9.1	'to Pillerton'
9.3	'to Pillerton Priors'
10.5	unsigned road, Pillerton Priors

Cue	
10.6	A422 'to Stratford'
10.9	'to Stow'
11.9	(20yd) unsigned road
13.4	'to Whatcote', Fulready
17.0	'to Brailes', Whatcote
17.1	B4035 'to Banbury', Upper Brailes
18.5	'to Sutton, Stourton'
19.1	'to Stourton' 'Sutton-under-Brailes'
19.5	'to Whichford', Stourton
	(30yd) 'to Whichford'
	'to Long Compton'
▲	0.5mi steep climb

Cue	
20.9	'to Long Compton'
21.8	dangerous bend on junction
22.2	'to Woodstock', Long Compton
23.0	'to Little Rollright'
23.0	1mi climb
23.8	'to Little Rollright'
24.1	'to Rollright Stones'
24.4	*Rollright Stones*
24.9	A3400/'to Great Rollright' (dogleg)
25.7	'to Great Rollright'
26.1	'to Hook N'ton', Great Rollright
27.2	'to Chipping Norton'
27.8	'to Chipping Norton'
28.0	'to Heythrop'
28.9	A361 'to Banbury'
31.4	'to the Tews'
31.6	'to Ledwell'
33.4	'to Sandford'
34.4	Sandford St Martin
34.7	'to Glympton'
39.0	'to Bletchingdon'
39.2	'to King's Head Inn', Wootton
39.3	unsigned road
40.2	'to Charlbury' (dogleg)
	Blenheim Palace 2mi ↻
40.7	'to Stonesfield'
41.8	'to Combe'
44.1	'to Long Hanborough'
44.7	Long Hanborough
44.8	A4095 'to Bicester'
44.9	'to Church Hanborough'
46.0	Church Hanborough
46.4	'to Eynsham'
48.1	↱ cross A40/B449 'to Standlake' (dogleg)
48.7	Eynsham
49.1	◇ B4044 'to toll bridge/Botley'
53.0	B4044 'to Oxford'
53.4	A420 'to city centre'
54.8	dismount & cross Worcester St
	thru passage to Gloucester Green
54.9	Oxford TIC

Elevation

CENTRAL ENGLAND

Warwick castle, one of the best in the country, lies 7mi north-east on the Warwick road.

Places to Stay About 1mi west along the lane to Luddington is the camping ground at **Stratford-upon-Avon Racecourse** (☎ 267 949), open March to November, where tent pitches start at £4.

Lodging in and around Stratford is abundant, but book ahead in the high season. The large **Stratford-upon-Avon (Hemmingford House) YHA** (☎ 297093, Alveston) is a Georgian mansion 1.5mi east of town, back across the river near Tiddington, where the £14.05 charge includes breakfast. It has a choice of different rooms, including rooms with bath.

B&B prices start at £15 at **Penshurst Guest House** (☎ 205259, 34 Evesham Place), 800m south-west of centre. **Eversley Bears Guest House** (☎ 292334, 37 Grove Rd), close to the middle of town, has a rich teddy bear culture and rooms from £22/44 for singles/doubles. Sue & Richard at **Quilt & Croissants** (☎ 267629, 33 Evesham Place) do rooms from £17/40, serve patisserie croissants for breakfast and have a children's bike buggy for hire. The 400-year-old **Stratheden Hotel** (☎ 297119, 5 Chapel St) is also central; it has TVs and antique furniture in rooms ranging from £40 to £62 for doubles only.

There are plenty of places near town too. If you've ever fancied staying in an en suite cow shed on a stud farm, this is your chance. **Oxstalls Farm Stud** (☎ 205277, Warwick Rd), a couple of miles north, has plenty of rooms where B&B costs from £17.50 per person. On the south side of Stratford in the little village of Clifford Chambers the **New Inn Hotel** (☎ 293402) charges £35/50 per room.

Places to Eat It's easy to carbo-load in Stratford's pubs, cafes and restaurants. The **Lemon Tree** (☎ 292997) does a varied menu during the day of baked potatoes and continental breads for £3 to £5. **Benson's** (☎ 261116, 4 Bard's Walk) does high-class lunches such as a fish platter for £7.95, including a glass of wine, and a roast turkey with French brie sandwich for £4.10. Unfortunately, it's closed in the evening.

Edward Moon Famous English Brasseries (☎ 267069, Chapel St) offers an English menu 'with influences', such as roasted lamb shanks for £9.95 and spinach and ricotta cannelloni for £7.95. (There's another branch in Leominster). For pizza, there's a branch of **Ask** (☎ 262440) off Bridge St, and a **Caffe Uno** on Wood St. One of the smartest places in town is the Michelin-rated **Marlowe's Restaurant** (☎ 204999, 18 High St), where dinner is served in an oak-panelled room from £20.

Day 4: Stratford-upon-Avon to Oxford

3½–6 hours, 54.9mi

The return leg to Oxford generally covers gentler farmland, with a couple of climbs to watch out for, one (19.5mi) beyond Stourton and the other (23.2mi) up to the **Rollright Stones**. These standing stones were erected during the Bronze Age and comprise a circle of stones on one side of the road, 'the King's Men' (who are said to dance at midnight) and a monolith, 'the King's Stone', on the other.

Spare an afternoon, if possible, to visit **Blenheim Palace** (☎ 01993-811325), the greatest of England's stately homes – it's a 2mi return side trip at the 40.2mi point; turn left onto the A44. Built in the 18th century, the Churchill family home was designed in a triumphant baroque style and set within 2500 acres of parkland. Highlights include the east gate, the Great Court and landscaping by the English master Capability Brown. Allow several hours to admire and wander. **Cafes** and **restaurants** are on site.

Watch out for a dangerous left-hand bend (21.8mi) on the fast descent after the Stourton climb. It is easy to overshoot, as there is a turn-off directly ahead, and you can end up flying into the path of oncoming cars. On the approach to Oxford it's impossible to avoid the traffic.

Chiltern Ridge

Duration	3–4½ hours
Distance	45.2mi
Difficulty	moderate
Start	Luton
End	High Wycombe

The Chiltern Hills is a lovely ridge that rises out from the plains around the north-west edge of London. It is easy to get to for a day trip, and it can be joined with the A

Cotswolds Triangle ride earlier in this chapter. The ride is especially memorable in the autumn when the beech forests cloak the slopes in a coppery blaze.

HISTORY
The route shares tracks with the prehistoric Ridgeway Path and the equally venerable Icknield Way, both popular with walkers.

NATURAL HISTORY
The slopes are a mixture of open chalk downland and ancient beech woodlands that have been worked for hundreds of years.

PLANNING
When to Ride
Spring fills the woods with bluebells. summer graces the fields with golden crops, but if there is one time to ride the Chilterns, it is autumn, when the turning leaves paint the hillsides glorious copper hues and the smell of woodsmoke is in the air.

On the weekends the lorry count on the main roads almost drops to nil, but near the picnic spots the day-trippers come out in force.

Maps
Recommended maps are OS Travelmaster maps (1:250,000) No 9, *South East England*; or No 6, *East Midlands and East Anglia*. OS Landranger maps (1:50,000) Nos 165 and 175 show a large bridleway network for mountain biking.

What to Bring
Although a mountain bike is best to negotiate the four sections of off-road bridleway, they can be negotiated on skinny-tyred bikes in the dry only.

GETTING TO/FROM THE RIDE
Luton
Train Luton, home to London's third airport, is well served by trains from London Kings Cross (£10 single, 35 minutes, every 15 minutes) from the Thameslink platform. Bikes go free, but can't be carried during the weekday evening rush period from 4.30 to 6.30 pm.

High Wycombe
See the A Cotswolds Triangle ride (p246) for details on getting to/from High Wycombe.

THE RIDE
Luton
☎ 01582
Luton is a sizable working town, with London's third airport and good connections to the capital. The TIC (☎ 401579) is in the bus station on Bute St and the closest store with bike parts is the Halfords Superstore (☎ 422525), on the retail park shopping area 1mi south of town on Kimpton Rd.

Places to Stay & Eat There is no camping ground nearby, but the nearest hostel is *Ivinghoe* (☎ 01296-668251), in an old brewhouse en route 7mi west of Dunstable along the B489. The hosts at *Belzayne* (☎ 736591, 70 Lalleford Rd) are used to cyclists, having put up the Irish national cycling squad three times. The double room is good value at £27 (total), singles are £18. The guesthouse is 1mi south of the station. The *Red Lion Hotel* (☎ 413881, Castle St) has rooms from about £30.

Near the bus and train station is the Italian restaurant *La Trattoria* (☎ 410291, 66 Bute St). It's open for lunch (except Sunday) and dinner. In the unlovely Arndale Shopping Centre is *Greenfields* (☎ 414954, 110 The Gallery), with a large and general menu. It closes early of an evening.

Chiltern Ridge
3–4½ hours, 45.2mi
The escarpment followed on this ride has long views out over Bedfordshire and Buckinghamshire; high spot Ivinghoe Beacon is popular with kite flyers and gliders who use the updraft as a launching place.

There are four sections of off-road bridleway, the first being the roughest – they all get quite boggy after wet weather.

The first 6mi through Luton and Dunstable are on fast roads that are best covered as quickly as possible. Things improve immediately after you turn-off the A5 to Sewell (6.0mi).

Ashridge Forest visitor centre (15.8mi), a little farther south, has information about walks and it offers refreshments. Good lunch-time *pubs* crop up at intervals in the pretty towns and villages including Aldbury (17.7mi). Cream teas are served at weekends in an old coach at the Chinnor & Princes Risborough **steam railway**, just before the final climb to Bledlow Ridge.

CENTRAL ENGLAND

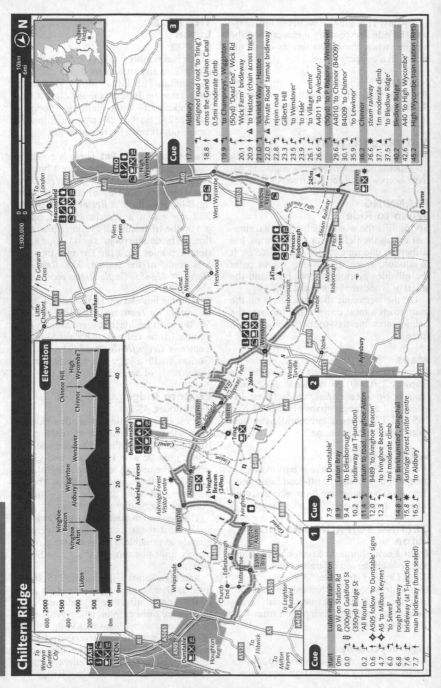

CENTRAL ENGLAND

Chiltern Ridge

Elevation

Cue		
start		Luton main train station
0.0		go W on Station Rd
		(200yd) Guildford St
		(350yd) Bridge St
0.2		'All Routes'
0.6		A505 follow 'to Dunstable' signs
4.7		A5 'to Milton Keynes'
6.0		'to Sewell'
6.8		rough bridleway
7.6		bridleway (at T-junction)
7.7		main bridleway (turns sealed)

Cue			2
7.9		'to Dunstable'	
8.9		Eaton Bray	
9.4		'to Edlesborough'	
10.2		bridleway (at T-junction)	
11.4		return to road, Ivinghoe Aston	
12.0		B489 'to Ivinghoe Beacon'	
12.3		'to Ivinghoe Beacon'	
14.8		1m moderate climb	
15.8		Ashridge Forest visitor centre	
16.5		'to Aldbury'	

Cue			3
17.7		Aldbury	
18.8		unsigned road (not 'to Tring')	
		cross the Grand Union Canal	
19.9		0.5mi moderate climb	
		'to Champneys', Wigginton	
20.1		(50yd) 'Dead End', Wick Rd	
20.9		'Wick Farm' bridleway	
21.0		'to Hastoe' (chain across track)	
		'Icknield Way', Hastoe	
22.0		'Private Road' tarmac bridleway	
22.8		rejoin road	
23.3		Gilberts Hill	
23.5		'to Wendover'	
23.9		'to Hale'	
26.1		'to Village Centre'	
26.6		A4011 'to Aylesbury'	
		(50yd) 'to P Risboro', Wendover	
29.6		A4010 'to Chinnor (B4009)'	
30.1		B4009 'to Chinnor'	
35.9		'to Lewknor'	
36.2		Chinnor	
36.6		steam railway	
37.1		'to Bledlow Ridge'	
37.5		'to Bledlow Ridge'	
40.2		Bledlow Ridge	
42.6		A40 'to High Wycombe'	
45.2		High Wycombe train station (RHS)	

High Wycombe
☎ 01494

Hemmed in by steep wooded hillsides, High Wycombe has an attractive setting. The town has a museum with a world-famous collection of chairs, and England's longest artificial ski slope at Wycombe Summit (☎ 474711), Abbey Barn Lane.

Information High Wycombe TIC (☎ 421 892) is on Paul's Row. Reflecting the depth of the local cycling community and the riding in the area, there are two good central bike shops: Bucks Cycle Centre (☎ 451972), 113 Oxford Rd; and Cycle Care (☎ 447908), 225 Desborough Rd.

Places to Stay The nearest camp site is at *Highclere Farm Country Park (☎ 874505; New Barn Lane, Seer Green)*, where a tent pitch is £7. The park is 7mi east along the main A40 road.

The small *Bradenham Youth Hostel (☎ 562929)* is open daily from May to September, catering for walkers on the Ridgeway Path. It lies just off the route, 5mi west of the finish.

En route 4mi before High Wycombe is *Old Callow Down Farm (☎ 01844-344416; Wigans Lane, Bledlow Ridge)*, a 16th-century farmhouse where Mrs Gee may do an evening meal by arrangement. Prices range from £30 to £44 for a twin room.

In High Wycombe, you get good views over the town from *Mrs Smails' (☎ 524310, 106 Green Hill)*, where singles/doubles cost £25/36. The *Bird in Hand (☎ 523502 or ☎ 459449, 81 West Wycombe Rd)* serves home-cooked food in its conservatory restaurant and charges from £45 for a room.

Places to Eat There is a small choice of eateries in Wycombe. The centrally located *Cafe Rouge (☎ 462762, 1 Church Square)* serves a good *gigot d'Agneau* (marinated lamb) for £9.75 alongside light meals and drinks.

Also central is the Italian *Francesco's (☎ 436346, 19 Octagon Parade)*, where a vegetarian pizza is £7.75 and fettucine carbonara is £6.95.

About 1.5mi west of town along the A40 is the *Clifton Lodge Hotel (☎ 440095, 210 West Wycombe Rd)*, where grilled trout will set you back £10.25.

The Long Mynd

MOUNTAIN BIKE RIDE

Duration	3–5 hours
Distance	12.4mi
Difficulty	moderate-hard
Start/End	Church Stretton

The bare hills of south Shropshire rise dramatically from verdant lowlands and make for great mountain biking.

The ride starts and finishes in the little town of Church Stretton in the Stretton Valley, and showcases the Long Mynd massif, which rises to almost 510m (1700ft). There are many miles' worth of bridleways that can be pieced together to cross the hills from Wenlock Edge in the east to the Stiperstones ridge in the west.

Whatever the time of year, you will meet walkers and horse-riders as well as other bikers on the tracks. Give way to everyone and pass slowly on the descents. When navigating, don't be waylaid by the miscellany of tracks that crisscross the route.

NATURAL HISTORY
The Long Mynd has been designated a Site of Special Scientific Interest (SSSI) because of its important wildlife habitats. Areas of heather and bilberry, and bogs and rivulets support a variety of birds and insects, but are threatened by the spread of bracken, which has been able to take hold following heavy sheep grazing over the centuries. To contain erosion and preserve the ecosystem, keep to the bridleways.

The uplands are also of geological interest, featuring some of England's oldest rocks.

PLANNING
When to Ride
An exposed plateau, the Long Mynd catches all the weather coming over from the Atlantic and the Welsh mountains. In winter, be prepared for anything, including snow. Periods of rain make the bridleways heavy going and will prolong the ride time. The summer months are warmer and drier, but it can still get very wet.

Maps
The OS Landranger map (1:50,000) No 137 *Ludlow, Wenlock Edge* is recommended. An

'access map' sketched by the National Trust and available from the TIC shows the different rights of way.

What to Bring

This is not a long ride and civilisation is never far away, but you should treat it as a day in the mountains: don't ride alone; carry a compass (in case of fog on the flat tops), rations, and warm, waterproof clothing; and note the weather forecast (dial ☎ 0891-333 111 plus the code for the Midlands ☎ 107).

GETTING TO/FROM THE RIDE
Church Stretton

Train For its rural location, Church Stretton is well connected. Services run direct to Shrewsbury (£3.40, 15 minutes), Manchester (Piccadilly; £13.70 return, 1½ hours) and Cardiff (£21.30 return, 1¾ hours).

Bicycle Church Stretton lies 4mi east of The Marches, Cheshire & Lancashire ride, earlier in this chapter – take the Burway west out of town over the hill to Bridges. It's also 12mi south of Shrewsbury on the Through the Midlands ride (also earlier in this chapter) along the busy A49.

THE RIDE
Church Stretton
☎ 01694

Plans by Edwardian developers to turn Church Stretton into a spa resort once the railways were built fell short of expectations and the place remains easy-going and comfortably old-fashioned.

Information The TIC (☎ 723133), Church St, is open from Easter to September, with the neighbouring library (☎ 722535) filling in to some extent during the months when it's closed. The year-round TIC at nearby Ludlow (☎ 01584-875053), on Castle St, can also help plug gaps.

Terry's Cycles (☎ 723302 or ☎ 724334), 6 Castle Hill, All Stretton, has permanent premises 1mi northwards along the B-road. It occupies a workshop in Burway Garage, on The Burway road, on Friday and Saturday from 10.30 am to 4.30pm. Hire mountain bikes, tandems, and child trailers/seats.

The Long Mynd mountain bike club can suggest other routes in the area. Telephone club secretary Tim Parker (☎ 724162).

Things to See & Do The town once promoted as 'Little Switzerland' has a quiet charm, with a cosy Thursday **market** that sells local cheeses and a **sweet shop** stacked with humbugs and toffees. **Antiques** and **curiosity shops** have also carved themselves a niche.

The town **church of St Lawrence** has a fine Norman nave and carving of a Saxon fertility symbol, a *Sheelagh Na Eigh*. As a reminder of stormier times in the region, make the trip 7mi south to the fine, fortified medieval manorhouse of **Stokesay Castle**, beyond Craven Arms.

Places to Stay & Eat The nearest camp site is *Small Batch (☎ 723358; Ashes Valley, Little Stretton)* 1.5mi south of Church Stretton. Open from Easter to the end of September, one/two adults in a tent cost £6/8 per night.

The nearest *youth hostel* is Bridges *(☎ 01588-650656)* in the valley that lies west of the Long Mynd, 5mi from Church Stretton over The Burway road. A bed costs £7.50.

Being a little place, accommodation in Church Stretton town is handy for both the centre and the hills. Rooms at *Highcliffe (☎ 722908, Madeira Walk)* are reasonable at £16 for a single/double. Stay in a family house at *Rheingold (☎ 723969)*, where Mrs Knight will do an evening meal for £9 by arrangement and rooms start at £16/35. The town hotel, the *Longmynd (☎ 722244, Cunnery Rd)* has a sauna and pool, and rooms from £55/100, which includes dinner if you stay for a weekend.

For after-ride refuelling in Church Stretton, there is no shortage of *teashops* and *cafes*. For dining in the evening, the three *pubs* offer decent fare, there are two *Indian restaurants* and a *pizza parlour* has recently opened. At *The Studio (722672, 59 High St)*, the Dutch chef Ed Van Doesburg cooks a modern European cuisine fresh on the premises. The most popular dish is fillet of Shropshire beef with a wild mushroom sauce (£13.25), with a veg dish also available daily.

The Long Mynd
3–5 hours, 12.4mi

The Long Mynd's bulk is penetrated by blind valleys such as Minton Batch where you climb 220yd up a track with narrow ledges and sections of portage. Once on top on the moorland and the ancient Portway road, the views are spectacular, especially at Pole Bank (516m/1692ft). The return leg downhill steers a course via the Cross Dyke earthwork and drops back to the road north of town.

Starting out from the Church Stretton TIC, make your way through town to the B4370; turn right (southwards) to Little Stretton. There, turn right at the telephone box next to the Ragleth Inn, and soon follow the road around to the left, then right at the farm in the fork. Continue and climb to Minton.

At **Minton** (2.5mi), follow the sign to Hamperley, then go right at the telephone box. After 400yd keep your eyes open for the signed bridleway on the right just before the road drops, and take it. Now off-road, follow the track, pass through two gates,

going to the right along the river. At the third gate turn right on to the dirt track. Follow this for about 150yd, stay right (signed 'path') at the farmhouse.

Follow the bridleway beside the stream up **Minton Batch**; watch your handling on the narrow ledges and you'll have to carry the bike in places. Towards the top where the land flattens, continue straight ahead as far as the paved path with the gliding club on the left (5mi).

Turn right onto this road, The Portway, and continue, climbing more gently for a little over 1mi. Pass woods on the left and after 100yd turn off-road left at the seven wooden posts. Climb to **Pole Bank** summit (7mi), which has a plate showing the neighbouring high points.

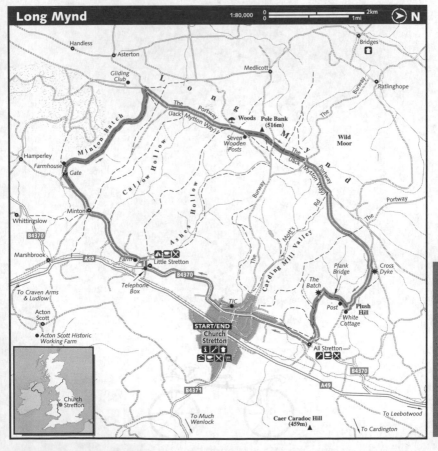

CENTRAL ENGLAND

Continue straight ahead, crossing first a dirt track then a paved road. After about 200yd at a junction with three tracks, take the middle one signed 'Duckley Nap'. Follow this path – ignore the first bridleway – to the right and take the second right shortly after. Follow the track round, cross the stream and make the short sharp climb on to the **Cross Dyke** (9.3mi). Turn right on the top of dyke and follow the track down the hill.

Turn right just before the white cottage (don't cross the cattle grid) and go past a

fenced field and head towards the post in the field. Fork right and follow the path in a lovely sweep down into the valley to the stream. There, turn left along the valley bottom and look for two plank bridges across the stream. These lead to a dirt track at the **Batch**, where you turn left.

With the ride almost over, follow the track to the paved road, then continue on the road to All Stretton (11.2mi). At the T-junction back at the B4370, turn right to return to Church Stretton.

Wales

There's an upbeat vibe in Wales these days, and why not? The economy is ticking along nicely, with Wales boasting the 'best business climate in Europe', the newly formed National Assembly is providing the Welsh people with a greater degree of autonomy, and Cardiff is still basking in the glow of hosting rugby's 1999 World Cup.

Even though Cardiff, having undergone a massive spruce-up, is looking better than ever, for the most part Wales' appeal lies not in its towns and cities, but in its beautiful countryside, making cycling the ideal way to fully appreciate its ample charms. Much of the finest scenery can be found within the borders of the Brecon Beacons, Pembrokeshire Coast and Snowdonia National Parks, although thanks to an abundance of precipitation, most of rural Wales, even in summer, is very green and exceedingly pleasant to pedal through.

As well as its natural attractions, Wales has an unsurpassed legacy of magnificent medieval castles and other historic attractions, providing lots to see and do off the bike.

HISTORY

The Celts arrived from their European homeland sometime after 500 BC. Little is known about them, although it is to their Celtic forebears that the modern Welsh attribute national characteristics like eloquence, warmth and imagination.

The Romans invaded in AD 43, and for the next 400 years kept close control over the Welsh tribes from their garrison towns at Chester and Caerlon. From the 5th century to the 11th, the Welsh were under almost constant pressure from the Anglo-Saxon invaders of England. In the 8th century, a Mercian king, Offa, constructed a dyke marking the boundary between the Welsh and the Mercians. Offa's Dyke can still be seen today – in fact you can walk its length.

The Celtic princes failed to unite Wales, and local wars were frequent. However, in 927, faced with the destructive onslaught of the Vikings, the Welsh kings recognised Athelstan, the Anglo-Saxon king of England, as their overlord in exchange for an alliance against the Vikings.

By the time the Normans arrived in England, the Welsh had returned to their war-

ring, independent ways. To secure his new kingdom, William I set up powerful feudal barons along the Welsh borders. The Lords Marcher, as they were known, developed virtually unfettered wealth and power and began to advance on the lowlands of South and Mid Wales.

Edward I, the great warrior king, finally conquered Wales in a bloody campaign. In 1302 the title of Prince of Wales was given to the monarch's eldest son, a tradition that continues today. To maintain his authority,

Edward built the great castles of Rhuddlan, Conwy, Beaumaris, Caernarfon and Harlech.

The last doomed Welsh revolt began in 1400 under Owain Glyndwr and was brutally crushed by Henry IV. In 1536 and 1543, the Acts of Union made Wales, for all intents and purposes, another region of England.

From the turn of the 18th century, Wales, with its plentiful coal and iron, became the most important source of Britain's pig iron. By the end of the 19th century, almost a third of the world's coal exports came from Wales, and an enormous network of mining villages, with their unique culture of Methodism, rugby and male-voice choirs, had developed.

The 20th century, especially the 1960s, 1970s and 1980s, saw the coal industry and the associated steel industry collapse.

Large-scale unemployment persists as Wales attempts to move to more high-tech and service industries. Tourism is now a major industry accounting for almost 10% of all jobs in the principality.

In 1997, in a wave of renewed nationalist sentiment, the Welsh people voted yes to a referendum to create a Welsh nationalist assembly with powers over Welsh domestic affairs. The National Assembly for Wales held its first session in Cardiff on 12 May 1999. Find out more at 🖳 www.wales.gov.uk.

NATURAL HISTORY

Some 8017 sq mi in area, 170mi long and 60mi wide, Wales is surrounded by the sea on three sides and England to the east – the English border still roughly runs along the

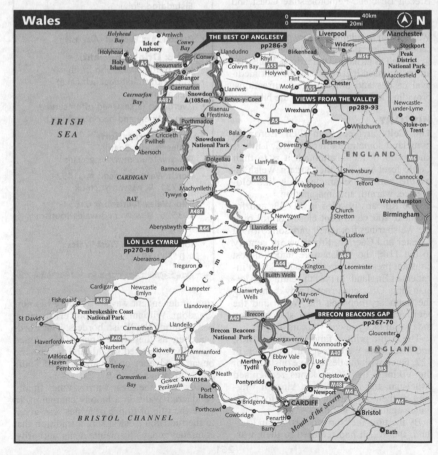

route of the historic Offa's Dyke (see History earlier).

There are two main mountain systems: the Black Mountains and Brecon Beacons in the south, and the more rugged glaciated mountains of Snowdonia in the north-west, deeply cut by narrow river valleys. These areas are joined by the hills and uplands of the Cambrian Mountains, which run north-south through much of central Wales. At 1085m (3650ft), Snowdon is the highest peak in England and Wales.

Rolling moorlands between altitudes of 180m (590ft) and 600m (1968ft) stretch from Denbigh in the north to the Glamorgan valleys in the south, ending on the west coast in spectacular cliffs and river estuary plains. With the exception of the island of Anglesey, there's no avoiding the hills on almost any tour through Wales.

The three national parks in Wales are uniquely different, each with much to offer. The Brecon Beacons National Park (🖳 www .breconbeacons.org) dominates the landscape of southern Mid Wales. With rolling hills, river valleys and picturesque lakes, it's a favourite destination of walkers and mountain bikers. The Pembrokeshire Coast National Park (🖳 www.pembrokeshirecoast .org), Britain's only coastal park, lies in the extreme south-west. It's characterised by rugged cliffs, windswept beaches, seabirds and old fishing ports. Some of Wales' most spectacular vistas, however, lie within the confines of the north-west Snowdonia National Park. Dramatic jagged peaks, a maze of walking trails and a spectacular 23mi stretch of coastline draw millions of visitors every year.

The population is mainly concentrated in the south-east of Wales, along the coast between Cardiff and Swansea and in the old mining valleys that run north into the Brecon Beacons National Park.

CLIMATE

Although Wales' weather is as unpredictable as anywhere in Britain, from the visitor's perspective it would be fair to say the region suffers from an excess of rainfall. Levels hover around 100mm a month from July to January, while the February to June rainfall is more like 60mm or 70mm a month.

Maximum temperatures in July average around 18°C with 11°C minimums, while in January the daily high hovers around 6°C, getting down to about 2°C.

The wind blows predominantly from the west and south-west, generally intensifying closer to the coast. The mountainous terrain throughout much of the country can produce dramatically different climatic conditions within relatively short distances.

INFORMATION
Maps
OS Travelmaster map No 7 (1:250,000), *Wales and West Midlands*, covers the whole of Wales in one sheet, providing an excellent resource for general navigation and route planning.

Books
Well worth collecting from any Welsh TIC is *Cycling Wales*, a free, glossy booklet describing cycling opportunities, tour operators and bike-friendly accommodation throughout the country. For comprehensive, general Welsh travel information, pick up Lonely Planet's *Britain*.

Before leaving home, bone up on Welsh culture and history: George Borrow's *Wild Wales* details his travels through the country in 1854 and is an entertaining, historical primer; *The Matter of Wales: Epic Views of a Small Country* by Jan Morris provides a more contemporary look. For exhaustive but readable detail, try *A History of Wales* by John Davies.

Information Sources
The Internet is a good place to start planning. The Wales Tourist Board (☎ 029 2049 9909, fax 2048 5031, 🖳 www.tourism.wales .gov.uk) Web site has loads of up-to-date information and lots of colour photos. Wales Calling at 🖳 www.wales-calling.com is another comprehensive tourist guide. An excellent source for news, sport and current events is Total Wales (🖳 www.totalwales .com), the online arm of the Trinity Mirror newspaper group.

Place Names
While many places in Wales have both an English and Welsh name, this guide tries to adopt the name most commonly used in the area. Where both names are widely used, we have included the Welsh equivalent in brackets.

What to Bring

With Wales' rainfall levels, quality rain gear and waterproof liners for your panniers are a wise investment before setting off on any of the rides.

GATEWAY CITIES
Cardiff
☎ 029

Much as Glasgow did in the early 1990s, the Welsh capital has of late been busy reinventing itself. With the 1999 Rugby World Cup and the new millennium providing the impetus for a massive building and redevelopment program, the city is looking better than ever.

The striking 72,500-seat Millennium Stadium (which hosted the Rugby World Cup final and will host the 2001 FA Cup final) and the massive Cardiff Bay redevelopment are the most tangible signs of Cardiff's transformation, but the city as a whole seems to be imbued with an enthusiasm for the 21st century.

Information The Cardiff Tourist Information Centre (TIC; ☎ 2022 7281), close to the central train and bus terminals on Wood St, has city maps and lots of brochures on Cardiff and the rest of Wales. It also sells the Cardiff Card, which provides free entry to a range of attractions (including Cardiff Castle, the National Museum and Techniquest) as well as free transport on local trains and buses. At £12 for a 48-hour pass, it's not hard to get your money's worth.

The Welsh Language

The one thing making Wales so distinctive is the survival of Welsh as a living language. With its weird-looking and seemingly unpronounceable chains of consecutive consonants, Welsh is an Indo-European language. It is part of the Celtic group of languages which also includes Scots Gaelic, Irish, Manx, Cornish and Breton. The language as it is spoken today, although later influenced by French and English, seems to have been more or less fully developed by the 6th century, making it one of Europe's oldest languages.

From around the 13th century, English attempts to colonise Wales (and their eventual success) had a detrimental effect on the language. Following the Act of Union in 1536, it was forbidden for people to hold high office unless they spoke English as well as Welsh. Bishop Morgan's translation of the Bible in 1588 is thought to have played an important part in keeping the language alive.

The decline of Welsh continued into the 19th century, when the Industrial Revolution brought a whole new class of industrial landlords and employers, few of whom spoke Welsh. By 1901 only 50% of the population spoke Welsh, and by 1991 this figure dropped to 19%, most of whom (75%) lived in north and north-west Wales.

Reasons for the decline are not hard to find: TV, better communications, emigration, mixed marriages and tourism are just some of those commonly cited. Perhaps what is more surprising is that so many people have continued to speak the language despite all these threats.

Since the 1960s, the importance of Welsh has been officially recognised, and in 1967 the Welsh Language Act ensured that Welsh-speakers could use their own language in court. Since then an increasing number of publications have been bilingual, Welsh-language TV and a radio station have been established, and it's rare nowadays to see a road sign in just one language.

In 1988, a Welsh Language Board was set up to advise the Secretary of State for Wales on everything to do with the language, while in 1994, a new Welsh Language Act gave equal validity to Welsh as a language for use in public-sector businesses – it's now illegal to discriminate against Welsh-speakers, in employment for example.

To those English visitors who get very hot under the collar when they have difficulty communicating in some areas, the Welsh-speakers point out that it's no different from going to any other country where, naturally, everybody speaks their own language. For non-British visitors it's a fascinating subject, but it's probably not wise to express strong opinions without first getting a good grip on the facts.

For spares and repairs, visit Reg Braddick Cycles (☎ 2049 0137), 59–61 Broadway. The YHA Adventure Shop (☎ 2039 9178), 13 Castle St, also sells a decent selection of panniers and touring accessories.

Check your email at the Cardiff Cyber Cafe (☎ 2023 5757), upstairs opposite the Castle on Duke St.

Things to See & Do The city's premier attraction, **Cardiff Castle**, sitting regally in the heart of the city centre, is hard to miss. The site has been occupied since Roman times, but most of the remaining structures are far more recent. The motte and bailey castle at the centre of the castle green dates back to Norman times, but the present Cardiff Castle is predominantly a 19th-century creation. The exterior is fairly unremarkable; it's only when you venture inside on a guided tour that the true splendour of the building becomes apparent. The outrageous William Burges interiors, showing medieval and Middle Eastern influences, are a sight to behold. Liberace would feel right at home!

The **National Museum of Wales**, near City Hall and the Law Courts in Cathays Park, is a great place to kick off a tour of Wales. The large collection contains some wonderful exhibitions on the evolution of Wales, providing a solid introduction to Welsh history that will enrich your experience and bring many of the sights to life. The natural history collections, complete with a

---

Welsh Pronunciation

All vowels except **y** can be short or long. A circumflex accent (eg, **ê**) lengthens the vowel sound.

a	long, as in 'far', *tad* (father)
a	short, as in 'ham', *mam* (mother)
e	long, as in 'whey', *hen* (old)
e	short, as in 'ten', *pen* (head)
i	long, as in 'marine', *mis* (month)
i	short, as in 'pin', *prin* (scarce)
o	long, as in 'more', *môr* (sea)
o	short, as in 'fond', *ffon* (walking stick)
w	long, as the 'oo' in 'moon', *swn* (sound)
w	short, as the 'u' in 'put', *gwn* (gun)
y	has three possible pronunciations: as the 'i' in 'marine', *dyn* (man); as the 'i' in 'pin', *cyn* (before); as the 'u' in 'run', *dynion* (men)
oe	as the 'oy' in 'annoyed', *coed* (wood)
u	as the 'i' in 'pimp', *pump* (five)

Welsh consonants are similar to their English counterparts, but there are a few exceptions:

c	always hard, as in 'cat', *cwm* (valley or corrie)
ch	as in Scottish *loch*, *fach* (small)
dd	as 'th' in 'them', *mynydd* (mountain)
f	as in 'of' (not as in 'if'), *fach* (small)
ff	as in 'off', *ffenestr* (window)
g	as in 'go', *gwyn* (white)
th	as in 'three', *byth* (ever)
ll	there is no exact equivalent sound in English; it's somewhere between the English 'l' and Scottish 'ch' (as in *loch*) – a little like the 'tl' in 'antler', *llyn* (lake)

Words & Phrases

If you're feeling brave, here are a few expressions you might try out in the Welsh-speaking parts of the country (word stress is usually on the second-last syllable in Welsh pronunciation):

Good morning.	*Bore da.*
Good afternoon.	*Prynhawn da.*
Good night.	*Nos da.*
How are you?	*Sut mae?* or *S'mae?*
Please.	*Os gwelch in dda.*
Thank you.	*Diolch.*
I don't understand.	*Dw i ddim in deall.*
Cheers!	*Iechyd da!*
Wales forever!	*Cymru am byth!*
(very) good.	*da (iawn).*

Women	*Merched*
Men	*Dynion*
Entrance	*Mynedfa*
Exit	*Allanfa*
Open	*Ar Agor*
Closed	*Ar Gau*

Check the Glossary for common words cyclists may encounter. For a more comprehensive guide to Welsh, get a copy of Lonely Planet's *British Phrasebook*.

humpback whale skeleton, are excellent, as is the 4th-floor art collection with works by Monet, Pisarro, Manet and Degas.

The fruits of the massive redevelopment of **Cardiff Bay** (once called Tiger Bay) are well worth taking a look at. On a sunny day it's a very pleasant place for a stroll, with works of sculpture dotted around the promenade. Specific sights include the **Welsh Industrial & Maritime Museum** and **Techniquest**, Britain's largest hands-on science exhibition. From the city centre, you can either cycle down Bute St, catch bus No 8 from the city centre or hop on a train to Cardiff Bay train station.

Places to Stay The best budget option is *Cardiff Backpacker* (☎ 2034 5577, 98 Neville St), a popular, well-run independent hostel about 1mi from the train station. Beds in small dorms cost £12.50. The *Cardiff YHA* (☎ 2046 2303; 2 Wedal Rd, Roath Park) has the cheapest beds in town at £10.15, although it's a little farther from the city centre.

Many of Cardiff's more moderately priced hotels and B&Bs are along leafy Cathedral Rd, just across the River Taff (Afon Taff), about 15 minutes' walk from the castle. The *Town House B&B Hotel* (☎ 2023 9399, No 70) has well-appointed, very comfortable rooms from £25 per person. It's very popular, so try and book ahead.

Also on Cathedral Rd, try the *Preste Garden Hotel* (☎ 2022 8607, No 181), occupying the old Norwegian consulate, with rooms from £18 per person. *Ferriers* (☎ 2038 3413, No 130) is a good-value B&B charging from £15.

If you're looking to splurge, the comfiest digs in town are at the new *Cardiff Hilton* (☎ 2064 6300), a stylish, modern hotel in a prime position near the castle. During the week, a room will set you back more than £100, but weekend packages are far more affordable, from £70 per room per night.

Places to Eat The *Cardiff Market* in the Hayes is a great place to stock up for a picnic lunch on the road, with dozens of stalls selling bread, cheeses and cold meats.

There are quite a few eateries along Church St and the top end of High St, including most of the well-known fast food, pizza and pasta chains. *Pierre Victoire* (☎ 2025 8188, 95 St Mary St) is a good-value French eatery with a two-course set menu for £7.95.

There's an abundance of Italian restaurants in Cardiff. *Topo Gigio* (☎ 2034 4794), near a couple of others on Church St, serves up a good selection of dishes for around £6.

The *Celtic Cauldron* (☎ 2038 7185), in the Castle Arcade, immediately opposite the castle, is a good place to try traditional Welsh favourites such as cawl (a thick vegetable broth, often flavoured with meat) and laverbread (a seaweed that is often served mixed up with oatmeal and bacon on toast) for under £5. It also has a good vegetarian selection.

Metropolis (☎ 2034 4300, 60 Charles St), a stylish bar and restaurant just off the Queen St mall, serves an excellent array of contemporary dishes and old favourites given the modern treatment. Expect to pay around £9 for mains such as steamed salmon on a bed of roasted vegetables.

Close to the B&Bs on Cathedral Rd, the *Poacher's Lodge* (☎ 2037 1599) enjoys a peaceful location on the edge of Sophia Gardens. Decked out as a country pub in the city, its large restaurant offers good pub fare for around £7.

Getting There & Away The Welsh capital is 155mi from London, 50mi from Bristol and 48mi from Swansea.

Air The airport (☎ 01446-711111, 🖳 www.cial.co.uk) is 12mi south-west of Cardiff's city centre. There are scheduled services on British Airways, KLM and smaller carriers to cities throughout the UK and continental Europe, including Glasgow, Edinburgh, Dublin, Paris, Amsterdam and Brussels.

Train Cardiff Central station, off Penarth Rd, is on the main InterCity London to Swansea route. For all inter-city services throughout the chapter, reserve a spot for your bike (each bike travels for £3) at the station or by calling ☎ 0845-7484950. All these services are frequent:

destination	one way	hours
Birmingham	£21.10	2¼
Liverpool	£38.90	3¾
London	£43.50	2
Manchester	£38.20	3¼
Nottingham	£43.90	3¾
Swansea	£7.80	1

Direct services also go to the ports at Portsmouth and Southampton.

Within Wales, trains connect Cardiff with Pembroke Dock via Tenby; Milford Haven via Haverfordwest; and Fishguard Habour (for Rosslare in Ireland). Cardiff Valley Lines has regional services (from Cardiff Central or Queen St) to Merthyr Tydfil, Aberdare, Pontypridd, Treherbert, Rhymney and Coryton.

Bicycle The route from Holyhead to Cardiff is described (in reverse) in the Lôn Las Cymru ride in this chapter.

Brecon Beacons Gap

MOUNTAIN BIKE RIDE

Duration	2½–4 hours
Distance	21.4mi
Difficulty	moderate
Start/End	Brecon

Suitable for mountain bike novices and experienced riders alike, this is an aptly named off-road ride climbing high into the heart of the Brecon Beacons National Park. The trail follows 'The Gap route', a former (possibly Roman) main road, between the barren peaks, starting and finishing in the attractive town of Brecon. After completing this ride it's not hard to see why off-road enthusiasts flock from all over southern Britain to the Brecon Beacons for a weekend thrash.

NATURAL HISTORY

Created in 1957, the Brecon Beacons National Park covers 522 sq mi of high, grassy ridge country interspersed with wooded valleys.

It also contains the highest mountain in southern Britain, the 886m (2096ft) Pen-y-Fan. Although they're referred to as mountains, the Brecon Beacons are hardly the Himalayas, and the countryside is less dramatic than Snowdonia to the north. Nevertheless, these bare escarpments are undeniably beautiful, rising in a series of great, green waves above the plains to the north and the former mining valleys to the south.

PLANNING
When to Ride

Cycling conditions are at their best in the summer months. If possible ride mid-week,

as many walkers and cyclists flock to the area on weekends. Be aware of the Brecon Jazz Festival in mid-August; it's one of Europe's largest jazz festivals and attracts thousands every year.

Maps

OS Outdoor Leisure Map No 12 (1:25,000), *Brecon Beacons National Park*, covers the ride in excellent detail and is a must if you intend to explore areas off the described route.

What to Bring

A sturdy mountain bike is a must for this ride. There are several good hire outlets in Brecon (see the Information section for Brecon). Leave your panniers in Brecon, it gets bumpy.

GETTING TO/FROM THE RIDE
Brecon

Brecon is 167mi from London, 45mi from Cardiff, 48mi from Bristol and 20mi from Abergavenny. As Brecon is not on the railway line, getting there on public transport with your bike can be problematic. Unless you intend to cycle to Brecon, a good option is to hire a mountain bike locally. See Information under Brecon for details.

Bus National Express (☎ 08705-808080) has daily links to Brecon from most parts of southern Britain via Cardiff (£2.60, 1½ hours). Stagecoach (☎ 01633-266336) runs a service between Brecon and Hereford via Hay-on-Wye five times a day (twice on Sunday). At present neither of these services carry bikes.

A welcome but limited 'cycle friendly' initiative is the Beacons Bus service (☎ 01873-853254), on Sunday and public holidays only (June to September). Buses with trailers connect various points within the national park to Brecon, Merthyr Tydfil, Abergavenny and Hay-on-Wye. An adult day pass costs £4.60 plus £2 per bike.

Train Brecon is not serviced by rail, but there are several daily services between Cardiff and Abergavenny (£7.30, 45 minutes) and Merthyr Tydfil (£3.40, 55 minutes).

Bicycle The ride along the Taff Trail from Cardiff is described in Day 1 of the Lôn Las Cymru ride later in this chapter.

WALES

THE RIDE
Brecon (Aberhonddu)
☎ 01874

The principal centre in the Brecon Beacons National Park, Brecon is an attractive, historic market town popular with weekend walkers and mountain bikers. The population swells dramatically in mid-August when the town hosts one of Europe's leading jazz festivals.

Information The helpful TIC (☎ 622485) sits in the corner of a shopping centre car park behind Lion St. The Brecon Beacons National Park visitor centre (☎ 623156) is in the same building. Information on the park itself can be found at the Park Authority's Web site (🖥 www.breconbeacons.org).

Brecon has a number of bike shops and hire outlets. The pick of them is the Brecon Cycle Centre (☎ 622651), on Ship St. Standard front-suspension hire bikes cost £10/15 for a half/full day, while more exotic fully suspended demo bikes are £30 per day.

There are numerous banks with ATMs in the town centre. Free Internet access is available at the public library.

Things to See & Do Built in the 11th century, **Brecon Cathedral** sits on a site above the River Honddu in the north of the town. Built on the site of an earlier church, all that remains of the Norman building is parts of the nave. There's an exhibition about the cathedral in the heritage centre (☎ 625222) housed in the restored tithe barn in Cathedral Close.

The **Brecknock Museum** (☎ 624121), on Glamorgan St, is one of the more interesting museums of the old county of Brecknockshire. Brecon was the county town, but the district has now been absorbed into Powys. Among other things, the museum has an old dugout canoe found in Llangorse Lake (Llyn Syfaddan; where *llyn* in Welsh means 'lake'), a recreated Welsh kitchen and the old town stocks.

The area's magnificent scenery is a mecca for walkers as well as cyclists. There are dozens of **great walks** of varying lengths and difficulty starting from or near the town. The TIC has details.

Places to Stay & Eat The *Ty'n-y-Caeau YHA* (☎ 665270, fax 665278) is in a large farmhouse at Groesffordd, about 3mi from Brecon. Dorm beds cost £8.35. Follow the Monmouthshire and Brecon canal path east from Brecon to the first lock, then continue on the road signed to Groesffordd – the hostel is about half a mile north of the village. The *Brynich Caravan Park* (☎ 623325), with tent pitches from £4 per person, is close by.

The *Beacons* (☎ 623339, 16 Bridge St) is a large guest house offering comfortable accommodation near the centre of town. B&B is from £18 per person. Close by, the *Welcome Stranger* (☎ 622188, 7 Bridge St) charges from £16 and is another good choice.

A little bit different and the best digs in town, the *Castle of Brecon Hotel* (☎ 624611, 🖥 www.breconcastle.co.uk) occupies the site and ruins of the town's Norman fortress. En suite rooms start at £27 per person, including breakfast.

The *George Hotel* (☎ 623421, George St) serves up some excellent food, with a very pleasant conservatory out the back; mains are around £8. Just across the courtyard is the *Mr Dickens Restaurant*, where a variety of tasty char-grilled meats, fish and poultry, accompanied by a help-yourself salad bar, also cost around £8. The popular *Camden Arms*, on The Watton, enjoys a reputation for having some of the best traditional pub grub in town, with most dishes under £6.

Brecon Beacons Gap
3½–4 hours, 21.4mi

The first half of the ride follows the Taff Trail to the head of the valley above the Talybont Reservoir. For the first few miles out of Brecon, follow the exceedingly pleasant cycle path alongside the canal, before taking a series of narrow country lanes via the villages of Llanfrynach and Pencelli to the Talybont Reservoir.

Across the dam wall, join a traffic-free path that climbs gently but steadily for the next 5.2mi (unsealed for 3.8mi). You could be forgiven for thinking you're in the Norwegian fjords, with fantastic vistas of pine-covered hillsides rising steeply from the water's edge.

After rejoining the road for a short stretch and reaching a summit, the route heads (right) down a gravel road, then onto a grassy bridleway through a series of gates, before finally parting company with the Taff Trail and continuing to climb along a stony track. At this

WALES

Brecon Beacons Gap

Cue	
start	Brecon TIC
0mi	go south thru Bethel Square
	(100yd) Lion St
0.1	The Watton
0.2	Rich Way 'to canal & theatre'
0.3	unsigned rd (past theatre)
	(40yd) join canal towpath
2.4	join road at Brynich Lock
2.8	'to Llanfrynach'
3.5	lane by churchyard, Llanfrynach
5.0	B4558, Pencelli
6.1	'Taff Trail'
6.9	'Taff Trail'
8.1	along dam wall
8.4	'Taff Trail'
	3.8mi dirt road
	5.2mi moderate climb
12.2	sealed road
	road (after cattle grid)
12.8	4.9mi dirt road & track
	(100yd) 'Taff Trail'
13.0	grassy track (thru gate)
13.8	stony track (at road)
14.3	The Gap & Pen-y-Fan trailhead
15.8	cross stream (steep dip)
17.5	thru gate
18.0	unsigned road
18.4	100yd after crossing bridge
20.6	B4601/Orchard St
21.1	Wheat St/B4520
21.3	Mount St (by supermarket)
21.4	Brecon TIC (end of car park)

Elevation

point you'll be glad you left your panniers in Brecon, as even on a fully suspended mountain bike, the softball-sized stones make for a bumpy ride.

Following a sharp dip to cross a stream, the track continues to climb steadily, with good views of the Upper Neuadd Reservoir away to the left. The barren, grassy landscape gives a great sense of solitude, although, as a popular route for walkers as well as cyclists, it's unlikely you'll be alone for long, especially on summer weekends.

A summit is reached at **The Gap**, a natural opening in the ridge of the central Beacons with marvellous views down the valley ahead. Various **walking tracks** lead to the summits of surrounding peaks. The path snaking away on the left winds its way via Cribyn (795m/2608ft) up to the highest point in Southern Britain, the summit of Pen-y-Fan (886m/2906ft) – a return walk of approximately 3mi. Away to the right is Fan-y-Big (719m/2358ft).

Beyond The Gap, it's downhill pretty much all the way back to Brecon. Although the gradients aren't steep, picking a fast route between the stones can be a tricky (and bone-jarring) exercise. Things get easier after 18.3mi when the track evolves into a sealed back road, a nice fast descent carrying you the final miles back into town.

Lôn Las Cymru

Duration	7 days
Distance	261.7mi
Difficulty	moderate-hard
Start	Cardiff
End	Holyhead

Spanning the length of the country from revitalised Cardiff in the south to the fertile flats of Anglesey and Holyhead, the Lôn Las Cymru (Greenways of Wales) provides a wonderful means of experiencing close-up much of the finest scenery Wales has to offer. One of the jewels in the crown of the National Cycling Network (NCN), the route is well signed with plenty of transport and accommodation options.

Predictably, this tour is fairly hilly throughout, especially in Mid Wales. With that in mind, the days are intentionally short. The described route starts in Cardiff;

an alternative route beginning in Chepstow (not described) meets the main route just outside Glasbury.

PLANNING
When to Ride

Try and get out over the summer months, which offer the longest and warmest days and the best chance of fine weather. The first day of the route is very popular with local cyclists and walkers, so avoid the weekends if possible. Also be aware that Brecon hosts one of Europe's leading jazz festivals over a weekend in mid-August. It's a great time to be in town, but book accommodation well in advance.

Maps & Books

Sustrans produces two excellent maps at 1:100,000 detailing the route, *Lôn Las Cymru – South*, from Cardiff or Chepstow to Builth Wells, and *Lôn Las Cymru – North*, from Builth Wells to Holyhead. They are available from TICs along the route or from Sustrans direct (💻 www.sustrans.org.uk).

For the first day, the Taff Trail is covered by a set of six pamphlets detailing the route, with maps and lots of information about sights encountered along the way. At just 40p each from TICs and bookshops, they are well worth picking up.

What to Bring

The route takes in a variety of surfaces, including sealed roads and long sections on off-road paths. These are generally smooth and in good condition and should not present too many problems for sturdy touring bikes, although for comfort and versatility, a good mountain bike would be the ideal choice.

GETTING TO/FROM THE RIDE
Cardiff

See the Gateway Cities section (pp264–7) for information about getting to/from Cardiff.

Holyhead

Ferry Regular ferry services travel between Holyhead and Dublin. Stena (☎ 0870-570 7070) and Irish Ferries (☎ 0870- 5134324) both have several crossings daily. Tickets are around £20 one way on the slower vessels and £35 on the high-speed services (99 minutes to Dun Laoghaire in Ireland). There are substantial discounts on day return tickets,

The Need for Speed

Feel like having a crack at a world record while cycling through the Welsh countryside? Not far from the Taff Trail, just west of Abergavenny, a stretch of the A465, known in cycling circles as 'the Bank', is the preferred destination of elite cyclists attempting to break the world time trial record. The current mark, set by British cyclist Bruce Bursford over a distance of 4.28mi, stands at an awesome average speed of 38.7mph. Bursford's record, set on 4 August 1999, smashed the previous mark set by fellow Brit and Olympic gold medalist Chris Boardman by more than 4mph.

Bursford rode to glory aboard a super high-tech machine known as the 'Ultimate Bike', a £25,000 aerodynamic, carbon fibre creation that tips the scales at less than 11lb (probably less than your handlebar bag!). Both Bursford's bike and aerodynamic helmet were awarded Millennium Products status by the British Design Council.

Not only did Bursford, who holds a host of cycling speed records, have a cutting edge kit and immensely powerful 36-inch thighs in his favour, but other worldly forces may have played a role in his remarkable ride. Trailing behind the cyclist during the record attempt, shouting encouragement through a loud-hailer (bull horn), was none other than spoon-bending, watch-stopping paranormalist and Ultimate Bike team member, Uri Geller.

Tragically Bruce Bursford won't, as he had hoped, get the chance to better his record ride. In February 2000, Bruce was knocked from his bike and killed while on a training ride near his home in Norfolk. His remarkable cycling achievements and the Ultimate Bike project live on.

with pre-dawn early bird fares from as little as £10 return. Bikes are free.

Train Thanks to the ferry terminal, there are frequent train services from Holyhead to Cardiff (£51.20, 5 hours), London (£75.50, 4½ hours) and several Welsh destinations. Reserve a spot for your bike (see the Gateway Cities section for details).

THE RIDE
Cardiff

See the Gateway Cities section (pp264–7) for information about accommodation and other services.

Day 1: Cardiff to Brecon
5½–7 hours, 51.0mi

Utilising a combination of traffic-free trails, rail and canal paths, as well as quiet country roads, the Taff Trail links the heart of Cardiff with the principal gateway of the wonderfully scenic Brecon Beacons National Park.

If only cycling out of all capital cities could be so easy! Once into leafy Bute Park, the path joins the River Taff and travels upstream, staying more or less beside the river until you're clear of Cardiff's urban fringe. The only hazard on the shady path are numerous dog-walking pedestrians also out enjoying the tranquil surroundings.

From the unremarkable village of Tongwynlais, the route climbs sharply up to spectacular **Castell Coch**, a fairy-tale fortress perched high on the wooded slopes behind the town. Predominantly a 19th-century creation by William Burges (also responsible for designing much of Cardiff Castle), the flamboyant interiors, like those in Cardiff, display a 'spare no expense' approach. It's a wealthy man's medieval fantasy.

From the castle car park, a steep path leads to the top of the wooded hillside before descending to join a rail trail that extends most of the remaining distance into Pontypridd. Unless you're in need of a drink or other supplies, however, it's easiest to stay on the A4054 instead of following the signed route through the town centre.

Near Abercynon turn off the A4054 (left) by a fire station and follow the Taff Trail as it parallels the river once more. The traffic-free path meanders through a very scenic wooded section before crossing the hump-backed Pontygwaith Bridge. Here, a flight of steps heads away from the Taff River and into more open scenery, passing a string of former coal-mining settlements along the valley below.

At 27.5mi, arrive in **Merthyr Tydfil**. During the 19th century, the town was home to one of the largest ironworks in the world. That's all long gone, but Merthyr, at the head of the Taff Valley, remains a sizeable

WALES

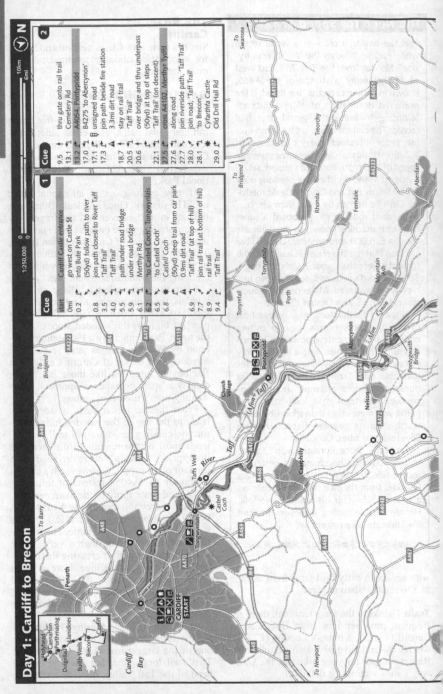

Day 1: Cardiff to Brecon

1:250,000

Cue	
start	Cardiff Castle entrance
0mi	go west on Castle St
0.2	(50yd) follow path to river into Bute Park
0.8	join path closest to River Taff
3.5	'Taff Trail'
4.0	'Taff Trail'
5.5	path under road bridge
5.9	under road bridge
6.1	Merthyr Rd
6.2	'to Castell Coch', Tongwynlais
6.5	'to Castell Coch'
6.8	Castell/ Coch (50yd) steep trail from car park
6.9	0.9mi dirt road 'Taff Trail' (at top of hill)
7.7	join rail trail (at bottom of hill)
8.9	rail trail
9.4	'Taff Trail'

Cue	
9.5	thru gate onto rail trail
13.1	Cemetery Rd
13.2	A4054, Pontypridd
17.0	B4275 'to Abercynon'
17.1	unsigned road
17.3	join path beside fire station 3.3mi dirt road
18.7	stay on rail trail
20.5	'Taff Trail'
20.6	over bridge and thru underpass (50yd) at top of steps
22.1	'Taff Trail' (on descent)
27.5	cross A4102, Merthyr Tydfil along road
27.6	join riverside path, 'Taff Trail'
27.7	join road, 'Taff Trail'
28.0	'to Brecon'
28.1	Cyfarthfa Castle
29.0	Old Drill Hall Rd

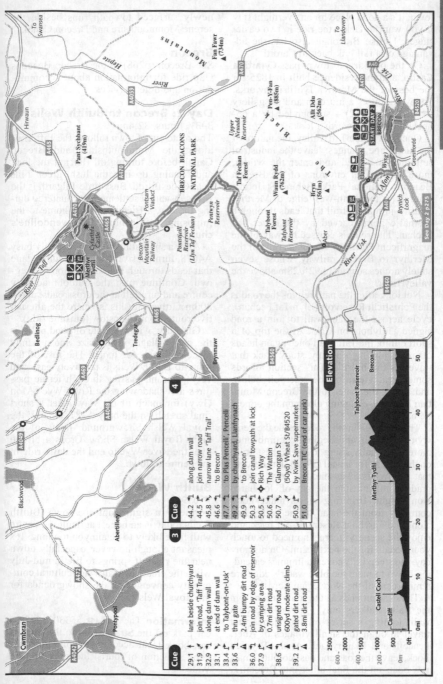

Cue		
29.1	↑	lane beside churchyard
31.9	↱	join road, 'Taff Trail'
32.9	↱	along dam wall
33.1	↱	at end of dam wall
33.4	↱	'to Talybont-on-Usk'
33.6	⤳	thru gate
		2.4mi bumpy dirt road
36.0	↱	join road by edge of reservoir
37.9	↱	by camping area
		0.7mi dirt road
38.6	↑	unsigned road
		600yd moderate climb
39.2	↑	gated dirt road
		3.8mi dirt road

Cue		
44.2	↱	along dam wall
44.5	↱	join narrow road
45.8	↘	narrow lane 'Taff Trail'
46.6	↱	'to Brecon'
47.7	↱	'to Plas Pencelli', Pencelli
49.2	↱	by churchyard, Llanfrynach
49.9	↱	'to Brecon'
50.3	↱	join canal towpath at lock
50.5	⬥	Rich Way
50.6	↱	The Watton
50.7	↱	Glamorgan St
		(50yd) Wheat St/B4520
50.9	↱	by Kwik Save supermarket
51.0	◁	Brecon TIC (end of car park)

Elevation

Cardiff · Castell Coch · Merthyr Tydfil · Talybont Reservoir · Brecon

town; it's a good place for an overnight stay if you want to tackle the ride in two easier stages. Unlike Brecon it also has the advantage of a rail link back to Cardiff.

On the outskirts of town, pass **Cyfarthfa Castle**, a grand residence built in 1825 for the boss of the Merthyr Tydfil ironworks. Today it houses a museum and art gallery (☎ 01685-723112) – surrounded by a 65-hectare park, it's worth a look.

Once out of the Taff Valley, the nature of the landscape changes: leave the industrial settlements behind and enter the wilder, more spectacular environs of the Brecon Beacons National Park. Behind St John's Church (at the north-west edge of Merthyr Tydfil), join a rail trail that leads through a dramatic gorge carved by the River Taf Fechan. The river is crossed by way of the magnificent **Pontsarn Viaduct**, a relic of the Merthyr to Brecon railway, whose seven stately arches soar up to 92ft/28m above the valley floor.

Not long after the path rejoins the road is the **Pontsticill Reservoir** (Llyn Taf Fechan); cycle across the dam wall to join a road signed 'Talybont-on-Usk'. At the top of a short climb, the Taff Trail once again heads off-road, joining a bumpy, stony track that traverses the hillside. This section affords some great views of the reservoir below, and across the water to the Brecon Mountain Railway, chugging along on the opposite bank.

The track rejoins the road beside the Pentwyn Reservoir and begins to climb once more, eventually rising to the highest point on the trail at Torpantau (39mi). The descent that follows is awesome, the very gradual gradient maximising the pay-off for hard-won height. Inspiring views make good company from the head of the valley and along the Talybont Reservoir. Sit back and enjoy the scenery; there's no need to touch your pedals for the next 5.2mi. On a sunny day, the steep hills covered in pines cascading down to meet the blue water's edge are reminiscent of the Norwegian fjords!

The descent ends as the route splits from the trail (walkers only), crosses the dam wall, joining a series of quiet lanes that travel through the small villages of Aber, Pencelli and Llanfrynach. At the Brynich Lock, leave the road and pass colourful narrow boats on the final miles into Brecon. A newly surfaced towpath runs beside the serene Monmouthsire and Brecon Canal.

Brecon

See Brecon (p268) in the Brecon Beacons Gap ride for information about accommodation and other services.

Day 2: Brecon to Builth Wells
3–3½ hours, 32.4mi

The route out of town follows the Taff Trail along the Monmouthshire and Brecon Canal, before turning off (left) at the lock and heading up into the lush, green hills near Groesffordd. Busy little Talgarth is the first substantial settlement encountered during the day, a friendly village home to the imposing 14th-century **St Gwendoline's church**.

After a short stint on the moderately busy A4078, turn back onto a quiet country lane that leads through Felindre and on to Tregoyd. Continue past the outdoor activity centre and turn left at the crossroads, about 800m farther on (this is where the alternative route from Chepstow joins the ride).

Glasbury, with a couple of good pubs, is the next village of any size and a handy place to break for lunch. The rest of the route to Builth Wells is relatively easy and very pleasant, passing through fertile pastures and shadowing the River Wye (Afon Gwy) for much of the way. After a short final stretch on the busy A481, pass by the Royal Welsh Showground, home of the giant Royal Welsh Show. Cross a bridge over the River Wye to end the day's ride in the centre of town.

Builth Wells
☎ 01982

Formerly a significant spa town, Builth Wells today is an honest agricultural centre with little likely to detain you too long. It's pleasant enough however, especially down near the river. It springs to life in mid-July when the cream of Wales' agricultural community converges on the showgrounds for the Royal Welsh Show.

Information The TIC (☎ 553307) is in a car park off the Strand, next to the river. It can book local accommodation and has a good selection of tourist literature on Mid Wales.

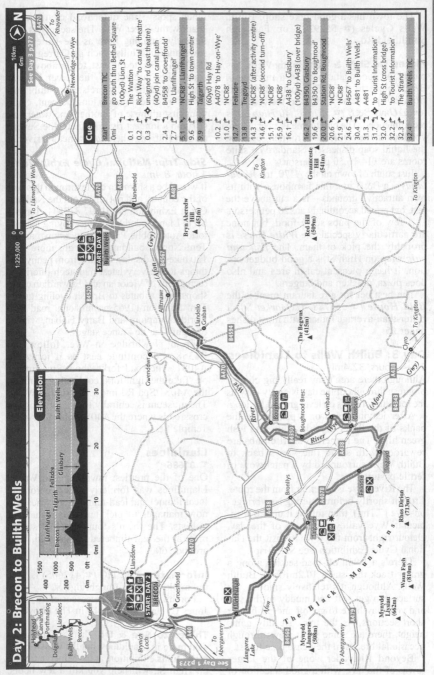

Day 2: Brecon to Builth Wells

Cue	
start	Brecon TIC
0mi	go south thru Bethel Square
	(100yd) Lion St
0.1	The Watton
0.2	Rich Way 'to canal & theatre'
0.3	unsigned rd (past theatre)
	(40yd) join canal path
2.4	B4558 'to Groesffordd'
2.7	'to Llanfihangel'
5.1	NCR8 'Llanfihangel'
9.6	High St 'to town centre'
9.9	Talgarth
	(60yd) Hay Rd
10.2	A4078 'to Hay-on-Wye'
11.0	'NCR8'
12.7	Felindre
13.8	Tregoyd
14.3	'NCR8' (after activity centre)
14.6	'NCR8' (second turn-off)
15.1	'NCR8'
15.9	'NCR8'
16.1	A438 'to Glasbury'
	(100yd) A438 (over bridge)
16.2	B4350, Glasbury
19.6	B4350 'to Boughrood'
20.0	Station Rd, Boughrood
20.6	'NCR8'
21.9	'NCR8'
24.6	B4567 'to Builth Wells'
30.4	A481 'to Builth Wells'
31.3	A481
31.7	'to Tourist Information'
32.0	High St (cross bridge)
32.2	'to Tourist Information'
32.3	The Strand
32.4	Builth Wells TIC

Elevation

The town has a good bike shop, Builth Wells Cycles (☎ 552923), on Fairleigh Smithfield Rd.

Places to Stay & Eat Builth Wells has plenty of good-value beds in a number of B&Bs close to the TIC. Most offer B&B from £14 per person. Right in the centre of town, *Owls B&B (☎ 552518, 40 High St)* is recommended. The bird theme is everywhere you look in the comfortable rooms – even on the liquid soap dispenser! Standard/en suite rooms are £14/16.50 per person.

Just south of town on the A470, the *Woodlands* – a B&B in a fine farmhouse with its own attractive grounds – is a cut above the rest, but priced accordingly at £20 per person.

A few of the pubs serve food, but none are particularly special; the *White Horse* is probably the pick of them. The *fish and chip shop* on High St is a good budget option. It has a pleasant eat-in area and also does pizza, chicken and burgers.

The best bet for a restaurant meal is the *Balti House (☎ 553788, 11 Market St)*, a better-than-average Indian with most dishes under £5.

Day 3: Builth Wells to Llanidloes
3½–4 hours, 32.4mi

Although there aren't any really big climbs, progress throughout the day is rarely easy as the route never stays on level ground for long.

After leaving town on a path along the banks of the River Wye, head up into lush green hills. The numerous short climbs are rewarded with some fine views back to Builth Wells surrounded by a patchwork of fertile pastures.

The River Wye is never far from the route. Cross it shortly before entering Newbridge-on-Wye (7.1mi), then follow it up the spectacular Wye valley for much of the day. Detour right from the town to visit the National Cycle Exhibition (see Side Trip).

There's a 1.9mi off-road section along a grassy track that starts 10.2mi from Builth Wells. Although it's relatively smooth, the surface can get soft and muddy in the wet and you may have to get off and push over short sections. As the track steadily gains height, there are some great views through occasional breaks in the dense pine forest.

Beyond Rhayader –one of the larger towns of the day, with a good selection of

lunch spots – the quiet road continues to shadow the River Wye. The scenery is particularly stunning here as the valley narrows and high hills, such as Garreg Lwyd (510m/1673ft) to the east, tower above. The route bids farewell to the River Wye at Llangurig. After a short steep climb, followed by an enjoyably long descent, catch your first glimpse of another fine waterway (Britain's longest river in fact), the Severn (Afron Hafren; where *afron* means 'river').

Side Trip: National Cycle Exhibition
1 hour, 8.4mi

It would be a shame to cycle through this part of the country and not check out the National Cycle Exhibition (☎ 01597 825531, Temple St) in Llandrindod Wells. Occupying the historic Automobile Palace, now known as the Tom Norton building, there are more than 120 bikes on display, ranging from penny farthings to the very latest high-tech offerings; recreations of Victorian and Edwardian cycle shops; and tributes to British cycling greats Tom Simpson (1965 professional road race world champion) and Barry Hoban, winner of eight Tour de France stages.

From Newbridge-on-Wye, follow the B4358 and continue east as it joins the A4081. The road forks about 2mi further on. Take the right fork, continuing south on the A4081/Spa Rd into Llandrindod Wells. The museum is centrally located, facing the crossroads where the A4081 joins the A483/Temple St.

Llanidloes
☎ 01686

One of the prettiest towns in Mid Wales, Llanidloes was formerly a centre for the local flannel and lead-mining industries, but now manages to pick up its fair share of tourists. The town's four principal streets meet at the half-timbered market hall, built around 1600.

Information The TIC (☎ 412605) is near the market hall on Longbridge St.

For bike parts and accessories, try Les Jones Cycles (☎ 412864), in The Grove.

Things to See & Do There's not a great deal to do in Llanidloes, but the **Welsh Heritage Quilts** exhibition, at the Minerva Centre on High St, will help you kill a few hours.

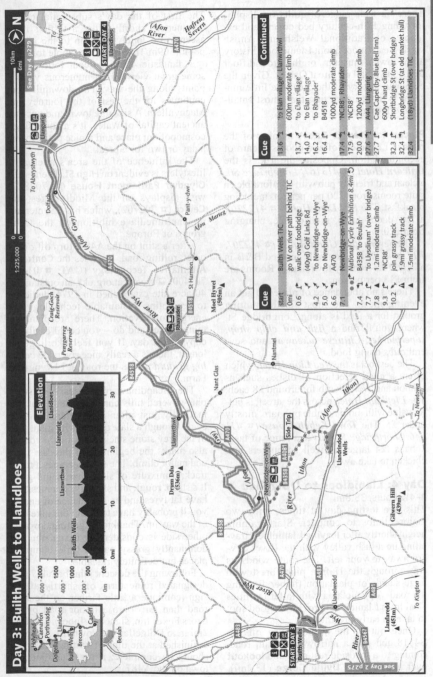

Day 3: Builth Wells to Llanidloes

Elevation

Cue		
start	Builth Wells TIC	
0mi	go W on river path behind TIC	
0.6	walk over footbridge	
	(40yd) Golf Links Rd	
4.2	'to Newbridge-on-Wye'	
5.0	'to Newbridge-on-Wye'	
6.6	A470	
7.1	Newbridge-on-Wye	
	National Cycle Exhibition 8.4mi	
7.4	B4358 'to Beulah'	
7.7	'to Llysdinam' (over bridge)	
7.8	1.2mi moderate climb	
9.3	'NCR8'	
10.2	join grassy track	
	1.9mi grassy track	
	1.5mi moderate climb	

Cue	Continued	
13.6	'to Elan village' Llanwrthwl	
	600m moderate climb	
13.7	'to Elan 'village'	
14.0	'to Elan village'	
16.2	'to Rhayader'	
16.4	B4518	
17.4	'NCR8' Rhayader	
	1000yd moderate climb	
17.9	'NCR8'	
	1200yd moderate climb	
20.0	A44, Llangurig	
27.6	Cae Capel (by Blue Bell Inn)	
27.7	600yd hard climb	
32.3	Shortbridge St (over bridge)	
32.4	Longbridge St (at old market hall)	
32.4	(18yd) Llanidloes TIC	

See Day 4 p229

See Day 2 p275

There's a wide range of quilts on display, including 17th-century bed covers and examples of traditional Welsh and Amish work. Learn more about Llanidloe's history at the town's **museum**, on the ground floor of the town hall on Great Oak St. Given the colourful history of the area, the little museum is more interesting than most small-town offerings.

Places to Stay & Eat A number of the pubs in Llanidloes offer a good standard of accommodation. Opposite the TIC is the *Unicorn Hotel* (☎ *413167, Longbridge St*), a clean and friendly pub with comfortable en suite rooms from £20 per person, including breakfast. The *Red Lion Hotel* (☎ *412270*), a few doors down, is also nice, charging from £20.

The *Severn View Guest House* (☎ *412207, 10 China St*) is a centrally located B&B in a large 19th-century townhouse. Rooms are from £18 per person.

There's no abundance of places to get an evening meal. The most fertile hunting ground for a feed is along Longbridge St, where you'll find a *fish and chip shop*, *supermarket*, *Chinese takeaway* and several *pubs* doing food.

The best bet is the *Red Lion Hotel*, which offers a good selection of dishes such as salmon and Welsh lamb for around £8 each. The *Elephant Hotel*, across the street, is better value with more humble pub fare, mostly under £5. The *Town Kebab House* (☎ *411 046, Shortbridge St*) serves a range of tasty kebabs (£4 large) as well as burgers and chicken to take away.

Day 4: Llanidloes to Dolgellau
4–4½ hours, 38.8mi

This is a testing day at times, with two major climbs to conquer. Start gaining height shortly after leaving Llanidloes, travelling up a lush valley with the River Severn away to your left. The route winds its way through the Hafren pine forest with large stands of plantation timber flanking the road. A picnic area with toilet facilities (7mi from Llanidloes) provides a good spot to take an early breather.

Once out of the woods, turn off the B4518 and join a narrow mountain road, coming to a roadside rest area and **lookout** over the dramatic **Dylife Gorge** (13.2mi).

The first of the day's substantial climbs commences shortly after: a testing 1.4mi ascent on a lonely road up to the highest point (509m/1669ft) of the whole tour.

A fantastic 4.3mi descent follows with some great views from numerous vantage points along the way. The downhill trend continues for the rest of the journey into Machynlleth. A sizeable town, and once the ancient capital of Wales, it's a surprisingly cosmopolitan place and a nice place to stay a day or two for a break.

The influence of the area's alternative lifestylers is evident on **High St**. There's also **Glyndwr Parliament House** (☎ 702827), with displays on the Middle Ages, and **Celtica** (☎ 702702), which has an entertaining multimedia exhibition on the Celtic groups of Europe.

After a stint on the A487, turn off onto a quiet, rolling road. It passes the **Centre for Alternative Technology** (CAT; ☎ 01654-702400, ⌨ www.cat.org.uk), an outstanding 40-acre site established in 1974, dedicated to promoting sustainable technology and energy conservation. There are plenty of things to see and do – you could easily occupy half a day. If you feel like lingering longer, there's a really nice riverside *camping ground* across the road at Llwyngwern Farm.

The 'Scandinavian' landscape of steep, pine-covered hills changes briefly but dramatically just after Aberllefenni as you cycle through a slate quarry with giant piles of the grey stone stacked beside the road. It also marks the beginning of the day's second major climb. The road becomes a rough track, a mixture of slate shards and grass. It's steep, rough and slippery, so unless you have fat tyres and an abundance of energy, you'll probably have to push your bike most of the way up. Thankfully, getting down the other side is considerably easier, the predominantly grassy path a little bumpy in places but definitely rideable.

Following the descent join the A487. The designated route turns off shortly after a sign (continue a little farther on the main road then turn onto a minor road by the Cross Foxes Inn, signed to Tabor). The final 2mi in to Dolgellau are downhill. Although unfinished at the time of writing, this route should be complete; if not, continue into town on the A487.

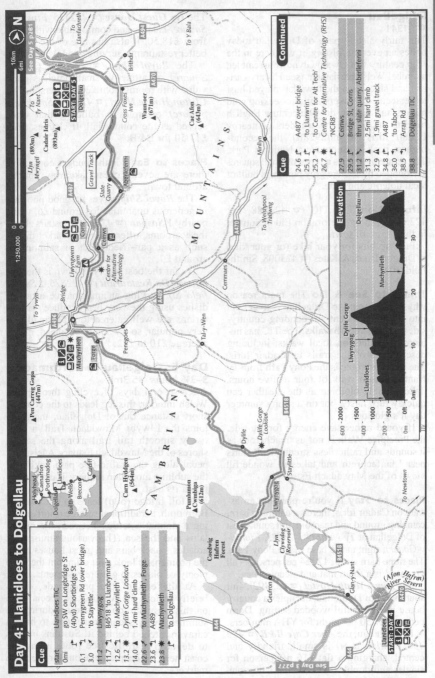

Day 4: Llanidloes to Dolgellau

Cue		
start	Llanidloes TIC	
0mi	go SW on Longbridge St	
	(40yd) Shortbridge St	↰ ↱
0.1	Pennygreen Rd (over bridge)	↰
3.0	'to Staylittle'	↱
11.2	Llwynygog	
11.7	B4518 'to Llanbrynmair'	↱
12.6	'to Machynlleth'	↰
13.2	*Dylife Gorge Lookout*	
14.0	1.4mi hard climb	↱
22.6	'to Machynlleth'; Forge	↱
23.6	A489	↰
23.8	Machynlleth	
	'to Dolgellau'	↱

Cue		
24.6	A487 over bridge	↰
25.1	'to Llanwrin'	↱
25.2	'to Centre for Alt Tech'	↱
26.7	*Centre for Alternative Technology (RHS)*	
	'NCR8'	↱
27.9	Ceinws	
29.5	Bridge St, Corris	↰
31.2	thru slate quarry, Aberllefenni	
31.3	2.5mi hard climb	↱
32.9	1.9mi gravel track	↰
34.8	A487	
36.0	'to Tabor'	↱
38.5	Arran Rd	↱
38.8	Dolgellau TIC	

Continued

Elevation

See Day 5 p281

See Day 3 p277

START: DAY 5

START: DAY 4

Dolgellau
☎ 01341

The fairly sleepy pace of Dolgellau today belies an eventful history. It was here in the 15th century that Owain Glyndwr assembled his rebel Welsh parliament (see History earlier) and since then the town has played host to persecuted Quakers, fortune-seeking gold miners and well-to-do 19th-century English tourists out to see the wonders of nearby Cadair Idris (893m/2928ft), the second-highest peak in Snowdonia National Park. The centre of town is a series of small squares surrounded by austere grey buildings built of local dolerite and slate.

Information The TIC (☎ 422888, fax 422576) is in Ty Meirion on Eldon Square, in the centre of town.

Pick up bits for your bike (or your kite) at Dragon Bikes & Kites (☎ 423008, Smithfield St).

Things to See & Do The main reason why people come to Dolgellau is to get out into the magnificent surrounding countryside on some superb **walks**. The TIC has numerous leaflets on local walks, including descriptions of the trails up Cadair Idris. The standard route is the **Pony Path** from Ty Nant, a return walk of four to five hours. Take suitable clothing as the weather can quickly turn nasty, but on a sunny summer day it's glorious.

If you'd rather save energy for the ride, the **Precipice Walk** is not as treacherous as it sounds and rather less strenuous. It starts near Llanfachreth and takes in wonderful views of the Mawddach Estuary.

Places to Stay If you're planning an assault on Cadair Idris, there's a camping barn, camping ground and tearoom 3mi south-west of Dolgellau at *Ty Nant* (☎ 423433, Ffordd-y-Gader), right at the base of the Pony Path. The stone barn sleeps 12 (£4 per person) – all you need is a foam mat and sleeping bag.

The *Kings Youth Hostel* (☎ 422392), 4mi south-west of Dolgellau, occupies a country house in a peaceful wooded setting. Dorm beds are £7.50 per night for YHA members.

In Dolgellau, the *Aber Cafe B&B* (☎ 422 460, Smithfield St) is small, friendly and central, charging a flat £16 per person for singles and doubles with shared bathroom.

The *Ivy Guest House* (☎ 422535, Finsbury Square) is large and comfortable with B&B from £18.50. It also has one of the town's better restaurants, serving good Welsh food.

The *Royal Ship* (☎ 422209, Queens Square), an attractive small hotel, is good value with rooms from £20 per person. The *Clifton House Hotel* (☎ 422554, Smithfield Square) occupies a building that once served as the county jail. It charges from £17.50 for B&B.

Places to Eat For the budget conscious, there are several cheap takeaway options around town.

The *Royal Ship* serves up good pub fare in generous quantities for around £6, while nearby *Y Sospan* (☎ 423174), upstairs above the tearooms, offers more upmarket dishes such as a pan-fried fillet of salmon for around £9.

By far the best eatery in town is the *Dylanwad Da Restaurant* (☎ 422870, 2 Smithfield St), serving an imaginative array of dishes using the very best produce – vegetarians are well catered for. It's small and very popular, so try and book ahead; mains average £10 to £12.

Day 5: Dolgellau to Porthmadog
3–3½ hours, 35.3mi

After several days of cycling through the Welsh interior, this leg leads to the coast. A short distance out of Dolgellau, the route joins the Llwybr Mawddach Trail, a relatively smooth rail trail along the scenic shores of the Mawddach Estuary. A leisurely pedal along the traffic-free path, taking in the sublime mountain scenery, is cycle touring at its best.

A toll bridge (60p) leads to the coast at Barmouth, a traditional seaside resort enjoying a dramatic setting between the mountains and the sea. The various amusement arcades, snack bars and guest houses along the promenade look a bit grim, but there are plenty of places to grab refreshments.

At the end of the promenade, climb briefly to join the A496. Take special care on this busy stretch of road as, during the summer, every second car seems to have a caravan hitched behind it! Sustrans intends to develop a traffic-free route along the coast here, so keep an eye out for the route markers.

WALES

Day 5: Dolgellau to Porthmadog

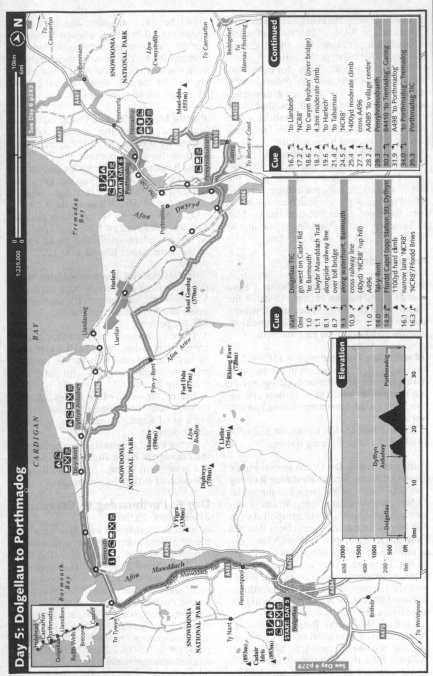

1:225,000

N

Cue

start	
0mi	Dolgellau TIC
1.0	go west on Cader Rd
1.1	'to Barmouth'
8.1	Llwybr Mawddach Trail alongside railway line
8.7	over toll bridge
9.3	along waterfront, Barmouth
10.9	cross railway line
	(40yd) 'NCR8' up hill'
11.0	A496
14.0	Tal-y-Bont
14.9	Ffordd Capel (opp Station St), Dyffryn
	1100yd hard climb
16.1	narrow lane 'NCR8'
16.3	'NCR8'/Ffordd Briws

Cue Continued

16.7	'to Llanbedr'
17.2	'NCR8'
18.6	'to Cwym Bychan' (over bridge)
18.7	4.3mi moderate climb
19.6	'to Harlech'
21.4	'to Talsarnau'
24.5	'NCR8'
25.4	1400yd moderate climb cross A496
27.1	A4085 'to village centre'
28.2	Penrhyndeudraeth
28.3	Penrhyndeudraeth
30.2	B4410 'to Tremadog', Garreg
31.9	A498 'to Porthmadog'
34.0	'to Porthmadog', Tremadog
35.3	Porthmadog TIC

Elevation

See Day 4 p279
See Day 6 p283

WALES

After following the coast, escape the congestion of the A496 at Dyffryn Ardudury, climbing on quiet lanes into sheep-grazing country, where the green hills are crisscrossed by a myriad of dry-stone walls. A multitude of gates can make progress frustrating at times. A nice descent through a lush patch of woods leads to the start of the major ascent of the day, a gradual 4.3mi climb providing great views over Tremadog Bay as you approach the summit.

Back on level ground, another toll bridge (free this time) crosses the River Dwyryd into Penrhyndeudraeth. Here, join the A4085 to start the easy, but indirect final leg into Porthmadog. A cycle-friendly route over the more direct but treacherous Cob embankment into Porthmadog is in the pipeline, so look for route markers.

Porthmadog
☎ 01766

Most noncyclists visit Porthmadog, a busy seaside town, for two reasons: to catch the Ffestiniog Railway to Blaenau Ffestiniog and to visit the nearby village of Portmeirion. The town makes a good base for both.

Information The Porthmadog TIC (☎ 512 981) is on High St, adjacent to the harbour. It offers an accommodation booking service and has a good selection of leaflets and information on the Snowdonia mountains and North Wales.

For bike bits, try KK Cycles (☎ 512310), 141 High St, near the train station.

Things to See & Do Of the several scenic railways in the region, the **Ffestiniog Railway** (☎ 512340) is probably the pick of them. The 13.5mi narrow-gauge line, which commenced operation in 1836 to transport slate to Port Madoc for export, departs from Blaenau Ffestiniog. It chugs its way through the spectacular scenery of Snowdonia down to Porthmadog. There are several services daily from March to October – trains leave from Porthmadog's Harbour Station. See the Ffestiniog Railway Web site (🖳 www.festrail.co.uk) for more information.

Located about 2mi from Porthmadog, **Portmeirion** is a private Italianate village created by the Welsh architect Sir Clough Williams-Ellis. Built between 1925 and 1927, it was intended to show that architecture could be fun, intriguing and interesting. There are 50 buildings clustered around a central plaza; some of the buildings were brought to the site to save them from destruction elsewhere. The village was used as the set for the cult 1960s TV series, *The Prisoner*. It's all quite bizarre.

Places to Stay & Eat Cheap bunkhouse beds and camp sites are available at **Tremadog Rocks** (☎ 512199), passed en route on the A498, opposite the Eric Jones Cafe. It caters mainly for rock climbers who scale the adjacent cliffs; you can get a mattress and a roof over your head for around £5.

The central **Mrs Williams B&B** (☎ 512 635, 12 Snowdon St) is reasonably priced at £18. **Yr Hen Fecws** (☎ 514625, 16 Lombard St) is an excellent, small B&B above a bistro of the same name. Rooms cost £22.50 per person.

The B&B **Royal Sportsman Hotel** (☎ 512 015, 131 High St), occupying a traditional Victorian coaching inn near the train station, offers comfortable rooms and charges from £26 per person.

Three of the better places in town to eat are on Lombard St. **The Ship** is a nice place to have an ale and also serves up some award-winning pub grub, with good-sized mains for around £7.

Nearby, the cosy **Yr Hen Fecws** bistro has an imaginative selection of dishes, including a good vegetarian selection, at reasonable prices.

At the top of the street opposite the park, the **Passage to India Tandoori** (☎ 512144) is a better-than-average Indian with a good selection of curries for around £6.

Day 6: Porthmadog to Caernarfon
2½–3 hours, 29.8mi

A short and relatively easy day providing plenty of time to explore Caernarfon and its magnificent castle, putting you within comfortable striking distance of Holyhead.

After a short backtrack to Tremadog, the route takes to quiet roads through the hills around Penmorfa, before meeting the coast at Criccieth, a relaxed seaside resort with a decidedly more genteel feel than Porthmadog. The main point of interest is the **13th-century castle** (☎ 01766-522227). While little of the original structure remains intact, the wonderful views over Cardigan Bay and the town

WALES

Day 6: Porthmadog to Caernarfon

Elevation

Cue		
start	Porthmadog TIC	
0mi		go north-west on High St
1.3		A487 to Caernarfon/Tremadog
2.2		Penmorfa
2.4		'to Hen Lôn'
		1400yd moderate climb
3.2		'NCR8'
5.0		'NCR8'
5.1		cross A487
7.3		B4411
8.5		Criccieth
8.7		Castle St
		Criccieth Castle
9.8		'NCR8' (bridge), Llanystumdwy
11.1		'NCR8', Llanystumdwy
11.5		'to Talhenbont Hall'
11.5		(40yd) 'to Talhenbont Hall'
12.6		'to Bryncir'
15.9		'NCR8'
16.7		'Llecheidd or U' (thru farm yard)
17.2		join Lôn Eifion rail trail
29.6		follow street around castle
29.8		Caernarfon TIC

justify the price of admission. The display on Welsh castles is also worth a look.

At Bryncir, join the Lôn Eifion rail trail, following the bed of a line closed in 1964. The surface is good, a combination of compacted gravel interspersed with bitumen sections. After a high point (at 20.8mi), the remainder of the day is wonderfully easy, a gradual downhill all the way to the end of the ride. Near Caernarfon, the path emerges from the trees with the awesome sight of Caernarfon Castle just a few hundred yards ahead.

Caernarfon
☎ 01286

Dominated by a magnificent castle that vies with Conwy's as the most impressive in Wales, Caernarfon is an attractive, historic market town well worth exploring.

Information The helpful Caernarfon TIC (☎ 672232) is opposite the entrance to the castle on Castle St. For bike parts and servicing, visit Beics Castel (☎ 677400, 33 High St) in the centre of town.

Things to See & Do Edward I wanted **Caernarfon Castle** to be the most impressive of his Welsh fortresses and it was modelled on the 5th-century walls of Constantinople. The castle was built between 1283 and 1301 as a part of a series of monumental forts constructed by Edward to keep the Welsh under control. It looks particularly impressive at night when its massive form is illuminated by floodlights. Inside, you can walk along the walls and climb to the top of the towers, which provide a magnificent view over the grounds, the Menai Strait and the town. The towers also contain a number of interesting exhibitions, including the excellent regimental museum of the Royal Welsh Fusiliers and displays on Prince Charles' 1969 royal investiture and Edward I's campaigns.

Places to Stay & Eat You can pitch a tent at *Cadnant Valley Camping & Caravan Park* (☎ 673196), about half a mile from the castle on Llanberis Rd (from £4.50 to £8 for a small tent). It's open from March to October.

The central *Totters* (☎ 672963, 2 High St), down towards the waterfront, is a comfortable, friendly independent hostel offering accommodation in four- or six-bed dorms for £9.50, including a help-yourself breakfast.

There are quite a few B&Bs around town, with a number clustered on Church St, just east of the castle. *Tegfan* (☎ 673703, No 4) has rooms from £14 per person, while just down the street, *Caer Menai* (☎ 672612, No 15) is friendly and comfortable with B&B from £17.

Hole in the Wall St has a number of places to eat. *Stone's Bistro* (☎ 671152, No 4) is a reasonable place with mains for around £9, including several vegetarian choices.

The *Black Boy Inn* (☎ 673604, Northgate St) has a bar serving good pub grub and a restaurant. Its set three-course dinner is tasty, and costs £11. The *Palace Vaults*, opposite the castle, is another good choice for a pub meal.

Courtenay's Bistro (☎ 677290, 9 Segontium Terrace) is one of the top places in town, showcasing fresh local produce in mains, reasonably priced from around £7 to £10.

Day 7: Caernarfon to Holyhead
3½–4 hours, 42.0mi

The exit from Caernarfon is traffic-free as you join the Lôn Las Menai rail trail down by Victoria Dock. It follows the route of the old Bangor to Caernarfon line, closed sine 1972. The easy, pleasant route travels along the shores of the Menai Strait (Afon Menai) and onto the road at the waterfront in Y Felinheli.

You soon join another shorter, traffic-free path, the Lôn Las Arfon, joining the road again at 5.6mi. Travelling on a series of quiet lanes, climb gently into the green hills behind Bangor. Watch for route markers here as navigation is tricky in places. Soon after crossing the A4087 is the Menai Suspension Bridge, designed by Thomas Telford. An engineering marvel when it opened in 1826, the bridge, at 579ft/176m long and 100ft/30m high, is still a most impressive sight. Once across the rushing tidal waters of the strait, you arrive in the imaginatively-named town of Menai Bridge, first port of call on the island of Anglesey – at 276 sq mi, the largest island in England and Wales.

Cycling along the moderately busy A4080, the view back across the Menai Strait, spanned by its two bridges and with the craggy peaks of Snowdonia in the background, is really a sight to behold. Just up the road is (take a deep breath) Llanfairpwll-gwyngyllgogerychwyrndrobwllllandysilio-gogogoch (Llanfair PG for short), the village

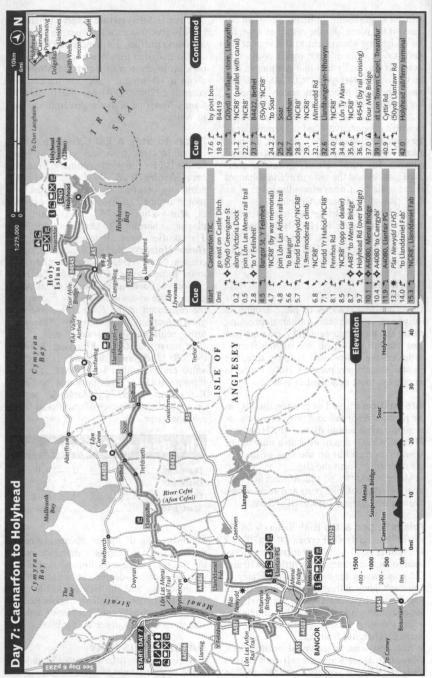

Day 7: Caernarfon to Holyhead

1:275,000

Cue

start		Caernarfon TIC
0mi	♦	go east on Castle Ditch
		(50yd) Greengate St
		along Victoria Dock
0.2	↰↱	join Lôn Las Menai rail trail
0.5	♦	'to Y Felinheli'
2.8	♦	Bangor St, Y Felinheli
4.5	↰↱	'NCR8' (by war memorial)
4.7	↰↱	join Lôn Las Afron rail trail
4.8	↰↱	'to Bangor'
5.6	↰↱	Ffordd Fodolydd/'NCR8'
5.7	◀	1.9mi moderate climb
6.8	↰↱	'NCR8'
7.1	↰↱	Ffordd Yr Hafod/'NCR8'
8.1	↰↱	Penrhos Rd
8.5	◇	'NCR8' (opp car dealer)
8.7	♦	A487 to Menai Bridge'
9.7	◇	Holyhead Rd (over bridge)
10.1	♦	A4080, Menai Bridge
10.4	↰↱	A4080 'to Caergybi'
11.9	✱	A4080, Llanfair PG
13.3	✱	Plas Newydd (LHS)
14.0	↰↱	'to Llanddaniel Fab'
15.3	↰↱	'NCR8, Llanddaniel Fab

Cue Continued

17.6	↰↱	by post box
18.9	↰↱	B4419
		(20yd) at village store, Llangaffo
21.2	↰↱	'NCR8' (parallel with canal)
22.1	↰↱	'NCR8'
23.7	♦	B4422, Bethel
		(50yd) 'NCR8'
24.2	↰↱	'to Soar'
25.2		Soar
26.7		Dothan
28.3	↘	'NCR8'
29.1	↰↱	'NCR8'
31.2	↰↱	Minffordd Rd
32.6		Llanfihangel-yn-Nhowyn
34.0	↰↱	'NCR8'
34.8	↰↱	Lôn Ty Main
35.6	↰↱	'NCR8'
36.1	↰↱	B4545 (by rail crossing)
37.0	◇	Four Mile Bridge
39.1	✱	at Lon Towyn Capel, Trearddur
40.9	↰↱	Cyttir Rd
41.4	↰↱	(50yd) Llanfawr Rd
42.0		Holyhead rail/ferry terminal

Elevation

Menai
Suspension Bridge

Soar

Holyhead

Caernarfon

0ft
200
400 — 200m
500
1000
1500

0mi   10   20   30   40

0m   0km

with the longest name in Britain. You can deviate off the route into the centre of town for the obligatory photo next to the sign at the train station – there's not much else worth seeing. If you really feel like stopping, a better bet is **Plas Newydd** (☎ 01248-714795), one of the most interesting stately homes in North Wales. It's en route at 13.3mi.

Anglesey is the flattest region in Wales, so with a cooperative wind the remainder of the route is relatively easy, passing on quiet country lanes through a succession of small villages. The rural serenity is briefly shattered just beyond the village of Llanfihangel as the route continues along the edge of an RAF (Royal Air Force) Airfield.

The Four Mile Bridge, which is actually much shorter, leads to Holy Island and the home stretch of the tour. Turn off the B4545 at Trearddur for the final few miles into Holyhead.

Holyhead
☎ 01407

There are few reasons to hang around in Holyhead, a drab and rather depressing place, and most people don't – pausing just long enough to roll on and off the ferries. Although the town itself is fairly dire, the coastal scenery on parts of Holy Island is among the most beautiful in Wales.

Information Instead of placing the TIC in the harbour-front rail and ferry complex, as common sense would dictate, the Holyhead TIC (☎ 762622) sits more than a mile out of town in a green hut on the side of the A5. It's not really worth the trip.

Motor World (☎ 761422, Market St) has a small selection of bike parts and accessories. There are numerous banks with ATMs.

Things to See & Do Both Stena (☎ 0870-5707070) and Irish Ferries (☎ 0870-513 4324) offer good-value **day trips** from Holyhead to Dublin, charging as little as £10 and £12 respectively for their early-bird fares. If you don't fancy getting up way before dawn, you'll have to pay a bit more. Stena, with its faster ferries and more flexible timetable, offers the most feasible post-dawn day-trip package, charging from £22.

Just 2mi west of town at South Stack (Ynys Lawd) are some magnificent coastal cliffs and a Royal Society for the Protection of Birds (RSPB) **nature reserve** where you can observe thousands of nesting sea birds, including puffins, guillemots and razorbills.

You can also follow a track from the car park up to the top of **Holyhead Mountain**, about a 30-minute walk. Surrounding the summit (220m/722ft) are the remains of **Caer-y-Twr**, one of the largest Iron Age sites in Wales.

Places to Stay & Eat Catering mainly to late-night ferry travellers, most of Holyhead's B&Bs are pretty ordinary. Your best bet is *Hendre* (☎ 762929, Porth-y-Felin Rd), a friendly, comfortable B&B with just three rooms, from £20. Closest to the ferry terminal, *Min-y-Don* (☎ 762718) is handy and pleasant, charging £15 per person for B&B. The comfiest rooms in town are at the *Boat House Hotel* (☎ 762094, Beach Rd), on the coast at Newry Beach, about a mile out of town. Expect to pay £30 each for B&B.

Greasy spoons aside, there's a real lack of good places to eat in town. One exception is the restaurant at the *Boat House Hotel*. A good selection of dishes, many of them featuring seafood, cost around £8 each.

In town, the *Omar Khayyam Tanddori* (☎ 760333, 8 Newry St) is a reliable, good-value choice with a wide range of curries for around £6. Another option is the *Crown Restaurant* (☎ 762706, Market St), serving up good-sized helpings of traditional fare at reasonable prices.

The Best of Anglesey

Duration	1½–2½ hours
Distance	16.9mi
Difficulty	easy
Start/End	Beaumaris

Following one of four signposted routes on the island, this is a fantastic short ride making the most of Anglesey's limited elevation to provide near 360-degree views of the Menai Strait, ocean and the island's fertile green fields. The historic buildings of holy Penmon Priory and magnificent Beaumaris Castle ensure there's plenty to see off the bike.

NATURAL HISTORY
Covering 276 sq mi, Anglesey (Ynys Môn) is the largest island in Wales and England.

It's the flattest part of Wales, although there are some rugged cliffs along the coastline, which has some excellent swimming beaches. The land is very fertile and the island is referred to as Môn Mam Cymru – Mother of Wales – because it provides wheat, cattle and other agricultural produce for North Wales.

PLANNING
When to Ride
This short ride can be enjoyed at any time of year.

Maps & Books
Be sure to pick up a copy of the *Rural Cycling on Anglesey* pamphlet, which describes this and three other signposted routes on the island. It's available from TICs. OS Landranger map No 115 (1:50,000), *Snowdon*, covers most of Anglesey and north-west Wales.

GETTING TO/FROM THE RIDE
Beaumaris
Beaumaris is on the eastern tip of Anglesey, 10mi from Bangor.

Train The closest train station is 6mi away at Llanfair PG, on the North Wales coastal railway line to Holyhead (the end town in the Lôn Las Cymru ride described earlier). About seven trains run from Cardiff per day (4–5½ hours); the 9.45 pm train takes 9 hours). Bangor train station, on the mainland, is almost as close; it's 4½–5 hours from Cardiff, with several services a day. There are several trains linking Holyhead with Llanfair PG (£4.20, 30 minutes). See the Gateway Cities section earlier this chapter for details on reserving a spot for your bike.

Bicycle Beaumaris is 4.3mi from the Menai Bridge, passed on the final day of the Lôn Las Cymru ride. If riding from Bangor, turn right at the roundabout just over the bridge and follow the moderately busy but very scenic A545 along the coast. Llanfair PG is only a short distance (west) from Menai Bridge on the A4080; turn left before the bridge.

Busy roads and numerous tunnels make the train the best option if travelling from the North Wales coast.

THE RIDE
Beaumaris
☎ 01248
Once the principal town and chief port of Anglesey, Beaumaris is now a popular holiday spot known for its fine castle, beautiful scenic setting and as a major sailing and water sports centre.

Information Beaumaris' small, unofficial TIC is in the middle of town on Castle St, the main thoroughfare. Pick up the *Rural Cycling in Anglesey* pamphlet here.

Beics Menai Cycles (☎ 811200, Castle St), in the Beaumaris Leisure Centre a few hundred yards from the TIC, has spares and accessories as well as hire bikes (£10 for half a day). There are several banks with ATMs on Castle St.

Things to See & Do On a flat site overlooking the Menai Strait, **Beaumaris Castle** is the last and largest of the castles built by Edward I. Started in 1295, construction was never fully completed, accounting for the remaining structure's somewhat squat appearance. With its water-filled moat complete with swans, double-walled symmetrical design and magnificently scenic location, it's not hard to see why it's a World Heritage List site.

Other attractions in town worth a look include the **Beaumaris Gaol**, a model prison when it opened in 1829, the **Courthouse** and the **Museum of Childhood**. Various companies operate **sightseeing cruises** out to Puffin Island and along the Menai Strait, departing from the pier.

Places to Stay & Eat The closest camping ground is *Kingsbridge* (☎ 490636), on Camp Rd about 1.2mi out of Llanfaes.

Swyn-y-Don (☎ 810794, 7 Bulkeley Terrace) is central and smart, with most of the en suite rooms offering great sea views. B&B is from £18 per person. Nearby *Hafan* (☎ 810481, Raglan St) charges from £17 per person.

The *White Lion* (☎ 810589), opposite the castle, offers basic pub accommodation from £17.50 and is your best bet for a reasonably priced single room, a scarce commodity around town.

The top place in Beaumaris is the *Bulkeley Hotel* (☎ 810415, Castle St), a rather

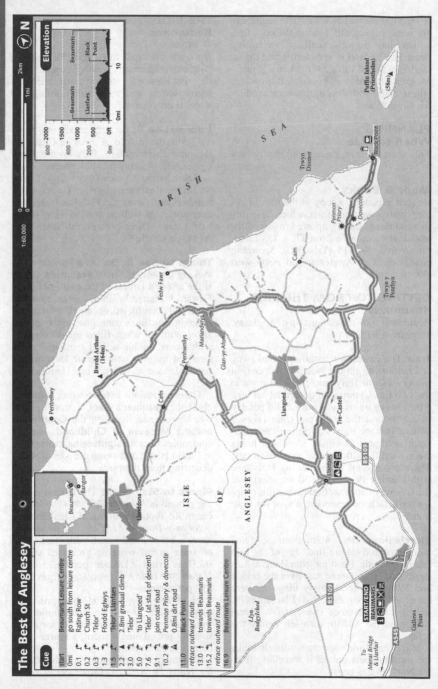

The Best of Anglesey

1:60,000

0   1mi
0   2km

N

Elevation

Cue	
start	Beaumaris Leisure Centre
0mi	go south from leisure centre
0.1	Rating Row
0.2	Church St
0.3	'Telor'
1.3	Ffordd Eglwys
1.5	'Telor', Llanfaes
2.2	2.8mi gradual climb
3.0	'Telor'
5.0	'to Llangoed'
7.6	'Telor' (at start of descent)
9.1	join coast road
10.2	Penmon Priory & dovecote
	0.8mi dirt road
11.0	Black Point
	retrace outward route
13.0	towards Beaumaris
15.2	towards Beaumaris
	retrace outward route
16.9	Beaumaris Leisure Centre

grand Georgian establishment. Most of the rooms enjoy spectacular views over the Menai Strait. Rooms start at £35 per person.

The old-world facade of the *Ye Olde Bulls Head Inn* (☎ 810329) hides a stylish, modern brasserie within. Most main dishes on the interesting and inventive menu are less then £8. There's also a very good, more formal restaurant upstairs.

The four-course set menu at the restaurant in the *Bulkeley Hotel* features an upmarket traditional selection and costs £17.50 a head.

The *Liverpool Arms*, on Castle St, and the *Sailor's Return*, on Church St, are the pick of the local watering holes, with decent pub grub for under £6.

The Best of Anglesey
1½–2½ hours, 16.9mi
The well-signed route begins from the Beaumaris Leisure Centre, a few hundred yards from the TIC on Castle St. The quiet lane, which climbs gently away from town towards Llanfaes, affords a spectacular view of Beaumaris Castle, with green fields in the foreground and the peaks of Snowdonia behind. High hazel hedges on either side of the road act as an effective buffer from the wind, which often blows hard.

A summit is reached on the outskirts of Llanddona, although the road continues to undulate. Head towards a tall communications mast, from where a spectacular vista of Red Wharf Bay, Menai Strait and the peaks of the mainland unfolds.

The fine view continues as the route gradually descends. Don't miss the turn-off on the left at 7.6mi, near the top of a steep descent. At 9.1mi turn left on to the road out to Black Point. This is a dead end, so you will have to backtrack to this point, but the sights encountered over the next few miles make it well worth the effort.

The road to Black Point soon meets the coast, before leading to a scattering of heritage buildings at the site of **Penmon Priory**. Along the way, enjoy fabulous views over the Menai Strait all the way to Llandudno's Great Orme, a spectacular limestone headland.

The former monastic outpost, which is still considered by many to be a very holy place, was initially established on nearby Puffin Island, but was moved to Penmon by the 6th-century head of the monastery, St

Seiriol. Many of the original buildings were razed by the Danes in the 10th century. The original wooden church was destroyed in 971, although its 12th-century replacement remains intact and is still used today. If you have a good look around the Penmon site you'll also see the ruins of the Priory refectory, the holy well and St Seiriol's cell.

A magnificent dome-roofed **dovecote**, built around 1600 to house a thousand pairs of birds, sits at the start of the short, dirt toll road (bikes free) out to Black Point, the easternmost point on Anglesey.

At the end of the road there's a small *cafe* from where you can relax and gaze out across the short stretch of water separating Puffin Island (Priestholm) from the mainland. Puffin Island is an important nesting site for a number of seabirds, including its namesake. For a closer look, jump on one of the tour boats that cast off from Beaumaris pier.

After backtracking to the Black Point turn-off, the lane turns inland and climbs briefly. Cross the B5109 and enter Llanfaes for the second time, retracing the first leg of the route back into Beaumaris. For a change of scenery, take the B5109 back into town. It's not as quiet but is fairly scenic, following the coast.

Views from the Valley

Duration	2 days
Distance	36.2mi
Difficulty	moderate-hard
Start/End	Conwy

Keeping to the scenic, wooded hills as much as the picturesque Conwy Valley itself, this short but challenging ride is a spectacular but manageable introduction to north-west Wales' mountainous interior.

The route is far from flat, however, with some very challenging sections on both days – accounting for the relatively short distances of each. The tour could be done as a strenuous day ride, especially if you leave your panniers in Conwy, but is best ridden as described, leaving plenty of time for some mountain biking or walks through the beautiful forests around Betws-y-Coed.

Much of the route follows the signposted (brown-and-white markers) Conwy Valley Cycle Route, which consists of two circuits originating from Llanrwst, one heading north to Conwy, the other south to Penmachno.

PLANNING
When to Ride
This is an enjoyable ride at most times of year, although summer obviously provides better opportunities for enjoying the many outdoor activities on offer. Betws-y-Coed is very popular, so book ahead, especially on weekends and during holiday periods.

Maps & Books
OS Landranger map No 115 (1:50,000), *Snowdon*, covers the Conwy Valley and northwest Wales, including most of Anglesey.

GETTING TO/FROM THE RIDE
Only selected Ffestiniog Railway (☎ 01766-512340) services have room for bikes (£3), so try to call ahead if you're using the service.

Conwy
Bus From London, there are two National Express (☎ 0870-5808080) services a day. There's also frequent buses between Llandudno, Bangor and Caernarfon. But only folding bikes in bags will be carried.

Train Conwy's small train station is now only used by regional trains. Llandudno Junction, about a mile away (just over the River Conwy), is the closest station on the North Wales coastal railway line to Holyhead. About five trains run from Cardiff a day (3¾–5¼ hours). There are a few trains a day from Conwy (£1.20, 4 minutes).

Betws-y-Coed
Train Betws-y-Coed is on the Conwy Valley railway line, connecting Llandudno and Llandudno Junction to Blaenau Ffestiniog. There are several services daily from Llandudno (£3.40, 39 minutes). It's possible to continue south from Blaenau Ffestiniog by catching the very scenic narrow-gauge Ffestiniog Railway through to Porthmadog, a port of call on the Lôn Las Cymru ride described earlier in this chapter.

THE RIDE
Conwy
☎ 01492
Conwy, at the mouth of the River Conwy, is a picturesque and interesting little town,

dominated by a superb castle, one of the grandest of Edward I's fortresses and a medieval masterpiece.

Information The Conwy TIC (☎ 592248), not to be confused with the Conwy Visitors Centre selling souvenirs by the train station, sits at the base of the castle and serves as the castle visitor centre and ticket office.

There's no bike shop in town – the closest being Aberconwy Cycles (☎ 573334, 47 Station Rd), over the river in Deganwy (a couple of miles away) – but Conwy Outdoor (☎ 593390, Castle St) hires bikes (£12/7 full/half day) and a few accessories.

Things to See & Do Even if you're all castled out, **Conwy Castle** is a must. Looking every bit like a castle should: massive, imposing and impregnable, Conwy's Castle vies with Caernarfon's as Wales' most spectacular fortress. It was built for Edward I from 1282 to 1287. The interior is mostly a ruin but there are some fantastic views from the top of the dizzyingly high towers. The informative guided tour is well worth the £1.

Conwy's **town walls** make it one of the finest remaining examples of a medieval walled town in Europe. Stretching for three-quarters of a mile, there are 22 towers and three original gateways. You can walk along a large section of them.

Other worthwhile activities include a look at **Aberconwy House**, a 14th-century timber and plaster building restored by the National Trust (NT), and a **walk** along the harbour front, more for the fetching river views than the various dubious amusements and much photographed **Smallest House in Britain**.

Places to Stay & Eat Camping sites are available at the *Conwy Touring Park (☎ 592 856)*, on the route about 1.2mi south of town on the B5106. Pitches cost £7 per night for two people.

The *Conwy YHA (☎ 593571, Sychnant Pass Rd)* seems disproportionately large for the size of the town, but that's no bad thing as it's a real beauty – spacious, well equipped and with some superb views. Dorms are small and all have showers; beds are £10.15. It's a short ride from the town centre.

For proximity to the castle, the *Town House (☎ 596454, Rosehill St)* is hard to beat, with B&B from £13.50 per person.

Pen-y-Bryn (☎ 596445), above the tea-rooms on High St, is excellent, with B&B from £17 per person (£19 with bath).

The **Castle Hotel** (☎ 592324, High St), the best in town, has singles/doubles for £65/75.

The **Galleon Fish and Chip Shop** (cnr High & Castle Sts) won the 1997 'Best Fish and Chip Shop in Wales' award. It's popular and has a nice eat-in area. Also on High St, **Edwards** is a bakery and deli with a tempting range of bread, cheese, pies and sandwiches – good for lunch or stocking up for a picnic.

There aren't many good places to eat. Try **Alfredo** (☎ 592381), on the square at the top of High St, for fairly standard but decent-value Italian fare; most dishes are under £6.

At the top end, the **Shakespeare** restaurant in the Castle Hotel offers an upmarket, traditional two-course set meal for £12.50. The bar meals are quite good and reasonably priced at under £6.

Day 1: Conwy to Betws-y-Coed
1¾–2½ hours, 16.1mi
You would think a ride along a valley would be pretty flat. Much of this leg, however, meanders through the hills to the east of the valley floor, making for a tough ride most of the way to Llanrwst.

The B5106 starts to climb shortly after leaving the TIC, and it's not long before the first of a series of brown-and-white markers sign the way to the Conwy Valley Cycle Route. Keep an eye out for these as the ride follows the signed route right through to Llanrwst.

The B5106 isn't particularly busy but it's nice all the same to turn off (at 2.5mi) onto a quiet lane that climbs steadily, providing some good views of the broad River Conwy (Afon Conwy) away to the left.

A swift descent brings you alongside the waterway after 4.3mi; cross to the other bank, entering the village of Tal-y-Cafn. This is where the killer hill of the day commences, an unrelenting 1.6mi climb, so steep in places you may have to get off and push.

Beyond the small lake, Llyn Syberi – a popular local fishing hole and a nice place to rest – the road emerges from the trees, providing an appreciation of the height you've gained. There are some fine views of the valley below and the bald high peaks of Snowdonia to the west. Most of the remaining miles to Llanrwst are mercifully downhill.

The main commercial centre of the Conwy Valley, Llanrwst is a pleasant, sizeable place without the touristy feel of its near neighbours. The shady park – just over the small humpbacked Pont Mawr bridge, attributed to the renowned architect and local lad, Inigo Jones – is an ideal place to break for lunch.

Just out of town is **Gwydir Castle** (13mi). More of a manor house than a true castle, it's the ancestral home of the Wynn family, still big landholders in the area. The early Tudor building, currently undergoing a lengthy restoration, is open to the public and makes an interesting stop if you're keen on stately homes.

The final few relatively flat miles into Betws-y-Coed along the B5106 pass quickly and it almost comes as a surprise to round a bend and see the sign welcoming you to town.

Betws-y-Coed
☎ 01690
Betus (as it's known and pronounced) has been Wales' most popular inland resort since Victorian days, and it still pulls in the crowds over summer. Walkers flock to the town to enjoy its picturesque woodland setting and tramp along the numerous trails snaking through the Gwydir Forest. The centre of town swells with sightseers enjoying cream teas and checking out the latest kit in the numerous outdoor equipment shops lining the main thoroughfare.

Information The TIC and the National Park Information Centre (☎ 710426) are in the Royal Oak Stables, at the far end of the playing fields past the train station.

Beics Betws (☎ 710766), in Tan Lan, behind the post office, has a good range of mountain bikes for hire (£16 per day) and does repairs.

Things to See & Do The best way to explore the **Gwydir Forest** is on a mountain bike. Forest Enterprise has commendably signposted two specific off-road routes, making use of the numerous trails that wind between the pines. The northern circuit starts just over the Pont-y-Pair bridge, with the southern ride starting a little farther down the road by Miners' Bridge. Permits to cycle in the forest are available from the TIC and

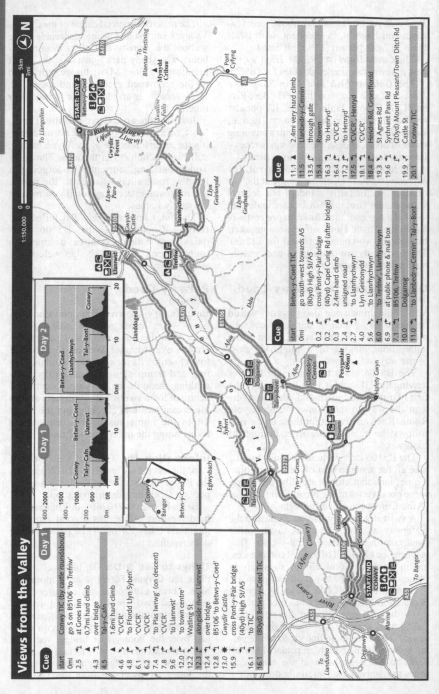

Views from the Valley

Day 1

Cue		
start		Conwy TIC (by castle roundabout)
0mi		go S on B5106 'to Trefriw'
2.5	◤	at Groes Inn
4.3	↰	0.7mi hard climb
		over bridge
4.5	↰	Tal-y-Cafn
		1.6mi hard climb
4.6	↱	'CVCR'
4.8	↱	'to Ffordd Llyn Syberi'
6.1	↰	'CVCR'
6.2	↱	'CVCR'
7.4	↰	'to Plas Iwrwg' (on descent)
7.8	↱	'CVCR'
9.6	↱	'to Llanrwst'
12.0	↰	'to town centre'
12.2	↱	Watling St
12.3		alongside river, Llanrwst
12.4	↰	over bridge
12.8	↱	B5106 to Betws-y-Coed
13.0	✳	Gwydir Castle
15.9	↱	cross Pont-y-Pair bridge
		(40yd) High St/A5
16.1	↰	'to TIC'
16.1		(80yd) Betws-y-Coed TIC

Cue		
start		Betws-y-Coed TIC
0mi		go south-west towards A5
		(80yd) High St/A5
0.2	↰	cross Pont-y-Pair bridge
0.2	↱	(40yd) Capel Curig Rd (after bridge)
0.3	↱	unsigned road
2.4		2.4mi hard climb
2.4	↰	'to Llanhychwyn'
2.7	↱	Llyn Geirionydd
4.0	↱	'to Llanhychwyn'
5.6	↰	'to Trefriw', Llanhychwyn
6.0	↰	at public phone & mail box
6.9	↱	B5106, Trefriw
7.1	↰	Dolgarrog
10.0		
11.0	↰	'to Llanbedr-y-Cennin', Tal-y-Bont

Cue		
11.1	◤	2.4mi very hard climb
11.5	↰	Llanbedr-y-Cennin
13.5	↱	through gate
15.4		Rowen
16.3	↱	'to Henryd'
16.4	↱	'CVCR'
17.2	↰	'to Henryd'
17.5	↱	'CVCR', Henryd
18.1	↰	'CVCR'
18.4		Hendre Rd, Groesffordd
19.3	↰	St Agnes Rd
19.6	↱	Sychnant Pass Rd
19.9		(20yd) Mount Pleasant/Town Ditch Rd
		Castle St
20.1		Conwy TIC

Beics Betws (see Information). Forest Enterprise also produces a map of the trails – pick one up from the TIC or Cotswold Outdoor, in town on the A5, for £2.

Most people come to Betws-y-Coed to walk and there is no shortage of great walks in the surrounding hills. The popular **Bridges & Rivers walk** is an easy walk that takes two to three hours, starting from outside the TIC. Pass the confluence of the Rivers Llugwy and Conwy and continue to Waterloo Bridge (built in 1815), then follow the river to Pont-y-Pair, the 15th-century Bridge of the Cauldron and finally to Miners' Bridge. Drop in at the TIC for details of many other local walks.

Places to Stay & Eat You can pitch a tent at the *Riverside Caravan & Camping Park* (☎ 710310), just behind the train station.

Betws-y-Coed has an enormous number of hotels and B&Bs, offering ample choice in most price brackets.

There aren't any youth hostels in town but two are relatively close, each about 5mi away. *Ledr Valley YHA* (☎ 750202, Pont-y-Pant) is on the A470 south-west of town (£8.35), and *Capel Curig YHA* (☎ 720225) is west of Betws-y-Coed on the A5, near the A4086 junction (£9.15).

In town, *Summer Hill* (☎ 710306) is a comfortable nonsmoking guest house in a nice central location overlooking the River Llugwy, just west of the Pont-y-Pair bridge. B&B costs £17 per person. The excellent *Bron Celyn Guest House* (☎ 710333, Llanrwst Rd) charges from £20 for B&B.

Ty Gwyn (☎ 710383), just over the Waterloo Bridge, is a 17th-century coaching inn with cosy rooms and a nice bar. Standard rooms are from £17, although you can pay up to £45 for one with a four-poster bed.

The town isn't as well endowed with places to eat as it is with places to stay. For a cheap feed try *Dil's Diner* (☎ 710346), by the train station entrance, which has generous serves of simple fare such as fish and chips for under £5.

The Stables (☎ 710219), attached to the Royal Oak Hotel, is a lively place with a large, relaxed outdoor area and a good selection of reasonably priced meals, mostly for around £7. There's also live jazz and a male voice choir a couple of nights a week.

The top place in town to eat is the restaurant at *Ty Gwyn*, which serves up superb gourmet dishes at around £12 for a main. The bar food is also excellent.

Day 2: Betws-y-Coed to Conwy
2–3 hours, 20.1mi

Like the Day 1 leg, this stage (although relatively short) can be tough at times, with a couple of steep, long climbs to tackle. Leave Betws-y-Coed via the Pont-y-Pair bridge. The quiet road shadows the River Llugwy as it climbs, steeply at times, up into the pines of the tranquil Gwydir Forest. The route levels and arrives at picturesque **Llyn Geirionydd**, an incredibly pretty lake surrounded by forest, popular with local waterskiers.

Hard-won height is shed rapidly on an exhilarating descent down from the hills, dropping back to the valley floor at the village of Trefriw. The next few miles of flat cycling along the B5106 give you a chance to catch your breath for the tough ascent ahead.

Leaving the B5106 behind at Tal-y-Bont, it's time to head for the hills yet again. If you're not feeling very energetic, turn right opposite the pub in Llanbedr-y-Cennin (11.5mi) and follow a less strenuous route (signed 'Conwy Valley Route') to Rowen.

Slogging up the hill, however, your extra efforts are soon rewarded with some memorable views back over the valley with the coast, Conwy and the bald higher peaks of Snowdonia's Carneddau Range all in view.

The tough 2.4mi climb propels you to a lofty 951ft/290m, summiting as you strike off along a gated road through pastures of grazing sheep. You can relax on the steep descent into Rowen – just keep an eye out for oncoming traffic on the narrow lane.

Rowen is a peaceful place with a simple *youth hostel* (☎ 01492 650089) if you feel like staying. Open from April to September, it charges £8.50 for a bed. Entering Rowen, turn left and follow the hostel sign; the hostel is just out of the village. Be warned, however, that it's at the top of a very steep hill. (So steep, in fact, that the caretaker has only ever seen one person successfully cycle up it – feeling fit?)

The remaining miles into Conwy are very pleasant and relatively easy; travel on quiet roads through the tiny settlements of Henryd and Groesffordd. A quick trip through busy streets leads back to the TIC, the magnificent castle and the end of the tour.

Northern England

The overall impression you get cycling through northern England is of rugged open space. Apart from Newcastle, Durham and Carlisle there are very few towns of any real size. The big attraction is the countryside itself, and cycling is the perfect way to explore.

As a rule the landscapes here are harder and more rugged than in the south – perhaps a reflection of history: just about every inch has been fought over. The central conflict was the long struggle between Scotland and England, with the battle lines shifting over the centuries.

The north-east is comprised of North Yorkshire, Durham and Northumberland, while over the Pennines, the county of Cumbria occupies England's north-west corner. Magnificent national parks abound. From North Yorkshire's world famous Yorkshire Dales and North York Moors, to the splendid isolation of Northumberland National Park and the legendary beauty of the Lake District, in this part of the world it's not hard to find yourself alone pedalling through some incredibly pretty scenery. Throw in Yorkshire's stately homes and abbeys, Northumberland's coast and castles, the urban vibrancy of Newcastle and World Heritage-listed Hadrian's Wall, and it's easy to see why this is a top cycling destination.

HISTORY

In the years before the Roman invasion, the area from the River Humber to the Firth of Forth was ruled by a confederation of Celtic tribes known as Brigantes. The Romans were the first to attempt to delineate a border with Hadrian's Wall in AD 122, but the struggle between north and south didn't end until the Act of Unity in the 18th century.

In the 9th century the Danes made York their capital and ruled the Danelaw (all of England north and east of a line between Chester and London). Later, William the Conqueror found the north to be rebellious and difficult, and responded with brutal thoroughness. After 500 knights were massacred at Durham, he burnt York and Durham and devastated the surrounding countryside. It took the north generations to recover.

In Summary

Terrain
Generally harder and more rugged than in the south: mostly hilly with larger peaks in the Northern Pennines, Yorkshire Dales and Lake District; gentle hills and low-lying plains along the east coast, with the exception of the high uplands of the North York Moors.

Special Events
- **Keswick Jazz Festival** (May)
- **Cockermouth Festival** (July)
- **Sunderland International Air Show** (July)
- **Great Yorkshire Show** (July), Harrogate
- **Alnwick International Music & Dance Festival** (August)

Food & Drink Specialities
- Cumberland sausage
- Yorkshire pudding
- Pan Haggerty (traditional Northumbrian supper)
- Wensleydale cheese
- Newcastle brown ale

Tourist Information
- **Yorkshire Tourist Board:** ☎ 01904-707961, 🖳 www.ytb.org.uk
- **Northumbria Tourist Board:** 🖳 www.ntb.org.uk
- Cumbria Tourist Board: 🖳 www .cumbria-the-lake-district.co.uk

Later the Normans left a legacy of spectacular fortresses and the marvellous Durham Cathedral. The region prospered on the medieval wool trade, which sponsored the great cathedral at York and enormous monastic communities, the remains of which can be seen at Rievaulx and Fountains Abbeys.

NATURAL HISTORY
The dominant geographic feature is the Pennine Hills that form a north-south spine

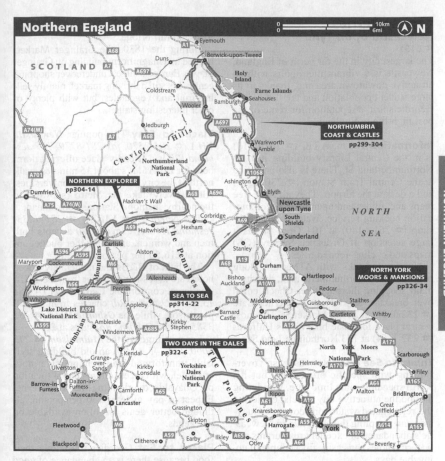

Northern England

0 ———— 10km
0 ———— 6mi

N

SCOTLAND

Eyemouth

Berwick-upon-Tweed

Duns

Coldstream

Holy
Island

Wooler

Bamburgh Seahouses

Farne Islands

**NORTHUMBRIA
COAST & CASTLES
pp299-304**

Jedburgh

Cheviot Hills

Alnwick

Warkworth
Amble

Northumberland
National
Park

A1

**NORTHERN EXPLORER
pp304-14**

Dumfries

Bellingham

Hadrian's Wall

Ashington

Blyth

Maryport

Carlisle

Haltwhistle

Hexham

Corbridge

Newcastle
upon Tyne

South
Shields

NORTH

Cockermouth

Alston

Stanley

Sunderland

Seaham

SEA

Workington

Penrith

Allenheads

**SEA TO SEA
pp314-22**

Bishop
Auckland

Durham

Hartlepool

Redcar

**NORTH YORK
MOORS & MANSIONS
pp326-34**

Whitehaven

Keswick

Appleby

Barnard
Castle

Middlesbrough

Guisborough

Staithes

Lake District
National Park

Ambleside

Kirkby
Stephen

Darlington

Castleton

Whitby

Windermere

Kendal

**TWO DAYS IN THE DALES
pp322-6**

Northallerton

North York Moors

Scarborough

Ulverston

Grange-
over-
Sands

Kirkby
Lonsdale

Yorkshire
Dales
National
Park

Thirsk

Helmsley

National Park

Pickering

Filey

Barrow-in-
Furness

Dalton-in-
Furness

Carnforth

Morecambe

Lancaster

Ripon

Malton

Bridlington

Fleetwood

Grassington

Skipton

Knaresborough

Harrogate

York

Great
Driffield

Blackpool

Clitheroe

Earby

Ilkley

Otley

Beverley

NORTHERN ENGLAND

dividing the region, with Cumbria and Lancashire to the west and Yorkshire, Durham and
Northumberland to the east. Even away
from the Pennines much of the region is
hilly with plenty of challenging climbs in
and around the Lake District, the Yorkshire
Dales and Moors, as well as Northumberland's Cheviot Hills. The Scottish border
traces a diagonal line south-west from
Berwick-upon-Tweed.

INFORMATION
Maps & Books

Northern England covers quite a large area,
but in conjunction with the maps in this
book, the OS Travelmaster series maps
(1:250,000) No 4, *Southern Scotland and
Northumberland*; and No 5, *Northern Eng-*

land, should prove more than adequate for
all the rides.

Information Sources

A number of the region's tourist authorities
have Web sites. The Northumbria Tourist
Board's is excellent (💻 www.ntb.org.uk)
with piles of tips on what to see and do, as
well as accommodation listings and general
information on the region. For information
specifically on cycle touring in Northumbria,
visit Cycle Northumbria's Web site (💻 www
.cyclenorth.org.uk). General information for
Yorkshire is at the Yorkshire Tourist Board's
site (💻 www.ytb.org.uk). For Cumbria and
the Lake District, visit 💻 www.cumbria-the-la
ke-district.co.uk, or the LakesNET Web site
at 💻 www.lakesnet.co.uk.

GATEWAY CITIES
Newcastle upon Tyne
☎ 0191

The largest city in the far north of England, Newcastle is a vibrant metropolis with an attractive downtown area and, thanks to its large student population and the fun-loving Geordie spirit, a reputation for some of the best nightlife in England.

Information The main TIC (☎ 261 0610) is in the Central Library building just off Northumberland St. There is also an office at the Central Train Station (☎ 230 0030) and a desk at the airport. They all have free maps and guides and operate an accommodation booking service. Waterstones bookshop (☎ 261 6140) at 104 Grey St has a large selection of Ordnance Survey (OS) maps and cycling-related titles.

Numerous banks with ATMs are along pedestrianised Northumberland St, the city's main shopping thoroughfare. Check email over breakfast at McNulty's Internet Cafe (☎ 232 0922) at 26–30 Market St. The most central place for basic bike bits is Halfords (☎ 232 1164) at 143 Northumberland St.

Things to See & Do Newcastle isn't overflowing with specific attractions, but it's worth spending some time here. Wandering around the attractive city streets, exploring the rejuvenated waterfront down at Quayside and sampling the local fare in Newcastle's abundance of excellent restaurants and watering holes can easily fill a couple of enjoyable days.

Castle Garth is the 'new castle' from which the city gets its name. The original was built from wood but the 'new' construction dates from 1168. Visit the well-preserved keep, which has some good views and interesting exhibits detailing the history of the city.

The best vantage point from which to take in the famous view of the **six bridges over the Tyne** is the water. Sightseeing cruises run from the Quayside pier – the TIC has details. Of the six spans, the **Tyne Bridge**, strongly resembling the Sydney Harbour Bridge in Australia and constructed at about the same time from 1925–28, is the most famous. Rail buffs however will be particularly interested in the **High Level Bridge** designed by Robert Stephenson, which, when opened in 1849, was the world's first combined road-and-rail bridge.

During the 1830s the **Grainger Market**, housed in a magnificent building on Grainger St, was Europe's largest undercover shopping centre. It's still a thriving market, mainly selling fruit and vegetables, but with plenty of other interesting stalls.

Places to Stay The popular *Newcastle YHA* (☎ 281 2570, fax 281 8779, 107 Jesmond Rd) is a friendly place offering dorm beds for £10.15. It's about 15 minutes' walk north of the city centre, past the universities. Alternatively, take the Metro (subway) to the nearby Jesmond Station. Book ahead.

The *North East YMCA* (☎ 281 1233, Jesmond House, Clayton Rd) accepts both men and women, and is another budget option at £16.50 per person.

The bulk of B&Bs and moderately priced hotels are in Jesmond, not far from the YHA. The large, comfortable *Cairn Hotel* (☎ 281 1358, 97 Osborne Rd) charges from £27.50 per person, while the *Osborne Hotel* (☎ 281 3385, 13–15 Osborne Rd) starts at £25.

For a splurge try the *Malmaison* (☎ 245 5000, fax 245 4545), an old building stylishly transformed into an impressive modern hotel, with an excellent central location on Quayside overlooking the River Tyne. Expect to pay at least £60 per person, although better deals are often available on weekends.

Places to Eat Geordies must love their food because there is an abundance of good places to eat. Dozens of restaurants run along Grey and Dean Sts, down to the waterfront at Quayside. Many offer early-bird specials before 7 pm.

For lunches, pick up everything you need for a tasty picnic at the *Grainger Market (Grainger St)*. The top floor of the *Monument Mall* shopping centre has a food court and all the *fast food* giants are represented along Northumberland and Grey Sts.

Most of the pubs down on Quayside also serve meals. Try *Flynns Bar*, the *Pump House*, *Bob Trollop* or the *Red House*, which have meals for around £3.

The *Fox Talbot Cafe* (☎ 230 2229, 46 Dean St) is a good place to grab a coffee, light lunch or an evening meal. The arty decor is complemented by friendly service and a good selection of wines. Lunch items are around £3 with evening mains from £6 to £9. Down on Quayside, *Casa* is an ultra-trendy bar-cafe with pasta around £6 and other mains from £6 to £9. The food is good, as is the view – sip a drink in one of their comfy lounge chairs while taking in the marvellous sight of the bridges over the Tyne. *The Metropolitan (☎ 230 2306, 35 Grey St)* is a modern, stylish brasserie housed in one of the handsome old office buildings lining the street. It boasts a modern, innovative menu with mains around £13. Early birds can enjoy a good selection of dishes for a very civilised £3.50, although servings can be a bit on the small side for a hungry cyclist.

Getting There & Away Newcastle is a major transport hub so there are plenty of ways to get in and out of the city. It's 275mi from London (about 5 hours by car), 105mi from Edinburgh and 57mi from Carlisle.

Air Newcastle international airport (☎ 286 0966) is 7mi north of the city, linked by the Metro subway system (folding or boxed bikes only) and 20 minutes by car off the A696. There are scheduled services to most major cities in Britain and Ireland as well as Oslo, Amsterdam, Brussels and Paris.

Train Newcastle is on the main London-Edinburgh line as well as the scenic Tyne Valley line west to Carlisle.

destination	one way	hours	frequency
Berwick	£10.00	¾	two/hr
Edinburgh	£29.50	1½	two/hr
Carlisle	£8.30	1¼	hourly
York	£10.50	1	two/hr
London	£72.00	3	two/hr

Sea Newcastle is one of England's major ferry ports with scheduled crossings to Scandinavia, Germany and the Netherlands. Color Line (☎ 0191-296 1313, 🖥 www.colorline .com) has two to three sailings per week to the Norwegian ports of Bergen, Stavanger and Haugesund. DFDS Seaways (☎ 0870-533 3000, 🖥 www.dfdsseaways.co.uk) has routes to Kristiansand, Gothenburg, Amsterdam and Hamburg. The ferry terminal is in North Shields.

Bicycle The route north along the coast to Berwick-upon-Tweed is described in the Northumbria Coast & Castles ride in this chapter. The route west to Whitehaven via Allenheads, Penrith and Keswick is covered in the Sea to Sea ride.

Carlisle
☎ 01228

Although modern-day Carlisle (population 72,000) may be a bit of a sleepy town, for 1600 years it defended either the north of England, or the south of Scotland, depending on who was winning. Today its strategic position and excellent rail links make it a good base for trips out to the nearby Lake District, Hadrian's Wall and Eden Valley.

Information The TIC (☎ 512444) in Town Hall Square is open year round and has piles of leaflets on Carlisle and nearby Hadrian's Wall. It also has a very handy secure bicycle

The Border Reivers

People who fret about the modern-day crime wave should thank their lucky stars they didn't live in the Border Lands during the 400 years when the rapacious Reivers were king.

The Reivers were brigands whose backgrounds differed but who had in common a complete disregard for the governments of England and Scotland. For the Reivers, sheep rustling and burning the homes of their enemies was a way of life. As a result, northern Cumbria and Northumberland, the southern Scottish Borders and Dumfries & Galloway are littered with minor castles and tower-houses, as people struggled to protect themselves.

It wasn't until James VI of Scotland succeeded Elizabeth I of England and united the two countries that order was finally reasserted.

The Reivers are credited with giving the words 'blackmail' and 'bereaved' to the English language. And if your surname is Armstrong, Carruthers, Dixon, Elliot, Nixon, Henderson, Johnstone, Maxwell, Scott, Taylor, Wilson or Young, genealogists would have us believe you could be descended from a Reiver.

storage area (£1.50 per day). There is a cluster of banks with ATMs on Bank St, just off pedestrianised English St, the main shopping thoroughfare. The train station is about 400yd south of Town Hall Square, just off Botchergate.

Palace Cycles (☎ 523142) at 122 Botchergate is well stocked and has a good workshop. Internet access is available in the public library, upstairs in the Lanes shopping complex.

Things to See & Do A well-preserved fortress that played a key role in numerous English/Scottish border disputes over the centuries, **Carlisle Castle** (☎ 591880, EH) is well worth exploring. There are some great views over the town from the walls and ramparts and the displays inside provide an informative history of the area's turbulent past. Mary Queen of Scots was briefly imprisoned here in 1568.

For a more complete history, the **Tullie House Museum** (☎ 534781), across the road from the castle, has a number of excellent collections detailing Carlisle's Roman past and the activities of the lawless Border Reivers (see the boxed text). The **Carlisle Cathedral**, a handsome red sandstone structure completed in 1133, is also well worth a look.

Places to Stay Pitch a tent from £6 at the **Dalston Hall Caravan Park** (☎ 710165), to the south of the city, just off the B5299. Although it's a fair ride out of Carlisle itself, the camping ground is well equipped and on the route to Cockermouth.

The **Carlisle YHA** (☎/fax 597352), on Bridge Lane, just west of the castle in the old Theakstons Brewery, operates during the summer (July to September) from the student residences of the University of Northumbria. Comfortable single rooms in self-contained flats cost £12 per night.

There are a number of B&Bs close to the centre of town. **Stratheden** (☎ 520192, 93 Warwick Rd) is small and friendly with pleasantly decorated rooms from £16 per person. Nearby **Cornerways Guest House** (☎ 521733, 107 Warwick Rd) is larger and does B&B from £14.

The upmarket **Crown and Mitre** (☎ 525 491) is pricey at £84/109 a single/double, but is rather grand and commands an excellent position overlooking the Town Hall Square.

Places to Eat There are several *fast food* places across from the train station. A number of restaurants offer happy-hour specials before 7 pm. Try **Zorba's Greek Taverna** (☎ 592227, 68 Warwick Rd) with early-bird mains under £4, or nearby **Casa Romana** (☎ 591969) where pizza and pasta mains average around £5; cheaper before 7 pm. **Le Gall** (☎ 818388, 7 Devonshire St) is a modern cafe-bar with an eclectic menu featuring Mexican, ribs and pasta for around £6 and various gourmet sandwiches at £3.95. The coffee is also good.

Getting There & Away Carlisle is 295mi from London, 98mi from Edinburgh, 95mi from Glasgow, 115mi from York and Manchester and 58mi from Newcastle upon Tyne.

Train Carlisle is a major regional train terminus serviced by all the main London-Glasgow, Leeds-Settle-Carlisle, Lakes, Tyne Valley and Cumbrian Coast lines. Services from Carlisle include:

destination	one way	hours	frequency
Edinburgh	£21.50	1½	hourly
Glasgow	£21.50	1½	hourly
Leeds	£25.80	3½	hourly
London	£79.00	4	hourly
Newcastle	£8.30	1¼	hourly
Whitehaven	£6.85	1	hourly

England's Far North

England's most northerly areas are among the least populated and, perhaps unfairly, among the least visited in the country.

While many visitors simply breeze through on their way to Scotland, on no account should cyclists follow suit as this is prime cycling country. Wild rugged landscapes, lonely roads and an absolute feast of historic attractions – a legacy of the area's strategic importance in the bitter border wars – make each of the three routes listed in this section – which can be ridden in a large continuous circuit – a must.

Northumbria Coast & Castles

Duration	2 days
Distance	107.0mi
Difficulty	easy-moderate
Start	Newcastle upon Tyne
End	Berwick-upon-Tweed

Northumberland is one of the wildest, least spoilt of England's counties, and thanks to its strategic position adjoining the Scottish border, home to more castles and battlefield sites than just about anywhere in the country. This relatively easy two-day ride heads north from Newcastle, following country lanes and coastal paths on the journey up to the border city of Berwick-upon-Tweed. Mighty fortresses at Warkworth, Alnwick, Dunstanburgh and Bamburgh provide ample sightseeing opportunities en route.

Although Day 1 of the ride provides a vivid insight into Tyneside's industrial heritage, the first half isn't particularly scenic. If you're short on time or want to skip straight to some excellent cycling country, catch the train from Newcastle to Widdrington station (£3.60, 30 minutes), and join the route as it runs along the coast at Druridge Bay. Alnmouth station (£5.20, 26 minutes), is the closest to Alnwick.

PLANNING
When to Ride

Although locals flock to the coast over summer, Northumberland's charms remain largely undiscovered by the rest of the country, making this a ride that can be enjoyed when roads in tourist hot spots such as the Lake District are choked with visitors. The longer daylight hours and warmer days between June and September offer the best touring conditions. The winter months can be bleak, with many attractions closed from November to March.

Maps & Books

If you're starting out from, or spending some time in, central Newcastle, the *Tyneside Cycling Map* by Cyclecity Guides is a handy and thorough companion. It details over 500mi of the most cycle-friendly routes throughout the city, simplifying the not-so-simple task of navigating the first leg of the

tour to Tynemouth. Look for it in bookshops or ask at local TICs.

The OS Map 14 Touring Map No 14 *Northumbria* (1:158,400), covers the whole region in excellent detail and is likely to prove invaluable for providing reassurance on some of the trickier navigational sections of the ride. Once in Berwick, pick up a copy of the lavish *Earth, Sea, Air, Fire* brochure from the TIC, containing extensive listings of accommodation in the surrounding area.

What to Bring

Several sections of the ride make use of bumpy bridleways (for use by walkers, horse riders and cyclists) and sandy coastal tracks. Although these are for the most part rideable on a touring bike, if you have the option, it's best to dust off your mountain bike for this ride.

GETTING TO/FROM THE RIDE
Newcastle

See the Gateway Cities section (pp296–7) for information on getting to/from Newcastle.

Berwick-upon-Tweed

Train Berwick is on the main east-coast London-Edinburgh line. There are frequent services north to Edinburgh and south to Newcastle and beyond. Most services require a reservation, arranged at the station, to be made for your bike at an additional cost of £3. Services from Berwick include:

destination	one way	hours
Edinburgh	£11.10	¾
London Kings Cross	£78.00	4
Newcastle	£10.00	¾
York	£29.00	1¾

Bicycle The route to Wooler, Bellingham, Carlisle, Cockermouth and Whitehaven from Berwick is described in the Northern Explorer ride later in this chapter.

Day 1: Newcastle to Alnwick

4½–6 hours, 55.0mi
Although today's ride isn't too physically taxing, navigation, especially on the first leg from the city centre to Tynemouth, can be confusing with myriad traffic-free paths and moderately busy roads to negotiate. So

NORTHERN ENGLAND

NORTHERN ENGLAND

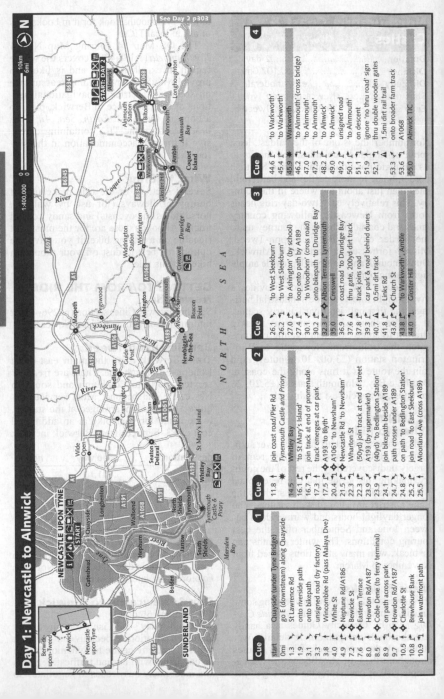

Day 1: Newcastle to Alnwick

See Day 2 p303

1:400,000

N

1

Cue	
start	Quayside (under Tyne Bridge)
0mi	go E (downstream) along Quayside
1.3	St Lawrence Rd
1.9	onto riverside path
3.1	onto bikepath
3.3	unsigned road (by factory)
3.8	Wincomblee Rd (pass Malaya Dve)
4.0	White St
4.9	Neptune Rd/A186
7.2	Bewicke St
7.6	Eastern Terrace
8.0	Howdon Rd/A187
8.5	Coble Dene (to ferry terminal)
8.9	on path across park
9.7	Howdon Rd/A187
10.5	Charlotte St
10.8	Brewhouse Bank
10.9	join waterfront path

2

Cue	
11.8	join coast road/Pier Rd
	Tynemouth Castle and Priory
14.5	Whitley Bay
16.1	'to St Mary's Island'
16.7	join track at end of promenade
17.3	track emerges at car park
17.5	A193 'to Blyth'
20.4	A1061 'to Newsham'
21.5	Newcastle Rd 'to Newsham'
22.3	Wharton St
22.3	(50yd) join track at end of street
23.9	A193 (by supermarket)
23.9	(40yd) to Bedlington Station'
24.1	join bikepath beside A189
24.7	path crosses under A189
24.8	on path 'to Bedlington Station'
25.2	join road to East Sleekburn'
25.5	Moorland Ave (cross A189)

3

Cue	
26.1	'to West Sleekburn'
26.2	'to West Sleekburn'
27.0	'to Ashington' (by school)
27.4	loop onto path by A189
30.1	'to Woodhorn' (cross road)
30.2	onto bikepath 'to Druridge Bay'
32.3	Albion Terrace, Lynemouth
35.0	Cresswell
36.9	coast road 'to Druridge Bay
37.6	thru gate, 200yd dirt track
37.8	track joins road
39.3	car park & road behind dunes
40.7	0.5mi dirt track
41.8	Links Rd
43.6	Church St
43.8	'to Warkworth', Amble
44.00	Gloster Hill

4

Cue	
44.6	'to Warkworth'
45.4	'to Warkworth'
45.9	Warkworth
46.2	'to Alnmouth' (cross bridge)
47.0	'to Alnmouth'
47.5	'to Alnmouth'
48.2	'to Alnwick'
49.0	'to Alnwick'
49.2	unsigned road
50.1	'to Alnmouth'
51.1	on descent
51.9	ignore 'no thru road' sign
52.1	thru double wooden gates
	1.5mi dirt rail trail
53.3	onto broader farm track
53.6	A1068
55.0	Alnwick TIC

long as you stick close to the River Tyne and keep heading east towards the coast, you can't go too far wrong. Keep an eye out for the blue No 72 and C2C markers that appear sporadically. As an alternative to the described route, you can also cycle along the southern bank of the Tyne, following the Keelmans way and C2C markers to Jarrow, where you cross back to the north bank using the Tyne Pedestrian Tunnel.

From Quayside, underneath the Tyne Bridge, follow the river-side path east past some new apartment and restaurant developments, with a brief stint on the road, before picking up the path again. The next few miles head through a rather bleak landscape of factories and industrial sites with occasional stretches on moderately busy roads.

Beyond the ferry terminal the route heads through North Shields before returning to the waterfront at Fish Quay. A pedestrian promenade leads the final mile to the official C2C end point marker, just across from **Tynemouth Castle and Priory** (☎ 0191-257 1090). The site, on a headland overlooking the mouth of the Tyne, contains the remnants of the castle walls and gatehouse within which stand the impressive remains of a Benedictine priory founded in 1090.

From Tynemouth, the road follows the coast through to the old-fashioned seaside resort of Whitley Bay. The wide promenade and the coast itself are rather nice but the string of hotels, boarding houses and restaurants on the opposite side of the road, like in so many English seaside resorts, look like they've seen better days. Pop music buffs will get a kick out of seeing the old amusement park, the Spanish City, the inspiration for a famous Dire Straits lyric.

The route follows the coast, passing **St Mary's Island** with its picture-perfect lighthouse (at low tide you can walk out to it), before turning inland through to Newsham, where a bumpy bridleway leads along the back of some houses, linking up with the A189.

A good cycle path, signed with blue NCN route markers, runs alongside the motorway, the signed route leading past various foul-smelling industrial installations to Lynemouth. Things finally start to look up when the route meets the coast, running just behind the dunes on quiet roads and scenic coastal tracks right through to Amble.

At Warkworth, see the first great **castle** (☎ 01665-711423) of the ride, a formidable 14th-century fortress with a large keep, full of narrow passageways and dark rooms to explore. The attractive village itself, situated on a loop of the River Coquet, is also well worth a look.

The route heads inland, climbing gently along quiet country lanes, following the cycle route signed to Alnmouth. Diverge from the marked route on the descent into Bilton (just short of Alnmouth train station), joining a bumpy railway path a short distance on that leads the remaining distance through to the outskirts of Alnwick.

Alnwick
☎ 01665

Alnwick (pronounced 'annick') is a charming market town that has grown up in the shadow of magnificent Alnwick Castle. The attractive old town still has a medieval feel with narrow cobbled streets and a market square.

Information Open year round, the Alnwick TIC (☎ 510665) is at the Shambles, in the central building opposite the market place. There are a number of banks with ATMs close by on Bondgate Within. Check email at the Barter Bookshop on South Rd or pick up bike spares at Geoff Saunders Cycles, close to the TIC at Pringles Yard.

Things to See & Do The Duke of the Northumberland's residence, **Alnwick Castle** (☎ 510777) is a must-see for castle fans. The home of the Percy family since 1309, it's the second-largest inhabited castle in England. The exterior looks much as it would have in the 14th century, but the magnificent state rooms are decorated in an Italian Renaissance style, with an impressive art collection featuring works by Titian, Canaletto and Van Dyck.

Alnwick also has one of Britain's largest second-hand bookshops. **The Barter Bookshop** (☎ 604888), in the old train station on South Rd opposite the hospital, has thousands of titles crammed into its expanse of shelves, priced from 30p. It's a browser's paradise.

Places to Stay & Eat A number of B&Bs and hotels are clustered on Bondgate Without, just outside the town's medieval gateway. The central ***Bondgate House Hotel***

(☎ *602025, 20 Bondgate Without)*, occupying a handsome Georgian building, offers B&B from £22 to £27 per person. *Aydon House (☎ 602218, South Rd)*, near the Barter Bookshop, has comfortable en suite rooms for £19 per person, and a tiny single for £17.

There are plenty of pubs in town serving food. The pick of them is the *Plough Hotel (☎ 602395, 20 Bondgate Without)*, which has a large meals area offering a good selection of generously proportioned meals, mostly under £6. A good place for a light meal, coffee or a drink is the *Wine Cellar*, a modern cafe attached to a liquor store near the TIC. Grab a bottle of wine off the well-stocked shelves and enjoy it at your table for an extra £2 corkage. Very civilised!

Day 2: Alnwick to Berwick-upon-Tweed
5–6 hours, 52.0mi

Although this is quite a long day, it's not too taxing with flat coastal terrain most of the way. Get an early start so you have plenty of time to enjoy the numerous sights along the route.

From Alnwick retrace back to Bilton, and beyond Boulmer join a coastal path to Craster, following (as for much of the day) the blue signs marking NCN 1. Although it is quite bumpy at times, the scenic traffic-free path running just behind the dunes is suitable for all but the most heavily laden of tourers. An alternative road route via Longhoughton is also signed.

After 12.5mi the route turns left towards Embleton although it's well worth making the 0.5mi side trip into Craster to visit **Dunstanburgh Castle** (☎ 1665-576231, EH; £1.80), a 14th-century fortress with a spectacular coastal backdrop. From Craster, it's a 1mi walk along a coastal path to the castle.

The route runs inland on a mix of traffic-free paths and quiet roads to Seahouses (25.4mi), a busy coastal resort and departure point for trips out to the Farne Islands, before following the coast to the seaside hamlet of Bamburgh.

Sitting atop a basalt crag rising from the sea, **Bamburgh Castle** (28.6mi; ☎ 01668-214515) is an awesome sight, its massive form dominating the coast for miles. Largely a late 19th-century creation of the Armstrong family, its interior isn't quite as impressive as some of the other castles of Northumbria.

Beyond Belford (34.8mi) navigation can be tricky with the route following a number of grassy bridleways and paths. At times you are literally riding through fields, making for a bumpy ride, especially if you don't have the benefit of fat tyres. Heavily laden tourers may prefer to stick to the on-road route between Belford and Detchant (37.9mi).

After crossing the A1 near Beal, follow a stony railway service road alongside the main Edinburgh line, before crossing (take care!) and following a road down to the Cheswick golf course. A grassy bridleway begins just before the rail line and runs parallel with it for around 1.9mi, emerging at a rough road by the coast. A short distance on, another very scenic bridleway heads along a narrow strip of grass hugging the tops of coastal cliffs, joining the bitumen again at Spittal (50.1mi).

The three bridges across the River Tweed make for an impressive first view of Berwick. Cross over the first, built in 1634, and after pushing your bike up one-way West St, emerge at Marygate, the town's prinicipal shopping street.

Side Trip: Holy Island
1 hour, 9.5mi return

Lying on the other side of a 3mi causeway and across fascinating muddy flats, tiny Holy Island is a beacon for tourists and can get very busy, even in the low season. St Aidan founded a monastery here in AD 635, and it became a major centre of Christianity and learning. The exquisitely illustrated *Lindisfarne Gospels*, which originated here can be seen in the British Library, in London. The two principal sights that everyone comes to see are **Lindisfarne Priory** (☎ 01289-389200, EH; £2.70/1.40), consisting of the remains of the priory's church and the 13th-century St Mary the Virgin Church; and **Lindisfarne Castle** (☎ 01289-389244, NT; £4), built in 1550 and restored by Sir Edward Luytens in 1903. The castle is open from April to October, Saturday to Thursday.

The island is cut off from the mainland when the causeway is submerged at high tide. Make sure to check the causeway notice board. Find out crossing times in advance by calling the Berwick TIC (☎ 01289 -330733). If you don't want to detour off the main

Day 2: Alnwick to Berwick-upon-Tweed

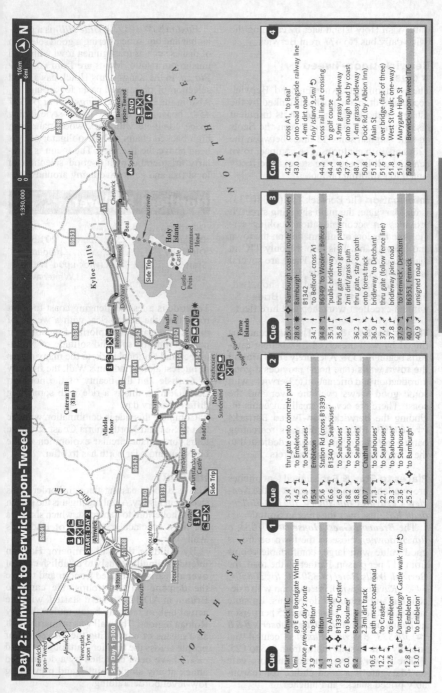

See Day 1 p300

Berwick-upon-Tweed

Alnwick

Newcastle upon Tyne

1:350,000

N

NORTH SEA

River Aln

NORTH SEA

Kyloe Hills

River Tweed

Holy Island

Farne Islands

Budle Bay

Cateran Hill ▲ 81m

Middle Moor

Ainmouth

Bilton

Boulmer

Longhoughton

Craster

Dunstanburgh Castle

Embleton

Beadnell

North Sunderland

Seahouses

Chathill

Bamburgh

Belford

Detchant

Fenwick

Beal

Causeway

Castle Point

Emmanuel Head

Castle

Cheswick

Spittal

Tweedmouth

Berwick-upon-Tweed END

A1

A698

B6353

B6349

B6341

A1068

B1340

B1339

B6347

B1341

B1342

B1340

Side Trip

Side Trip

NORTHERN ENGLAND

Cue 1

Cue		
start		Alnwick TIC
0mi		go E on Bondgate Within
		retrace previous day's route
3.9	↱	'to Bilton'
4.1		Bilton
4.3	◇↰	'to Ainmouth'
5.0	◇↱	B1339 'to Craster'
6.0	↱	'to Boulmer'
8.2		Boulmer
10.5	↰	path meets coast road
12.2	↱	'to Craster'
12.5	↱	'to Embleton'
12.8	●↰	*Dunstanburgh Castle walk 1mi* ↺
13.0	↱	'to Embleton'

Cue 2

Cue		
13.4	↰	thru gate onto concrete path
14.5	↱	'to Embleton'
15.3	↱	'to Seahouses'
15.4		Embleton
16.5	↱	Station Rd (cross B1339)
16.6	↱	'to Seahouses'
16.9	↱	'to Seahouses'
18.2	↰	'to Boulmer'
18.8	↱	'to Seahouses'
20.7		Chathill
21.3	↱	'to Seahouses'
22.1	↰	'to Seahouses'
23.6	↰	'to Seahouses'
25.2	◇↰	'to Bamburgh'

Cue 3

Cue		
25.4	◇	'Bamburgh coastal route', Seahouses
28.6	✳	Bamburgh
34.1		B1342
34.8	↱	'to Belford', cross A1
35.1		B6349 'to Wooler', Belford
35.8	↱	'public bridleway'
	↱	thru gate onto grassy pathway
36.2		2mi dirt/grass path
36.4	↰	thru gate, stay on path
36.9	↱	onto forest track
37.4	↰	bridleway to Detchant'
37.8	↰	thru gate (follow fence line)
37.9	↱	bridleway joins road
40.7	↱	'to Fenwick', Detchant
40.9	↰	B6353, Fenwick
		unsigned road

Cue 4

Cue		
42.2	↰	cross A1, 'to Beal'
43.0	↱↺	onto road alongside railway line
	●●●	*Holy Island 9.5mi* ↺
44.2		1.4mi dirt road
44.4	↰	cross rail line at crossing
45.8	↱	to golf course
47.7	↰	1.9mi grassy bridleway
48.7	↱	onto rough road by coast
50.8	↱	1.4mi grassy bridleway
51.5	↱	Dock Rd (by Albion Inn)
51.6	↱	Main St
51.8	↰	over bridge (first of three)
51.9	↱	West St (walk, one-way)
52.0		Marygate High St
		Berwick-upon-Tweed TIC

route, visit Holy Island later by catching the twice-daily bus No 477 from Berwick.

Berwick-upon-Tweed
☎ 01289

The northernmost town in England, Berwick occupies a dramatic position flanked by the estuary of the River Tweed. In its turbulent history the town passed between the Scots and the English some 13 times between the 12th and 15th centuries. The compact town centre, built largely from stone, is perfectly suited to exploring on foot.

Information The Berwick TIC (☎ 330733) is on Marygate, the main shopping street. It provides an accommodation booking service and has lots of information on the town and Holy Island. It is also the only TIC in the area open year round. There are several banks with ATMs on Hide Hill.

Berwick has a very good bike shop, Brilliant Bicycles (☎ 331476), on Bridge St, with an excellent workshop and hire fleet.

Things to See & Do The city centre is ringed by well-preserved Elizabethan ramparts begun in 1558. A leisurely **stroll around the town walls** (one hour) provides a good introduction and orientation to Berwick, with some good views over the river and the coast. There are several small museums including the **Berwick-upon-Tweed Barracks** (☎ 304493, EH), with displays recreating barrack room life and a section dedicated to the King's Own Scottish Borderers.

Places to Stay & Eat Limited tent pitches are available from £5 per night at the **Seaview Caravan Club Site** (☎ 305198, Billendean Rd), just over the river in Spittal.

The **Breacon Guest House** (☎ 307883, 8 Ravensdowne), close to the town centre, is good value with large, comfortable rooms from £17 per person. Farther up the road, the **Berwick Walls Hotel** (☎ 330770, fax 308304, 34–36 Ravensdowne), is a cosy inn with a decent bar and restaurant downstairs. En suite singles and doubles start from £25 per person including breakfast. **Jeanette Blaaser's B&B** (☎ 305323, 3 Scott's Place) is central and friendly with en suite rooms from £18 to £25.

The **Bakers Oven** with an in-store cafe on Marygate is a good choice for reasonably priced snacks and lunches.

Foxton's (☎ 303939, Hide Hill) is a popular bar and brasserie offering a good selection of dishes such as roast guinea fowl with wild mushroom risotto. Mains are from £6. **Cafe Piazza**, in the Kings Arms Hotel, has a good selection of pizzas and pasta for around £5. Also in the hotel is the **Kings Room** (☎ 307 454), boasting a country-house-style dining space complete with dark wood panelling, high-backed chairs and the obligatory stag's head above the fireplace. The menu is similarly aristocratic with a good selection of local fish and game, averaging around £10.

Northern Explorer

Duration	5 days
Distance	201.5mi
Difficulty	moderate
Start	Berwick-upon-Tweed
End	Whitehaven

This ride is a less challenging coast-to-coast route than the Sea to Sea, with a wealth of things to see and do exploring England's far north. From the splendid solitude of Northumberland National Park, to the many places of interest along Hadrian's Wall, the fine city of Carlisle and the beauty of the northern Lake District, this is a ride with something different every day.

Complete this ride in combination with the Sea to Sea and Northumbria Coast & Castle tours for a giant circular exploration of the best England's far north has to offer.

HISTORY
This is a route passing through border lands steeped in history. A real highlight is the stretch from Chollerford to Lanercost, which shadows the most spectacular sections of Hadrian's Wall.

By building the wall, Emperor Hadrian intended simultaneously to establish control over a clearly delineated frontier and reduce the demand on the troops. He came to Britain in AD 122 to see it started, with the actual task of building being undertaken by Roman legions. The wall was primarily built as a means of controlling the movement of people across the frontier – although it could easily have been breached by a determined attack at any single point – and preventing low-level border raiding.

Cross the drawbridge and explore Cardiff Castle, Wales.

CADWCH GYMRU'N DACLUS

EWCH Â'CH SBWRIEL GYDA CHI

PLEASE TAKE YOUR LITTER HOME

KEEP WALES TIDY

COSB UCHAF £1000 MAX PENALTY

Litterbugs not welcome here.

Cycle across the dam wall at Pontsticill Reservoir, near Merthyr Tydfil, Wales.

Rest up at a Barmouth local.

Enjoy the solitude on the Lôn Las Cymru near Aberllefenni, Wales.

IAN DUCKWORTH

Criccieth Castle, Wales.

DENNIS JOHNSON

Wander around Caernarfon's market, Wales.

IAN DUCKWORTH

Hold a spelling bee at Llanfair PG, the town with the longest name in Britain (58 letters).

PETER HINES

Take a ride around Anglesey to see Beaumaris' moated castle.

BRYN THOMAS

Squeeze! Conwy's tiny house.

No one knows when the troops finally abandoned their posts; it's most likely that around AD 400 Britain was simply set adrift as the Roman Empire fragmented. When pay stopped arriving the soldiers remaining on the wall would simply have left for greener pastures.

PLANNING
When to Ride
Much of the ride, especially through Northumberland, is well off the beaten track so with the possible exception of Cockermouth, you shouldn't have too many problems finding accommodation even during peak periods. If possible, try and ride the leg from Bellingham to Carlisle mid-week as the B6318 can carry a lot of tourist traffic on weekends. Summer, with its warm weather and light nights is the pick of the seasons, while many attractions will be closed from November to March.

Maps & Books
Navigation is fairly straightforward throughout this ride, especially from Carlisle where the ride follows the well-signed Reivers cycle route. The free *Hadrian's Wall: Frontier of the Roman Empire* pamphlet, produced by EH and available from TICs in the area, is worth picking it up. It provides a history of the wall and has a map detailing all the major points of interest. Two route maps available from Sustrans and local TICs, the *Hadrian's Wall Country Tyne Valley Cycle Map* and the *Reivers Route Map* are useful if you intend a more thorough exploration of the area.

What to Bring
With so many historic sights to visit, consider getting an EH membership (see Useful Organisations in the Facts for the Cyclist chapter); it will entitle you to free entry at all EH properties.

GETTING TO/FROM THE RIDE
Berwick-upon-Tweed
See Getting To/From the Ride (p299) in the Northumbria Coast & Castles ride for details on getting to/from Berwick.

Whitehaven
Train Whitehaven is a stop on the Cumbrian Coast line which runs from Carlisle to Barrow-in-Furness and inland east to Lancaster. Both Lancaster and Carlisle are on the main Glasgow-London line. Fares from Whitehaven are:

destination	one way	hours	frequency
Carlisle	£6.85	1	hourly
Glasgow	£29.00	2½	several daily
Lancaster	£14.20	2½	hourly
London	£95.50	5½	hourly

Bicycle The route from Whitehaven to Newcastle, via Keswick, Penrith and Allenheads is described in the Sea to Sea ride later in this chapter.

THE RIDE
Berwick-upon-Tweed
See Berwick (p304) in the Northumbria Coast & Castles ride for information about accommodation and other services.

Day 1: Berwick to Wooler
2½–3½ hours, 29.9mi
This is a short and relatively easy day, heading briefly over the border into Scotland and finishing at the foot of the rolling green Cheviot Hills. The route crosses into Scotland on the way to Paxton, shortly after turning off the A1. England awaits close by, however, on the other side of the River Tweed, crossed via a small suspension bridge at the 7.1mi point.

Norham Castle (11.4mi; ☎ 01661-881 297), built in 1160, stands as a vivid reminder of the centuries of hostilities the towns along the border have witnessed. Much of the original structure has been destroyed but there is still enough standing to make it a good stopping-off point, especially with the self-guided audio tour. Etal (18.4mi) also has a castle, but while the visitor centre's **display on border warfare** is quite good, not much of the fortress itself remains.

Heading towards Ford turn off the main road after 20.1mi and cycle past a farm where the road becomes rougher and eventually turns into a bumpy track through some woods. It's quite sandy and may be unrideable in a few short sections. Emerge back on to sealed road after 22.3mi, heading for Doddington, the rolling B6525 leading the remaining distance into Wooler.

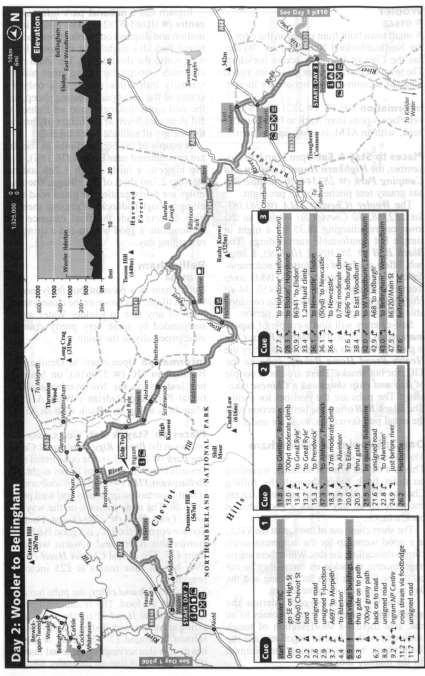

Day 3: Bellingham to Carlisle
6–7 hours, 58.6mi

This long day heads along the most interesting sections of Hadrian's Wall, with lots of historic sites along the way. Brampton (turn off at 39.6mi, Lanercost Priory) makes a good alternative to Carlisle if you want to explore at a more leisurely pace.

The countryside south of Bellingham is scenic and very lush, with the road passing green fields and numerous pockets of woods as it follows the course of the River North Tyne. The road rolls along throughout the day with a few moderate climbs to tackle from time to time.

Near Chollerford the route joins the B6318, the road that most closely follows the course of Hadrian's Wall. It can be quite busy with tourist traffic, especially on summer weekends, but it isn't too stressful to cycle on, offering a direct route to all the best sights of the wall, the first of which is reached almost immediately.

Chesters Roman Fort & Museum (13.8mi; ☎ 01434-681379, EH) houses the remnants of a Roman cavalry fort. Wander around and explore the foundations of the barracks and bathhouse, complete with an extraordinary under-floor heating system. The museum, with its extensive collection of Roman artefacts and inscribed stones, is a good place to start. Like most of the wall sites however don't expect to see any buildings largely intact – it helps to have a vivid imagination!

The next major site is **Housesteads Roman Fort & Museum** (22.2mi; ☎ 01434-344396, EH). The ruins aren't quite as extensive or well preserved as Chesters, but its setting, perched high on a ridge, is spectacularly dramatic.

Not far down the road is Once Brewed (25.0mi), a settlement with a national park visitor centre, youth hostel and other accommodation. The **Vindolanda** site (☎ 01434-344277, EH), where the remains of a fort and accompanying civil buildings are still being excavated, is a 3mi return side trip, signposted from the visitor centre.

Beyond Greenhead (31.2mi), much of the traffic is thankfully lost to the A69, with the route continuing on the much quieter B6318 to Gilsland. Cycle past an impressive, largely intact section of the wall containing the **Birdoswald Fort** (35.0mi; ☎ 016977-

47602, EH), a well-preserved fort overlooking the beautiful Irthing Gorge, plus a visitor centre, before arriving at Lanercost (39.6mi) where the feast of historic sites continues. Visit the **priory** (☎ 01697-73030), from where Edward I briefly ruled the kingdom. At Lanercost it's also time to decide whether you want to press on to Carlisle or call it a day in Brampton, an attractive market town just 2.5mi away.

From Lanercost the route to Carlisle follows quiet roads through Walton, Hethersgill and Smithfield, a bridge over the M6 leading into Houghton on the outskirts of Carlisle itself. Traffic increases on the approach to the city centre so it's a good idea to use the dual-use paths where possible.

Carlisle
See Gateway Cities (pp297–8) for accommodation and other services in Carlisle.

Day 4: Carlisle to Cockermouth
4–5 hours, 46.7mi

The route out of town leads along the banks of the River Eden on a traffic-free, bumpy pathway. A flight of steps leads away from the river on to an industrial estate, but the urban clutter is soon left behind as the road, flanked by hedgerows, heads out to the picturesque Cumbrian countryside.

A number of small villages punctuate the route, the *tearooms* at Hesket Newmarket (27.6mi) providing a good spot to break for lunch and sample some home-made pasties. Beyond the village the ride becomes a little hillier, with a number of small climbs to negotiate. The landscape is one of green pastures, dry stone walls and woolly sheep.

As the route climbs up towards the Caldbeck Fells the countryside takes on a less manicured, exposed appearance with sheep grazing on the common land beside the road. Some classic Lake District views over Bassenthwaite Lake can be enjoyed as you pass through Fellend Farm, a nice descent heading down to the A591.

After crossing the River Derwent there's a short steep climb to negotiate before the final downhill stretch into Cockermouth.

Cockermouth
☎ 01900

Best known as the birthplace of William Wordsworth, Cockermouth is an attractive

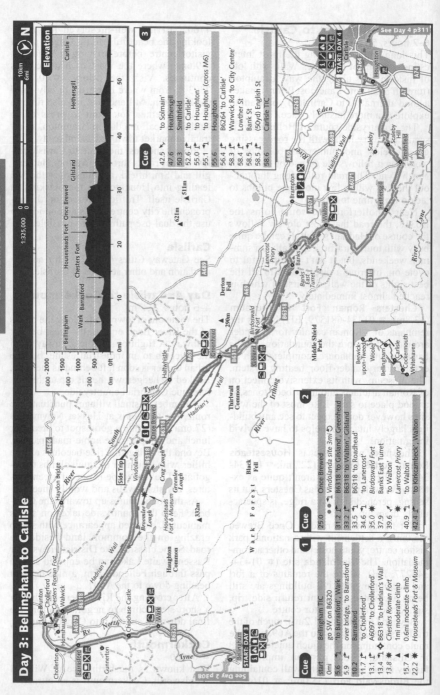

Day 3: Bellingham to Carlisle

Elevation

N

1:325,000

NORTHERN ENGLAND

Cue		
start	0mi	Bellingham TIC
		go SW on B6320
5.6		'to Barrasford', Wark
5.9		over bridge, 'to Barrasford'
10.2		Barrasford
11.7		'to Chollerford'
13.1		A6097 'to Chollerford'
13.4		B6318 'to Hadrian's Wall'
13.8	◇	Chesters Roman Fort
15.7	▲	1mi moderate climb
	▲	0.6mi moderate climb
22.2	◆	Housesteads Fort & Museum

Cue		
25.0		Once Brewed
	●●	Vindolanda site 3mi ↻
31.2		B6318 'to Gilsland' Greenhead
33.2		B6318 'to Walton', Gilsland
33.5		B6318 'to Roadhead'
34.6		'to Lanercost'
35.0	✳	Birdoswald Fort
37.9		Banks East Turret
39.6	✳	'to Walton'
	✳	Lanercost Priory
40.9		'to Walton'
42.4		'to Kirkcambeck', Walton

Cue		
42.5		'to Solmain'
47.6		Heathersgill
50.3		Smithfield
52.6		'to Carlisle'
55.0		'to Houghton'
55.1		'to Houghton' (cross M6)
55.6		Houghton
56.4		B6264 to Carlisle
58.3		Warwick Rd 'to City Centre'
58.4		Lowther St
58.5		Bank St
58.5		(50yd) English St
58.6		Carlisle TIC

See Day 2 p308

See Day 4 p311

START: DAY 4
Carlisle

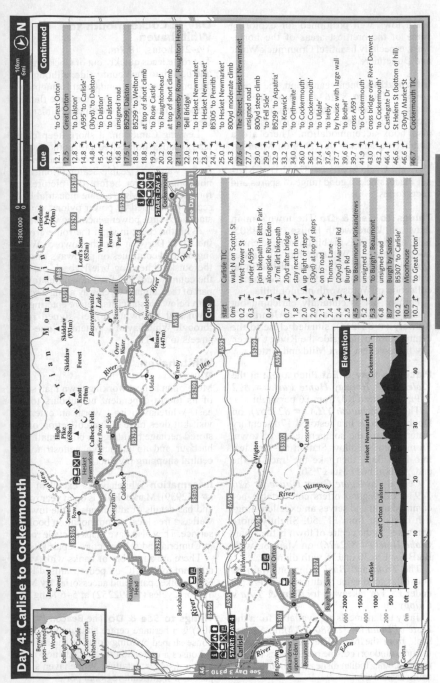

Day 4: Carlisle to Cockermouth

START DAY 4
Carlisle

See Day 3 p310

START DAY 5
Cockermouth

See Day 5 p313

NORTHERN ENGLAND

1:300,000 N 10km / 6mi

Inglewood Forest
Cumbrian Mountains
Skiddaw (931m)
Skiddaw Forest
High Pike (658m)
Knott (710m)
Lord's Seat (552m)
Grisedale Pike (790m)
Whinlatter Forest Park
Binsey (447m)
Bassenthwaite Lake
Over Water
River Ellen
River Wampool
River Eden
River Caldew
River Derwent
River Cocker

Berwick-upon-Tweed, Wooler, Bellingham, Carlisle, Cockermouth, Whitehaven

Cue

start		Carlisle TIC
0mi	↑	walk N on Scotch St
0.2	↰	West Tower St
0.3	↑	under A595
		join bikepath in Bitts Park
0.4	↑	alongside River Eden
		1.7mi dirt bikepath
0.7	↑	20yd after bridge
1.8	↑	stay next to river
2.0	↑	up flight of steps
2.0	↰	(30yd) at top of steps
2.1	↑	on to road
2.4	↑	Thomas Lane
2.4	↰	(20yd) Marconi Rd
2.5	↰	Burgh Rd
4.5	↱	'to Beaumont', Kirkandrews
5.2	↑	unsigned road
5.3	↱	'to Burgh', Beaumont
6.8	↑	unsigned road
8.7	↑	Burgh by Sands
10.2	↱	B5307 'to Carlisle'
10.5	↱	Moorhouse
10.7	↰	'to Great Orton'

Cue Continued

12.1	↰	'to Great Orton'
12.5		Great Orton
12.8	↱	'to Dalston'
14.8	↑	A595 'to Carlisle'
14.8	↰	(30yd) 'to Dalston'
15.4	↱	'to Dalston'
16.2	↰	'to Dalston'
16.8	↱	unsigned road
17.5	↰	B5299, Dalston
18.5	↱	B5299 'to Welton'
		at top of short climb
18.8	↱	'to Rose Castle'
19.3	↱	'to Raughtonhead'
20.2	↱	at top of short climb
20.8	↱	'to Sowerby Row', Raughton Head
21.1	↱	'Bell Bridge'
22.0	↰	'to Hesket Newmarket'
23.3	↱	'to Hesket Newmarket'
23.6	↱	B5305 'to Penrith'
24.7	↱	'to Hesket Newmarket'
25.0	↰	800yd moderate climb
26.3	↱	The Street, Hesket Newmarket
27.6	↱	unsigned road
27.7	↰	800yd steep climb
29.0	↱	'to Fell Side'
29.5	↰	B5299 'to Aspatria'
32.9	↱	'to Keswick'
33.2	↱	'to Orthwaite'
34.0	↱	'to Cockermouth'
36.0	↰	'to Cockermouth'
36.2	↱	'to Uldale'
37.4	↰	'to Ireby'
37.6	↰	by house with large wall
37.7	↱	'to Bothel'
39.6	↑	cross A591
39.7	↰	'to Cockermouth'
41.9	↱	cross bridge over River Derwent
43.0	↑	'to Cockermouth'
43.2	↱	Castlegate Dr
46.4	↰	St Helens St (bottom of hill)
46.6	↱	(30yd) Market St
46.7		Cockermouth TIC

Elevation

Carlisle — Great Orton — Dalston — Hesket Newmarket — Cockermouth

See Day 3 p310
See Day 5 p313

small town well positioned for exploring some of the prettiest areas of the north-west, especially beautiful Crummock Water and Buttermere.

Information Open year round, the Cockermouth TIC (☎ 822634), on Market St, has a good range of pamphlets detailing local activities and a few cycle routes. They also book accommodation. There are a number of banks with ATMs on Main St, Cockermouth's principal thoroughfare. Derwent Cycle Sports (☎ 822113), 4 Market Place, stocks a good range of spares and accessories.

Things to See & Do The town's main drawcard, **Wordsworth House** (☎ 824805, NT), on Main St, is the birthplace and childhood home of William and his sister Dorothy. Built in 1745, it's furnished in an authentic 18th-century style and contains a collection of Wordsworth memorabilia.

Perhaps not as culturally enriching but equally enjoyable is a tour of **Jenning's Brewery** (☎ 823214), situated close to the centre of town alongside the River Cocker. Try the excellent Dark Mild and Bitter.

Places to Stay & Eat Pitch a tent at the *Violet Bank Holiday Home Park (☎ 822 169),* off Lorton Rd, from £6 per night.

The *Cockermouth YHA (☎ 822561),* on Double Mills, is in a restored 17th-century water mill on the southern edge of town. From Main St follow Station St, turn left into Fern Bank then take the track at the end. A dorm bed costs £7.50.

Central *Castlegate Guest House (☎ 826 749, 6 Castlegate)* offers comfortable accommodation and serves an excellent English breakfast from £17.50. Slightly more upmarket, in the centre of town is the smart *Globe Hotel (☎ 822126),* on Main St, with B&B for £26.50 or £35 with dinner.

The *Trout* and *Bush* pubs on Main St both offer good value traditional bar fare for under £5. For takeaway try *Tony & Tina's Chippy*.

Tasty Indian meals are available from the *Taste of India (☎ 822880, 72 Main St),* set back from the road. The extensive menu features tandoori cuisine but also has a large range of other Indian dishes with mains averaging around £7.

Day 5: Cockermouth to Whitehaven
1½–2½ hours, 18.7mi
The route leads quickly out of Cockermouth and back into the countryside, although the pastoral scenery beyond Great Broughton is briefly interrupted as the quiet lane flanks a barbed wire fence protecting a Ministry of Defence (MOD) magazine.

Leaving Camerton, a short steep climb leads onto a traffic-free rail path (6.4mi), passing under a number of old stone bridges on the way into sizeable Seaton (7.6mi). It's not long however before the picturesque rural scenery yields to a more industrial landscape, punctuated by power pylons, smokestacks and large power generating windmills.

With the coast in sight the route crosses the River Derwent into the town of Workington, and continues on pathways through the outskirts heading briefly back out into the countryside. The final few miles follow part of the Cumbria Cycleway along a scenic path below coastal cliffs, before entering the town and following a well-signed route through Whitehaven's system of one-way streets to the TIC.

Whitehaven
☎ 01946
More of an honest working town than some of its tourist-dependent neighbours to the east, Whitehaven isn't worth an extended visit but does have a fine collection of restored heritage buildings, a busy small boat harbour and an attractive pedestrianised central shopping precinct.

Information Whitehaven's excellent TIC (☎ 852939), Market Hall, is open year round and has details of attractions in the town as well as a free local accommodation booking service. They also have maps of cycle routes in Cumbria and sell puncture repair kits.

There are a number of banks with ATMs adjacent to the TIC on pedestrianised King St. For bike spares and accessories try Mark Taylor Cycles (☎ 692252) at 5–6 King St.

Things to See & Do The Beacon (☎ 592 302) is a heritage centre situated in a lighthouse-shaped building down by the harbour. It houses a collection of artefacts and interactive displays detailing Whitehaven's rich past as a significant regional port.

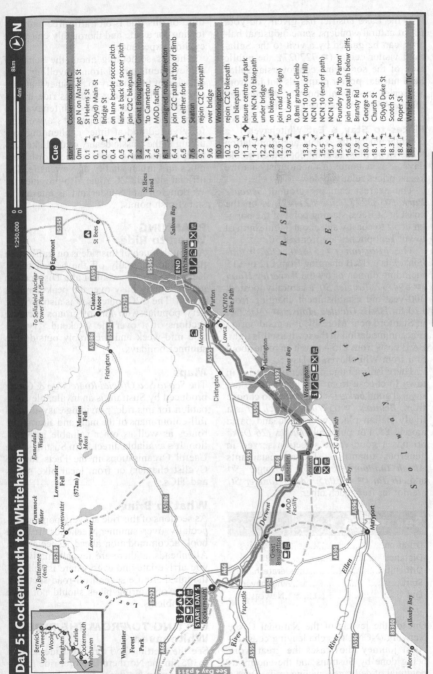

Day 5: Cockermouth to Whitehaven

1:250,000

0   4mi   8km

N

Cue	
start	Cockermouth TIC
0mi	go N on Market St
0.1	St Helens St
0.1	(30yd) Main St
0.2	Bridge St
0.4	on lane beside soccer pitch
0.5	lane at back of soccer pitch
2.4	join C2C bikepath
3.2	Great Broughton
3.4	'to Camerton'
4.6	MOD facility
6.1	unsigned road, Camerton
6.4	join C2C path at top of climb
6.5	on either fork
7.6	Seaton
9.2	rejoin C2C bikepath
9.6	over bridge
10.0	Workington
10.2	rejoin C2C bikepath
10.9	on bikepath
11.3	leisure centre car park
11.4	join NCN 10 bikepath
12.2	under bridge
12.8	on bikepath
12.9	join road (no sign)
13.0	'to Lowca'
13.8	0.8mi gradual climb
14.7	NCN 10 (top of hill)
15.5	NCN 10 (end of path)
15.7	NCN 10
15.8	Foundry Rd 'to Parton'
16.6	join coastal path below cliffs
17.9	Bransty Rd
18.0	George St
18.1	Church St
18.1	(50yd) Duke St
18.3	Scotch St
18.4	Roper St
18.7	Whitehaven TIC

NORTHERN ENGLAND

If the Lake District has given you your fill of natural wonders, some industrial balance can be gained by a visit to the Sellafield visitor centre (☎ 727027), the public face of the somewhat controversial **Sellafield nuclear power plant**. It's not far from Seascale, about 9mi south of Whitehaven off the A595. Whitehaven TIC has details.

Places to Stay & Eat Whitehaven is a commercial centre, so its accommodation tends to be most heavily booked on weekdays – as a bonus its nontouristy nature keeps prices relatively low.

The nearest camping ground, *Seacote Park (☎ 822777, fax 824442)*, is on the coast at St Bees, starting point of the popular coast to coast walk, about 3.7mi south of town. Tent pitches are from £8.50.

The *Mansion (☎ 61860, Old Woodhouse)*, is a B&B charging from £12 or £15 including dinner, or try the *Waverley Hotel (☎ 694337, Tangier St)*, a centrally located, 300-year-old establishment charging from £20 for B&B. *Glenlea House (☎ 693873)*, in Stanford near Moresby, is a good option if accommodation in the town itself is tight. B&B costs from £15 – pass it en route about 5mi from Whitehaven on Day 5.

There isn't a huge number of eateries in town to choose from. For lunch, there are several good *bakeries* on King St to choose from. *Bruno's (☎ 65270, 9 Church St)* is a lively Italian place with pizza and pasta around £5. For pub grub, *Dukes (26 Duke St)* has a good-value selection served in generous quantities. Indian restaurants *Akash Tandoori (☎ 691171, 3 Tangier St)* and *Ali Taj (☎ 693085, 34–35 Tangier St)* are not far from each other.

Sea to Sea

Duration	4 days
Distance	130.6mi
Difficulty	moderate-hard
Start	Whitehaven
End	Newcastle

One of the jewels of the National Cycle Network (NCN), this challenging coast-to-coast journey showcases the great work being done by Sustrans and the enormous potential of dedicated cycling trails. Over a third of this ride is on traffic-free paths allowing for a safe and thoroughly enjoyable cycling experience.

There's something about the sense of achievement gained from travelling from one side of the country to the other that captures the imagination, and this ride travelling west to east from Whitehaven to Newcastle is no exception. It's a wonderfully varied and at times challenging tour taking in the classic beauty of the Lake District, solitude and space of the North Pennines and urban vitality of Newcastle. The official signed C2C route also provides for Workington and Sunderland as alternative start/finish points.

PLANNING
When to Ride
Although much of this ride is on traffic-free paths and generally off the beaten track, Keswick and the whole Lake District can get extremely busy over the peak summer period. The C2C route itself is also proving very popular with lots of groups tackling sections of it over the weekend. Try and ride mid-week and preferably outside the summer holidays.

Maps
The *Sea to Sea Official Route Map & Guide* produced by Sustrans is an invaluable companion for this ride, providing easy-to-read full-colour maps of the main and alternative routes as well as other valuable information. It's available direct from Sustrans (see Useful Organisations in the Facts for the Cyclist chapter) or from local bike shops and TICs.

What to Bring
As sections of this ride are very popular, especially over summer weekends, try and book accommodation ahead, especially in Allenheads as there are few alternatives if you arrive late and everywhere is full. Although there are several off-road sections, cyclists on touring bikes should not have any problems.

GETTING TO/FROM THE RIDE
Whitehaven
See the Getting To/From the Ride section (p305) in the Northern Explorer ride for information on getting to/from Whitehaven.

Newcastle

See Gateway Cities (pp296–7) for information on getting to/from Newcastle.

THE RIDE
Day 1: Whitehaven to Keswick
3–4 hours, 32.1mi

It doesn't take long to pedal from the somewhat industrial Cumbrian coast to some of the prettiest countryside in England. The route out of Whitehaven follows the signed C2C trail along a series of pathways, a great traffic-free start to the ride although the multitude of paths can make navigation difficult at times. Climb gradually but steadily as the bikepath, part of the West Cumbrian Cycle Network, follows the bed of an old mineral railway. A number of interesting sculptural trail-markers punctuate the route.

Beyond Kirkland (10.9mi) the gradual ascent continues, following quiet country lanes by fields of sheep as you pass Keltonfell Top. A nice descent leads down alongside Loweswater, the quiet road bordered by forest on one side and an expanse of water on the other, providing some inspiring **Lake District views**.

Just after Low Lorton (21.6mi) a testing steep climb reaches the high point of the day near the **Whinlatter Forest Visitor Centre** (25.3mi; ☎ 017687-78469), which has an audio-visual presentation about the surrounding forest. From here an exhilarating, fast descent ends at the village of Braithwaite (27.6mi). Beyond Ullock, a very peaceful lane through the forest leads the final mile into Portinscale, nestled on the banks of Derwent Water. The access road leading into Keswick's town centre is reached after a brief stint on a pathway alongside the A66.

Keswick
☎ 017687

As the main northern centre for the Lakes, Keswick is a bustling place full of Gore-Tex-clad walkers peering through the windows of the town's numerous outdoor shops. It enjoys a picturesque setting sandwiched between the great rounded peak of Skiddaw and the very lovely Derwent Water.

Information The Keswick TIC (☎ 72645) in Market Square is open year round. It's a busy place stocking all manner of maps, books and leaflets on local attractions and the Lakes. Given the popularity of the town, especially on summer weekends, the free local accommodation booking service is a valuable one.

There are a number of banks with ATMs adjacent to the TIC in Market Square. Check email at U-Compute, inside the post office on Market Square. For bike bits try Lakeland Pedlar (☎ 75752) in Hendersons Yard, down a lane off the Market Square, or see the Keswick Mountain Bike Centre (☎ 75202), just behind the pencil museum (see the Things to See & Do section), for mountain bike hire.

Things to See & Do Fact: the lead pencil was invented in Keswick. If you want to know everything else there is to know about pencils and also see the world's largest, you'll want to visit the town's **pencil museum** (☎ 73626). It's down Southey Lane, attached to the factory that turns out world-famous Derwent colour pencils.

A very pleasant way to see picturesque Derwent Water is to cruise around it on the **Keswick Launch** (☎ 72263). The small wooden vessel stops at various points along the way, taking around 50 minutes for a complete circumnavigation. Another nice way to see the lake and to stretch your legs off the bike is to take a **stroll** along the pathway that runs along the water's edge. Access to the lake is via Lake Rd, a five-minute walk from the TIC.

Places to Stay Pitch a tent at the ***Braithwaite Camping Site*** (☎ 78343), about 5mi from Keswick in the village of Braithwaite, passed on Day 1, from £5.

The ***Keswick YHA*** (☎ 72484, Station Rd), a short walk from the TIC, is open daily from mid-February through December. Beds are £10.15 a night. If it's full, ***Derwentwater YHA*** (☎ 77246) is just 2mi away in Borrowdale.

Keswick is chock full of B&Bs and hotels but things can still get tight on summer weekends. The ***Strathmore Guest House*** (☎ 72584; 8 St John's Terrace, Ambleside Rd) is a short walk from the TIC and offers comfortable rooms and a hearty breakfast from £17.50. Another good bet is the ***Bridgedale Guest House*** (☎ 73914, 101 Main St) with B&B for a very reasonable £15, or £12 without breakfast.

NORTHERN ENGLAND

Day 1: Whitehaven to Keswick

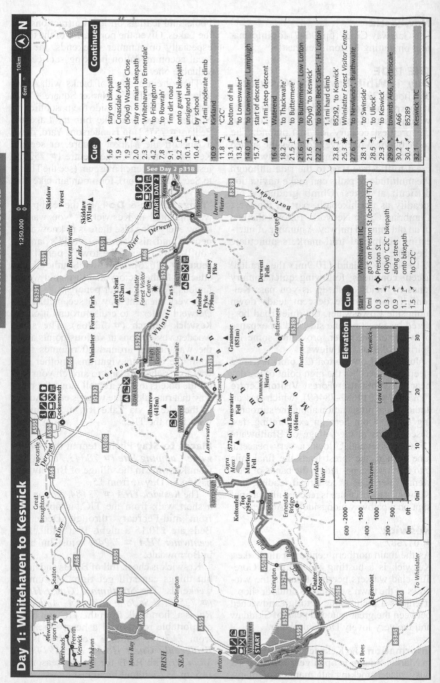

1:250,000

N

0   6mi

0   10km

Continued

Cue	
1.6	stay on bikepath
1.9	Croasdale Ave
1.9	(50yd) Wasdale Close
2.0	stay on main bikepath
2.3	'Whitehaven to Ennerdale'
4.2	'to Frizington'
7.8	'to Rowrah'
9.1	1mi dirt road
9.1	onto gravel bikepath
10.1	unsigned lane
10.4	by school
	1.4mi moderate climb
10.9	Kirkland
11.8	'C2C'
13.1	bottom of hill
13.5	'to Loweswater'
14.0	'to Loweswater', Lamplugh
15.7	start of descent
	1.1mi steep descent
16.4	Waterend
18.2	'to Thackwaite'
21.5	'to Buttermere'
21.6	'to Buttermere', Low Lorton
21.6	(50yd) 'to Keswick'
22.2	'to Boon Beck Scales', H. Lorton
	1.1mi hard climb
23.8	B5292, 'to Keswick'
25.3	Whinlatter Forest Visitor Centre
27.6	'to Newlands', Braithwaite
28.1	'to Swinside'
28.5	'to Ullock'
29.3	'to Keswick'
29.9	towards A66, Portinscale
30.2	A66
30.4	B5289
32.1	Keswick TIC

Cue

Cue	
start	Whitehaven TIC
0mi	go S on Preston St (behind TIC)
0.3	Preston St
0.3	(40yd) 'C2C' bikepath
0.9	along street
1.1	onto bikepath
1.5	'to C2C'

Elevation

600 - 2000
400
1500
1000
200
500
0m   0ft

Whitehaven · Low Lorton · Keswick

0mi   10   20   30

See Day 2 p318
START DAY 2
Keswick

Skiddaw Forest
Skiddaw (931m)

Bassenthwaite Lake

River Derwent

A591

B5291

B5289

Derwent Water

Borrowdale

Grange

Cockermouth

Papcastle
A594
A595

Great Broughton

A66

River Derwent

Lord's Seat (552m)
Whinlatter Forest Park
Whinlatter Forest Visitor Centre
Whinlatter Pass
B5292
High Lorton
Low Lorton
B5292

Braithwaite
B5292

Grisedale Pyke (790m)
Causey Pike
Grasmoor (851m)
Derwent Fells

Buttermere
B5289

Thackthwaite
Lorton Vale

Loweswater
Waterend
Fellbarrow (415m)
Loweswater Fell
Loweswater
Crummock Water
Great Borne (616m)
Buttermere

Lamplugh
Cogra Moss
Murton Fell
Kirkland
Kelton Fell Top (295m)
Ennerdale Bridge
Ennerdale Water

A5086

Dyke
Frizington
B5294
B5295
C2C
Cleator Moor
B5086

Egremont
A595
B5345

To Whinlatter

IRISH SEA

Mass Bay

Parton

Seaton

Distington
A597

A595

B5345
St Bees

Whitehaven
START

Newcastle upon Tyne
Allerheads
Penrith
Keswick
Whitehaven

Places to Eat Self-caterers will find the large *Lakes Foodstore* on Tithebarn St. For lunches try one of the *bakeries* close to the TIC in Market Square. The rather grand *Bryson's Tea Room (38 Main St)* has excellent traditional cakes, buns and other goodies.

Many of Keswick's pubs offer reasonable value evening meals. The *Dog & Gun (cnr Market Square & Lake Rd)* does a good job with a range of traditional favourites such as Cumberland sausage and mash, as well as a few Indian dishes, most under £6. For a full Indian meal try the popular *Maharaja (☎ 74799)*, upstairs just off Main St. Most dishes on the extensive menu are under £7. They also do takeaway.

Day 2: Keswick to Penrith
2½–3 hours, 23.9mi

The route out of Keswick follows a traffic-free rail trail along the tranquil River Greta. There are some steep steps to negotiate as well as a few gates, but despite these obstacles it makes for tremendous cycling with many of the original rail bridges and shelters still intact along the shady, wooded pathway.

Shortly after emerging at the A66 the route passes the turn-off (3.6mi) to the **Castlerigg Stone Circle**, a sacred Bronze Age meeting place, before continuing to Threlkeld (4.2mi). Beyond the village the quiet country lane climbs briefly, passing farms and sheep grazing on the hillsides. Minor roads and short stretches alongside the A66, eventually lead to the village of Greystoke (16.9mi). The **Greystoke Castle**, closed to the public and hidden behind high walls, is linked with the legend of Tarzan, the chest-beating, fictional jungle hero created by Edgar Rice Burroughs. The final stretch into Penrith, along a public bridleway emerges at busy Scotland Rd, a short distance from the town centre.

Penrith
☎ 01768

Once the capital of Cumbria, the bustling market town of Penrith, built of red sandstone, is still the principal northern gateway to the Lake District and the North Pennines.

Information Penrith TIC (☎ 867466, fax 891754) is next to the museum, near the centre of town on Middlegate. Bike parts and accessories are available from Arragons Cycle Centre (☎ 890344) at 2 Brunswick Rd. Market day is Tuesday.

Things to See & Do Much of Penrith's appeal lies in exploring the various small squares and laneways running through the central shopping precinct. The ruins of **Penrith Castle**, former home of Warwick the Kingmaker and the Duke of Gloucester, later Richard III, are worth a quick look. They lie in a park close to the train station.

Penrith Museum (☎ 864671), next to the TIC, is housed in a former girls' charity school dating from 1670. It contains a good collection of exhibits providing an introduction to the history of Penrith and the Eden district.

Places to Stay & Eat A large historic house, the *Friarage (☎ 863635, Friargate)* is a comfortable B&B near the town centre, charging from £15. *Albany House (☎ 863 072, 5 Portland Place)* is also well equipped and central with B&B from £17.

For a splurge, the *George Hotel (☎ 862 696, Devonshire St)*, with its wood panelling and antique furnishings, provides a comfortable, dignified retreat in the heart of Penrith. B&B is from £31.

Gianni's Ristorante Pizzeria (☎ 891791, 11 Market Square) dishes out generous helpings of pizza and pasta, perfect for carbo loading, at around £5 a dish, cheaper during happy hour (5.30 to 7 pm). The *White Horse*, on Great Dockray, is a good bet for pub grub with a roast of the day and all the usual favourites for under £6. *Chataways Bistro (☎ 890233)*, on the lane running alongside St Andrews Churchyard, offers a good selection of traditional English dishes served with contemporary flare. The four course set menu costs £12.95.

Day 3: Penrith to Allenheads
4½–5½ hours, 33.5mi

This is a tough day involving numerous testing climbs, heading away from the lakes and up into the ruggedly beautiful northern Pennines. Setting the tone for the day, it starts with a climb on quiet roads, through Edenhall to the village of Langwathby (4.9mi). A little farther on, just out of Little Salkeld, are a couple of **ancient stone circles** signed just

NORTHERN ENGLAND

Day 2: Keswick to Penrith

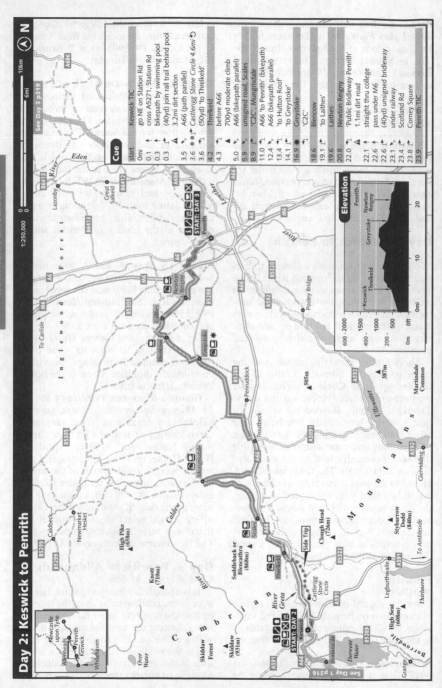

Cue	
start	0mi	Keswick TIC
0.1	go NE on Station Rd
0.3	cross A5271, Station Rd
0.3	bikepath by swimming pool
	(40yd) join rail trail behind pool
3.5	3.2mi dirt section
3.5	A66 (path parallel)
3.6	Castlerigg Stone Circle 4.6mi ↻
3.6	(50yd) 'to Threlkeld'
4.2	Threlkeld
4.3	before A66
5.0	700yd moderate climb
5.9	A66 (bikepath parallel)
8.9	unsigned road, Scales
8.9	'C2C', Mungrisdale
11.0	A66 'to Penrith' (bikepath)
12.4	A66 (bikepath parallel)
13.4	'to Hutton Roof'
14.1	'to Greystoke'
16.9	Greystoke ✳
	'C2C'
18.6	Blencow
19.1	'to Laithes'
19.6	Laithes
20.8	Newton Reigny
22.0	'Public Bridleway Penrith'
22.1	1.1mi dirt road
22.6	straight thru college
22.6	pass under M6
	(40yd) unsigned bridleway
23.1	under railway
23.4	Scotland Rd
23.8	Corney Square
23.9	Penrith TIC

Elevation

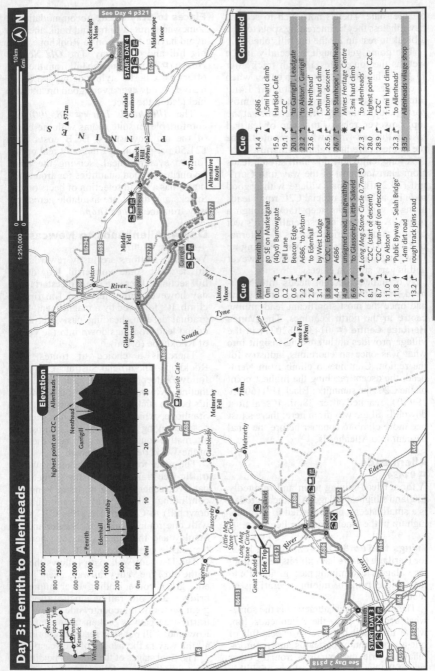

Day 3: Penrith to Allenheads

Elevation

highest point on C2C

Allenheads
Nenthead
Garrigill
Langwathby
Penrith
Edenhall

Cue	
start	Penrith TIC
0mi	go SE on Marketgate
0.0	(40yd) Burrowgate
0.2	Fell Lane
0.6	Beacon Edge
2.2	A686, 'to Alston'
2.6	'to Edenhall'
3.1	by West Lodge
3.8	'C2C'; Edenhall
4.4	A686
4.9	unsigned road, Langwathby
6.6	'to Glassonby', Little Salkeld
7.1	Long Meg Stone Circle 0.7mi
8.1	'C2C' (start of descent)
8.7	'C2C' turn-off (on descent)
11.0	'to Alston'
11.8	'Public Byway - Selah Bridge'
	1.4mi dirt road
13.2	rough track joins road

Cue		
14.4		A686
15.9	▲	Hartside Cafe
19.1		'C2C'
20.1		'to Garrigill', Leadgate
23.2		'to Alston', Garrigill
23.6		'to Nenthead'
26.5		1.9mi hard climb
		bottom descent
26.7	✳	Mines Heritage Centre
		'to Stanhope', Nenthead
27.3		'to Allenheads'
28.0	▲	highest point on C2C
28.9		'C2C'
32.3	▲	'to Allenheads'
33.5		Allenheads village shop

Continued
1.5mi hard climb
1.3mi hard climb
1.1mi hard climb

NORTHERN ENGLAND

off the route. There's not much to see but nevertheless they're interesting spots to take a break to rest up for the big hills ahead.

The going gets tough, especially in the wet, as the route joins a rough track after 11.8mi. Things don't get much easier when it emerges back on to the bitumen 1.4mi later, at the start of a long, but for the most part gradual, climb up Hartside. Once at the top, however, relax with a cup of tea and take in the view from what is reputed to be the highest *cafe* in England (15.9mi).

A long, enjoyable downhill stretch leads from Hartside most of the way into Garrigill (23.2mi), a small village with a good *pub*. From here the official C2C route leads along a very rough, steep track through a quarry. A better option, especially if it's wet or you're on a touring bike, is the alternative sealed route described here, leading up Dowgang Hush. It's still no picnic however and is very steep in places.

A breakneck descent heads into Nenthead, one of the highest villages in England and once the most significant lead-mining centre in the north Pennines. The **Mines Heritage Centre** (☎ 01434-382037) in the village provides an interesting insight into what was once an enormous industry for the region. Continue to climb from Nenthead, the ascent reaching the highest point on the C2C, the summit of Black Hill (609m/ 1998ft), reached after 28mi. It's almost downhill all the way from here; there's just one more climb to conquer before the final descent into Allenheads.

Allenheads
☎ 01434
A former lead-mining town and reputedly England's highest village, Allenheads today is a small, sleepy place nestled in a valley, high up in the lonely northern Pennines.

Things to See & Do Well worth a look, the **Heritage Centre** has exhibits recounting the village's lead-mining past, giving life to the various ruins of mining operations en route.

The only other real attraction is the somewhat **eccentric pub**, the Allenheads Inn, where the small bars are so chock full of bric-a-brac, smutty postcards and memorabilia that retrieving your drink from the other side of the bar becomes a real test of skill.

Places to Stay & Eat Accommodation is somewhat limited so try and book ahead to avoid having to slog on to Rookhope, up a big hill and 6mi away. The *Old School House* (☎ 685040), up the hill from the pub, offers basic hostel style lodging at a rather hefty £14, however a very good breakfast is included in the price.

The *Allenheads Inn* (☎ 685200) has comfortable en suite rooms with the bonus of the bar downstairs. B&B costs from £21.50 per person. It's the only real option for an evening meal, serving the usual favourites in good quantities for around £5. It also has a broad selection of beers on tap. Snacks and drinks are available across the way from the *village shop*.

Day 4: Allenheads to Newcastle
4–5 hours, 41.1mi
Yesterday's efforts are justly rewarded on this leg with some wonderful, long downhill sections. There's a strenuous start to the day however with a testing 1.1mi first-up climb. It's followed by a magnificent, long, gradual descent, heading past long abandoned lead workings down into the village of Rookhope (6.1mi).

There is a choice of routes from Rookhope. The official Sustrans C2C route follows a steep, rough path up an old railway incline. Without a mountain bike however it's best to stick to the less jarring route via Stanhope, which is touring-bike friendly, despite having a couple of stiff climbs. The alternative routes meet again near the start of the Waskerley Way bikepath.

The route follows the Waskerley Way, a traffic-free trail taking in the rugged, expansive scenery of the northern Pennines, continuing all the way (predominantly downhill) to Consett. Here the C2C splits with one route heading to Sunderland via Stanley and the other (described here) to Newcastle via Rowlands Gill.

The Derwent Walk path follows the bed of the old Tyne Valley railway, a very pleasant, green route leading over numerous bridges and old rail viaducts, affording great views of the countryside below. The traffic-free path is broken momentarily at Rowlands Gill but soon resumes continuing all the way to the fringes of Newcastle.

The final stages of the ride can be difficult to navigate at times, following the Keelmans

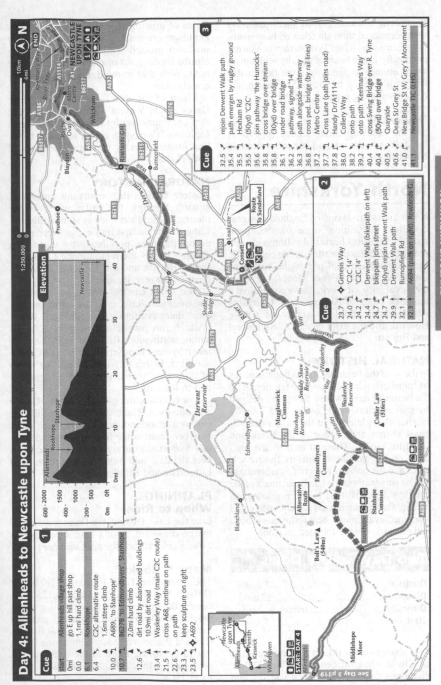

Day 4: Allenheads to Newcastle upon Tyne

1:250,000

Elevation

Cue ①

Start	Allenheads village shop
0mi	go E up hill past shop
0.0 ▲	1.1mi hard climb
6.1	Rookhope
6.4 ⌄	C2C alternative route
	1.6mi steep climb
10.0 ⌄	A689, 'to Stanhope'
10.7 ⌄	B6278 'to Edmondbyers' 'Stanhope
	2.0mi hard climb
12.6 ⌄	dirt road by abandoned buildings
	10.9mi dirt road
13.4 ⌄	Waskerley Way (main C2C route)
21.5	cross A68, continue on path
22.6 ⌄	on path
23.3 ⌄	keep sculpture on right
23.5 ⌄ ✦	A692

Cue ②

23.7 ✦	Genesis Way
24.0 ⌄	'C2C 14'
24.2 ⌄	'C2C 14'
24.4 ⌄	Derwent Walk (bikepath on left)
24.7	bikepath joins street
24.7 ⌄	(30yd) rejoin Derwent Walk path
29.9	Derwent Walk path
32.1	Burnopfield Rd
32.3 ⌄	A694 (path on right), Rowlands G.

Cue ③

32.5 ⌄	rejoin Derwent Walk path
35.4	path emerges by rugby ground
35.5 ⌄	Hexham Rd
35.5 ⌄	(50yd) 'C2C'
35.6 ⌄	join pathway 'the Hurrocks'
35.8	cross bridge over stream
35.8 ⌄	(30yd) over bridge
36.1	under road bridge
36.2 ⌄	pathway, signed '14'
36.3 ⌄	path alongside waterway
36.8 ⌄	cross ped. bridge (by rail lines)
37.2	Metro Centre
37.7 ⌄	Cross Lane (path joins road)
37.8 ⌄	Handy Dr/A1114
38.0 ⌄	Colliery Way
38.2 ⌄	onto path
38.2 ⌄	onto path 'Keelmans Way'
40.4 ⌄	cross Swing Bridge over R. Tyne
40.4 ⌄	(50yd) over bridge
40.5 ⌄	Quayside
40.6 ⌄	Dean St/Grey St
41.0 ⌄	New Bridge St W, Grey's Monument
41.1	Newcastle TIC (LHS)

START DAY 4
Allenheads

See Day 3 p.319

NORTHERN ENGLAND

Way along a succession of small pathways with occasional short stretches on busy roads. Once across the River Tyne, however, you are practically in the heart of the city with only a short distance to pedal from the fashionable Quayside area up to Grey's Monument, the central shopping precinct and the TIC.

Newcastle

See the Gateway Cities section (pp296–7) for accommodation and other services in Newcastle.

North Yorkshire

North Yorkshire is one of England's largest counties, containing some of the finest monuments, most beautiful countryside and most spectacular coastline in the country. It includes two national parks (the Yorkshire Dales and the North York Moors), the great medieval city of York, the extraordinary monastic ruins of Rievaulx and Fountains Abbeys, the classical beauty of Castle Howard, and the grim castles of Richmond and Bolton.

NATURAL HISTORY

In the west the Pennines, including the peaks of Ingleborough and Pen-y-ghent, dominate the beautiful dales whose flanks are defined by snaking stone walls overlooked by wild heather-clad plateaus. In the east, stone villages shelter at the foot of the bleak and beautiful moors. These stretch to the high cliffs on the east coast with its fishing villages and the holiday resort of Scarborough.

The winter climate is harsh and much of the countryside lends itself to sheep grazing, an activity that has continued largely unchanged from medieval times. Great fortunes – private and monastic – were founded on wool.

Two Days in the Dales

Duration	2 days
Distance	66.8mi
Difficulty	moderate-hard
Start/End	Ripon

This short circular ride is a great introduction to the magnificent Yorkshire Dales. Picturesque valleys, dry stone walls, green fields of grazing sheep and charming market towns are features of the ride. It is rarely on level ground with several challenging climbs leading out of one dale and into the next. With that in mind, each day is deliberately short.

Much of the ride follows the Yorkshire Dales Cycle Way, a 128mi circular route that continues south to Skipton and east to Ingleton. It's easy to construct some excellent longer rides by combining sections of both routes.

NATURAL HISTORY

Austere stone villages; streams and rivers cutting through the hills; wide, empty moors; and endless lines of stone walls dividing the landscape into a checkerboard of green pastures populated by wandering sheep – this is the region made famous by James Herriot and the TV series *All Creatures Great and Small*.

The dales can be broken into northern and southern halves: in the north the two main dales (valleys), Swaledale and Wensleydale, run parallel and east-west. In the south, north-south Ribblesdale is the route taken by the Leed-Settle-Carisle (LSC) railway line, which provides access to a series of attractive towns. Wharfedale is parallel and to the east.

The overwhelming impression is of space and openness. The high tops of the hills are exposed moorland, and the sheltered dales between them range from narrow and sinuous Swaledale through to broad and open Wensleydale and Wharfedale and rugged Littondale and Ribblesdale.

PLANNING
When to Ride

Like the Lake District, the Dales are a major tourist drawcard, so it's best if possible to avoid weekends and the peak summer period.

Maps & Books

The Yorkshire Tourist Board's *Yorkshire Dales Official Tourist Map* (1:125,000) covers the area in excellent detail and has most attractions and camping grounds marked. The *Yorkshire Dales Cycle Way* by Richard Peace is a handy companion if you intend exploring more of the route than is covered on this ride. It's available from local TICs.

What to Bring

There are no banks or ATMs in Kettlewell so grab some extra cash in Ripon.

GETTING TO/FROM THE RIDE
Ripon

Train The closest rail links are at Thirsk and Harrogate. There are frequent trains from York to Thirsk, a stop on the main Edinburgh line. The 20-minute journey costs £6.60 one way. The 30-minute trip from York to Harrogate or from Leeds to Harrogate costs £3.40 one way.

Bicycle Ripon is an easy 28.5mi ride from York. Follow the route out of York detailed in Day 1 of the North York Moors & Mansions ride (pp327–9) and continue on back roads through Linton-on-Ouse, Lower Dunsforth, Boroughbridge and Skelton.

From Thirsk avoid the A61 by cycling the back roads through Sowerby, Dalton, Topcliffe, Rainton and Sharrow, an easy ride of 16.1mi (see also the Day 1 map for the North York Moors and Mansions ride; p328).

THE RIDE
Ripon
☎ 01765

A busy market town with a magnificent cathedral and a history dating back to the 7th century, Ripon is an ideal base for exploring the dales.

Information The Ripon TIC (☎ 604625) is on Minster Rd opposite the cathedral. There are several banks with ATMs surrounding the market place. A limited range of cycling spares and accessories are available from Motorworld (☎ 606600) on Westgate.

Things to See & Do Yorkshire's only World Heritage–listed site, **Fountains Abbey** (☎ 608888) lies just 3.7mi from Ripon off the B6265. The magnificent, and largely intact ruins of the 12th-century Cistercian abbey are surrounded by extensive parklands and the Studley Royal water garden. Take your bike with you through the gates.

Impressively large **Ripon Cathedral** has been a place of worship for over 1300 years, since St Wilfred built one of England's first stone churches on the site in 672. Today's structure is a product of several periods of building and reconstruction over the centuries

although the crypt remains virtually unchanged from St Wilfred's time. The entrance is opposite the TIC.

Keep an ear out at 9 pm, when every night a horn is blown in the market square as part of the thousand-year-old setting of the watch ceremony.

Places to Stay & Eat The well-equipped *River Laver Holiday Park* (☎ 692015, fax 690508), is about a mile out of town just off the B6265 on the way to Fountains Abbey. Tent pitches are £8.50.

The *Riverside Hotel* (☎ 603864, 20–21 Boroughbridge Rd) is a small but comfortable guesthouse charging from £20, including breakfast. The *Unicorn Hotel* (☎ 602 202) is smarter and ideally located overlooking the market place, but priced accordingly at £47/67 for singles/doubles.

A number of pubs do evening meals. The *Black Bull* (☎ 602755), on Queen St, serves a good roast of the day for £4.75 and has Yorkshire puddings with a choice of fillings for around £3.50. *Prima Pizzeria* (☎ 602 034), on Kirkgate, is a popular eatery serving a good selection of pizzas and pastas at around £6. Over the road on Duck Hill, the *Ali Raj Balti House* (☎ 690885), fills the street with the fragrant aroma of the treats served within – a good selection of curries and other dishes for under £6.

Day 1: Ripon to Kettlewell
3½–4½ hours, 35.5mi

This is a reasonably short but strenuous day leading high into the heart of the dales. The rolling hills start soon after leaving Ripon, the narrow road to Masham carrying a moderate amount of traffic. Beyond Grewelthorpe, there are fewer cars to contend with as the narrow country lane travels a postcard dales landscape of rolling green fields, dry stone walls and grazing sheep.

Shortly after a fairly tough climb out of Healey is **Jervaulx Abbey** (17.0mi; ☎ 01677 -460226). A profusion of wildflowers (over 200 species) bloom in between the stones of the privately owned Cistercian ruins, which date back to 1156. It's a pleasant place to take a break and there's a small *cafe* over the road at the visitor centre.

A fine church marks your arrival in East Witton (18.7mi), a pretty village with a pub and small *store*, the last for quite a distance.

Two Days in the Dales

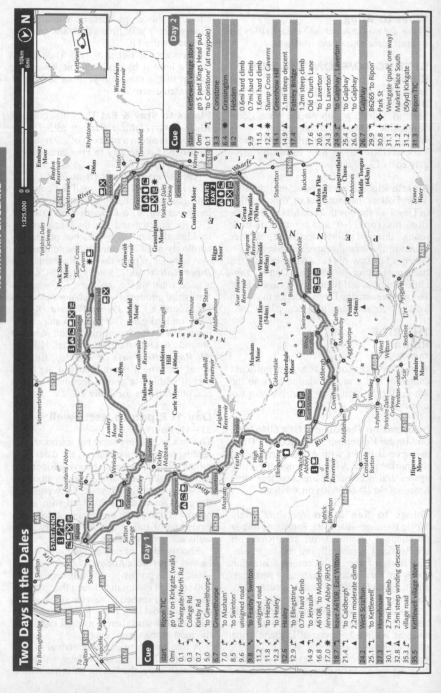

Day 1

Cue		
start		Ripon TIC
0mi		go W on Kirkgate (walk)
0.1	↰	Fishergate/North Rd
0.3	↰	College Rd
0.7	↱	Kirkby Rd
5.0	↱	'to Grewelthorpe'
6.7		Grewelthorpe
7.0	↰	'to Masham'
8.5	↱	'to Swinton'
9.6		unsigned road
9.8	↰	'to Fearby', Swinton
11.2		unsigned road
11.8	↱	'to Healey'
12.3	↱	'to Healey'
12.6		Healey
12.9	↰	'to Ellingstring'
14.9		0.7mi hard climb
16.8	↱	'to Jervaulx'
17.0		A6108, 'to Middleham'
18.7		Jervaulx Abbey (RHS)
21.4	↰	leave A6108, East Witton
		2.2mi moderate climb
24.2	↱	'to Caldbergh'
25.1	↱	West Scrafton
27.3	↱	'to Kettlewell'
30.1	▲	Horsehouse
32.8	▲	2.7mi hard climb
35.3	▲	2.5mi steep winding descent
35.5		village road
		Kettlewell village store

Day 2

Cue		
start		Kettlewell village store
0mi		go S past Kings Head pub
0.1	↱	'to Conistone' (at maypole)
3.3		Conistone
6.4		Grassington
8.2		Hebden
9.9	▲	0.6mi hard climb
11.5	▲	0.7mi hard climb
12.4	▲	1.6mi hard climb
		Stump Cross Caverns
14.1	*	Greenhow Hill
14.9	▲	2.1mi steep descent
17.4		Pateley Bridge
		1.2mi steep climb
17.6	↰	Old Church Lane
20.6	↱	'to Laverton'
24.3	↰	'to Laverton'
24.9	↱	'to Galphay', Laverton
25.4	↱	'to Galphay'
26.7	↰	'to Galphay'
		Galphay
29.9	↱	B6265 'to Ripon'
30.8	◆	Park St
31.1		Westgate (push, one way)
31.2		Market Place South
31.2	↰	(50yd) Kirkgate
31.3		Ripon TIC

The hills get larger as the day progresses, the quiet lane climbing steadily, leaving the lush green pastures behind for a wilder landscape of open grazing land roamed by wandering livestock.

The day's biggest ascent starts a short distance out of Horsehouse and continues, steeply at times, for a considerable 2.7mi. Care is needed to keep your speed under control on the final twisting descent into Kettlewell, which at times boasts a frighteningly steep, brake-block-burning gradient of one in four.

Kettlewell
☎ 01756

A picture-perfect village popular with walkers, cyclists and other outdoor enthusiasts, Kettlewell is a great place to take it easy for a few days, with numerous opportunities for some day rides in the magnificent surrounding countryside. The village is a stop on both the Dales Way footpath and the Yorkshire Dales Cycleway.

Information A small selection of bike spares and accessories are available from the outdoor store, Over & Under (☎ 760871). There are no banks or ATMs in the village.

Places to Stay & Eat The *Kettlewell YHA* *(☎ 760232, fax 760402)* is excellent. It's in the centre of the village in a fine old stone building, boasting modern amenities and a secure bike storeroom. The charge for a bed is £9.15 and dinner/breakfast is also available for £4.60/3.10.

There are three pubs in Kettlewell, all offering accommodation. *Blue Bell (☎ 760 230)* offers the best value with comfortable singles/doubles from £21/36.

The *Littlebeck B&B (☎ 760378)* occupies a fine Georgian house in a central position opposite the village maypole. Comfortable en suite rooms cost £25 per person; £5 single supplement. The *Elms (☎ 760224)*, on Middle Lane, offers B&B in a roomy Victorian home from £22.

Self-caterers will find a small selection of groceries at the village *store*. Dining options, apart from the *YHA* are limited to the village's three pubs, but they do offer a good selection. The *Blue Bell* has the best choice with a number of daily specials supplementing the substantial menu. Most dishes are under £6.

Day 2: Kettlewell to Ripon
3–3½ hours, 31.3mi

From Kettlewell a quiet, gently rolling lane runs parallel with the River Wharfe, through Conistone to Grassington, a sizeable village and home to the **National Park Centre** (☎ 01756-752774), boasting all the usual TIC services as well as piles of information relating specifically to the Yorkshire Dales National Park.

The route splits from the Yorkshire Dales Cycleway at Hebden (8.2mi), from where the B6265 begins to climb, with a number of stiff ascents over the next 5mi. The **Stump Cross Caverns** (12.2mi, ☎ 01423-711282) is a good place to take a well-earned break. The limestone caves, in which animal remains as old as 90,000 years have been found, are open for self-guided and guided tours. If speleology isn't your thing, grab a drink in the *cafe*.

The road continues to climb beyond the caves, with the steady gain in altitude gradually reflected in the transition to an open moors landscape. A high point is reached at the aptly named settlement of Greenhow

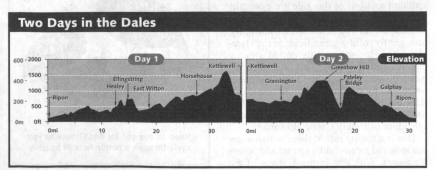

Two Days in the Dales

Hill (14.1mi), beyond which numerous roadside vantage points provide excellent views out over Nidderdale. Hard-won height is quickly shed on the enjoyable, but at times frighteningly steep descent into Pateley Bridge (17.4mi).

A bustling dales town straddling the River Nidd, Pateley Bridge has a good selection of shops and *food outlets*, as well as a TIC, fronting its narrow and exhaustingly steep high street.

The climb out of Pateley Bridge will test the strongest of riders, and although you'll more than likely have to get off and push in places, the brutal gradient does provide a mercifully direct and a relatively short route out of the valley.

At the top your hard work is rewarded with some stunning views of Nidderdale and the rooftops of Pateley Bridge below. The lonely road travels along the open heather-topped moor beside dry stone walls and fields of woolly sheep, before descending into greener countryside near Laverton (24.9mi).

The final miles, with the exception of a small climb just beyond Galphay, are fairly easy, bringing you out on to the moderately busy B6265 near the outskirts of Ripon. Follow the well-signed route into the centre of town.

North York Moors & Mansions

Duration	4 days
Distance	139.7mi
Difficulty	moderate-hard
Start/End	York

The contrasts between the northern and southern sections of this ride are dramatic, with each day presenting a fresh series of landscapes. As you pedal farther north, the lush, gently rolling green fields of the Hambleton and Howardian Hills, dotted with numerous stately homes, are replaced by isolated stone cottages and remote villages weathered by the harsh environment of the stark but beautiful North York Moors. The route returns via Pickering and the palatial splendour of stately Castle Howard.

This is a testing ride at times with numerous long and steep climbs up into and across the moors. With that in mind, many of the days described below are intentionally short. Much of the route from York to Swainby is on the Sustrans *White Rose* Hull to Middlesbrough cycle route (No 65, 66). Keep an eye out for the blue and white route markers.

NATURAL HISTORY

Only Exmoor, Dartmoor and the Lake District can rival the beauty of the 553 sq mile North York Moors National Park. More expansive than Dartmoor and far less crowded than the Lake District, the park's network of

Heather & Grouse

The North York Moors have the largest expanse of heather moorland in England. You can see three species: ling is the most widespread, has a pinkish-purple flower, and is most spectacular in late summer; bell heather is deep purple; and cross-leaved heather (or bog heather) prefers wet ground, unlike the first two, and tends to flower earlier. Wet, boggy areas also feature cotton grass, sphagnum moss and insect-eating sundew plants.

The moors have traditionally been managed to provide an ideal habitat for the red grouse – a famous game bird. The shooting season lasts from the 'Glorious Twelfth' of August to 10 December. The heather is periodically burned, giving managed moorland a patchwork effect – the grouse nests in mature growth, but feeds on the tender shoots of new growth.

KATE NOLAN

Keep an eye out for Red Grouse as you cycle through a purple haze of heather.

lonely roads connects small stone villages across vast tracts of open moors.

The western boundary is a steep escarpment formed by the Hambleton and Cleveland Hills, with the coastal cliffs between Scarborough and Staithes marking the western extremity. Rainwater escapes from the Moors down deep parallel dales to the Rivers Rye and Derwent in the south and the River Esk in the north.

PLANNING
When to Ride
The North York Moors are at their best from July to early September when the heather blooms in an explosion of purple.

Maps
If you're looking to construct some of your own rides, the OS Touring Map No 2, *North York Moors* (1:63,360) provides an excellent overview of the area. The *North York Moors Cycling Map*, available from local TICs, may also be useful with several tours and cycle friendly roads marked.

GETTING TO/FROM THE RIDE
York
Air Although it doesn't have its own airport York is serviced by several in the vicinity. The closest are Leeds/Bradford, Humberside (near Scunthorpe) and Teesside (near Middlesbrough). The nearest servicing international destinations beyond Europe is Manchester airport, conveniently connected to York by the Trans-Pennine Express rail service (two hours, £7.80).

Train York is well served by rail. There are numerous trains to/from London's King's Cross (two hours, £57.50) and points north including Newcastle (one hour, £13.90) and Edinburgh (2½ hours, £47). Local trains to Scarborough take 45 minutes and cost £9.10. For Whitby (three hours, £16.50) it's necessary to change at Middlesbrough (one hour, £11.90). Trains to/from the west and north-west go via Leeds (30 minutes, £6.20).

Bicycle See Days 7 & 8 (pp219–23) of the Central England Explorer ride in the Central England chapter for maps and a description of the route from York to Haworth and Lancaster.

THE RIDE
York
See York (pp217–19) in the Central England Explorer ride in the Central England chapter for information about accommodation and other services.

Day 1: York to Thirsk
3½–4½ hours, 39.3mi
This is a relatively easy day, but like most on this ride, there's plenty to see and do off the bike. The exit from York is very cycle friendly, travelling the first few miles on a path alongside the River Ouse.

After 9mi, pass stately **Beningbrough Hall** (☎ 01904-702021, NT), one of many fine homes in the area that's open to the public. Keep an eye out for the turn-off before Linton-on-Ouse, which unlike the many low-flying RAF planes from the nearby air base, is easy to miss. A short stretch on a bumpy public bridleway and quiet country lanes leads to Easingwold (20.3mi), a busy Georgian market town with its own TIC and plenty of places around the central grassed square to grab some lunch.

Out of Easingwold the route becomes hillier, nothing too serious but plenty of taxing little ups and downs. One of the off-bike highlights of the day is **Newburgh Priory** (26.0mi; ☎ 01347-868435), a fine stately home built on the site of an Augustinian priory. The house, reputed to hold the entombed body of Oliver Cromwell, is surrounded by impressive gardens. A little farther down the road, not far from the picture perfect village of Coxwold, is **Byland Abbey** (☎ 01347-868614, EH), an historic site providing a fine example of the later development of Cistercian churches.

Following the *White Rose* low-level route pass through Kilburn (32.0mi) and get a close-up view of the famous **White Horse**, first laid out by the local schoolmaster on the hillside in 1857. Kilburn is also where Robert Thompson produced his famous, fine oak furniture complete with the trademark mouse carved into each handcrafted piece. The furniture factory is still going strong and you can learn all about the man and the furniture at the **Mouseman visitor centre** (☎ 01347-868222), in Thompson's original workshop.

Leave the *White Rose* route (33.0mi), continuing through Bagby and over the

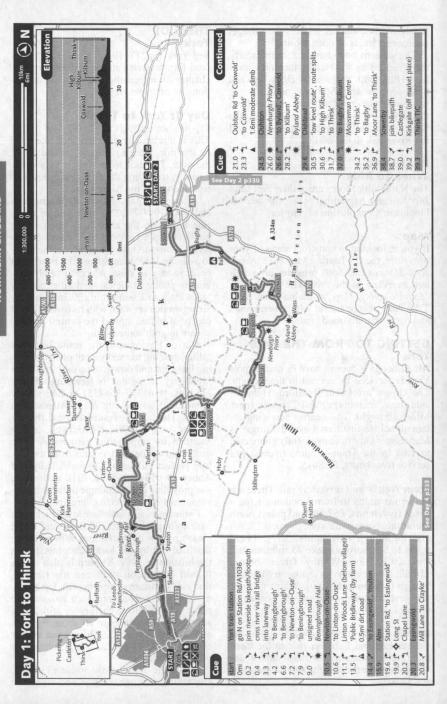

NORTHERN ENGLAND

Day 1: York to Thirsk

Elevation

	Cue
start	York train station
0mi	go N on Station Rd/A1036
0.2	join riverside bikepath/footpath
0.4	cross river via rail bridge
3.3	into laneway
4.2	'to Beningbrough'
6.6	'to Beningbrough'
7.2	'to Newton-on-Ouse'
7.9	'to Beningbrough'
9.0	unsigned road
	Beningbrough Hall
10.5	Newton-on-Ouse
10.6	'to Linton-on-Ouse'
11.1	Linton Woods Lane (before village)
13.5	'Public Bridleway' (by farm)
	0.5mi dirt road
14.4	'to Easingwold' Youlton
15.9	Alne
19.6	Station Rd, 'to Easingwold'
19.9	Long St
20.2	Chapel Lane
20.3	Easingwold
20.8	Mill Lane 'to Crayke'

	Cue Continued
21.0	Oulston Rd 'to Coxwold'
23.3	'to Coxwold'
	1.6mi moderate climb
24.5	Oulston
26.0	Newburgh Priory
26.6	'to Byland, Coxwold
28.2	'to Kilburn'
	Byland Abbey
	Oldstead
29.6	'low level route', route splits
30.6	'to High Kilburn'
31.7	'to Thirsk'
32.0	'to Bagby', Kilburn
	Mouseman Centre
34.2	'to Thirsk'
35.2	'to Bagby'
36.9	Moor Lane 'to Thirsk'
38.4	Sowerby
38.7	join bikepath
39.0	Castlegate
39.2	Kirkgate (off market place)
39.3	Thirsk TIC

See Day 2 p330

See Day 4 p333

busy A19, to enter Thirsk via Sowerby on quiet but unremarkable back roads.

Thirsk
☎ 01845

A typical, busy Yorkshire market town, Thirsk is best known as the home of the late James (Alf) Wight, the vet who penned the hugely popular autobiographical James Herriot stories that have become synonymous with rural Yorkshire.

Information The Thirsk TIC (☎ 522755, fax 526230) is at 25 Kirkgate. The staff here can provide information on local attractions and accommodation.

Virtually all services, including numerous banks with ATMs, are around the central market place. The town's bike shop, the Cycle Centre (☎ 527444), is across from the TIC on Kirkgate.

Things to See & Do The big attraction in town is the recently opened **James Herriot Experience** (☎ 524234), next to the TIC in the vet's Skeldale House surgery. Learn all about the goings on of a rural vet practice through a number of well-presented exhibits featuring multimedia displays, original veterinary instruments and period furnishings. Tickets are sold in the TIC and provide a pre-booked admission time. **St Mary's**, one of the finest Gothic churches in Yorkshire is also well worth a look. Just continue down Kirkgate past the TIC.

Places to Stay Pitch a tent at the *York House Caravan Park* (☎ 597495), in Balk on the Day 1 route about 3.1mi south of Thirsk, from £5.80.

For location, the *Lavender House B&B* (☎ 522224), next to the TIC on Kirkgate, is hard to beat. It charges from £16 per person. *Fourways Guest House* (☎ 522601, fax 522 131), on Town End, a large B&B in a handsome building close to the centre of town, also charges from £16.

The *Three Tuns Hotel* (☎ 523124), overlooking Market Place, has comfortable en suite rooms from £40/60 for a single/double including breakfast.

Places to Eat There are a number of good bakeries including a *Bakers Oven* and *Thomas the Baker* around the square, as well as a *Kwik Save* supermarket. The *White Horse Cafe*, next to the clock in the middle of Market Place, is a popular choice for sit-down fish and chips, and the like.

The *Golden Fleece Hotel* (☎ 523108), on Market Place, boasts a surprisingly good bar menu featuring such varied dishes as risotto and couscous with mains averaging around £7. For more of a restaurant atmosphere *Charles* (☎ 527444), on Baker's Alley, is a good choice. It's a small bistro with an interesting menu, mains around £10.

Day 2: Thirsk to Castleton
3½–4½ hours, 37.7mi

Despite a short initial stretch on busy Stockton Rd, it's not long before you're away from the traffic, cycling along quiet hedgelined lanes and up into the Hambleton Hills. Beyond Kepwick the route enters the Silton Forest pine plantation and climbs sharply on a gravel forestry road, emerging to reveal a dramatically different landscape.

Welcome to the North York Moors National Park, a lonely open expanse of heather-carpeted hills. It's wild and bleak, but undeniably beautiful. Your first taste of the moors is a brief one though, with the route descending back to greener surrounds at Cod Beck Reservoir on the way in to Swainby.

Following a short stretch on the busy A172 the ride is largely level to Great Broughton (24.6mi) but becomes increasingly hilly beyond it. Just out of Battersby an 18m **obelisk** erected in honour of Captain James Cook is visible atop Easby Moor. This is Captain Cook country; the famous explorer was born in Marton, now a suburb of Middlesbrough, and educated in nearby Great Ayton.

A couple of tough climbs around Kildale (30.4mi) and out of Commondale lead back into characteristic moors scenery, with a final ascent from the Castleton train station (a stop on the scenic Middlesbrough-Whitby (Esk Valley) line) heading in to the village.

Castleton
☎ 01287

A small village of stone cottages, Castleton boasts a reasonable number of services for its size. There's not much to do but rest your weary legs, although the parish church, with **furniture** by Robert 'Mouseman' Thompson, is worth a look.

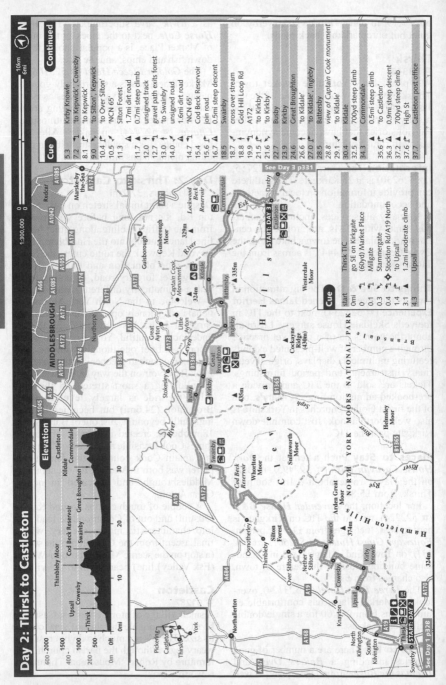

NORTHERN ENGLAND

Day 2: Thirsk to Castleton

Cue — Continued

5.3		Kirby Knowle
7.2	↰	'to Kepwick', Cowesby
8.1	↱	'to Kepwick'
9.0	↰	'to Silton', Kepwick
10.4	↱	'to Over Silton'
10.5	↗	'NCN 65'
11.3	↖	Silton Forest
11.7	◀	0.7mi steep climb
12.0	◀	unsigned track
12.7	↱	gravel path exits forest
13.0	↱	'to Swainby'
14.0	↰	unsigned road
	◀	1.6mi dirt road
14.7	↰	'NCN 65'
15.4		Cod Beck Reservoir
15.6	↳	join road
16.7	◀	0.5mi steep descent
18.5		Swainby
18.7	◀	cross over stream
18.8	↟	Gold Hill Loop Rd
19.9	↰	A172
21.5	↱	'to Kirkby'
21.6	↰	'to Kirkby'
22.7		Busby
23.9		Kirkby
24.6		Great Broughton
26.6	↱	'to Kildale'
27.0	↰	'to Kildale', Ingleby
28.5		Battersby
28.8		view of Captain Cook monument
29.1	↗	'to Kildale'
30.4		Kildale
32.5	◀	700yd steep climb
34.3		Commondale
	◀	0.5mi steep climb
35.6	↳	'to Castleton'
36.3	◀	0.9mi steep descent
37.2	◀	700yd steep climb
37.6	↳	High St
37.7		Castleton post office

See Day 3 p331

Cue

start		Thirsk TIC
0mi	↱↱↰	go SE on Kirkgate
0.1	↰↙	(60yd) Market Place
0.3	↱	Millgate
0.4	↰↙	Stammergate
	↱↰	Stockton Rd/A19 North
1.4	↰	'to Upsall'
3.1	◀	1.2mi moderate climb
4.3		Upsall

Elevation

Day 2: Thirsk to Castleton

Scale 1:300,000

Day 3: Castleton to Pickering

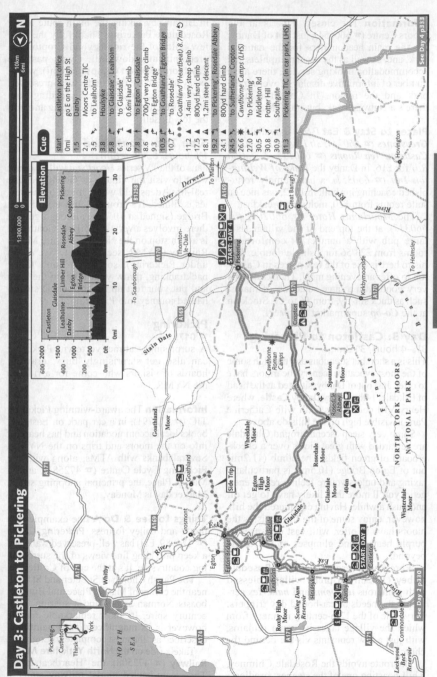

NORTHERN ENGLAND

Cue		
start	0mi	Castleton post office
		go E on the High St
1.5		Danby
2.1		Moors Centre TIC
3.5	↗	'to Lealholm'
3.8		Houlsyke
5.8	↰	'to Glaisdale', Lealholm
6.1	↰	'to Glaisdale'
6.3	◀	0.6mi hard climb
7.8	↰	'to Egton', Glaisdale
8.6	◀	700yd very steep climb
9.3	↰	'to Egton Bridge'
10.5	↰	'to Goathland', Egton Bridge
10.7	↰	'to Rosedale'
	●●●	Goathland (Heartbeat) 8.7mi
11.2	◀	1.4mi very steep climb
17.5	◀	800yd hard climb
18.1	◀	1.2mi steep descent
19.2	↰	'to Pickering', Rosedale Abbey
24.1	◀	800yd hard climb
24.5	↰	'to Sutherland', Cropton
26.6	✳	Cawthorne Camps (LHS)
27.0	↰	'to Pickering'
30.5	↗	Middleton Rd
30.8	↗	Potter Hill
30.9	↘	Southgate
31.3		Pickering TIC (in car park, LHS)

Elevation

Information The closest TIC is at the Moors Centre (☎ 660654), just out of Danby. It's the main headquarters for the national park, and, as well as the usual pamphlets and accommodation booking service, there are a number of informative displays covering the park and the region. In Castleton itself there's a Natwest bank, but no ATM.

Places to Stay & Eat B&B is available at *Greystones* (☎ 660744, 30 High St) or at the *Castleton Tea Rooms* (☎ 660135, 2 Station Rd) for £16. In Danby the *Duke of Wellington Inn* (☎ 660351), a handsomely refurbished coaching inn built in 1732, has nice en suite rooms from £20, including breakfast.

The *Moorlands Hotel* (☎ 660206, fax 660317), at the top end of the village, is a large pub with a number of comfortable rooms from £23/56 for a single/double. The bistro here is one of the few places in Castleton to offer an evening meal. Thankfully it's very good with a large selection of mains, such as duck stir-fry, from £6 to £9. Stock up at the *Co-op* supermarket *(High St)*.

Day 3: Castleton to Pickering
3½–4 hours, 31.3mi
This is a short but strenuous day through some of the most evocative scenery the moors have to offer. Just out of Danby, situated at the head of Eskdale, 14th-century **Danby Castle**, where Henry VIII courted his sixth wife Catherine Parr, is visible high on the hillside above.

Some very steep ascents around Glaisdale are rewarded with great views over a checkerboard of green fields. The climb (11.2mi) out of Egton Bridge (10.5mi) is particularly taxing and unless you're feeling really energetic, you'll more than likely have to get off and push a while. Having conquered the hill, however, enjoy some of the finest vistas the moors have to offer, with vast expanses of purple heather and glimpses of the ocean beyond.

A breakneck descent heads into **Rosedale Abbey** (19.2mi), a pretty village blessed with numerous *tearooms* and *bakeries* servicing the needs of car-bound day trippers. Very little of the 12th-century nunnery from which the village takes its name remains, with just a few remnants visible behind the church.

The route avoids the Rosedale Chimney, a hill boasting one of the steepest gradients in Britain, by taking the main route along Rosedale to Pickering. Thankfully the final few miles of the ride beyond Cropton are predominantly downhill. Cycle past the **Cawthorne Roman Camps** (26.6mi), where excavations have revealed a well-preserved Roman settlement, before descending from the hills on to the Vale of Pickering and into the town itself.

Side Trip: Goathland
1½ hours, 8.7mi return
Fans of the TV series *Heartbeat* will no doubt want to visit the village of Goathland, the real-life Adensfield where much of the series is filmed. It's around 4.3mi from Egton Bridge (signed at 10.7mi) although getting there involves a very stiff climb. Goathland is also a stop on the North Yorkshire Moors Railway (NYMR; see Things to See & Do under Pickering), so if you don't fancy backtracking, throw your bike on the train and put your feet up for the scenic steam-hauled journey into Pickering.

Pickering
☎ 01751
A surprisingly attractive town, Pickering can also get surprisingly busy, drawing hoards of visitors who come for a ride on the NYMR.

Information The award-winning Pickering TIC (☎ 473791), in a car park on Eastgate, books local accommodation and has heaps of info on the moors and trips on the NYMR. Several banks with ATMs, along with the Pickering Cycle Centre (☎ 472581), are on Market Place, the principal shopping street. Market day is Monday.

Things to See & Do A fine example of a motte and bailey fortress, **Pickering Castle** (☎ 474989, EH) has well-preserved walls and a keep providing fine views of the surrounding countryside. It's at the end of Castlegate.

The Parish Church of St Peter and St Paul, near the corner of Market Place and Burgate, boasts Norman arches and a soaring 14th-century spire. Its most remarkable feature however is its **magnificent wall paintings**, described as 'the most complete in England'.

Take a ride on the **North Yorkshire Moors Railway** (☎ 472508), the 'Heartbeat train'. The steam-hauled tourist railway stops at

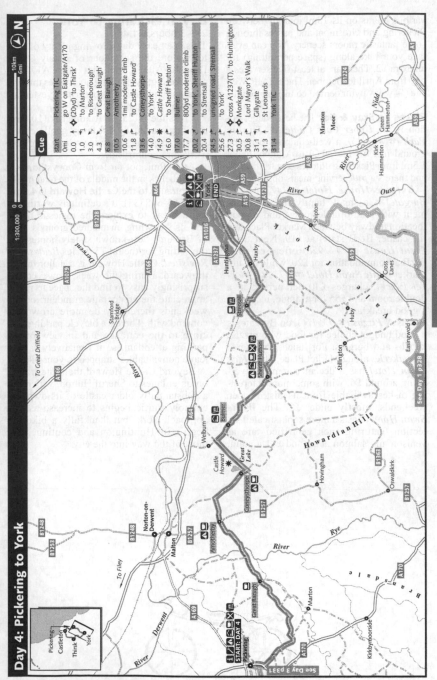

Day 4: Pickering to York

Cue		
start		Pickering TIC
0mi		go W on Eastgate/A170
0.0	◇←↑	(20yd) 'to Thirsk'
1.0	↙	'to Marton'
3.0	↗	'to Riseborough'
4.3	↗	'to Great Barugh'
6.8	←	Great Barugh
10.5	◄	Amotherby
10.6	◄	1mi moderate climb
11.8	↗	'to Castle Howard'
13.6	←	Coneysthorpe
14.0	↓	'to York'
14.9	✳	Castle Howard
16.0	↓	'to Sheriff Hutton'
17.0		Bulmer
17.7	◄	800yd moderate climb
20.2	↗	'to York', Sheriff Hutton
20.4	↗	'to Strensall'
24.5		unsigned road, Strensall
25.6	↓	'to York'
27.3	◇↓	cross A1237(T), 'to Huntington'
30.5	↓	Monkgate
30.8	↓	Lord Mayor's Walk
31.1		Gillygate
31.3		St Leonards
31.4		York TIC

various points on its 18mi journey between Pickering and Grosmont and passes through some fantastic moors scenery. You can even take your bike along (space permitting) for an extra £2. There are at least five services a day from April to October. The NYMR Web site (🖳 www.nymr.demon.co.uk) has details.

Places to Stay & Eat The best budget option is the *Upper Carr Chalet & Touring Park* (☎ *473115)*, a well-equipped camping ground just off the A169 to Malton, about 1.5mi from Pickering. Pitches cost from £5.50 and there's a *pub* serving meals opposite.

Burgate House Hotel (☎ *473463, 17 Burgate)* is a small, family run establishment with comfortable rooms and a good location midway between Market Place and the castle. B&B starts at £19. Next door, *Clent House* (☎ *477928)* offers en suite B&B accommodation for £20, while the upmarket *White Swan Hotel* (☎ *472288, Market Place)*, charges £40 per person in a double room and £55 for a single, including a good breakfast.

Bits N Pizzas (☎ *475116)*, on Burgate, is a good budget choice for food with pizzas, kebabs and burgers. For lunch, try one of the *bakeries* along Market Place. The *Black Swan Hotel* has a decent bar menu averaging around £6, with some more interesting dishes available from its bistro, open weekends, mostly under £8. The *White Swan Hotel* boasts a more sophisticated selection featuring such gentrified fare as venison and salmon at around £11 a main.

Day 4: Pickering to York
2½–3 hours, 31.4mi
This is an easy day allowing plenty of time to explore the splendour of stately Castle Howard. After a brief stint on the A170 out of Pickering, cycle along quiet lanes through pleasant and, in stark contrast to yesterday, relatively flat rural scenery.

Cross the B1257 at Amotherby (10.5mi) and begin a steady but fairly gentle climb, providing some nice views back over the Yorkshire countryside.

At 14.9mi, not far from Coneysthorpe, a large obelisk in the middle of the road marks the entrance to the **Castle Howard** (14.9mi; ☎ 01653-648333). It's definitely worth taking a break to explore the majestic house and its sprawling, manicured grounds. One of Britain's best-known stately homes and the setting for the hit TV series *Brideshead Revisited*, Castle Howard is a major tourist drawcard. During the week, however, it's surprisingly easy to find the space to really appreciate the aristocratic grandeur; on the weekends there may be more crowds to contend with. There's a bicycle parking area close to the entrance and in view of the parking attendant, so it's relatively safe to leave nonvaluables strapped to your bike.

Beyond Castle Howard the route travels on quiet lanes to Sheriff Hutton, which has a substantially older castle of its own. Inevitably traffic begins to increase as you approach York, but thankfully a bikepath begins in Huntington and continues for most of the way into the city.

Scotland

If you think of cycling in Britain, remote and wild country isn't generally what springs to mind. Scotland, however, is more lightly populated than the rest of Britain and it is here, particularly in the Highlands, that narrow, winding single-track roads undulate across lonely purple moors, alongside long and narrow lochs, and around the convoluted coast. Here, sheep and shaggy Highland cattle own the roads and pretty white crofters' cottages dot the hillsides. Especially in more settled areas, the countryside is littered with evidence of earlier times – from ancient forts and monuments to beautiful old abbeys and castles.

The weather can be unpredictable – as rugged and wild as the landscape or as warm and hospitable as the people. The Scots have a strong sense of their cultural identity – traditional dress is worn with pride, and traditional music is widely played. (Also readily available, of course, is traditional home baking and plenty of single-malt whisky...)

HISTORY

It's believed that the earliest settlement of Scotland was undertaken by hunters and fishers 6000 years ago. They were followed by the Celtic Picts, whose loose tribal organisation survived to the 18th century in the clan structure of the Highlands. They never bowed to the Romans, who retreated and built Hadrian's Wall. Another Celtic tribe, the Gaels (or Scots), arrived from northern Ireland (Scotia) in the 6th century. By the time the Normans arrived, most of Scotland was loosely united under the Canmore dynasty.

Despite almost continuous border warfare, it wasn't until a dispute over the Canmore succession that England's Edward I attempted the conquest of Scotland. Beginning with the siege of Berwick in 1296, fighting finally ended in 1328 with the Treaty of Northampton, which recognised Robert the Bruce as king of an independent Scotland. Robert, more Norman than Scottish in his ancestry, cemented an alliance with France that would complicate the political map for almost 400 years.

In 1542 Scotland's James V died, leaving two-week-old daughter Mary a heir. Henry VIII of England decided she would make a

suitable daughter-in-law, and his armies ravaged the Borders and sacked Edinburgh in a failed attempt to force agreement from the Scots (called the Rough Wooing).

At 15, Mary married the French dauphin and duly became Queen of France as well as Scotland. Mary was later forced to abdicate in favour of her son, James VI. Mary was imprisoned but escaped and fled to England's Queen Elizabeth (her cousin), who locked her in the Tower of London. Nineteen years later, at the age of 44, Mary was beheaded for allegedly plotting Elizabeth's death. When the childless Elizabeth died in 1603, Mary's son united the two crowns for the first time as James I of England and James VI of Scotland.

In 1707, after complex bargaining (and buying a few critical votes), England persuaded the Scottish Parliament to agree to the union of the two countries under a single parliament. The Scots received trading privileges and retained their independent church and legal system. The decision was unpopular from the start, and the exiled Stuarts promised to repeal it. Jacobites (Stuart supporters) led two major rebellions – in 1715 and in 1745, when Bonnie Prince Charlie failed to extend his support beyond the Catholic Highland clans. The Jacobite cause was finally buried at the Battle of Culloden

(1746), after which the English set out to destroy the clans, prohibiting Highland dress, weapons and military service.

In the mid-19th century overpopulation, the collapse of the kelp industry, the 1840s potato famine and the increased grazing of sheep by the lairds (landowning aristocrats) led to Highlanders being forced off their land – the Highland Clearances. After WWI Scotland's ship, steel, coal, cotton and jute industries began to fail, and, though there was a recovery during WWII, since the 1960s they have been in terminal decline.

In the 1970s and 80s, North Sea oil (Scottish oil, as the Scots saw it) gave the economy a boost. Despite the bonanza, Thatcherism failed to impress the Scots. From 1979 to 1997, Scotland was ruled by a Conservative

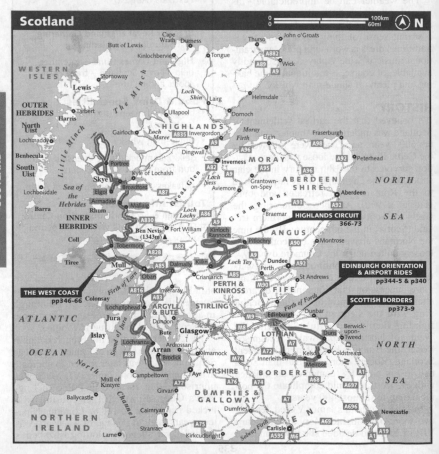

Edinburgh Castle is the jewel of Scotland's capital...

...and the pubs aren't bad either.

Catch a ferry from Scotland's west coast to the azure – and almost tempting – waters of the Isle of Iona.

Lochranza village, Isle of Arran.

Stock up on supplies in the busy fishing village of Tarbert.

How to beat Scotland's wind.

Gateway to the Scottish Isles, the Highland port of Oban.

Look out for seals at night in the harbour of the lively fishing village of Mallaig, Scotland.

At last! The John o'Groats pedestal in northern Scotland.

Fuel stop: a Gifford bakery.

government for which the majority of Scots didn't vote. Following the victory of the Labour Party in May 1997, a referendum on the creation of a Scottish Parliament was overwhelmingly supported by voters. For the first time since 1707, the Scottish Parliament opened in Edinburgh on 1 July 1999.

NATURAL HISTORY

About half the size of England, Scotland is often described in terms of three regions. The Southern Uplands are the fertile coastal plains and ranges from the English border to Edinburgh and Glasgow. Within the triangle from Glasgow to Edinburgh and Dundee are the Central Lowlands, containing the industrial belt and most of the population. The northern two-thirds of the country comprise the Highlands and Islands.

Among the Highland mountain ranges of sandstone, granite and metamorphic rock are almost 300 peaks over 900m (3000ft), known as 'Munros', after the man who listed them. At 1343m (4406ft) Ben Nevis, in the western Grampians, is Britain's highest mountain. The Great Glen is a fault line running north-east from Fort William to Inverness, containing a chain of freshwater lochs, including Loch Ness.

Of Scotland's 790 islands, 130 are inhabited. The inner and outer Hebrides are off the west coast; to the north are the Orkney and Shetland groups.

Despite its wild, uncultivated appearance, the Scottish countryside has been dramatically altered by humans. Much of Scotland was once covered by Caledonian forest (a mix of Scots pine, oak, birch, willow, alder and rowan), though only 1% now remains. Today almost three-quarters of the country is uncultivated bog, rock and heather. Peat covers almost two million acres. Fast-growing conifer plantations have been encouraged in recent decades, despite ecological drawbacks.

The ubiquitous heather brings a purple haze to the moors in August. Other summer flowers include bluebells (Scotland's national flower), thistles (also a common emblem), yellow flag, wild thyme, yarrow and gorse.

Changes to the environment and hunting have taken their toll on native animals, many of which are now rare or extinct. Some of the more common species include the red deer, Highland cattle, red squirrels, foxes, hares and minks.

Grouse graze the heather on the moors, which gamekeepers burn to encourage new shoots and attract birds. Less common is the black, turkey-like capercaillie, largest of the grouse family, which prefers heavily wooded areas.

Scotland, with 80% of Britain's coastline, is also home to millions of seabirds, including comical puffins. Whales and seals are frequently seen in Scottish waters, while Scottish salmon, along with trout, is found in many rivers and lochs.

CLIMATE

With a cool temperate climate, Scotland has changeable and localised weather. The west is considerably wetter than the east. Rainfall in the Highlands can be up to 3000mm (prompting the wry observation: 'If you can see the mountains, it's about to rain, if you can't, it already is'). May and June are generally the driest months, but be prepared for rain any time.

Its proximity to the Gulf Stream means that the west coast is milder than the east (the average summer high being around 19°C). Considering its northerly latitude, the whole country's climate is relatively mild.

Warnings

Be conscious of the following when cycling in Scotland:

- Take particular care if you're cycling or walking off-road during the grouse hunting season, which opens on August 12. Avoid areas where shooting is in progress (look out for signs or check with local TICs).

- Deer stalking also takes place from August to October. Pick up a free Hill Phones brochure, available from TICs, and call the relevant number before heading off-road.

- Scottish weather can change quickly and dramatically. It's essential to carry adequate protective clothing and food, particularly in the Highlands.

- Outside the main tourist season (Easter to October), services and accommodation may close. Especially in remote areas, it's advisable to phone ahead.

SCOTLAND

Getting to/from Edinburgh Airport

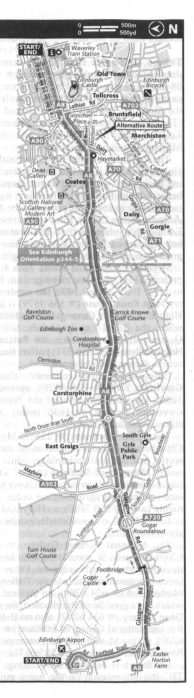

Edinburgh airport is about 8mi west of the centre of Edinburgh and the direct route from the airport to the city centre (Edinburgh TIC) is via main roads. The ride is quick and easy, if not especially scenic and takes up to an hour. See also the Edinburgh Orientation ride map (pp344–5) for greater detail of central Edinburgh.

Airport to City

Although the route runs entirely along busy main roads, there are shared bicycle paths or Greenway (bike/bus) lanes for much of the way.

Between the airport and the Maybury Rd intersection (3mi) cyclists are required to use the sometimes-bumpy shared footpath along the A8. Initially the path is only on the south side of the road. It continues on the north side after crossing a footbridge (2mi).

From Maybury Rd, Greenway (bike/bus) lanes continue to the city.

Take particular care at roundabouts, especially at the massive Gogar roundabout (2.6mi) and in shopping areas, where the Greenway disappears to make way for parking.

City to Airport

When riding to the airport from the city, detour onto George St (via St David St) to avoid Princes St – there is no bike lane on the north side of Princes St and traffic can be particularly heavy. Particular care is needed at the one-way section through Torpichen Place and Morrison St (1.2mi). Use the middle lane, but beware of heavy traffic.

The Edinburgh skyline on a summer day.

BETHUNE CARMICHAEL

up to £30. If you're single, try **Mrs Ross** (☎ *557 9368; 3a Clarence St, Stockbridge)*, where B&B is £17 per person for singles and doubles/twins.

Private hotel accommodation in Edinburgh is expensive. At the pleasant, central **Greens Hotel** (☎ *337 1565, fax 346 2990, 24 Eglington Crescent)*, B&B starts at £60 for a single and £110 for a double or twin. The bistro's two-course set meal is good value at £6.95.

Thrums Hotel (☎ *667 5545; fax 667 8708; 14 Minto St, Newington)* charges £35/80 for singles/doubles. Fairly standard mains in the small restaurant start at £5.50.

Places to Eat Princes St is the best spot for fast food, with international chains and food courts in the Waverley Market and St James shopping centres.

The groovy, off-beat **Elephant House** (☎ *2205355, 21 George IV Bridge)* is deservedly popular. Good coffee can be had here, as well as pastries and mains like chilli con (or sin) carne for £3.65, or lasagne and salad for £4.75. **Elephant's Sufficiency** (☎ *220 0666; 170 High St, Royal Mile)* – no relation – has lunch burgers, salad and baked potatoes. Takeaway starts at £2.25, more if you eat in. **Common Grounds** (☎ *226 1416, North Bank St)* has good cheap food, but don't go for the coffee.

Parrots (☎ *229 3252, 3 Viewforth, Bruntsfield)*, off Brunstfield Place, has great-value evening meals and lots of parrots. Try the moussaka for £3.95. Down the hill, **Filfila** (☎ *622 7319, 60 Home St)* serves inexpensive, large, mostly Middle Eastern lunches. Opposite the church spire, **Scott's Delicatessen & Continental Bakers** (cnr Leven St & Gillespie Crescent)* has excellent bread and melt-in-the-mouth 59p almond croissants.

Towards the west end of town, try **Pizza Express** (32 Queensferry St)* for good pizzas between £4.25 and £6.45. The Italian-style chain **Costa** (☎ *229 9328, Shandwick Place)* is reliable for decent coffee and reasonable food. Good-sized, delicious two-course dinners at the cosy **French Corner Bistro** (☎ *226 1890, 17 Queensferry St)* cost around £12.

Good veg restaurants include the long-established, **Henderson's** (☎ *225 2131; 92 Hanover St)*, a well-run, cafeteria-style restaurant in the city. Main plus salad or potatoes is around £7. The daytime deli

sells good bread and takeaway lunches. Near the university, **Susie's Wholefood Diner** (☎ *667 8729, 51 West Nicholson St)* is less slick and better value.

Getting There & Away There are plenty of air, train and bus options for getting to and leaving from Edinburgh.

Air Edinburgh airport (☎ *333 1000)*, 8mi west of the city, has numerous services to other UK cities, Ireland and Europe, and some to Africa, the Middle East and Asia. North American flights arrive via Glasgow. See the boxed text 'Getting to/from Edinburgh Airport' for directions and a map covering the route into the city.

Airbus Express (☎ *556 2244, 🖳 www.guidefriday.com)* runs every 15 minutes from the airport to the city. The 25-minute trip is £3.60 one way and bikes (carried at the driver's discretion) are free. LRT buses (which also service the airport) do not carry bikes.

A taxi to the city centre costs between £12 and £15.

Train The main train station is Waverley, near the TIC (also accessible from Waverley Bridge). For rail inquiries, contact Scotrail (☎ *0845-748 4950, 🖳 www.scotrail.co.uk)*.

There are many services to and from London (anything from £28 to £85, five- to six-hours) and services to Glasgow at least hourly (£7.30 one way, 50 minutes). Trains run from Edinburgh to Inverness (through Fife and Aberdeen); west-bound trains travel via Glasgow.

Bikes travel free on Scotrail services, but space may be limited. Reservations are not available for bicycles on some services, but are compulsory on others. See Scotrail's *Cycles on Train* brochure for details.

Bus Bikes – other than folding bikes – are not officially carried on buses in Scotland. However, depending on who you talk to, they may be taken (free) at the driver's discretion. Since buses are considerably cheaper than trains, it may be worth checking, especially if you're on a tight budget, but don't rely on them. Scottish Citylink (☎ *0900-505050, 🖳 www.citylink.co.uk)* links Edinburgh to towns all over Scotland and also connects to England and Wales.

Glasgow

☎ 0141

The third most-popular destination for foreign visitors to the UK (after London and Edinburgh), Glasgow is a large and lively city. Though it was known for its high unemployment levels, economic depression and urban violence in the 1970s, the city has since reinvented itself, rediscovering rich cultural roots. By 1990 it was elected 'European City of Culture'. With appealing Victorian architecture, Glasgow has some excellent art galleries and museums, countless restaurants and bars, and a lively arts scene.

Though larger, more hilly and less charming than Edinburgh, the city is reasonable for cycling, with bike parking around inner areas and cycle routes within and surrounding the city. Here, too, cycling facilities are improving in preparation for Velocity 2001.

Information The main TIC (☎ 204 4400, e TourismGlasgow@ggcvtb.org.uk), 11 George Square, opens Monday to Saturday from 9 am to at least 6 pm; and Sunday from 10 am to 6 pm, Easter to September. There's another branch at the airport (☎ 848 4440).

For information and guides to cycling routes, pick up the free *Fit for Life* pamphlet or the series of *Glasgow and Clyde Coast Cycle Routes* pamphlets available from TICs and libraries. For more information, phone Glasgow City Council's cycling line (☎ 287 9171).

Dales Cycles (☎ 332 2705), 150 Dobbies Loan, hires hybrids, mountain bikes and road bikes from £50 a week. West End Cycles (☎ 357 1344) is at 16 Chancellor St.

Laundrettes include Grosvenor Laundrette (☎ 339 8385) at 17 Dowanhill St, and the Garnethill Laundrette at 33/39 Dalhousie St.

Luggage can be left during the day in lockers at Central Station and Buchanan Bus Station. Charges start from £2.

Things to See & Do The Glasgow Cathedral (☎ 552 6891) is the only mainland Scottish cathedral to have survived the Reformation. The Gothic architecture of the current building dates from the 15th century. In the Cathedral precinct are the award-winning St Mungo's Museum of Religious Life & Art (☎ 553 2557) and Glasgow's oldest house, Provand's Lordship (☎ 552 8819), built in 1471.

The UK's City of Architecture and Design in 1999, Glasgow has numerous fine buildings. Many of note are between the TIC and the cathedral in The Merchant City, an area developed by 18th-century Tobacco Lords.

Look out for the distinctive Art Nouveau buildings designed by Scottish architect Charles Rennie Mackintosh. The Glasgow School of Art (☎ 353 4526), on Renfrew St, is recognised as his greatest triumph. Contact the Charles Rennie Mackintosh Society (☎ 946 6600) about building tours.

The unique Burrell Collection (☎ 649 7151) is in Pollok Country Park, 3mi south of the city centre. It's Glasgow's top attraction.

Other recommended galleries include the Gallery of Modern Art (☎ 229 1996), on Queen St, and the Kelvingrove Art Gallery & Museum (☎ 287 2700), on Argyle St, for its excellent Scottish and European collection.

The surprisingly interesting Museum of Transport (☎ 287 2720), on Argyle St, includes cars, railway locos, trams, ships and bikes. Don't miss The Barras (☎ 552 7258), on Gallowgate, Glasgow's weekend flea market.

Walks include the woodland trails around Pollok Country Park, and the Kelvin Walkway encompassing the Botanic Gardens, Kelvingrove and Dawsholm Parks.

Off-road cycle routes surrounding Glasgow include the Sustrans National Cycle Network sculpture trail to Greenock/Gourock via Paisley, and Glasgow to Loch Lomond.

Places to Stay About 6mi east of the city is *Craigendmuir Caravan Park* (☎ 779 4159; *Campsie View, Stepps*). It's £8.50 per tent for one or two, including showers.

West of the city, the excellent *SYHA Hostel (332 3004, 7 Park Terrace)* has mainly four-bed dorms for £13.25 per person including continental breakfast. Also popular is *Glasgow Backpackers Hostel (332 9099, 17 Park Terrace)*, open from July to September. It's £10.20 per person in a three- to five-bed dorm and £11.80 per person for a twin.

The University of Strathclyde's *Baird Hall* (☎ *332 6415,* e *baird.hall@strath.ac.uk, 460 Sauchiehall St)* offers B&B (with laundry) at £16/19 per person for twins/singles from mid-June to mid-September.

Renfrew St has many guesthouses, including the bright, pleasant en suite rooms at *The*

Old School House (☎ 332 7600, 194 Renfrew St), which cost £30 for singles and £24 per person for doubles or twins. Also comfortable, the *Willow Hotel (☎ 332 2332, 228 Renfrew St)* has singles/doubles starting at £27/44.

Friendly *Mrs Bennett (☎ 337 1307; 107 Dowanhill St, West End)* does B&B for £20/35. *Rosewood Guest House (☎ 550 1500, 4 Seton Terrace)* caters for vegetarians, with B&B at £18/16 per person. *Amadeus Guest House (☎ 339 8257, 411 North Woodside Rd)* charges £18/20per person.

Places to Eat Daytime cafes close to the TIC in Royal Exchange Square include the Italian-style chain *Costa (☎ 221 9305)*, reliable for decent coffee and reasonable food, and *The Jenny (☎ 204 4988)* for wicked fudges, cakes, coffee. Breakfast starts at £2.85.

Bradfords Bakery (245 Sauchiehall St) serves reasonably priced light meals (breakfasts from £3.85) in its upstairs tearoom until 5.45 pm. Wholesome, mostly veg lunch at *The Granary (☎ 226 3770, 82 Howard St)* costs around £4 a main.

Next to Baird Hall, in Sauchiehall St, are the good value *Mr Chips* with pizza from £2.75, and the *Noodle Bar* with £4.95 mains. *Ristoro Ciao Italia (☎ 332 4565, 441 Sauchiehall St)* has pastas, risottos and pizzas from around £6 and steaks from £14.

Across the motorway, *Antonious (☎ 221 7636, 523 Sauchiehall St)* has souvlaki and kebabs from £4.30 and mains for between £4.50 and £8.50. There's an all-you-can-eat buffet at *Cafe India (☎ 248 4074, 171 North St)*, which costs £5.95 for lunch, and £9.95 in the evening Monday to Friday (£12.95 on weekends).

Janssens (☎ 334 9682, 1355 Argyle St) is a licensed restaurant opposite Kelvingrove Park. It has a pleasant and casual feel to it. International and veg mains start around £6; pizzas start from £4. There are dozens of restaurants in West End, on Byres Rd and Ashton Lane. Locals recommend the Belgian *Bar Brel (☎ 342 4966, 37 Ashton Lane)*.

For reasonably priced pub food in the city, try *Auctioneers (☎ 229 5851; North Court, St Vincent Place)* or *Drum & Monkey (☎ 221 6636, 93 St Vincent St)*.

Getting There & Away There are plenty of options for getting to/from Glasgow.

Air Glasgow airport (☎ 887 1111) is 10mi west of the city and about 2mi north-west of Paisley, along Inchinnan Rd.

Trains from Paisley Gilmour St station to Glasgow Central cost £1.95 (bikes free).

The Glasgow to Paisley cycle route (9mi) from Saucehill Park on Causeyside (continue south along Gilmour St) ends at Bell's Bridge, about 1.5mi from the city centre (follow the river east from here). The free *Glasgow to Paisley* brochure in the Glasgow and Clyde Coast Cycle Routes series details the route. It's available at the airport TIC.

CityLink (☎ 332 9644) operates a fixed-route, 25-minute coach service between the airport and the city (£3 one way). However, bikes are not officially carried.

Train Trains to/from England, Wales and southern Scotland generally use Central Station on Argyle St, while Queen St Station (about five minutes' ride away) serves trains to/from Edinburgh and the north. To reach Glasgow Central from Queen St Station, exit onto the corner of George and Queen Sts, take Queen St, go right at St Vincent Place, left at Renfield/Union St and right onto Argyle St.

Scotrail (☎ 0845-748 4950, 🖳 www.scotrail .co.uk) services include Glasgow to Mallaig (£29.20, 5¼ hours) and Inverness (£29.60, 3½ hours).

Bikes travel free on Scotrail services, but space may be limited. Reservations are not available for bicycles on some services, but are compulsory on others. See Scotrail's *Cycles on Train* brochure for details.

Bus For information about buses to Glasgow, see the Bus entry in the Edinburgh section, earlier in this chapter.

Edinburgh Orientation

Duration	1½–2½ hours
Distance	15.7mi
Difficulty	easy
Start/End	Edinburgh TIC

Edinburgh is a compact, bike-friendly city with plenty of green space in the heart of town. This easy introduction squeezes the historic Old Town, wide open spaces, city views and leafy bikepaths into less than 16mi.

SCOTLAND

Edinburgh Orientation

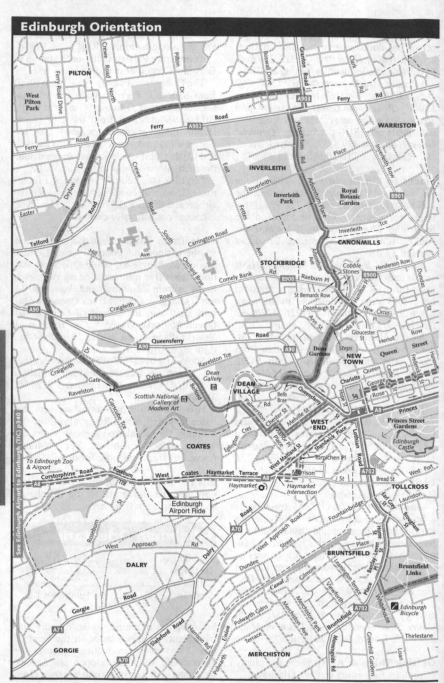

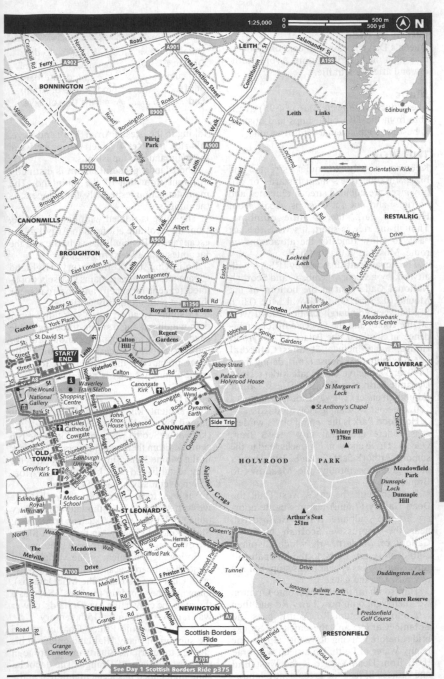

1:25,000
0   500 m
0   500 yd
N

Edinburgh

⟵ Orientation Ride

LEITH

BONNINGTON

Leith Links

RESTALRIG

PILRIG

Pilrig Park

CANONMILLS

BROUGHTON

Royal Terrace Gardens

Lochend Loch

Sleigh

WILLOWBRAE

Gardens

Regent Gardens

Calton Hill

Marionville

Meadowbank Sports Centre

START/ END

Waterloo Pl

Abbeyhill

Spring Gardens

The Mound

National Gallery

Waverley Train Station

Shopping Centre

Canongate Kirk

Abbey Strand

Palace of Holyrood House

St Margaret's Loch

St Anthony's Chapel

Bank St

High

John Knox House

Horse Wynd

Dynamic Earth

Whinny Hill 178m

Meadowfield Park

St Giles Cathedral

Cowgate

Holyrood

CANONGATE

Side Trip

Dunsapie Loch

Dunsapie Hill

OLD TOWN

Grassmarket

Chambers

Edinburgh University

HOLYROOD   PARK

Greyfriar's Kirk

Medical School

Salisbury Crags

Arthur's Seat 251m

Edinburgh Royal Infirmary

ST LEONARD'S

Hermit's Croft

Queen's

The Melville

Meadows

Meadowbank

Queen's

Drive

Duddingston Loch

The Meadows

Drive

Tunnel

Innocent Railway Path

Nature Reserve

SCIENNES

NEWINGTON

Scottish Borders Ride

Prestonfield Golf Course

PRESTONFIELD

Grange Cemetery

See Day 1 Scottish Borders Ride p375

SCOTLAND

PLANNING
When to Ride
Queen's Drive is closed to cars on Sunday, making it the best riding time. Avoid morning and afternoon traffic.

Maps
The *Edinburgh Bicycle Map* (£4.95) available from the TIC, bike shops and hostels, is best for supplementary information.

THE RIDE
Keeping mostly to quiet streets and bikepaths, the ride's main hazards or annoyances are cobbled streets, chicanes and barriers, and one set of steps. Apart from Holyrood Park, there's little climbing. Though the ride is short, it's wise to start early to allow time for the attractions en route. Most are in the first half.

The **Royal Scottish Academy** (RSA), with artwork by academy members, and **Scottish National Gallery** sit at the bottom of the Mound (0.25mi). On the Royal Mile (High St), between **Edinburgh Castle** (300yd west off the route) and the Queen's official residence in Scotland, the **Palace of Holyrood House**, sights include: **St Giles Cathedral** (0.6mi); **John Knox House** (1mi), dating from 1490; and attractive **Canongate Kirk** (1.1mi). **Dynamic Earth** (see Things to See & Do for Edinburgh under Gateway Cities, earlier) is a 160yd-detour west along Holyrood Rd.

Holyrood Park is the central city's wilderness. There are great city views from Queen's Drive and walking tracks lead to the summit, **Arthur's Seat** (251m/823ft). There's more greenery, through the Meadows to Bruntsfield.

Back through the city's West End, the **Dean Gallery** (7.5mi) features contemporary art and sculpture. It's on Belford Rd, near the impressive **Scottish National Gallery of Modern Art**, which displays 20th-century art. Entry to the bikepath off Ravelston Dykes is near a bus stop, but not obvious. Use the gate.

Turn south off the bikepath onto Granton Rd, then right onto busy Ferry Rd and then left into Arboretum Rd. You'll pass the **Botanic Garden** and the cafes of Stockbridge before walking down the steps by the bonny Water of Leith. Up a steep wee brae (hill) from Dean Village is the West End and Princes St (use the green centre lane).

The West Coast

Duration	10 days
Distance	424.7mi
Difficulty	moderate-hard
Start	Brodick (Isle of Arran)
End	Armadale (Isle of Skye)

Taking in the Isles of Arran, Mull and Skye, this ride involves five ferry trips between the mainland and the islands.

The islands' peaceful charm is distinctly different from that of the mainland. The main detraction, especially for campers, is the midges.

The route is riddled with historical lore, from the neolithic artefacts in Argyll to the escapades of Bonnie Prince Charlie and the Jacobites in the Western Highlands.

Following the 18th-century Highland Clearances, the area remains sparsely populated (except by sheep) and the roads, for the most part, are lightly trafficked.

In sunny weather, there's nothing finer than winding along a single-track loch-side road, around awe-inspiring mountains or looking across the sea to the islands. But come prepared – this is the west (or wet) coast. Sunny weather is not guaranteed.

HISTORY
The ancient kingdom of Dalriada was named by Gaelic-speaking Irish settlers (known as Scotti) who claimed it in the 6th century. From their headquarters at Dunadd, in the Moine Mhor (in present day Argyll), they established the kingdom of Alba, which eventually became Scotland.

Vikings took over and controlled the western seaboard from the late 8th century until 1263. Place names, such as Trotternish, Staffin and Flodigarry (on the Isle of Skye) are evidence of the early Norse presence.

Following the defeat of the Vikings, the western seaboard became ruled by the powerful Clan Donald (later, the MacDonalds), known as the 'Lords of the Isles'. Seen as a threat to the crown, the MacDonalds' power was removed late in the 15th century.

In 1745, Bonnie Prince Charlie gained the support of many Highland chiefs in his attempt to return the Stuarts to the throne in place of William of Orange. The Jacobite campaign ended in spectacular defeat at the

Battle of Culloden in 1746, after which the fugitive prince dodged English government troops across the Highlands before escaping to France from the west coast.

Following the Jacobite defeat, the clan system fell apart and Highland culture was outlawed by the English government. Over the next century, Highlanders were forced off the land to make way for sheep farming, in an attempt to draw profit from the land.

NATURAL HISTORY

Scotland's Western Highlands is the wettest part of Europe. Things don't get too cold, however, and particularly on the more southerly islands, the mild, moist conditions give rise to lush vegetation. Much of the area is covered in peat bogs, which act as a sponge, absorbing run-off from the hills.

Widespread sheep grazing and conifer plantations have taken their ecological toll on the Highlands' indigenous forests. Remnants of ancient oak forests can be seen on the Ardnamurchan peninsula, by Loch Moidart. This area – only lightly grazed by sheep and deer – still supports animals such as pine martins, otters and wildcats. The Natural History Centre near Kilchoan has more information on local fauna (see Day 6).

One local insect impossible to miss during the summer period is the midge – a relative of the mosquito. They're particularly prevalent in the early evening, in still, sheltered conditions, and are attracted to dark colours.

Not surprisingly, the west coast and islands are home to thousands of seabirds; seals and whales can also be seen.

The famous Scottish wild salmon are threatened by disease and gene-pool dilution from commercial salmon farms, while shellfish and mackerel are in danger of being overfished.

PLANNING
When to Ride

Plan to ride between May and September. The weather is most settled in summer (June to August), but this is the busiest tourist (and midge) season. Ferries and many other services decrease or close down between October and April.

Maps

The OS Travelmaster series (1:250,000) is best. The area is covered by No 3, *Western*

Scotland & Western Isles; and No 4, *Southern Scotland & Northumberland*.

What to Bring

Don't go without weatherproof gear or a reliable midge-repellent containing DEET or DMP, especially if you're camping.

Wild Camping in Scotland

Wild camping is relatively common in Scotland and a cheap way to go. You can camp free on public land (unless it's specifically protected) and, in many instances, on private land.

Wild camping is generally accepted in most areas, provided: it's away from houses and cultivated land; permission has been given by the landowner (where possible); it's unobtrusive; and the area is left in the condition in which it was found.

If you are camping wild:

- Practise minimum impact camping.

- Avoid camping immediately beside water courses.

- Be scrupulous about toilet hygiene: bury excrement; go at least 30yd from water; and carry out tampons and sanitary pads.

- Carry out all rubbish.

- Use fuel stoves rather than lighting wood fires.

- Minimise disturbance to vegetation and wildlife.

For more information, contact the Mountaineering Council of Scotland (☎ 01738-638227) and ask for their Wild Camping brochure.

GETTING TO/FROM THE RIDE
Brodick

Train & Ferry Scotrail (☎ 0845-748 4950, 🖳 www.scotrail.co.uk) trains from Glasgow Central station (Argyle St) to Ardrossan harbour (£4.30, 1¼ hours) connect with the ferry to Brodick, several times daily. Phone Scotrail for train times or collect a *Glasgow-Ardrossan* timetable from major train stations. Connecting services are also shown in CalMac's ferry timetable.

Trains also from to Ardrossan from Edinburgh (£10.30, 1 hour, hourly).

Caledonan MacBrayne (CalMac; ☎ 01475-650100 or ☎ 01294-463470, 💻 www.calmac.co.uk) is Scotland's major ferry operator. Its packaged 'Island Hopscotch' tickets are cheaper than buying individual tickets for the five ferry crossings. Buy a 'Hopscotch 5' (Ardrossan-Brodick, Lochranza-Claonaig) for £7.15, and a 'Hopscotch 8' (Oban-Craignure, Tobermory-Kilchoan, Mallaig-Armadale) for £8.30; bikes travel free.

Bicycle It's possible to cycle from Glasgow to Ardrossan via the NCN (39mi). Use either the free *Glasgow to Paisley* or the *Paisley to Irvine & Ardrossan* pamphlets, available at TICs, libraries and council offices; or the Sustrans map *Glasgow to Carlisle Cycle Route* (£5.99).

Armadale
Train & Ferry The return ferry from Armadale to Mallaig, on the west coast (not included in 'Hopscotch 8'), is £2.60 (bikes free). Ferries sail seven times daily (Sunday from June to mid-September only).

Scotrail runs daily services from Mallaig to Glasgow (£29.20, 5¼ hours) and Edinburgh, two of which connect with the ferry daily (outside July and August it's only one on Sunday). Leave the train at Crianlarich (3¼ hours from Mallaig) to start the Highlands Circuit ride.

THE RIDE
Brodick
☎ 01770
Easily accessible (by train and ferry) from Glasgow, Arran is a traditional Glaswegian holiday destination, particularly during the 'Glasgow Fair' – the holiday period over the middle two weeks in July (during which time Arran's weather is reputedly bad). The island is often called 'Scotland in miniature' – rolling hills and pastures in the south, with the mountainous north more reminiscent of the Highlands. Brodick sits south of Arran's highest peak, Goatfell (874m/2867ft). The town is largely geared towards accommodating visitors, but it's still fairly laid back.

Information Arran's only TIC (☎ 302140, 💻 www.arran.uk.com), at the Brodick pier, opens from 9 am to 7.30 pm Monday to Saturday and 10 am to 5 pm on Sunday, June through September.

Brodick Cycles (☎ 302460), opposite the village hall on Shore Rd, is open daily. It's the only place for repairs on the island. Branches of the Bank of Scotland and Royal Bank of Scotland (with ATMs) are on Shore Rd.

Things to See & Do The small **Heritage Museum** (☎ 302636), 1.5mi north at Rosaburn, has social history, archaeological and geological displays. Handsome **Brodick Castle** (☎ 302202), 2.5mi north of town, and its **woodland gardens** date, in part, from the 13th century.

Walks around Brodick include woodland trails around the castle and Goat Fell (from the car park near Cladach sawmill). Pick up the Forest Enterprise *Isle of Arran Forest Walks* brochure (50p) from the TIC. Make sure you're adequately equipped on mountain trails. Forest Enterprise (☎ 302218) also runs seasonal **guided walks** to more remote areas.

Hire gear for **boating**, **fishing** and **windsurfing** from Brodick Boat & Cycle Hire (☎ 302868), on Brodick Beach. You can also sail on the world's last sea-going **paddlesteamer**, the *Waverley* (☎ 0141-243 2224). Ask at the Brodick TIC for details of day and afternoon cruises around the **Mull of Kintyre** and **Holy Island**.

Places to Stay & Eat The *Glen Rosa Farm Site* (☎ 302380), 2mi north-west of the pier (turn right off The String Rd), charges £4 for a tent and two people (wash basins and cold water only – and take the midge repellent!). The nearest hostel is the *Whiting Bay Youth Hostel* (☎ 700339; Shore Rd, Whiting Bay), 7.5mi south on Day 1. Beds are available from March to October for £8.

Friendly *Glenard* (☎ 302380), near the football field, does B&B for £17/18 per person for singles/doubles or twins. Bikes can be stored in a garden shed. The *Kingsley Hotel* (☎ 302226, Shore Rd) welcomes cyclists, and charges £28 per person for B&B. Bikes are locked in a hut behind the hotel. Adjoining the hotel is *Duncan's Bar*, which serves standard pub food.

Co-op and *All Days* supermarkets are on Shore Rd, and the *Good Food Shop* (grocer, deli, tearoom) is over the bridge past the rugby field. Try the fish and chips from *The*

Ferry Fry by the pier, or have a light meal until 8 pm at *Wooleys Bakers (Shore Rd)* – don't miss the excellent oat cakes.

Best for pub food is the friendly *Ormidale Hotel (☎ 302293)*, behind the football field on Knowe Rd. Generous home-style mains (including veg) start at £5.65 and there's often live folk music. You can also stay here – B&B costs £23.

Day 1: Brodick to Lochranza

3½–5½ hours, 42.4mi

Arran is blessed with mild temperatures that, along with a relatively high rainfall, make the island quite lush. The east coast is more sheltered than the west – the main towns (Brodick, Lamlash and Whiting Bay) are here, as is most of the traffic. Rolling farmland prevails in the west.

There are some moderate climbs to negotiate, particularly in the east and south, and excellent coastal views – benches have been thoughtfully placed at scenic points along the road.

Arran is known for its cheeses, made at the **Torrylin Creamery** (☎ 870240; 16.5mi), with a shop and displays. There's a good *tearoom* in shady Lagg (16.9mi), right before a short steep climb. **Blackwaterfoot** is the largest village on the west coast – it has a small *store*, a *bakery* and a *tearoom*.

A 1.5mi walking track (at 27.7mi) to the impressive **Machrie Moor standing stones**, erected around 6000 years ago. The *Machrie Bay Tearooms/Golf Club* (28.5mi), less than 1mi on, has delicious light meals and great country atmosphere.

Apart from a short steep climb (32.9mi), the terrain into Lochranza is relatively flat, with nice views of the Kintyre Peninsula. Approaching Lochranza, the mountainous north unfolds and there's some attractive rocky coastline. Look out for the **Twelve Apostles** at Catacol – 12 whitewashed cottages built to house people who were cleared from the land to make way for sheep.

Lochranza

☎ 01770

Lochranza is a beautiful little spot tucked alongside a narrow bay and surrounded by mountains. The ruined Lochranza Castle on its tiny peninsula is the central focus of the town.

Try the hostel (☎ 830631) or the post office for other tourist information.

Things to See & Do The Isle of Arran Distillery (☎ 830364, 🖳 www.arranwhisky.com), at the eastern end of town, is Scotland's newest. You can visit **Lochranza Castle** (free) – collect the key at the village store.

Walks from Lochranza include the **Cock of Arran** running south-east along the coast. Ask at the hostel for details.

Places to Stay & Eat Through the village, *Lochranza Golf Caravan & Camping Site* (☎ 830273) charges £5/8 per tent with one/two people. The very good *Lochranza Youth Hostel* (☎ 830631) is open February to early January. A bed costs £9 and there's a bike shed, laundry and drying room.

Once a church, *Castlekirk* (☎ 830202), opposite the castle, is now a B&B and art gallery. It costs £18 to stay. Bikes go indoors, and washing, drying and veg breakfasts are available. Also overlooking the bay, *Caberfeidh* (☎ 830255), with spa and garage, offers B&B for £20/22 per person a single/double or twin room.

Butt Lodge (☎ 830240) is a small private hotel 1mi off the main road. B&B costs £42.50/32.50 per person for singles/doubles. Laundry facilities and bike storage are provided, and a three-course (set menu) dinner is £15.

The Lochranza *store* sells basic food supplies. *Pier Tearoom & Licensed Restaurant* serves moderately priced breakfasts, lunches and evening meals. Also recommended is the *Catacol Bay Hotel* (☎ 830231), 2mi west of Lochranza. *Lochranza Hotel* (☎ 830223) has bar meals from £5.30 (including veg). Restaurant mains start at £9.50 (or £15 for a three-course meal).

Day 2: Lochranza to Lochgilphead

4–6 hours, 44.7mi

Day 2 starts with a 30-minute ferry trip to Claonaig. Ferries to Kintyre (April to mid-October; several daily) leave from the pier at the western end of Lochranza. Check the timetable by the pier or phone the Brodick terminal (☎ 302166).

Apart from two short main-road sections, the route is on undulating single-track roads.

Day 1: Brodick to Lochranza

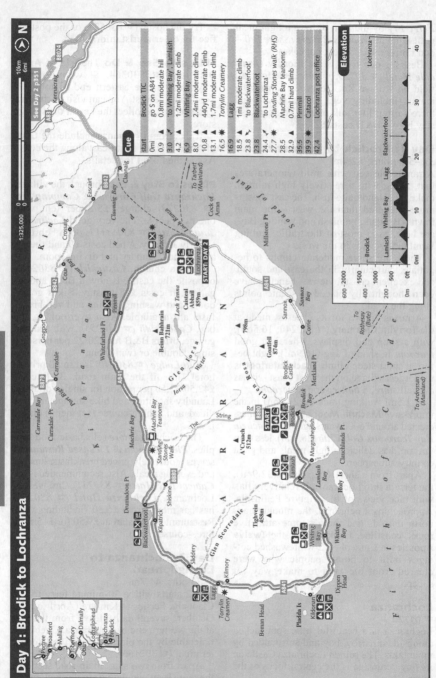

See Day 2 p351

Cue

start	0mi	Brodick TIC
	0.9	go S on A841
	0.9	0.8mi moderate hill
	3.0	'to Whiting Bay', Lamlash
	4.2	1.2mi moderate climb
	6.9	Whiting Bay
	8.0	2.4mi moderate climb
	10.8	440yd moderate climb
	13.1	1.7mi moderate climb
	16.5	Torrylin Creamery
	16.9	Lagg
	18.5	1mi moderate climb
	23.8	'to Blackwaterfoot'
	23.8	Blackwaterfoot
	24.4	'to Lochranza'
	27.7	Standing Stones walk (RHS)
	28.5	Machrie Bay tearooms
	32.9	0.7mi hard climb
	35.5	Pirnmill
	39.9	Catacol
	42.4	Lochranza post office

Elevation

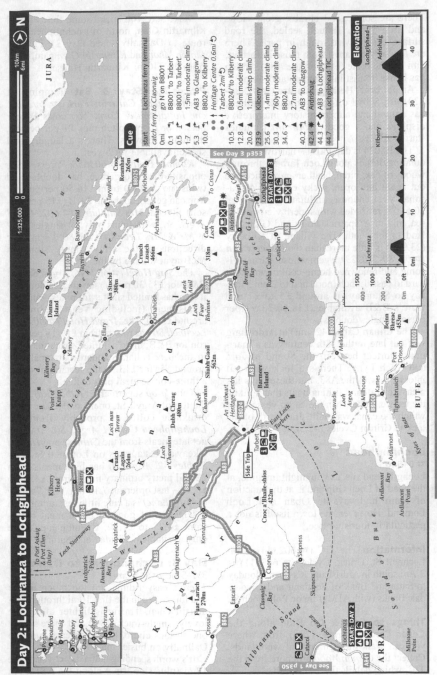

Day 2: Lochranza to Lochgilphead

N

1:325,000

0   5   10km
0   5   6mi

Cue

start	Lochranza ferry terminal
	catch ferry to Claonaig
0mi	go N on B8001
0.1	B8001 'to Tarbert'
0.5	B8001 'to Tarbert'
1.7	1.5mi moderate climb
5.3	A83 'to Glasgow'
10.0	B8024 'to Kilberry'
	Heritage Centre 0.6mi ↺
	Tarbert 2mi ↺
10.5	B8024 'to Kilberry'
12.8	0.5mi moderate climb
20.6	1.1mi steep climb
23.9	Kilberry
25.6	1.4mi moderate climb
30.3	760yd moderate climb
34.6	B8024
	2.7mi moderate climb
40.2	A83 'to Glasgow'
42.4	Ardrishaig
44.3	A83 'to Lochgilphead'
44.7	Lochgilphead TIC

See Day 3 p353

Elevation

Lochgilphead
Ardrishaig

Kilberry

Lochranza

1500
1000
500
0ft

400
200
0m

0mi   10   20   30   40

SCOTLAND

There are some good climbs, great views and little traffic. Though sealed, the road surface is somewhat rough in parts. There are few services apart from those in Tarbert, 1mi off the route (east, on the A83), which has banks, tourist information and shops.

An Tairbeart Heritage Centre (☎ 01880-820190), 500yd off-route towards Tarbert, has natural and human history interpretive displays and a good *restaurant* (lunches start at £3.95).

The B8024 is delightful – narrow and undulating, it runs along **Loch Tarbert**, through woods of oak, birch, heather and spruce and out again into open, rocky country. A reasonably strenuous, undulating climb at 20.6mi is rewarded with superb views out to sea, and of Ardpatrick Point and Gigha Island to the south. The village of Kilberry (23.9mi) is little more than the *Kilberry Inn* (☎ 01880-770223), a gem whose warm welcome and renowned home-cooking make it hard to pass. Lunch (noon and to 2 pm Monday to Saturday) is around £5 to £7 and there's B&B available (£38.50/33.50 per person singles/doubles).

The **Crinan Canal** (42.4mi) at Ardrishaig was cut late in the 18th century as a maritime shortcut between the Sound of Jura and Loch Fyne. There's a lock where it intersects with the A83, but these days it's pleasure craft and fishing boats that hold up the traffic, rather than the cargo vessels for which the canal was built. Just north of the lock is Crinan Cycles (42.5mi; ☎ 603511).

Lochgilphead
☎ 01546

Lochgilphead sits, as you might imagine, at the head of Loch Gilp and is at the junction of main highways to Oban and Loch Lomond. However, the town itself is not a particularly touristy place.

Information The TIC (☎ 602344) is on Lochnell St. Crinan Cycles (☎ 603511) is 2.2mi south in Ardrishaig; it's open Monday to Saturday. Bank of Scotland and Clydesdale Banks (with ATMs) are on Poltalloch St.

Things to See & Do Ride along the **Crinan Canal** to Crinan (7mi), from where you can **walk** through ancient woodlands. Collect the *Crinan Wood* brochure from the TIC, which details the 1.5mi trail.

Make sure you spend some time around **Kilmartin Glen**, north of Lochgilphead (en route to Dalmally – see Day 3). Pick up *Moine Mhor* and *Kilmartin Glen* pamphlets from the TIC or Kilmartin House.

Places to Stay & Eat Camping at *Lochgilphead Caravan Park* (☎ 602003, cnr Poltalloch & Lorne Sts)* costs £4 per person or £7 per pitch plus £1 per person, including showers. There's a laundry and shelter available for bikes.

Kilmory House (☎ 603658, Paterson St), opposite the Esso garage, has doubles and twins (no singles) from £16.50 per person. You can get cheap, basic B&B (£15 per person) either at *Mrs Sinclair's* (☎ 602244, 38 Argyll St), with twins only; or singles only at *Mr & Mrs Lear's* (☎ 602808) – ask for directions at the army supply store on McBrayne's Lane by the TIC.

The *Stag Hotel* (☎ 602496, Argyll St) has B&B for £35/30 per person singles/doubles; it also has limited shelter for bikes – and bar meals here (including veg) are mostly around £5.50. The *Argyll Hotel* (☎ 602221, Lochnell St) has rooms from £19/18 per person for B&B; there's limited space for bikes in the beer cellar. Standard bar meals are around £5; for £13.95 the restaurant offers a three-course meal plus coffee.

The *Co-op* supermarket (Oban Rd), near the top of Argyll St, opens daily. The most drinkable coffee is probably from the *Lochgilphead Cafe (1 Argyll St)*. You can get late meals from the *Chinese* and *Indian* takeaway restaurants on Lochnell St. *The Stables (48 Argyll St)* has light meals from £2 and pretty ordinary mains from £4.25 to £6.50 – last orders at 7.15 pm. *The Smiddy (Smithy Lane)* is a cute little restaurant with a selection of good veg and meat mains from £4.25 to £7.30. Evening meals are only available on Friday and Saturday.

Day 3: Lochgilphead to Dalmally
3½–5 hours, 41.0mi

There's easy riding, not too much traffic and lots to see in the first 10mi through Kilmartin Glen. Traffic is lighter along the lovely, single-track B840 and there's only one serious climb, before an easy run into Dalmally on busier main roads.

It's worth spending half a day covering the 10mi (plus side trips) along the A816. An information board (3.5mi) describes the attractions around Kilmartin Glen, the first of which is **Dunadd**, the fort at the centre of the ancient kingdom of Dalriada – an access road (4.8mi) leads to a 10-minute walk to the fort. Dunadd was home to the Scotti, a Celtic tribe whose kingdom was the beginning of modern Scotland. It was allegedly the location of the Stone of Destiny, upon which Scottish kings and queens were crowned. Prehistoric rock carvings still remain. The fort overlooks the 'great moss', **Moine Mhór Nature Reserve**, which is one of the few remaining raised peat bogs in Britain. A boardwalk through the moss is just west of the route (side trip at 6.3mi). Look out for the Ballymeanoch standing stones to the west on the way to **Dunchraigaig** (6.9mi), where there's a burial mound and more rock carvings.

An alternative route (go left at 7.5mi, then right 'to Slockavullin') passes more standing stones at **Lady Glassary Wood**, the **Temple Wood stone circle** and the **Nether Largie chambered cairn** – it's 1.3mi back to the main road, and adds 1mi in total.

At the village of Kilmartin, the churchyard has some 10th-century Celtic crosses and many medieval graveslabs. The archaeological centre **Kilmartin House** (☎ 01546-510278, 🖳 www.kht.org.uk) has excellent audiovisual and fixed displays and welcomes cyclists; its *cafe* serves good espressos and baked goods. For a more substantial meal, *The Cairn Restaurant* (☎ 01546-510254) serves sandwiches from £2.50 and has lunch mains around £6. North of Kilmartin are the extensive remains of 16th-century **Carnassarie Castle** (9.6mi).

Leaving the A816, the route heads towards the Highlands. It undulates gently by the side of beautiful **Loch Awe** (the longest in Scotland) for 19mi, dipping through wee wooded glens and alongside bubbling burns, before climbing to meet the A819. The main road is busier, but the remaining 6.3mi to Dalmally are not challenging.

Dalmally
☎ 01838

The village of Dalmally is relatively spread out. The closest thing to a 'village centre' is the post office-cum-pharmacy (☎ 200465), set off the main road near the train station. There's also a store and the small 'suburb' of Glenview about 1mi east.

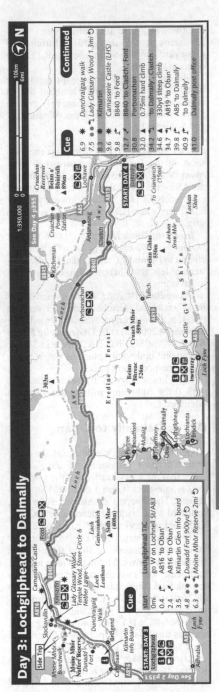

Day 3: Lochgilphead to Dalmally

Cue

start	Lochgilphead TIC
0mi	go W on Lochnell St/A83
0.4	A816 to Oban'
2.4	A816 to Oban'
3.5	Kilmartin Glen info board ↰
4.8	Dunadd Fort 900yd ↰
6.3	Moine Mhór Reserve 2mi ↰

Cue (Continued)

6.9	Dunchraigaig walk
7.5	Lady Glassary Wood 1.3mi ↰
8.3	Kilmartin
9.6	Carnasserie Castle (LHS)
9.8	B840 to Ford'
12.7	B840 'to Cladich'; Ford
30.8	0.75mi hard climb
32.0	'to Dalmally'; Cladich
34.2	330yd steep climb
34.6	A819 'to Oban'
34.7	A85 'to Dalmally'
39.8	'to Dalmally'
40.9	Dalmally post office
41.0	

Otherwise, there ain't much here – wander through the delightful **church** and **graveyard** (on the Stronmilchan Rd/B077) or go to the **pub**.

Glenorchy Lodge Hotel is probably the best bet for information; it's about 500yd east of the post office. Alternatively, try the post office (closed after 1 pm Wednesday and Saturday).

Places to Stay & Eat Camp by the loch shore at the *Drishaig Restaurant & Tearoom (☎ 200241)*. To get there, turn left onto the A85 – it's 0.9mi from the turn-off. A tent pitch costs £3 plus £1 for showers and toilets. There's also B&B for £20/18 per person single/double.

Inveraray Youth Hostel (☎ 01499-302454, Dalmally Rd), open April to October, is closest to Dalmally (turn right at Cladich, instead of left; from here it's 9mi on the A819 to Inveraray).

Orchy Bank (☎ 200370, Stronmilchan Rd/ B8077) is a lovely farmhouse on the river with B&B for £18 per person. Across the road, *The Smiddy (☎ 200245)* is £15. *Glenorchy Lodge Hotel (☎ 200312)* has B&B for £35/30 per person and is the only place to eat in town. Meals are moderately priced.

The closest *store* is 1mi east along the A85 (turn right and follow the signs to Glenview).

Day 4: Dalmally to Oban
2–3 hours, 26.6mi

About half of today's ride is on the busy (but otherwise pleasant and easy) A85. After that the main 'traffic' on the undulating, single-track Glen Lonan Rd is four-legged. The steepest climb is a short one, followed by a winding descent into Oban. There are no services after leaving the A85.

It's a scenic day, beginning in the mountains and then travelling along the northern shores of **Loch Awe**. Mountain views are best to the east, so it's worth stopping periodically to look back. Buried beneath Ben Cruachan (1126m/3693ft) is the **Cruachan hydroelectric power station** (8.4mi); the visitor centre (☎ 01866-822618) runs tours underground and has displays. The spillway (10.9mi) is a good spot to watch salmon jumping.

After the A85 Glen Lonan is 'Glen lonely'. Its green rolling hills are very pretty and there are plenty of sheep to contend

with, as well as the slow, eminently photogenic 'heilan coos' (Highland cows). There are more farm animals at the **Oban Rare Breeds Farm Park** (☎ 01631-770608), near the top of the last steep climb (24.2mi) before the swoop down to Oban.

Oban
☎ 01631

Often dubbed 'The Gateway to the Isles', Oban is the most important ferry port on the west coast. Built around the harbour, it's a pretty town, if a bit touristy, and is one of the largest in the Highlands.

Information The busy TIC (☎ 563122) is in the old church on Argyll Square. From May to September it's open daily from 9 am until at least 5 pm.

Banks (with ATMs) are on George St; Oban Cycles (☎ 566996), on Craigard Rd, is just off George St (on the uphill side).

The CalMac ferry terminal (☎ 566688) is at the harbour's southern end (east of the TIC).

Things to See & Do On Stafford St near North Pier, **Oban Distillery** (☎ 572004) has produced single malt since 1794. As well as running tours, the distillery has a small exhibition. The Colosseum-like **McCaig's Tower**, overlooking Oban, was built late in the 19th century by the philanthropic John Stuart McCaig. Though never finished, its purpose (apart from glorifying the McCaig name) was to keep local stonemasons gainfully employed. The views from here are worth the climb – they're reputedly even better from **Pulpit Hill** at the bay's southern end.

Bowmans (☎ 563221) run day **ferry tours** from Oban including trips to Iona, where St Columba set up an early Christian mission in the 6th century; Staffa, location of a huge natural cavern that inspired Mendelssohn's 'Hebrides Overture'; and **puffin colonies** on the Treshnish Isles.

Places to Stay The *Gallanachmore Farm Caravan Park (☎ 562425, Gallanach Rd)* is 2.5mi from south-west of town. A tent site is £4.50/8.00 for one/two, including showers. There's a basic kitchen with stove top, and a laundry.

The friendly and comfortable *Oban Backpackers (☎ 562107, Breadalbane St)* is part of the excellent Scotland's Top Hostels

Days 4 & 5: Dalmally – Oban – Tobermory

N ⊙
1:375,000
0 — 10km
0 — 6mi

Day 4

Cue	
start	Dalmally post office
0mi	go E on main access road
0.4	A83 'to Crianlarich'
0.6	B8077 'to Stronmilchan'
0.9	over bridge
4.1	A85 'to Oban'
4.7	Lochawe
8.4	Cruachan Power Station
14.5	Glen Lonan Rd (no sign)
16.0	1.9mi moderate climb
23.6	7mi of cattle grids & sheep unsigned road
24.0	'to Oban'
24.2	0.7mi steep climb
24.4	Rare Breeds Park
24.7	1.2m steep/winding descent
26.4	Soroba Rd/Combie St
26.6	Argyll Square
26.6	Oban TIC

Day 5

Cue	
start	Oban ferry terminal
	catch ferry to Mull
0mi	go NW on A849
0.0	Craignure
9.1	celtic cemetery
11.2	B8035 'to Gruline', Salen
13.7	B8073 'to Calgary'
27.0	1.9mi steep climb
33.0	1.7mi hard climb
33.2	Calgary
37.5	Heritage Centre 1.5mi ↺
38.1	Dervaig
41.0	1.4mi hard climb
45.1	1.2mi steep climb
45.4	A848 'to Salen'
45.4	across river
45.5	Main St
45.5	650yd steep descent
46.1	Tobermory TIC

SCOTLAND

chain. Dorm beds cost £10 (including linen); there's a £2.50 laundry service, Internet facility, and continental breakfast is £1.60. The larger **Oban Youth Hostel** (☎ 562025, *Corran Esplanade)* is also good. Beds (plus continental breakfast) are £11.75 (£12.75 in July and August).

Close to the ferry pier, **Carnbahn** (☎ 570 617, Albany St) does B&B for £12.50 per person. **Glen Cottage** (☎ 563420, Longsdale Rd) offers doubles and twins only at £15 per person. Small and friendly, it's halfway up the hill. **Glenara Guest House** (☎ 571125, Rockfield Rd) is very comfortable, but is also up the hill. En suite rooms cost £27 per person.

The **Glenburnie Hotel** (☎/fax 562089, Corran Esplanade) does B&B from £30 per person. It's smoke-free and has a garage and drying facilities.

Places to Eat The *Tesco* and *Co-op* supermarkets are in Soroba Rd south of Argyll Square; buy good bread and gourmet items from **Kitchen Garden** (14 George St) delicatessen and coffee shop.

The popular **Oban Inn** (Stafford St) does good bar meals from around £4.60. The 1950s-style **Pancake Place** (☎ 562593, 95–97 George St) serves chilli and pasta, as well as standard Scottish fare for around £5 to £6. Across the road, **Onorios** (☎ 563736) does takeaway fish and chips, or pizza. There's a nightly Scottish show at **McTavish's Kitchens** (George St), where evening mains start at £6.95.

The **Gallery Restaurant** (☎ 564641, cnr Combie & Market Sts) serves Scottish produce and veg options, with mains around £10; or, for the best of local produce and preparation (at a price), try **Heatherfield House** (☎ 562681, Albert Rd).

Day 5: Oban to Tobermory
4–6 hours, 46.1mi

Beginning with a scenic 40-minute ferry trip (6–8 daily) to Craignure, Day 5 is scenically stunning (weather permitting). With quiet, mostly single-track roads, cute villages and sandy beaches, the Isle of Mull is cycling heaven. (At least, heaven *seems* closer after the hills in the ride's second half.)

The Craignure TIC (☎ 01680-812377) opens daily from 9 am (10.30 am Sunday), and has free maps of Tobermory; the village also has a small *store*, post office, *hotel*, *restaurant*, and the well-equipped **Shieling Holidays Campsite** (☎ 01680-812496), which also has hostel accommodation.

The two-way A849 to Salen (10.5mi) is easy riding. Look out for the **celtic cemetery** (9.1mi). In Salen, On Yer Bike (☎ 01680-300501) is the last repair opportunity. After Salen there are few services until Tobermory.

Traffic is almost non-existent off the main road, yet the views to the mountains across Loch na Keal and Loch Tuath are superb. Like Arran, Mull grows green and lush.

Riding becomes more strenuous as the road heads north-west. The first climb (17.7mi) is not too bad, but a swim in beautiful **Calgary Beach** (32.6mi) could be in order after sweating up the second (27mi). Calgary is barely a town, but it has an **art gallery** (and *tearoom*) and a *hotel*.

The **Old Byre Heritage Centre** (☎ 01688-400229), open 10.30 am to 6.30 pm Easter to October, has exhibitions on Mull's human and natural history and a film. There's also a good *tearoom*. It's a 1.5mi return side trip (37.5mi) just before Dervaig – take the Torloisk turn-off; then the first left.

Two serious hills lie between Dervaig and Tobermory. There's a welcome **lookout**

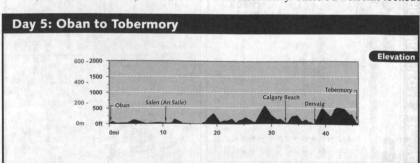

Day 5: Oban to Tobermory

Elevation

Oban Salen (An Saile) Calgary Beach Dervaig Tobermory

(39mi) shortly before the first summit; views are also good just before the top of the second. After that, it's downhill to the sea at Tobermory.

Tobermory
☎ 01688

Tobermory rises steeply from its colourful, much photographed harbour. Mull's capital is a picturesque fishing village, home to about two-thirds of the island's population and the centre for most services. It can be busy, so it pays to book ahead.

Information The TIC (☎ 302182, 💻 www .zynet.co.uk/mull/), at the ferry terminal, opens daily between April and October until at least 5 pm. The Clydesdale Bank (with ATM) is Mull's only bank (other than travelling banks).

Browns Ironmonger (☎ 302020), 21 Main St, does bike repairs.

Things to See & Do The **An Tobar Arts Centre, Gallery & Cafe** (☎ 302211), on Argyll Terrace, has national and local exhibitions plus concerts and ceilidhs (traditional music and dancing) on Tuesday and Friday. The **Tobermory Distillery** (☎ 302645) runs weekday tours from Easter to October. Local history is on display at the **Mull Museum** on Main St.

The Hebridean waters are home to a variety of marine mammals – check them out at the **Whale & Dolphin Centre** (☎ 302620), 28 Main St. Information about **wildlife tours** is available here, at the TIC or at Tackle & Books (☎ 302336), 7 Main St. Information is also available here about **fishing** and **diving** trips from Tobermory (minimum numbers apply). **Mountain bike** rides on Mull are described in *Isle of Mull Bike Rides*, available for £3 from The Coffee Pot in Salen (☎ 01680-300555) or Tackle & Books.

Places to Stay The *Tobermory Campsite* (☎ *302525; Dervaid Rd, Nervdale*) is around 1.7mi east of town. Tent sites cost £5 for two people.

Book ahead for the central *Tobermory Youth Hostel* (☎ *302481, Main St*), which is open from March to October. Beds are £8.50 and there's a laundry, drying room and secure bike storage.

Copeland House (☎ *302049, Jubilee Terrace)* is a friendly place with great views. B&B is £25 for singles, and £23 per person for doubles and twins. Also up the hill is *Callicvol* (☎ *302396, 8 Strongarbh Park)*, a small and friendly B&B that costs £15 per person. The *Harbour Guest House* (☎ *302209, 59 Main St*) is right on the waterfront. B&B is £19.50 per person (£22 with en suite).

Harbour Heights Hotel (☎ *302430, Western Rd*) is good value – not least for the manager's humour. B&B costs £25 for singles, and £20 per person for doubles and twins (more in August). It's equipped with a laundry, a basement and a large lounge.

B&B at the *Tobermory Hotel* (☎ *302091, Main St*) starts at £39 for singles and £35 per person for doubles and twins.

Places to Eat Tobermory's waterfront restaurants can be busy – avoid waiting by booking ahead.

The *Co-op* supermarket opens 8 am to 8 pm daily (12.30 to 7 pm Sunday). Along with its excellent bread, the *Island Bakery (26 Main St)* sells other delicious takeaway foods and groceries.

For cheap meals, try the *MacDonald Arms Hotel* (☎ *302011, Main St)*, *Posh Nosh* (☎ *302499, Calmac Pier)* or the *Fish and Chip Van (Fisherman's Pier)*.

Gannets Restaurant (☎ *302313, Main St*) has good cycling food, including a decent veg selection. Mains are around £6 to £10. The *Anchorage* (☎ *302313, 28 Main St*) is a little pricier (mains start at £7.95) but the food is excellent.

Day 6: Tobermory to Mallaig
5½–8 hours, 61.2mi

Scenic and sparsely populated, Scotland's 'empty quarter' offers quiet roads all the way to Lochailort.

It's wise to catch an early ferry for the long and reasonably strenuous ride through Ardnamurchan. Ferries depart Tobermory (☎ 302660) from 7.20 am (10 am Sunday). Traffic increases somewhat on the Road to the Isles (A830). The serious climbing is in the ride's first half. Arisaig is the main centre between Lochailort and Mallaig.

It is possible to break the journey around Acharacle (22.4mi) and Mingarry (24.4mi), where B&Bs include *Yuzan* (☎ 01967-431384); or, after the main hills, the *Glenuig*

SCOTLAND

Day 6: Tobermory to Mallaig

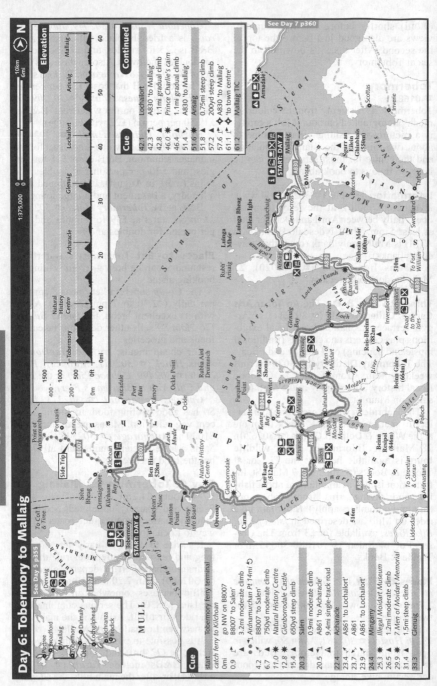

Elevation

| | Natural History Centre | Tobermory | Acharacle | Glenuig | Lochailort | Arisaig | Mallaig |

Cue

start	Tobermory ferry terminal
	catch ferry to Kilchoan
0mi	go NW on B8007
0.9	B8007 'to Salen'
	3.2mi moderate climb
4.2	Ardnamurchan Pt 14mi ↺
	B8007 'to Salen'
6.7	750yd moderate climb
11.0	Natural History Centre
12.8	Glenborrodale Castle
15.4	650yd steep climb
20.3	Salen
	0.9mi moderate climb
20.5	A861 'to Acharacle'
	9.4mi single-track road
22.4	Acharacle
23.4	A861 'to Lochailort'
23.7	A861
23.9	A861 'to Lochailort'
24.4	Mingarry
25.3	Illegal Moidart Museum
26.5	1.2mi moderate climb
29.9	7 Men of Moidart Memorial
31.4	1.5mi steep climb
33.3	Glenuig

Cue Continued

42.1	Lochailort
42.3	A830 'to Mallaig'
42.8	1.1mi gradual climb
46.0	*Prince Charlie's cairn*
46.4	1.1mi gradual climb
51.4	A830 'to Mallaig'
51.6	Arisaig
51.8	0.75mi steep climb
57.2	200yd steep climb
57.6	A830 'to Mallaig'
61.1	'to town centre'
61.2	Mallaig TIC

See Day 7 p360

See Day 5 p355

START: DAY 6

START: DAY 7

Sound of Arisaig

Sound of Mull

ARDNAMURCHAN

MOIDART

ARISAIG

MORAR

SLEAT

Loch Nevis

North Morar

Loch Morar

South Morar

Loch nan Uamh

Loch Ailort

SUNART

MOIDART

1:375,000

Inn (34.2mi; ☎ 01687-470219). Kilchoan TIC (☎ 01972-510 222) has more details.

Ardnamurchan Point is the British mainland's most westerly point, seven undulating miles west of Kilchoan. The lighthouse complex (☎ 01972-510210) includes an interactive **museum** and *cafe*.

Ben Hiant (528m/1732ft), Ardnamurchan's highest mountain, sits dramatically on the shores of Loch Sunart. Settled by families for thousands of years, the surrounding fertile volcanic soils now support mainly sheep and cattle, following the eviction of families during 18th-century Highland Clearances.

Riding is surprisingly hard along the undulating shore of Loch Sunart. Local wildlife can be seen at the well-regarded **Natural History Centre** (11mi; ☎ 01972-500254), which sells snacks and lunches. **Glenborrodale Castle** (12.8mi) was formerly owned by Jesse Boot, pharmacist and founder of the Boots chemist chain.

The *Burger Bite* takeaway at Acharacle sells bread and great fruit pies. At Mingarry is the **Illegal Museum** (25.3mi) of poaching and distilling, while over the hill on Loch Moidart is a memorial to the **Seven Men of Moidart** who joined Bonnie Prince Charlie in the ill-fated 1745 uprising. The MacDonalds who lived here were some of the Prince's strongest supporters. The indigenous forest on the steep hills beside the loch is significant for the richness of plant and animal species.

Riding is easier along the sublime Loch Ailort and the Road to the Isles. Bonnie Prince Charlie's arrival and departure point in 1745–46 was at Loch nam Uamh – there's a **cairn** marking the start of a walk to his escape point in 1746. Natural and social history is interpreted at Arisaig's **Land, Sea & Islands Centre** (☎ 01687-450266). Between here and Mallaig are **beaches** known as the 'Silver Sands of Morar'.

Mallaig
☎ 01687

Primarily a fishing village rather than a tourist town, Mallaig is linked via ferry to Skye and the Small Isles.

The TIC (☎ 462170) on Main St opens 9 am to 8 pm Monday to Saturday (10 am to 5 pm on Sunday) from June to August, with shorter hours at other times. Banks (with

ATM) are on Main St. The ferry terminal (☎ 462403) is 550yd north-east of the TIC.

Mallaig Marine World (☎ 462292) is an aquarium that keeps mainly local aquatic species. Exhibits at the **Mallaig Heritage Centre**, by the train station, include crofting, the Highland Clearances, steam trains and the fishing industry.

Look out for seals as you watch the evening action at the **harbour**. Minch Charters (☎ 462304) runs **wildlife-watching cruises** during summer.

Places to Stay & Eat While there is no official camping area in Mallaig, several do exist along the 'Silver Sands of Morar', east of Mallaig. *Silversands Portnaluchaig* *(☎ 450269)* is 7.1mi south of Mallaig.

Advance booking is advised for accommodation in Mallaig. *Sheena's Backpacker's Lodge (☎ 462764, Harbour View)* has beds in comfortable mixed dorms for £9.50. The owners also run the popular *Teagarden Cafe*, which has coffee and light meals from £2 until around 6 pm.

Cyclists often stay at *The Moorings (☎ 462 225, East Bay)*. Smoke-free B&B is £18/16 per person for singles/doubles with en suite. *Springbank (☎ 462459, East Bay)* charges £16 per person.

The grand *West Highland Hotel (☎ 462 210)*, up the hill from the TIC, charges £36 for singles and £35 per person for doubles and twins in the high season.

Inexpensive bar meals are available from *Tigh-a-Chlachain*, opposite the *Spar* supermarket on the hill. *The Cabin (☎ 462207)*, opposite the TIC, has good-value fish dinners. Mains (including pastas, curries and steaks) are mostly between £7 and £9. The *fish and chip window* is next door. Meals from the pleasant *Cornerstone Cafe*, across the road, are slightly cheaper. The seafood meals at the *Marine Hotel (☎ 462217, Main St)* start at £6.45 in the lounge bar.

Day 7: Mallaig to Broadford
1½–2½ hours, 27.5mi

Armadale (Armadal), the southern entrance to the Isle of Skye, is a 30-minute ferry trip from Mallaig. (See Day 10 (pp364–6) at the end of this ride for details about Armadale.)

The easy, short run from Armadale to Broadford is interrupted with a more challenging section – and more scenic – by detouring

SCOTLAND

SCOTLAND

Days 7 & 8: Mallaig – Broadford – Portree

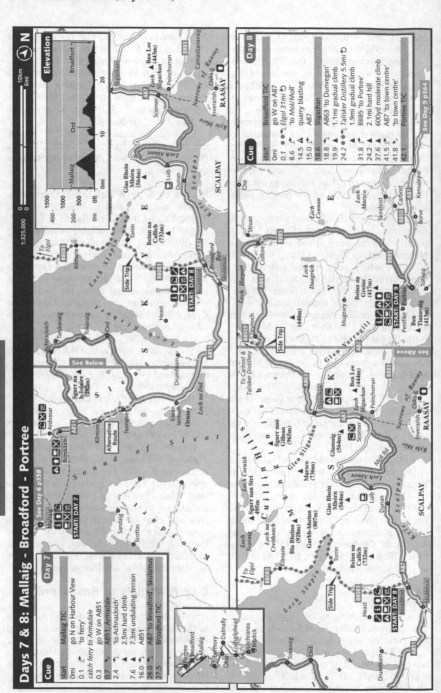

Elevation

	Mallaig	Ord	Broadford

1500
1000
500
0ft

400
200
0m

0mi   10   20

6mi

N

1:325,000

0   10km
0   6mi

Cue — Day 7

start	Mallaig TIC
0mi	go N on Harbour View
0.1	'to ferry'
	catch ferry to Armadale
0.3	go W on A851
0.7	A851 'Armadale'
2.4	'to Achnacloich'
	2.5mi hard climb
	7.3mi undulating terrain
7.6	A851
16.0	A851
26.0	A87 'to Broadford, Skulamus'
27.5	Broadford TIC

Cue — Day 8

start	Broadford TIC
0mi	go W on A87
0.1	Elgol 31mi
8.6	'to Mol/Moll'
14.5	quarry blasting
15.0	A87
18.6	Sligachan
18.8	A863 'to Dunvegan'
19.9	1.1mi gradual climb
24.2	Talisker Distillery 5.5mi
	1.9mi gradual climb
31.8	B885 'to Portree'
24.2	2.1mi hard hill
37.6	600yd moderate climb
41.5	A87 'to town centre'
41.8	'to town centre'
42.1	Portree TIC

See Day 9 p364

via the hilly (but virtually traffic-free) Ord road to the western side of the Sleat Peninsula (pronounced 'slate'). It offers great views of the Sound of Sleat to the east and the Cuillins mountain range to the west (beware of cattle grids). Traffic is busiest on the A851 at ferry times. The last 9mi of the A851 is a new two-lane road, but parts of the pleasant old road (adjacent) are still accessible to bicycles (keep an eye out for access points). The final 1.5mi to Broadford are via the busy A87.

Most of the road signs on Skye are in Gaelic as well as English – it's spoken by half the island's residents – and there's a Gaelic college a couple of miles from Armadale pier.

Referred to as 'The Garden of Skye', the **Sleat Peninsula** is wooded and less rugged than other parts of the island, and contains most of Skye's tallest and rarest trees.

Broadford (An T-Ath Leathann)
☎ 01471

Broadford is one of Skye's two main towns – the other being Portree. On the main highway (the A87), it's 8mi from Kyleakin and the bridge to the mainland at Kyleakin.

Information The TIC (☎ 822361), next to the Esso petrol station, opens Monday to Saturday between April and October from 9 am to 5 pm, and Sunday in July and August.

Fairwinds Cycle Hire (☎ 822270), on the Elgol Rd, has limited spares and does repairs from 9 am to 7 pm. The Bank of Scotland (with ATM) and post office are across the bridge towards Portree.

Most shops close early on Wednesday.

Local attractions include a **picture gallery** and a **wool spinner and dyer** by the old pier, 250yd east of the TIC. You can see and touch a variety of snakes at the **Serpentarium** (☎ 822209), at the Old Mill.

Places to Stay & Eat Almost 3mi east of the TIC on the A87, *Campbell's Cuillin View Camping & Caravan Park* (☎ 822 248) is fairly basic. Tent pitches cost £2.20 per night.

The *Hostel* (☎ 822442) – cross the bridge and turn right – costs £9 per bed. The small *Fossil Bothy* (☎ 822644/297, 13 Lower Breakish), east of Broadford, is £7.50 per person.

Friendly, nonsmoking *Fairwinds* (☎ 822 270) does B&B as well as cycle hire; doubles and twins cost £20 per person. Also nonsmoking, the pleasant *Ptarmigan* (☎ 822744), on the A87, overlooks the sea. B&B costs £21 for singles and £25 per person for doubles and twins. B&B at *The Shieling* (☎ 822533) is £17 per person.

At the *Hebridean Hotel* (☎ 822486) B&B starts at £19.50, or a bed only is £15. Mains in the pleasant bistro area are around £6.

There are good bread and pastries available from the *bakery* near Elgol Rd (not open Sunday) and a large *Co-op* supermarket next to the TIC. The *Harbour Grill* has standard meat and fish mains as well as burgers from £4.30. Locals recommend bar meals at the *Claymore* (☎ 822333), which cost around £6 (more in the restaurant). The nonsmoking *Fig Tree Restaurant* (☎ 822 616), across the bridge, is also recommended – mains are mostly around £8.

Day 8: Broadford to Portree
3½–5½ hours, 42.1mi

Skye's Cuillin mountains dominate the skyline, but the busy A87 remains relatively flat until Sligachan (18.6mi). Escape the traffic by taking the coastal Moll Rd

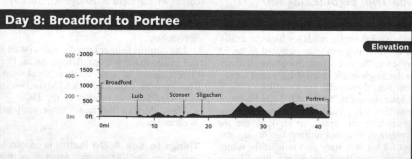

Day 8: Broadford to Portree

Roads in Scotland: Know your A, B, Single-Track

One of the joys of the Scottish Highlands and islands is cycling on isolated single-track roads. The joy is firstly the scenery – it is, invariably, delightful – and secondly the relative absence of cars.

In a world obsessed with going faster, motorists generally avoid the long winding drive along a single-track B-road (where one is forced to drive slowly) in favour of the blink-and-miss-it sprint along a straight, boring, evenly-graded A-road.

Evenly-graded, however, is what B-roads are not. While most A-road hills are long, steady climbs at worst, narrow B-roads and unclassified roads typically rock and roll with steeper gradients.

Courtesy has special significance on a single-track road – it's important to know your single-track protocol. Passing places, which are located at regular intervals, are the only spots wide enough for two road users to pass (even, in many cases, when one is a bicycle). The accepted practice is for the road user closest to the passing place to pull over to the left (never to the right), allowing the other to pass. You're also legally required to pull over to enable a closely following vehicle to pass. Do take care, however, not to be driven off the road by somebody overtaking at a place not designated for passing.

(8.6mi). The A863 from Sligachan is considerably quieter than the A87, yet still A-road in character, with relatively fast traffic and gentler gradients. In contrast, the B885 to Portree (31.8mi) is single-track, lightly trafficked, winding and constantly undulating with steeper grades.

Sligachan is a good base from which to explore the Cuillins. Apart from a bustling *hotel* (with good cheap bar meals that cater mainly to climbers and walkers), there's not much else here – or anywhere, until Portree.

Skye's **Talisker Distillery** (☎ 01478-640314) is a short side trip away at Carbost – go left at 24.2mi and follow the B8009 – in the pretty crofting valley around Loch Harport. It involves some short hills and affords more excellent views of the Red and Black Cuillins. Tours of the distillery are £3 and they run from 9 am to 4 pm weekdays (also on Saturday from July to September).

Side Trip: Elgol (Ealaghol)
2½–4 hours, 31mi return
Escaping the main traffic on Skye means getting off the main roads – which generally means returning via your outward route. In any case, the marvellous mountain scenery on the single-track Elgol Rd is worth seeing from both directions.

Take the Elgol Rd/B8083, 240yd west of Broadford TIC, and follow it through pleasant crofting countryside to Elgol. There are a couple of hills, but nothing too taxing, except for the very steep first mile of the return journey from the Elgol wharf. **Elgol** has a

shop, a *tearoom* and a *fish and chip van*. *Coruisk House* (☎ 01471-866330), at the narrow end of town, does B&B for £25 per person (£40 including dinner).

Closer to Broadford, the skyline is dominated by the smooth slopes of the 'red hills'. The striking jagged black peaks that come into view around the village of Torrin and Loch Slapin are exquisite; but it's at the end of the road, right down at the Elgol wharf that the spectacular main Cuillin Range is best viewed.

Portree (Port Righ)
☎ 01478
Port Righ is Gaelic for King's Harbour, which the area was named after James V called here in 1540 to pacify local clan chieftans. The attractive, lively town is Skye's largest settlement.

Information The TIC (☎ 612137), on the corner of Bayfield & Bridge Rds, opens 9 am to at least 5.30 pm Monday to Saturday and 11 am to 4 pm Sunday, from April to September.

The helpful folk at Island Cycles (☎ 613 121), downstairs from Bridge St at The Green, have a well-stocked workshop. There are three banks (with ATMs) – two in Somerled Square, another by the TIC.

Many Portree businesses close early on Wednesday.

Things to See & Do Portree is an excellent place for **live music**. Apart from the central hotels that regularly have free gigs (try the Isles, Caledonian, Tongadale and Royal), the nonsmoking **Aros Centre** (☎ 613 649), on Viewfield Rd (A87), has music or films every summer evening. During the day the **Aros Experience**, an exhibition at the Aros Centre, is a lively introduction to Skye life. There's also a good *restaurant*. The modern **An Tuireann Art Centre** (☎ 613 306), on Struan Rd, hosts contemporary art exhibitions and has a licensed *cafe*.

Places to Stay It's advisable to book accommodation, especially in July and August.

The well-run *Torvaig Caravan & Camp Site* (☎ 612209, Staffin Rd) is 1.2mi uphill from town. It's £3 per person to camp, including showers.

Portree Backpackers Hostel (☎ 613641, Dunvegan Rd), opposite the Co-op supermarket, charges £4 per person to camp, £8.50 in pleasant 4- or 5-bed dorms or £10 per person in a twin. The *Portree Independent Hostel* (☎ 613737, Bridge Rd), near the square, has larger, noisier dorms for £8.50 and Internet access. Neither has inside bike storage.

B&B at the comfortable, nonsmoking *Givendale Guest House* (☎ 612183, Heron Place), off Viewfield Rd, includes homemade bread. High season rates are £25 for singles, and £20 to £24 per person for doubles and twins. Also welcoming to cyclists, *Oronsay* (☎ 612192, 1 Marsco Place) charges £19 per person (no singles). *Rosebank Guest House* (612282, Springfield Rd) does B&B for £20 per person. The newly refurbished *Caledonian Hotel* (☎ 612641, Wentworth St) charges £30 per person for B&B.

Places to Eat The *Safeway (Bank St)* and *Co-op (Dunvegan Rd)* supermarkets both

close on Sunday, as does *Jackson's Wholefoods (Park Lane)*.

The *Granary (Somerled Square)* is an excellent bakery with adjoining coffee shop serving light meals until 7 pm.

Bar meals at the *Tongadale Hotel (Wentworth St)* cost around £6. Locals recommend *The Isles Inn* (☎ 612129, Somerled Square), where mains (including pasta) are mostly around £8 to £11. Burgers start from £5.50.

The *Ben Tianavaig Bistro* (☎ 612152, 5 Bosville Terrace) serves plenty of carbohydrates. Veg mains are £8.95, and the two-course seafood menu starts at £13.95.

Day 9: Portree to Portree
4–6 hours, 49.7mi

The lonely Trotternish Peninsula offers some dramatic scenery north of Uig and, particularly, along the west coast. Traffic is reasonably light, especially after the Dunvegan turn-off (4.2mi), and the climbing is mostly in the second half.

Uig (15.5mi) is the main town on the peninsula's west side, and the departure point for ferries to the outer Hebrides – of which there are good views, following the climb out of Uig. The TIC, wharf and *cafes* are 0.8mi off the main route.

There are few services until Staffin (31.6mi), but it's worth stopping for delicious homemade food at *Whitewave* (☎ 01470-542414) in Linicro (19.9mi), a small cafe and outdoor centre that also does folk music, and offers B&B.

The recommended **Skye Museum of Island Life** (22.0mi; ☎ 01470-552206) depicts traditional crofting lifestyle. A monument to **Flora MacDonald** (who helped Bonnie Prince Charles escape his defeat at the Battle of Culloden) is nearby in the cemetery.

Day 9: Portree to Portree

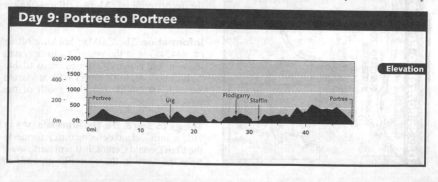

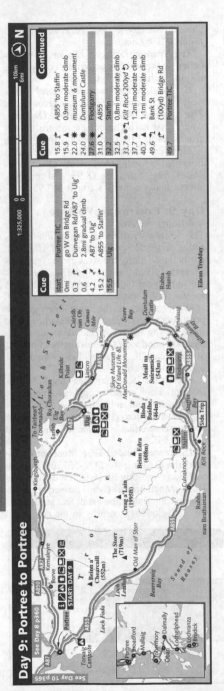

Cue (Continued)

15.8	↱	A855 'to Staffin'
15.9	◄	0.9mi moderate climb
22.0	✱✱	museum & monument
27.6	✱✱✱	Duntulum Castle
31.0	◄	Flodigarry
32.2	▲	Staffin
32.5	◄	0.8mi moderate climb
33.7	●●↱	Kilt Rock 200yd ↻
37.7	◄	1.2mi moderate climb
40.7	◄	1.1mi moderate climb
49.6	↰	Bank St
	↱	(100yd) Bridge Rd
49.7		Portree TIC

Cue

start		Portree TIC
0mi	↱	go W on Bridge Rd
0.3	↰ ◄	Dunvegan Rd/A87 'to Uig'
0.6	◄	2.8mi gradual climb
4.2	↗	A87 'to Uig'
15.2	↱	A855 'to Staffin'
15.5		Uig

At 23.4mi, the ruins of **Duntulum Castle** sits on a point that looks out to sea and the outer Hebrides (three minutes' walk from the road).

It's a stark landscape around the peaty moors of the peninsula's northern end. At the site of Flora MacDonald's home in **Flodigarry** (28.4mi), brooding grey cliffs stand like a fort to the west, the weather-worn folds in the rock like the rouched skirts of austere Victorian aunts.

The hills are more significant after Staffin (32.2mi), but the stunning scenery continues to back Portree. Stop to see spectacular **Kilt Rock** (a side trip at 34.3mi) and look out for the dramatic spike of the **Old Man of Storr** (41.7mi), as well as **Loch Leathan** (43.5mi) and the Island of Raasay, to the east.

Day 10: Portree to Armadale
3¼–5½ hours, 43.4mi

The return to Armadale via the A87 is straightforward, easy riding but with more traffic.

There's a long, gradual climb to 113m (371ft) altitude after leaving Portree – a pretty unmemorable road until the descent into Sligachan when, suddenly, it's surrounded by moors and mountains.

Though the Moll Rd detour (at 13.5mi) is more pleasant, the most direct route between Sligachan and Broadford is via the A87, but it involves a moderate climb to 130m (426ft).

Likewise, between Broadford and Armadale stay on the A85 instead of detouring through Ord.

Armadale (Armadal) & Ardvasar
☎ 01471

Armadale is a scattering of services around the ferry terminal. More 'village-like' is Ardvasar, 0.6mi from the ferry terminal.

Information The CalMac booking office (☎ 844248) is at the wharf. Coin-operated showers and laundry facilities are available 24 hours (Easter to October) at Sleat Marine Services (☎ 844216), 150yd south of the Ardvasar store.

Things to See & Do The Armadale (☎ 844 305, ✉ info@cland.demon.co.uk), formerly the Clan Donald Centre, is 0.6mi north-west from the ferry in the beautiful grounds of

Day 10: Portree to Armadale

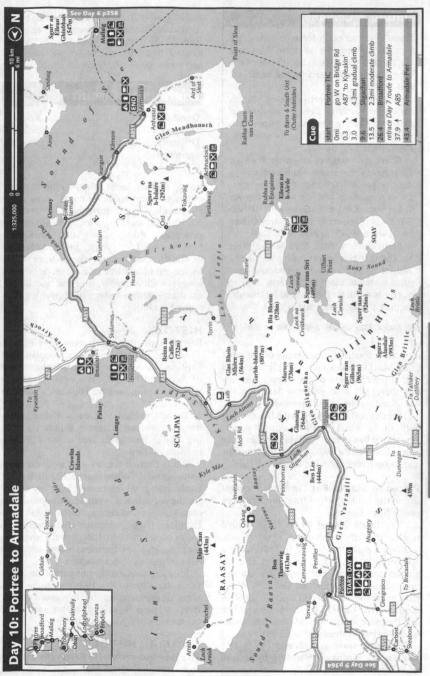

Cue		
start		Portree TIC
0mi		go W on Bridge Rd
0.3	◣	A87 'to kyleakin'
3.0	◣	4.3mi gradual climb
9.6	▲	Sligachan
13.5	▲	2.3mi moderate climb
26.4	◀	Broadford
37.9	◀	retrace Day 7 route to Armadale
43.4	◀	A85
		Armadale Pier

SCOTLAND

Culture & Ceilidhs

If you're out to catch some contemporary Scottish culture, the Western Isles and Highlands is the place to be. It's one of the richest areas in Scotland for live music, art and festivals.

Even the most sleepy-looking villages come alive, whether through regular local sessions, touring shows, or impromptu *ceilidhs* (informal gatherings for entertainment, music and dance).

Check out village pubs – often the spot for regular jam sessions – and keep an eye out for posters advertising touring gigs. Other venues to look up include the **An Tobar Arts Centre & Gallery** (☎ 01688 302211) in Tobermory and the **Aros Centre** (☎ 01478 613649) in Portree on Skye.

Festivals such as the **Skye Festival** (Feis an Eilein) – two weeks of music, poetry and more, held annually in mid July – are great places to catch quality acts. They're put on as much for the locals as for tourists, so there's quite a community spirit.

Armadale Castle, former home of the powerful MacDonald Clan. The clan story is told at the **Museum of the Isles** in the castle; there are also **walking trails** in the woodland gardens, and *tearooms*.

There's good **swimming** at the beach 1.7mi north of the wharf; and look out for posters advertising **live music** – ceilidhs, or gigs at the pub or Sabhal Mòr Ostaig, the Gaelic college, and its new venue, Arainn Chaluim Chille.

Places to Stay & Eat There's free *camping* in the woods 440yd from the ferry, opposite Skye Batiks.

The *Youth Hostel* (☎ 844260), 380yd north of the ferry terminal, has £8 dorm beds.

Home Leigh (☎ 844361), in Ardvasar, is a comfortable B&B charging from £28 for singles and £16.50 per person for doubles and twins. B&B is £50 for singles and £40 per person for doubles and twins at the *Ardvasar Hotel* (☎ 844233). This is a social hub and the place for bar meals where mains start at £6.95 (basket meals from £3.90).

The small *store* at Ardvasar closes at 5 pm. Try the *Ardvasar Hotel* for basic supplies after hours.

The *Galley Restaurant* (☎ 844252) by the Armadale Pier has traditional and veg mains from £5.20. The tiny *Pasta Shed* at the pier has fish and chips for £4.50, pizza from £4 and pasta for £6.50. It's open until 7 pm.

Highlands Circuit

Duration	3 days
Distance	126.8mi
Difficulty	moderate
Start/End	Killin

Long, narrow lochs, purple moors, rocky mountains and bubbling burns – this is the Highlands. Once a stronghold of the clans, who farmed and fought for centuries its now peaceful, middle-of-nowhere atmosphere makes it ideal for cycling and walking.

The three-day circuit takes in three scenic lochs, the oldest tree in Europe, Scotland's longest and, arguably, loveliest and loneliest glen – plus a village so happening they named it Dull.

HISTORY

Breadalbane, the region from Aberfeldy to Tyndrum, literally means 'the uplands of Scotland'. Located at the geographic centre of Scotland, it links the west Highlands with the north, and the Highlands with the Lowlands.

There's evidence of early Celtic settlement. According to legend, St Fillan, a healing monk, lived in the area with a wolf who befriended him.

Clans farmed the area up until the mid-18th century. Following the 1746 Battle of Culloden, in which many clansmen fought for the Jacobites, government troops burned clan villages and destroyed crops. After the Highland Clearances, rich landowners who were keen on field sports, built shooting lodges, developed grouse moors and bred deer in place of sheep farming.

Forestry was another important industry from the 17th to the 19th centuries. Logs were transported on the Tay and Tummel Rivers. These days the rivers are used in the production of hydroelectricity.

NATURAL HISTORY

The Ben Lawers Nature Reserve is home to some rare alpine flora – for more information, visit the National Trust for Scotland visitor centre (see Day 3).

A rare stand of ancient Caledonian Pine forest can be seen at the Black Wood of Rannoch (just west of the Rannoch School – see Day 2).

Other things to watch for include birds of prey and, in forested areas, red deer, squirrels and pine martens. Salmon and trout are found in the lochs and rivers, the most spectacular example of which is the salmon swimming up the Pitlochry fish ladder.

PLANNING
When to Ride
Ride between May and September – it's best during summer, especially later in summer when heather turns the moors purple. Beware of grouse and deer hunting from mid-August to October if you're heading off-road.

Maps
The ride falls on the boundaries of the OS Travelmaster (1:250,000) maps No 2, *Northern Scotland* and No 4, *Southern Scotland*. Perhaps better (and practically essential for mountain biking or walking) are the OS Landranger (1:50,000) maps, Nos 51 and 52.

GETTING TO/FROM THE RIDE
This ride can be linked up from the end of the West Coast ride by catching the train from Mallaig to Crianlarich (14mi from Killin). Killin is one day's ride from Perth, which is connected to Edinburgh by train.

Killin
Train & Bicycle The Scotrail (☎ 0845-748 4950, ☐ www.scotrail.co.uk) West Highland Line between Glasgow and Oban/Mallaig stops at Crianlarich, which is 1¾ hours from Glasgow and 3¼ hour from Mallaig (£17.90). At least two trains run daily from Mallaig, at least four to/from Glasgow, with connections to/from Edinburgh.

Crianlarich to Killin is an easy 14mi ride. Go north from the station and turn right (east) onto the busy A85, signed 'to Perth'. Take the A827 (left) to Killin at 11.6mi. The Breadalbane Centre & TIC is on the left after crossing the bridge into Killin.

Bicycle Killin to Perth is around 47mi; go via Lochearnhead (south of Lock Earn to St Fillans) and Crieff, turning right ('to Madderty')

near the top of the hill. The minor road rejoins the busy A84 just before Perth.

THE RIDE
Killin
☎ 01567
The pretty village of Killin sits by the River Dochart, just west of Loch Tay. With more services and charm than Crianlarich, it's a better base from which to ride.

Information The TIC in the Breadalbane Folklore Centre (☎ 820254), by the bridge, opens daily from 10 am to 6 pm or longer between June and September. It has a bureau de change and there's a Bank of Scotland (with ATM) in the village.

Tay Cycles (☎ 01887-830439, ☐ taycycles @heirs.demon.co.uk) is a keen cycle tourer's home business, 13.5mi away on Loch Tay (see Day 1), near Acharn. It's best to phone ahead – repairs are mostly done in the evenings (they will come to Killin by arrangement). Good rigid-fork mountain bikes are available for hire along with route directions. The Killin Outdoor Centre (☎ 820652), on Main St, is also worth a try.

Things to See & Do The Breadalbane Folklore Centre is an old mill overlooking the Falls of Dochart. It has displays on local clans and an exhibition and film on St Fillan, a 7th-century missionary. The unusual 1744-built church near the Killin Hotel has a remarkable font believed to be 1000 years old.

The TIC has information about walks in and around the village. The area is also popular for Munro-bagging. Ben Lawers, at 1214m (3982ft), is one of several Munros in the area. Ask at the hostel for walking advice and take an OS map (Landranger No 51, *Loch Tay & Glen Dochart*). There's also good mountain biking – Tay Cycles (see Information) has information about routes.

Places to Stay & Eat The closest camping site is *Shieling Accommodation* (☎ 820 334, Aberfeldy Rd), 1.9mi north-east of the TIC. Tent sites are £3.50 plus £1 for showers.

The small, friendly *Youth Hostel* (☎ 820 546), at the village's northern end, charges £8.50 between March and October.

Breadalbane House (☎ 820134, ☐ stay @breadalbane48.freeserve.co.uk, Main St) is a comfortable, smoke-free place that offers a good breakfast. It's £30 for a single and £20 per person for doubles and twins. *Fairview House (☎ 820667, Main St)* charges £24 per person plus £14 for a pre-ordered three-course evening meal; book ahead. B&B starts at £16 (no singles) at *Craigbuie Guesthouse (☎ 820 439, Main St)*.

The *Coach House Hotel (☎ 820349)*, towards the north end of town, has folk music on weekends and good bar meals (most mains around £5 to £7.50). B&B starts at £28 for a single and £23 per person in a double or twin (bike storage is unsheltered).

The *Wee Bake Shop (Main St)* opens daily. The *fish and chip van* in the village hall car park opens till around 10 pm, as does the *Co-op* supermarket opposite the post office.

Capercaillie (☎ 820355, Main St) has a lovely outlook over the River Dochart. It serves standard fare (lasagne, haddock etc) for between £6 and £8. *Shutters Restaurant & Coffee Shop*, opposite the post office, is similar and has some delicious home-baked goods.

Day 1: Killin to Kinloch Rannoch
3–4½ hours, 33.4mi

Day 1 begins with the quiet, single-track road along the south of Loch Tay, the second half, via the slightly busier B846, heads over the shoulder of Schiehallion before a cracking descent through the heather to Kinloch Rannoch.

The road beside Loch Tay undulates constantly for the 16.8mi to Kenmore. The surprisingly strenuous riding is tempered by pleasant surrounds. Look out for squirrels and other critters in the shady woods. Ben Lawers (the ninth-highest peak in Scotland) sits above the loch to the north.

The reconstructed crannog at the **Scottish Crannog Centre** (16.4mi; ☎ 01887-830583) features fine example of the ancient defensive homesteads built on lochs throughout Scotland and Ireland.

By the eastern end of the loch, Kenmore (16.8mi), the main settlement en route, is a good lunch spot. Baguettes at the *Kenmore Hotel (☎ 01887-830205)* start at £3.60; full mains from £7.25. Check out the Burns poem in the bar, apparently written onto the wall by his own hand. There's also a *bakery* in the post office, and light meals at the *Taymouth Trading Co*.

The countryside feels more remote towards the end of the 4mi climb up the

shoulder of Schiehallion. A **cairn** 2.2mi along Schiehallion Rd commemorates the Reverend Nevil Maskelyn, an astronomer who used the Schiehallion's symmetry to calculate the Earth's mass.

Kinloch Rannoch
☎ 01882

A peaceful backwater, the village of Kinloch Rannoch sits at the east end of Loch Rannoch. Crofting is evident around the village, but the largest employers are the exclusive Rannoch School and the time-share resort.

Information There's a tourist information board at the village square, and maps and tourist brochures are available from the Spar store south of the bridge. It's open daily from 8 am to 8 pm (9 am to 5 pm Sunday).

Things to See & Do The **Rannoch Forge** (☎ 632219), 1mi east of the village on Schiehallion Rd, uses traditional blacksmith techniques.

Walks in the area are described in the *Welcome to Rannoch* (10p) brochure. An OS Landranger map is recommended, especially for serious climbs such as Schiehallion. Check for grouse and deer shooting activities before setting out.

The **Loch Rannoch Outdoor Activity Centre** (☎ 632303), west of the village on the B846, is part of the time-share resort open to the public. As well as supervised activities, there's an indoor climbing wall, plus squash and tennis courts.

Places to Stay & Eat Tent sites are £3 at the secluded *Kilvrecht (☎ 01350-727284)* camping ground. Turn off onto a 0.7mi unsealed road, 3mi from Kinloch Rannoch on the loch's south side.

The food at *Glenrannoch House (☎ 632 307)* is the drawcard, except to hard-core carnivores. Veg B&B is £18.50 to £20.50. Prebooked dinner (£14.50) and breakfast (£6.50) are also available to nonguests; packed lunches are available for £3.50.

Riverside (☎ 632282) does B&B for £23 for singles and £18 per person for doubles and twins. Chinese-style evening meals are available with advance notice.

The *Loch Rannoch Hotel (☎ 632201)*, at the resort on the north Loch Rannoch Rd, has good mid-priced meals (pastas and pizzas

Days 1 & 2: Killin – Kinloch Rannoch – Pitlochry

1:325,000

N

Elevation

600 – 2000
400 –
1500
1000
200 –
500
0m 0ft

Schiehallion Rd
Kinloch Rannoch
Ardeonaig
Kenmore
Acham
Killin

See Day 3 p372

0mi   10   20   30

SCOTLAND

Day 1

Cue		
start		Killin TIC
0mi		go S over bridge
0.1	↰	'to South Loch Tay' (dogleg)
7.6	▲	0.75mi steep climb
12.3	▲	400yd moderate climb
15.1		Acham
16.4		Crannog Centre
16.7	↰	'to Killin'
16.8		Kenmore
17.3	↱	'to Kinloch Rannoch'
19.8	↰	B846 'to Kinloch Rannoch'
20.4	▲	4mi moderate climb
24.2	↰	Schiehallion Rd
26.4	✳	Maskelyn cairn
32.6	↰	unsigned road
33.4		Kinloch Rannoch village square

Day 2

Cue		
start		Kinloch Rannoch village square
0mi		go S over bridge
0.1	↰	'to south Loch Rannoch'
5.2	✳	Rannoch School
12.0	↱	B846 'to Kinloch Rannoch'
	●●● ↰	Rannoch Station 10mi ↰
16.2		Talladh-A-Bheithe Lodge
23.2	↰	B846, Kinloch Rannoch
25.9	↱	'to Tummel Bridge'
26.4	▲	850yd steep climb
31.1	▲	1.2mi moderate climb
32.4	↱	'to Foss'
36.9	▲	440yd gradual climb
37.6	▲	550yd steep climb
39.6	▲	550yd steep climb
40.4	▼	800yd steep descent
41.1		Coronation Bridge walk
41.5		Lin of Tummel walk
43.8		thru gate to bikepath
44.0		thru gap in fence on bikepath
44.3		join Foss Rd
44.9	↰	Bridge Rd
45.1	↱	'to Pitlochry'
45.4		Pitlochry TIC

To Perth
River Tummel
A924
Loch Faskally
Moulin
Dunfallandy
Stone
Logierait
A9
A827
B898
Pitlochry START DAY 3
Cammoch Hill
Queen's View
Loch Derculich
Coronation Bridge & Lin of Tummel Walks
START·DAY 3
Tressait
Loch Tummel
Loch Bhac
Loch Tummel
B8019
Foss
Loch Kinardochy
Tummel Bridge
Farragon Hill (788m)
Weem
Aberfeldy
Edradynate
Strathtay
River Tay
B846
Dull
River Lyon
Keltneyburn
Fortingall
B846
Dunalastair Water
B847
Schiehallion (1083m)
Carn Mairg (1042m)
Glen Lyon
START·DAY 2
Kinloch Rannoch
Kilvrecht
Carn Gorm (1029m)
Inverwar
River Lyon
Maskelyn Cairn
Garrow
Loch Hoil
Cranog Centre
Kenmore
Acham
A827
Crеаgаn na Beinne (887m)
River Almond
Pitlochry
Killin
Edinburgh
Loch Lednock
Fearnan
Ardtalnaig
Lawers
NTS Visitor Centre
Loch Tay
Ben Lawers (1214m)
Lochan na Lairige
Ardeonaig
Loch Breaclaich
Creag Gairbh (637m)
B846
Black Wood Of Rannoch
Talladh-A-Bheithe Lodge
Killichonan
Loch Rannoch
Rannoch School
Loch Eigheach
Bridge of Gaur
Rannoch Station
Side Trip
Morenish
Lochan Breaclaich
B e n   L a w e r s
Killin
START/END

0   10km
0   6mi

start under £6). B&B is £45 for singles and £35 for doubles and twins. Somewhat cheaper for singles is the *Bunrannoch Hotel* (☎ *632367)*, where B&B costs £30 per person (bikes are stored outside). Evening mains are mostly around £7. The *Spar* supermarket is just across the road.

Day 2: Kinloch Rannoch to Pitlochry
3½–5½ hours, 45.4mi

A quiet, easy 23mi circuit around Loch Rannoch begins the ride, followed by some climbing – parts of it steepish, though nothing extended.

There's more traffic during the ride's second half, especially between Kinloch Rannoch and the village of Tummel Bridge (30.4mi), but no services.

Now virtually uninhabited – apart from a handful of dwellings on the north side – the land surrounding Loch Rannoch was once occupied by eight different clans – who, it seems, were less than neighbourly. **Clan trail** information boards (beginning at 0.6mi) around the loch illustrate the warring Highland lifestyle.

The area couldn't be more peaceful now, however. Alongside birch, bracken and bluebells, the south side offers beautiful views of the loch. The exclusive **Rannoch School** (5.2mi) is one of the few buildings on this side.

For more back-of-beyond before heading east, take a side trip at 12.0mi to the end of the road – **Rannoch Station** – on the edge of the wild Rannoch Moor (10mi return).

The north bank of the loch is more open and dotted with sandy beaches; at 16.2mi, gracious *Talladh-A-Bheithe Lodge* (☎ *633 203)*, once the Clan Menzies hunting lodge, is now run by a German family who bake delicious cakes (B&B starts at £22).

Leaving Kinloch Rannoch for the second time, the riding becomes more strenuous, but the surroundings are no less attractive. The much photographed **Queen's View** looks west from Loch Tummel's busier north bank (the view from the lightly trafficked south bank is also pretty special).

Also spectacular is the descent through the gorge to Pitlochry. Short five-minute walks to **Coronation Bridge** (41.1mi) and the **Lin of Tummel** (41.5mi) provide opportunities to linger.

Approaching Pitlochry, the route passes under the A9 and gets a bit complicated – after 600yd follow the bike signs left and through a gate onto a bikepath that leads to the town's access road.

Pitlochry
☎ 01796

Though it's packed with accommodation and tourist shops, Pitlochry is more than just a junky tourist town – probably because it's been a holiday destination since the 1860s.

Information The TIC (☎ 472215), 22 Atholl Rd, opens daily from 9 am to 8 pm between late May and mid-September.

Banks (with ATMs) are on Atholl Rd. Escape Route bike shop (☎ 473859), 8 West Moulin Rd, has helpful staff. Ask about local mountain bike rides; it's open seven days Easter to October.

Things to See & Do Pitlochry's two whisky distilleries are **Bell's Blair Atholl Distillery** (☎ 472234) on the corner of Bridge and Perth Rds, and Scotland's smallest, **The Eradour** (☎ 472095), 2.5mi northeast on the A924 (offering free tours).

The highly regarded **Pitlochry Festival Theatre** (☎ 484626) has productions showing most nights between May and October.

Walk west from the theatre to the **fish ladder**, constructed to allow salmon to swim up to their spawning grounds. May and June are the best months to see the fish. The **Scottish Hydroelectric Visitor Centre** (☎ 473152) has an audiovisual interactive presentation of 'The Salmon Story'.

The TIC has information about local **walks**, or you can climb a **Munro** with Strathbraan Treks (☎ 01350-723201). Qualified guides lead **mountain bike** rides (bookings required) and the local mountain bike club has Friday night rides – ask at Escape Route (see Information) for details.

Places to Stay It's advisable to phone ahead to *Faskally Caravan Park* (☎ *472 007)*, 2mi north of Pitlochry on the B8019. A tent site costs £6.15 for one plus 80p per extra person. On-site facilities include a large store, indoor pool, spa, sauna, bar and restaurant (mains mostly £4 to £7). Alternatively, you can try the *Milton of Fonab*

Caravan Site (☎ *472882, Bridge Rd*), where tents cost £7/8 for one/two people.

The congenial *Pitlochry Youth Hostel* (☎ *472308, Knockard Rd*), overlooking the town, charges £10.75 a bed including continental breakfast.

Cyclists are welcomed and well-fed at the smoke-free *Carra Beag Guest House* (☎ *472835, 16 Toberargan Rd*). B&B is £22 per person. Booking ahead is advised. Close by, the elegant *Craigroyston House* also caters for cyclists. Expect to pay £28 per person in August (no singles). The owners of the *Poplars Hotel* (☎ *472129, 27 Lower Oakfield Rd*), as well as providing B&B (£30 for singles and £55 per room for doubles and twins), offer instruction for outdoor activities including mountain biking.

B&B at the *Moulin Hotel* (☎ *472196*), 1mi north of town (take the Moulin Rd), starts at £55/60 a single/double.

Places to Eat Next to the bike shop on West Moulin Rd is *Penny's Supermarket*. It's open daily, as is *Treasure Island Wholefoods* (115 Atholl Rd).

Bakers Oven (Atholl Rd) has cafeteria-style light meals plus baked goods. For fish and chips try *The Plaice to Be* (☎ *473737, 4/8 West Moulin Rd*).

Luigis (☎ *472292, 40 Bonnethill Rd*) serves traditional Italian meals. Pizzas start at £4.25, pastas at £5.50, and the espresso is excellent. Locals also recommend the coffee at *Victoria's* (☎ *472670, 45 Atholl Rd*), where mains (traditional Scottish as well as pizzas, fajitas etc) are between £8 and £9. For good home cooking, try *The Old Smithy* (☎ *472356, 154 Atholl Rd*). Mains range from £7.25 to £11.75. A mile north of town (take the Moulin Rd), the 300-year-old *Moulin Inn* (☎ *472196*) has a good atmosphere and home-brewed ales. Good bar meals (including veg) start at £4.95.

Day 3: Pitlochry to Killin
4–6 hours, 48.0mi

Initially undulating, Day 3 flattens out along the wide Tay Valley. Apart from a brief busy stretch after Logierait (4.9mi) traffic is not intrusive.

The highlight is the climb through beautiful Glen Lyon (22.4mi) – Scotland's longest and, some say, loneliest glen – and over the shoulder of Ben Lawers. The

The Stone of Destiny

Alleged to have accompanied the Scots in all their mythical journeys, the original Stone of Destiny (the Fatal Stone) was a carved block of sandstone on which the Scottish monarchs placed their feet during the coronation.

Stolen by Edward I in 1296, this venerable talisman was incorporated into the Coronation Chair used by English (and later British) monarchs in London's Westminster Abbey. Apart from being taken to Gloucester during air raids in WWII, the Stone lay undisturbed for centuries.

On Christmas Eve 1950, a plucky band of Scottish students drove from Glasgow, jemmied the door of Westminster Abbey and stole the Stone. English officialdom was outraged. The border roads were blocked for the first time in 400 years, but while Scots living in London jeered the English police as they searched the Serpentine Lake and the River Thames, the Stone was being smuggled back to Scotland.

King George VI was 'sorely troubled about the loss', but the students issued a petition affirming their loyalty to him, stating they would return the Stone if it remained on Scottish soil. The authorities refused to negotiate and, three months after it was stolen, the Stone turned up on the altar of the ruined Abbey of Arbroath. It was here, in 1320, that the Arbroath Declaration was signed, reaffirming the right of Scots to self-rule and independence from England. Before the public were aware the Stone had even been found, it was back in London. No charges were brought and Ian Hamilton, the student who led this jolly caper, published his story in *The Taking of the Stone of Destiny*.

Many Scots, however, hold that the original Stone is safely hidden somewhere in Scotland, and that Edward I was fobbed off with a shoddy imitation. This is possibly true, for descriptions of the original state that it was decorated with carvings, not that it was a plain block of sandstone. However, given that Scottish nationalism is running high, this powerful symbol of Scotland would surely have been brought out by now.

Imitation or not, in 1996 the sandstone block was returned to Edinburgh Castle with much pomp and circumstance.

Day 3: Pitlochry to Killin

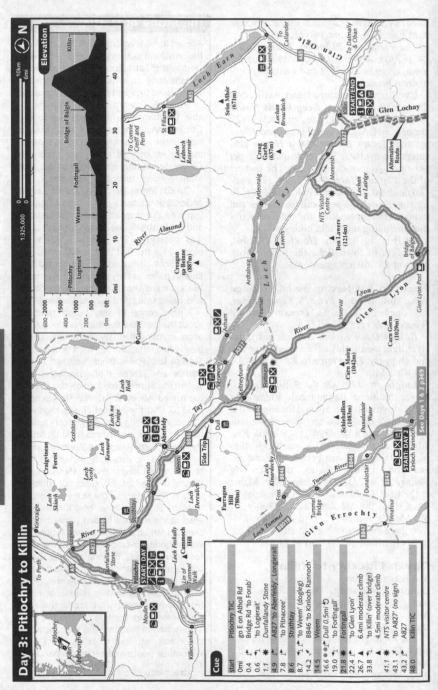

Elevation

Cue

Start		Pitlochry TIC
0mi	↑	go E on Atholl Rd
0.4	↙	Bridge Rd 'to Forab'
0.6	↙	'to Logierait'
1.1	✻	*Dunfallandy Stone*
4.9	↙	A827 'to Aberfeldy, Longieralt
7.8	↙	'to Pitnacree'
8.6		Strathtay
8.7	↙	'to Weem' (dogleg)
14.2	↙	B846 to Kinloch Rannoch'
14.5		Weem
16.6 ●✻↺		*Dull 0.5mi* ↺
19.0	↗	'to Fortingall'
21.8		Fortingall
22.4	↖	'to Glen Lyon'
26.7	◢	6.4mi moderate climb
33.8	◢	'to Killin' (over bridge)
		4.5mi moderate climb
41.1	✻	NTS visitor centre
43.1	↙	'to A827' (no sign)
43.2	↗	A827
48.0		Killin TIC

steady but mostly gentle (at least until the final 4.5mi) climb is lightly trafficked and gloriously scenic. (Note that camping is restricted through Glen Lyon).

Just over 1mi from Pitlochry are the ancient Pictish carvings of the **Dunfallandy Stone**.

The names are the most delightful aspect of some tiny Tay Valley villages. Weem (14.5mi), is deliciously whimsical; but Dull (16.6mi) takes the cake. Appropriately, not much happens at **Dull**, but they say it was once the capital of Perthshire (as the location of Perthshire's first church). The small, unassuming **church** (not open to the public) is visible from the main road, but better seen on a wee detour (0.5mi return) through the village.

Some claim that Dull also held the 'real' Stone of Destiny (see the boxed text) – that is, until it was taken into hiding in the mid-1990s (there are several Stones floating around Britain, some of which must be fakes).

Delightful for its character is the village of Fortingall (21.8mi), famous for the **3000-year-old yew** in the churchyard – probably the oldest tree in Europe. Fortingall is the last meal opportunity, apart from the quaint *Glen Lyon POST (☎ 01887-866221)* at 33.7mi.

From the POST, it's possible to detour farther up the Glen and return to Killin via the hydro road and Glen Lochay. Some claim the top of the glen is the nicest, as it becomes more open. Others say it's been spoiled by hydroelectric pylons. The alternative route is 8mi longer.

Break the descent to Killin to explore natural history at the **NTS visitor centre** (41.1mi).

Scottish Borders

Duration	3 days
Distance	125.6mi
Difficulty	moderate
Start/End	Edinburgh

It may not be Scotland's major drawcard, but the Scottish Borders' relative anonymity and quiet roads make it ideal for cycling. The region lies between the Cheviot Hills along the English border and the heather moors of the Pentland, Moorfoot and Lammermuir Hills south of Edinburgh.

Undulating, but without the mountains of the north, the rolling hills of patchwork green

and yellow are bisected by hedge-trimmed country lanes. The Borders is characterised by quaint burghs (towns), stately homes, abbeys and, of course, the River Tweed meandering its dignified way through the middle.

Don't leave without trying the Border country speciality, Selkirk Bannock, a rich, yeasted fruit bun that makes excellent cycling food.

HISTORY
Historically, southern Scotland was the buffer between the imperialist English and the equally unruly Scots, surviving centuries of war and plunder.

Although today's inhabitants are proudly and indisputably Scottish, they are unique – like but unlike the Scots farther to the north, and like but unlike the northern English to the south.

Romans invaded the area in the first century – evidence of their forts can still be seen. Unsuccessful in their attempted conquest, the Romans marked the bounds of their territory with Hadrian's Wall.

The fertile Valley of the River Tweed has been a wealthy region for 1000 years, with the population concentrated in a number of towns that also supported large and wealthy monastic communities. These provided an irresistible magnet during the border wars and were destroyed and rebuilt numerous times.

The monasteries met their final fiery end in the mid-16th century, burnt by the English yet again, but this time English fire combined with Scottish Reformation and they were never rebuilt.

The towns thrived once peace was established and traditional weavers provided the foundation for a major textile industry, which still survives.

The Scottish Borders was also home to the great writer Sir Walter Scott, who was influential in reinventing and romanticising Scottish culture.

NATURAL HISTORY
Scotland and England are thought to have been part of separate continents until they collided around 400 million years ago, bringing about the formation of the Southern Uplands.

While 16% of the Borders is covered in forest, much is plantation timber – only a tiny proportion of ancient woodland remains.

SCOTLAND

Forest conservation laws were passed as early as the 14th century, following the destruction during wars against the Romans.

Other important ecosystems include bogs, rich in plant and insect diversity, and the flower-filled grasslands. In the uplands, heather-covered moors are burnt to encourage grouse, which feed on the new shoots.

Lifeblood of the region, the River Tweed and its tributaries form Britain's fourth-largest river system. Once the victim of industrial pollution, it is now one of Britain's least polluted major rivers, supporting 16 fish species, otters, water voles and various other fauna.

Find out more about the region in *The Nature of the Borders* (£1.50 from TICs).

PLANNING
When to Ride

The moors are prettiest in August, when the heather is flowering. However, the ride is pleasant any time between April and September.

Maps & Books

Use the OS Travelmaster (1:250,000) No 4, *Southern Scotland*.

For additional detail, use the *Spokes Edinburgh Cycle Map*, along with OS Landranger (1:50,000) Nos 73 and 74.

The Scottish Tourist Board (STB; ☎ 0131-472 2035; 🖳 www.visitscotland.com) produces two useful booklets, *Cycling in the Scottish Borders* (free) and the *4 Abbeys Cycle Route Guide* (£1.50), available from TICs or the STB.

GETTING TO/FROM THE RIDE

See Gateway Cities (pp340-7) for details on getting to/from Edinburgh.

THE RIDE
Edinburgh

See the Gateway Cities section (pp338-41) for information on accommodation and other services.

Day 1: Edinburgh to Duns

3–5 hours, 40.3mi

After winding through the city streets join the attractive Innocent Railway bikepath (1.9mi). It starts with a 550yd tunnel – bizarrely buried in a residential car park. Once through the suburbs, the ride to Duns

is via quiet country lanes. It's quite hilly farming country, with several hefty climbs between Musselburgh and East Saltoun.

Last services before Duns are in the gorgeous leafy village of **Gifford** (17.5mi). The *Goblin Ha Hotel* (☎ *01620-810244*) does good counter meals; turn right at the village green for the *bakery* and the toilets.

After leaving Gifford, there's a long climb, steep in parts, through the heather moors of the **Lammermuir Hills**.

Duns
☎ 01361

Duns is a small burgh on the edge of the Lammermuir Hills. Now a peaceful village, it has been destroyed and rebuilt at least three times over the centuries. The original settlement stood on the slopes of nearby Duns Law (see Things to See & Do), from which it gets its name.

Information The Cherry Tree Tea Room (☎ 882089), on Market Square, has limited tourist information. It's open daily from 9 am (11 am Sunday) to 4.45 pm. There's also an information board by the Whip & Saddle (see Places to Stay & Eat).

Banks (with ATMs) are in Market Square.

Things to See & Do About 2mi east of Duns on the A6150, Edwardian **Manderston House** (☎ 883450) is a classic stately home set in 56 acres of beautiful gardens.

The 190-acre Duns Castle **nature reserve** has nature trails and 'Hen Poo' – a lake whose name means 'the haunt of wildfowl'. The castle itself is not open to the public. Also in the Castle Estate is **Duns Law** (218m/715ft), the summit of which offers good views and holds the **Covenanters' Stone**, which marks the spot of the Covenanting army's camp in 1639. To get there, follow Castle St up from the square.

More information on **walks** around Duns is contained in the free brochure *Walks around Duns & Places of Interest* available from the Cherry Tree Tea Room (see Information earlier).

Places to Stay & Eat For value, try *Miss Black's* (☎ *883553, 37 Castle St*), where B&B is £15 per person (twin or single). Smoke-free *St Albans* (☎ *883285, Clouds*) is a very comfortable old manse whose

Day 1: Edinburgh to Duns

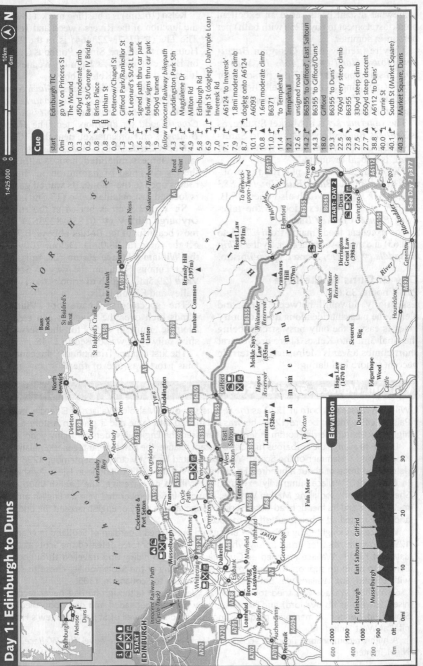

Cue		
start		Edinburgh TIC
0mi		go W on Princess St
0.3	↑	The Mound
0.3	↖	450yd moderate climb
0.5	⌂	Bank St/George IV Bridge
0.8	⌂	Bristo Place
0.8	↑	Lothian St
0.9	↑	Potterow/Chapel St
1.3	↖	Gifford Park/Rankeillor St
1.5	↖	St Leonard's St/St L Lane
1.6	↖	signed path thru car park
1.8		follow signs thru car park
1.9	↖	550yd tunnel
		follow Innocent Railway bikepath
4.3	↑	Duddingston Park Sth
4.4	↖	Magdalene Dr
4.9	◀	Milton Rd
5.8	↑	Edinburgh Rd
6.9	↗	High St (dogleg), Dalrymple Loan
7.0	◀	Inveresk Rd
7.1	◀	A6124 to Inveresk'
7.9	↖	1.8mi moderate climb
8.7	↗	dogleg onto A6124
10.1	↗	A6093
10.8	↖	1.6mi moderate climb
11.0	◀	B6371
11.4	↖	'to Templehall'
12.1		Templehall
12.6	↗	unsigned road
14.2	↖	B6355 to Gifford', East Saltoun
14.3	↖	B6355 to Gifford/Duns'
18.0		Gifford
19.3	↗	B6355 'to Duns'
22.5	↖	760yd very steep climb
23.8	◀	B6355
27.5	↖	330yd steep climb
27.7	◀	650yd steep descent
38.8	↗	A6112 'to Duns'
40.0		Currie St
40.1	↖	South St (Market Square)
40.3		Market Square, Duns

Elevation

SCOTLAND

See Day 2 p 377

somewhat distant hosts serve an excellent breakfast. Expect to pay £25 (with bath) per person in summer.

They're friendly at the Georgian *Barniken House Hotel* (☎ *882466, 18 Murray St*). En suite rooms are £27 per person. Bar meals (including a good veg selection) are £5.25 to £8.95 and there's a choice of 100 malt whiskies.

The *supermarket* is in Market Square, as is *Trotters Bakers* (open Monday to Saturday). *Luca's Icecream*, at the west end of town, is a local favourite.

The cheapest standard pub food is probably at the smaller *Black Bull Hotel* (☎ *883 379, Black Bull St*), which also does B&B, starting at £22.50. Next door is the takeaway *Fish & Chicken Bar*.

For excellent food (mains from £7.65 to £12.65) and award-winning beer, try the *Whip & Saddle* (☎ *883215, Market Square*) bistro.

Day 2: Duns to Melrose

2½–4 hours, 33.6mi

Essentially downhill between Duns and Kelso, the pleasant ride along quiet country lanes is easy – the only busy stretch being the final 3mi into Kelso. There are several short climbs towards Melrose as the terrain becomes more undulating.

Kelso (16.2mi) is a bustling market town at the junction of the Rivers Tweed and Teviot. The TIC (☎ 01573-223464) is in the Town House on the square. Simon Porteous Cycles, on Bridge St, closes at 1 pm on Wednesday. It's near the ruined Kelso Abbey.

Places to eat include the cosy *Black Swan Hotel* (☎ *01573-224563, 7 Horsemarket) or the Cottage Garden Tearooms (7 Abbey Court)*, good for afternoon tea. The *Home Bakery* is on Horsemarket, near the TIC.

Floors Castle (☎ 01573-223333), is Scotland's largest inhabited house, although there's no sense of habitation in the 10 rooms open to the public. Its walled garden is located just outside Kelso (17.5mi).

Sir Walter Scott is buried at the ruined **Dryburgh Abbey** (☎ 01835-822381), the most beautiful of the Border abbeys, 0.75mi off the route (at 28.0mi). Detour 200yd to the **William Wallace statue** (28.4mi), another famous Scot, on the way to **Scott's View** (29.5mi), which overlooks the Tweed Valley and Eildon Hills.

The spectacular **Leaderfoot Viaduct** stands high over the River Tweed east of Melrose. Built in 1865, for the Berwickshire railway, it was closed in 1948.

The first-century Trimontium ('three mountains') fort was one of the Romans' most

William Wallace, Scottish Patriot

William Wallace was born in 1270 as the second son of Sir Malcolm Wallace of Elderslie, near Paisley. Little-known before 1296, he was catapulted into fame and a place in history as a highly successful guerrilla commander who harassed the English invaders for many years.

Driven to avenge the barbarous rule of his distant relative, the Edward Plantagenet (England's King Edward I, Hammer of the Scots), Wallace secured his first victory in September 1296 by defeating a troop of about a hundred English soldiers at the battle of Loudoun Hill in Ayrshire. In May 1297, Wallace summarily executed Sir William de Hazelrigg, the English-imposed Sheriff of Lanark, for killing Marion Wallace, his wife. In September that year an English army met Wallace and his friends head-on at Stirling Bridge; a large party of English crossed the bridge and were routed after being cut off by the Scots.

Wallace was knighted by Robert the Bruce and proclaimed Guardian of Scotland in March 1298. However, disaster struck in July when Edward's superior force defeated the Scots at the Battle of Falkirk. Wallace resigned as Guardian, went into hiding and travelled throughout Europe to drum up support for the Scottish cause. Many of the Scots nobility chose to side with Edward, and Wallace was betrayed after his return to Scotland in 1305.

Sir William Wallace was tried for treason at Westminster (although he had never recognised Edward as his overlord) and he was cruelly hanged, beheaded and disembowelled at Smithfield, London. A memorial plaque is incorporated in the wall of St Bartholomew's Hospital at West Smithfield.

A highly recommended fictional account of Wallace's exploits is the novel *The Wallace*, by Nigel Tranter.

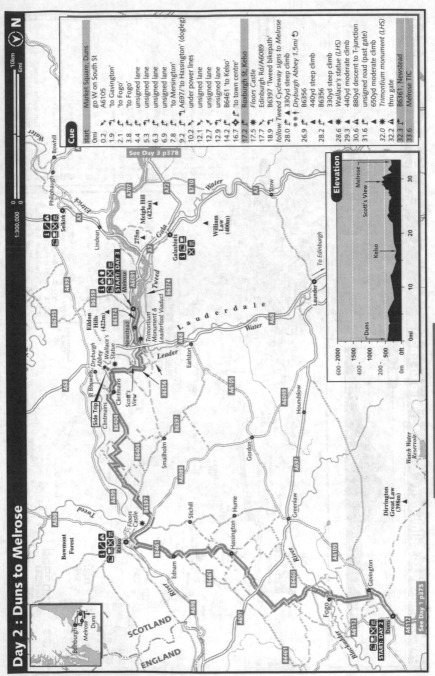

Day 2 : Duns to Melrose

Cue

start	0mi	Market Square, Duns go W on South St
0.2		A6105
1.9		'to Gavington'
2.1		'to Fogo'
3.8		'to Fogo'
4.4		unsigned lane
5.3		unsigned lane
6.3		unsigned lane
6.9		unsigned lane
7.8		'to Mersington'
9.2		A697/'to Hassington' (dogleg)
10.2		under power lines
12.1		unsigned lane
12.7		unsigned lane
12.9		unsigned lane
14.2		B6461 'to Kelso'
16.7		'to town centre'
17.2		Roxburgh St, Kelso
17.5		Floors Castle
17.7		Edinburgh Rd/A6089
18.9		B6397 'Tweed bikepath'
		follow Tweed Cycleway signs to Melrose
28.0		330yd steep climb
		Dryburgh Abbey 1.5mi
26.9		B6356
28.2		440yd steep climb
		B6356
		330yd steep climb
28.6		Wallace's statue (LHS)
29.3		440yd moderate climb
30.6		880yd descent to T-junction
31.6		unsigned road (past gate)
		650yd moderate climb
32.0		Trimontium monument (LHS)
32.2		thru gate
32.3		B6361, Newstead
33.6		Melrose TIC

Elevation

SCOTLAND

SCOTLAND

Day 3: Melrose to Edinburgh (& Day 13: End to End)

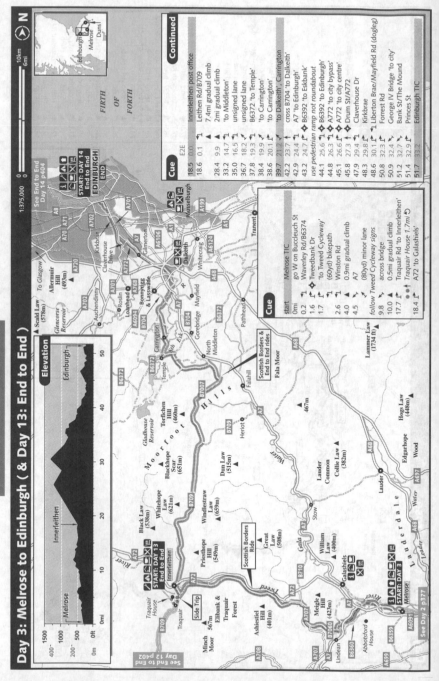

Elevation

Melrose — Innerleithen — Edinburgh

Continued

Cue	E2E	
18.5		Innerleithen post office
18.6	0.1	Leithen Rd/B709
28.4	9.9	7.4mi gradual climb
33.2	14.7	2mi gradual climb
35.0	16.5	'to Middleton'
36.7	18.2	unsigned lane
37.8	19.3	B6372 'to Temple'
38.4	19.9	'to Carrington'
38.6	20.1	'to Carrington'
39.7	21.2	'to Dalkeith', Carrington
42.2	23.7	cross B704 'to Dalkeith'
42.9	24.4	A7 'to Edinburgh'
43.2	24.7	B6392 'to Eskbank'
		use pedestrian ramp not roundabout
44.1	25.6	B6392 'to Edinburgh'
44.8	26.3	A772 to city bypass'
45.1	26.6	A772 to city centre'
45.8	27.3	Drum St/A772
47.9	29.4	Claverhouse Dr
48.3	29.8	Kirkbrae
48.6	30.1	Liberton Brae/Mayfield Rd (dogleg)
50.8	32.3	Forrest Rd
50.9	32.4	George IV Bridge 'to city'
51.2	32.7	Bank St/The Mound
51.4	32.9	Princes St
51.7	33.2	Edinburgh TIC

Cue	
start	Melrose TIC
0mi	go W on Buccleuch St
0.2	Waverley Rd/B6374
1.6	Tweedbank Dr
1.7	'to Tweed Cycleway'
	(60yd) bikepath
2.6	Winston Rd
4.0	0.9mi gradual climb
4.5	A7
	(80yd) minor lane
	across bridge
	follow Tweed Cycleway signs
9.8	0.5mi gradual climb
10.0	Traquair Rd 'to Innerleithen'
17.7	Traquair House 1.7mi
18.4	A72 to Galashiels'

important. The **Trimontium monument** (31.9mi) marks the site of Roman occupation.

Melrose
☎ 01896

Melrose is the most charming of the Border towns, lying at the foot of the three Eildon Hills. It's spic-and-span with a classic market square and one of the great abbey ruins.

Information The TIC (☎ 822555), on Abbey St, opens 10 am to at least 5.30 pm Monday to Saturday (to 2 pm Sunday) from June to September. It sells some good publications about history, nature and walks in the area.

There are banks in Market Square and High St.

Things to See & Do Founded in 1136, Melrose Abbey (☎ 822526) was repeatedly destroyed by the English in the 14th century. Robert the Bruce's heart was buried here after he rebuilt the abbey.

The interesting **Trimontium Exhibition** (☎ 822651) in the square focuses on the Roman 'three hills' fort and local archaeological digs. There's also a **guided walk** to nearby Roman sites.

Abbotsford (☎ 752043) is about 3mi west of Melrose between the Tweed and B6360. It was home to Sir Walter Scott and has an extraordinary collection of his possessions.

Walking in the Eildon Hills is described in the *Eildon Hills Walk* booklet (£1), available from the TIC.

Places to Stay & Eat Tent sites at *Gibson Park (☎ 822969, High St)* cost £3 plus £4 per person.

The *Melrose Youth Hostel (☎ 822521)* is a Georgian mansion overlooking the abbey. Dorm beds cost £10.75 with continental breakfast.

Friendly and down-to-earth, *Birch House (☎ 822391, High St)* charges £22 for singles and £18 per person for doubles and twins (£22 with en suite). *Braidwood (☎ 822 488, Buccleuch St)* is very comfortable. B&B costs between £19 and £22 per person for doubles and twins.

The High St hotels are not cheap, but they are of a high standard – you will need to book ahead. Try *George & Abbotsford*

(☎ 822308), which charges £53 for singles and £47.50 per person for doubles and twins.

For self-caterers, there's a *Co-op* supermarket, *fruit shop* and two *bakeries* on High St, plus a *poulterer and fishmonger*, as well as delicatessen goodies at the *Country Kitchen* on the square.

Russell's Restaurant (☎ 822335) is good for daytime light meals (ploughman's platter is £4.50) and high teas (closed Thursday and Sunday). Or there's fish and chips at *Haldane's (Scott's Place)*; closed Wednesday.

Hotels in Melrose are excellent for evening meals. The cosmopolitan menu at the *Kings Arms (☎ 822143)* includes a good veg selection and real ales. Mains start around £5.50.

Treat yourself at *Melrose Station Restaurant (☎ 822546)*. Evening meals are available from Thursday to Saturday, and bookings are recommended. Mains range from £6.95 to £13.50.

Day 3: Melrose to Edinburgh
4–6½ hours, 51.7mi

Beginning on bikepaths and quiet roads by the River Tweed, the route follows the signed Tweed Cycleway to Innerleithen (18.4mi). From here the long, gradual climb (starting at 18.6mi) over the Moorfoot Hills is not difficult. Traffic is heavier in the last 9mi through Edinburgh; roads have some cycle lanes. Take particular care at the large roundabouts and major intersections.

Though it's relatively long, the ride is easy and pleasant. The flower-filled pastures and forests by the river contrast with the rocky heather hillsides later in the day. There are good views of Edinburgh and the Firth of Forth from the Moorfoot Hills (31.7mi).

Traquair House (☎ 01896-830785), a quarter mile from the Innerleithen turn-off (17.7mi) claims to be the oldest inhabited house in Scotland. It makes a good picnic spot and there's a *restaurant* in the pleasant walled garden.

There are no services between Innerleithen and the outskirts of Edinburgh. In Innerleithen, the *Corner Hotel (☎ 01896-831181, cnr High & Chapel Sts)* has generous mains starting at £4.25; there's *fish and chips* and a *bakery (High St)*, or the *Riverbank Restaurant* (with mains around £6).

Land's End to John o'Groats

Travelling from Land's End to John o'Groats – from the extreme south-west tip to the north-east corner of the British Mainland – is an ambition harboured by many. Around 3000 people cycle the thousand-odd miles every year.

The route detailed here, one of many possible, balances quiet roads and scenery with accommodation choice and ease of navigation. Though it keeps mostly to quiet roads, there are some busier sections, especially around larger towns. The 1051.2mi route is broken into 20 days, averaging 52.6mi per day, but could be varied according to fitness and time restraints.

Alternative routes include the CTC's (Cyclists' Touring Club) three 1000mi (or so) routes: a main road route; a scenic, Youth Hostel-based route, divided into 14 or 15 days; and a scenic B&B-based route. Some of the trip could also be done via Sustrans' National Cycle Network.

Cyclists traditionally do the ride from Land's End to John o'Groats. Not only are the winds more likely to be favourable, there's no riding into the midday sun.

Heading south to north is apparently psychologically uphill – at least if you believe north is higher than south. It's probably not the best factor on which to base a directional decision. However, check the long-range forecast (see Weather Forecasts in the Facts for the Cyclist chapter) and consider travelling north to south if, as rarely happens, the wind is predominantly from the north.

Raising money for charity is very common among end-to-enders – it's estimated that around 80% of those undertaking the trip (most of them locals) raise money – whether it's the primary purpose of the trip, or just an added extra (see the Information section later in this chapter).

HISTORY
The first person to travel from one end of the British mainland to the other was Eliuh Burritt, an American, who walked from John o'Groats to Land's End in 'several weeks'. Robert Carlisle, who pushed a wheelbarrow to John o'Groats, was the first Briton on record to have made the journey. It was first cycled around 1880.

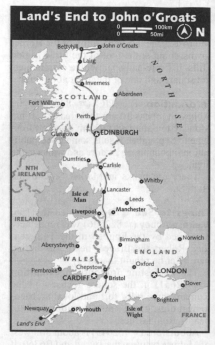

Land's End to John o'Groats

But the end to end craze didn't really gain momentum until the 20th century, with the advent of the motor car. Both bikes and cars were popular vehicles for the trip. With waves of end-to-enders coinciding with the release of new models, it appears that Land's End to John o'Groats became something of a test route.

Entries in the John o'Groats House Hotel's visitor book chronicle the development of motor cars and bicycles. Some of them, virtual essays (in beautiful copperplate), detail journeys made in little-known models brought out from the US or Germany.

The 20-odd visitor books are now held by the End to End Club, which is developing Miles of Memories – an end to end hall of fame. Unfortunately, the records that were stored at Land's End were destroyed by a fire in 1985.

CLIMATE
Generally speaking, the temperature becomes cooler heading north. The coldest section is

likely to be through the Grampian Mountains in Scotland, especially on the high passes.

Rainfall is greatest in the west and in hilly areas, for example, around the Pennines. However, in Britain, it can rain anywhere, anytime.

The prevailing wind is from the southwest, though it's possible to get periods of north-easterlies.

INFORMATION
Maps & Books

The best supplementary maps are the Ordnance Survey (OS) 1:250,000 Travelmaster series. The ride is covered by sheets eight, seven, five, four and two (£4.25 each), available from tourist information centres (TICs), and map and book shops. The OS Landranger series maps (1:50,000; £5.25) are useful for providing detail in some areas.

The excellent 1:50,000 route maps for the Sustrans National Cycle Network (£5.99 each) are available from bookshops, TICs, Youth Hostels, bike shops or by mail order from Sustrans (see Information Sources, following).

There are numerous books about journeying from Land's End to John o'Groats. Try browsing the Waterstones catalogue at 🖥 www.waterstones.co.uk.

Information Sources

The CTC (☎ 01483-417217) Land's End to John o'Groats pack (£12.50, free to members) contains directions for three different end to end routes, plus a record sheet, information and T-shirt order forms.

Also worth contacting is the End to End Club (☎ 01736-871501, ext 346), Custom House, Lands End (🖥 www.landsend-landmark.co.uk). The club provides advice or assistance for those doing the ride for charity. It also records who's out there and will raise the alarm when someone doesn't show at the other end. You can join the club after completing the trip.

End to End Records

Around 4000 people each year complete the journey from one end of Britain to the other, an estimated 75% of whom do it by bike. Most cyclists do the trip in two or three weeks.

Andy Wilkinson was much less patient – in 1990, he cycled 874mi from Land's End to John o'Groats in one day, 21 hours, two minutes and 18 seconds, beating the previous record by 53 seconds. Pauline Strong holds

THE ABANDONED ATTEMPT ON THE END-TO-END RECORD.
G. A. Olley (in trousers) and some of his followers, with spare Rudge-Whitworth "Speedirons." Next to Olley is Harry Andrews, the old trainer. Olley has just got up from a three hours' nap.

The End-to-End record has been enticing cyclists for decades.

PAUL FARREN COLLECTION

the women's cycling record of two days, six hours, 49 minutes and 45 seconds. An early cycling record to be recognised was by GP Mills who, in 1891, rode the distance in four days, 11 hours and 17 minutes.

Special Records

With so many people making the journey these days, you have to do something extra special to be noticed. People have spiced up the journey – and the record books – in all manner of ways: Steve Gilkes has done it several times on a motorised toilet (one wonders whether he was linked with the motorised bar stool); another used a supermarket trolley. It's been done in a battery-powered Sinclair C5 in 80 hours and on roller skates in 9½ days. Penny farthings are relatively common, as are tricycles and tandems. In 1990, it was run in 26 days and seven hours by Arvind Pandya – no great record in itself, apart from the fact that he was running backwards! If you're in a real hurry, you'd better take a harrier jump jet – that'll get you there in 47 minutes.

Sustrans (☎ 0117-929 0888, 💻 www.sust rans.org.uk) has up-to-date information on the National Cycle Network (NCN).

Various end-to-enders have immortalised their trips in cyberspace. For a series of long-winded personal accounts, look up the Trento Bike Pages (💻 www-math.science .unitn.it/Bike/Countries/Great_Britain /#LandsEnd).

Recording the Trip
Both the CTC and End to End Club provide certificates on evidence of completion. Use the official record or transit sheet (or equivalent) to collect hostel stamps or date stamps from places of accommodation.

CTC's certificate is free providing you buy a T-shirt or cloth badge; End to End Club charges £5, which includes a year's membership of the club.

PLANNING
When to Ride
Although most people have ridden end to end in the dead of winter, the ideal time is between April and mid-September. June is perhaps the best month: the roads – and accommodation – are less crowded than in July and August, the days are long, and the weather is more likely to be on your side than in spring or autumn. By mid-September, there can be snow on the Grampian's high passes.

What to Bring
Make sure that your bike is in good working order – have it serviced before you go. Check that there is plenty of wear left in the tyres, rims and chain, and take some chain

Warning

While most of the route is via quiet roads, there are some short sections on busy highways. These are highlighted in the ride descriptions as areas in which to take particular care.

Sections of the route such as through the Grampian Mountains and in the far north of Scotland are exposed and remote. Be sure to carry adequate food, water and clothing through these areas. Outside the summer, check the weather forecast before riding (see the boxed text 'Telephone Weather Services' in the Facts for the Cyclist chapter).

lubricant and a rag to keep it clean and oiled throughout the ride, plus emergency repair tools (see the Your Bicycle chapter).

Don't leave without decent weatherproof gear and clothing – including sunscreen and sunglasses. A helmet is highly recommended.

Remember to bring and fill out your transit or record sheet, to qualify for an official certificate.

GETTING TO/FROM THE RIDE
Land's End
Unless you can convince a friend to drive you to Land's End, the best option is to catch the train to Penzance, about 9mi from Land's End, and ride west from there. We suggest riding the fastest route from Penzance – via the often busy A30 – since Day 1 of our End to End ride returns to Penzance via more scenic (and quieter) B-roads.

Train The train journey from London to Penzance takes about five hours and a standard one-way fare is £65 (considerably cheaper if you book; call ☎ 0845-7484950 a week in advance). On Great Western services, up to six bicycles are carried on each train; bikes booked at least two hours before departure cost £1. They're £3 if you book under two hours before departure.

John o'Groats
From John o'Groats, the nearest train station is at Wick, about 17mi of gently undulating roads south. From the Seaview Hotel, follow the A99 all the way to Wick. Although it's the main highway, traffic is not too heavy. Alternatively, backtrack 21mi to Thurso.

Bikes are not carried on the Highland Country Buses (☎ 01847-893123) service from John o'Groats to Wick. However, a local taxi (☎ 01955-611314) will carry up to four bikes in a mini bus. Expect to pay around £12 to £15.

Train Scotrail (☎ 0345-484950) services run from Wick and Thurso to Inverness (£20, 4 hours, up to three per day); and from Inverness to Edinburgh and Glasgow (£30, 3½ hours, several daily). (Check the timetable carefully: some Wick trains travel via Thurso, others run direct). Services also run from Inverness to Kyle of Lochalsh (£24, 2½ hours, up to four per day) in the Western Highlands.

Reservations for bikes (which travel free) are essential on these services. Though Wick to Inverness trains carry six bikes per carriage, places fill up quickly on services from Inverness to Edinburgh and Glasgow, which only carry two per carriage.

Book at least a week ahead if your travel date is critical. However, once purchased, a ticket cannot be changed, except at the station from which it was purchased. Instead, a new ticket must be bought (though a partial refund of the original cancelled ticket may be available). See the Gateway Cities Section in the Scotland chapter for information on getting to/from Edinburgh and Glasgow.

End to End

Duration	20 days
Distance	1051.2mi
Difficulty	hard
Start	Land's End
End	John o'Groats

THE RIDE
Land's End
☎ 01736

While its name conjures up images of wild isolation, Land's End is in fact a much-visited and none-too-pretty tourist trap. Certainly some of the attractions at the **theme park development** (☎ 01736-871501) are interesting and informative, but mostly they sully the rugged cliffs overlooking the Atlantic Ocean.

All end to end riders start their journey at the famous signpost (a photo by the resident concession holder will set you back £5), which is a stone's throw from the Land's End Hotel, the nearest accommodation option. However, there's cheaper accommodation strung out from St Just-in-Penwith (about 6mi by road from Land's End) to Sennen, the village nearest Land's End.

See St Just (p173) in the Southern England chapter for information about accommodation and other services in the Land's End–Sennen–St Just area.

Day 1: Land's End to Newquay
6–7 hours, 51.1mi

This is a nice warm-up day, mostly on B-roads, featuring some lovely ocean views and interesting towns and villages. While

St Michael's Mount

In 1070 St Michael's Mount was granted to the same monks who built Mont St Michel off Normandy. Though not as dramatically sited as its French counterpart, St Michael's Mount is still impressive. High tide cuts the island off from the mainland, and the NT-run **priory buildings** (☎ 01736-710507) rise loftily above the rocks. During the Middle Ages it was an important place of pilgrimage, but since 1659 the St Aubyn family have lived here.

At low tide, you can walk across the causeway to the Mount from Marazion, but at high tide in summer a ferry (☎ 01736-710265) lets you save your legs for the stiff climb up to the house, which is open from April to October, Monday to Friday, 10.30 am to 5.30 pm; entry is £4.40.

there are no major climbs, there's a fair bit of the up-and-down terrain typical of Cornwall.

From Land's End to Penzance you'll see Cornwall countryside and the ocean off to the south and east. Along the Penzance waterfront and extending to Marazion there are wonderful **views of Mount's Bay** and historic **St Michael's Mount** (see the boxed text). Just past Marazion (15.6mi) the route slices inland and, for about 15mi, follows quiet B-roads. Be careful through Redruth; there can be quite a bit of traffic in the town centre, near the train station, and again on the short stretch on the A30 and A3075 in the 38 to 40mi range.

A return to the coast, after the exhilarating downhill into Perranporth, precedes a steady climb and another niggling up-and-down before you rejoin the A3075 about 3mi from Newquay. Be careful of traffic over this last section, especially in mid-summer.

Newquay
See Newquay (p169–71) in the Southern England chapter for information about accommodation and other services.

Day 2: Newquay to Launceston
5½–6½ hours, 49.8mi

Another full day in Cornwall yields wonderful cycling both on- and off-road. A busy morning for traffic is broken by a stint on the

Day 1: Land's End to Newquay

1:300,000 N

Cue

Start	Land's End signpost
0mi	go E from signpost to A30
0.7	B3315
2.7	Trethewey
4.7	B3315
10.5	Newlyn
11.1	Penzance
12.7	A30 'to Redruth' (50yd) New St
13.3	'to Long Rock'
13.9	'to Marazion'
14.6	'to Marazion'
15.6	Marazion
17.4	Goldsithney
20.7	Townshend
21.8	Leedstown
24.2	Praze-an-Beeble
24.3	'to Redruth'
26.1	'to Redruth'
28.2	'to Redruth'
28.6	Four Lanes
31.0	Redruth

Continued

Cue

31.1	Clinton Rd
31.7	Station Rd
31.9	Fore St/East End
32.0	Drump Rd
32.4	North St/Close Hill
32.8	'to Porthtowan'
32.9	'to Portreath'
34.2	'to Mawla'
35.5	unsigned road
35.7	unsigned road
37.7	B3277
37.9	A30
38.4	A3075
39.5	'to Perranporth'
40.4	B3284
43.4	High St, Perranporth
43.7	'to Newquay'
44.6	'to Mount'
46.0	'to Mount'
47.0	'to Newquay'
47.7	A3075
49.8	A392
50.4	Trevemper Rd
50.6	Trevance Rd
50.9	Mount Wise
51.0	Marcus Hill
51.1	Newquay TIC

See Day 2 p385

START: DAY 2

See below

ATLANTIC OCEAN

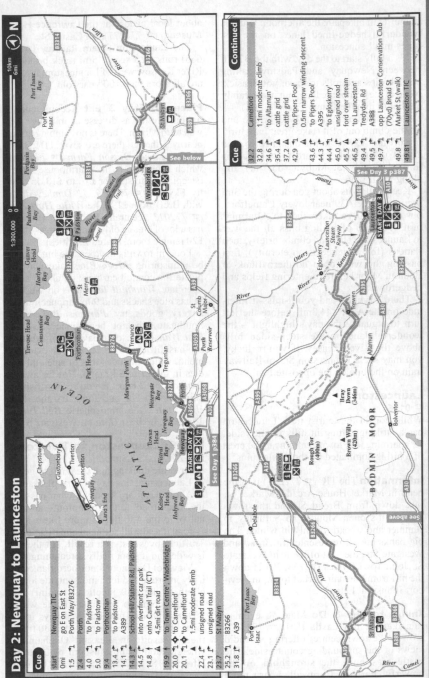

Day 2: Newquay to Launceston

Cue		
start		Newquay TIC
0mi	→	go E on East St
1.5	←	Porth Way/B3276
2.4		Porth
4.0	←	'to Padstow'
5.0	←	'to Padstow'
9.4		Porthcothan
13.4	←	'to Padstow'
14.1	←	A389
14.3		School Hill/Station Rd, Padstow
14.5	←	into riverfront car park
14.8	←	onto Camel Trail (CT)
		4.5mi dirt road
19.9	←	'to Town Centre', Wadebridge
20.0	◇←	'to Camelford'
20.1	◇←	'to Camelford'
		1.5mi moderate climb
22.4	←	unsigned road
23.1	←	unsigned road
23.7		St Mabyn
25.2	←	B3266
31.8	←	A39

Cue		Continued
32.2		Camelford
32.8	◄	1.1mi moderate climb
34.6	←	'to Altarnun'
35.4		cattle grid
37.2		cattle grid
42.9	◄	'to Pipers Pool'
		0.5mi narrow winding descent
43.6	←	'to Pipers Pool'
44.3		A395
44.4	←	'to Egloskerry'
45.0		unsigned road
45.5		ford over stream
46.5	←	'to Launceston'
49.4		A388
49.5	←	opp Launceston Conservation Club
49.7	←	(70yd) Broad St
49.8	←	Market St (walk)
49.81		Launceston TIC

Camel Trail bikepath; the afternoon features wonderful hedge-lined lanes on the last miles into Launceston.

It's a hilly start to the day, with the B3276 between Newquay and Padstow taking enough dips and rolls to make you seasick. None of the climbs are long, but it's certainly a relief to join the Camel Trail (14.8mi).

Expect some traffic in Wadebridge and on the climb out of it (take great care turning off the A39 on to the unsigned road at 22.4mi), but look forward to quiet going through lovely St Mabyn (23.7mi) and along the B3266.

Keep your wits about you during the 3mi section on the A39 near lovely Camelford, but once you've taken the 'to Altarnun' turn, it's 15mi of cycling bliss all the way to Launceston. The road climbs briefly, then flattens (for what seems an eternity), first passing the wide-open northern flank of Bodmin Moor before re-entering fields and hedgerows.

There's a blink-and-you'll-miss-it interlude on the A395 (44.3mi) before the left turn to arguably the day's highlight – the wonderful lane on the steep-sided hills above the River Kensey. If you're lucky, you may see a Launceston Steam Railway train on the line on the opposite bank.

Launceston
☎ 01566

While not on the tourist trail, Launceston has a striking setting in hilly countryside. Its charming, old town centre near the crest of a hill is dominated by the castle ruins.

Information The TIC (☎ 772231) is at the bend in Market House Arcade, Market St, just down from Broad St and the town square; it's open Monday to Saturday in summer and weekdays only in winter. The big banks are all represented in Broad and Westgate Sts; the post office is in Westgate St. John Towl Cycles (☎ 774220) is down the hill from the main part of town, in Newport Industrial Estate.

Things to See & Do Majestic even in ruin, **Launceston Castle** (EH; ☎ 772365) crowns the town centre, offering splendid views of the surrounding countryside. The castle was once the stronghold of the powerful Earls of Cornwall. Learn more

about local history at the **Lawrence House Museum** (☎ 773277), on Castle St.

The **Launceston Steam Railway** (☎ 775 665) runs on a scenic 5mi track beside the River Kensey, west of Launceston; its locos are all more than 100 years old.

Places to Stay & Eat Accommodation options are not as diverse as in a big Cornwall tourist town. There is no camping ground nearby, although there are several B&Bs, including *Lower Dutson Farm* (☎ 776 456), which offers B&B in a farmhouse annexe (sleeping up to six) for £16 to £18. In town, try Skylark (☎ 775779, 11 Dunheved Rd), with B&B from £19. The *White Hart Hotel* (☎ 772013), centrally located on Broad St, has a lot of creaky old rooms; charges start at £20 (single room, shared facilities).

Food in town is inexpensive but tends to be uninspiring. *Mega Bites* takeaway, opposite the council car park, is cheap and is open late. *Windmill Tearooms* on Westgate St has nice snacks and 90p cappuccinos; for bakery goods try *Parkers Bakery*, on Southgate – baking here since 1804. The *Sun Wah* Chinese takeaway, on Westgate St, has little above £5 on its extensive menu, which includes lots of rice and noodles in the £1 to £2 range. Not far away is *Launceston Fryers* if you're in a fish and chips mood. For pub food, try the *White Hart Hotel*, the atmospheric *Bell Inn* on Tower St, or *West Gate* on Westgate St.

Day 3: Launceston to Tiverton
5½–7 hours, 52.3mi

After some ducking and weaving to get out of Launceston, this day is very pleasant.

About 12mi are spent on what passes as the 'back road' to Okehampton – an alternative to the A30 that is more like a minor A-road it's so well surfaced and maintained. Traffic moves fast as a result, but the road is wide and it's not really threatening.

Views of Dartmoor's northern flank gradually improve and for a moment, the single climb to the A30 junction (16.4mi) feels like it's going to continue all the way to 2038ft-high (621m) High Willhays mountain. After a brief blast from the A30 traffic, there's respite in pleasant Okehampton, where a stop at the **Museum of Dartmoor Life** (☎ 01837-52295) tells of the bleak expanse of Dartmoor and its inhabitants.

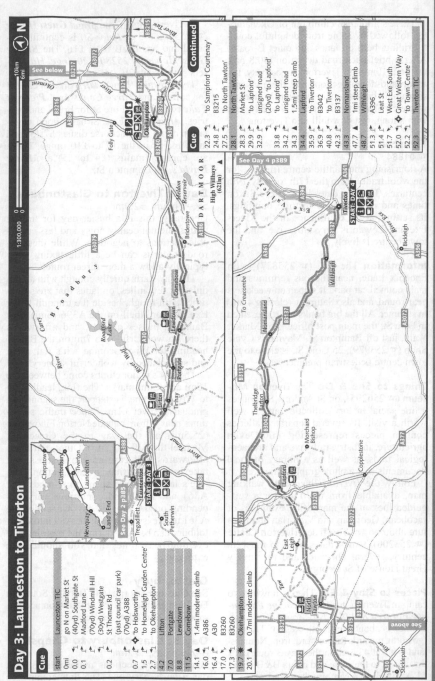

Day 3: Launceston to Tiverton

Cue		
start	Launceston TIC	
0mi	go N on Market St	
0.0	(40yd) Southgate St	↰
0.1	Madford Lane	↰
	(70yd) Windmill Hill	↱
0.2	(30yd) Westgate	↰
	St Thomas Rd	↱
	(70yd) A388	↱
	(past council car park)	
0.7	'to Holsworthy'	◇
1.5	'to Homeleigh Garden Centre'	↱
2.7	'to Okehampton'	↱
4.2	Lifton	↰
7.0	Portgate	↰
8.8	Lewdown	↰
11.5	Comebow	↰
14.1	1.4mi moderate climb	◀
16.0	A386	↰
16.4	A30	↱
17.0	B3260	↱
17.3	B3260	↱
19.7	Okehampton	✳
20.1	0.7mi moderate climb	◀

Cue		
Continued		
22.3	'to Sampford Courtenay'	↱
24.8	B3215	↱
27.5	'to North Tawton'	↱
28.1	North Tawton	
28.3	Market St	↰
29.9	'to Lapford'	↱
32.9	unsigned road	↱
	(20yd) 'to Lapford'	↱
33.8	'to Lapford'	↱
34.2	unsigned road	↱
34.3	1.5mi steep climb	◀
34.4	Lapford	
35.9	'to Tiverton'	↱
36.9	B3042	↰
40.8	'to Tiverton'	↱
42.3	B3137	↱
43.3	Nomansland	◀
47.7	1mi steep climb	◀
48.7	Withleigh	
51.3	A396	↰
51.4	Leat St	↱
51.7	West Exe South	↱
52.0	Great Western Way	◇
52.2	'to Town Centre'	↱
52.3	Tiverton TIC	◀

There's a longish climb out of Okehampton followed by some truly delightful country riding, both on lanes and quiet B-roads. After a brief back-road deviation (40.8 mi), the final 10mi into Tiverton can be busy. It's an up-and-down section, and there's some slow uphill corners on the way into Withleigh, where care's especially needed. The day ends with a long, fast downhill into Tiverton.

Tiverton
☎ 01884

A flourishing mercantile centre (mainly for the wool trade) from the 17th to early 19th centuries, Tiverton dates back to pre-Saxon times and retains many historic buildings. Its setting, at the confluence of the Rivers Exe and Lowan is very attractive, and the town centre is lively.

Information The TIC (☎ 255827) is on Phoenix Lane, near the bus terminus and main council car park. It's open on weekdays year-round, and also Saturday (closing 4 pm) in summer. All the big banks are represented in Fore St; the main post office is on Market Walk, just off Bampton St. Maynards Cycle Shop (☎ 253979), 25 Gold St, is close to the town centre pedestrian precinct.

Things to See & Do The **Tiverton Museum** (☎ 256295), on St Andrew St, houses a fine social history collection and is well worth a visit. Its several separate galleries contain pieces representing mid-Devon agriculture, industry, railways and archaeological finds, as well as a library of local documents and a photographic archive.

Follow the *Tiverton Town Trail* walking map, available from the TIC, for a self-guided look at the many fine examples of Jacobean, Georgian and Victorian **architecture** about town. You'll see **Tiverton Castle** (☎ 253200), which dates back to the 12th century, several churches and the lovely Great House of St George.

Places to Stay & Eat There's nowhere to camp in Tiverton itself; **Creacombe Parsonage Farm** (☎ 881441; *Two Moors Way, Creacombe*) is about 9mi north-west of Tiverton (go north, towards Rackenford, from Nomansland – it's at 43.3mi on the Day 3 route). It's the closest to the route and offers B&B (from £17) as well as a camping barn and sites.

In Tiverton itself, the **Angel Guest House** (☎ *253292, 13 St Peter St*) is centrally located and has B&B from £16. The **Bridge Guest House** (☎ *252804, 20 Angel Hill*) offers singles at £20.

Try **Upstairs Downstairs** on Angel Hill for coffee, and **Three Cooks** or **A Piece of Cake** bakeries on Fore St for bread and pastries. **Arrivals** on Fore St has a good vegetarian menu (main course dishes £7.25) and meat mains in the £7 to £10 range. There are cheaper mains (£4 to £5) at **Mister David's**, on Bampton St.

Day 4: Tiverton to Glastonbury
5½–7 hours, 52.9mi

Generally, this is a busier day for traffic, with some noticeably noisy and less enjoyable sections to negotiate. While these A-road sojourns can be a little taxing, they typically allow a more direct route.

The day starts quietly enough with an undulating few miles, on lanes that are sometimes a bit rough, beside the tranquil River Exe. A short spell on the A396 (6mi) near Bampton passes quickly, and afterwards there's a wonderful 6 to 7mi on the B3227 heading for Wiveliscombe – it's flat, wide and surrounded by wonderful scenery.

The day's major climbs come between the 15mi and 22mi marks. The first, leading up to Wiveliscombe, is steeper; the second is a gradual rise over 3.1mi. Expect traffic, sometimes heavy, from outside Norton Fitzwarren (25.5mi) all the way to the Creech St Michael turn-off (31.2mi). Quiet, flat lanes afterwards will ease any road-stress, but take care navigating in this section. The ride's last 12mi are spent on A-roads (the A361 and A39) and conditions vary depending on the time of day. Generally the A361 traffic isn't too bad; the A39 into Glastonbury can be busy during the morning and evening peak times and you should take extra care.

Glastonbury

See Glastonbury (pp164–7) in the Southern England chapter for information on accommodation and other services.

Day 5: Glastonbury to Chepstow
6–7½ hours, 57.4mi

Extended flat sections make this longish day a fairly easy one. The flats commence

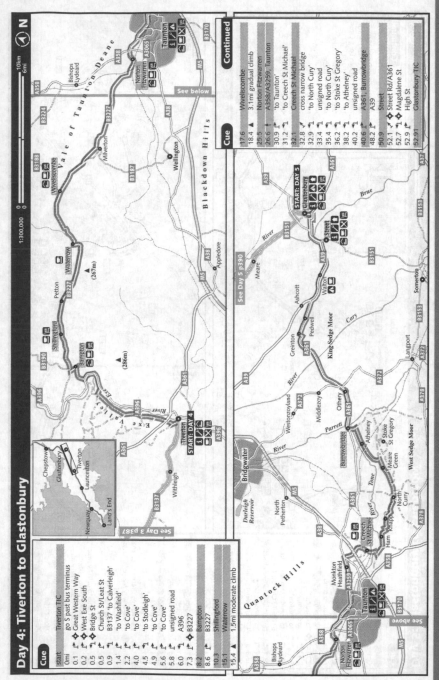

Day 4: Tiverton to Glastonbury

Cue

start		Tiverton TIC
0mi		go S past bus terminus
0.1	↰↱	Great Western Way
0.2	↰↱	West Exe South
0.5	◇	Bridge St
0.5		Church St/Leat St
0.9		B3137 'to Calverleigh'
1.4	↰↱	'to Washfield'
2.2	↰↱	'to Cove'
4.0	↰↱	'to Stodleigh'
4.5	↰↱	'to Cove'
4.9	↰↱	'to Cove'
5.6	↰↱	unsigned road
6.0		A396
7.3		B3227
8.2		Bampton
8.6		B3227
10.3		Shillingford
15.1		Waterrow
15.4	▲	1.5mi moderate climb

Cue

17.6		Wivelliscombe
18.4	▲	3.1mi gradual climb
25.5		Norton Fitzwarren
26.6	↰↱	A358/A3259, Taunton
30.9	↰↱	'to Taunton'
31.2	↰↱	'to Creech St Michael'
32.1		Creech St Michael
		cross narrow bridge
32.8	↰↱	'to North Cury'
32.9	↰↱	unsigned road
33.4	↰↱	'to North Cury'
35.4	↰↱	'to Stoke St Gregory'
36.2	↰↱	'to Athelney'
38.2	↰↱	unsigned road
40.6		A361, Burrowbridge
48.2		A39
50.9		Street
52.1	◇	Street Rd/A361
52.7	◇	Magdalene St
52.9	↰↱	High St
52.91		Glastonbury TIC

Continued

See Day 3 p387

See Day 5 p390

Day 5: Glastonbury to Chepstow

Cue	
start	Glastonbury TIC
0mi	go W on High St
0.4	(50yd) Northload St
	◇ B3151
2.7	Meare
4.7	Westhay
6.9	0.6mi steep climb
8.6	Wedmore
8.7	◇ 'to Cheddar'
8.9	'to Cheddar'
9.1	'to Cheddar'
12.5	'to Cheddar Leisure Centre'
12.9	B3135 'to Cheddar Gorge'
13.1	'to Cheddar Gorge', Cheddar
13.4	'to Cheddar Gorge'
13.8	4.7mi moderate climb
16.8	B3371 'to Compton Martin'
20.3	0.7mi narrow winding descent
21.1	A368
	(40yd) Tinkers Lane
22.2	unsigned road
22.6	B3314
24.7	Chew Stoke
25.0	'to Bristol'
25.9	1.7mi steep climb
28.7	Withywood (Bristol)
29.4	Church Rd
29.7	St Peters Rise
29.8	join Malago Greenway bikepath
	follow Malago Greenway bikepath 'to city'
32.5	Coronation Rd
	(50yd) shared bridge
32.6	NCN 4
32.7	down ramp to path by river
	across old railway bridge
33.5	NCN 4, Ashton & Pill Path
34.1	3.7mi dirt bikepath
34.2	Clifton Suspension Bridge
37.8	Hospital Rd
38.4	Ham Green/Eirene Terrace, Pill
38.7	Mt Pleasant/Marine Parade
39.2	Avon Rd

Cue	Continued
39.3	NCN 4
39.6	Avonmouth Bridge Bikepath
40.7	Avonmouth Rd/Lower High St
40.9	Kings Weston Ave/Long Cross
42.4	Lawrence Weston Rd
43.4	past refuse transfer centre
43.9	Kings Weston Lane
44.6	A403
51.1	NCN 4
52.3	A403 'Cycle track Chepstow'
52.4	under road overpass
52.5	Severn Bridge bikepath
56.6	A48 'to TIC'
56.9	'to town centre'
57.1	thru gate to hill bottom
57.4	into car park
	(50yd) Chepstow TIC

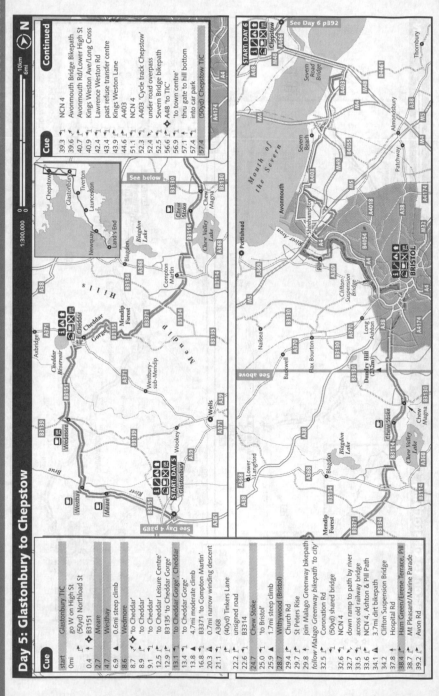

on the route out of Glastonbury. The B3151 is level and also very straight for extended sections; as a consequence traffic moves fast, but vision is good and the situation isn't worrying. The stiff pinch uphill into Wedmore comes as a bit of a shock, but it's easy going again from there to Cheddar.

The 4.7mi climb up through striking **Cheddar Gorge** (13.8mi) sounds daunting, but it's a gradual rise and you're conscious of the strain in only a few places. Once atop the **Mendip Hills** the views are splendid. Take care descending (20.3mi) and save some breath for the last climb – the nasty, rearing ascent of Dundry Hill (25.9mi).

It's slow going through Bristol on the cycle paths but worth it to miss the city traffic. Once on NCN 4 (39.3mi) it's flat riding practically all the way to Chepstow – the biggest climbs are on bridge cycle paths. Several new sections of cycle path in the Avonmouth to Severn Beach section

Thrill at the Severn Bore

For something like 24 days a year, a spectacular wall of water sweeps up the Severn estuary carrying surfers, canoeists and branches alike. One of the best tidal waves, or bores, in the world, it is formed because the funnel shape of the broad estuary can't dissipate the sudden volume of water quickly enough. With a good spring tide, low inland water and a wind coming off the sea, the wave can rise as high as 6.5ft (2m) as it rushes in noisily at 10mph. For the surfers, it's the longest rollers they've ever caught, swooshing them as far as the tidal weirs at Gloucester. For spectators, it's an excuse for a picnic and a chance to get your feet wet if you get too close.

There's a good view of the full bore at Minsterworth, Stonebench or Overbridge. Get there early to nab a spot if it's a weekend or bank holiday. The nascent bore can also be spotted en route on Day 6 at Newnham (17.4mi).

The bore is best during the lunar cycles of January, February, March, April, July, August, September and October. The Gloucester TIC (☎ 01452-421188) has times or visit the Environment Agency Web site (🖥 www.environment-agency .gov.uk.envinfo/index.htm).

(43mi to 51mi) should be completed soon, and will make for a more pleasant ride. The A403 is a fine alternative only if it's ridden on the weekend, when the road's free of lorries – it should be avoided at other times.

Chepstow
See Chepstow (pp224–5) in the Central England chapter for information about accommodation and other services.

Day 6: Chepstow to Worcester
4–6½ hours, 58.6mi
This route tracks the course of the River Severn as it changes from a broad tidal estuary at the Welsh border to a gentle water-meadow flowing through Gloucestershire.

The first 20mi are on the fast and narrow A48 – riding here will take nerve, for the road carries heavy lorry traffic. A recommended alternative, if you have time, is to follow Day 1 of the Marches, Cheshire & Lancashire ride in the Central England chapter to Coleford; then take very hilly B4226 to Cinderford, through the Forest of Dean; and the A4151 to join the A48 not far from the Westbury-on-Severn turn-off.

Riverside viewpoints on the way often feature a drinking hole or two. Good pubs en route can be found in **Newnham** (17.4mi); **Ashleworth quay**, a side trip to the right just eastward of Ashleworth at 34.4mi; and **Upton upon Severn** (47.5mi).

Westbury Court Garden (20.1mi; ☎ 014 52-760461), a 17th-century Dutch-style water garden, is worth a visit in good weather. About 10mi on, **Hartpury mill** (not open to the public) and **church** enjoy an idyllic setting.

Worcester
☎ 01905
Worcester straddles the River Severn, with the city centre on the eastern bank dominated by a handsome cathedral. It has everything you need for an overnight stay but, apart from a handful of historic buildings and the famous porcelain works, little else will distract you from your journey.

Information The TIC (☎ 726311) is inside the Guildhall and opens Monday to Saturday from 8.30 am to 4.30 pm year-round. Two of several central bike shops are Single Track

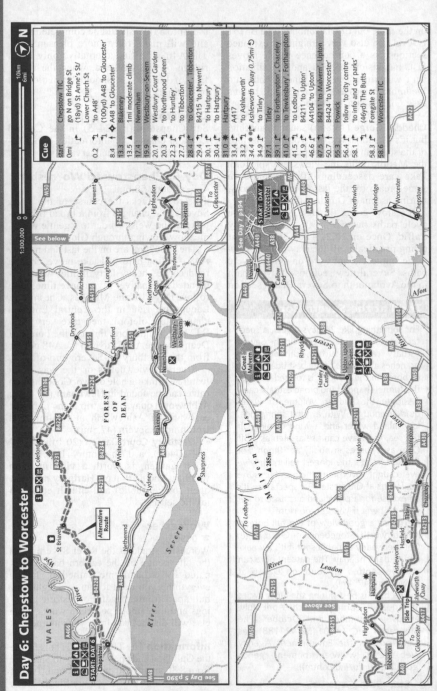

Day 6: Chepstow to Worcester

Cue		
start		Chepstow TIC
		go N on Bridge St
0mi		(18yd) St Anne's St/
		Lower Church St
0.2		'to A48'
		(100yd) A48 'to Gloucester'
8.4		A48 'to Gloucester'
13.3	◄	Blakeney
13.5	▲	1mi moderate climb
17.4		Newnham
19.9		Westbury-on-Severn
20.1	✳	Westbury Court Garden
20.3		'to Northwood Green'
22.3		'to Huntley'
27.7		'to Tibberton'
28.4		B4215 'to Gloucester', Tibberton
29.4		'to Hartpury'
30.1		'to Hartpury'
30.4		'to Hartpury'
31.0	✳	Hartpury
33.4		A417
33.2		'to Ashleworth'
34.4 ●●●	⚓	Ashleworth Quay 0.75mi
34.9		'to Tirley'
37.1		Tirley
39.1		'to Forthampton', Chaceley
41.0		'to Tewkesbury', Forthampton
41.5		'to Upton'
41.9		B211 'to Upton'
46.6		A4104 'to Upton'
47.5		B211 'to Malvern', Upton
50.7		B4424 'to Worcester'
55.3		Powick
56.4		follow 'to city centre'
58.1		'to info and car parks'
		(46yd) The Butts
58.3		Foregate St
58.6		Worcester TIC

(☎ 619000), in Pump St just off High St, and F Lewis Cycles (☎ 26455), in New St.

Things to See & Do The city's main draw is the **cathedral** (☎ 28854). It was begun in 1084, with further additions in the 13th century. Buried in the 13th-century choir is King John, whose treachery towards his brother Richard left the country in turmoil upon his death.

Other buildings of note include the gilt-decorated **Guildhall**, which was designed by a pupil of Christopher Wren and dates back to 1722; **Commandery Civil War Centre**, a splendid Tudor building used as Charles II's headquarters during the fighting in the 17th century; **Trinity House**, on The Trinity just off The Cross; and **King Charles House**, 29 New St, where the king is said to have hidden. Friar St is lined with Tudor and Elizabethan architecture, including the fully restored 1480 **Greyfriars**, run by the National Trust.

For more than 250 years the **Royal Worcester Porcelain Works** has been producing fine china for tables high and low. Factory tours (book in advance; ☎ 21247) include the world's largest collection of Worcester porcelain.

Places to Stay A pitch at the *Ketch* camp site (☎ 820430, A38 Bath Rd), 2.5mi south on the A38, costs £7. The nearest hostel – the *Malvern Hills* (☎ 01684-569131) – is 8mi away in Malvern Wells (south-west), part of the handsome spa town Great Malvern. A bed costs £9.80.

There are several B&Bs north of Worcester centre in Barbourne Rd. The *Shrubbery Guest House* (☎ 24871, No 38) starts at £20/38 for a single/double. The tariff is similar at the *Barbourne* (☎ 27507, No 42), with a few pounds more for an en suite.

An easy three minute ride from the cathedral at the courtyard is the *Loch Ryan Hotel* (☎ 351143, 119 Sidbury), where en suite rooms start from £45/60.

Places to Eat Worcester has a good choice of restaurants, some in interesting locations. Funky *RSVP* (☎ 723035, The Cross), in the converted St Nicholas church, does crusty baguettes for £4.50 daytime, and Vietnamese stir fry for £5.50 in the evening. The traditional *King Charles House* (☎ 22449, 29

New St) does theme nights such as Olde English night, when staff dress up to serve mulled wine with a gamey four-course dinner for £21.95. The *Lemon Tree* (☎ 27770, 12 Friar St) offers a varied Modern British menu, including vegetarian. The gelée of mixed mushrooms in chive sauce goes for £10.

Day 7: Worcester to Ironbridge
2½–4 hours, 40.5mi

The River Severn enters Shropshire, traversing a landscape of valleys and forest as far as the spectacular Ironbridge Gorge.

The riding is persistently hilly, gaining height numerous times between streams that feed the Severn and towns that bridge it. A satisfying 16mi stretch between the red sandstone towns of Bewdley and Bridgnorth starts with a steady climb through the **Wyre Forest** and continues with a rollercoaster road and good views before a long descent into Ironbridge.

Beware of heavy traffic leaving Worcester on the A-roads, and the right turn at 7.7mi. Thereafter, things are quieter.

Ironbridge
☎ 01952

As 'the birthplace of the industrial revolution', Ironbridge sounds grim, yet the little town that grew up around the first iron bridge in the world is a beautiful and fascinating place. A fixture on the tourist trail; accommodation and eats are plentiful, yet the ambience is friendly and unhurried.

Abraham Darby I first smelted iron ore and coke at Coalbrookdale, down the road, in 1709. His grandson Abraham Darby III refined the process and erected the bridge in 1779 to demonstrate the material's potential.

Information The TIC (☎ 432166) is just down the hill on the town side of the gorge. You can hire bikes at the tollhouse on the bridge, but the nearest bike shop is in Broseley, just before Ironbridge. There is also a Halfords chainstore at the Telford Bridge retail park in Telford.

The nearest banks are in Madeley, 1.5mi up the Silkin Way (see Things to See & Do).

Things to See & Do In good weather it's as satisfying just kicking back in Ironbridge as it is getting a handle on its fascinating history. The graceful 100ft bridge spans the

LAND'S END TO JOHN O'GROATS

Day 7: Worcester to Ironbridge

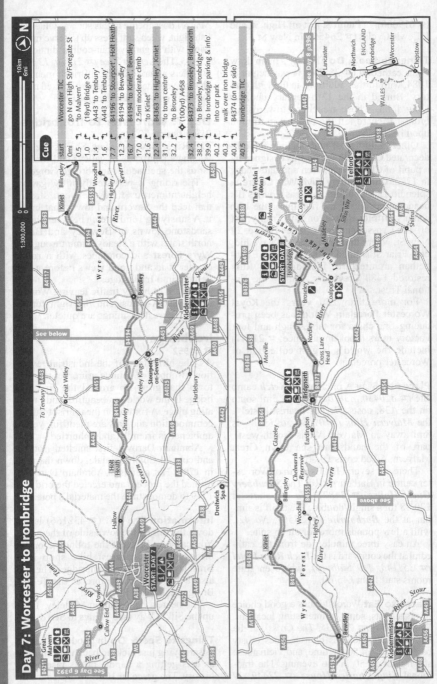

Cue	
start	Worcester TIC
0mi	go N on High St/Foregate St
	'to Malvern'
0.5	(18yd) Bridge St
1.0	A443 'to Tenbury'
1.4	A443 'to Tenbury'
1.6	B4196 'to Stourport, Holt Heath
7.7	B4194 'to Bewdley
12.3	B4194 'to Kinlet, Bewdley
16.7	2.5mi moderate climb
17.0	B4363 'to Highley, Kinlet
21.6	'to kinlet'
22.4	'to Broseley'
31.7	(100yd) A458
32.2	'to Broseley, Bridgnorth
32.4	B4373 'to Broseley, Ironbridge'
38.2	'to Ironbridge parking & info'
39.9	into car park
40.2	walk over iron bridge
40.3	B4374 (on far side)
40.4	Ironbridge TIC
40.5	

gorge above the slow flowing River Severn, lined with **walks** and **picnic spots**. Quaint shops, cafes, restaurants and a unique museum occupy the World Heritage List site.

From the south side of the bridge it is possible to pick up the **Silkin Way**, a walking/ cycle route that follows a disused railway and canal into Telford, which has all facilities and some progressive architecture. Follow signs for NCN 81.

Visits to the nine museums and sites of the **Ironbridge Gorge Museum** (☎ 432166) can be paid for individually or with a passport ticket (£9.50). Pick up a leaflet from the TIC, with details of the **Museum of Iron** (see the original furnace), the **Blists Hill Victorian Town** (pay in old money) and the **Tar Tunnel** (a natural source of bitumen).

The **Hay Plane Incline**, 1mi east along the gorge, is an extraordinary hoist once used to lift boats from the river to the Shropshire Canal above.

Places to Stay A pitch at the *Severn Gorge* camp site (☎ 684789; *Bridgnorth Rd, Tweedale*) is £4. It's 1.5mi towards Telford, beyond Madeley.

Ironbridge Gorge Youth Hostel (☎ 588 755) has two sites 3mi apart. The one in High St, Coalport, downstream, has an all-day restaurant. The other is in Paradise Rd, Coalbrookdale. Both charge £10.15.

A B&B very close to the bridge is *Eley's* (☎ 432541, *10 Tontine Hill*), which also runs the neighbouring *pork pie shop*. Singles/ doubles are from £35/45. *Grove Farm House* (☎ 433572; *Leighton Rd, Buildwas*) is 2.5mi west of town, with prices from £36 for a twin or double with shared facilities. The rather upmarket *Library House* (☎ 432299, *11 Severn Bank*) is up the pathway from the main road below the bridge, where cyclist George Maddocks offers a filling, healthy breakfast and singles/doubles for £45/55.

Places to Eat There are cafes at the *Museum of Iron*, *Blists Hill* and the *China Museum*. The unpretentious *Central Cafe*, near the bridge, does good-value hot food and teas during the day. *Peacocks Pantry* does similar with half-curtained windows. *Oliver's Vegetarian Bistro* (☎ 433086), next to the Central, has main dishes from £6, but restricted evening opening hours are usually from 7 to 9.30 pm (10 pm Friday

and Saturday). The *Meadow Inn* just west of town along the river has a reputation for good pub food. A reader recommended another pub, the *Coalbrookdale Inn* near the Coalbrookdale hostel north-west of town, which has real ale and tasty pub grub.

Day 8: Ironbridge to Northwich
4–6½ hours, 60.4mi
Day 8 is distinguished by a major early ascent, a Cold War relic and idyllic country lanes.

With a 180m, 5mi climb directly out of Ironbridge up the side of The Wrekin, the route leaves the Severn valley for good. Between Waters Upton (15.2mi) and Audlem (35.2mi) are 20mi of pretty rural lanes along the Rivers Tern and Weaver – cars are a rarity.

Detour (follow the signs to the left) to the recently declassified **Hack Green Secret Nuclear Bunker** (40.0mi; ☎ 01270-629219). It was set up for 130 officials to hide out in, in post-Bomb north-west England. In the middle of rural Cheshire, experience a 4-minute warning, watch genuine pre-strike TV broadcasts and see the decontamination room. Entry costs £4.90 per adult.

The route skirts the centre of Nantwich, which has all facilities, to an overnight stop at Northwich.

Northwich
☎ 01606
Northwich lies between the Rivers Weaver and Dane and has four historic bridges, and a marina. An otherwise ordinary little town, it was once part of the only large-scale salt mining operation in the country. The numerous lakes (or 'flashes') around the town are collapsed mines.

Information The TIC (☎ 353 5341), The Arcade, is open standard hours and can provide further accommodation details. All the major banks have branches in the town centre. The town's main bike shop is Jack Gee Cycles (☎ 43029), 136 Witton St.

Things to See & Do The **Salt Museum** (☎ 41331), half a mile south at 162 London Rd, tells the interesting story of the town's briny past.

About 2mi north-west, the giant derelict **Anderton Boat Lift** will soon once more be

Day 8: Ironbridge to Northwich

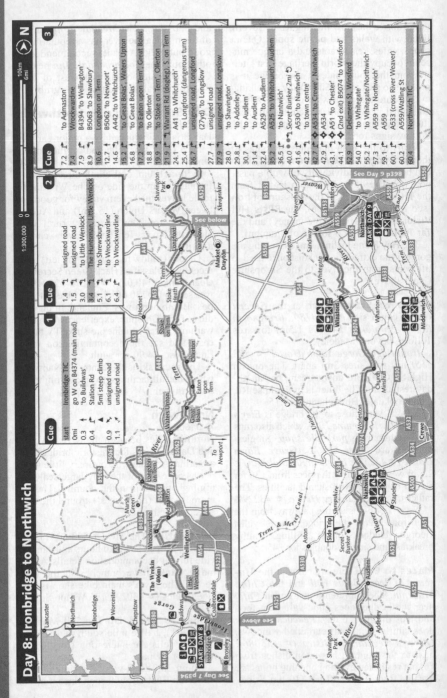

1:300,000

Cue	
start	Ironbridge TIC
0mi	go W on B4374 (main road)
0.3	'to Buildwas'
0.4	Station Rd
	5mi steep climb
0.9	unsigned road
1.1	unsigned road

Cue	
1.4	unsigned road
1.5	unsigned road
3.0	'to Little Wenlock'
3.4	The Huntsman, Little Wenlock
5.1	'to Shrewsbury'
6.1	'to Wrockwardine'
6.4	'to Wrockwardine'

Cue	
7.2	'to Admaston'
7.4	Wrockwardine
7.9	B4394 'to Wellington'
8.9	B5063 'to Shawbury'
10.6	Longdon on Tern
12.7	B5062 'to Newport'
14.6	A442 'to Whitchurch'
15.2	'to Great Bolas', Waters Upton
16.8	'to Great Bolas'
17.2	to Eaton upon Tern', Great Bolas
18.8	'to Ollerton'
19.9	'to Stoke on Tern', Ollerton
21.9	Warrant Rd (dogleg), S. on Tern
24.1	A41 'to Whitchurch'
25.4	'to Longford' (dangerous turn)
26.7	unsigned road, Longford
	(27yd) 'to Longslow'
27.7	unsigned road
27.9	unsigned road, Longslow
28.0	'to Shavington'
29.8	'to Adderley'
30.7	'to Audlem'
31.4	'to Audlem'
32.4	A529 'to Audlem'
35.2	A525 'to Whitchurch', Audlem
36.5	'to Nantwich' ↻ Secret Bunker 2mi
40.0	A530 'to Nantwich'
41.6	'to town centre'
42.2	A534 'to Crewe', Nantwich
42.7	A534
42.9	A51 'to Chester'
43.1	B5074 'to Winsford'
44.1	(2nd exit) B5074 'to Winsford'
52.9	Delamere St, Winsford
54.0	'to Whitegate'
55.2	'to Whitegate/Northwich'
57.3	A559 'to Northwich'
59.1	A559
60.1	A533 (cross River Weaver)
60.2	A559/Watling St
60.4	Northwich TIC

See Day 9 p398

hoisting boats in dual troughs between the River Weaver and the Trent & Mersey Canal. On Sunday you can see it by boat on a **river trip** from Northwich Marina with the Big Dutch Barge company (☎ 76204).

Places to Stay & Eat Accommodation in central Northwich is limited, so you may have to stay a few miles out of town. The 17th-century thatched *Clock Cottage (☎ 891 271; Heild Lane, Aston by Budworth)* has rooms for £20 per person B&B. It lies a couple of miles north-east near the Day 9 route. In a similar direction along the A559 is the *Slow & Easy Hotel (☎ 42148; Manchester Rd, Lostock Gralam)*, which charges £30/40 for en suite singles/doubles. *Park Villa (☎ 74533; Park Rd, Winnington)*, 1mi north-west along the A533, charges from £22.50/35. Bang in the centre on the marina is the luxury floating *Quality Hotel (☎ 44443)*; where rates start from £70/81.50.

While there are plenty of good pubs in the area, eating out in the centre is a plainer choice of Italian, Indian and Chinese; the hotel menus are also worth a look. A good Italian is *De Souza's (☎ 46131; The Bull Ring, High St)* near Town Bridge. The carvery at the *Quality Hotel* is £14.50 and there's a la carte main courses from £9. The *Cheshire Tandoori (☎ 871040, 45 Chester Rd)* is a popular local Indian restaurant.

Day 9: Northwich to Lancaster
5–8½ hours, 78.8mi

There are few distractions during this long journey through the north-west's urban sprawls, where there's plenty of traffic for company. It's best to get your head down and bag it.

It is possible to split the day into two shorter ones, stopping at Preston (49.8mi) or Garstang (64.7mi).

From Northwich there's countryside as far as Warburton, with the only rural crossing of the Manchester Ship Canal (11.9mi) for miles. Thereafter, continue for 17mi from Culcheth (18mi) to Shevington (34.3mi). Here things go rural again until the fast A-road-approach to Preston – which at least has a cycle lane.

Take great care on the last section into Preston, to the point of dismounting and walking along the verge where the A59 dual

carriageway joins: two fast lanes of traffic must be crossed to exit.

Preston TIC (☎ 01772-253731), Guildhall Arcade, Lancaster Rd, can provide accommodation options if you want to split the journey here. For budget accommodation in the town centre, the *University of Central Lancashire student residences (☎ 01772-982650; Foster Building, off Corporation St)* has rooms in self-catering flats for £12.50 per night from mid-May to mid-September. The office closes at 5 pm. *Stanley Guest House (☎ 01772-253366, 7 Stanley Terrace)* has single/double rooms for £20/32.

In Garstang, *Mrs Heaton's Guesthouse (☎ 01995-602022; Castle View, 42 Bond St)* has single rooms at £20 and twins at £35.

In Preston, pick up the Southport to Lancaster route at the 17.8mi mark on that cue sheet (follow the E2E cues on p233; Day 5 of the Marches, Cheshire & Lancashire ride in the Central England chapter), which becomes more pleasant again on the Lancashire plain to Lancaster. Save time and a mile or two by continuing straight on to Lancaster on the A588 (72.3mi) instead of turning left to Glasson.

A short side trip (at 74mi) leads to **Glasson** and its historic dock and lighthouse. This interesting town had its heyday in the 18th century, when the local canal from Lancaster ran to its dock basins, which remains the oldest existing tidal dock in England.

Lancaster
See Lancaster (p223) in the Central England chapter for details of accommodation and other services.

Day 10: Lancaster to Kirkby Stephen
4½–6 hours, 53.0mi

This day passes through three different counties and a variety of picturesque landscapes. The magnificent scenery encountered along Dentdale and Mallerstang Common in the Yorkshire Dales National Park is particularly memorable.

The day's major climb is a testing 2.5mi ascent from Cowgill (36.5mi), which is followed by a frighteningly steep descent to Garsdale Station.

Kirkby Lonsdale (15.2mi) is a charming Cumbrian market town in the heart of the

Day 9: Northwich to Preston (Part 1)

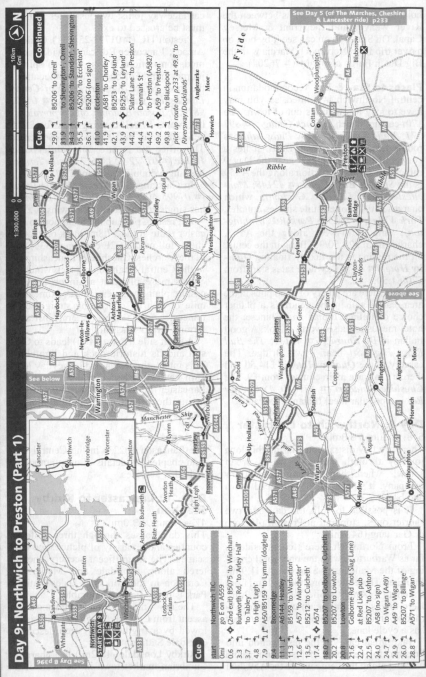

Cue (Continued)

29.0	♦	B5206 'to Orrell'
31.9		'to Shevington'; Orrell
34.3		B5206 'to Standish'; Shevington
35.5		A5209 'to Eccleston'
36.1		B5206 (no sign)
41.0		Eccleston
41.9		A581 'to Chorley'
42.1		B5253 'to Leyland'
43.9		B5253 'to Leyland'
44.2		Slater Lane 'to Preston'
44.4		Denmark St
44.5	♦	'to Preston (A582)'
49.2		A59 'to Preston'
49.8	♦	'to Blackpool'
		pick up route on p233 at 49.8 to Riversway/Docklands'

See Day 5 (of The Marches, Cheshire & Lancaster ride) p233

Cue

start		Northwich TIC
0mi		go E on A559
0.6	♦	(2nd exit) B5075 'to Wincham'
3.3		Budworth Rd, 'to Arley Hall'
3.7		'to Tabley'
4.8		'to High Legh'
7.9		A50/B5159 'to Lymm' (dogleg)
9.4	♦	Broomedge
11.1		A6144, Heatley
11.3		B5159 'to Warburton'
12.6		A57 'to Manchester'
13.5		B5212 'to Culcheth'
17.4	♦	A574
18.0		B5207 'to Golborne' - Culcheth
20.2		B5207 'to Lowton'
20.8		Lowton
21.6		Golborne Rd (not Slag Lane) at Red Lion pub
22.4		B5207 'to Ashton'
22.5		A58 (no sign)
24.0		'to Wigan (A49)'
24.7		A49 'to Wigan'
24.9		B5207 'to Billinge'
26.0		A571 'to Wigan'
28.8		

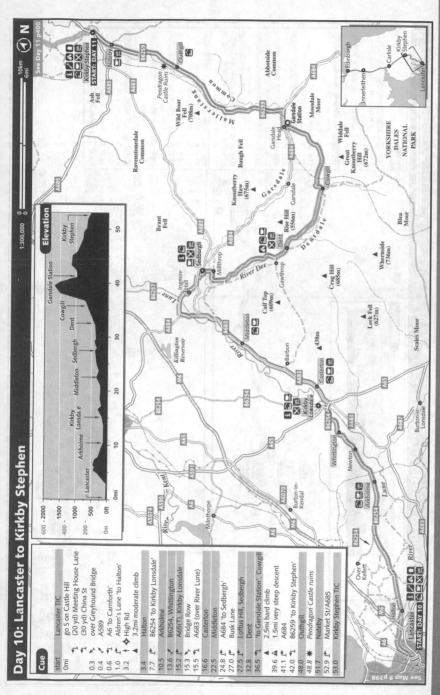

Day 10: Lancaster to Kirkby Stephen

See Day 11 p400

Elevation

Cue		
start	Lancaster TIC	
0mi	go S on Castle Hill	
	(20 yd) Meeting House Lane	
0.3	(30 yd) China St	
0.4	over Greyhound Bridge	
0.6	A589	
1.0	A6 to Carnforth'	
3.2	Aldren's Lane 'to Halton'	
	High Rd	
	3.2mi moderate climb	
3.4	Halton	
7.7	B6254 'to Kirkby Lonsdale'	
10.5	Arkholme	
13.6	B6254, Whittington	
15.2	A65(T), Kirkby Lonsdale	
15.3	Bridge Row	
15.5	A683 (over River Lune)	
16.6	Casterton	
22.5	Middleton	
24.8	A684 'to Sedbergh'	
27.0	Busk Lane	
27.5	Loftus Hill, Sedbergh	
32.8	Dent	
36.5	'to Garsdale Station', Cowgill	
	2.5mi hard climb	
39.6	1.5mi very steep descent	
41.1	A684	
42.0	B6259 'to Kirkby Stephen'	
48.0	Outhgill	
48.8	Pendragon Castle ruins	
51.7	Nateby	
52.9	Market St/A685	
53.0	Kirkby Stephen TIC	

Day 11: Kirkby Stephen to Carlisle

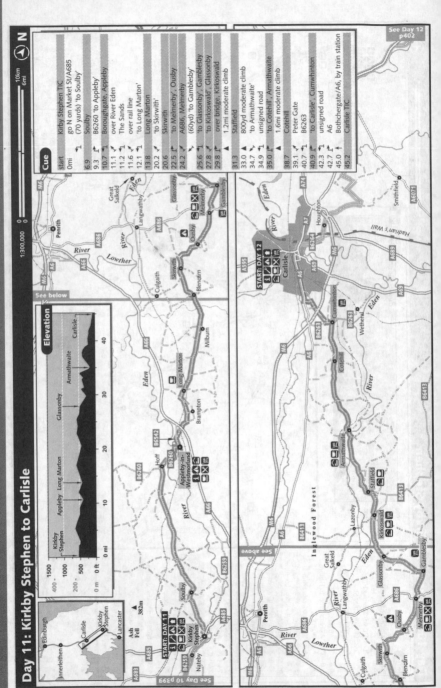

Cue		
start		Kirkby Stephen TIC
		go N on Market St/A685
0mi		(70 yards) 'to Soulby'
6.9		Soulby
9.3		B6260 'to Appleby'
10.7		Boroughgate, Appleby
11.1		over River Eden
11.2		The Sands
11.6		over rail line
12.1		'to Long Marton'
13.8		Long Marton
20.2		'to Skirwith'
20.6		Skirwith
22.5		'to Melmerby', Ousby
24.2		A686, Melmerby
		(60yd) 'to Gamblesby'
25.6		'to Glassonby', Gamblesby
27.8		'to Kirkoswald', Glassonby
29.8		over bridge, Kirkoswald
		1.2mi moderate climb
31.3		Staffield
33.0		800yd moderate climb
34.7		'to Armathwaite'
34.9		unsigned road
35.0		'to Cotehill', Armathwaite
		1.6mi moderate climb
38.7		Cotehill
39.1		Peter Gate
40.7		B6263
40.9		'to Carlisle', Cumwhinton
42.3		unsigned road
42.7		A6
45.0		Bothchergate/A6, by train station
45.2		Carlisle TIC

See Day 12
p402

Elevation

(elevation profile: Kirkby Stephen, Appleby, Long Marton, Glassonby, Armathwaite, Carlisle; 0 ft / 500 / 1000 / 1500; 0 m / 200 / 400; 0 mi 10 20 30 40)

See Day 10 p399

See below

See above

See Day 12

START: DAY 11

START: DAY 12

Lune Valley – a very pleasant place to rest. On Sunday, look out for the motorcyclists who gather by the old bridge to show off their hardware.

The River Lune is followed upstream, joining the River Dee at Sedbergh (27.5mi) for the journey through picturesque Dentdale. There's steady climbing up the valley to Cowgill before the final ascent to a lofty exposed summit.

The road shadows the rail line for much of the remaining distance to Kirkby Stephen, the B6259 winding its way down the wildly beautiful dale of Mallerstang. The ruin of 12th-century **Pendragon Castle** (48.8mi) was reputedly the home of King Arthur's father. Its inhabitants today aren't quite as regal (a flock of curious sheep), but nonetheless it's an interesting ruin in a beautiful setting.

Kirkby Stephen
☎ 017683

Kirkby Stephen is a classic market town with stone Georgian-style houses fronting an attractive High St. There's nothing remarkable about the place but that's part of its charm. Unlike nearby towns in the Lakes and the Dales it's not inundated with visitors, although you're likely to meet plenty of walkers passing through on the popular Coast to Coast trek.

Information The TIC (☎ 71199) is on Market St, the town's main thoroughfare. A Barclays Bank (with ATM) is a few doors down. For a bike shop, HS Robinson (☎ 71519) is at 2 Market St.

Places to Stay & Eat On the southern fringes of town, the *Pennine View Caravan & Camping Park (☎ 71717, Station Rd)*, has tent pitches from £8. The *Kirkby Stephen YHA (☎ 71793)* is centrally located in a former Church on Market St, charging £8.35. The evening meal is filling and tasty – unbeatable value at £4.60 for three courses.

The *Old Court House (☎ 71061, High St)* has excellent B&B from £15 – and yes, it did formerly host the town's judiciary.

Limited dining options include several *pubs*, *fish and chip* shops and a *Chinese takeaway*. A decent bar menu at the *Pennine Hotel (☎ 71382, Market St)* offers basic fare such as the regional speciality, Cumberland sausage (around £5).

Day 11: Kirkby Stephen to Carlisle
4–5 hours, 45.2mi

This excellent day travels on a series of quiet country lanes, through lush grazing land. This sea of green is testimony to the region's reputation as one of England's wettest. Although the barren tops of the lofty Pennines loom close for most of the day, the ride itself is relatively flat, skirting the base of the bigger peaks, along the picturesque Eden Valley.

For much of the way to Appleby-in-Westmorland (10.7mi), the route undulates along part of the 280mi Cumbria Cycleway.

Appleby, the largest settlement encountered all day, is a picturesque, bustling market town on the River Eden. The **Norman castle** (☎ 017683-51402), extensively renovated in the 17th century, is worth a visit. It's at the top of Boroughgate, the principal shopping street.

Most of the villages en route are very small. Melmerby (24.2mi) is a good lunch spot. There's a *bakery* and the *Smithfield Inn* serves excellent pub grub.

Sheep farming dominates the Cumbrian landscape, through the scenic Eden Valley. Neatly divided by dry stone walls, the countryside looks remarkably like that of the nearby Yorkshire Dales.

On the outskirts of Carlisle quiet country lanes are left for the busy A6 for a short final leg into the centre of town.

Carlisle
See the Gateway Cities section (pp297–8) in the Northern England chapter for information about accommodation and other services.

Day 12: Carlisle to Innerleithen
5–8 hours, 67.3mi

Quickly leaving Carlisle's suburbs for gently undulating country lanes, this route then joins the not-too-busy A7, crossing the Scottish border (14.9mi) before returning to quiet roads again.

Undulations become more pronounced over the border, with some short steep hills. The River Esk is followed for most of its length to the watershed in the Eskdalemuir Forest. The long, gradual, undulating climb to this point begins after Langholm (23.4mi). The day's highest point (385m), however, is a little farther on (55.2mi).

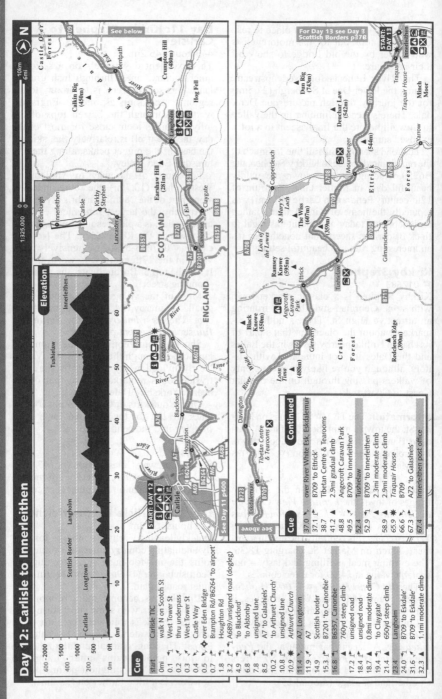

Day 12: Carlisle to Innerleithen

1:325,000

Elevation

Carlisle — Longtown — Scottish Border — Langholm — Tushielaw — Innerleithen

Cue

start	Carlisle TIC
0mi	walk N on Scotch St
0.1	West Tower St
0.2	thru underpass
0.3	West Tower St
0.4	Castle Way
0.5	over Eden Bridge
0.7	Brampton Rd/B6264 'to airport'
1.8	Houghton Rd
3.2	A689/unsigned road (dogleg)
4.9	'to Blackford'
6.8	'to Alstonby'
7.8	unsigned lane
8.5	A7 'to Galashiels'
10.2	'to Arthuret Church'
10.8	unsigned lane
10.9	Arthuret Church
11.4	A7, Longtown
11.9	A7
14.9	Scottish border
15.3	B7201 'to Canonbie'
16.8	B6357, Canonbie
17.2	760yd steep climb
18.4	unsigned road
18.7	0.8mi moderate climb
19.4	'to Claygate'
21.4	650yd steep climb
23.4	Langholm
24.0	B709 'to Eskdale'
31.6	B709 'to Eskdale'
32.3	1.1mi moderate climb

Cue — Continued

37.0	over River White Esk, Eskdalemuir
37.1	B709 'to Ettrick'
38.7	Tibetan Centre & Tearooms
41.2	2.9mi gradual climb
48.8	Angecroft Caravan Park
49.5	B709 'to Innerleithen'
52.4	Tushielaw
52.9	B709 'to Innerleithen'
	2.3mi moderate climb
58.9	2.9mi moderate climb
65.9	Traquair House
66.6	B709
67.3	A72 'to Galashiels'
67.4	Innerleithen post office

See below

For Day 13 see Day 3 Scottish Borders p378

START: DAY 13

See Day 11 p400

START DAY 12

Castle Over Forest

Bentpath

Crampton Hill (480m)

Calkin Rig (450m)

Hog Fell

Langholm

B709

B7068

Earnshaw Hill (281m)

Esk

Claygate

Canonbie

B6318

B6318

B720

B6357

Edinburgh — Innerleithen — Carlisle — Kirkby Stephen — Lancaster

SCOTLAND

ENGLAND

River Esk

Eden

River

Blackford

Houghton

Carlisle

A7

A74

A6071

A69

A595

A7

Longtown

River Lyne

River White Esk

Davington

Eskdalemuir

Tibetan Centre & Tearooms

B723

Loom Tima (488m)

Craik Forest

Glenkerry

Redcleuch Edge (390m)

B709

Ettrick

Black Knowe (550m)

Angecroft Caravan Park

Ramsey Knowe (595m)

Tushielaw

B711

Ettrick Forest

Gilmanscleuch

Loch of the Lowes

St Mary's Loch

The Wiss (607m)

A708

A708

Mountbenger

Deuchar Law (542m)

Yarrow

Traquair House

Traquair

Innerleithen

Minch Moor

Dun Rig (743m)

B709

N

0 10km
0 6mi

The peace and relative remoteness of the open hills is captivating, however there are few services between Langholm and Innerleithen. At 38.7mi, there's the *Samye-Ling Tibetan Centre & Tearooms*. The welcoming *Tushielaw Inn* (52.4mi; ☎ *01750-62205*) serves lunch (from £4) between 12 and 2.15 pm; B&B is £21/25 per person for a double or twin/single. The Inn or the adjacent *Kirkbrae* (☎ *01750-62208*), with B&B for £14, make good alternative stopovers. The *Angecroft Caravan Park* (☎ *01750-62251*), 3.6mi earlier, is in a pretty spot. Tent sites are £4 (including showers) and you can buy basic supplies.

Early in the day, look out for the **Arthuret Church** (10.9mi) on the unsigned lane entering Longtown. According to legend, King Arthur's head is buried here. Somewhat grander is **Traquair House** (65.9km; ☎ 01896-830785), which claims to be the oldest inhabited house in Scotland.

Innerleithen
☎ 01896
Situated on the River Tweed at the base of the Moorfoot Hills, Innerleithen – a small mill town – has the air of a working class town, albeit one where the hospitality is honest and friendly.

Information There's no TIC, but the post office (☎ 830364), High St, may be able to help. There's also a Bank of Scotland (with ATM) on High St. Bikesport Innerleithen (☎ 830880), on High St 50yd west of the Traquair Rd turn-off, is also the contact for guided mountain bike tours.

Things to See & Do Attractions at Innerleithen include Robert Smail's **Printing Works** (☎ 830206), High St, where typesetting is still done by hand; and **St Ronan's Well** (☎ 830660), on Well's Brae, a natural spa. There's also good **mountain biking** in the nearby Moorfoot Hills – Bikesport Innerleithen (☎ 830880) can suggest 50 routes from the shop, or can organise half/full day tours for £40/60 including a bike and qualified guide (up to 8 people). Mountain bike hire only is £13.50 per day.

Places to Stay & Eat Follow signs from the eastern end of town to *Tweedside Caravan Park* (☎ *831271, Montgomery St)*, where tent sites cost £3.50 to £5, plus £2 key deposit. Laundry facilities and showers are coin operated.

The very comfortable *Caddon View Guest House* (☎ *830208, 14 Pirn Rd)* has a sauna and offers en suite B&B at £26 per person for doubles or twins and £35 for singles. Pay an extra £16 for a three course French meal ('made with love', according to the chef).

The *Corner House Hotel* (☎ *831181, cnr High & Chapel Sts)* has friendly B&B for £23 per person and good, generous bar meals starting at £4.25 (the dining room is nonsmoking). The *Traquair Arms Hotel* (☎ *830229, Traquair Rd)* is a little grander – and a little pricier: Meals start at £5.30, expect to pay £30 to £40 for B&B (more for singles).

The *Co-op* supermarket *(Chapel St)* is open till 8 pm. There's *fish and chips* or *Chinese takeaway* on High St, plus the *Jackie Lunn Bakery* next to the post office. The cafe-style *River Bank Restaurant* (☎ *831 221, 1 Leithen Rd)* has evening meals on Friday to Sunday. Smallish pasta-based mains are £5 to £6 (ask for extra potatoes).

Day 13: Innerleithen to Edinburgh
2½–4 hours, 33.2mi
See Day 3 (pp378–9) of the Scottish Borders ride in the Scotland chapter for a map and description of this ride. Innerleithen starts at 18.2mi (from the post office, go NE on the A72 and then pick up the E2E cues on the Scottish Borders map).

Edinburgh
See the Gateway Cities section (pp338–41) in the Scotland chapter for information about accommodation and other services.

Day 14: Edinburgh to Perth
3½–6 hours, 48.1mi
After leaving behind Edinburgh's leafy north western suburbs the **Forth Road Bridge** (11.4mi), suspended high above the water, provides spectacular views en route to the Kingdom of Fife.

Thereafter, the route undulates through the countryside surrounding Inverkeithing, Dunfermline and Kinross with a number of short steep hills. After Kinross, the route continues north, undulating on quiet roads to Bridge of Earn (43.4mi) where it joins Old Edinburgh Rd for the final run into Perth.

Day 14: Edinburgh to Perth

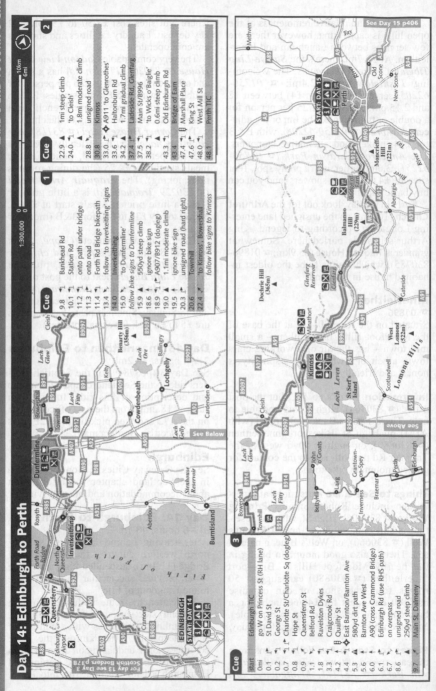

N

1:300,000

0 — 10km
0 — 6mi

For day 13 see Day 13 p379 Scottish Borders

Cue

0mi	Edinburgh TIC
0.1	go W on Princess St (RH lane)
0.2	St David St
0.7	George St
	Charlotte St/Charlotte Sq (dogleg)
0.8	Hope St
0.9	Queensferry St
1.1	Belford Rd
1.8	Ravelston Dykes
3.3	Craigcrook Rd
4.2	Quality St
4.4	East Barnton/Barnton Ave
5.3	580yd dirt path
5.6	Barnton Ave West
6.0	A90 (cross Crammond Bridge)
6.1	Edinburgh Rd (use RHS path)
6.7	on overpass
8.6	unsigned road
9.7	250yd steep climb
	Main St, Dalmeny

Cue

9.8	Bankhead Rd
10.1	Station Rd
11.2	onto path under bridge
11.3	onto road
11.4	Forth Rd Bridge bikepath
	follow 'to Inverkeithing' signs
13.4	Inverkeithing
14.0	'to Dunfermline'
	follow bike signs to Dunfermline
15.0	550yd steep climb
15.9	ignore bike sign
18.6	A907/B912 (dogleg)
18.9	1.1mi moderate climb
19.0	ignore bike sign
19.5	unsigned road (hard right)
20.3	Townhill
20.6	'to Kinross,' Bowershall
22.4	*follow bike signs to Kinross*

Cue

22.9	1mi steep climb
24.0	'to Cleish'
	1.8mi moderate climb
28.8	unsigned road
30.8	Kinross
33.0	A911 'to Glenrothes'
33.6	Haltonburn Rd
34.2	1.7mi gradual climb
37.4	Ladeside Rd, Glenfarg
37.5	Main St/B996
38.2	0.6mi steep climb
	'to Wicks o'Baiglie'
43.3	Old Edinburgh Rd
43.4	Bridge of Earn
47.4	Marshall Place
47.6	King St
48.0	West Mill St
48.1	Perth TIC

See Day 15 p406

Superseded by the motorway, Edinburgh Rd is not especially busy, but traffic is fast.

Much of the route is on quiet roads and, from the bridge to Kinross, follows part of the signed Fife Millennium Cycleway. Care is required, however, on busy sections in central Edinburgh; on Edinburgh Rd (6.1mi), where bikes are requested to use the footpath; and the dogleg across the A907 (18.9mi) by Dunfermline. There's also an easily-negotiated 580yd dirt path (5.3mi) in Edinburgh.

Perth
☎ 01738

Set on the River Tay, Perth is a busy trading town and was once Scotland's capital. Its rise to importance derives from Scone (pronounced 'scoon'), 2mi north, to where Kenneth MacAlpin, first king of a united Scotland, brought the Stone of Destiny (on which kings and queens were crowned) in the 9th century.

Information The TIC (☎ 627958), Lower City Mills, West Mill St, opens daily (Sunday from 11 am to 4 pm) between March and October. It has a bureau de change, and there are banks (with ATMs) at the eastern end of High St.

JM Richards Bikeshop (☎ 626860), 44 George St, is well regarded. The Fair City Laundry (☎ 631653) is at 44 Methven St.

Things to See & Do See Day 15 for details about **Scone Palace**, 2mi north on the route.

The recommended **JD Fergusson Gallery** (☎ 441994), corner of Marshall Place and Tay St, shows work by the Scottish colourist (free entry). Also free is the military **Black Watch Museum** (☎ 621281), Balhousie Castle, Hay St. **Lower City Mills** (☎ 627

958), by the TIC, is a working Victorian oatmeal mill.

Places to Stay It's advisable to book accommodation ahead in Perth, especially during August.

Cleeve Caravan Park (☎ 639521, Glasgow Rd), 1.2mi east of town, has limited tent sites for £2.10 plus £2.30 per person.

The *Perth Youth Hostel* (☎ 623658, 107 Glasgow Rd) offers good local information. Beds cost £9.

Small and homely, the *Arran Guest House* (☎ 634216, 2 Pitcullen Crescent) charges £20 per person B&B. The friendly *Beeches* (☎ 624486, cnr Pitcullen Crescent & Comely Bank) charges the same. More central, the *Heidl Guesthouse* (☎ 635031, 43 York Place) does B&B for £16 to £20.

The central *New County Hotel* (☎ 623 355, 26 County Place) has refurbished en suite rooms for £32.50/40 per person for doubles or twins/singles.

Places to Eat Perth has a good choice of eateries. There's a *Safeway* supermarket *(cnr Glasgow & Caledonian Rds)* and a bulk store *Scoop 'n' Save (135 South St)*. *Daniels* takeaway on County Place has kebabs, chicken, lasagne and pizza.

Bakeries include *Goodfellow & Steven* (☎ 630327) with branches at 50 High St and 13 Scott St. For coffee, *Costas* (☎ 643522, cnr High & Scott Sts) is reliable. It also has sandwiches, pasta (£4.95) and pizza (£5.95). The *Willows Coffee Shop & Restaurant* (☎ 441175, 12 St Johns Place) serves £4.50 breakfasts from 7.30 am (8.30 am Sunday).

High Teas (£7.50 to £9.50) are very popular at the *Grampian Hotel* (☎ 621057, 37 York Place). *Louis' Restaurant* (☎ 447999,

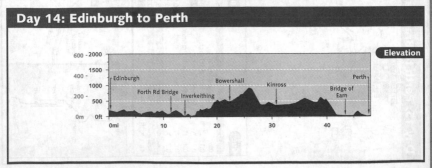

Day 14: Edinburgh to Perth

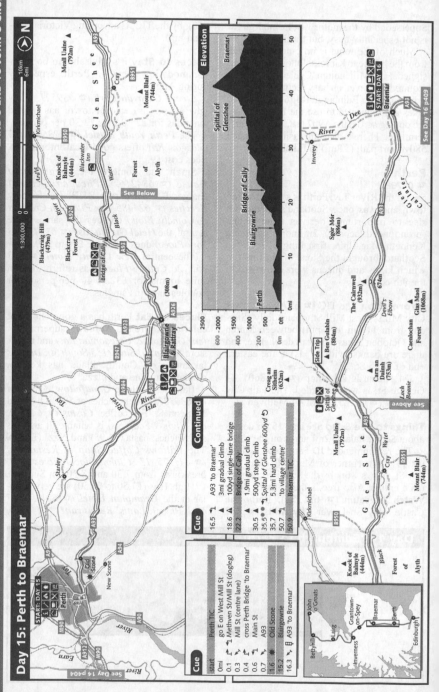

181 South St) is hip and comfortable and includes carbo-based and vegetarian meals. Mains are £4.95 to £11.95. Irish pub *Mucky Mulligans (☎ 636705, 97 Canal St)* is good value with mains from £2.75 to £3.95. *Le Cafe Kashmir (☎ 441313, 173 South St)* does four-course buffets for £8.95 weekdays.

Day 15: Perth to Braemar

4–6½ hours, 50.9mi
Heading into the mountains, the ride presents some challenging climbing. Though it's all on the A93, traffic is not too intrusive and dissipates to a trickle north of Bridge of Cally (22.2mi). The busiest section, to twin towns Blairgowrie and Rattray (15.2mi) is easy riding.

Just out of town in Old Scone, **Scone Palace** (1.6mi; ☎ 552300) houses a superb collection of French furniture, including Marie Antoinette's writing table.

Blairgowrie is the last major centre before Braemar, with *bakeries*, *supermarkets* and a bank (with ATM). Crighton's Cycles (15.8mi; ☎ 01250-374447), 87 Perth St, is en route.

The route from Blairgowrie to Braemar is increasingly undulating, though apart from the climb through Glenshee (30.5mi), there's nothing too steep. Initially wooded and then rolling farmland, the landscape becomes rugged moors towards the Grampian Mountains. After the Spittal of Glenshee (a side trip at 35.5mi) is the big one – a long, demanding climb, very steep for the last 3mi – followed by 10mi of downhill to Braemar.

If it all seems too hard, try tapping into the local ambience: Glenshee is literally the 'valley of peace' from the Gaelic *glen* (valley), *shee* (peace).

The *Blackwater Inn (26.4mi; ☎ 01250-882286)* is one of a few isolated pubs. Lunch (except on Monday) is under £4. The *Spittal of Glenshee Hotel (☎ 01250-885215)* is a good spot to refuel before the climb. Bar lunches (until 5.30 pm), including home-made bread, are £5 to £6.

Braemar

☎ 01339
Braemar is an attractive village, famous for the Braemar Gathering (see the boxed text), which inundates the town in early September.

Information The TIC (☎ 741600), The Mews, Mar Rd, opens daily from 10 am to

---

Braemar Gathering

There are Highland games in many towns and villages throughout the summer, but the best known is the Braemar Gathering, which takes place on a 12-acre site on the first Saturday in September. It's a major occasion, annually organised by the Braemar Royal Highland Society since 1817, drawing international athletes. Events include highland dancing, pipers, tug-of-war, a hill race up Morrone, tossing the caber, hammer and stone throwing, and the long jump.

These types of events took place informally in the Highlands for many centuries as tests of skill and strength, but they were formalised around 1820 due to rising pseudo-Highland romanticism caused by people like King George IV and Sir Walter Scott. Queen Victoria attended the Braemar Gathering in 1848, starting the tradition of royal patronage which continues to this day.

---

5 pm (later in summer and, from October to May, opens at noon on Sunday). The TIC has a bureau de change and there's a Bank of Scotland ATM in The Mews.

There's no bike shop but ask nicely and the helpful Braemar Mountain Sports (☎ 741 242) at the village entrance may assist in an emergency. There's also a good range of outdoor clothing and equipment.

Things to See & Do Just north of the village (on the Day 16 route) is **Braemar Castle** (☎ 741219). It was a government garrison after the 1745 Jacobite rebellion, before becoming a family home.

Braemar Mountain Sports provides route advice, maps and hires decent rigid bikes for **mountain biking** in the area. Ask them about the alternative mountain bike route to Tomintoul. The TIC has information about local **walks**. Be sure to carry good maps and to check for deer stalking (☎ 013397-41911) and grouse shooting (keep to main paths).

Places to Stay Book ahead for accommodation in August and September.

There are great views from the *Invercauld Caravan Club Site (☎ 741373)*, south of the village on Glenshee Rd. Tent pitches are £2 plus £4 per adult, including showers and drying room.

Rucksacks (☎ *741517, 15 Mar Rd*) is a clean and well-run – if basic – hostel and the manager has excellent knowledge of local walks and mountain biking. Dorm beds are £8.50 (£7 with own bedding). The *Youth Hostel* (☎ *741659, 21 Glenshee Rd*) charges £9.

Homely and comfortable *Mayfield House* (☎ *741238, 11 Chapel Brae*) is a long-running family business, charging £17.50 per person B&B.

Pleasant *Balnellan House* (☎ *741474, Balnellan Rd*) offers B&B for £22 per person for doubles or twins, and £30 for singles.

Callater Lodge (☎ *741275, 9 Glenshee Rd*) is a small and friendly hotel with B&B for £28 (most with en suite). Evening meals (by arrangement) are £14 to £16, packed lunches £5 (catering for a range of diets).

Overlooking the Highland Games park, *Moorfield House Hotel* (☎ *741244*), off Chapel Brae, charges £16 B&B. Basic pub meals are £5 to £7.

Places to Eat There's an *Alldays* supermarket in Mar Rd; and *Braemar Takeaway* (*14 Invercauld Rd*) is recommended locally.

Gordon's Tearoom & Restaurant (*Mar Rd*) has standard mains from £4.95 to £6.95. Next door, excellent home baking and light meals are available from *The Old Bakery Coffee Shop*. Finer fare is found at *Braemar Lodge* (☎ *741627, Glenshee Rd*), where mains (traditional – scampi, venison, lamb – and vegetarian) range from £6.95 to £12.95.

Day 16: Braemar to Grantown-on-Spey

4–6 hours, 46.6mi

Arguably the hardest day of the lot, the ride through the heart of the Grampians involves seven significant hills, three of them steep.

It's possible to break the ride at Tomintoul (32.5mi) – the only town en route. The TIC (☎ 01807-580285) is in the square. *Camp* for free by the Glen Livet Estate information centre (☎ 01807-580283) at the south end of town. Beds at the *Tomintoul Bunkhouse* (☎ 01807-580206) are £7; or try *Morinsh* (☎ 01807-580452, 26 Cults Drive), £14; or the *Glen Avon Hotel* (☎ 01807-580218), from £17.50 for B&B.

Climbing begins 9mi from Braemar with the turn onto the single-track B976. For

---

The Malt Whisky Trail

Roughly 45 of Scotland's famous whisky distilleries are open to the public and you should certainly try to visit one while in Scotland.

In some, showing tourists around has become a slick marketing operation, complete with promotional videos, free drams (whisky measures), gift shops that rival the distillery in size and an entry charge of around £3.

Regions renowned for their whisky production include Speyside, east of Inverness and the Isle of Islay (pronounced 'isle-ah'), west of Kintyre.

Eight Speyside distillers – Glenfiddich, Cardhu, Glenfarclas, Glen Grant, The Glenlivet, Strathisla, Tamdhu and Tamnavulin – promote themselves in the Malt Whisky Trail (although visiting all eight might be overkill).

Pick up the Tourist Board's free *The Malt Whisky Trail* brochure, which shows the distilleries on a map. The closest lie around 20mi east (downstream) of Grantown-on-Spey.

Recommended tours include: Glenfiddich, The Glenlivet and Strathisla on Speyside; any of the Islay distilleries; and Highland Park on Orkney, one of the few distilleries where you still see the barley malting process.

---

procrastinators, there is an opportunity to dally with a side trip to the Queen's summer residence, **Balmoral Castle** (☎ 01339-742334; £3 entry), the entrance to which is about 0.5mi further on the A93. An information kiosk, toilets and the Crathie Kirk are nearby.

The undulating first climb passes from woodland to open moor, distinctively striped with scars of burnt heather (to encourage grouse), a characteristic of much of the ride.

A *tearoom* (20.8mi) offers a refuelling opportunity before the mother of the day's climbs, which is 2mi on, just past **Corgaff Castle** (☎ 01975-651460). Take consolation in the roadside footprints and wheel marks of cyclists who've *walked* before you. A tough (but rideable) hill to Lecht Pass (637m/2089ft) follows immediately, before a long, steep descent into Tomintoul.

Day 16: Braemar to Grantown-on-Spey

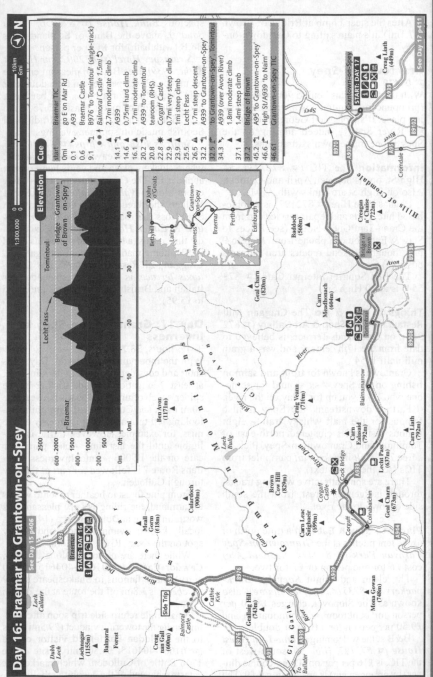

Cue		
start		Braemar TIC
0mi		go E on Mar Rd
0.1	↖	A93
0.6		Braemar Castle
9.1	⤹	B976 'to Tomintoul' (single-track)
	●●●●	*Balmoral Castle 1.5mi* ↻
14.1		2.7mi moderate climb
14.6	↖	A939
16.1		0.75mi hard climb
20.2	↰	1.7mi moderate climb
		A939 'to Tomintoul'
20.8		*Corgarff Castle* tearoom (RHS)
22.8	✳	*Corgarff Castle*
22.9	↰	0.7mi very steep climb
23.9		1mi steep climb
25.5		Lecht Pass
26.5		1.7mi steep descent
32.2	↰	A939 'to Grantown-on-Spey'
32.5	↱	'to Grantown-on-Spey', Tomintoul
34.3		A939 (over Avon River)
37.1		1.8mi moderate climb
37.2		1.4mi steep climb
		Bridge of Brown
45.2	↰	A95 'to Grantown-on-Spey'
46.6	↱	High St/A939 'to Nairn'
46.61		Grantown-on-Spey TIC

Elevation

Braemar / Tomintoul / Lecht Pass / Bridge of Brown / Grantown-on-Spey

1:300,000

After the steep climb at Bridge of Brown (37.1mi), it's plain sailing to Grantown-on-Spey.

Grantown-on-Spey
☎ 01479

With the Grampians behind you, Grantown (pronounced 'gran-ton') is a welcome resting place. It's a pleasant Georgian town on the River Spey – indeed angling on the Spey is one of the town's attractions.

Information The TIC (☎ 872773), 54 High St, opens between April and October. Also on High St are banks with ATMs.

Logans Bike Hire (☎ 872197) is a home-based hire, parts and repair service run from the Crann-Tara Guest House (see Places to Stay & Eat; you can phone from 9 am to 9 pm, though weekend repairs aren't always possible).

The Red Squirrel Internet Cafe (☎ 873 554) is at 20 High St.

Things to See & Do The Craggan Mill Restaurant Craft Shop & Art Gallery (☎ 872 288), on Woodlands Terrace, is believed to date from the 17th century and was a grain mill until 1954.

Grantown is known for **trout and salmon fishing** on the Spey. Ask around for someone who'll kit you up for a day on the river.

Farther downstream, the Spey is also famous for the **malt whisky trail** – eight famous distilleries clustered north-east of Tomintoul and Grantown-on-Spey. Pick up a free *The Malt Whisky Trail* pamphlet from TICs (see the boxed text).

There are some attractive **walking** tracks, through indigenous forest, from the south side of town to the river.

Places to Stay & Eat Half a mile north of town, tent pitches at the *Grantown-on-Spey Caravan Park* (☎ 872474, *Seafield Ave)* cost £6 for one person or £7 for two.

The clean and bright *Speyside Backpackers* (☎ 873514, *16 The Square)*, also known as The Stopover, charges £8.50 per person for bunkroom accommodation and £9.50 per person for a twin or double.

B&B at the welcoming *Crann-Tara Guest House* (☎ 872197, *High St)*, south-west of the TIC, is £16 per person. Three-course dinner (by arrangement) is an additional £9. The

spacious *Bank House* (☎ 873256, *1 The Square)*, above the Bank of Scotland, does B&B (with bath) for £17 per person.

Strathspey Hotel (☎ 872002, *cnr High St & the A939)* does B&B in pleasant en suite rooms for £22/25 per person for a double or twin/single (ask for a bath). The bar has a good selection of mains (pasta £5.75, up to £13.25 for steak) and there's traditional Scottish music on summer evenings.

Smiffy's Fish and Chips (☎ 872400, *36 The Square)* has takeaway and a restaurant, where chicken, pizza and vegie burgers start at under £5. The *Co-op* supermarket is a few doors along. *Walkers Bakery*, makers of Walkers shortbread, is near the TIC on High St. Across the road is the *Ice-Cream Parlour & Coffee House*, which has excellent daytime meals (a huge salad plate plus bread is £3), home-made ice cream and gateaux. *Craggan Mill Restaurant* (☎ 872288, *Woodlands Terrace)* is locally recommended for Italian and British cuisine (pastas are £4.95 to £5.95).

Day 17: Grantown-on-Spey to Inverness
3–4½ hours, 38.7mi

With the mountains behind you, Day 17 is short and considerably easier – terrain-wise, at least. Navigation is made trickier by the spider's web of unsigned roads between the 10mi mark and Culloden – the insignificant-looking left turn at 10.5mi is an easy one to miss, for example. However, traffic is negligible until the last 5mi – take particular care on the B9006 – into Inverness. Sustrans Route 7 is followed for part of the way through Culloden.

From pine forest to heather moor to woods to farmland, the riding is very pleasant. It's worth lingering at **Dulsie Bridge** (14.2mi), a locally known swimming hole and beauty spot on the rocky River Findhorn.

While there are no towns along the way, **Cawdor Castle** (☎ 01667-404615; £5.60 entry), made famous in Shakespeare's play *Macbeth*, is 1.8mi off the route at the 23.5mi point.

A half-mile return side trip soon after cycling under the towering viaduct (29.5mi) goes to the **Culloden Battlefield visitor centre** (☎ 01667-404615; £3.50 entry), site of the 1746 Battle of Culloden, which marked the catastrophic end of the Jacobite rebellion.

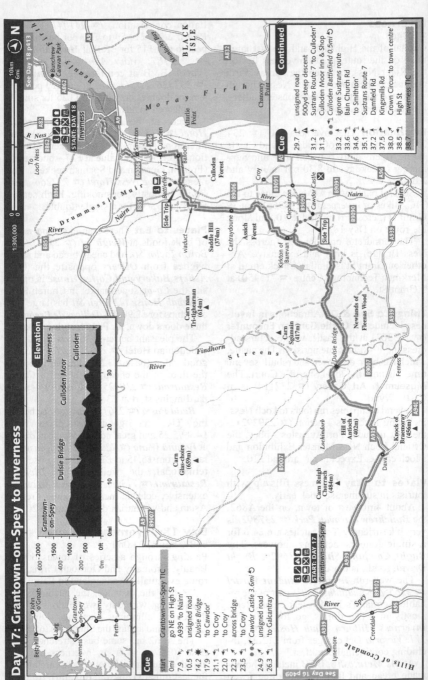

Day 17: Grantown-on-Spey to Inverness

Elevation

Grantown-on-Spey	Dulsie Bridge	Culloden Moor	Culloden	Inverness

600 - 2000
400 - 1500
200 - 1000
500
0m 0ft
0mi 10 20 30

1:300,000

0 10km
0 6mi

N

Cue

start	Grantown-on-Spey TIC
0mi	go NE on High St
7.9	A939 'to Nairn'
10.5	unsigned road
14.2	*Dulsie Bridge*
17.9	'to Cawdor'
21.1	'to Croy'
22.0	'to Croy'
22.3	across bridge
23.5	'to Croy'
	Cawdor Castle 3.6mi ↻
24.9	unsigned road
26.3	'to Galcantray'

Cue Continued

29.7	unsigned road
31.2	500yd steep descent
31.3	Sustrans Route 7 'to Culloden'
	Culloden Moor Inn & Shop
	Culloden Battlefield 0.5mi ↻
	ignore Sustrans route
33.2	Bain Church Rd
33.6	Sustrans Route 7
34.6	'to Smithton'
35.1	Damfield Rd
37.2	Kingsmills Rd
37.5	Crown Circus 'to town centre'
38.0	High St
38.5	Inverness TIC
38.7	

Side Trip

START DAY 17
Grantown-on-Spey

START DAY 18
Inverness

See Day 18 p413
See Day 16 p409

Inverness
☎ 01463

Capital of the Highlands and the last large town on the route, pretty Inverness lies on the River Ness, between the Moray Firth and the northern end of Loch Ness. Though inundated with tourists and monster hunters, it remains a pleasant spot.

Information The Inverness TIC (☎ 234 353), on the corner of Bridge St and Castle Wynd, opens daily between June and September (weekdays to 8.30 pm in July and August).

Several banks with ATMs are close to the TIC. Bikes of Inverness (☎ 225965) is at 39 Grant St (across Friars Bridge), 0.8mi along the route on Day 18.

The laundrette on Young St (across the Ness Bridge) is busy and expensive. Another on Grant St is similar. Check email at Merkinch Technology Centre (☎ 715450) at 2 Grant St.

Things to See & Do Attractions in Inverness include the **Castle Garrison Encounter** (☎ 243363) at the castle, where actors address the 1746 Jacobite uprising. The castle, which has been destroyed and rebuilt several times, is now the local Sheriff's Court. The **Museum & Art Gallery** (☎ 237114) is at Castle Wynd.

Several companies run tours to **Loch Ness**, including Inverness Traction (☎ 239292) – the tour includes Fort Augustus Abbey, the Official Loch Ness Monster Exhibition and a loch cruise. Expect to pay around £10.

Places to Stay Inverness fills up with tourists so book early.

About 4mi west of town, on the A862, the *Bunchrew Caravan Park (☎ 237802)* is very bike-friendly. Tent pitches are £4/6 for a single/double, including showers. The *Bught Camping Site (☎ 236920, Bught Drive)*, south, is closer.

The well-run *Inverness Student Hostel (☎ 236556, 8 Culduthel Rd)* is part of the reliable 'Scotland's Top Hostels' chain. Beds, mostly in 6-bed dorms, go for £10. The *Inverness Milburn Youth Hostel (☎ 231 771, Victoria Dr)* charges from £12.25, including continental breakfast.

At *Ms McIntosh's,* B&B includes homemade bread and Italian-style coffee (even

Italian conversation) *(☎ 241041, 9 Lovat Rd)*. It costs £14.50 to £20 per person. Expect to pay £15 for B&B at *Mary Ann Villa (☎ 230187; Mary Ann Court, Ardross Place)*. B&B at comfortable *Sunnyholm (☎ 231336, 12 Mayfield Rd)* is £19 per person for doubles or twins, and £25 for singles – book well in advance.

Decor at the *MacDougall Clansman Hotel (☎ 713702, 103 Church St)* looks unintentionally retro but, for the central location, B&B is great value at £27 – book early (French, German and Spanish spoken). The pleasant *Brae Ness Hotel (☎ 712266, Ness Bank)* is mostly nonsmoking. High season B&B is £33/39 for a single/double.

Places to Eat There's an excellent range of bulk foods at *Weigh In (☎ 237414, 40 Baron Taylor St)*, and cheap bread and sandwiches from *Olivers* opposite the TIC. *Ashers Bakery and Coffee House* is opposite the *Co-op* supermarket in Church St.

Kebab House (42 High St) has large fish and chips for £2.90. Try *Délices de Bretagne,* three doors down, for French-style breakfast.

The pleasant buffet-style *Arts Bar* at the Caledonian Hotel *(☎ 235181, Church St)* is good value (pasta £3.50). People queue at the door of the cheap and cheerful *Castle Restaurant (☎ 230925, 41 Castle St)* – standard mains start at £3.30.

Bella Pasta (☎ 230138, Bridge St), below the TIC, has good pasta/pizza from £4.99/5.25 and great coffee. Mexican dishes at *Iguana Wana (☎ 729362, 19 Queensgate)* range from £5.45 to £7.65. Calling itself international, the well-regarded *Dickens Restaurant (☎ 713111, 77 Church St)* has an extensive, eclectic menu including French, Asian and vegetarian dishes from £6.20.

Day 18: Inverness to Lairg
5–8½ hours, 71.0mi

Passing through a series of towns on the Beauly, Cromarty and Dornoch Firths, this route eventually heads inland to Lairg.

Despite the distance, the terrain is not challenging, with only two sections of (not difficult) climbing: leaving Dingwall (22.3mi), and around the Shin Falls (65.3mi).

The A862 has some busy stretches – the first 10mi or so from Inverness are best avoided during peak hour. Take care also in the last mile to Dingwall (20.3mi); from the

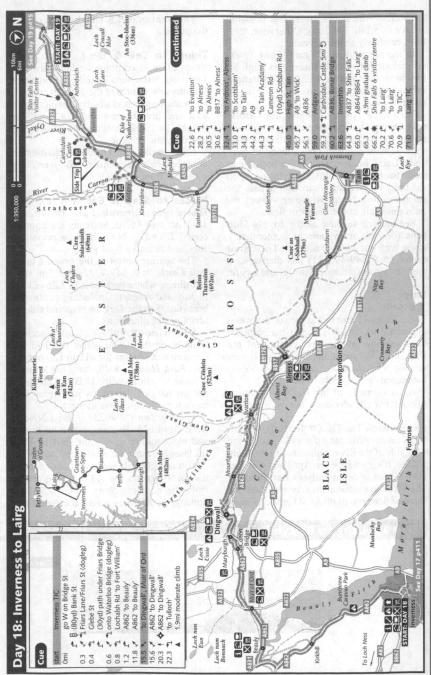

Day 18: Inverness to Lairg

Cue

start		Inverness TIC
0mi	↱	go W on Bridge St
	⬆🚲	(80yd) Bank St
0.3	↱↰	Friars Lane/Friars St (dogleg)
0.4	↰	Glebe St
0.6	↰	(30yd) path under Friars Bridge
	↱	onto Waterloo Bridge (dogleg)
0.8	↰	Lochalsh Rd 'to Fort William'
1.2	↰	A862 'to Beauly'
11.8	↰	A862 'to Beauly'
15.5		'to Dingwall', Muir of Ord
15.6	↱	A862 'to Dingwall'
20.3	◆↰	A862 'to Dingwall'
22.3	↰	'to Tulloch'
	▲	1.9mi moderate climb

Cue (Continued)

22.6	↱↰	'to Evanton'
28.2	↱↰	'to Alness'
30.5	↱↰	'to Alness'
30.6	↱↰	B817 'to Alness'
32.4	↱↰	'to Ardross', Alness
33.0	↱↰	'to Scotsburn'
34.3	↱↰	'to Tain'
44.2	↰	A9
44.3	↱↰	'to Tain Acadamy'
44.4	↱↰	Cameron Rd
		(10yd) Scotsburn Rd
45.0	↱↰	High St, Tain
45.7	↰	A9 'to Wick'
56.1	↰	A836
59.0		Ardgay
59.3	●●●↰	🏰 Carbisdale Castle 5mi ↺
60.2	↰	A836, Bonar Bridge
63.6		Invershin
64.3	↱↰	A837 'to Shin Falls'
65.0	↰	A864/B864 'to Lairg'
65.3	▲	4.9mi gradual climb
66.2	✱	Shin Falls & visitor centre
70.2	↰	'to Lairg'
70.6	↰	'to Lairg'
70.9	↰	'to TIC'
71.0		Lairg TIC

See Day 19 p415
START DAY 19

See Day 17 p411
START DAY 18

turn-off to Alness (28.2mi); and crossing the A9 into Tain (44.2mi). Otherwise, traffic is relatively unintrusive.

In the pretty town of Tain (45mi), eateries include *Harry Gow Bakery* on High St, for cheap light meals. The **Glen Morangie Whisky Distillery** (☎ 01862-892477) is 1mi north of town.

Turn left at Ardgay (59.3mi) for **Carbisdale Castle**. The imposing castle, which sits across the Kyle of Sutherland from Invershin, is now a hostel (see Places to Stay under Lairg, following). It's also possible to reach the hostel from Invershin train station (63.6mi) by walking your bike across the narrow railway bridge with care – check the train timetable at the platform first.

See salmon leaping at the lovely **Shin Falls** (66.2mi) from June to September – along with bus loads of tourists. The visitor centre (☎ 01549-402231) has displays on the life cycle of Atlantic Salmon and a *cafe*.

Lairg
☎ 01549

The village of Lairg lies at the southern end of Loch Shin. In 1807, Lairg parishioners became some of the first victims of the Highland Clearances, but the village is now famous for its annual August Lamb Sale – the largest one-day sale in Europe.

As is common in the Highlands, many (though not all) services close on Sunday.

Information The TIC (☎ 402160), including a countryside ranger service, is on the west side of the River Shin – not in the main village. It's open between April and October from 10 am to 5 pm daily (4 pm Sunday). The TIC can exchange money and there's a Bank of Scotland (with ATM) in the village.

The caravan park's laundrette is open to the public.

Things to See & Do Lairg's a pretty sleepy place – except for the day of the lamb sale – but attractions include the **Ferrycroft Countryside Centre** at the TIC. Its museum has audiovisuals and displays exploring the past and present environment, including Stone Age inhabitants and the Loch Shin hydroelectric scheme.

Local **walks** and **cultural activities** are described in a free leaflet, *Discover Lairg*, available from the TIC.

Places to Stay & Eat Tent pitches at *Dunroamin Caravan Park* (☎ 402447, Main St) cost £5.50. Showers are coin operated. It's advisable to book, especially in July, and to arrive by 4 pm.

The nearest hostel is the grand *Carbisdale Castle* (☎ 01549-421232), 7.5mi south at Culrain, where beds cost £12.25 (£13.25 in July and August), including continental breakfast. See the Day 18 map and ride description for directions.

Loch View (☎ 402578), 400yd north of Main St on the A836, offers B&B in spacious en suite rooms for £17 to £20 per person. *Park House* (☎ 402208), off Main St, is more luxurious with B&B at £26/36 per person for doubles or twins/singles (£14 more for a three-course dinner).

The *Nip Inn* (☎ 402243, Main St) does B&B from £25. Evening mains in the bar and nonsmoking restaurant start at £6.95 for lasagne (most are around £7 or £8).

You can get fish and chips after 5 pm at the *Shin Fry* on the A836 and groceries from the adjacent *Spar* supermarket (on Sunday, the *BP store* across the river opens

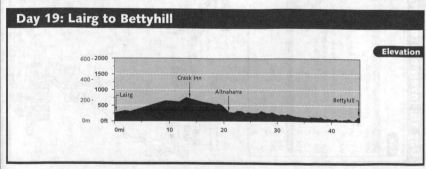

Day 19: Lairg to Bettyhill

until 4 pm).The licensed *Crofters Restaurant* in Main St has standard mains (including vegetarian) from £4.95 to the £7.95 poached salmon fillet.

Day 19: Lairg to Bettyhill
3–5½ hours, 45.3mi

North of Lairg, the countryside is increasingly remote, with only occasional cars along the single-track road. It's bleakly beautiful country, but pretty exposed – pray for a southerly wind.

There's a gentle 10mi gradual climb from just out of Lairg into the open moors, after which it's downhill overall – albeit undulating through Strathnaver – until the final 1.2mi into Bettyhill.

The cosy *Crask Inn* (☎ *01549-411241)*, 13.7mi north of Lairg, is a lone landmark in a sea of green and purple – a welcoming traveller's rest, with meals for £6 and B&B for £20 (free camping is also permitted).

The only other services are at Altnaharra (20.9mi), where there's the *Bed & Breakfast* (☎ *01549-411258, 1 Macleod Crescent)* and the *Altnaharra Hotel* (☎ *01549-411222)*. Book ahead if you're planning to stay in the area: beds are few and far between.

Though maps show settlements through Strathnaver, since the clearances, sheep are the main company through the valley.

Bettyhill
☎ 01641

Bettyhill is a crofting community, named after Elizabeth, Countess of Sutherland, who resettled her tenants here after clearing them out of Strathnaver to make way for (more-profitable) sheep.

The village's Gaelic name – Am Blaran Odhar – means 'The Grey Place'. Yes, it's bleak, though the beach is impressive.

Information The TIC (☎ 52132), at the bottom of the hill, opens between April and September for several hours to 5 pm daily (Sunday only in August). Alternatively, try phoning Thurso TIC (☎ 01847-892371), which has slightly longer hours. A travelling bank is available on Friday from 10 am to noon by the public hall.

Things to See & Do The **Strathnaver Museum** (☎ 521418), in an old church near the TIC, tells the sad story of the Strathnaver

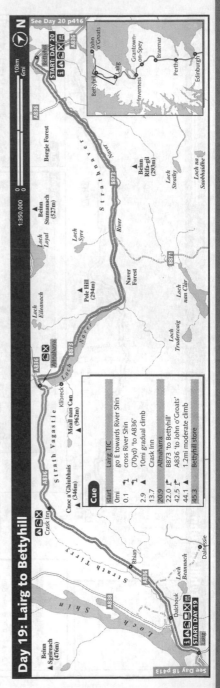

Cue		
start		Lairg TIC
0mi	←	go E towards River Shin
0.1	←	cross River Shin
	◄	(70yd) 'to A836'
2.9	◄	10mi gradual climb
13.7	◄	Crask Inn
20.9		Altnaharra
22.0	←	B873 to Bettyhill
42.5	←	A836 to John o'Groats'
44.1	◄	1.2mi moderate climb
45.3	◄	Bettyhill store

Day 19: Lairg to Bettyhill

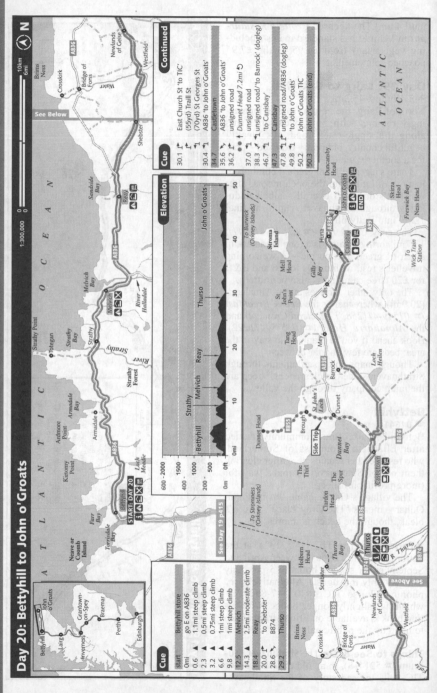

Clearances. It also contains the Farr Stone, an ancient Celtic cross from Christianised Pictish times, and Clan Mackay memorabilia.

Try the **surf** – if you can stand the cold water – or swim at the village **pool**.

Places to Stay & Eat There are only three options, so book ahead. Arrange camping (£2 to £5 per tent) through friendly *Dunveaden House* (☎ 521273), which has B&B for £16. The *Bettyhill Hotel* (☎ 521352) has great views of the beach. B&B is £15 (some rooms with bath). Bar meals start at £4.75.

The village *store* opens daily (limited hours on Sunday).

Day 20: Bettyhill to John o'Groats

4–6½ hours, 50.3mi
The final 50mi of the tour begins with six tough climbs in 17mi – and some great coastal views – before settling into less taxing, unremarkable farming country.

With more cars than Day 19, the road becomes two-way east of Melvich (12.5mi); between Thurso and John o'Groats, traffic on the A836 is fast and fairly heavy. It's largely avoided (as is the Dounreay nuclear power station, east of Reay) on the country lanes between Reay and Thurso and from Castletown to Canisbay.

There are small *stores* at Melvich (12.5mi) and Reay (18.4mi), but Thurso (29.2mi) is the main service town.

Thurso TIC (☎ 01847-892371), Riverside Rd (turn left at 30.2mi and ride 65yd), opens between April and October, until 5 pm Monday to Saturday (and to 4 or 5 pm on Sunday from June to September). Leisure Activities bike shop is on the corner of Princes St and Cowie Lane. There's a range of accommodation and eateries, including *Reid's Bakery* in the pedestrian mall and *Sandra's Snack Bar & Takeaway* (☎ 894575, 24 Princess St). The *Co-op* supermarket (*Grove Lane*) is next to the post office.

Although John o'Groats is the farthest town from Land's End, it is not the mainland's most northerly point. That honour is claimed by **Dunnet Head**, a few miles west. To get there, stay on the A836 at 36.2mi and turn left to Dunnet Head around 2.5mi on.

The John o'Groats finish line is by the turreted **John o'Groats House**. Congratulations!

John o'Groats
☎ 01955

It may be the most northerly settlement on the British mainland, but there's nothing spectacular about John o'Groats. The village is named after a Dutchman, Jan de Groot, who ran ferries to Orkney in 1496.

About 2mi east, Duncansby Head is the most north-easterly point, known for its seabird colonies.

Information The TIC (☎ 611373) opens between April and October from 11 am to 5 pm (closed Sunday; longer hours in summer).

Things to See & Do The touristy **Last House** (☎ 611250), near the finish line, is a souvenir shop and historical museum.

A **John o'Groats signpost** and platform by the hotel is just waiting for the 'I made it!' photograph. From £5, a photographer will take the shot – ask at the adjacent booth or phone ☎ 611254.

Register your journey in the **record book** (in the John o'Groats House hotel public bar, open from 11 am to 11 pm) to get a certificate from the End to End Club (☎ 01736-871501, ⓔ info@landsend-landmark.co.uk).

Look for **seals** off the John o'Groats coast or watch **seabirds** at Duncansby Head, 2mi east of John o'Groats (take the turn-off just south of the Seaview Hotel). A path from here leads south to **Duncansby Stacks**, impressive rock formations off the coast.

Places to Stay & Eat Right by the finish line, *John o'Groats Caravan & Camping Site* (☎ 611329) has tent pitches for £4/5 per single/double, with coin operated showers.

In Canisbay, 3mi west, *John o'Groats Youth Hostel* (☎ 611424) has beds for £8.

Book ahead at the *Caber Feidh Guest House* (☎ 611219), at the junction, which offers B&B for £17 for singles and £18 per person for doubles or twins, including an official end-to-end stamp and certificate. It also provides a la carte evening meals (mains £4 to £6), which are available to nonguests too (phone first).

Standard B&B at *Seaview Hotel* (☎ 611220), at the junction, costs £14.50/25 per person for doubles/singles. Restaurant meals start from £7.50; bar meals are cheaper.

The small *store* (*Wick Rd*) opens until 6 pm Monday to Saturday.

Glossary

aber – estuary (Wales)
afon – river (Wales)
aye – yes; always (Scotland)

bach – small (Wales)
bailey – outermost wall of a castle
bairn – baby (Newcastle & Scotland)
bangers – sausages
bar – gate (York)
barrow – see *tumulus*
ben – mountain (Scotland)
bent – not altogether legal
bevvy – a drink (originally northern England)
bitter – beer
black pudding – a type of sausage made from dried blood (Scotland)
blatherskite – boastful or talkative person (northern England)
bloke – man
bodge job – poor-quality repairs
bothy – hut or mountain shelter (Scotland)
brae – hill (Scotland)
bridleway – path that can be used by walkers, horse riders and cyclists
broch – defensive tower (Scotland)
Brummie – Birmingham accent
bryn – hill (Wales)
burgh – town (Scotland)
burn – creek, stream (Scotland)
bwlch – pass (Wales)

cadair – stronghold/chair (Wales)
caer – fort (Wales)
capel – chapel (Wales)
carnedd – mountain (Wales)
carreg – stone (Wales)
carry-out – takeaway (Scotland)
cashpoint – ATM (automatic teller machine)
ceilidh – (pronounced 'kaylee') informal evening of entertainment and dance (Scotland)
cheers – goodbye
chips – French fries
circus – a junction of several streets, usually circular
clogwyn – cliff (Wales)
clun – meadow (Wales)
ccoch – red (Wales)
coed – forest/wood (Wales)
Corbett – mountain of between 762m (2500ft) and 914.0m (2999ft) in height
couchette – sleeping berth in a train/ferry
crannog – artificial island settlement

cream tea – afternoon tea typically including scones with jam and cream
crisps – potato chips
croft – plot of land with adjoining house worked by the occupiers
crofting – subsistence farming
cromlech – burial chamber (Wales)
cwm – cirque/corrie/valley (Wales)

de – south (Wales)
din (dinas) – fort (Wales)
dolmen – chartered tomb
downs – rolling upland, characterised by lack of trees
duvet – doona
dyffryn – valley (Wales)

Eisteddfod – festival in which competitions are held in music, poetry, drama and the fine arts (Wales)
evensong – daily evening service (Church of England)

fagged – exhausted
fawr – big (Wales)
fell – hill or section of upland moor (northern England and Scotland)
fen – drained or marshy low-lying flat land
ffordd – road (Wales)
ffynnon – spring (Wales)
firth – estuary (Scotland)
footpath – sidewalk (cycling not permitted)

gate – street (York)
ginnel – alleyway (Yorkshire)
glan – shore (Wales)
glas – blue (Wales)
glen – valley (Scotland)
glyn – valley (Wales)
greasy spoon – cheap cafe
gwrydd – green (Wales)
gwyn – white (Wales)

haar – fog off the North Sea (Scotland)
High Street – British term for main street
Highland Clearances – period in the 19th century where Highlanders were forced off their land by the English government to make way for sheep farming
Hogmanay – New Year's Eve (Scotland)

inn – pub with accommodation

keep – main tower within the walls of a medieval castle or fortress
kirk – church (Scotland)
kyle – narrow strait

laird – estate owner (Scotland)
ley – clearing
linn – waterfall (Scotland)
llan – enclosed place or church (Wales)
llyn – lake (Wales)
loch – lake (Scotland)
lock – part of a canal or river that can be closed off and the water levels changed to raise or lower boats

Martello tower – small, circular tower used for coastal defence
mawr – great (Wales)
mere – marsh, lake
merthyr – burial place of a saint (Wales)
midge – a mosquito-like insect
moel – hill (Wales)
moor – exposed upland, usually heath-covered
moss – marsh, peat bog (northern England and Scotland)
motorway – freeway
motte – mound on which a castle was built
Munro – mountain of at least 914.4m (3000ft)
Munro-bagger – someone who reaches the top of a *Munro*
mynydd – mountain (Wales)

nant – valley/stream (Wales)
neeps – turnips (Scotland)
newydd – new (Wales)

ogof – cave (Wales)

pee – pence
pen – headland (Wales)
pend – arched gateway (Scotland)
pete – fortified houses
Pict – early Celtic inhabitants
pint – beer
pistyll – waterfall (Wales); also rhaeadr
pitch – playing field; also camp site
plas – hall/mansion (Wales)
pont – bridge (Wales)
postbus – bus that follows postal delivery route
pub – short for 'public house'; a bar usually with food, sometimes with accommodation
punter – customer
pwll – pool (Wales)

quid – pound

rail trail – disused railway line converted for walking and cycling
ramble – to go for a short walk
rhaeadr – waterfall (Wales); also pistyll
rhiw – slope (Wales)
rhos – moor/marsh (Wales)
roll-up – roll-your-own cigarette
rood – alternative word for crucifix, especially one at the entrance to a church
rugger – rugby

Sassenach – an English person or a lowland Scot (Scotland)
sett – tartan pattern
shout – to buy a group of people drinks, usually reciprocated
shut – partially covered passage
snicket – alleyway (York)
sporran – purse (Scotland)
steaming – drunk (Scotland)
strath – valley (Scotland)
subway – underpass

ta – thanks
takeaway – takeout or carry-out food
thwaite – clearing in a forest
toastie – toasted sandwich (Scotland)
tor – Celtic word describing a high hill (often shaped like a wedge)
torch – flashlight
towpath – path running beside a river or canal
traveller – nomadic, new-age hippy
tre – town (Wales)
tron – public weighbridge
tube – the London Underground (subway)
tumulus – a heap of earth placed over one or more prehistoric tombs; also *barrow*
twitchers – bird-watchers
twitten – passage, small lane
twr – tower (Wales)
ty – house (Wales)

uisge-bha – the water of life: whisky (Scotland)
Underground – subway

verderer – officer upholding law and order in the royal forests

way – a long-distance trail
wold – open, rolling country
wych – a hamlet or village (Old English)
wynd – lane (Scotland)

ynys – island (Wales)

ACRONYMS

The British love their acronyms; here's a guide to those you're likely to encounter en route:

AONB – Area of Outstanding Natural Beauty
ATM – automatic teller machine
AUK – Audax United Kingdom
B&BRP – Bristol & Bath Railway Path
BABA – Book-A-Bed-Ahead scheme
BCF – British Cycling Federation
BOATS – Byways Open to All Traffic; legal for cycling
BTA – British Tourist Authority
C2C – Sea to Sea (Sustrans) ride
Cadw – Welsh Historic Monuments agency
CC – Countryside Commission
CCW – Countryside Council for Wales
CTC – Cyclists' Touring Club
CTC(S) – Cyclists' Touring Club (Scotland)
E2E – End to End (Lonely Planet) ride
EH – English Heritage
EN – English Nature
ESA – Environmentally Sensitive Area

FC – Forestry Commission
FNR – Forest Nature Reserve
HI – Hostelling International
OS – Ordnance Survey
NCN – National Cycle Network
NNR – National Nature Reserve
NSA – National Scenic Area (Scotland)
NT – National Trust
NTS – National Trust for Scotland
NYMR – North Yorkshire Moors Railway
RSA – Royal Scottish Academy
RUPPS – Roads Used as Public Paths; legal for cycling
SNH – Scottish National Heritage
SSSI – Site of Special Scientific Interest
STB – Scottish Tourist Board
SYHA – Scottish Youth Hostel Association
TIC – Tourist Information Centre
TOC – train operating company
UCR – unclassified country road
VAT – value-added tax, levied on most goods and services, currently 17.5%
WTB – Wales Tourist Board
YHA – Youth Hostel Association

This Book

Ian Connellan was the coordinating author of *Cycling Britain*; he wrote the introductory chapters as well as the London and Southern England chapters. Nicola Wells wrote the Scotland chapter and coordinated the Land's End to John o'Groats chapter, to which all the authors contributed. Nicky Crowther wrote the Eastern England and Central England chapters, while Ian Duckworth wrote the Northern England and Wales chapters.

The Your Bicycle chapter was written by Darren Elder with contributions by Nicola Wells, Neil Irvine and Sally Dillon. The Health & Safety chapter was written by Ian Connellan, Dr Isabelle Young and Kevin Tabotta. Material from the 3rd edition of Lonely Planet's *Britain* guide, by Bryn Thomas, Tom Smallman and Pat Yale, was used for parts of this book. Material was also used from the 1st edition of Lonely Planet's *Scotland* guide, by Tom Smallman and Graeme Cornwallis.

FROM THE PUBLISHER

Cycling Britain, the third in Lonely Planet's new series of cycling guides, has been a long time in the making. The series was developed by a team from Lonely Planet's Outdoor Activities Unit in Melbourne, including Emily Coles, Sally Dillon, Teresa Donnellan, Chris Klep, Andrew Smith, Nick Tapp and series editor Darren Elder, assisted by Paul Clifton and Nicola Wells. The cover design for the series was developed by Jamieson Gross, who also designed this book's cover.

Thalia Kalkipsakis and Darren Elder joined forces to coordinate the editing of this book; while Andrew Smith coordinated the mapping and design, with Michael Blore and Teresa Donnellan overseeing operations. Janet Brunckhorst, Emily Coles, Brigitte Ellemor, Adam Ford, Angie Phelan and Nicola Wells assisted with editing; Sonya Brooke, Heath Comrie, Tony Fankhauser, Simon Tillema, John Shippick and Glenn van der Knijff assisted with mapping.

Andrew Smith and Mathew Burfoot designed the book, and Angie Phelan coordinated editorial matters during layout. Glenn van der Knijff designed the colour pages. Geoff Rasmussen wrote computer programs to automate our processes. The staff of LPI, in particular Fiona Croyden, Brett Pascoe and Annie Horner, lent valuable assistance. Matt King (also of LPI) coordinated the illustrations; drawn by Martin Harris and Don Hatcher.

Thanks to Mike Collins and Edward Freeman from Sustrans for the colour map, all their enthusiasm and help throughout. Thanks also to all the regional route coordinators who helped our authors on the road.

Jeff Crowe from Sport: The Library shot the photographs used in the Your Bicycle chapter. A crew from Cannondale USA and Cannondale Australia provided the bicycles for the Your Bicycle chapter; thanks to Nick Goljanin, Bill Conradt, Tom Armstrong and Matt Moon. Christie Cycles, Hawthorn, and Swim Bike Run, St Kilda, assembled the bicycles and provided technical assistance; thanks to Ian and Richard, in particular.

LONELY PLANET

Guides by Region

Lonely Planet is known worldwide for publishing practical, reliable and no-nonsense travel information in our guides and on our Web site. The Lonely Planet list covers just about every accessible part of the world. Currently there are 16 series: Travel guides, Shoestring guides, Condensed guides, Phrasebooks, Read This First, Healthy Travel, Walking guides, Cycling guides, Watching Wildlife guides, Pisces Diving & Snorkeling guides, City Maps, Road Atlases, Out to Eat, World Food, Journeys travel literature and Pictorials.

AFRICA Africa on a shoestring • Cairo • Cape Town • Cape Town City Map • East Africa • Egypt • Egyptian Arabic phrasebook • Ethiopia, Eritrea & Djibouti • Ethiopian (Amharic) phrasebook • The Gambia & Senegal • Healthy Travel Africa • Kenya • Malawi • Morocco • Moroccan Arabic phrasebook • Mozambique • Read This First: Africa • South Africa, Lesotho & Swaziland • Southern Africa • Southern Africa Road Atlas • Swahili phrasebook • Tanzania, Zanzibar & Pemba • Trekking in East Africa • Tunisia • Watching Wildlife East Africa • Watching Wildlife Southern Africa • West Africa • World Food Morocco • Zimbabwe, Botswana & Namibia
Travel Literature: Mali Blues: Traveling to an African Beat • The Rainbird: A Central African Journey • Songs to an African Sunset: A Zimbabwean Story

AUSTRALIA & THE PACIFIC Auckland • Australia • Australian phrasebook • Australia Road Atlas • Bushwalking in Australia •Cycling New Zealand • Fiji • Fijian phrasebook • Healthy Travel Australia, NZ and the Pacific • Islands of Australia's Great Barrier Reef • Melbourne • Melbourne City Map • Micronesia • New Caledonia • New South Wales & the ACT • New Zealand • Northern Territory • Outback Australia • Out to Eat – Melbourne • Out to Eat – Sydney • Papua New Guinea • Pidgin phrasebook • Queensland • Rarotonga & the Cook Islands • Samoa • Solomon Islands • South Australia • South Pacific • South Pacific phrasebook • Sydney • Sydney City Map • Sydney Condensed • Tahiti & French Polynesia • Tasmania • Tonga • Tramping in New Zealand • Vanuatu • Victoria • Walking in Australia • Watching Wildlife Australia • Western Australia
Travel Literature: Islands in the Clouds: Travels in the Highlands of New Guinea • Kiwi Tracks: A New Zealand Journey • Sean & David's Long Drive

CENTRAL AMERICA & THE CARIBBEAN Bahamas, Turks & Caicos • Baja California • Bermuda • Central America on a shoestring • Costa Rica • Costa Rica Spanish phrasebook • Cuba • Dominican Republic & Haiti • Eastern Caribbean • Guatemala • Guatemala, Belize & Yucatán: La Ruta Maya • Healthy Travel Central & South America • Jamaica • Mexico • Mexico City • Panama • Puerto Rico • Read This First: Central & South America • World Food Mexico • Yucatán
Travel Literature: Green Dreams: Travels in Central America

EUROPE Amsterdam • Amsterdam City Map • Amsterdam Condensed • Andalucía • Austria • Baltic States phrasebook • Barcelona • Barcelona City Map • Berlin • Berlin City Map • Britain • British phrasebook • Brussels, Bruges & Antwerp • Brussels City Map • Budapest • Budapest City Map • Canary Islands • Central Europe • Central Europe phrasebook • Corfu & the Ionians • Corsica • Crete • Crete Condensed • Croatia • Cycling Britain • Cycling France • Cyprus • Czech & Slovak Republics • Denmark • Dublin • Dublin City Map • Eastern Europe • Eastern Europe phrasebook • Edinburgh • Estonia, Latvia & Lithuania • Europe on a shoestring • Finland • Florence • France • Frankfurt Condensed • French phrasebook • Georgia, Armenia & Azerbaijan • Germany • German phrasebook • Greece • Greek Islands • Greek phrasebook • Hungary • Iceland, Greenland & the Faroe Islands • Ireland • Istanbul • Italian phrasebook • Italy • Krakow • Lisbon • The Loire • London • London City Map • London Condensed • Madrid • Malta • Mediterranean Europe • Mediterranean Europe phrasebook • Moscow • Munich • the Netherlands • Norway • Out to Eat – London • Paris • Paris City Map • Paris Condensed • Poland • Portugal • Portuguese phrasebook • Prague • Prague City Map • Provence & the Côte d'Azur • Read This First: Europe • Romania & Moldova • Rome • Rome City Map • Russia, Ukraine & Belarus • Russian phrasebook • Scandinavian & Baltic Europe • Scandinavian Europe phrasebook • Scotland • Sicily • Slovenia • South-West France • Spain • Spanish phrasebook • St Petersburg • St Petersburg City Map • Sweden • Switzerland • Trekking in Spain • Tuscany • Ukrainian phrasebook • Venice • Vienna • Walking in Britain • Walking in France • Walking in Ireland • Walking in Italy • Walking in Spain • Walking in Switzerland • Western Europe • Western Europe phrasebook • World Food France • World Food Ireland • World Food Italy • World Food Spain
Travel Literature: Love and War in the Apennines • The Olive Grove: Travels in Greece • On the Shores of the Mediterranean • Round Ireland in Low Gear • A Small Place in Italy • After Yugoslavia

LONELY PLANET

Mail Order

Lonely Planet products are distributed worldwide.They are also available by mail order from Lonely Planet, so if you have difficulty finding a title please write to us. North and South American residents should write to 150 Linden St, Oakland, CA 94607, USA; European and African residents should write to 10a Spring Place, London NW5 3BH, UK; and residents of other countries to Locked Bag 1, Footscray, Victoria 3011, Australia.

INDIAN SUBCONTINENT Bangladesh • Bengali phrasebook • Bhutan • Delhi • Goa • Healthy Travel Asia & India • Hindi & Urdu phrasebook • India • Indian Himalaya • Karakoram Highway • Kerala • Mumbai (Bombay) • Nepal • Nepali phrasebook • Pakistan • Rajasthan • Read This First: Asia & India • South India • Sri Lanka • Sri Lanka phrasebook • Tibet • Tibetan phrasebook • Trekking in the Indian Himalaya • Trekking in the Karakoram & Hindukush • Trekking in the Nepal Himalaya
Travel Literature: The Age of Kali: Indian Travels and Encounters • Hello Goodnight: A Life of Goa • In Rajasthan • A Season in Heaven: True Tales from the Road to Kathmandu • Shopping for Buddhas • A Short Walk in the Hindu Kush • Slowly Down the Ganges

ISLANDS OF THE INDIAN OCEAN Madagascar & Comoros • Maldives • Mauritius, Réunion & Seychelles

MIDDLE EAST & CENTRAL ASIA Bahrain, Kuwait & Qatar • Cairo City Map • Central Asia • Central Asia phrasebook • Dubai • Hebrew phrasebook • Iran • Israel & the Palestinian Territories • Istanbul • Istanbul City Map • Istanbul to Cairo on a shoestring • Jerusalem • Jerusalem City Map • Jordan • Lebanon • Middle East • Oman & the United Arab Emirates • Syria • Turkey • Turkish phrasebook • World Food Turkey • Yemen
Travel Literature: Black on Black: Iran Revisited • The Gates of Damascus • Kingdom of the Film Stars: Journey into Jordan

NORTH AMERICA Alaska • Boston • Boston City Map • California & Nevada • California Condensed • Canada • Chicago • Chicago City Map • Deep South • Florida • Great Lakes • Hawaii • Hiking in Alaska • Hiking in the USA • Honolulu • Las Vegas • Los Angeles • Los Angeles City Map • Louisiana & The Deep South • Miami • Miami City Map • New England • New Orleans • New York City • New York City City Map • New York City Condensed • New York, New Jersey & Pennsylvania • Oahu • Out to Eat – San Francisco • Pacific Northwest • Puerto Rico • Rocky Mountains • San Francisco • San Francisco City Map • Seattle • Southwest • Texas • USA • USA phrasebook • Vancouver • Virginia & the Capital Region • Washington DC • Washington, DC City Map • World Food Deep South, USA • World Food New Orleans
Travel Literature: Caught Inside: A Surfer's Year on the California Coast • Drive Thru America

NORTH-EAST ASIA Beijing • Beijing City Map • Cantonese phrasebook • China • Hiking in Japan • Hong Kong • Hong Kong City Map • Hong Kong Condensed • Hong Kong, Macau & Guangzhou • Japan • Japanese phrasebook • Korea • Korean phrasebook • Kyoto • Mandarin phrasebook • Mongolia • Mongolian phrasebook • Seoul • Shanghai • South-West China • Taiwan • Tokyo
Travel Literature: In Xanadu: A Quest • Lost Japan

SOUTH AMERICA Argentina, Uruguay & Paraguay • Bolivia • Brazil • Brazilian phrasebook • Buenos Aires • Chile & Easter Island • Colombia • Ecuador & the Galapagos Islands • Healthy Travel Central & South America • Latin American Spanish phrasebook • Peru • Quechua phrasebook • Read This First: Central & South America • Rio de Janeiro • Rio de Janeiro City Map • Santiago • South America on a shoestring • Trekking in the Patagonian Andes • Venezuela
Travel Literature: Full Circle: A South American Journey

SOUTH-EAST ASIA Bali & Lombok • Bangkok • Bangkok City Map • Burmese phrasebook • Cambodia • Hanoi • Healthy Travel Asia & India • Hill Tribes phrasebook • Ho Chi Minh City • Indonesia • Indonesian phrasebook • Indonesia's Eastern Islands • Jakarta • Java • Lao phrasebook • Laos • Malay phrasebook • Malaysia, Singapore & Brunei • Myanmar (Burma) • Philippines • Pilipino (Tagalog) phrasebook • Read This First: Asia & India • Singapore • Singapore City Map • South-East Asia on a shoestring • South-East Asia phrasebook • Thailand • Thailand's Islands & Beaches • Thailand, Vietnam, Laos & Cambodia Road Atlas • Thai phrasebook • Vietnam • Vietnamese phrasebook • World Food Thailand • World Food Vietnam

ALSO AVAILABLE: Antarctica • The Arctic • The Blue Man: Tales of Travel, Love and Coffee • Brief Encounters: Stories of Love, Sex & Travel • Chasing Rickshaws • The Last Grain Race • Lonely Planet Unpacked • Not the Only Planet: Science Fiction Travel Stories • On the Edge: Extreme Travel • Sacred India • Travel with Children • Travel Photography: A Guide to Taking Better Pictures

LONELY PLANET

You already know that Lonely Planet produces more than this one guidebook, but you might not be aware of the other products we have on this region. Here is a selection of titles that you may want to check out as well:

Walking in Britain
ISBN 0 86442 478 7
US$17.95 • UK£11.99 • 140FF

Britain
ISBN 0 86442 578 3
US$25.95 • UK£15.99 • 190FF

British phrasebook
ISBN 0 86442 484 1
US$5.95 • UK£3.99 • 40FF

London City Map
ISBN 1 86450 008 5
US$5.95 • UK£3.99 • 39FF

London Condensed
ISBN 1 86450 043 3
US$9.95 • UK£5.99 • 59FF

London
ISBN 0 86442 793 X
US$15.95 • UK£9.99 • 120FF

Scotland
ISBN 0 86442 592 9
US$15.95 • UK£9.99 • 120FF

Ireland
ISBN 0 86442 753 0
US$19.95 • UK£11.99 • 160FF

Walking in Ireland
ISBN 0 86442 602 X
US$17.95 • UK£11.99 • 140FF

Europe on a shoestring
ISBN 1 86450 150 2
US$24.99 • UK£14.99 • 179FF

Read this first: Europe
ISBN 1 86450 136 7
US$14.99 • UK£8.99 • 99FF

Western Europe
ISBN 1 86450 163 4
US$27.99 • UK£15.99 • 189FF

Available wherever books are sold

Index

Bold indicates maps.

425

Bold indicates maps.

Boxed Text

ABOUT LONELY PLANET GUIDEBOOKS

Lonely Planet published its first book in 1973 in response to the numerous 'How did you do it?' questions Maureen and Tony Wheeler were asked after driving, busing, hitching, sailing and railing their way from England to Australia.

Written at a kitchen table and hand collated, trimmed and stapled, *Across Asia on the Cheap* became an instant local bestseller, inspiring thoughts of another book.

Eighteen months in South-East Asia resulted in their second guide, *South-East Asia on a shoestring*, which they put together in a backstreet Chinese hotel in Singapore in 1975. The 'yellow bible', as it quickly became known to backpackers around the world, soon became the guide to the region. It has sold well over half a million copies and is now in its 10th edition.

Today an international company with offices in Melbourne (Australia), Oakland (USA), London (UK) and Paris (France), Lonely Planet has an ever-growing list of books and other products, including: travel guides, walking guides, city maps, travel atlases, phrasebooks, diving guides, wildlife guides, healthy travel guides, restaurant guides, world food guides, first time travel guides, condensed guides, travel literature, pictorial books and, of course, cycling guides. Many of these are also published in French and various other languages.

In addition to the books, there are also videos and Lonely Planet's award winning Web site.

Some things haven't changed. The main aim is still to help make it possible for adventurous travellers to get out there – to explore and better understand the world.

At Lonely Planet we believe travellers can make a positive contribution to the countries they visit – if they respect their host communities and spend their money wisely. Since 1986 a percentage of the income from each book has been donated to aid projects and human rights campaigns.

> Lonely Planet gathers information for everyone who's curious about the planet – and especially for those who explore it first-hand. Through guidebooks, phrasebooks, activity guides, maps, literature, newsletters, image library, TV series and Web site we act as an information exchange for a worldwide community of travellers.

LONELY PLANET OFFICES

Australia
Locked Bag 1, Footscray, Victoria 3011
☎ 03 9689 4666 fax 03 9689 6833
ⓔ talk2us@lonelyplanet.com.au

USA
150 Linden St, Oakland, CA 94607
☎ 510 893 8555 or ☎ 800 275 8555 (toll free)
fax 510 893 8572
ⓔ info@lonelyplanet.com

UK
10a Spring Place, London NW5 3BH
☎ 020 7428 4800 fax 020 7428 4828
ⓔ go@lonelyplanet.co.uk

France
1 rue du Dahomey, 75011 Paris
☎ 01 55 25 33 00 fax 01 55 25 33 01
ⓔ bip@lonelyplanet.fr
🖳 www.lonelyplanet.fr

World Wide Web: 🖳 www.lonelyplanet.com *or* AOL keyword: lp
Lonely Planet Images: ⓔ lpi@lonelyplanet.com.au